KU-770-047

PRIMA Official Game Guide

Written by Stephen Stratton with David Knight

Prima Games
An Imprint of Random House, Inc.

3000 Lava Ridge Court, St. 100
Roseville, CA 95661
www.primagames.com

Senior Product Manager: Mario De Govia
Associate Product Manager: Shaida Boroumand
Design & Layout: Marc W. Riegel
Manufacturing: Stephanie Sanchez, Suzanne Goodwin

Special thanks to the team at Nintendo: Staci Antich, Tim Casey, Dave Casipit, Shawn Gates, Kindra Timmerwilke, James Kim, Ann Lin, Teresa Lillygren, Noriko Matsunaga, Byron Munford, Josh Newman, and Michael Ottaviano.

Stephen Stratton has authored over 40 guides in his seven years with Prima. His personal favorites include *Resident Evil 4: Wii Edition*, *Mercenaries: Playground of Destruction*, *Mass Effect*, and pretty much every guide he's written that has either "Mario" or "Zelda" in its title.

Steve is a lifelong video gamer who attended the Rochester Institute of Technology in Rochester, NY. In addition to his Prima Games guides, he also held a staff position with Computec Media and managed the strategy section of their incite.com video game website.

Steve would like to thank Noriko Matsunaga and all the good people of Nintendo for their tremendous help and hospitality. Special thanks to Mike Keough and Dave Casipit at Nintendo for taking the time to bail me out whenever things became dicey. Happy Holidays to all my family and friends, and all my love to Jules.

We want to hear from you! E-mail comments and feedback to sstratton@primagames.com.

ISBN: 978-0-307-46593-1
Library of Congress Catalog Card Number: 2009911156
Printed in the United States of America
09 10 11 12 LL 10 9 8 7 6 5 4 3 2 1

Contents

Introduction

The Legend Reborn

The Legend of Zelda: Spirit Tracks is the latest in a long line of adventures featuring a green-clad sword-wielding hero named Link. This game is set approximately 100 years after the events of *Phantom Hourglass*, the previous installment of *Zelda* on the Nintendo DS. That means *Spirit Tracks'* star is a different Link than the hero of *Phantom Hourglass*—and as you've no doubt discovered by watching the game's opening, he's not alone. For the first time ever in this beloved and long-standing series, Princess Zelda, the game's titular character herself, fills a major role throughout the adventure and becomes a playable ally!

The Legends of Zelda

The Legend of Zelda, 1987 (NES)

Many consider the original *Legend of Zelda*, released for the 8-bit Nintendo Entertainment System (NES) in July 1987, to be the title that took video games to a new level. It was the first nonlinear adventure game, meaning that gamers weren't led by the nose to the next objective. They could spend hours exploring the overworld if they wanted to and could continually discover new and unexpected things.

The *Legend of Zelda* established most of the major game elements that have since appeared in every *Zelda* game to date. It featured Link, the boy hero dressed in green; Zelda, the imperiled Princess of Hyrule; and Ganon, the monstrous archenemy who tried to bring darkness to Hyrule. Link's main objective was to assemble the eight shards of Zelda's Triforce of Wisdom and defeat Ganon in his Death Mountain lair.

Best of all, when you finished the game, you could play through a wholly different second version, in which the placement of the dungeons had been switched around. You could also jump straight into the second version of the quest by entering "ZELDA" as your name.

The Adventure of Link, 1988 (NES)

The only *Legend of Zelda* game not to have the word "Zelda" in the title, *The Adventure of Link* was a dramatic departure from the original game. Although there was a top-down overworld perspective in the game, most of the action took place in a side-scrolling platform.

However, many of the original game's elements were retained for the new game. Link quested through dungeons in search of a piece of an artifact of great power (shards of a Magic Crystal, rather than pieces of the Triforce of Wisdom), all to save Princess Zelda, who was put into an enchanted sleep. Instead of Ganon, Link fights his own shadow at the game's climax!

While some of the *Adventure of Link's* innovations were discarded (such as Link's ability to earn experience points and raise his skill level), some remained, including the ability to learn new sword techniques.

The Legend of Zelda: A Link to the Past, 1992 (SNES)

Link's third adventure, *A Link to the Past*, was his first adventure on the Super Nintendo Entertainment System (SNES). Released in April 1992, *A Link to the Past* was a return to the original game's top-down, dungeon-crawling, overworld-exploring formula. During his quest, Link gathered magic amulets and crystals to rescue Zelda, free Hyrule, and stop the evil plans of Ganon and his accomplice, Agahnim.

A Link to the Past was the first _Zelda_ game to imply that each game featured a different Link. It was described as a prequel to the original _Legend of Zelda_, taking place long before the events of the first game.

A Link to the Past drew inspiration from the original *Legend of Zelda*, but thanks to the power of the 16-bit SNES, it had twice as much of everything: more detailed graphics, more dungeons, more enemies and bosses, more items—even two overworlds that Link could warp between!

A Link to the Past was one of Super Nintendo's most popular games, and it is remembered as one of the greatest *Zelda* games ever created. Its timeless appeal was proved by its successful rerelease as a Game Boy Advance game in December 2002, *The Legend of Zelda: A Link to the Past/Four Swords.*

The Legend of Zelda: Link's Awakening, 1993 (Game Boy)

Link's Awakening was Link's first adventure on the original Game Boy, and it proved that the grand adventure of the *Zelda* series worked perfectly on the Game Boy's small black-and-white screen. Shipwrecked on Koholint Island, Link recovered the eight Instruments of the Sirens to awaken the Wind Fish and return to the land of Hyrule.

When the Game Boy made way for the Game Boy Color, *Link's Awakening* was rereleased in December 1998 as the full-color *Link's Awakening DX,* with an additional hidden dungeon.

The Picto Box/Nintendo Gallery side-quest of _The Wind Waker_ was inspired by a similar photo-taking side-quest in _Link's Awakening,_ in which there were 12 photo opportunities. After you took a photo in _Link's Awakening,_ you could print it with a Game Boy Printer!

The Legend of Zelda: Ocarina of Time, 1998 (N64)

After alternating between two-dimensional perspectives for four adventures, Link broke into the third dimension in November 1998 with *Ocarina of Time*. The first Zelda game for the 64-bit Nintendo 64, *Ocarina of Time* brought the lush landscapes of Hyrule to life in an epic quest for the power of the Seven Sages of Hyrule.

The story line of *Ocarina of Time* was divided between two time periods—one featured Link as a boy, and the other was set seven years later, featuring Link as a young man. It had all the action and adventure of the previous *Zelda* games, but many gamers loved *Ocarina* for the detail it brought to Link, Zelda, Ganon, and the kingdom of Hyrule and all its major races.

Ocarina of Time introduced several new gameplay mechanics into the *Zelda* franchise, including a robust targeting system, the ability to play notes on an instrument and to wear masks, and side-quests for hundreds of hidden items! As the first 3-D *Zelda* game, *Ocarina* has become the standard against which all other 3-D adventure games are judged.

Ocarina of Time featured two eras, but it was neither the first nor the only _Zelda_ game to use the "two worlds" concept. _A Link to the Past_ had a Light World and a Dark World that Link could warp between with the Magic Mirror, and The Wind Waker and the original _Legend of Zelda_ could be played through a second time for a different gameplay experience.

The Legend of Zelda: Majora's Mask, 2000 (N64)

A follow-up to *Ocarina of Time*, *Majora's Mask* found Link in a parallel version of Hyrule called Termina, into which the moon was going to crash within 72 hours! Fortunately, Link retained his time-warping talents from *Ocarina* (and learned a few new ones) that allowed him to travel through time to save the day. By the end of the game, Link had recovered his horse, Epona, and his Ocarina of Time from the Skull Kid, who had misused the power of the Majora's Mask to pull the moon from its orbit.

Majora's Mask was the first (and so far only) Zelda game to set time limits on Link's quest. Much of the overworld exploration of earlier Zelda titles became a different sort of adventuring in *Majora's Mask*. Every area in the game changed, from the beginning of the 72-hour deadline to the end, with different people to talk to and different side-quests to explore.

The Legend of Zelda: Oracle of Seasons/Oracle of Ages, 2001 (Game Boy Color)

Oracle of Seasons and *Oracle of Ages*, two Game Boy Color games, took the "two worlds" concept to a new level. Both were released on May 14, 2001. In *Ages*, Link found himself in the distant land of Labrynnia, where he had to defeat Veran, the Sorceress of Shadows, by recovering the eight Essences of Time. In *Seasons*, Link's adventure took place in Holodrum, where he had to defeat the power-hungry General Onox by collecting the eight Essences of Nature.

The games were complete adventures individually, but players could also link up the games and transfer secret items and information between them to unlock new items, abilities, and a hidden ending featuring Ganon!

The Legend of Zelda: A Link to the Past/Four Swords, 2002 (Game Boy Advance)

The first *Zelda* game for the Game Boy Advance, *A Link to the Past/Four Swords* was a pixel-perfect translation of the SNES classic to Nintendo's latest portable console. It also included *Four Swords*, the first multiplayer *Zelda* game. Two to four players could link up their Game Boy Advances, cooperating and competing across four worlds to rescue Zelda from the clutches of Vaati, the Wind Sorcerer.

As a bonus, performing certain feats in *Four Swords* unlocked hidden side-quests in *A Link to the Past*, such as a scavenger hunt and the Palace of the Four Swords. Similarly, achieving certain goals in *A Link to the Past* gave a *Four Swords* player new abilities, such as the power to fire magical blasts from his or her sword!

The Legend of Zelda: The Wind Waker, 2003 (GameCube)

Carrying the *Zelda* franchise to new heights, *The Wind Waker* shocked fans with its beautiful-yet-controversial cell-shaded graphics and with its dramatic departure from the overworld norm. Set at least 100 years after the conclusion of *Ocarina of Time*, the overworld was completely flooded in *The Wind Waker*, transforming the entire land of Hyrule into a gigantic ocean! Instead of traversing a vast land on foot or with the aid of Link's trusty steed, Epona, players ventured between 49 individual islands via a small sailboat, the *King of Red Lions*, in their quest to rescue Link's sister and save the land from the clutches of Ganon once more.

The combination of its whimsical graphical style and watery overworld antics threw many fans for a loop, but those who gave *The Wind Waker* a chance found that it was indeed worthy of the critical acclaim it received. Refining the control scheme of its 3-D predecessors, the *The Wind Waker's* combat system was second to none, allowing Link to roll circles around his enemies, attacking them from all sides with the timely press of a button. The enemies were a treat for franchise fans to encounter, as many were brilliantly imagined evolutions of classic franchise foes, including Octoroks, Darknuts, and Wizzrobes.

As the first GameCube *Zelda*, expectations were high for *The Wind Waker*. After the game's release, many fans pined for a more realistic graphical style, while others begged for more cell-shaded genius. With the releases of *Twilight Princess*, *Phantom Hourglass*, and now *Spirit Tracks*, both wishes have at last been fulfilled!

The Legend of Zelda: Four Swords Adventure, 2004 (GameCube)

Taking full advantage of the connectivity between the Game Boy Advance (GBA) and the GameCube, *The Legend of Zelda: Four Swords Adventure* provided one of the GameCube's most unique gameplay experiences. Up to four players could connect their GBAs to a GameCube, each assuming the role of one of four different-colored Links. In many ways, the game was similar to the *Four Swords* portion of *A Link to the Past/Four Swords* on the GBA, but it was larger in every detail, and players worked together to solve brain-teasing puzzles and defeat imaginative foes as they ventured deep into danger-filled dungeons.

Although the GBA-to-GameCube connectivity wasn't required to play *The Legend of Zelda: Four Swords Adventure*, the game was meant to be enjoyed that way. When linked up, the action seamlessly shifted from the TV display to a player's GBA screen each time they entered a house or delved into an underground cavern. Similarly, all text-based messages and dialogue with nonplayer characters occurred on the GBA screen, leaving the TV display clear and the action uninterrupted. The many ways in which the game utilized this unique connectivity were truly impressive, making *The Legend of Zelda: Four Swords Adventure* a testament to the gaming goodness that can be achieved when handhelds and consoles are linked together.

The Legend of Zelda: The Minish Cap, 2005 (Game Boy Advance)

Borrowing from the innovative gameplay mechanics and robust graphical style displayed in the *Four Swords* portion of the GBA's *A Link to the Past/Four Swords* outing, *The Minish Cap* pushed the boundaries of Nintendo's former handheld system to astonishing heights. Featuring the same fundamental gameplay of its 2-D predecessors, *The Minish Cap* piled on the mind-bending puzzles and top-down, dungeon-delving fun that series fans have come to love.

The chief villain from the GBA's *Four Swords* adventure, Vaati, made his evil return in *The Minish Cap* when he cursed Princess Zelda and turned her to stone! Aided by a comical talking cap that shrank Link down to itty-bitty proportions that allowed him to explore his surroundings in a whole new way, the boy hero set out to search for four sacred elements that could help him break Zelda's curse and punish the wicked Vaati. Link got additional help in his quest by the Minish, a race of miniature beings with whom Link could interact whenever he shrank down to his tiny size.

The Legend of Zelda: Twilight Princess, 2006 (GameCube, Wii)

Unquestionably the most ambitious and profound *Zelda* title thus far, *Twilight Princess* finally gave hardcore *Zelda* fans the epic adventure they'd been dreaming of since the GameCube's debut. Boasting hyper-realistic graphics, a massive overworld, nine labyrinthine dungeons, and a host of hard-to-find collectibles, *Twilight Princess* simply piled on the gameplay. Its incredible production value and rich plotline satisfied even the hungriest of *Zelda* series fans. You might still be playing it now!

The Legend of Zelda: Phantom Hourglass, 2007 (DS)

The first *Zelda* to release on Nintendo's current handheld platform, the Nintendo DS, *Phantom Hourglass* departed from one of the franchise's long-standing traditions by serving as a direct sequel to *The Wind Waker*. This had never been done before in the series; every *Zelda* up to *Phantom Hourglass* had been a completely separate and self-contained adventure sporting a fresh cast of characters—a different Link, Zelda, and villain every time. But *Phantom Hourglass* took place shortly after the end of *The Wind Waker*, picking up right where that sweeping adventure left off. Its charming cell-shaded graphics fit the DS perfectly, and its simplistic all-stylus control scheme made the title easy for anyone to pick up and enjoy.

The Legend of Zelda: Spirit Tracks, 2009 (DS)

We could try to sum up the wonder of *Spirit Tracks* in a couple of paragraphs, but we've got the rest of this guide to cover it in glorious detail! In short, with the addition of Zelda as a playable character and a whole new means of exploring the overworld, this massive adventure is one of the best handheld *Zelda* games to date. We hope you enjoy playing it as much as we enjoyed crafting its guide!

 How to Use This Book 

Thank you for purchasing Prima's Official Game Guide to *The Legend of Zelda: Spirit Tracks.* We've crammed this guide full of vital tips and strategy to help you get the most out of your time in Link's world. First, let's quickly review what you'll find in each major section of this guide.

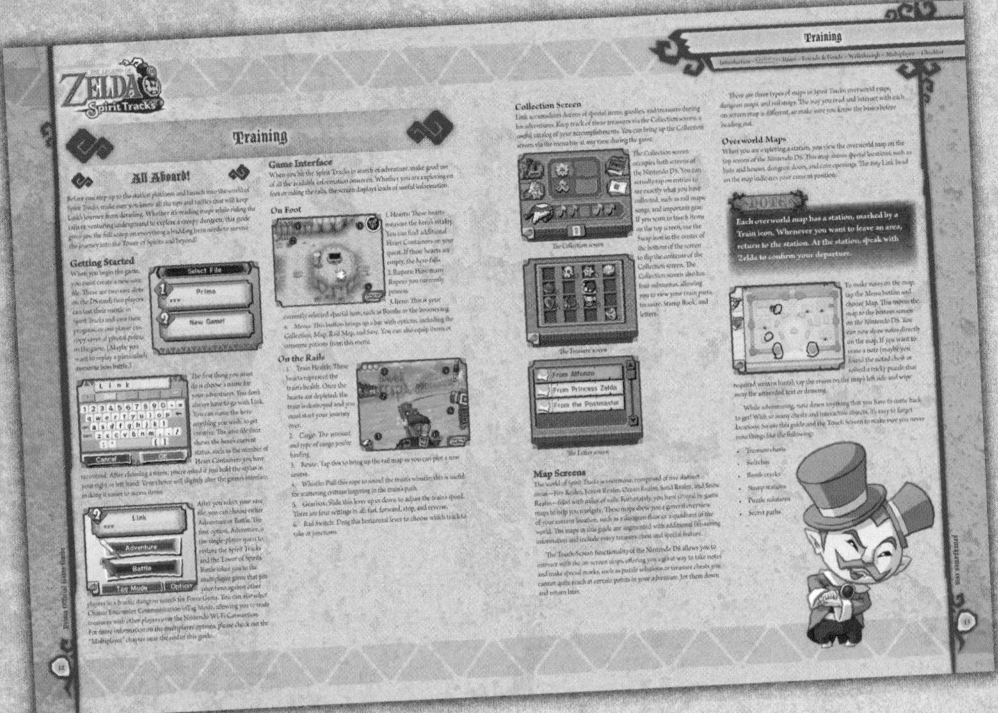

Training

Spirit Tracks features a stylus-based control scheme, and depending on whether you've played *Phantom Hourglass* before, this new method of controlling Link may take a bit of getting used to! When you grow accustomed to using the stylus, though, we think you'll agree that it's the best way to adventure on the DS. Before you sound your whistle and roll off into the world of *Spirit Tracks,* make sure to flip through our detailed training section. Here we discuss the ins and outs of the controls, along with all the major actions and interactions Link can perform.

Items

Link discovers a wide variety of wondrous and unique items as he explores his vast new world. Some items are common and found regularly, while others are unique and vital to our hero's progress. This section of the guide details every special item and tool that Link can find.

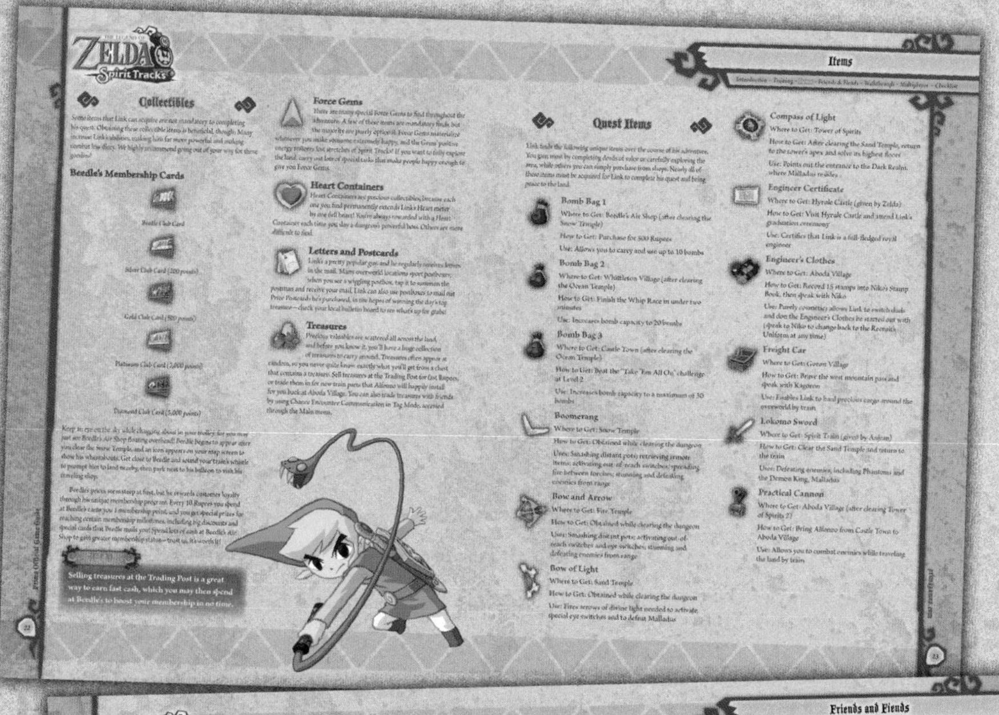

Items

Collectibles

Beedle's Membership Cards

Force Gems

Heart Containers

Letters and Postcards

Treasures

Selling treasures at the Trading Post is a great way to earn fast cash, which you may then spend at Beedle's to boost your membership in no time.

Quest Items

Bomb Bag 1

Bomb Bag 2

Bomb Bag 3

Boomerang

Bow and Arrow

Bow of Light

Compass of Light

Engineer Certificate

Engineer's Clothes

Freight Car

Lokomo Sword

Practical Cannon

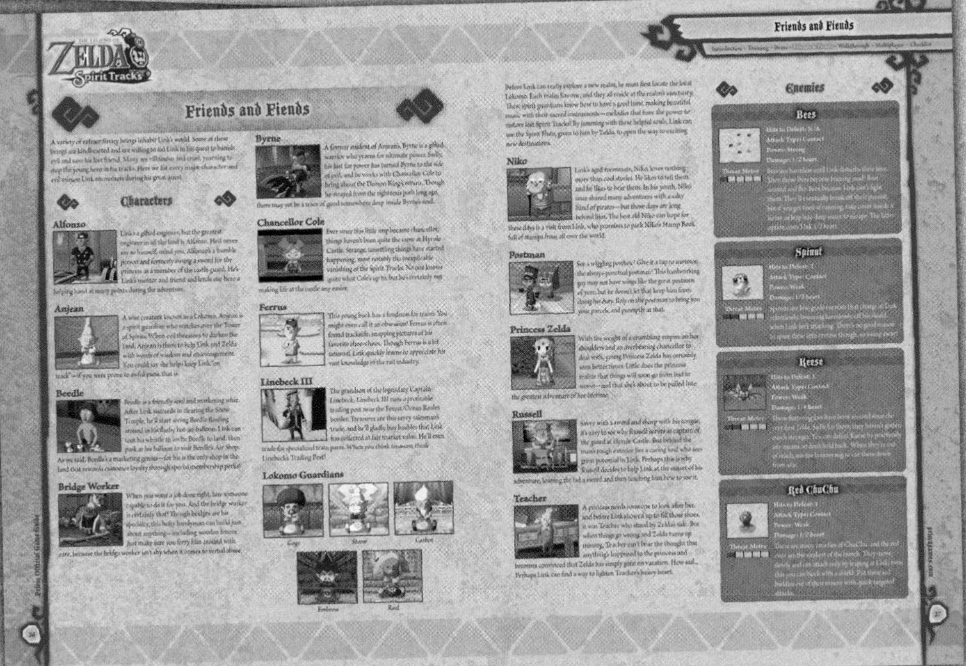

Friends and Fiends

Characters

Alfonzo

Anjean

Beedle

Bridge Worker

Byrne

Chancellor Cole

Ferrus

Linebeck III

Lokomo Guardians

Niko

Postman

Princess Zelda

Russell

Teacher

Enemies

Bees

Spinut

Keese

Red ChuChu

Friends and Fiends

The land Link calls home is populated by an assortment of extraordinary beings. Many of these beings are simple folk going about their daily lives, while others are willing to aid Link in his heroic quest. And, of course, there are plenty of villainous monsters that exist merely to stop the young hero dead in his tracks! Here we provide descriptions and information on every character and hostile entity Link encounters.

Walkthrough

The vast majority of this sizable tome is devoted to the walkthrough: a step-by-step guide through Link's second sweeping adventure on the DS! Our walkthrough provides a complete journey through Link and Zelda's epic quest, revealing all the tips and tricks you need to prevail over even the most challenging of obstacles. Because so much of what you can see and do in Link's world is purely optional, we've implemented a number of "Missing Links" sidebars to show you the best times to complete all optional side-quests and obtain every beneficial collectible. The sometimes sizable Missing Links sidebars inform you when optional tasks become available to you, while at the same time keeping these elective activities separate from the game's main path. Adventurers who aren't interested in pursuing such optional ventures can simply ignore the sidebars until they feel up to a bit of ancillary exploring!

Heart Meter

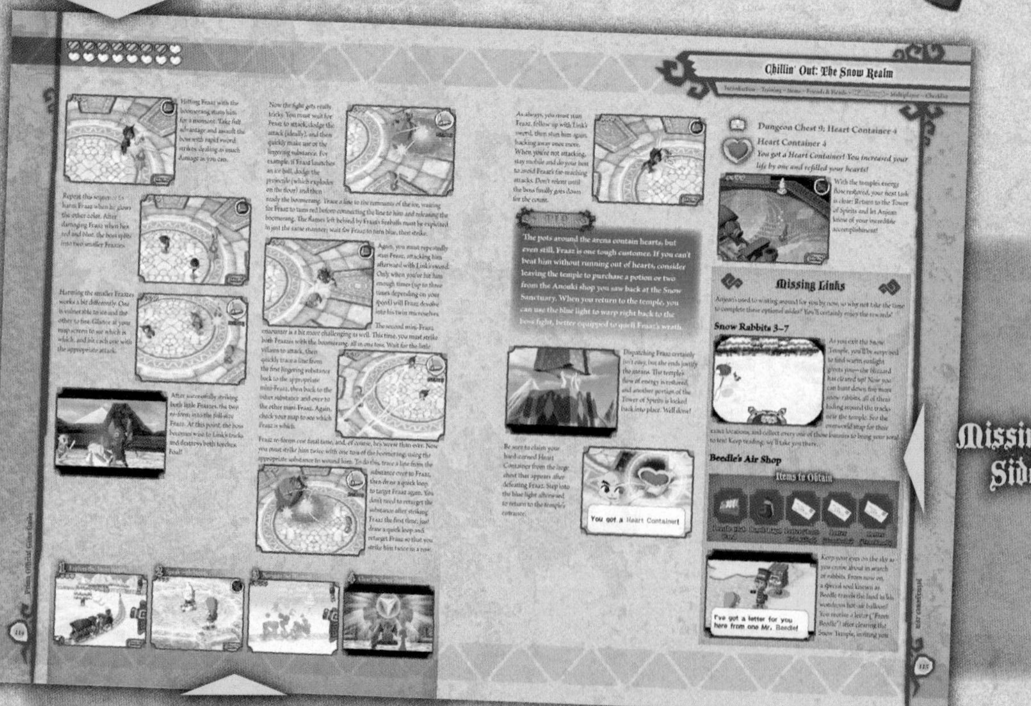

Missing Link Sidebar

Task Bar

Multiplayer

Did we mention *Spirit Tracks* contains a rich and addictive multiplayer option as well? In Battle Mode, up to four players can compete via DS Wireless Play, facing off in one of six unique stages and battling for supremacy over a collection of Force Gems. Each player controls a different Link, and it's every Link for themselves! Trigger traps, collect power-ups, and dodge those freaky Phantoms as you hoard Force Gems for the high score. It's a wild game that offers hours of laughs and challenging entertainment, and our in-depth "Multiplayer" section offers you unbeatable tips and tactics for every board.

The Legendary Checklist

With a vast land to roll through and over 20 unique stations to visit, there's plenty to see and do all across the overworld. It's easy to become lost if you aren't keeping track, so be sure to use the handy checklists at the back of the guide. Each time you accomplish a task, earn a reward, or find an important item, mark it off in the appropriate checklist. Check off everything in each of these lists to consider yourself a master explorer!

Training

All Aboard!

Before you step up to the station platform and launch into the world of *Spirit Tracks*, make sure you know all the tips and tactics that will keep Link's journey from derailing. Whether it's reading maps while riding the rails or venturing underground to explore a creepy dungeon, this guide gives you the full scoop on everything a budding hero needs to survive the journey into the Tower of Spirits and beyond!

Getting Started

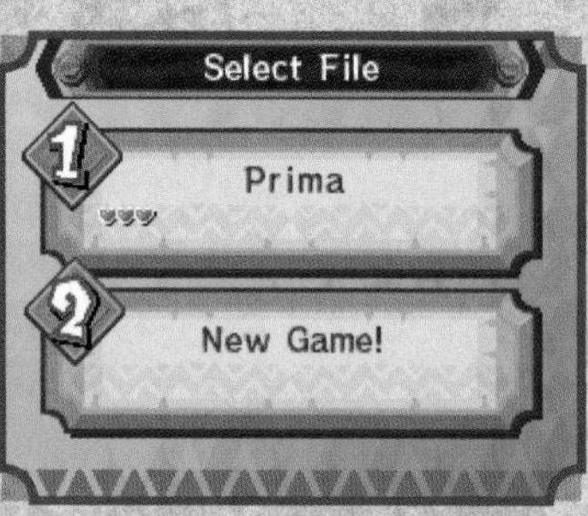

When you begin the game, you must create a new save file. There are two save slots on the DS card; two players can test their mettle in *Spirit Tracks* and save their progress, or one player can copy saves at pivotal points in the game. (Maybe you want to replay a particularly awesome boss battle.)

The first thing you must do is choose a name for your adventurer. You don't always have to go with Link. You can name the hero anything you wish, so get creative. The save file then shows the hero's current status, such as the number of Heart Containers you have recovered. After choosing a name, you're asked if you hold the stylus in your right or left hand. Your choice will slightly alter the game's interface, making it easier to access items.

After you select your save file, you can choose either Adventure or Battle. The first option, Adventure, is the single-player quest to restore the Spirit Tracks and the Tower of Spirits. Battle takes you to the multiplayer game that pits your hero against other players in a frantic dungeon search for Force Gems. You can also select Chance Encounter Communication in Tag Mode, allowing you to trade treasures with other players over the Nintendo Wi-Fi Connection. For more information on the multiplayer options, please check out the "Multiplayer" chapter near the end of this guide.

Game Interface

When you hit the Spirit Tracks in search of adventure, make good use of all the available information onscreen. Whether you are exploring on foot or riding the rails, the screen displays loads of useful information.

On Foot

1. Hearts: These hearts measure the hero's vitality. You can find additional Heart Containers on your quest. If these hearts are empty, the hero falls.
2. Rupees: How many Rupees you currently possess.
3. Item: This is your currently selected special item, such as Bombs or the boomerang.
4. Menu: This button brings up a bar with options, including the Collection, Map, Rail Map, and Save. You can also equip items or consume potions from this menu.

On the Rails

1. Train Health: These hearts represent the train's health. Once the hearts are depleted, the train is destroyed and you must start your journey over.
2. Cargo: The amount and type of cargo you're hauling.
3. Route: Tap this to bring up the rail map so you can plot a new course.
4. Whistle: Pull this rope to sound the train's whistle; this is useful for scattering critters lingering in the train's path.
5. Gearbox: Slide this lever up or down to adjust the train's speed. There are four settings in all: fast, forward, stop, and reverse.
6. Rail Switch: Drag this horizontal lever to choose which track to take at junctions.

Collection Screen

Link accumulates dozens of special items, goodies, and treasures during his adventures. Keep track of these treasures via the Collection screen, a useful catalog of your accomplishments. You can bring up the Collection screen via the menu bar at any time during the game.

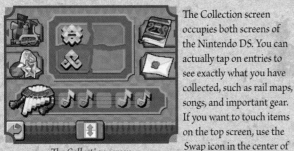

The Collection screen

The Collection screen occupies both screens of the Nintendo DS. You can actually tap on entries to see exactly what you have collected, such as rail maps, songs, and important gear. If you want to touch items on the top screen, use the Swap icon in the center of the bottom of the screen to flip the contents of the Collection screen. The Collection screen also has four submenus, allowing you to view your train parts, treasure, Stamp Book, and letters.

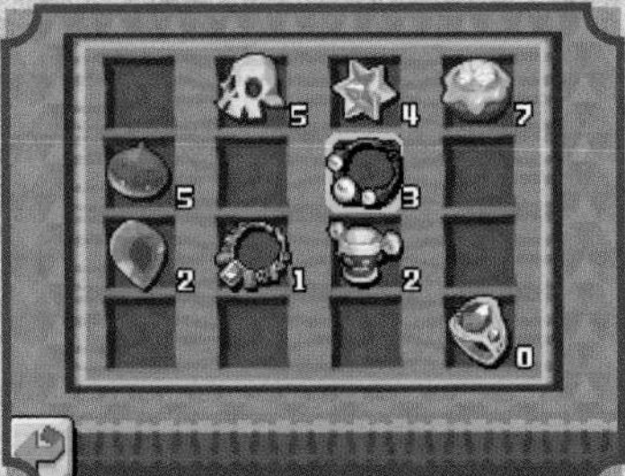

The Treasure screen

The Letter screen

Map Screens

The world of *Spirit Tracks* is enormous, comprised of five distinct areas—Fire Realm, Forest Realm, Ocean Realm, Sand Realm, and Snow Realm—filled with miles of rails. Fortunately, you have several in-game maps to help you navigate. These maps show you a general overview of your current location, such as a dungeon floor or a quadrant of the world. The maps in this guide are augmented with additional life-saving information and include every treasure chest and special feature.

The Touch-Screen functionality of the Nintendo DS allows you to interact with the on-screen maps, offering you a great way to take notes and make special marks, such as puzzle solutions or treasure chests you cannot quite reach at certain points in your adventure. Jot them down and return later.

There are three types of maps in *Spirit Tracks*: overworld maps, dungeon maps, and rail maps. The way you read and interact with each on-screen map is different, so make sure you know the basics before heading out.

Overworld Maps

When you are exploring a station, you view the overworld map on the top screen of the Nintendo DS. This map shows special locations, such as huts and houses, dungeon doors, and cave openings. The tiny Link head on the map indicates your current position.

Each overworld map has a station, marked by a Train icon. Whenever you want to leave an area, return to the station. At the station, speak with Zelda to confirm your departure.

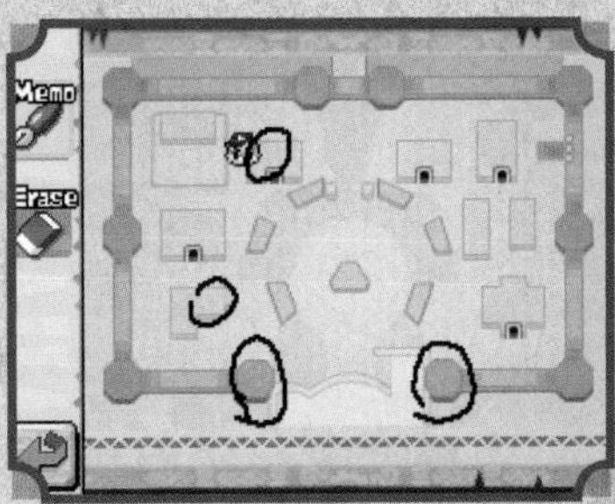

To make notes on the map, tap the Menu button and choose Map. This moves the map to the bottom screen on the Nintendo DS. You can now draw notes directly on the map. If you want to erase a note (maybe you found the noted chest or solved a tricky puzzle that required written hints), tap the eraser on the map's left side and wipe away the unneeded text or drawing.

While adventuring, note down anything that you have to come back to get! With so many chests and interactive objects, it's easy to forget locations. So use this guide and the Touch Screen to make sure you never miss things like the following:

- Treasure chests
- Switches
- Bomb cracks
- Stamp stations
- Puzzle solutions
- Secret paths

Dungeon Maps

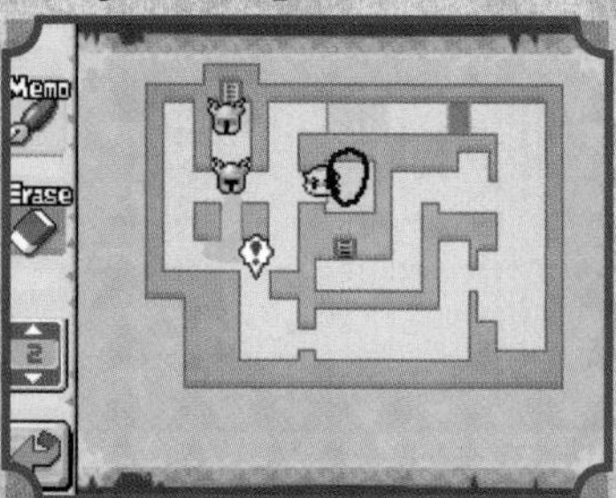

Inside a dungeon, you will see a map of the current floor on the top screen. This map shows the available exits. In the Tower of Spirits, the map shows the location of enemies like the Phantoms. Other dungeon maps do not show enemy locations, but we'll point those bad guys out for you! The dungeon maps don't show the location of switches and other interactive items, so you may want to scribble those in as you explore the dungeon—or simply rely on the maps in this guide.

To make notes on a dungeon map, select the Menu option. Choose Map to pull the dungeon map down to the lower screen. You can make and delete notes on the dungeon map the same way you do on an overworld map. However, unlike an overworld map, you can tap on the Floor label (on the left) to see the dungeon's different floors. You can view maps of only the floors you have visited. After you visit a floor for the first time, you can always see the map.

Rail Maps

Link must operate a train to travel between the world's various locations, and the rail map shows the layout of all available Spirit Tracks, helping you plot a course from point A to point B. The dark lines on the rail map represent open tracks, which are accessible to your train; the light-colored tracks are off-limits. At the start of Link's journey, only a few Spirit Tracks are available. But as the adventure continues, more tracks appear as you discover Force Gems and new rail maps.

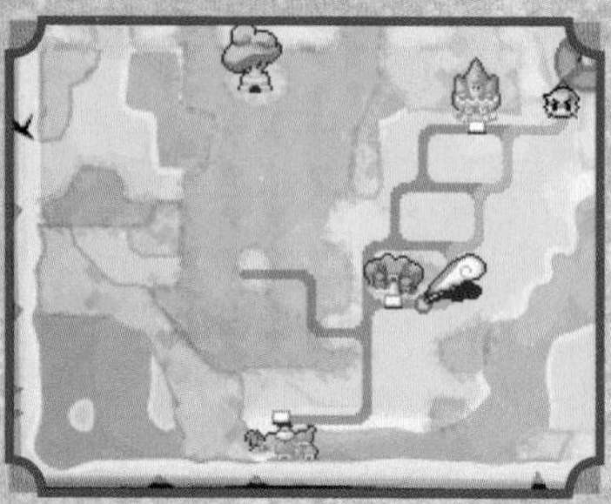

So how does the rail map work? As you leave a station, the rail map automatically appears, prompting you to plot a course. Simply use the stylus to draw the path you wish to take, starting at the purple Jewel icon and dragging it along the tracks. Your plotted route appears on the map as an orange line. Once you've plotted a route, select OK to begin the journey.

Drawing a route on the rail map automatically activates the necessary switches to reach the destination, allowing you to focus on other matters during the trip, such as obstructions or enemies. But you don't have to follow the original course. At any time, you can throw a switch and deviate from the original route; sometimes this is necessary to avoid collisions with other trains. Or if you wish to set a new course, select the Route option in the touch screen's bottom-left corner and plot a new course.

Link's Moves and Abilities

If you played *The Legend of Zelda: Phantom Hourglass*, you'll be quite familiar with the controls in *Spirit Tracks*. But if you missed out on the previous installment, you're in for a pleasant surprise. Instead of moving Link with a traditional directional pad or control, you direct the hero via the touch screen. No more pressing a button to lunge forward with a sword attack. Now you tap or draw short lines to engage the enemy. It's totally different, but within minutes, you will be well on your way to legendary hero status.

Basic Moves on Land

Movement

To make Link go, move the stylus across the touch screen. Dragging the stylus just ahead of the hero makes him move at a more measured pace. Quickly moving the stylus ahead of the hero initiates a sprint. Practice this technique at the starting location, Adoba Village. Various situations call for all sorts of movement speeds. Need to carefully negotiate a narrow bridge? Gingerly and deliberately drag the stylus right in front of Link, carefully directing him across the screen. Need to dodge an enemy's blow? Place the stylus a good distance from Link and start drawing his course well ahead. Link springs into motion, running toward the spot where you have the stylus.

CAUTION

Link cannot swim, so be careful near the edges of islands. If our hero topples into the drink, he loses half a heart.

Combat

After Link has acquired the Recruit's Sword from Hyrule Castle, he can engage enemies in battle. There are four different ways you can attack an enemy (these all become available once you acquire the sword). Each attack has its benefits and shortcomings.

- Thrust: Tap a nearby enemy to make Link perform a fast stab. This is a great way to quickly target an enemy as it gets close, but it is not Link's strongest attack.

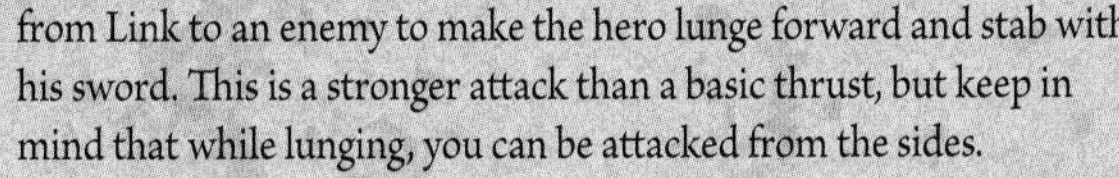

- Targeted Attack: Quickly draw a short line from Link to an enemy to make the hero lunge forward and stab with his sword. This is a stronger attack than a basic thrust, but keep in mind that while lunging, you can be attacked from the sides.
- Side Slash: Draw a short line that divides Link from a nearby enemy. Link swipes at the enemy with his sword. This is a good attack, but you leave yourself open while drawing the line.
- Spin Attack: Draw a quick circle around Link to make him spin on his heels with the sword outstretched. You will hit any enemy within range (the range is noted by a green blur along the sword's path). If you ever get surrounded, this is a great attack. However, if you use the spin attack more than three times in rapid succession, Link gets dizzy and must take a small breather. During his rest, you are completely vulnerable to attack.

As you quest, you discover which attacks are best against Link's different enemies. You can dispatch smaller foes, like Red ChuChus, with a quick stab. But against tougher monsters, like Zora Warriors, you may need stronger attacks like the lunge.

Did we say *four* attack techniques? Well, Link actually has five, but you must complete a quest for Niko to unlock the final power. However, you don't need to use a different stylus motion to unleash it.

Items

In addition to his sword and shield, Link also has a variety of special items he uses during his adventure, such as a boomerang or Bombs. If you're a *Legend of Zelda* fan, you surely have experience with many of these items, but controlling them with the Nintendo DS Touch Screen is very different from using a traditional controller.

To select an item, tap the Menu button. This brings up a bar along the screen's bottom. Tap the item you want to equip. The selected item then appears in the lower screen's upper-right corner. Tap the on-screen item icon to use the item or put it away.

You can use L and R to equip the currently selected item. The item can be easily unequipped in any instance by clicking L or R again.

Spirit Flute

You got the Spirit Flute!

Link receives the Spirit Flute from none other than Princess Zelda herself. The ornate pan flute is a prized family heirloom dating back to the origins of Hyrule. Playing the flute allows Link to reveal some of the world's most obscure secrets and treasures. During his journeys, Link is taught new songs to play on the flute, each with its own unique effect. The flute also plays a role in recharging the Spirit Tracks, allowing Link to explore new realms.

Once you equip the flute, play it by blowing into the Nintendo DS's microphone and dragging the flute horizontally with the stylus. The flute consists of different colored tubes, each producing a unique note. To play different notes, line up the orange vertical line (in the top screen) with the appropriate colored tube in the bottom screen. Once the proper tube is selected, blow into the microphone to produce the note. The various songs Link learns along the way require him to play several consecutive notes. To do this, continue blowing into the microphone while sliding the flute left or right. It's certainly a unique interface, but with some practice, playing the flute becomes second nature.

The Whirlwind

You got the Whirlwind!

The Whirlwind is one of Link's earliest discoveries, allowing him to generate a powerful cyclone. Use this to blow out torches, activate Windmill Switches, daze enemies, or repel projectiles. It can also come in handy as a clever form of propulsion—when Link is standing on a floating object, use the Whirlwind to sail in any direction.

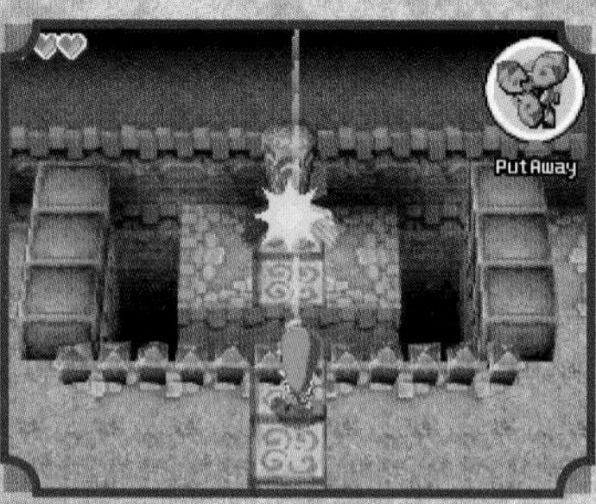

After you equip the Whirlwind, a solid yellow line appears on the screen, representing the path the Whirlwind will take once generated. Use the stylus to rotate Link and aim the Whirlwind at the intended target. When you're ready, blow into the microphone to generate the Whirlwind—once you use this item, it automatically is stowed; you must equip it to use it again. Take care when using this item, as Link is vulnerable to attacks while aiming the device. When possible, eliminate all nearby threats before giving this object a whirl.

If you're having trouble playing the Spirit Flute or operating the Whirlwind, move the DS closer to your face so you're blowing directly into the microphone.

Boomerang

You got the boomerang!
This item follows the path
you draw on the screen!

This handy item doubles as both a weapon and a retrieval device. If you throw the boomerang at a pot, it shatters it and brings back the pickup, like a heart or Rupee. As a weapon, the boomerang can be thrown to stun or dispatch an enemy depending on the strength of the target. You can also activate orbs and torches by hitting them with the boomerang.

To throw the boomerang, you can either tap the boomerang with the stylus to select it, or hold R then tap the nearest target or draw a path for the item. Draw a line from Link to the target. You can arc the boomerang around the screen—this is how you throw the boomerang behind an enemy and hit it in the back (it's an effective technique against enemies with armor). You can target multiple objects, too, by drawing a line from Link to the various targets. Maybe you need to hit four orbs to open a door? Draw the line around the room, touching each orb.

Be economical with your boomerang throws. Don't draw lengthy lines between targets unless absolutely necessary, as the boomerang can go only so far.

While throwing the boomerang, you are helpless. Be mindful of your surroundings before you let fly. Take care of enemies first, then use the boomerang to activate an orb or smash a pot.

Bombs

As soon as you get bombs, you can use them to attack foes or to blow open bomb cracks. Tapping the equipped Bomb icon raises a bomb over Link's head. Activate the bomb by throwing it or setting it down. To throw a bomb, tap the target destination. Link cannot heave a bomb across the entire screen; he can throw it only a short distance. When a bomb turns red, you know it's about to explode.

Not every bomb spot is marked with a crack. Look for discoloration or a break in scenery patterns as a hint.

You can carry only as many bombs as your Bomb Bag allows. The maximum is 30. To conserve bombs, look for bomb flowers. Tap a bomb flower to pick up the explosive and then throw it like a regular bomb.

Whip

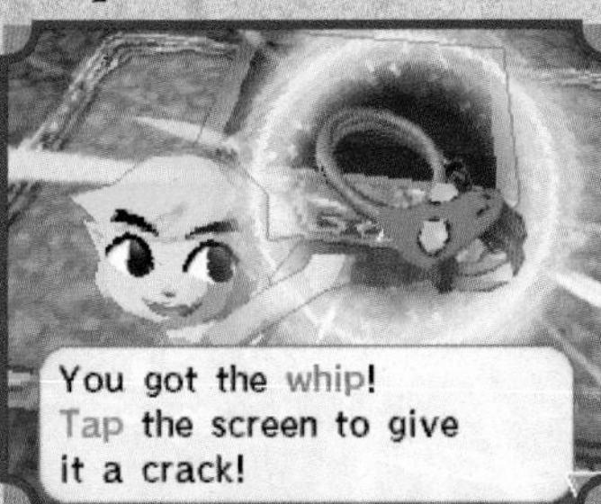

You got the whip!
Tap the screen to give it a crack!

When you're first starting out, you will notice overhead wooden posts sticking out over ledges. There is little you can do with them until you acquire the whip, at which point you can use these posts to cross gaps and access previously unreachable areas. The whip can latch on to more than just posts. Use it to activate switches, pull handles, or retrieve loose items.

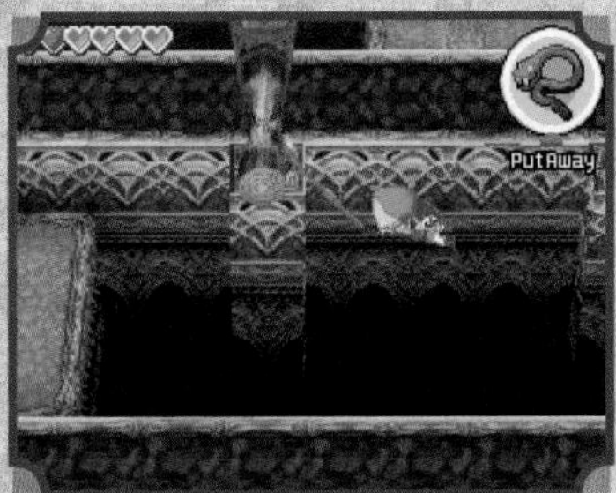

With the whip equipped, tap a post to swing across. During the swing, you can tap new posts as they appear; this allows you to latch on and continue your whip-assisted journey over pits or lava pools. The whip is a handy offensive weapon, too, capable of dazing and even eliminating some enemies. Also, look for opportunities to snatch shields from Geozards, leaving them defenseless.

Bow and Arrow

After you pick up the bow, you can shoot arrows over great distances. Use arrows to attack enemies from a safe distance or target their weak spots, such as their faces or the symbols on their backs. You can also use arrows to trigger switches. Look for eye symbols on the walls of dungeons and caves. Fire an arrow into the eye and you'll see different effects like materializing treasure chests or mysteriously appearing bridges.

To use the bow, equip it and then tap on your target. Link automatically nocks an arrow and sends it flying. Every time you tap somewhere on the screen, Link shoots an arrow in that direction. To deselect the bow, tap the bow icon in the upper-right corner.

If you're running low on arrows, look for Item Bulbs and smash them to replenish your supply.

Sand Wand

You got the Sand Wand!
Tap any sandy area to raise the sand into a wall!

When it comes to manipulating sand, there's no better tool than the Sand Wand. This item allows Link to raise walls of sand, which is useful for blocking, raising, and rolling objects. However, the wand's power over the sand is only temporary, causing the sandy walls to crumble after a few seconds. Still, it costs nothing to erect a fresh wall of sand, as the wand never runs out of power.

To harness the wand's power, equip it and simply drag the stylus over a sandy floor. As you drag, a wall of sand rises from the surface. You can even use it to raise Link to higher elevations. Simply target the sand beneath Link's feet to create a type of elevator. Or try targeting the sand beneath an object to make it roll. Mastering this skill is vital in defeating Skeldritch and solving the block puzzles at Disorientation Station.

Railway Moves

Basic Engineering

Plotting a route on the rail map is easy enough, but that's not all there is to being an engineer. It's up to you to set the train's speed and make any last-second course corrections to avoid a show-stopping collision. Start by dragging the gearbox lever on the screen's right side—think of this as the train's throttle. There are four gearbox settings: fast, forward, stop, and reverse. Trains are heavy and incapable of stopping quickly, so plan ahead and begin slowing down before you reach your destination. As you near a station platform, stop the train and let it coast the rest of the way. In some instances, it may be necessary to stop more abruptly, so set the engine in reverse to drastically reduce the forward momentum. Quick stops like this are more efficient if you're in a hurry, but it may unsettle any passengers onboard.

Need to repair your train? Simply stop at a station, then hop back on board—your train's health is fully restored! Stopping at stations is also a good way to orient your train in a new direction.

As you approach track junctions, you're prompted to choose which track to take by manipulating the horizontal switch lever at the screen's bottom. The currently selected track appears orange, making it easier to determine where you're headed. If you plotted a course on the rail map, all the switches are already set to get you to your destination. But sometimes Dark Trains and other obstacles get in your way, forcing you to detour. So keep an eye on the rail map and make any necessary course corrections as you go.

Not all obstacles are complete showstoppers, but they can still damage your train. Watch out for Moinks and other creatures lingering about the tracks ahead. If you sense an impending collision, sound the train's whistle. Early on, this is the only way to scare creatures away from the train. Sounding the train's whistle is also necessary to open warp gates and summon Beedle's balloon.

Cannon

Sometimes the whistle just isn't enough to keep your train safe. Fortunately, Alfonzo equips Link's ride with a powerful cannon. The cannon is as easy to use as the bow—simply tap your target to fire a blazing cannonball in its direction. The cannonball flies at high speed, but sometimes it's still necessary to lead your target, firing where the target is going to be instead of where it currently is. This is important when targeting fast-moving creatures. You can also use the cannon to destroy incoming projectiles fired by Tanks, Bulbins, and Cannon Boats. Simply locate and target the incoming red projectile and blast it out of the sky before it can damage your train.

In addition to shooting hostile creatures, you can also target rocks and barrels with the cannon to earn hearts and Rupees.

Passengers

From time to time, Link must ferry passengers between locations. While transporting passengers, you must exhibit your best engineering skills; otherwise you'll reach the destination with some very unhappy customers. When a passenger is on board, a Face icon appears over the train, representing the passenger's mood. Your goal is to keep the passenger smiling throughout the journey. Accomplish this by paying close attention to the signs lining the track. Some signs require you to slow down, others require you to speed up, and some prompt you to sound the whistle. As long as you do what each sign says, your passenger will remain in a good mood.

But that's not all. You must also protect your train from attack. If the train is damaged during the journey, it will adversely affect the mood of your passenger. So keep those enemy units at bay! Finally, when you approach the final destination, bring the train to a gentle stop at the station—never throw the gearbox into reverse for an emergency stop.

So what's the point of keeping your passengers happy? Some passengers merely thank Link for such a smooth ride. But others are so grateful that they hand over some Rupees or other treasures. Therefore, treat all of your passengers like the precious cargo they are; you never know what you might receive for your efforts.

Cargo

Speaking of cargo, you can also transport goods on your train once you acquire the Freight Car from the Gorons. Unlike passengers, cargo doesn't care whether you obey the rules posted on the railway signs. You can even screech to a halt without protest. However, you must still protect the train from attack. Every hit taken reduces your cargo by one unit. If you sustain too much damage, you might not have enough cargo left to fulfill a quest's requirements. Furthermore, some cargo is sensitive to certain environments: Ice melts when transported outside the Snow Realm, and Dark Ore disintegrates when exposed to prolonged sunlight. When hauling such volatile cargo, it's even more important to protect your train from attack—even if you arrive at your destination untouched, you'll still end up with less cargo than you began the trip with.

Warp Gates

Need to get somewhere fast? Consider using one of the many warp gates to magically transport your train from one realm to another. These gates encircle certain pieces of track, but they won't function until activated. To activate a gate, fire your cannon at the green triangle at the top. This turns the triangle yellow, indicating that the gate is operational. For each pair of gates, there is one gate that you must activate before commencing warp travel. If you come across a gate that has no triangle at the top, it can't be activated—you must find and activate its corresponding gate elsewhere. Once a gate is activated, roll toward it and blow the train's whistle to trigger a yellow warp portal. Zoom directly into the portal to warp your train to a different realm.

Warp-gate travel is essential when undertaking time-sensitive quests such as when transporting ice or Dark Ore.

Rabbit Rescue

As the name implies, the Rabbit Rescue (in the Forest Realm) is a refuge for rabbits. Upon visiting this location and speaking with its eccentric proprietor, you're given a rabbit net that you will use to collect rabbits during your journey. While traveling along the rails, look out for rabbit ears poking over the tops of rocks or barrels. Take this as your cue to blast away the rabbit's hiding spot with your cannon—don't worry, you won't injure the rabbit. Once the rabbit is on the run, a minigame begins tasking you with catching a rabbit in your net. These little creatures hop around in predictable patterns, so study their movements before attempting to drop the net on them. But you have only 10 seconds to catch the rabbit, so don't wait too long. There are a total of 50 loose rabbits scattered throughout the world, so keep your eyes peeled. Once you've captured a few rabbits, return to the Rabbit Rescue for a reward. Capture them all to receive the Sword Beam!

Interactive Objects

As you explore the world, you interact with a host of objects, such as doors and switches. Many of these objects are quite familiar to *Legend of Zelda* fans. (Everybody knows you slash through grass to discover hidden Rupees and hearts, right?) Some objects require further explanation.

Common Interactions

Cutting grass reveals hidden Rupees and hearts.

Lift pots or rocks to throw them at enemies or break them apart. You can also strike pots to shatter them and reveal hidden goodies.

Just tap a treasure chest to make Link open it and claim the prize inside.

Tap a movable object like a block to make Link grab it. Then tap the arrow indicating the direction you wish to push or pull it.

Switches are often connected to puzzles or hazards. For example, striking a switch can lower spikes or make an invisible treasure chest appear.

Walk over floor switches to trigger them.

Hey, Link!
Today's your graduation ceremony, right?

Tap on people to initiate a conversation.

Tap on wall maps to read the inscriptions and then copy them to your own maps.

Locked Doors

Throughout your dungeon exploration, you stumble across locked doors that halt your progress. You must find Small Keys to open these doors. Small Keys are sometimes dropped by enemies or stashed inside treasure chests. After you retrieve a Small Key, you can open a locked door. However, Small Keys can be used only once—so once you unlock a door, the key is lost forever.

Boss Key blocks are tougher obstacles that lock you out of boss lairs. These require special Boss Keys that are typically hidden deep inside a dungeon. Boss Keys are heftier than Small Keys. You must carry the Boss Key overhead as you traverse the dungeon to the Boss Key block. While holding the key, you cannot attack or defend yourself. If you encounter an enemy, tap the screen to drop the Boss Key. Now you can fight. When the battle is over, tap the Boss Key to pick it up again and resume your travel to the Boss Key block. Tap on the block to toss the key inside.

Postboxes

Almost every station has a bright red postbox. When you have mail waiting for you, the postbox bounces back and forth, almost like it's waving hello. Tap on the postbox and the postman flutters in to deliver your special letter. Some letters are just cordial greetings or notes containing useful quest information, but some island citizens send you presents to show gratitude.

Stamp Stations

Once you acquire Niko's Stamp Book, you can interact with these stations. There are 20 stamp stations in all, each possessing a unique stamp. After tapping the station, the book opens and prompts you to place a new stamp on a blank page. Tap a blank page in the Stamp Book to mark the page with a colorful design—the date also appears beneath each stamp. Flip through the pages in the book to view all the stamps you've collected—and be sure to show Niko too!

Force Gems

In *Spirit Tracks*, Force Gems are generated by pure happiness. So go out of your way to please everyone you encounter. This often requires you to perform some task, such as transporting a passenger or cargo. Once a Force Gem is generated, a new set of Spirit Tracks becomes accessible somewhere in the world. To unlock all the tracks, you must collect all 20 Force Gems.

Air Stones

These odd-looking statues emit tiny colorful orbs of light, hinting at the tune it wishes you to play on your Spirit Flute. Memorize the colors, then play the same tune on the Spirit Flute to learn a new song. There are five songs to learn in all, each with its own unique power. Here's a quick rundown of the songs:

- Song of Awakening: Play to awaken a Gossip Stone
- Song of Healing: Restores health
- Song of Birds: Call a bird and hitch a ride to reach a higher elevation
- Song of Discovery: Causes long-lost treasures to rise to the surface
- Song of Light: Illuminates crystals, pointing the way to secrets

Gossip Stones

These statues closely resemble Air Stones, but they serve an entirely different purpose. Before you can interact with these statues, you must first wake them up by playing the Song of Awakening on your Spirit Flute. Once awake, the statue will offer valuable clues, sometimes even revealing the locations of all hidden treasure chests on a dungeon floor.

In most dungeons, you can find a Gossip Stone on each floor that tells you how many treasure chests are still on the floor. This information isn't free, though. These statues charge Rupees for their secrets, so if you pony up for the goods, make sure you write down the hidden chest locations. Of course, we call out every treasure chest on the maps in this guide, so feel free to save your Rupees....

Blue Light

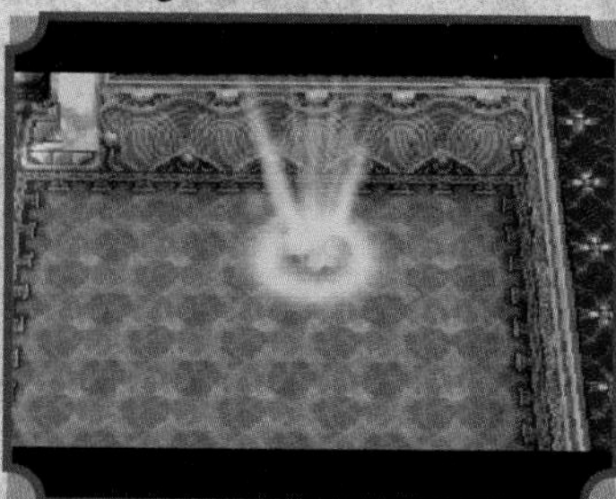

When you reach certain milestones inside a dungeon, such as the room just before the boss lair, you uncover blue circles of light. These circles are warps that take you back to the dungeon entrance. When you warp to the starting point, another blue light is waiting to send you back to the bottom of the dungeon. Use these blue lights to shop for useful potions or replenish spent items (like bombs or arrows) before going into battle against a fearsome boss.

Lava Geysers

On their own, these violent eruptions of lava aren't much of a help. In fact, it's best to stay away from them. But if you happen to find a stone disc, these geysers can serve as a makeshift elevator. Simply toss the stone disc onto the geyser, then hop aboard for a quick ride skyward.

Arrow Aimers

These tricky devices are capable of catching an arrow shot from your bow and redirecting it in a new direction. This is useful when trying to hit eye switches and other objects that Link doesn't have a direct line of sight on. Arrow aimers can be relocated and rotated, allowing for a variety of different firing configurations. Try setting up multiple arrow aimers to pull off some truly remarkable trick shots.

Items

Link discovers all manner of unique and wondrous items as he explores his vast new world. This chapter details every special item and tool the young hero can find.

Refer to the "Legendary Checklist" portion of this guide for handy checklists of all items and collectibles in *Spirit Tracks*. Use them to keep track of everything you've found and to quickly locate goodies you may have missed!

Common Items

Some items are found all over the place. Link commonly discovers items when smashing pots, rocks, and barrels and when cutting down tall grass and slaying evil monsters. He can also purchase common items from shops and vendors he meets in his travels.

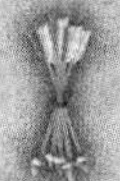

Arrows

Arrows provide ammunition for the bow. You can't use one without the other!

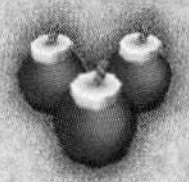

Bombs

Bombs are optional throughout most of the adventure, but toward the end, you need them to progress. Once you've scored a Bomb Bag (see the "Quest Items" section for details), you'll be able to carry and use bombs, and you'll occasionally find bombs while breaking pots and such. You can also buy bombs from shops.

Rupees

Rupees are big, shiny pieces of currency. Link keeps them safe in his wallet, and he can hold *a lot* of Rupees in there! Here's what each one's worth:

 Green = 1 Rupee

 Big Green = 100 Rupees

 Blue = 5 Rupees

 Big Red = 200 Rupees

 Red = 20 Rupees

 Big Gold = 300 Rupees

Dungeon Items

The following items are primarily found within dungeons, dark places filled with danger that Link must brave to bring peace to his world. Any temple or structure that's more complex than a simple house or cavern is considered a dungeon in this guide.

Boss Key

Nearly every dungeon features a Boss Key. These giant items are too big for Link to stash in his pack, so he must carry them overhead instead! Bring a dungeon's Boss Key to its Boss Key door (a giant, scary-looking block), and then tap the door to make Link heave the key into it, thereby removing the obstacle. If danger lurks nearby, tap the touch screen to make Link set down or toss a Boss Key so that he may draw his sword.

Small Key

Small Keys are common and exist within most dungeons. Link stores these items on his person and uses them to open locked doors within the dungeon; simply tap a locked door to open it. Once used, a Small Key is removed from Link's inventory. Any Small Keys Link is carrying are shown at the lower-right corner of the map screen.

Tear of Light

Each section of the Tower of Spirits features three Tears of Light that you must collect to power up Link's sword. Once you've obtained all three Tears, Link can strike a Phantom in the back, stunning it so Zelda can possess the creature. After Link obtains the Lokomo Sword, he no longer needs to use Tears of Light—the sword itself is infused with divine energy.

 Collectibles 

Some items that Link can acquire are not mandatory to completing his quest. Obtaining these collectible items is beneficial, though: Many increase Link's abilities, making him far more powerful and making combat less dicey. We highly recommend going out of your way for these goodies!

Beedle's Membership Cards

Beedle Club Card

Silver Club Card (200 points)

Gold Club Card (500 points)

Platinum Club Card (2,000 points)

Diamond Club Card (5,000 points)

Keep an eye on the sky while chugging about in your trolley, for you may just see Beedle's Air Shop floating overhead! Beedle begins to appear after you clear the Snow Temple, and an icon appears on your map screen to show his whereabouts. Get close to Beedle and sound your train's whistle to prompt him to land nearby, then park next to his balloon to visit his traveling shop.

Beedle's prices seem steep at first, but he rewards customer loyalty through his unique membership program. Every 10 Rupees you spend at Beedle's earns you 1 membership point, and you get special prizes for reaching certain membership milestones, including big discounts and special cards that Beedle mails you! Spend lots of cash at Beedle's Air Shop to gain greater membership status—trust us, it's worth it!

Selling treasures at the Trading Post is a great way to earn fast cash, which you may then spend at Beedle's to boost your membership in no time.

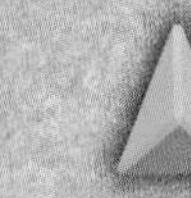

Force Gems

There are many special Force Gems to find throughout the adventure. A few of these items are mandatory finds, but the majority are purely optional. Force Gems materialize whenever you make someone extremely happy, and the Gems' positive energy restores lost stretches of Spirit Tracks! If you want to fully explore the land, carry out lots of special tasks that make people happy enough to give you Force Gems.

Heart Containers

Heart Containers are precious collectibles, because each one you find permanently extends Link's Heart meter by one full heart! You're always rewarded with a Heart Container each time you slay a dungeon's powerful boss. Others are more difficult to find.

Letters and Postcards

Link's a pretty popular guy, and he regularly receives letters in the mail. Many overworld locations sport postboxes; when you see a wiggling postbox, tap it to summon the postman and receive your mail. Link can also use postboxes to mail out Prize Postcards he's purchased, in the hopes of winning the day's top treasure—check your local bulletin board to see what's up for grabs!

Treasures

Precious valuables are scattered all across the land, and before you know it, you'll have a huge collection of treasures to carry around. Treasures often appear at random, so you never quite know exactly what you'll get from a chest that contains a treasure. Sell treasures at the Trading Post for fast Rupees, or trade them in for new train parts that Alfonzo will happily install for you back at Aboda Village. You can also trade treasures with friends by using Chance Encounter Communication in Tag Mode, accessed through the Main menu.

Quest Items

Link finds the following unique items over the course of his adventure. You gain most by completing deeds of valor or carefully exploring the area, while others you can simply purchase from shops. Nearly all of these items must be acquired for Link to complete his quest and bring peace to the land.

Bomb Bag 1

Where to Get: Beedle's Air Shop (after clearing the Snow Temple)

How to Get: Purchase for 500 Rupees

Use: Allows you to carry and use up to 10 bombs

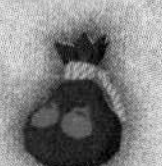

Bomb Bag 2

Where to Get: Whittleton Village (after clearing the Ocean Temple)

How to Get: Finish the Whip Race in under two minutes

Use: Increases bomb capacity to 20 bombs

Bomb Bag 3

Where to Get: Castle Town (after clearing the Ocean Temple)

How to Get: Beat the "Take 'Em All On" challenge at Level 2

Use: Increases bomb capacity to a maximum of 30 bombs

Boomerang

Where to Get: Snow Temple

How to Get: Obtained while clearing the dungeon

Uses: Smashing distant pots; retrieving remote items; activating out-of-reach switches; spreading fire between torches; stunning and defeating enemies from range

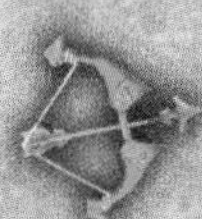

Bow and Arrow

Where to Get: Fire Temple

How to Get: Obtained while clearing the dungeon

Uses: Smashing distant pots; activating out-of-reach switches and eye switches; stunning and defeating enemies from range

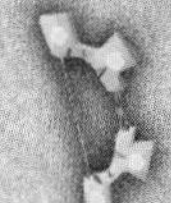

Bow of Light

Where to Get: Sand Temple

How to Get: Obtained while clearing the dungeon

Use: Fires arrows of divine light needed to activate special eye switches and to defeat Malladus

Compass of Light

Where to Get: Tower of Spirits

How to Get: After clearing the Sand Temple, return to the tower's apex and solve its highest floors

Use: Points out the entrance to the Dark Realm, where Malladus resides

Engineer Certificate

Where to Get: Hyrule Castle (given by Zelda)

How to Get: Visit Hyrule Castle and attend Link's graduation ceremony

Use: Certifies that Link is a full-fledged royal engineer

Engineer's Clothes

Where to Get: Aboda Village

How to Get: Record 15 stamps into Niko's Stamp Book, then speak with Niko

Use: Purely cosmetic; allows Link to switch duds and don the Engineer's Clothes he started out with (speak to Niko to change back to the Recruit's Uniform at any time)

Freight Car

Where to Get: Goron Village

How to Get: Brave the west mountain pass and speak with Kagoron

Use: Enables Link to haul precious cargo around the overworld by train

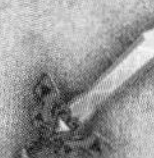

Lokomo Sword

Where to Get: Spirit Train (given by Anjean)

How to Get: Clear the Sand Temple and return to the train

Uses: Defeating enemies, including Phantoms and the Demon King, Malladus

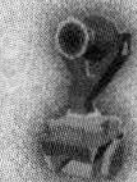

Practical Cannon

Where to Get: Aboda Village (after clearing Tower of Spirits 2)

How to Get: Bring Alfonzo from Castle Town to Aboda Village

Use: Allows you to combat enemies while traveling the land by train

Prize Postcard

Where to Get: Various shops

How to Get: Buy with Rupees (usually 100 for 10 cards)

Use: Mail these at a postbox for a chance to win the treasures of the day (check a town's bulletin board to see what's available)

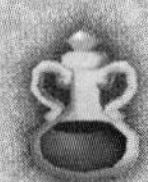

Purple Potion

Where to Get: Various shops

How to Get: Buy with Rupees (usually costs 150)

Use: Restores up to eight of Link's hearts; automatically used when Link is about to fall in battle

Quiver 1

Where to Get: Goron Village (after clearing the Fire Temple)

How to Get: Purchase from shop for 2,000 Rupees

Use: Increases arrow capacity to 30 arrows

Quiver 2

Where to Get: Pirate Hideout (after rescuing the Papuchia prisoner)

How to Get: Earn less than 4,000 points when replaying the challenge

Use: Increases arrow capacity to 50 arrows

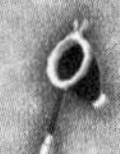

Rabbit Net

Where to Get: Rabbitland Rescue

How to Get: Speak with the rescue's owner and agree to hunt for rabbits

Use: Allows you to catch trackside rabbits

Rail Maps
(Fire, Forest, Ocean, and Snow)

Where to Get: Tower of Spirits

How to Get: Scale the tower, section by section

Use: Each rail map reveals lost Spirit Tracks to its associated realm

Recruit's Sword

Where to Get: Hyrule Castle (given by guard captain)

How to Get: Speak with Russell, the guard captain, after Zelda's suggestion

Uses: Defeating monsters; activating statues and switches; cutting tall grass and skinny trees, etc.

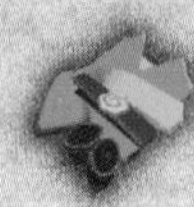

Recruit's Uniform

Where to Get: Hyrule Castle

How to Get: Given by Zelda during secret meeting following Link's graduation ceremony

Use: Allows Link to blend in with the castle's guards, facilitating Zelda's escape

Red Potion

Where to Get: Various shops

How to Get: Buy with Rupees (amount varies)

Use: Restores up to six of Link's hearts when used

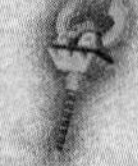

Sand Wand

Where to Get: Sand Temple

How to Get: Obtained while clearing the dungeon

Use: Raises walls of sand that help Link overcome obstacles in a variety of ways

Shield of Antiquity

Where to Get: Aboda Village

How to Get: Collect 10 stamps for Niko, then speak with him

Use: Allows Link to wield a more antiquated-looking shield (speak to Niko to change back to the Wooden Shield at any time), cannot be eaten by Like Likes.

Song of Awakening

Where to Get: Forest Sanctuary

How to Get: Mimic the Air Stone's melody on the Spirit Flute

Use: Play near Gossip Stones to wake them and chat

Song of Birds

Where to Get: Papuchia Village

How to Get: Mimic the Air Stone's melody on the Spirit Flute

Use: Play near birds and Cuccos to attract them to you

Song of Discovery

Where to Get: Anouki Village

How to Get: Mimic the Air Stone's melody on the Spirit Flute

Use: Play to reveal nearby hidden objects

Song of Healing

Where to Get: Forest Temple

How to Get: On the Spirit Flute, mimic the Air Stone's melody near the entrance

Use: Play in any dungeon to summon a fairy that fully restores Link's health, but only one time

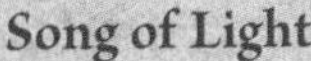

Song of Light

Where to Get: Trading Post

How to Get: Mimic the Air Stone's melody on the Spirit Flute

Use: Play to activate dark crystals, causing them to light up and emit guiding laser beams

Spirit Flute

Where to Get: Hyrule Castle

How to Get: Given by Zelda after she becomes a spirit

Uses: Equip and blow into the microphone to sound the instrument's color-coded notes, completing songs and melodies for a variety of purposes throughout the adventure

Stamp Book

Where to Get: Aboda Village (after Tower of Spirits 2)

How to Get: Speak with Niko after bringing Alfonzo home

Use: Allows you to record stamps from stamp stations you discover on your journey

Swordsman's Scroll 1

Where to Get: Rabbitland Rescue

How to Get: Catch all 50 rabbits and speak to the rescue's owner

Use: Grants Link the Sword Beam ability, which causes beams of energy to fly out from his sword

Swordsman's Scroll 2

Where to Get: Aboda Village

How to Get: Plant all 20 stamps into Niko's Stamp Book, then return to Niko

Use: Grants Link the great spin attack, a very powerful but exhausting maneuver

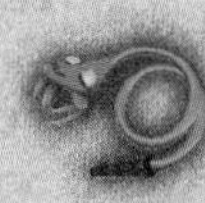

Whip

Where to Get: Ocean Temple

How to Get: Obtained while clearing the dungeon

Uses: Yanking on handles; swinging on overhead posts; retrieving out-of-reach items; stunning and defeating enemies from medium range

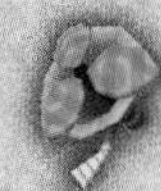

The Whirlwind

Where to Get: Forest Temple

How to Get: Obtained while clearing the dungeon

Uses: Blowing enemies away and stunning them; clearing out poisonous fog; blowing distant objects into easy reach; casting objects into other objects; blowing out torches

Wooden Shield

Where to Get: Sold at various shops

How to Get: Buy for 80 Rupees

Use: Automatically defends against weak frontal attacks just by holding it

Yellow Potion

Where to Get: Papuchia Village shop

How to Get: Buy for 200 Rupees

Use: Restores all of Link's hearts when used

Friends and Fiends

A variety of extraordinary beings inhabit Link's world. Some of these beings are kindhearted and are willing to aid Link in his quest to banish evil and save his lost friend. Many are villainous and cruel, yearning to stop the young hero in his tracks. Here we list every major character and evil minion Link encounters during his great quest.

Characters

Alfonzo

Link's a gifted engineer, but the greatest engineer in all the land is Alfonzo. He'd never say so himself, mind you. Alfonzo's a humble person and formerly swung a sword for the princess as a member of the castle guard. He's Link's mentor and friend and lends our hero a helping hand at many points during the adventure.

Anjean

A wise creature known as a Lokomo, Anjean is a spirit guardian who watches over the Tower of Spirits. When evil threatens to darken the land, Anjean is there to help Link and Zelda with words of wisdom and encouragement. You could say she helps keep Link "on track"—if you were prone to awful puns, that is.

Beedle

Beedle is a friendly soul and marketing whiz. After Link succeeds in clearing the Snow Temple, he'll start seeing Beedle floating around in his flashy hot-air balloon. Link can toot his whistle to invite Beedle to land, then park at his balloon to visit Beedle's Air Shop. As we said, Beedle's a marketing genius—for his is the only shop in the land that rewards customer loyalty through special membership perks!

Bridge Worker

When you want a job done right, hire someone capable to do it for you. And the bridge worker is certainly that! Though bridges are his specialty, this hefty handyman can build just about anything—including wooden fences. Just make sure you ferry him around with care, because the bridge worker isn't shy when it comes to verbal abuse.

Byrne

A former student of Anjean's, Byrne is a gifted warrior who yearns for ultimate power. Sadly, his lust for power has turned Byrne to the side of evil, and he works with Chancellor Cole to bring about the Demon King's return. Though he strayed from the righteous path long ago, there may yet be a trace of good somewhere deep inside Byrne's soul.

Chancellor Cole

Ever since this little imp became chancellor, things haven't been quite the same at Hyrule Castle. Strange, unsettling things have started happening, most notably the inexplicable vanishing of the Spirit Tracks. No one knows quite what Cole's up to, but he's certainly not making life at the castle any easier.

Ferrus

This young buck has a fondness for trains. You might even call it an obsession! Ferrus is often found trackside, snapping pictures of his favorite choo-choos. Though Ferrus is a bit unusual, Link quickly learns to appreciate his vast knowledge of the rail industry.

Linebeck III

The grandson of the legendary Captain Linebeck, Linebeck III runs a profitable trading post near the Forest/Ocean Realm border. Treasures are this savvy salesman's trade, and he'll gladly buy baubles that Link has collected at fair market value. He'll even trade for specialized train parts. When you think treasure, think Linebeck's Trading Post!

Lokomo Guardians

Gage

Steem

Carben

Embrose

Rael

Before Link can really explore a new realm, he must first locate the local Lokomo. Each realm has one, and they all reside at the realm's sanctuary. These spirit guardians know how to have a good time, making beautiful music with their sacred instruments—melodies that have the power to restore lost Spirit Tracks! By jamming with these helpful souls, Link can use the Spirit Flute, given to him by Zelda, to open the way to exciting new destinations.

Niko

Link's aged roommate, Niko, loves nothing more than cool stories. He likes to tell them, and he likes to hear them. In his youth, Niko once shared many adventures with a salty band of pirates—but those days are long behind him. The best old Niko can hope for these days is a visit from Link, who promises to pack Niko's Stamp Book full of stamps from all over the world.

Postman

See a wiggling postbox? Give it a tap to summon the always-punctual postman! This hardworking guy may not have wings like the great postmen of yore, but he doesn't let that keep him from doing his duty. Rely on the postman to bring you your parcels, and promptly at that.

Princess Zelda

With the weight of a crumbling empire on her shoulders and an overbearing chancellor to deal with, young Princess Zelda has certainly seen better times. Little does the princess realize that things will soon go from bad to worse—and that she's about to be pulled into the greatest adventure of her lifetime.

Russell

Savvy with a sword and sharp with his tongue, it's easy to see why Russell serves as captain of the guard at Hyrule Castle. But behind the man's rough exterior lies a caring soul who sees great potential in Link. Perhaps this is why Russell decides to help Link at the outset of his adventure, loaning the lad a sword and then teaching him how to use it.

Teacher

A princess needs someone to look after her, and before Link showed up to fill those shoes, it was Teacher who stood by Zelda's side. But when things go wrong and Zelda turns up missing, Teacher can't bear the thought that anything's happened to the princess and becomes convinced that Zelda has simply gone on vacation. How sad... Perhaps Link can find a way to lighten Teacher's heavy heart.

Enemies

Bees

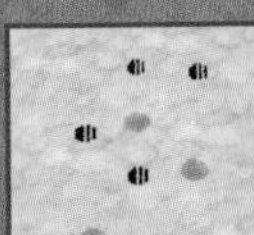

Threat Meter

Hits to Defeat: N/A
Attack Type: Contact
Power: Strong
Damage: 1/2 heart

Bees are harmless until Link disturbs their hive. Then those Bees become buzzing mad! Run around and flee Bees, because Link can't fight them. They'll eventually break off their pursuit, but if you get tired of running, take cover inside a house or leap into deep water to escape. The latter option costs Link 1/2 heart.

Spinut

Threat Meter

Hits to Defeat: 2
Attack Type: Contact
Power: Weak
Damage: 1/2 heart

Spinuts are low-grade enemies that charge at Link relentlessly, bouncing harmlessly off his shield when Link isn't attacking. There's no good reason to spare these little cretins, though, so swing away!

Keese

Threat Meter

Hits to Defeat: 1
Attack Type: Contact
Power: Weak
Damage: 1/4 heart

These fluttering foes have been around since the very first *Zelda*. Sadly for them, they haven't gotten much stronger. You can defeat Keese by practically any means, so don't hold back. When they're out of reach, use the boomerang to cut them down from afar.

Red ChuChu

Threat Meter

Hits to Defeat: 1
Attack Type: Contact
Power: Weak
Damage: 1/2 heart

There are many varieties of ChuChu, and the red ones are the weakest of the bunch. They move slowly and can attack only by leaping at Link; even this you can block with a shield. Put these sad baddies out of their misery with quick targeted attacks.

Rat

Hits to Defeat: 1
Attack Type: Contact
Power: Weak
Damage: 1/2 heart

Threat Meter

Zelda gets a good scare from Rats, who often creep out from holes in the walls. Though fast and frightening to the princess, Rats pose little threat to Link. Come to your maiden's rescue, valiant hero, and slay the foul beasts with righteous steel.

Phantom

Hits to Defeat: 1 (with powered-up sword)
Attack Type: Contact
Power: Strong
Damage: 1 heart

Threat Meter

Phantoms are giant armored guardians entrusted with the Tower of Spirit's security. The Demon King's servants have possessed these noble soldiers, however, and they now serve to hinder Link's progress. Should a Phantom spy Link, it chases him down with great speed and focus. Flee to a safe zone, where Phantoms cannot travel. Collect three Tears of Light from each section of the tower to power up Link's sword; then attack a Phantom from behind to stun it. Zelda can possess any Phantom Link stuns; simply tap the brute to have the princess take control.

Crow

Hits to Defeat: 1
Attack Type: Contact
Power: Strong
Damage: 1/2 heart

Threat Meter

Heads-up: Dangerous Crows often lurk in the treetops, ready to swoop down and strike. These annoying birds steal Link's Rupees, so don't let them get too close! Though you can defeat Crows by many methods, they're fast and tough to target. It's usually best to simply outmaneuver Crows—they're quick to give up the chase.

Vengas

Hits to Defeat: 1
Attack Type: Contact
Power: Weak
Damage: 1/2 heart

Threat Meter

Vengas live in the Forest Temple. They take just one hit to defeat and bounce harmlessly off Link's shield. However, Vengas leave a cloud of noxious poison behind when they're defeated—don't touch the stuff! If necessary, use the Enginee to blow the stuff away.

Bubble

Hits to Defeat: 1
Attack Type: Contact
Power: Strong
Damage: 1/2 heart

Threat Meter

Bubbles don't aggressively pursue Link, but they're also resistant to his sword. Use the Whirlwind to stun and ground these frothing foes; then tap their flapping skulls to finish them off with Link's steel.

Mothula

Hits to Defeat: Multiple
Attack Type: Contact
Power: Strong
Damage: 1/2 heart

Threat Meter

The Mothula is a foe with unique attacks. Wait for a Mothula to spawn a Bubble, then quickly cast out a cyclone to catch the Bubble and send it crashing back into its creator. This stuns the fiend; rush forward and give it a thrashing with Link's blade.

Don't fire cyclones at a Mothula when no Bubbles are about, because vacant cyclones rebound off the Mothula, heading back toward Link! Drop the Whirlwind quickly and flee when you see a cyclone coming your way.

Blastworm

Threat Meter

Hits to Defeat: 1
Attack Type: Contact
Power: Weak
Damage: 1/2 heart

Creepy crawlers known as Blastworms reside in the Forest Temple. Strike one with Link's sword to make it curl up into a spiky ball that's dangerous to touch. Once curled, a Blastworm is moments away from detonating, just like a bomb. Use the Whirlwind to knock these beasts into remote switches, bomb blocks, and enemies for explosive results!

Key Master

Threat Meter

Hits to Defeat: 3
Attack Type: Contact
Power: Strong
Damage: 1/2 heart

Beware when carrying a Boss Key around: There's a good chance that vile Key Masters will appear! When Key Masters materialize, tap anywhere near Link to set down the Boss Key; then attack the villains without mercy. The Key Masters' goal is to capture the Boss Key and return it to its holding chamber, so don't let them past your guard. The creatures aren't all that difficult to defeat if you're quick with your swordplay.

Octorok

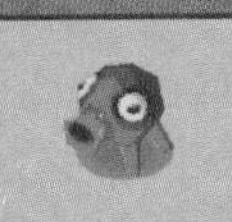

Threat Meter

Hits to Defeat: 2
Attack Type: Contact and Range
Power: Weak
Damage: 1/2 heart

These classic baddies have been around since the dawn of *Zelda*. They strut about and spit rocks from their snouts at high speed. Block their projectiles with Link's shield, and hack these minor threats apart once you've closed in.

Geozard

Threat Meter

Hits to Defeat: Multiple
Attack Type: Sword
Power: Strong
Damage: 1/2 heart

These formidable fish-folk are well versed in the use of sword and shield. Geozards block all frontal attacks until Link tears their shield away with his trusty whip, making them vulnerable. But until Link finds the whip, he and Phantom Zelda must work together to penetrate these villains' defenses. First, have Zelda engage a Geozard by tracing a line between her and the creature. While the Zora's attention is focused on battling Zelda, Link can slip around behind the monster and assault its vulnerable backside.

Mounted Miniblin

Threat Meter

Hits to Defeat: 1
Attack Type: Spikes
Power: Strong
Damage: 1/2 heart

These high-riding Miniblins cruise around atop giant Armos statues, making for a truly peculiar sight. At first, Link and Phantom Zelda must work together to defeat Mounted Miniblins. Link must leap from a high ledge to land atop Zelda's shoulders, leveling the playing field. From this height, Link can use the Whirlwind to knock a Mounted Miniblin from its Armos steed, or he can defeat the creature outright with the whip, the boomerang, or an arrow. Once you best a Miniblin, its Armos companion is also destroyed.

Ice ChuChu

Threat Meter

Hits to Defeat: 1
Attack Type: Contact
Power: Strong
Damage: 1/2 heart (contact); 1/4 heart (freeze)

Even fluffy snow can hide its share of dangers. Ice ChuChus commonly pop up from the powder. Touching these frosty foes encases Link in ice. Rub the stylus across the screen to break free, and defeat these enemies from a safe range with items such as the Whirlwind, boomerang, whip, or bow and arrow.

White Wolfos

Hits to Defeat: 2 each
Attack Type: Contact
Power: Weak
Damage: 1/4 heart

Threat Meter

They say trouble comes in threes, and that saying is accurate when speaking about White Wolfos. These hungry hunters bound up from the snow, surrounding Link in a blink. Best them quickly by unleashing spin attacks, or Link will soon become a tasty treat.

Octive

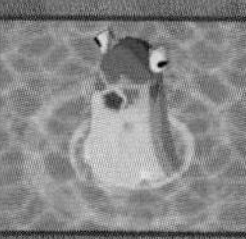

Hits to Defeat: 1
Attack Type: Range
Power: Weak
Damage: 1/2 heart

Threat Meter

Octives prefer the icy waters of the Snow Temple. They emerge when Link draws near and spit spiky projectiles at him. Block these projectiles with Link's shield, then quickly take up the Whirlwind and use it to repel the next one back at the monster, defeating it with a taste of its own medicine. Or simply pick them off with the bow.

Freezard

Hits to Defeat: 2
Attack Type: Contact
Power: Weak
Damage: 1/2 heart

Threat Meter

Freezards are best avoided. You can defeat them by melting their icy armor, which you do by passing a boomerang through a torch, then onto the villain. Attacking a Freezard without first melting its armor often causes them to skate about at high speed, becoming dangerous obstacles. However, once exposed to heat, Freezards are reduced to garden-variety Octoroks and are vulnerable to Link's sword. You can also chip away at their icy armor with sword attacks. Once the armor is removed, they can be defeated.

Ice Keese

Hits to Defeat: 1
Attack Type: Contact
Power: Strong
Damage: 1/4 heart (freeze)

Threat Meter

Ice Keese radiate a bitter chill that freezes Link in place if he gets too close. Rub the stylus on the screen to break free, then use items such as the Whirlwind, whip, boomerang, or bow to wipe out these fluttering frosties from a safe range.

Fire Keese

Hits to Defeat: 1
Attack Type: Contact
Power: Strong
Damage: 1/4 heart

Threat Meter

Fire Keese can't be harmed by Link's sword; their flames singe him when he gets too close. Wipe out these pesky fliers with long-range weapons such as the boomerang and whip.

Nocturn

Hits to Defeat: 1 (once stunned)
Attack Type: Contact
Power: Strong
Damage: 1/2 heart

Threat Meter

Fear the dark, friends, because it's often home to Nocturns! These poor lost souls attack Link ferociously if he wanders near, but they shun the light and won't pursue Link out of the pitch-dark. Only Torch Phantom Zelda can best these dreary spirits.

Torch Phantom

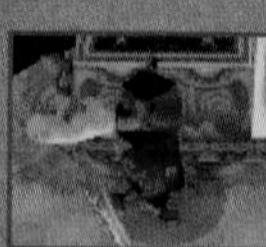

Hits to Defeat: 1 (with powered-up sword)
Attack Type: Contact
Power: Strong
Damage: 1 heart

Threat Meter

Torch Phantoms are similar to regular Phantoms in every way, except the fiery blades they carry provide them a bit of light in dark areas. Once Zelda possesses a Torch Phantom, she can light the way with her burning blade and can light up torches.

Geozard Chief

Hits to Defeat: Multiple

Attack Type: Contact and Range

Power: Strong

Damage: 1/2 heart (both attacks)

Threat Meter

Geozard Chiefs are bigger, badder versions of Geozards. In addition to strong defenses and vicious sword attacks, Chieftains also bound around and spit out far-reaching streams of flame. Tackle these worthy foes as you would a Geozard, directing Zelda to attack the creature from the front, then quickly circling Link around to punish its rear. Or simply whip away their shields and assault them from the front with Link's steel.

TIP

Phantom Zelda can block a Geozard Chief's flames, sheltering Link.

Like Like

Hits to Defeat: Multiple

Attack Type: Range (inhale)

Power: Strong

Damage: 1/4 heart (digest)

Threat Meter

These wormlike foes will suck Link up if he gets too close, so toss bombs at them from afar instead. If bombs aren't an option, use the boomerang to stun Like Likes before moving close to attack with Link's sword. Beware jiggling pots and chests as well—they're bound to contain Like Likes!

CAUTION

Being swallowed by a Like Like can cost Link his shield. These things will eat *anything*! Quickly rub your stylus across the screen to break free before the shield is lost.

Lobarrier

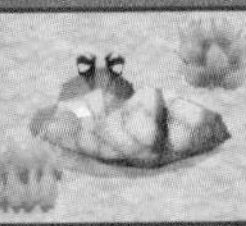

Hits to Defeat: 1

Attack Type: Swipe (claw)

Power: Strong

Damage: 1/2 heart

Threat Meter

Hiding behind their one massive claw, Lobarriers act like impenetrable roadblocks. Use the whip to disarm these foes and make them vulnerable. If you don't have the whip, keep your distance and toss the boomerang around Lobarriers, whacking them from behind to knock them silly. Then get behind them and finish them off with Link's sword.

Miniblin

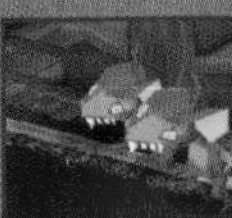

Hits to Defeat: 1

Attack Type: Swipe (pitchfork)

Power: Strong

Damage: 1/2 heart

Threat Meter

Miniblins are tiny, fragile monsters that only become dangerous when encountered in large groups. When Miniblins swarm in, unleash rapid spin attacks to wipe them all out in short order.

Big Blin

Hits to Defeat: Multiple

Attack Type: Swipe (club)

Power: Strong

Damage: 1/2 heart

Threat Meter

Don't get greedy while battling a burly Big Blin. Slip in, land a few hits, then dart out of range before it unloads a heavy blow. Big Blins are relentless and can take *a lot* of punishment, so repeat this sequence to keep the Big Blin at bay and eventually drop the brute.

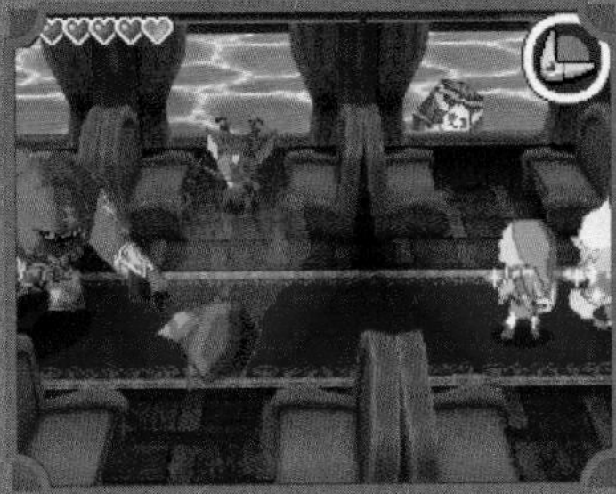

Yellow ChuChu

Hits to Defeat: 1
Attack Type: Contact
Power: Strong
Damage: 1/2 heart

Threat Meter

Yellow ChuChus regularly become electrically charged, zapping Link if he touches them while they're all sparked up. Wait for their current to fade before striking, or stun them with the boomerang if you're in a hurry.

Snapper

Hits to Defeat: Multiple
Attack Type: Contact and Range
Power: Strong
Damage: 1/2 heart

Threat Meter

As their name implies, Snappers lash out at Link with their whips, potentially snaring our hero by the waist. Not good! When Link's tied up, wait for the Snapper to pull Link close, then trace straight lines from Link to the villain to make Link thrust forward with his sword. Do this quickly and Link will stab the Snapper as he's being reeled in, breaking free of the whip's grip. Don't give a Snapper a chance to snare Link again; stay in its face, slashing away with Link's blade.

Helmet ChuChu

Hits to Defeat: 1
Attack Type: Contact
Power: Weak
Damage: 1/2 heart

Threat Meter

These little creeps are practically invincible while wearing their giant spiked helmets, so use the whip to relieve them of their defensive gear. After snatching off a Helmet ChuChu's helmet, it's reduced to a garden-variety Red ChuChu—easy pickings!

Blue ChuChu

Hits to Defeat: 1
Attack Type: Contact
Power: Strong
Damage: 1/2 heart

Threat Meter

These charged-up foes can be tough to handle, but not if you have bombs. Just heave a bomb at a Blue ChuChu to destroy the villain in short order. If you don't have bombs, look around for objects to hurl at them with the whip. Phantom Zelda can also dispatch Blue ChuChus without a problem; just steer her into range.

Phantom Eye

Hits to Defeat: 1
Attack Type: N/A
Power: N/A
Damage: N/A

Threat Meter

Beware all those little eyeballs you see on your map while exploring the Tower of Spirits' higher floors. They represent new adversaries called Phantom Eyes, which act as sentries for Warp Phantoms. If you need to defeat a Phantom Eye, try stunning it by tossing the boomerang from around a corner. The Whirlwind can also stun a Phantom Eye—and since stunned Phantom Eyes can't call for backup, Link can safely slip past or dispatch them with Link's sword.

Many Phantom Eyes reincarnate, returning to duty moments after you defeat them.

Warp Phantom

Hits to Defeat: 1 (with powered-up sword)

Attack Type: Contact

Power: Strong

Damage: 1 heart

Threat Meter

As their name implies, Warp Phantoms can instantly teleport to any Phantom Eye the moment the sentry catches sight of an intruder. So keep well out of sight! Once Zelda possesses a Warp Phantom, she can warp to any Phantom Eye on the map; simply trace a line to the sentry to warp her there.

Fire Baba

Hits to Defeat: 2

Attack Type: Contact and Range

Power: Strong

Damage: 1/2 heart (both attacks)

Threat Meter

These carnivorous plants are native to the Fire Realm. Though rooted to the ground, Fire Babas spit searing flames at Link from range. The flames can't be blocked, so stay mobile and hurl bombs at these menaces to quickly eliminate them. Better yet, learn to tap them the moment they sprout up to dispatch Fire Babas in one fast, long-range leap attack.

Stalfos

Hits to Defeat: Multiple

Attack Type: Contact and Range

Power: Strong

Damage: 1/2 heart

Threat Meter

Stalfoses are skinny skeletons that toss bones at Link from afar. They're too agile to attack directly, so whip them repeatedly to defeat them, or use bombs or arrows to bust them up even faster.

Moldola

Hits to Defeat: N/A

Attack Type: Contact

Power: Strong

Damage: 1/2 heart

Threat Meter

Keep away from Moldolas that slink along the walls; they'll give Link a nasty shock if he touches one. Only an arrow from the bow can defeat these mindless wanderers.

Heatoise

Hits to Defeat: Multiple

Attack Type: Contact

Power: Strong

Damage: 1/2 heart

Threat Meter

When Link first encounters a Heatoise, he's unable to attack it directly and must trick the creature into slamming into a roaming Moldola to stun the beast. Once Link acquires the bow, he can stun Giant Turtles by firing arrows directly into the gem on their forehead. Once it is stunned, quickly assault a Giant Turtle's exposed head to dispatch it before the monster recovers.

Wrecker Phantom

Hits to Defeat: 1 (with powered-up sword)

Attack Type: Contact

Power: Strong

Damage: 1 heart

Threat Meter

Wrecker Phantoms chase Link down with great speed by turning into huge wrecking balls. It's best to keep well out sight when one of these rolling guardians lurks nearby. Once Zelda has possessed a Wrecker Phantom, she's able to smash through bomb blocks, Armos statues, and many other obstacles. She can even slam other Phantoms around, knocking them dizzy while Link sprints past!

Gerune

Hits to Defeat: Special
Attack Type: Contact
Power: Strong
Damage: 1/2 heart

Threat Meter

The Sand Wand is your go-to tool against Sandmen. Equip the Sand Wand and target a Gerune, working the wand's magic on the creature as it attempts to flee. Keep affecting the Gerune with the Sand Wand until it at last hardens, becoming solid and vulnerable. Now's your chance! Stop using the Sand Wand and tap the Gerune to make Link lift the monster over his head; then tap anywhere else to make Link throw his foe, damaging it when it strikes the ground. Repeat as needed until the Gerune crumbles to dust.

Stalfos Warrior

Hits to Defeat: Multiple
Attack Type: Contact (sword)
Power: Strong
Damage: 1/2 heart

Threat Meter

Stalfos Warriors are challenging adversaries who attack with great ferocity. Don't give these undead soldiers a chance to build up speed; shred them with arrows or blast them with bombs to quickly put them to rest.

Ergtorok

Hits to Defeat: Multiple
Attack Type: Range
Power: Weak
Damage: 1/2 heart

Threat Meter

Ergtoroks are similar to Octives, rising up to fire spiky balls at Link from afar. However, Ergtoroks can move about underground, and they're smart enough to retreat when Link sends their projectiles back at them with the Whirlwind. To defeat an Ergtorok, first stun it by using the Sand Wand on the creature while it's moving underground—target the telltale puffs of sand. After stunning an Ergtorok, raise Link up to its level and then quickly close on the creature, hacking away before it recovers.

Train Enemies

Moink

Hits to Defeat: N/A
Attack Type: Contact
Power: N/A
Damage: 1 heart

Threat Meter

The whistle is more than just a fun thing to play with. You can also use it to scatter Moinks that lie in the track! Ramming into Moinks is bad, because it brings your ride to a short stop—and brings down upon you the full wrath of an enraged bovine!

Snurgle

Hits to Defeat: 1 (scatter with whistle)
Attack Type: Contact
Power: N/A
Damage: 1 heart

Threat Meter

You can't defeat Snurgles when Link first encounters them; instead, you must scatter them by blowing the whistle. However, once the Spirit Train has been outfitted with a cannon, Snurgles can be blasted from the sky instead. Be especially wary of these flying fiends when transporting cargo, as they love nothing more than ruining your precious payloads.

Skulltula

Hits to Defeat: 1 (scatter with whistle)
Attack Type: Contact
Power: N/A
Damage: 1 heart

Threat Meter

Scary Skulltulas descend from the forest's roof as you motor through thick, wooded areas. Scatter these giant spiders with your whistle when you first see them, and blast them with the cannon once it's installed.

Dark Train

Hits to Defeat: N/A
Attack Type: Contact
Power: N/A
Damage: Insta-squish

Threat Meter

These possessed transports are no joke, so adjust your course and keep far away from them. Monitor your map to see which direction Dark Trains will turn at junctions, and be sure you're not in their path. Don't be afraid to slam it into reverse if necessary—being rammed by a Dark Train instantly destroys your ride!

Bullbo

Hits to Defeat: 3
Attack Type: Contact
Power: N/A
Damage: 1 heart

Threat Meter

Bullbos will make short work of your train if you don't hurry up and blast them with the cannon. These monsters usually appear in pairs, so alternate your attacks to keep them from charging. Being hit interrupts a Bullbo's charge.

Rocktite

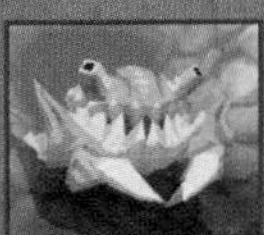

Hits to Defeat: Multiple
Attack Type: Contact
Power: N/A
Damage: 1 heart

Threat Meter

A Rocktite's weakness is its giant yellow eye, found within its mouth. Unleash your cannon the moment you spy that eye, and don't hesitate to pick your shots—just keep those cannonballs flying! After suffering several direct hits, the Rocktite collapses in a heap, giving you a chance to catch your breath. Watch for that glowing eyeball to appear in the distant darkness, and resume fire the moment you see it. Repeat until the Rocktite is forced to give up the chase.

Sir Frosty

Hits to Defeat: 2 (head and torso)
Attack Type: Range
Power: N/A
Damage: 1 heart

Threat Meter

Sir Frosties have a rep for being friendly and fun, but the ones you encounter in the Snow Realm are neither. They toss their heads at your train, trying to derail your progress! Listen for the telltale sound of Sir Frosties springing up, and be quick to blast their inbound heads from the sky. Nail their torsos afterward to put these immobile foes on ice.

Bulblin

Hits to Defeat: 3
Attack Type: Contact and Range
Power: N/A
Damage: 1 heart (both attacks)

Threat Meter

Bulblins use Bullbos to chase Link's train, lobbing bomb arrows at Link's ride. To eliminate these threats, blast their bomb arrows from midair, and then punish the Bullbos mounts with multiple cannon shots. If you face two or more Bulblins at once, alternate your shots, pounding one and then the other to prevent them both from getting off a shot.

Ocean Octorok

Hits to Defeat: 3
Attack Type: Range (ink)
Power: N/A
Damage: None

Threat Meter

Ocean Octoroks reside deep underwater; you encounter them only en route to the Ocean Temple. They attack by spitting dark clouds of ink that blot out your vision. Defeat these potential menaces by pounding them with three cannon shots before they have a chance to ink you over.

Armored Train

Hits to Defeat: N/A
Attack Type: Contact
Power: N/A
Damage: Insta-squish

Threat Meter

Armored Trains are a lot like Dark Trains, only they pursue Link with greater speed and tenacity, often stopping and reversing direction if he gives them the slip. Also, as their name implies, Armored Trains are covered in thick plating and are completely immune to the cannon. Since Armored Trains are also faster than the Spirit Train, Link must outsmart these menaces by mixing them up at junctions. Trick these trains into thinking you're going one way, then back up and take a different route!

Cannon Boats

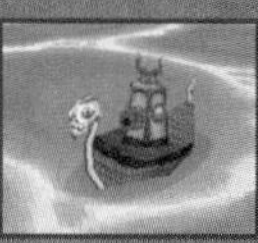

Hits to Defeat: 2 each
Attack Type: Range
Power: N/A
Damage: 1 heart

Threat Meter

Take care while roaming the Ocean Realm, for battalions of Cannon Boats patrol its waters. These ships often appear in threes and aren't shy about bombarding Link's train with cannonballs. Blast their inbound fire from the sky, and counter at once to destroy these dangerous threats, sinking each ship in turn.

Tanks

Hits to Defeat: 2 each
Attack Type: Range
Power: N/A
Damage: 1 heart

Threat Meter

Snurglar

Hits to Defeat: N/A
Attack Type: Contact
Power: N/A
Damage: 1 heart

Threat Meter

Charge Snurglars head-on, and when you get close to one, blow your train's whistle. Anything with ears *that* big has to be sensitive to sound! After stunning a Snurglar with the whistle, blast it with the cannon to score a direct hit and bring the beast down.

Malgyorg

Hits to Defeat: 1
Attack Type: Contact
Power: N/A
Damage: 1 heart

Threat Meter

Go carefully while traveling the Sand Realm, for dangerous Malgyorgs survive the desolate place by preying upon the unwary. Whenever you see shark fins emerge from the sand near your trolly, you know that Malgyorgs are on the hunt! Malgyorgs are immune to attacks while traveling underground, and they strike very suddenly by leaping out of the ground and slamming your train. Blast a Malgyorg while it's airborne to defeat it before its attack lands—or better yet, sound your train's whistle to force all nearby Malgyorgs to jump, giving you a chance to blast them before they strike!

Rocktite

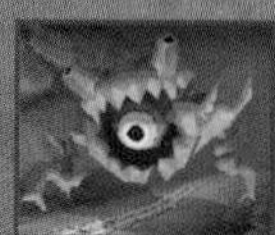

Hits to Defeat: Multiple
Attack Type: Contact
Power: N/A
Damage: 1 heart

Threat Meter

Tackle this giant cave crawler just as you did the Rocktite in the snow: Pound its glowing eyeball with relentless cannon fire. Keep whaling away on the Rocktite's eye until it collapses, falling behind into the pitch. Be ready to resume fire the moment you see its eye start to glow again.

Eventually, you start passing explosive barrels that are lodged in the cave wall. At this point, the Rocktite closes its mouth, and you must catch the beast with at least one explosive barrel to make it open up and expose its eye again. Just blast each barrel you pass to detonate it, hoping to harm the Rocktite. Then feed its eye a steady diet of cannonballs.

Tektite

Hits to Defeat: 1
Attack Type: Contact
Power: N/A
Damage: 1 heart

Threat Meter

Tektites appear only in train tunnels, running all around and leaping at Link's ride. Blast these little creeps with the cannon before they get too close, leading them a bit as they circle the tunnel's walls.

Bosses

Stagnox, Armored Colossus

Hits to Defeat: Multiple

Attack Type: Contact

Power: Strong

Damage: 1/2 heart (charge); 1/4 heart (poison)

Threat Meter

Stagnox looks big and mean, but he's by far the easiest boss Link faces. Simply run circles around the monster, aiming to sneak behind him. Be careful not to touch the poison fumes pluming out from the creature's rear—use the Whirlwind to blow out the fumes instead!

Without its poison fumes, Stagnox's behind is primed for stabbing. Land as many blows as you can before the beast recovers. Repeat this sequence until Stagnox takes flight, raining Blastworms down upon the arena. Quickly run around and stab each minion to curl it up into a spiky bomb. After curling up all of the Blastworms, run toward the foreground, then turn to face Stagnox. Equip the Whirlwind and blow a Blastworm at the boss as he swoops down, knocking him to his back. While Stagnox is down, rush forward and score as many hits as you can before the boss recovers. Repeat this process until Stagnox succumbs to the power of good.

Fraaz, Master of Icy Fire

Hits to Defeat: Multiple

Attack Type: Contact and Range

Power: Strong

Damage: 1/2 heart (fire); 1/2 heart (ice); 1/4 heart (freeze)

Threat Meter

Fraaz can assault Link with both fire and ice, and his attacks can be tough to avoid. Keep your distance and watch Fraaz as he inhales—his color determines his forthcoming attack and his current vulnerability. Expect ice attacks when he's glowing blue and fire attacks when he's red.

Avoid Fraaz's attacks and wound him by tossing your boomerang into either the blue or red torch, then hitting Fraaz. Strike Fraaz with a fiery boomerang when he's glowing blue, and hit him with a frosty boomerang when he's glowing red. Hitting Fraaz with the boomerang stuns him for a moment. Take full advantage and assault the boss with rapid sword strikes, dealing as much damage as you can. Repeat this sequence to harm Fraaz when he glows the other color.

After damaging Fraaz when he's red and blue, the boss splits into two smaller Fraazes. One is vulnerable to ice and the other to fire. Glance at your map screen to see which is which, and hit each one with the appropriate attack. After successfully striking both little Fraazes, the two re-form into the full-size Fraaz.

continued

At this point, the boss becomes wise to Link's tricks and destroys both torches. You must wait for Fraaz to attack, dodge the attack (ideally), and then quickly use the substance left behind. Should Fraaz launch an ice ball, dodge the projectile and then ready the boomerang. Trace a line to the remnants of the ice, waiting for Fraaz to turn red before connecting the line to him and releasing. The flames left behind by Fraaz's fireballs must be exploited in just the same manner; wait for Fraaz to turn blue, then strike. Again, you must stun Fraaz when he's blue and when he's red, and you must attack him afterward with Link's sword both times. Only then will Fraaz devolve into his twin microselves again.

In the second mini-Fraaz encounter, you must strike both Fraazes with the boomerang, all in one toss. Wait for the little villains to attack, then quickly trace a line from the first lingering substance back to the appropriate mini-Fraaz, then back to the other substance and over to the other mini-Fraaz. Again, check your map to see which Fraaz is which.

When Fraaz at last re-forms, you must strike him twice with one toss of the boomerang, using the appropriate substance to wound him. To do this, trace a line from the substance over to Fraaz, then draw a quick loop to target Fraaz again. Stun Fraaz when he's blue, follow up with Link's sword, then stun him again when he's red, and hack away once more. Don't relent until the boss finally goes down for the count.

Phytops, Barbed Menace

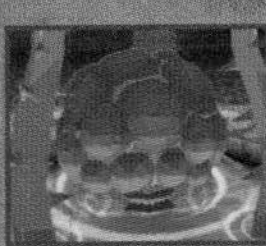

Hits to Defeat: Multiple

Attack Type: Contact

Power: Strong

Damage: 1/2 heart

Threat Meter

In this fight, Link must scale a tall cliff before Phytops reveals himself. Use the whip to swing along the posts, and watch out for Phytops to periodically spew toxic gunk, which will rain down around you. Be patient if the gunk lands in your way; it'll evaporate after a moment. Each time you face a giant tentacle, use the whip to rip off one of its thorns, then toss the thorn at the tentacle's yellow eye to remove the obstacle. Keep going until you reach Phytops.

Dodge the toxic gunk Phytops continues to spit, and avoid being crushed by the tentacles. After a tentacle crashes to the ground, quickly lash it with the whip to tear off a thorn. Toss the thorn at one of the two purple sacs just above Phytops's mouth. Burst both sacs with thrown thorns to expose the fiend's weak spot: his eye! Heave a third thorn at the creature's eye to stun the brute, causing his head to crash down. Race over and bring the full weight of Link's sword to bear on the exposed eyeball. Repeat this sequence until you achieve victory.

Cragma, Lava Lord

Hits to Defeat: Multiple
Attack Type: Contact
Power: Strong
Damage: 1/2 heart

Threat Meter

Cragma attacks by slamming the ground with his gigantic stone fists. Run to one side or the other, double-tapping the screen to make Link somersault away from these crushing blows. As Cragma lifts a fist in preparation to strike, he reveals a weak spot somewhere along the base of his torso. Watch for a glowing patch of skin, and quickly strike this area with an arrow from Link's bow.

After Cragma slams the ground with both fists, run around and locate a fallen boulder. Trick the boss into smashing the boulder with a heavy blow, reducing the boulder to a stone disc. Quickly place the stone disc onto the northeast fire geyser, then cross the disc to reach the nearby mine cart.

Hop into the cart to begin circling Cragma. Look for more glowing weak spots, and strike each one with an arrow. Do your best not to miss or you'll need to make multiple trips around the boss and will risk running out of arrows before you reach the top. If you run out of arrows, you can acquire more from rocks that fall from the ceiling.

Make it all the way up to the highest rail by striking all of Cragma's weak spots. When you reach the top, aim and fire an arrow into Cragma's giant eyeball. Time this well or your arrows may be deflected when Cragma raises an arm or blinks.

Cragma collapses when you shoot his eye, and Link is deposited onto the arena's floor. Run up and unleash the full fury of Link's blade against the glowing weak spot located atop the boss's head. Repeat this sequence a second time, following the exact same steps to stun and collapse Cragma so you can deliver more punishment. Become one with the mine cart and the bow to at last bring the Lava Lord down.

Byrne

Hits to Defeat: Multiple
Attack Type: Contact and Range
Power: Strong
Damage: 1/4 heart (all attacks)

Threat Meter

During the first stage of this fight, keep control of Link and run around, avoiding Byrne's ranged attacks. Zelda will block his energy beams, so try to keep her between Link and Byrne. Hearts may appear if the princess blocks several beams in a row.

continued

Eventually, the camera will pan down low, and Byrne will prepare to launch his retractable gauntlet. Dodge the attack, then quickly switch to Zelda and direct her to grab his gauntlet while it's stuck in the ground. Zelda yanks Byrne to the floor; switch to Link and strike. Repeat this sequence after Byrne recovers to bring him down a second time and inflict more damage.

After walloping Byrne for a second time, the battle moves to its third phase, during which Byrne remains on the ground and swipes furiously at Link with his heavy gauntlet. Dodge and wait for a moment when Byrne isn't attacking, then unleash a fast sword combo with Link. Byrne blocks every blow, then leaps back and begins to glow with power. Quickly move Link behind Zelda so that Byrne charges into Zelda, locking up with the princess. While Zelda and Byrne are locked in a struggle, have Link attack Byrne's vulnerable backside. Repeat this sequence as needed—it won't be long before Byrne has had enough.

Skeldritch, Ancient Demon

Hits to Defeat: Multiple
Attack Type: Contact and Range
Power: Strong
Damage: 1/2 heart (all attacks)

Threat Meter

First, run circles around Skeldritch, waiting for the fiend to fire a series of boulders. Get the timing down, and then use the Sand Wand to stop the last boulder in its tracks. Quickly maneuver the boulder you've captured onto one of the many hammer devices that border the arena. Once the boulder is in place, whack the trigger switch to send it flying at Skeldritch, smashing the first of its many vertebrae. Repeat this sequence to destroy all of Skeldritch's vertebrae, one after the other.

Skeldritch's upper vertebrae are covered by thick armor, but each one is missing a chink. Circle the boss to find those weak points, then load a hammer device with a boulder and circle around the boss again, tricking Skeldritch into turning away from the loaded device. Lure Skeldritch into exposing its rear weak spot to the boulder, and when Skeldritch is facing in the proper direction, quickly hurl the boomerang around the boss, striking the hammer device's switch. If your aim is true, the boulder crashes into the exposed bone, destroying another vertebra. Note that Skeldritch's final vertebra's weak spot is not directly behind the boss but slightly off to the side.

After you've severed all vertebrae, Skeldritch's massive skull starts hopping around on its own, chasing Link. Run away to gain some distance, then use the Sand Wand to raise the earth, surrounding the boss in solid walls of sand. When Skeldritch is completely surrounded, it starts struggling to free itself. Now's your chance! Raise Link up with the Sand Wand and then dart behind Skeldritch, whaling away on the giant jewel atop its massive skull. Keep freezing Skeldritch in place and then unleashing Link's blade on its vulnerable jewel until the fiend is destroyed.

Demon Train

Hits to Defeat: Multiple

Attack Type: Contact and Range

Power: N/A

Damage: 1 heart

Threat Meter

To tackle this boss, blast all of the barrel launchers on one side of the Demon Train, then blast all the ones on the other side. Be ready to slam on the brakes at any moment—the Demon Train crosses between the tracks at will, and you don't want to be running alongside it when it moves over. To advance to the next stage of the battle, destroy every barrel launcher before you run out of track.

The battle's second phase is much like the first, with you racing alongside the Demon Train and destroying its weapon systems. This time, the Demon Train employs laser cannons. The lasers have a limited firing arc, so simply keep back a bit and you should be able to blast each one without exposing yourself to much danger.

Destroy all of the Demon Train's laser cannons to advance to the third and final phase. Now the Demon Train has abandoned all defenses and unleashes a wide spread of rotating laser beams that strike out in all angles. Do your best to avoid being sliced by the lasers as you race alongside the Demon Train, blasting the blue crystals from which the lasers emanate.

The Demon Train shudders and slows dramatically once you've hit all crystals. Race forward and unload on the fiend's face! Keep your train in high gear and just keep pounding away until the terrible train is at last derailed.

Cole

Hits to Defeat: N/A

Attack Type: Summon (Rats)

Power: Strong

Damage: 1/2 heart (Rat)

Threat Meter

Possessed Zelda

Hits to Defeat: 1 (Bow of Light)

Attack Type: Range

Power: Strong

Damage: 1/2 heart

Threat Meter

This fight is brutal until you realize how simple it is. For the most part, just ignore Malladus—Cole is the real threat here. Direct Zelda to walk north along the train; then switch to Link and focus on wiping out the white Rats that Cole spawns. It's bad news if one of Cole's Rats manages to touch Zelda, for Cole seizes control of the princess when this occurs, steering her actions like a puppeteer.

continued

Whenever Cole takes control of Zelda, immediately toss out the boomerang, guiding it around and behind the princess, with the intent of severing the magical strings Cole's using to control her. Cut the cords and Zelda returns to normal.

Prevent Cole from possessing Zelda while also keeping Zelda moving north, toward her possessed body. Zelda must lead the way, because only she can withstand the powerful laser Malladus fires as you approach. Keep Link behind Zelda at all times, and keep his sword swinging away at those Rats. Battle all the way up to Malladus, then steer Zelda into contact with her possessed body.

Zelda grabs hold of Malladus tightly, and the two soar off into the sky. While Zelda and Malladus are locked in a struggle, whip out the Bow of Light and hold the stylus on the screen to charge up an arrow. Aim at Malladus and fire when he (she?) spins around and you have a clear shot. A single light arrow brings the fight to a close.

Malladus, Demon King

Hits to Defeat: Multiple

Attack Type: Contact and Range

Power: Strong

Damage: 1/2 heart (all attacks)

Threat Meter

Stand before Zelda and swing Link's sword to batter away each demonic fireball Malladus spits forth. While you're getting down the timing, try swinging in advance of each fireball—swing just after you see it appear at the top of the touch screen. Just keep knocking those fireballs away from Zelda until she finally summons the power she needs. The great spin attack is ideal for thwarting the fireballs, provided you've learned the move from Niko.

Take up the Spirit Flute when Zelda prompts you to, and play a challenging song with the princess. Make quick strokes of the stylus to skip past certain notes as you steadily blow into the microphone, acing the song to summon the spirits of the many Lokomo guardians you've met on your travels. The song has the desired effect, wounding Malladus with its purity and revealing a shimmering weak point on his back.

The goal now is simple: Run up to Malladus and assault him with a barrage of sword strikes until he finally rounds on Link. Then run away screaming and glance at the top screen to view the world through Zelda's eyes. When at last the Demon King's back is within her sight, Zelda's purple targeting crosshair changes to a yellow burst. Now! Tap the Bow of Light icon at the bottom of your screen to make Zelda fire, striking Malladus's weak spot with a light arrow. Repeat this sequence, pumping Malladus full of light arrows until the villain at last collapses. Then sprint to the glowing red gemstone on Malladus's head, and hack at it with Link's sword until the Demon King regains his senses.

Eventually, Link's blade becomes lodged inside of Malladus's forehead gemstone. You can't give up! Rub the stylus back and forth across the screen as fast as you can, helping Link wedge his sword deeper and deeper into Malladus's head. Keep rubbing that stylus until you at last destroy the Demon King.

All Aboard: The Journey to Castle Town

Aboda Village

Legend

1 Stamp station

2 Train station

Link's newest adventure begins humbly, dear friends, in the quiet town of Aboda Village. Excitement's at an all-time low down here by the water, but big things are on the horizon—for today is the day of Link's graduation ceremony. Yes, that's right! Link is poised to earn his stature as Hyrule's youngest official train engineer, and none other than Princess Zelda herself will be the one to bestow this great honor upon him!

Enemies Encountered

Bees | Moinks

Items Already Acquired

Engineer's Clothes

Items to Obtain

Red Rupee | Treasure

A Link to the Present

Task 1: Travel to Castle Town

Humble Aboda

After snoozing through his roommate Niko's magnum opus, Link is rudely awakened by his mentor, the great engineer Alfonzo. The burly man reminds Link that he's got a big day ahead—for today is the day that Link becomes an official royal engineer!

1 Travel to Castle Town

2 Speak with Princess Zelda

3 Reach the Tower of Spirits

4 Retrieve the Forest Rail Map

Alfonzo tells Link to meet him at the village's train station so they can depart for the castle. Niko gives Link a few parting words of advice.

When you gain control of Link, try moving him around. Tap and hold the stylus on the location on the screen where you'd like him to go. The farther away from Link you tap and hold, the faster he'll run.

Tap the small blue pot to make Link lift it over his head. To carry the pot around, tap and hold the stylus on the screen. To toss the pot, tap the screen in the direction you want Link to throw it; it smashes apart, revealing whatever might be hidden inside. Simply contact whatever goody pops out to collect it.

Smashing pots often reveals useful items, such as hearts and Rupees. Collect hearts to restore Link's life energy. Collect Rupees to increase your wealth. Tap the Menu button in the lower-right corner to view your total Rupees (shown on the left) and other quick-menu options.

Step outside and sprint along the Aboda shore. It's okay to run along the water's edge like this, but be careful not to leap off a cliff and into the water—Link doesn't like getting wet and will lose life energy!

Try lifting a big stone next. Just tap one to make Link lift it like a pot. He's so strong! Carry the boulder around if you like, then toss it to smash the stone and discover hidden goodies.

NOTE

Rarely, valuable treasures will pop out of pots and boulders. Link gets excited when he finds treasure, and he stores them in his inventory. Tap Menu and then tap Collection to call up the Collection screen. Next, tap the Treasure icon on the left to view your stash of valuables. You can't do much with treasures at first, but they become important later in the adventure.

Press SELECT to call up the Collection screen even faster.

Village People

Alfonzo urged you to meet him at the station, but it would be rude not to take a moment to meet your neighbors first. Speak to the farmer near the empty stable to learn that he has an unusual interest in chickenlike fowls called Cuccos. He hopes to raise a bunch of them someday. Perhaps one day you can help him realize this lofty goal!

Listen closely to everything people say, even if it seems unimportant. Even mundane conversations can hold secret clues!

This is a stamp station.
Menu

Next, tap the odd stone pedestal north of the farmer to examine it. It's a stamp station, but you can't use it just yet. Remember where you saw it for future reference.

Jot down notes on your map so you don't forget things. Tap Menu, then tap Map to bring your map down to the touch screen so you may scribble on it. Scratch an S near your current location to label the stamp station you've just found.

You may also press Ⓑ or ✚ to call up the map even faster.

Nasty Prank

If you want to prove me wrong, go roll into that tree over there!
Menu

Run right and speak to the boy near the tree with the beehive next to it. He dares Link to somersault into the nearby tree. Kid's play!

Simply double-tap the screen to make Link somersault, gaining a boost of speed. Ignore the buzzing bees and roll into the tree near the boy to wow him with your somersaulting skill.

Uh-oh, those bees are buzzing mad! Disturbing beehives in any fashion is certain to draw the ire of their swarming inhabitants. Tap and hold the stylus far away from Link to make him bolt around the village, outrunning the bees as they give chase. Their stingers are no joke!

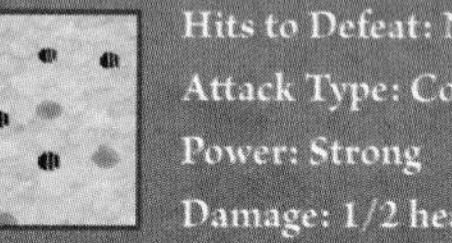

Bees will eventually break off their pursuit, but if you get tired of running, take cover inside a house or leap into deep water to escape. The latter option hurts Link, so use this as a last resort.

Bees

Hits to Defeat: N/A
Attack Type: Contact
Power: Strong
Damage: 1/2 heart

Threat Meter

Fear not, friends, there's a reason to live daringly. Return to the boy and speak with him to receive a reward for your bravery: a valuable treasure!

Let me give you something to make up for it!
Menu

Treasure

You got a treasure! Check it out on the Collection screen!

Manual Labor

If you'd like to earn a Red Rupee, speak to the girl near the central house, who calls out to Link when he passes by. She needs help; someone has piled a bunch of stones in front of her house!

Tap each stone to lift it, then toss it away. Smash them all to collect a few items and prove that Link is an upstanding member of his community.

Like bravery, hard work has its rewards. Speak to the girl after removing all of the stones to receive a sparkling Red Rupee! This moola will come in handy when you reach Castle Town.

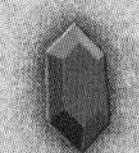

Red Rupee

You got a Red Rupee! It's worth 20 Rupees!

NOTE

Rupees come in various colors, some more valuable than others. Here's the breakdown:

- Green Rupees are worth 1 Rupee.
- Blue Rupees are worth 5 Rupees.
- Red Rupees are worth 20 Rupees.
- Big Green Rupees are worth 100 Rupees.
- Big Red Rupees are worth 200 Rupees.
- Big Gold Rupees are worth 300 Rupees.

On to Castle Town

That's enough dallying for now—you've got a train to catch! Head north to the train station, where Alfonzo greets Link by rolling up on his very own choo-choo.

Alfonzo has a surprise in store: As a final exam, he asks Link to drive to the castle. Can do! Hop aboard to start off toward the big ceremony.

Training Day

You must reach Castle Town Station in under 300 seconds, but that's plenty of time. Follow Alfonzo's instructions and kick the train into high gear by sliding the stylus upward along the gearbox lever to the right.

Cruising in the train couldn't be easier. For now, just keep the speed set to maximum. If you like, drag the stylus down along the cord above the gearbox to sound the steam whistle, and tap the edges of the screen to view the scenery as you enjoy the ride.

The whistle is more than just a fun thing to play with. It's also used to scatter Moinks that lie on the track. Ramming into Moinks is bad, because it brings your ride to a short stop—and it brings the full wrath of an enraged bovine down upon you!

Moink

Hits to Defeat: N/A
Attack Type: Contact
Power: Strong
Damage: 1 heart

Threat Meter

Your train has a Life meter separate from Link's. It's game-over if either the train's or Link's Life meter falls to zero hearts, so do your best to avoid hazards!

Course Correction

Nearing a fork in the rail, Alfonzo warns Link that they'll soon be sharing the track with other trains. Look at your map to view the other trains, and use the rail switch that pops up at the screen's bottom to pick the proper route. In this case, slide the lever to the right to avoid a head-on collision with a train headed your way.

You speed past a station after turning right, but there's no time to stop. Link's graduation ceremony won't wait!

If you've been making good time, you should be able to veer left at the next fork, ahead of a second train. If you're afraid you might hit the train, hit the brakes and let it pass, then quickly follow along behind it.

To continue toward Castle Town, make a right at the next junction, followed by a left at the next. Alfonzo points out the breathtaking Tower of Spirits, which dominates the horizon not far from the castle.

Stopping at the Castle Town Station is your final test. It takes the train quite a while to stop, so reduce your speed well in advance. If you're going too fast, slam it into reverse to apply the emergency brake—not the ideal way to stop, but, hey, it's your first time!

The train must be put into park (second option from the bottom of the gearbox) to stop at a station.

Castle Town

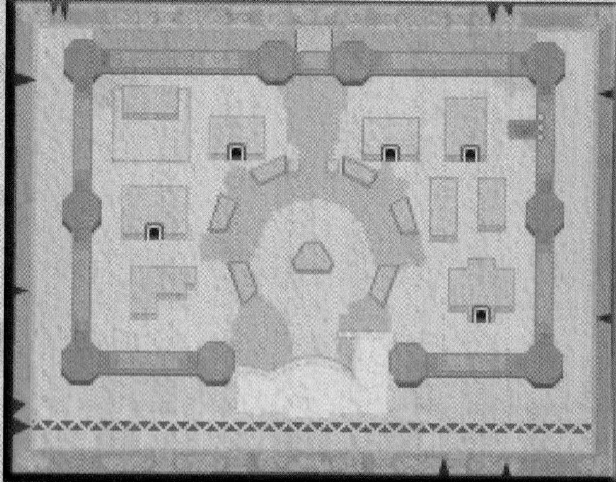

Castle Town

1 Travel to Castle Town

2 Speak with Princess Zelda

3 Reach the Tower of Spirits

4 Retrieve the Forest Rail

Items to Obtain

Letter ("From Postmaster")

Big City

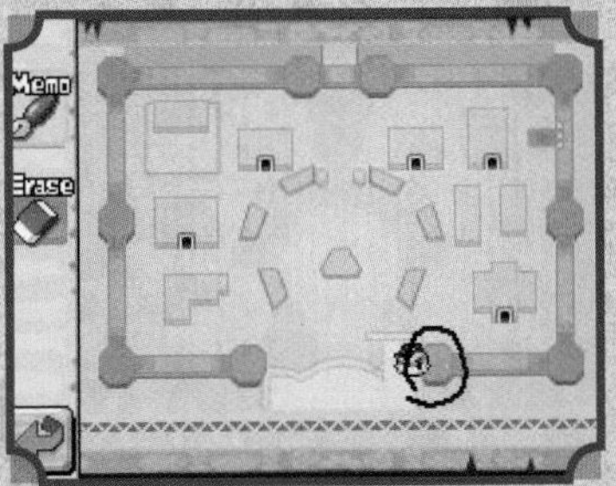

Castle Town may be the crown jewel of the kingdom, but there isn't much you can do here at present. Several treasure chests taunt you from high perches about the town, but you've no way to reach them. Make notes on your map so you don't forget where they sit.

Check out the bulletin board near the central fountain. You'll find such signs at many major locales you visit. Bulletin boards inform you of the current prizes of the day, along with noteworthy Battle Mode battle reports. Again, you can't do much with this yet.

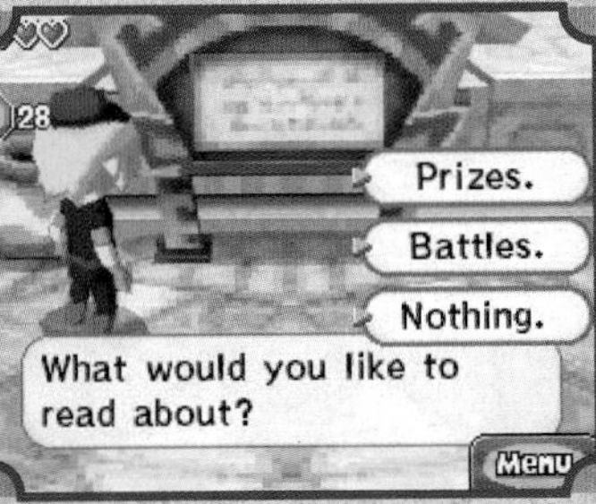

NOTE

Check the "Training" and "Multiplayer" chapters of this guide for more on prizes and Battle Mode, respectively.

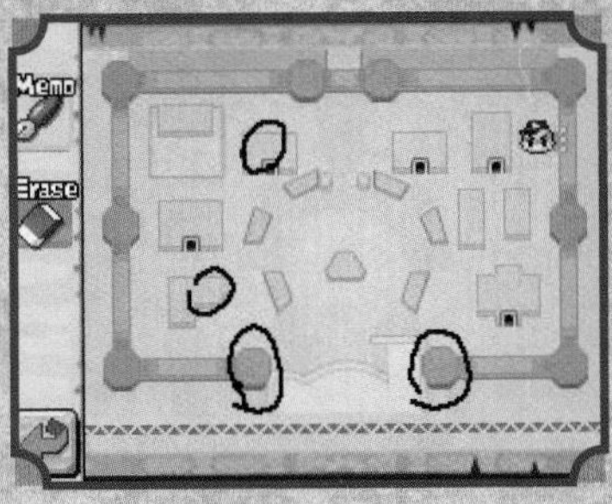

Some cracked blocks bar the east steps leading to the town's ramparts. These are bomb blocks, and they can be destroyed only with bombs. Make a note on your map of where you saw them for future reference.

Castle Town Shop

Pay a quick visit to the local shop. Various items are for sale, all of which are completely out of your current price range. That shield sure looks spiffy though, eh? It will be yours soon enough.

No Kids Allowed

The mysterious-looking shop to the southeast seems quite intriguing, but its mistress doesn't enjoy entertaining children. Perhaps you can do more here later.

The Postman Cometh

As you make your way north to the castle, tap the wiggling postbox for a brief chat with your local postman. The postman isn't much for words these days, but he'll gladly deliver you your first piece of mail: a letter from the postmaster himself!

Letter

You got a letter from the postman! Go to the Collection screen to read it!

Each time you get a new letter, call up the Collection screen, then tap the Letter icon to check your mail. Be sure to read every letter you get; some are quite important!

Tip

Many towns and villages sport postboxes. Always tap those wiggling boxes to claim your mail.

That's all Castle Town has to offer you at the moment. Hurry through the north gate to reach the grounds of Hyrule Castle!

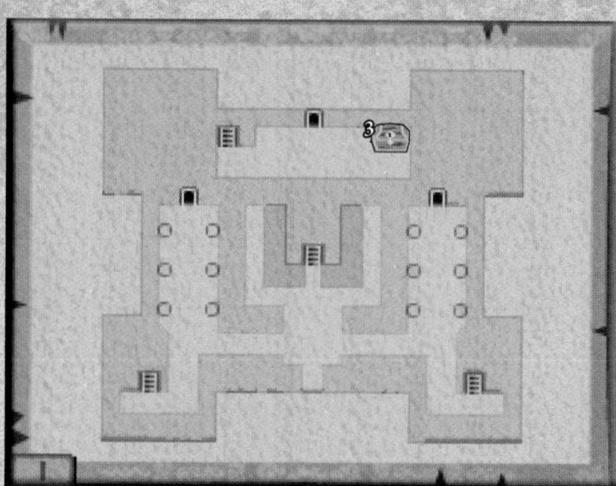

Hyrule Castle First Floor

Hyrule Castle

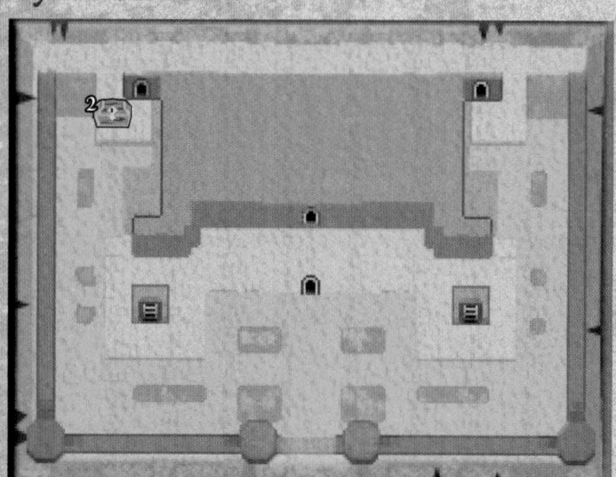

Hyrule Castle Grounds

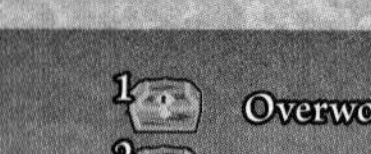

Legend

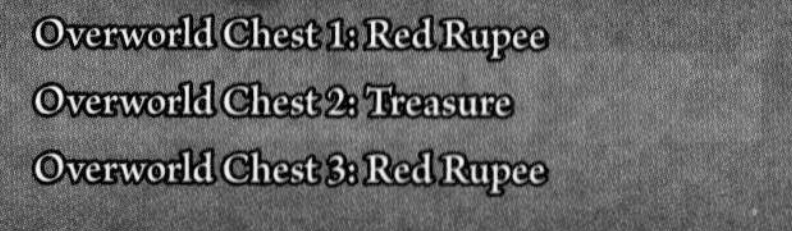

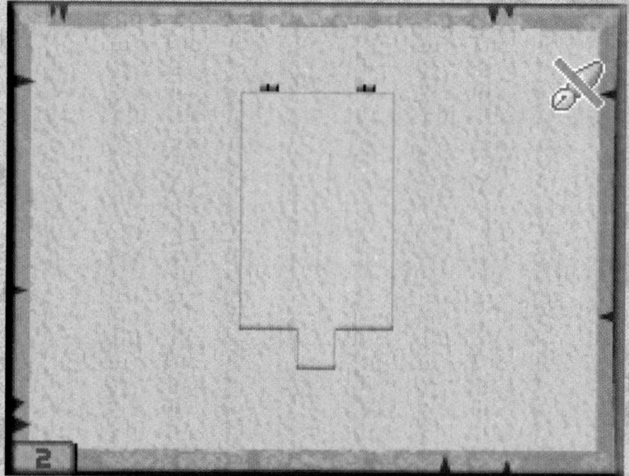

Hyrule Castle Throne Room

Items to Obtain

Engineer Certificate
Letter ("From Zelda")
Recruit's Sword
Recruit's Uniform
Red Rupee x2
Spirit Flute
Treasure
Wooden Shield

1 Travel to Castle Town

2 Speak with Princess Zelda

3 Reach the Tower of Spirits

4 Retrieve the Forest Rail Map

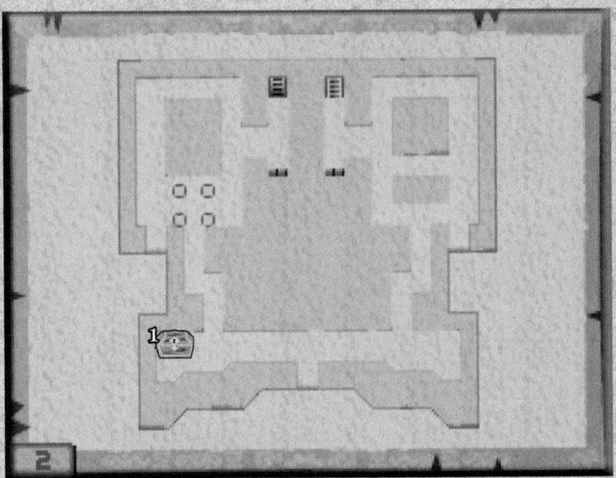

Hyrule Castle Second Floor

Cold Welcome

Aside from a beehive and a few stones, there's not much to interact with around the grounds. Speak to the burly guard at the north gate to gain entry to the castle proper.

The next guard doesn't let Link pass so easily. However, an odd-looking fellow named Chancellor Cole appears and barks at the guard, ordering him to let Link pass. He seems eager to get the ceremony over with, calling it a waste of time. What a creep!

Smash the pots to the side of the stairs before following Chancellor Cole up to the throne room. After all, breaking stuff is always fun—and usually profitable!

Sinister Ceremony

At last, you've come to the ceremony. Time to see what all the hoopla's been about!

None other than Princess Zelda herself appears to conduct the ceremony and award Link his very own Engineer Certificate. Our hero is now a royal engineer in Hyrule's service!

Engineer Certificate

You got your royal Engineer Certificate! Now you're a full-fledged engineer!

That's not to say the ceremony goes off without a hitch. Chancellor Cole interjects at various points, aiming to speed the process along. Something's clearly not right here—a suspicion that's proven true when the princess leans in and whispers to Link that she needs his help!

Shh--take this. No! Don't say a word right now.

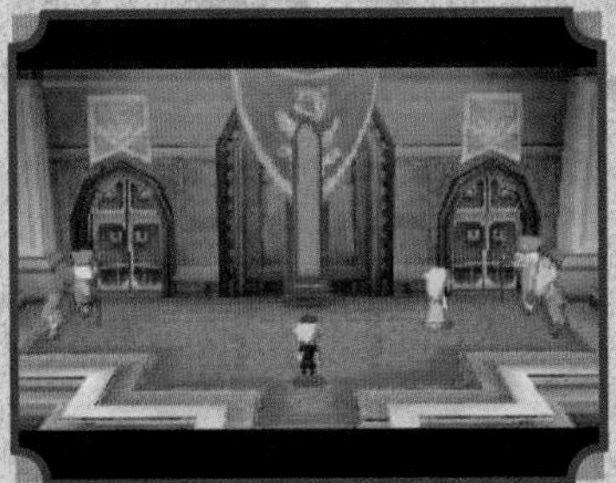

Zelda hands Link a letter and urges him to read it in privacy. She warns him to beware of the chancellor, then retires to her chambers. Say, what's going on around here, anyway?

Letter

You got a letter from the princess! Go to the Collection screen to read it!

Chancellor Cole departs next, flashing Link a terrible, toothy grin as he leaves. Beware the chancellor, indeed.

The door leads to the castle's second floor. This area's totally off-limits, even to royal engineers, so don't let anyone see you! Move directly toward the northeast stairs, which lead up to Zelda's chambers.

Task 2: Speak with Princess Zelda

Helping Zelda

Read Zelda's letter to learn that she'd like to talk to you in private. The princess asks you to sneak along a secret passage to visit her personal quarters. She has outlined the passage on a crude map for you to follow. Tap the Map button to call up your map and copy Zelda's notes onto it.

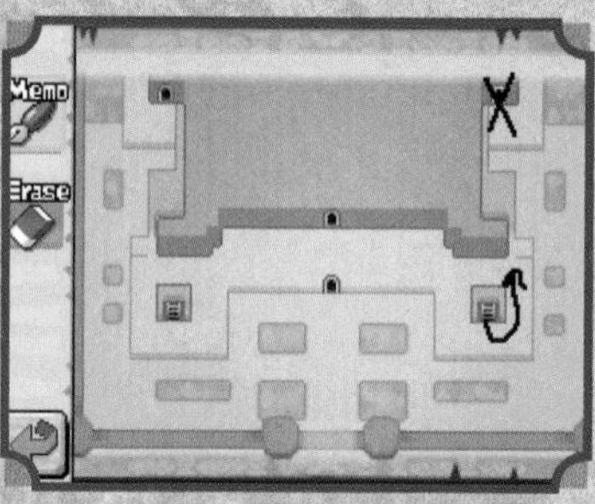

Link finds Zelda playing a somber tune on an ornate pan flute. What an interesting young woman!

Return to the castle's first floor. You can explore more of this area now, as the guards have left their posts to patrol the halls instead. There isn't a whole lot to see at the moment, however, so sprint right and go up the southeast stairs.

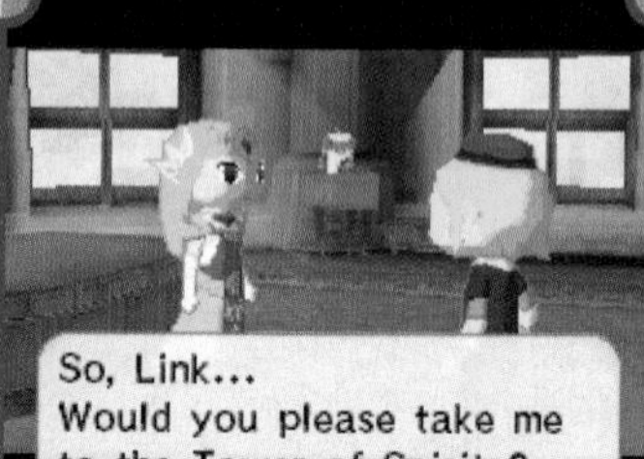

Zelda thanks Link for coming and quickly describes how all of the land's Spirit Tracks are vanishing. She believes the problem must have something to do with the Tower of Spirits, into which the Spirit Tracks flow, and asks Link to ferry her to the tower by train so she might investigate further.

The stairs lead back out to the grounds, but you're up on the ramparts now. Follow the path Zelda gave you, slipping through a small opening in the wall to reach the northeast door.

Agree to bring the princess to the tower, and she'll be overjoyed. Sneaking out of the castle won't be easy, though: Chancellor Cole has restricted Zelda's movements due to "safety concerns," and the guards have strict orders to keep her cooped up inside the castle. The princess hands Link a Recruit's Uniform, thinking the disguise may help them flee the scene without raising an alarm.

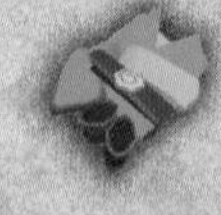

Recruit's Uniform

You got a Recruit's Uniform! Wearing this, you can pose as a soldier and move freely about the castle!

1 Travel to Castle Town

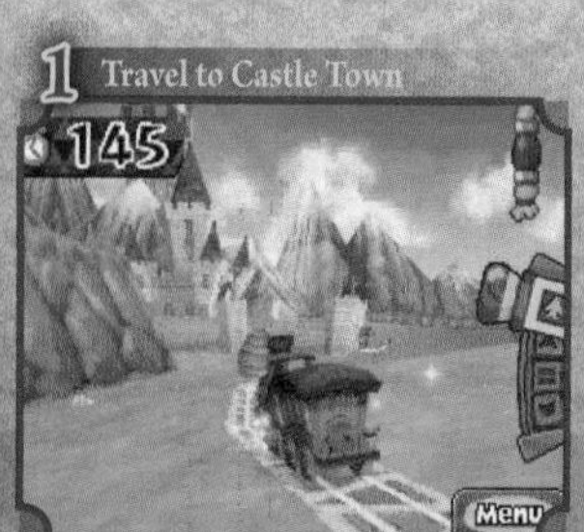

2 Speak with Princess Zelda

3 Reach the Tower of Spirits

4 Retrieve the Forest Rail Map

Task 3: Reach the Tower of Spirits

Engineering an Escape

Follow Zelda back downstairs. Numerous guards now patrol the castle's second floor, and each one is shown on your map. The orange cone emanating from each guard represents his field of vision. Remember: Zelda must not be seen!

Sneaking through the second floor is fairly easy. Just wait for the guards to wander off, then dash up and around the hallway, heading for the east door—the same one you took to get here. No need to order Zelda about; just have her follow Link as you move through.

Tap the Call icon if Zelda ever stops following Link, and she'll hurry to his position.

Don't you have work to do, rookie? Why don't you go cut the grass or something?

At the castle grounds, stationary guards present a greater challenge. You'll need to get creative to slip past them. Have Link distract the closest guard by moving behind him and tapping the guard to start up a conversation.

While the guard is speaking to Link, tap the Switch icon to take control of Zelda. Tap the marker at her feet, and trace a line to the middle of the two small hedges to the guard's south.

If you issue Zelda an incorrect move order, simply tap the marker at her feet to make her stop. Hey, it happens!

Some guards may seem a bit creeped out by Link's extended presence, but don't worry; they won't do anything to him.

Nice work! Once Zelda is hidden between the two hedges, regain control of Link by tapping the Switch icon again or by tapping anywhere on the screen other than the marker at Zelda's feet. Send Link south to distract the next guard ahead while leaving Zelda in place.

Again, sidle up behind the guard and tap him to start chatting. With the guard facing west, switch to Zelda and direct her toward the long hedge south of the second guard's position. Put her close to the hedge's west edge, but keep her out of sight.

The third guard isn't so easily distracted. He won't stop to chat with Link; he's focused on his duty of looking straight ahead. It's important work! You wouldn't understand.

The first rule of patrol duty is vigilance, even when people are talking to you.

To distract this stalwart starer, collect one of the large stones behind him and toss it westward, close to the castle gate. The noise forces the guard to move and investigate.

Immediately switch to Zelda after tossing the rock. Trace a line west, between the two hedges, and then south, leading her out of the castle grounds and into Castle Town. While Zelda's in motion, you can switch back to Link and toss another rock to keep the guard distracted if need be.

Royal Escort

Having escaped the castle in grand fashion, Link and Princess Zelda waste no time rushing to the train station. Alfonzo is shocked to see the princess, and Link is surprised to learn the two know each other. It turns out Alfonzo was formerly a great swordsman and officer of the castle guard.

Oh! Hello, Your Highness!
What are you doing here?

Please come with us to the
Tower of Spirits!

At Zelda's request, Alfonzo agrees to accompany the pair on their journey to the Tower of Spirits. After all, who better to have by your side than a gifted swordsman when venturing into the perilous unknown?

Vanishing Tracks

Sadly, the trio don't quite make it to their intended destination. As they steam along their way, the Spirit Tracks suddenly vanish out from underneath them, and the train derails in a heap!

The terrible crash ruins Alfonzo's train and does a number on poor Link. Apparently, royal engineers are not required to wear safety belts.

As if the vanishing tracks weren't bad enough, a darkness soon covers the land. Thick clouds blanket the sky, and a sinister force envelopes the tower, shattering it into pieces and suspending them in the sky!

A scary-looking train suddenly descends from on high, soaring through the air and nearly plowing into Link and Zelda. The train speeds off, leaving none other than Chancellor Cole in its wake.

1 Travel to Castle Town

2 Speak with Princess Zelda

3 Reach the Tower of Spirits

4 Retrieve the Forest Rail Map

My goodness, pretending to be human is exhausting.

With a burst of rage, the chancellor transforms his appearance, revealing his true form: a double-horned fiend! Cole isn't alone, either; a burly ruffian saunters up beside him, glowering with menace.

The other man's name is Byrne, and he has no qualms against fighting Alfonzo. Talented though he is, the former swordsman is no match for the brute's might. With a powerful blow, Alfonzo is quickly knocked unconscious.

Though he steps up heroically in Zelda's defense, Link proves to be even less of a challenge for Byrne, who knocks him aside without pause. Cole then unleashes his wicked power at the princess, subduing her.

Guards to the Rescue

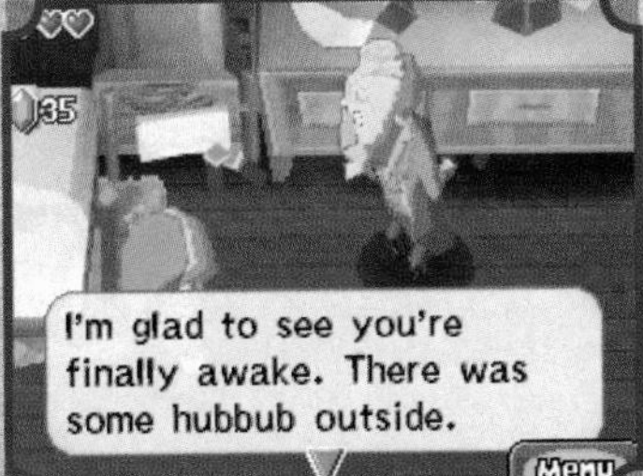

I'm glad to see you're finally awake. There was some hubbub outside.
Menu

Link awakens in the guard's quarters of Hyrule Castle, none the worse for wear. An old man known only as Teacher is there to greet him, and he informs Link that the castle guard found both him and Alfonzo lying unconscious when they went to investigate the disturbance outside. Unfortunately, Alfonzo is still quite injured and bedridden for the time being. It's been a rough day for that guy!

Teacher is horrified to learn that Zelda has been kidnapped, which is the last thing Link saw before he fell unconscious. He clings to the hope that the princess is simply off on an adventure somewhere and not in the clutches of evil.

So...what you're saying is...the princess has been kidnapped!
Menu

Noble Ghost

...Can any of you see me? I need your help!

Step out of the guard's quarters to see a haunting sight: the spirit of Princess Zelda! The princess's ghost floats up to the throne room, distraught that the guards don't acknowledge her presence. Follow after her!

Link watches Zelda's spirit float through the door leading toward her chambers. That's where she must be headed! Tap the large door to open it and give chase, hurrying up the stairs beyond.

Sure enough, Link finds Zelda's ghost lingering in her quarters. She is surprised that Link can see and hear her but is dismayed that the chancellor managed to fool her so easily.

...Can you...see me, Link?

This Spirit Flute is a prized family heirloom.

Struggling to put it all together, Zelda finally realizes that she must visit the Tower of Spirits, now more than ever. Before setting off, she asks Link to take her Spirit Flute, certain that the ancient instrument is meant to protect her.

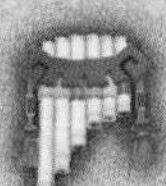

Spirit Flute

You got the Spirit Flute! This pan flute will probably come in very handy!

I've heard that there's a path from the castle to the tower...

As Link begins to leave Zelda's quarters, the princess suddenly realizes that they cannot get to the Tower of Spirits by train. However, she recalls that there used to be a path running behind the castle that led to the tower.

Finding the Path

You can explore the entire second floor now, so go ahead and do so. Tap the chest you discover in the floor's southwest corner to claim a shiny Red Rupee.

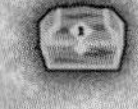

Overworld Chest 1: Red Rupee

Red Rupee

You got a Red Rupee! It's worth 20 Rupees!

Next, sprint to the floor's northwest corner, and smash three pots for three valuable star fragment treasures.

Treasure

You got a treasure! Check it out on the Collection screen!

Run south a bit and exit through the nearby door to reach the courtyard ramparts. Pop open another chest here to claim a treasure.

Overworld Chest 2: Treasure

Treasure

You got a treasure! Check it out on the Collection screen!

Return through the door and make your way to the northern stairs, which lead down to the first floor. There you discover the back door that Princess Zelda thought might lead to the old path to the tower; however, the guard standing watch won't let you through without a sword.

It's not the kind of place
you want to go without

Gearing Up

Zelda thinks that the captain of the guard, Russell, just might lend you a sword. It's worth a shot! But before you leave, take a moment to open the nearby treasure chest and collect a Red Rupee.

Overworld Chest 3: Red Rupee

Red Rupee

You got a Red Rupee! It's worth 20 Rupees!

Some swordsman you are,
running around with no
sword!

Russell stands in the guards' training room, which is located on the right side of the castle's first floor. Go there and speak with the burly man to score some sharp steel. Now you're playing with power!

Recruit's Sword

You got the Recruit's Sword! Tap an enemy or slide the stylus to attack.

1 Travel to Castle Town

2 Speak with Princess Zelda

Swordplay Training

If Russell is to give a sword to such a young man, he needs to know the kid can use it properly. Complete his brief sword training by first tapping all of the soldiers twice to strike them with one targeted attack each.

Targeted attacks are ideal, as they have the least chance of missing. Furthermore, if Link is a good distance away from the enemy, he'll perform a leaping attack, dealing double damage.

Next, attack each soldier with a slide-slash. Perform the move by tracing a line sideways across the screen in the direction of the enemy (as if you were swinging the sword horizontally at them). Hit each guard with two side-slashes to advance.

Side-slashes are great defensive attacks, as they can hit practically anything that stands within range in front of Link.

Lastly, perform a powerful spin attack by tracing a circle around Link. Whack each guard with two spin attacks to complete the training.

TIP

Spin attacks are incredibly powerful, inflicting twice the damage of a normal attack and striking anything and everything around Link. However, Link becomes dizzy if you perform too many of these special attacks in a row.

The one attack Russell doesn't cover is the forward stab, which you execute by drawing a straight line directly toward Link's target. Forward stabs inflict normal damage and are ideal for keeping less-mobile foes at bay.

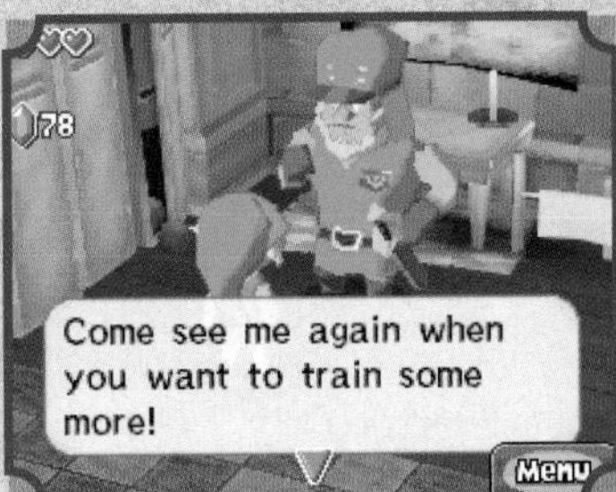

78
Come see me again when you want to train some more!
Menu

Impressed with Link's aptitude for the blade, Russell has no qualms with letting the lad run about with such a dangerous weapon. He even invites Link to return later for more training—keep this generous offer in mind!

Score a Shield

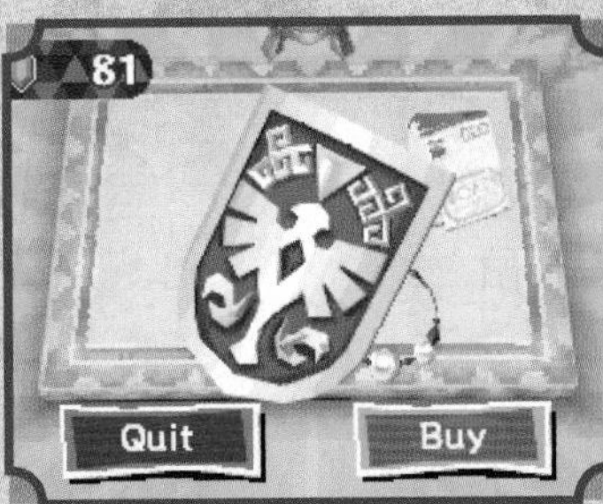

You're ready to venture off toward the Tower of Spirits now, but before you go, consider popping into Castle Town's shop to pick up a shield. It costs only 80 Rupees, and the defensive benefits are well worth the price!

If you're a bit short on funds, run around and break stuff until you scrape together 80 Rupees. Now that you have a sword, you can cut grass to find loose Rupees, too!

Wooden Shield

You got the Wooden Shield! Defend yourself from minor attacks just by holding it!

Now you're ready to handle yourself out there. Return to the castle and take the second floor's northwest stairs down to reach the northern section of the first floor. Seeing you're armed and dangerous, the guard lets you pass without incident. Time for some good ol' adventuring!

Oh, I see you got yourself
a weapon. All right then.
Be careful out there!
Menu

Trek to the Tower

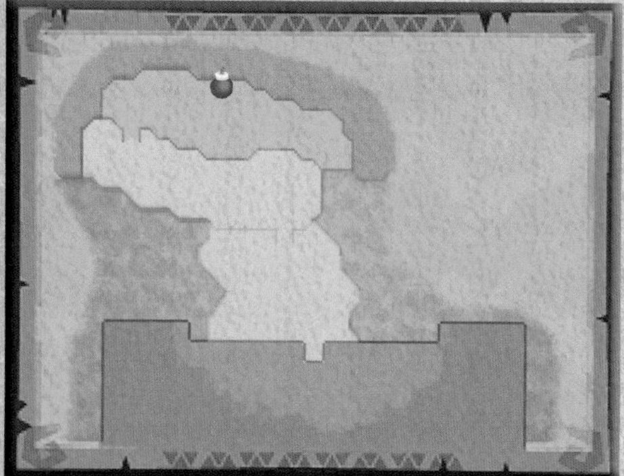

Path to the Tower

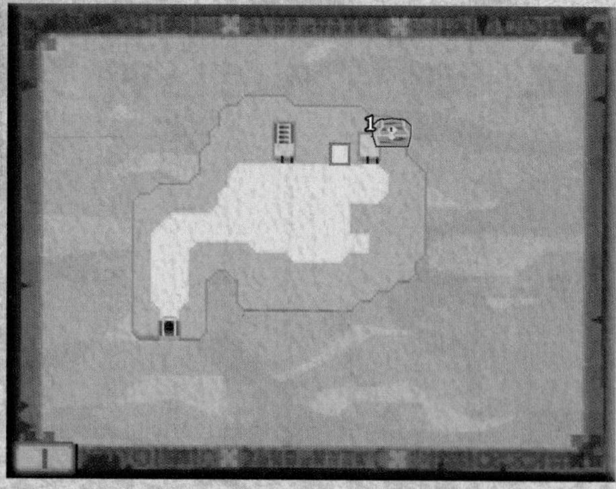

Tunnel to the Tower, First Floor

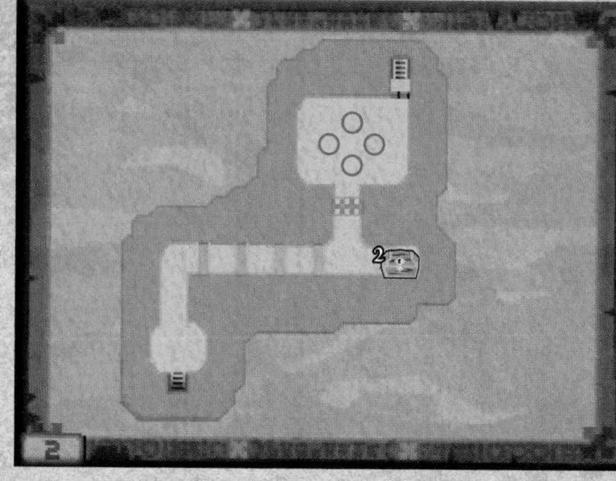

Tunnel to the Tower, Second Floor

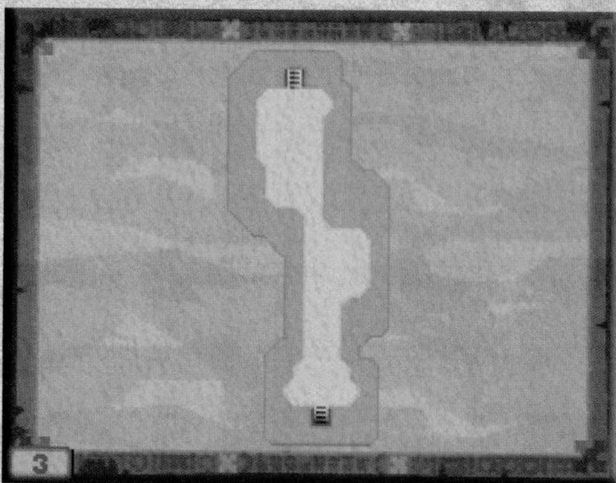

Tunnel to the Tower, Third Floor

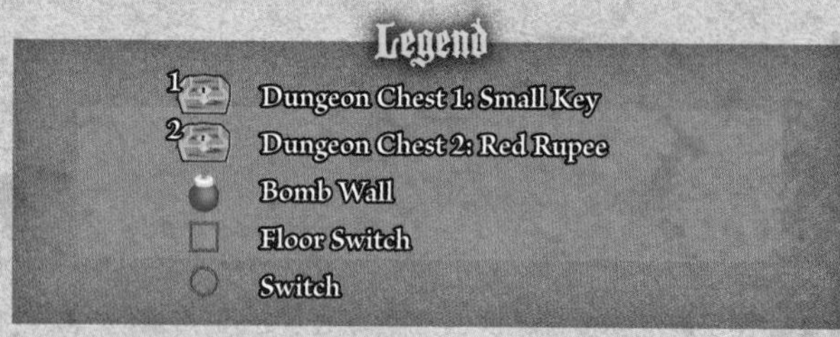

Items to Obtain

Red Rupee

Small Key

Path to the Tower

You'll instantly appreciate having the Wooden Shield at the ready—that is, if you picked it up from the Castle Town shop. The Spinuts you encounter along the path charge at Link relentlessly, but they bounce harmlessly off his shield if you don't swing at them. 'Course, there's no good reason to spare these little cretins, so swing away!

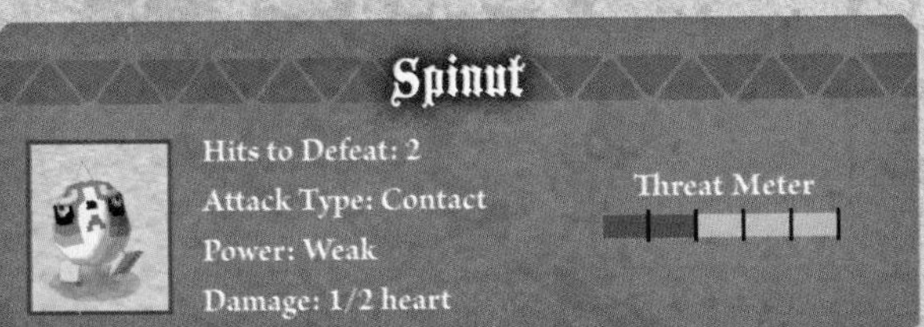

A Call for Backup

Just ahead, a guard is being overwhelmed by Spinuts. Looks like *someone* didn't come prepared with a shield. Dispatch the monsters to save the guard and earn his thanks.

Well, there was a path up that way, but recently the rockfalls have closed it off.

The guard has some valuable information: The entrance to the tunnel that leads to the tower has been covered up by a rockslide. There's no trace of the tunnel's mouth anymore, but it merits a closer look.

Fun with Bomb Flowers

There's little of interest at the trail's north end save a couple of Bomb Flowers. These are your ticket inside the cave! Tap the Bomb Flower to snatch up a bomb, then quickly run east and toss the bomb near the middle of the northern rock wall. Don't worry if your aim is off; Bomb Flowers indefinitely produce replacement bombs, so you can just keep trying.

Boom! The bomb blows a hole through the rock wall, revealing the entrance to the tunnel. Hurry inside, young hero!

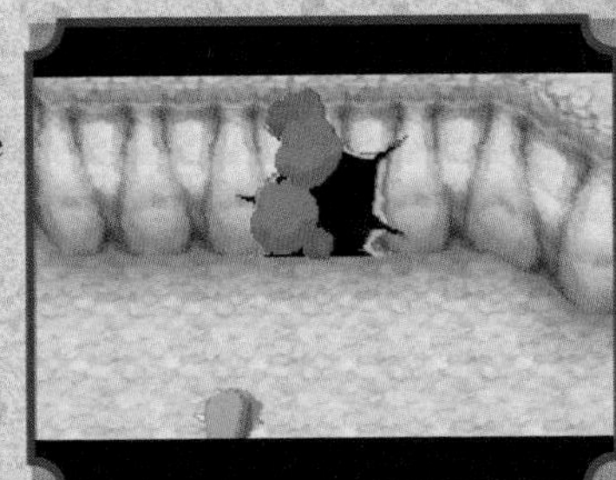

Tunnel to the Tower: First Floor

The tunnel is dark and damp—and filled with foes. Tread lightly as you tap each Keese and Red ChuChu, slaying the fiends in short order.

Tip

Don't hesitate to collect hearts dropped by defeated enemies. They don't linger for long, so grab 'em while they last.

Keese

Hits to Defeat: 1
Attack Type: Contact
Power: Weak
Damage: 1/4 heart

Threat Meter

Red ChuChu

Hits to Defeat: 1
Attack Type: Contact
Power: Weak
Damage: 1/2 heart

Threat Meter

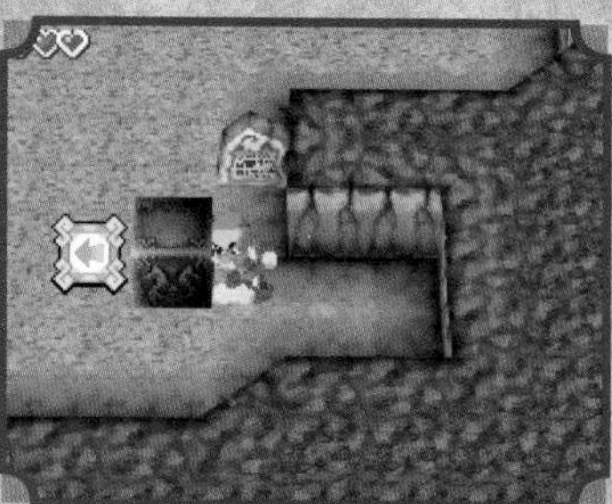

Tap the nearby stone sign to read it for a clue: You can push a nearby block. Stand to the right of the block and tap it to grab a hold; then tap the Arrow icon that appears to slide the block to the left.

Once you're past the stone sign, stand south of the block and slide it north toward a floor switch. Maneuver the block onto the switch to open the sealed door to the right, revealing a treasure chest.

You got a small key!
Use this key to open
locked doors!

Open the chest to claim a Small Key. With this, you can now tap the locked door to the left and open it. Proceed up the stairs beyond to reach the tunnel's second floor.

NOTE

Any Small Keys you're carrying are shown at the lower-right corner of the Map screen.

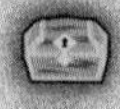

Dungeon Chest 1: Small Key

Small Key

You got a Small Key! Use this key to open locked doors!

Tunnel to the Tower: Second Floor

16
The door won't open if you
just hit the switches in
a circle.
Menu

Pause to read the second floor's stone signs for clues on how to proceed. Don't worry if the clues seem cryptic; they'll make sense soon enough.

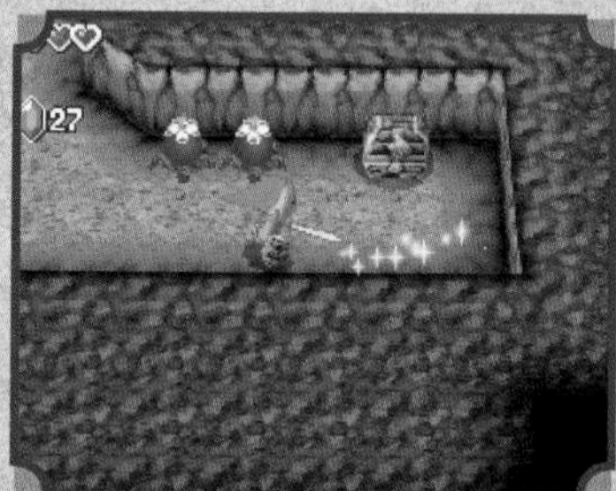
27

Flip the lid of the chest to the right for a Red Rupee. You'll refill your wallet in no time!

Dungeon Chest 2: Red Rupee

Red Rupee

You got a Red Rupee! It's worth 20 Rupees!

1 Travel to Castle Town

145
Menu

2 Speak with Princess Zelda

3 Reach the Tower of Spirits

4 Retrieve the Forest Rail Map

Pluck bombs from the nearby bomb flowers and place them near the cracked blocks ahead to blast open the way forward.

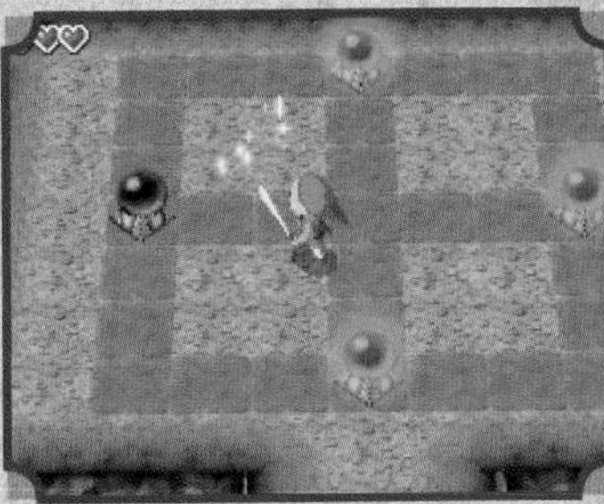

Aha! You've found the switches those signs were describing! Do you recall the pattern? Hit the switches in this order: east, north, south, west. This opens the north door, allowing you to reach the tunnel's third floor.

Tunnel to the Tower: Third Floor

Zelda gets a good scare as you speed through the final floor. Rats slither out from a hole in the wall, really freaking the princess out! Aw, how cute. Come to your maiden's rescue, valiant hero, and slay the foul beasts with righteous steel.

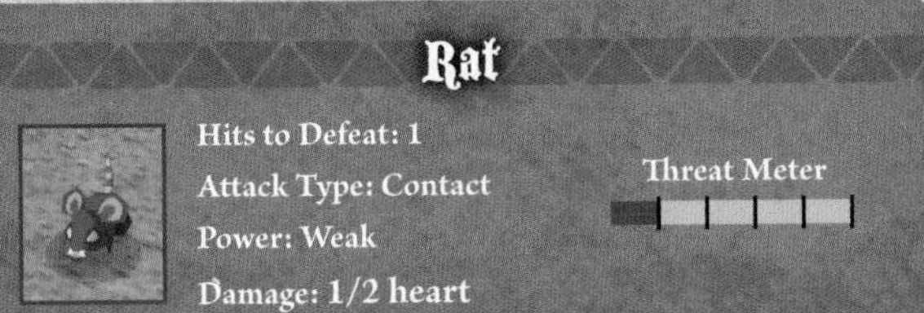

Rat

Hits to Defeat: 1
Attack Type: Contact
Power: Weak
Damage: 1/2 heart

Threat Meter

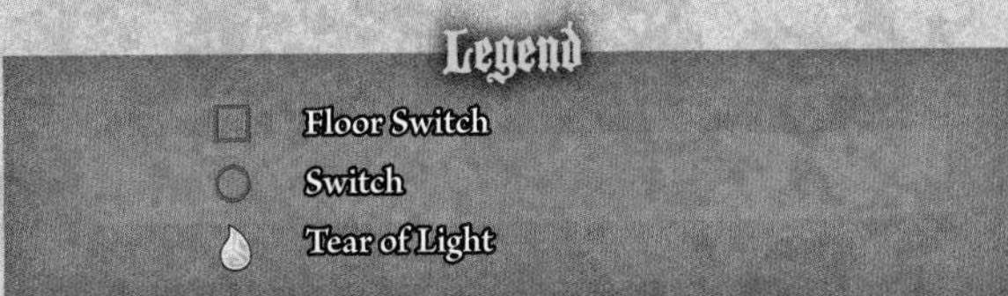

Legend

Floor Switch
Switch
Tear of Light

Items to Obtain

Forest Rail Map
Tear of Light x3

Enemies Encountered

Spinut
Phantom
Rat

Task 4: Retrieve the Forest Rail Map

The Tower of Spirits

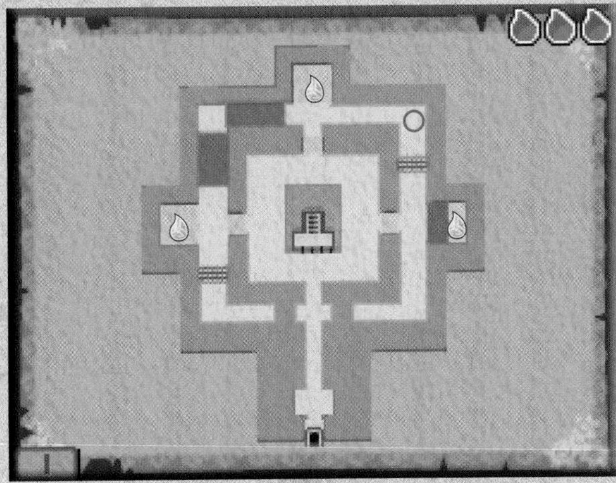

Tower of Spirits, First Floor

Tower of Spirits, Second Floor

Tower of Spirits, Third Floor

Zelda and Link arrive at the base of the tumultuous tower, watching in awe as the majority of the structure spins in midair, broken into several sections. What a mess!

Perhaps even more amazing is a train the duo discover sitting nearby. How could this have gotten here?

Are you...the wise one?

The answer comes from a mysterious voice: An odd-looking old woman rolls up on wheels, informing the two that the vehicle is none other than the Spirit Train. The woman goes on to explain everything that's going on: how the tower itself is a powerful seal against evil, powered by the Spirit Tracks that run from four temples, one at each corner of the land. Only by restoring the Spirit Tracks that link the temples to the tower can the land be saved.

59
You must ascend the tower and retrieve the rail maps!
Menu

The woman's name is Anjean, and she's an ancient guardian of the Spirit Train. She says that, to restore the tracks that lead to the first temple, Link and Zelda must brave the tower—what's left of it, at least—and retrieve the first of four special rail maps. The rail maps will help them travel to the temples, where they must go to reenergize the Spirit Tracks and restore the tower.

There's no time to waste! Sprint up the north steps to enter the tower's staircase, then run up the stairs and into the only door.

Tower of Spirits: First Floor

Unfortunately, Link and Zelda's first trip up into the tower isn't very successful. A monstrous creature of armor materializes out of thin air, stalks Link, and sends him back to the tower's base with a swipe of its magical sword.

Back So Soon

Returning to Anjean, the two learn the nature of the creature: It is a Phantom, one of the tower's more formidable guardians. Though Phantoms are supposed to hunt the wicked, it's likely that an evil spirit has possessed them, which explains this one's attack on Link.

Sounds like a Phantom, my dear. They're the guardians of the Tower of Spirits.

Anjean advises Link to collect three special objects called Tears of Light, which can infuse his sword with righteous power. Once Link's blade is fully charged, one swipe to a Phantom's unarmored back should be enough to banish the evil spirit.

1 Travel to Castle Town

2 Speak with Princess Zelda

3 Reach the Tower of Spirits

4 Retrieve the Forest Rail Map

Fair enough! Armed with your new knowledge of how to handle Phantoms, head back to the tower.

Tower of Spirits: First Floor Revisited

Your next trip into the tower is far more eventful. The Phantom's still about, but it's on patrol duty now, stalking the central halls. You can see the Phantom's location and field of vision on your map. Keep your distance and run west to find the first Tear of Light (also shown on your map).

Phantom

Hits to Defeat: 1 (with powered-up sword)

Attack Type: Contact

Power: Strong

Damage: 1 heart

Threat Meter

En route to the west Tear of Light, Link must cross a special floor tile known as a *safe zone*. Anjean's voice suddenly rings out, informing Link that Phantoms can't harm him as long as he stands within a safe zone. Good to know!

Continue west and collect the first Tear of Light. Two more to go!

Tear of Light

You got a Tear of Light! Gather three of them to power up your sword!

Return to the central hall and make for the north Tear of Light; it is north of the central hall and within easy reach. Just be sure that Phantom doesn't spot you! Hurry to a safe zone if it does, and the brute will quickly lose track of you.

Tear of Light

You got a Tear of Light! Gather three of them to power up your sword!

With two Tears of Light in your possession, check the northeast corner of the floor to discover a dark crystal. These objects are known as switches; hit the switch with Link's sword to light it up.

Activating the switch extends a bridge to the final Tear of Light. Return to the central halls and run east to claim this final item.

Tear of Light

You got a Tear of Light! Gather three of them to power up your sword!

Anjean was as good as her word. Now that Link has collected all three Tears of Light, his sword begins to glow with power. Time for some payback!

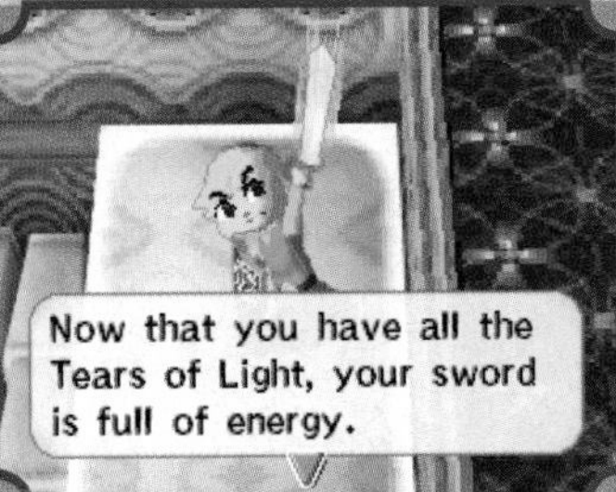

Run up behind the Phantom (don't worry, it can't hear Link's footfalls) and attack its back with Link's sword. The monster freezes for a moment, then rounds on its attacker.

Seeing the Phantom poised to retaliate, Princess Zelda acts on instinct to protect her friend. She flies at the Phantom, passing into the monster just as its sword comes speeding toward Hyrule's youngest engineer. With a flash of light, the Phantom suddenly halts its attack—much to Link's relief!

It's me! It's Zelda!

Incredibly, Zelda has somehow managed to merge with the Phantom, taking total control of the creature. This could come in handy!

You're now able to control Phantom Zelda in the same manner as you did when escaping the castle. Approach the massive double door at the floor's center, then draw a line from the marker at Zelda's feet to one half of the door. Take control of Link and tap the other half of the door, and the two will shove it open and advance upstairs.

Tower of Spirits: Second Floor

Spikes block Link's progress through the second floor, but they pose little threat to Phantom Zelda. Direct Zelda past the spikes, and watch as she walks across them without suffering harm. There's no denying it: Phantoms make handy friends!

Trace another line to a nearby switch, and Zelda will approach it and smack it with her sword. This retracts the floor spikes, allowing Link to progress.

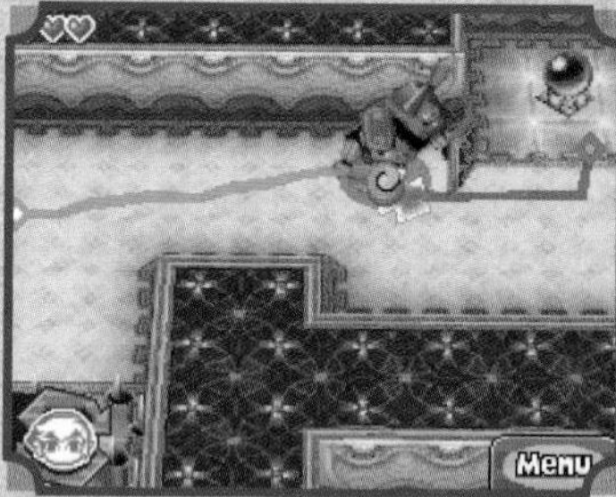

The north pit is too wide to cross, so venture south and wipe out the Spinuts that lie in wait. Position Link and Zelda on each of the two floor switches here to open the nearby sealed door.

Uh-oh, Rats! Even when covered in mega-thick armor, Zelda is still terrified of these dirty vermin. Have Link eliminate the pests, then shove the nearby block to seal off the Rat hole.

1 Travel to Castle Town
145

2 Speak with Princess Zelda

3 Reach the Tower of Spirits

4 Retrieve the Forest Rail Map

Lead Zelda across the next patch of floor spikes. Another Phantom guards the staircase ahead, and it's not leaving its post anytime soon. It won't take much notice of Zelda, though, so send her trudging past the guardian and have her whack the switch beyond.

The switch drops the floor spikes back near Link. Before switching control, issue Zelda one last move order. Trace a line directly to the Phantom, and she'll strike up a conversation with the ancient creature. The lonely Phantom turns its back to Link to speak with its "comrade."

Now's your chance! Switch to Link and run up behind the enemy Phantom. Slash its back with your powered-up sword to defeat the evil spirit that's controlling the creature, then tap the stunned Phantom to have Zelda leave her current host and take up a new one. This eliminates the threat and clears the way upstairs.

Tower of Spirits: Third Floor

Ahhh... It's nice to get out of that clanky outfit and back to my old self.

Entering the tower's third floor, Zelda is forced out of her Phantom suit, and the light fades from Link's sword. You've come to the rail map's holding chamber!

Bolt up to the central platform to obtain the first of four rail maps you must collect from the Tower of Spirits. Excellent work! Anjean is sure to be pleased with your success.

Forest Rail Map

You got the Forest Rail Map! Some of the lost Spirit Tracks on it are reappearing!

TIP

No need to truck it back down the tower; simply step into the blue light that appears nearby to warp back down to Anjean.

Getting Lost: The Forest Temple

Working together, Link and Zelda have succeeded in scaling a portion of the Tower of Spirits and claiming the first rail map. This great success has reenergized some of the Forest Realm's Spirit Tracks! Now, the duo must venture forth to the Forest Temple so they may reestablish the link between the temple and the Tower of Spirits. Reaching the temple won't be easy, though; a confounding forest known as the Lost Woods stands in the way.

Enemies Encountered

Moink	Snurgle

A Link to the Present

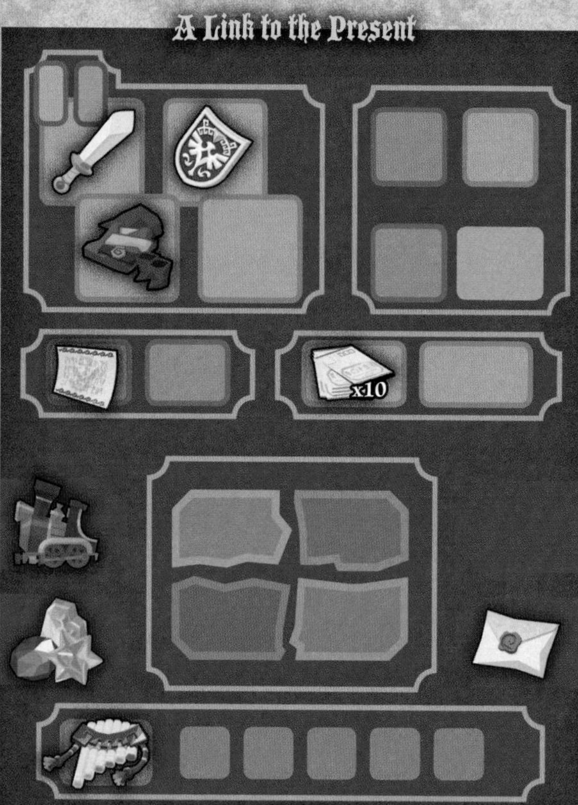

Items Already Acquired

Engineer Certificate	Forest Rail Map	Recruit's Sword	Recruit's Uniform	Spirit Flute	Wooden Shield

Task 1: Visit Whittleton Village

Words of Wisdom

But I don't think you can make it to the temple as things are right now.

Anjean is thrilled to hear of Link and Zelda's success in finding the first rail map. Though the newly formed Spirit Tracks don't lead all the way to the temple, the old Lokomo informs the two that another spirit guardian named Gage might be able to help. Gage lives at the Forest Sanctuary, and Anjean kindly points to its location on the map.

I'm sure the spirits wouldn't mind lending it to you.

Now our heroes know where to go, but how are they to get there? Realizing the gravity of the situation at hand, Anjean graciously allows them to take the Spirit Train. Thanking Anjean, Link and Zelda depart without further ado.

When your rail map appears, trace a line along the tracks, plotting a course toward the station you passed before on your way to Castle Town. Tap "Go" to set off toward your destination.

1 Visit Whittleton Village

2 Pass Through the Lost Woods

3 Speak with Gage

4 Clear the Forest Temple

Should you decide to change your destination, simply tap Route at the screen's bottom left to plot a new course.

You may now view your rail map at any time. Just tap Menu, then Rail Map for a large-scale view of the land. You can scribble notes on the rail map, and you can tap any place you've visited to call up its local area map. Handy!

Blow 'Em Away

Remember to use your whistle to scatter Moinks from the tracks.

New enemies accost you on your way to the station: Snurgles! You can't defeat these monsters at present, so whenever one appears, toot the whistle to make it flee.

Snurgle

Hits to Defeat: 1 (scatter with whistle)
Attack Type: Contact
Power: N/A
Damage: 1 heart
Threat Meter

As you near the station, put your train in park so that it begins to slow. Again, if you're moving too fast, slam it into reverse to apply the emergency brake. Just be sure to put it in park when you're ready to detrain.

Task 2: Pass Through the Lost Woods

Whittleton Village

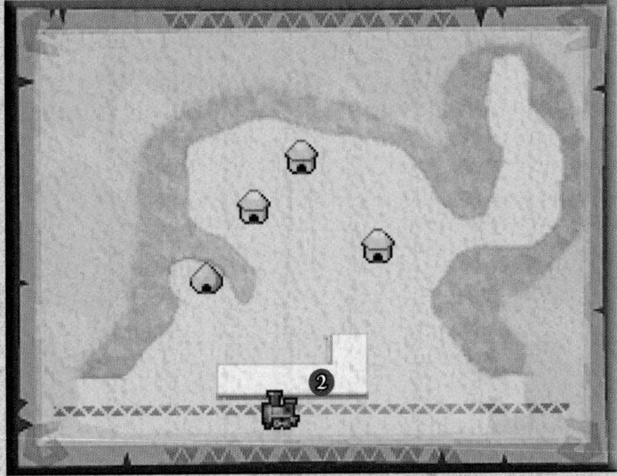

Whittleton Village

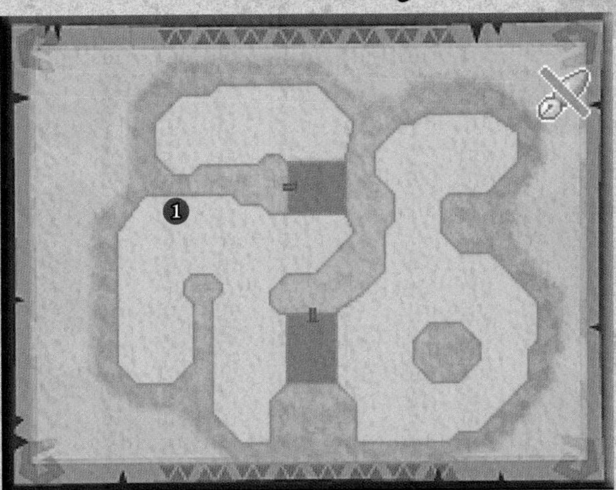

Whittleton Village North

Legend

1 Stamp station
2 Train station

Enemies Encountered

Spinut

Lost Woodsmen

Welcome to Whittleton, seat of intrigue and excitement! Well, not really. Things are pretty humdrum here, but take a moment to say hi to folks. Everyone's glad you've managed to restore the Spirit Tracks, as their lumber trade was beginning to rot without them.

The village shop has a few interesting goods, including a Wooden Shield. Definitely pick one up if you haven't yet!

Gage, the forest guardian, lives in those parts.
Menu

Speak with the village elder, who lives in the northernmost hut. The elder confirms that Gage does indeed live in the nearby forest, but he warns that it's easy to get turned around in the place. That's why everyone calls it the Lost Woods!

Just don't listen to that fourth tree. It has no sense of direction.
Menu

The elder advises you speak with the Whittleton villagers again for clues on how to navigate the Lost Woods. It's sound advice, for the villagers know that the forest's old trees point out the proper route. However, one villager warns you not to listen to the fourth tree, because its sense of direction is all whacky.

But you don't have a stamp book...
Menu

Right! Now that you've learned how to navigate the Lost Woods, you'd best be on your way. You can explore the northern region of the village if you like, where you'll encounter a few Spinuts and discover another stamp station. You still can't use stamp stations, but mark this one's location for future reference.

NOTE

You'll return to the northern portion of Whittleton later with a special item that'll allow you to explore this area more fully.

Through the Woods

Return to your train and speak with Zelda when she materializes. Tell her you wish to head out, and you'll be on your way. Plot a course west, heading straight into the Lost Woods.

The Lost Woods sure are creepy, but it's not that hard getting through. Pay attention to the old, bare trees; you pass one before each junction. Whichever way these trees' limbs point is the way you must go.

TIP

Remember to ignore that fourth tree! Whichever way its limb points, go the opposite direction.

1 Visit Whittleton Village

2 Pass Through the Lost Woods

3 Speak with Gage

4 Clear the Forest Temple

Task 3: Speak with Gage

Forest Sanctuary

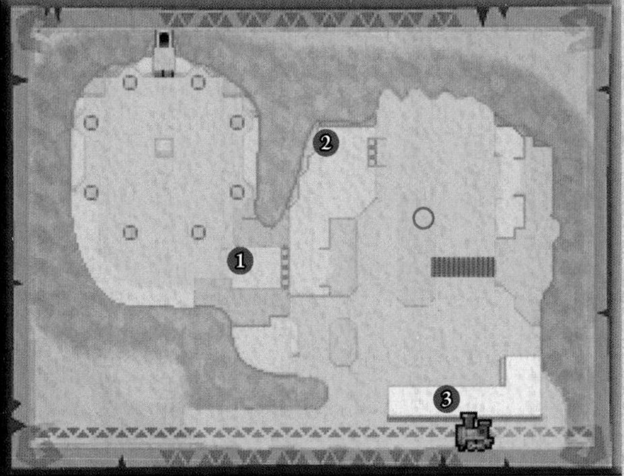

Forest Sanctuary

Legend

- 1 Air Stone
- 2 Stamp station
- ○ Switch
- 3 Train station

Items to Obtain

Song of Awakening

Enemies Encountered

Spinut | Crow | Red ChuChu

Seeking Gage

This place may be called a sanctuary, but it's crawling with monsters. Cut down those Spinuts, and make a note of the treasure chest you see on a high ledge, which you can't reach right now.

Heads-up: Dangerous Crows lurk in the treetops here, ready to swoop down and attack. These annoying birds steal your Rupees, so don't let them touch you! It's usually best to outmaneuver Crows rather than try to fight them.

Crow

Hits to Defeat: 1
Attack Type: Contact
Power: Strong
Damage: 1/2 heart

Threat Meter

Bombs and Bridges

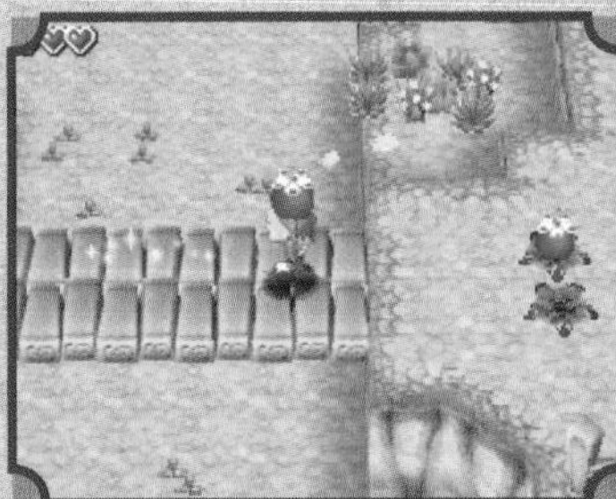

A bit of cunning is needed to reach the sanctuary's west half. Run up the northeast steps to locate a pair of Bomb Flowers. Pluck a bomb from one of them, then sprint across the nearby bridge.

Quickly throw the bomb next to the darkened switch beyond the bridge, then run back across. Grab another bomb from the other plant.

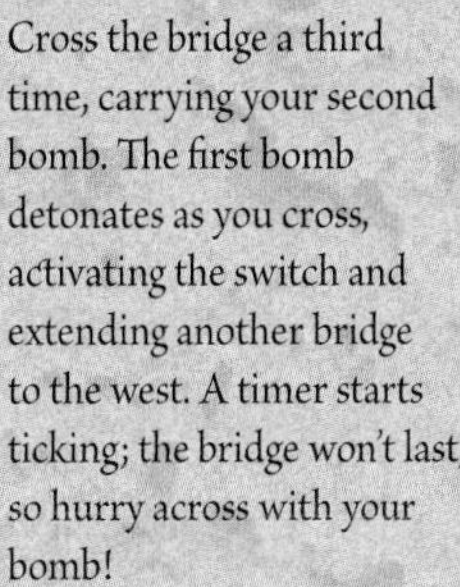

Cross the bridge a third time, carrying your second bomb. The first bomb detonates as you cross, activating the switch and extending another bridge to the west. A timer starts ticking; the bridge won't last, so hurry across with your bomb!

Toss the bomb next to the cracked blocks beyond the bridge to blow them away, opening the way forward.

TIP

If you're having trouble tossing bombs close to objects, try running up close to the object and then tapping the ground near Link's feet. This makes Link set the bomb down with greater care.

Great work! You can ignore the northern set of bomb blocks for now; there's really no need to destroy them at present. But take note of yet another stamp station that stands nearby.

The Statue's Song

Beyond the bomb blocks stands an odd stone statue. Pause near the statue to hear faint music coming from it. How strange! Tap the statue for a closer look, then wait as you begin to see colored balls drift out of the statue's mouth.

The statue is trying to tell you something. Tap Menu, then tap the Spirit Flute to make Link take up the ancient instrument. Tap and hold the stylus on the Spirit Flute, then slide the stylus so that the instrument's blue pipe is centered on the screen. Blow into the microphone, and keep blowing as you slide the stylus to play the orange note next.

Imitating the statue's song makes it spring to life. Incredible! The statue informs you that you've just learned the Song of Awakening, which you may play to awaken anything that sleeps nearby. This should come in handy!

106
That song you just played is called the Song of Awakening.
Menu

Check your Collection screen to review the songs you've learned. Tap a song to call up its melody in case you've forgotten it.

Song of Awakening

You've learned the Song of Awakening! Play it to wake up anything that's asleep.

1 Visit Whittleton Village

2 Pass Through the Lost Woods

3 Speak with Gage

4 Clear the Forest Temple

Here's Looking at You

Defeat the Red ChuChus to the west, then tap the sign in the center of the ring of stone statues. The sign instructs you to connect the two stone statues that face each other—but you'll have to examine them first.

Run around and check out the statues. Sure enough, two of them are looking right at each other. Return to the sign and trace a line between these two statues to solve the puzzle and open the north door.

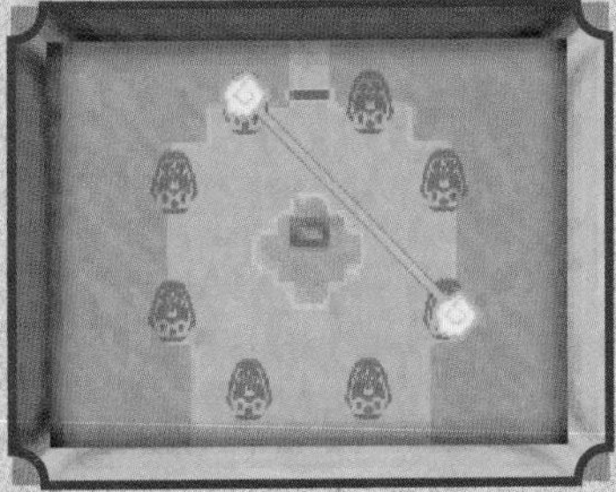

Playing with Gage

To restore the tracks that disappeared, you need to know a special song.

Gage awaits you in the chamber beyond the door. He greets Zelda and Link and tells them they must play a special song to restore the Spirit Tracks leading toward the Forest Temple. No problemo, Lokomo!

Gage teaches you your part of the song first. This is just for practice, so don't worry if you make any mistakes—we won't tell. Use the Spirit Flute as you did before, tapping and holding the stylus and sliding it as you blow into the microphone. Sound the notes in rhythm to the beat.

Ah, what lovely music you make! When you're ready to try the real thing, tap the Back Arrow icon at the screen's bottom left. Gage tells you that, for the real song, his part is different than yours. Don't let his part mess you up! Bob your head to keep the timing if it helps, and play your part after Gage plays his.

Complete the song with Gage to restore even more of the Forest Realm's Spirit Tracks. Great work! Now you can reach the temple!

To the Temple

Enemies Encountered

Skulltula

Frightening Forest

Bid Gage a fond farewell and return to your train. Plot a northward course to the Forest Temple. The Spirit Tracks must be reenergized!

Scary Skulltulas descend from the forest's roof as you motor toward the temple. Scatter these giant spiders with your whistle before you strike them, and continue on your way without pause.

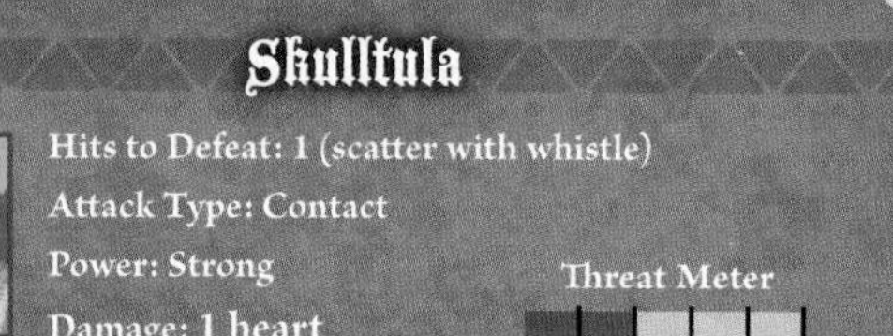

Skulltula

Hits to Defeat: 1 (scatter with whistle)

Attack Type: Contact

Power: Strong

Damage: 1 heart

Threat Meter

Task 4: Clear the Forest Temple

Forest Temple

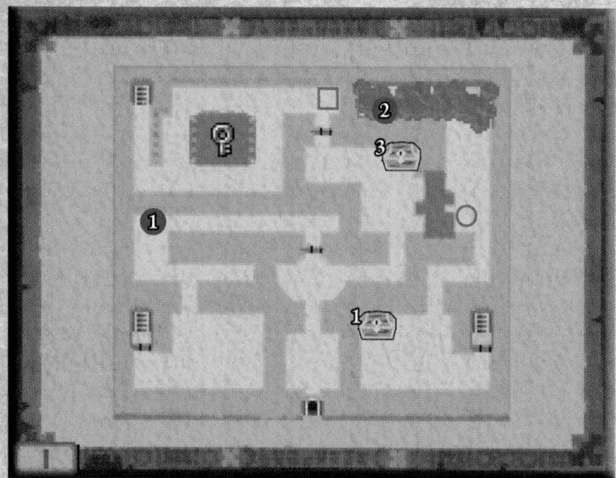

Forest Temple, First Floor

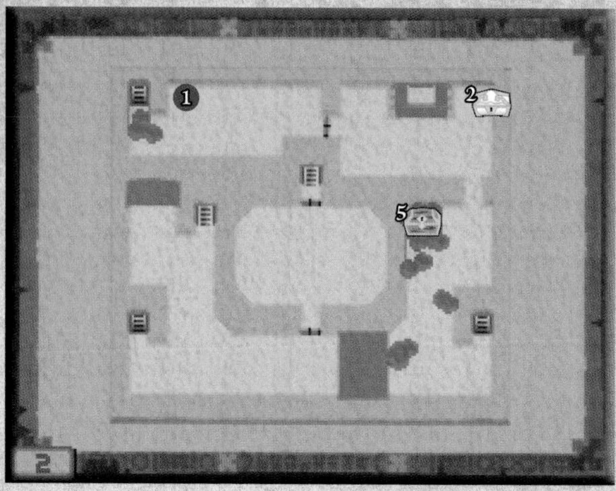

Forest Temple, Second Floor

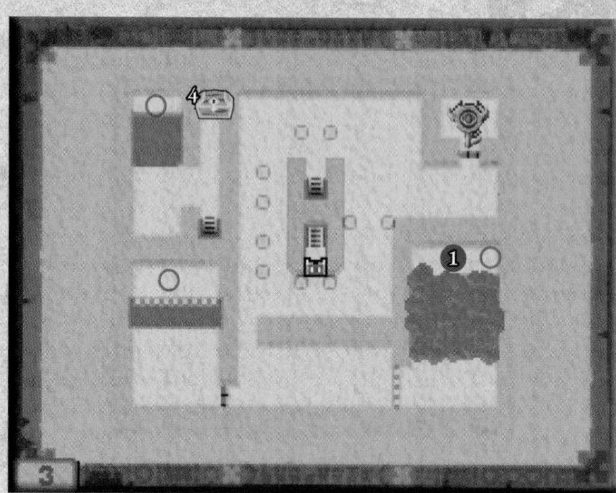

Forest Temple, Third Floor

Items to Obtain

1 Visit Whittleton Village

2 Pass Through the Lost Woods

3 Speak with Gage

4 Clear the Forest Temple

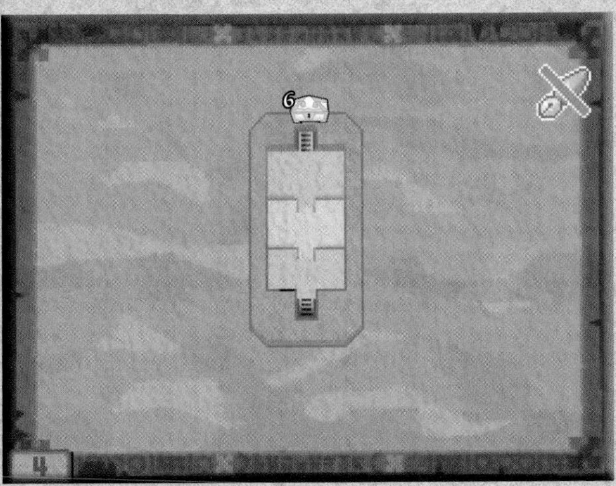

Forest Temple, Fourth Floor

Legend

- 1 Dungeon Chest 1: Big Green Rupee
- 2 Dungeon Chest 2: The Whirlwind
- 3 Dungeon Chest 3: Treasure
- 4 Dungeon Chest 4: Big Green Rupee
- 5 Dungeon Chest 5: Small Key
- 6 Dungeon Chest 6: Treasure
- 7 Dungeon Chest 7: Heart Container 1
- Boss Key
- Floor switch
- 1 Gossip Stone
- 2 Stamp station
- Switch

Forest Temple: First Floor

After exiting the train, run up the steps to find an Air Stone. Imitate the statue's melody on your Spirit Flute to score another song: the Song of Healing!

The Song of Healing will restore all of Link's hearts, but you can play it only once, and only in a place of strong energy, such as a temple or the Tower of Spirits. Therefore, it's best to save it until later in the adventure, when you'll get more benefit out of using it.

Song of Healing

You got the Song of Healing! Play it in a dungeon to restore your hearts one time.

After learning the Song of Healing, proceed upstairs to the temple's first floor. A locked door bars your progress north, so head east to discover a pair of Item Bulbs. Whack the plants for goodies, then watch in awe as they regrow after a few moments.

Collect one of the Item Bulbs by tapping it, then run to the east pit. Tap the switch on the far side to heave the Item Bulb at the switch, triggering the switch and extending a narrow bridge.

Cross the bridge and run south. A door rises behind Link, trapping him in a room with numerous Spinuts. Defeat the cretins to unseal the room and reveal a treasure chest. Open the chest to claim a Big Green Rupee!

Dungeon Chest 1: Big Green Rupee

Big Green Rupee

You got a Big Green Rupee! It's worth 100 Rupees!

That's all you can do on this floor for now, so head up the nearby stairs to reach the second level.

Forest Temple: Second Floor

Avoid the plumes of poison gas as you explore the second floor. Enter the northern room, and the door seals behind you, trapping you in with a group of gnarly Vengas!

Vengas

Hits to Defeat: 1
Attack Type: Contact
Power: Weak
Damage: 1/2 heart

Threat Meter

Vengas take just one hit to defeat and bounce harmlessly off Link's shield. However, they leave a cloud of noxious poison behind when you defeat them—don't touch the stuff!

You got the Whirlwind!

Slay all the Vengas to unseal the room and reveal a giant treasure chest. Way to go! Flip the chest's lid to claim a powerful new tool: the Whirlwind!

Dungeon Chest 2: The Whirlwind

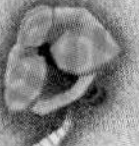

The Whirlwind

You got the Whirlwind! Blow into the mic to send a cyclone in the direction you're facing!

Let's try out your new toy. Tap the Item icon in the screen's upper right to equip the Whirlwind; then use the stylus to aim at the poison clouds the Vengas so unceremoniously left behind. Blow into the microphone to cast out a cyclone that clears away the fumes. Neat!

Put Away

Next, aim at the odd object that's out of reach due to a surrounding pit. Use the Whirlwind to activate the object, which is called a Windmill Switch. Once activated, the Windmill Switch opens the west door—but don't go through just yet. Instead, backtrack to the poison fog you ran past a moment ago.

Clear out the fog in the hall here to reveal a treasure chest. Sneaky! Open the chest to claim a treasure.

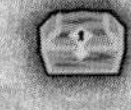

Dungeon Chest 3: Treasure

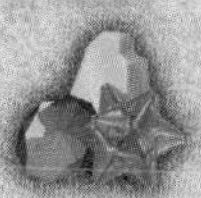

Treasure

You got a treasure! Check it out on the Collection screen!

Now return to the door you opened by activating the Windmill Switch, and clear out the fog near the northwest stairs. Wake the Gossip Stone if you like, but it's not necessary; its purpose is to show you hidden treasure chests, but you've already found all the chests on this floor.

Forest Temple: First Floor Revisited

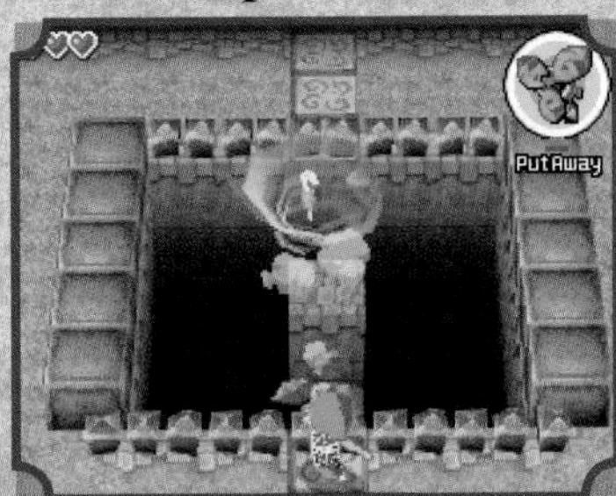

The stairs lead back down to the first floor. Position Link to the south of the key that's surrounded by a wide pit; then use the Whirlwind to blow it north, across the pit and within your reach. Circle 'round and collect the key.

Small Key

You got a Small Key! Use this key to open locked doors!

There's more fog you must disperse to the northeast. Head there, but watch out for Vengas along the way. Clear out the fog to reveal a stamp station and a floor switch. You can't interact with the stamp station, but step on the switch to reveal a hidden chest back near the bugs.

TIP

Use the Whirlwind to stun enemies and make them easier to handle.

Go to the chest and open it for another Big Green Rupee. This whole adventuring gig is starting to pay off!

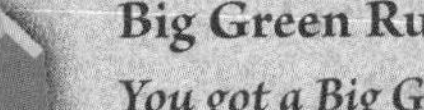

Dungeon Chest 4: Big Green Rupee

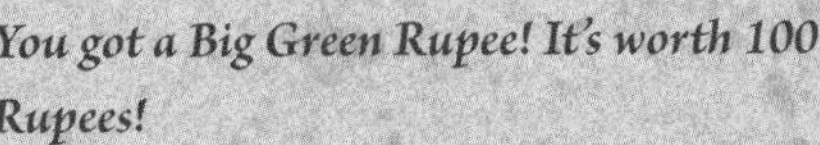

Big Green Rupee

You got a Big Green Rupee! It's worth 100 Rupees!

Now run south and open the locked door you noticed when you first entered. Ignore the Gossip Stone—there are no chests for it to reveal—and proceed to the southwest room. You become trapped here and must fight a pair of dangerous Bubbles.

Bubble

Hits to Defeat: 1 (stun with the Whirlwind)

Attack Type: Contact

Power: Strong

Damage: 1/2 heart

Threat Meter

Bubbles don't aggressively pursue Link, but they're also resistant to his sword. Use the Whirlwind to stun and ground these frothing foes, then tap their flapping skulls to finish them off with Link's steel. Dispatch both Bubbles to open the way upstairs.

Forest Temple: Second Floor Revisited

This is a short visit to the second floor. Wipe out the Vengas and loot the place. Also, take note of the locked door to the south. Head up the northern stairs to reach the third level.

Forest Temple: Third Floor

Link notices a switch across a pit up here, but it's well out of his reach. But not the Whirlwind's! Stand just south of the Item Bulb that's south of the switch, then cast out a cyclone. The cyclone carries the Item Bulb across the pit, smacking into the switch and activating it. Clever!

Activating the switch reveals a chest. Open it to claim another small key.

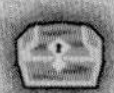

Dungeon Chest 5: Small Key

Small Key

You got a Small Key! Use this key to open locked doors!

Forest Temple: Second Floor, Third Visit

Backtrack downstairs and use your newfound key to open the locked door you noticed earlier. Step into the chamber beyond to initiate a tough fight against a Mothula.

Mothula

Hits to Defeat: Multiple
Attack Type: Contact
Power: Strong
Damage: 1/2 heart

Threat Meter

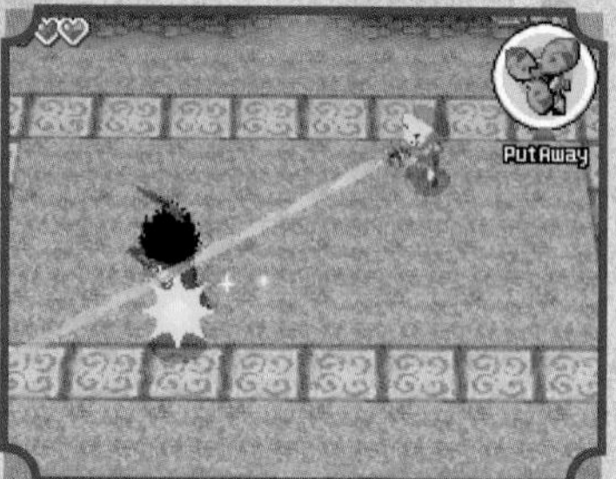

The Mothula is the toughest foe you've faced thus far, so stay mobile. Wait for the Mothula to spawn a Bubble, then quickly cast out a cyclone to catch the Bubble and send it crashing into its creator.

Don't fire cyclones at the Mothula when no Bubbles are about. Empty cyclones rebound off the Mothula, heading back in your direction! Quickly drop the Whirlwind and flee when you see a cyclone headed your way.

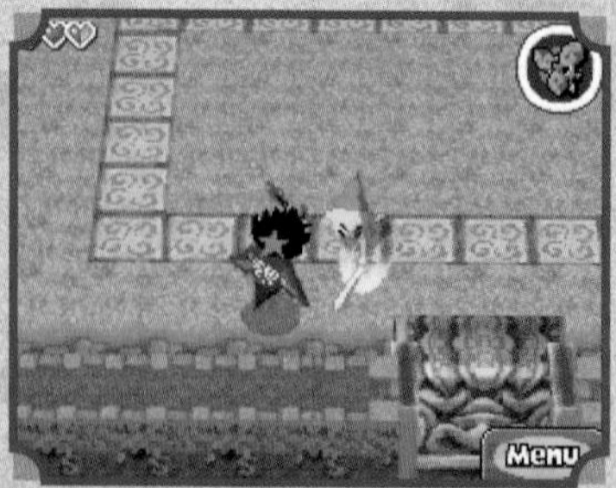

Knocking a Bubble into the Mothula stuns the fiend. Now's your chance! Rush forward and assault the Mothula with rapid sword strikes by tapping it relentlessly with the stylus.

1 Visit Whittleton Village

2 Pass Through the Lost Woods

3 Speak with Gage

4 Clear the Forest Temple

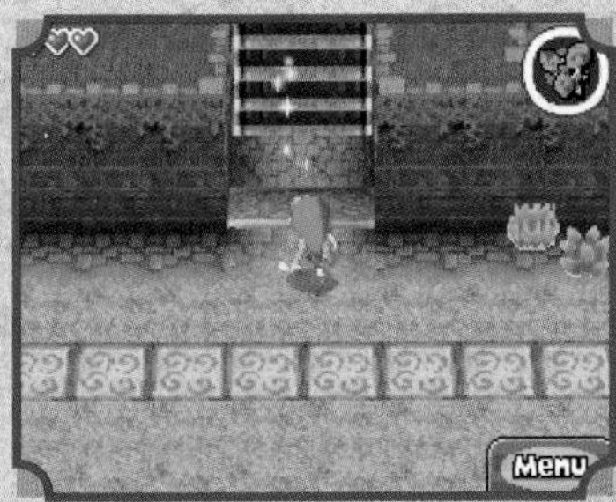

Keep stunning and slashing the Mothula until you finally defeat it. The room's doors then open, allowing you to continue onward. Loot the room and then sprint up the staircase to return to the third floor.

Forest Temple: Third Floor Revisited

You've done well to make it this far, hero—but you're not finished here yet! Explore this floor's south hall, where you encounter creepy crawlers known as Blastworms. Strike one with Link's sword to make it curl up into a spiky ball that's dangerous to touch.

Blastworm

Hits to Defeat: 1
Attack Type: Contact
Power: Weak
Damage: 1/2 heart

Threat Meter

Keep a distance from a curled-up Blastworm; it's about to explode! Since you can't safely pick up these living bombs, use the Whirlwind to knock one into the east bomb blocks instead, which makes them the blocks and the Blastworms explode. The little guys will just keep falling from above, so don't worry if it takes a few tries to line things up.

With the bomb blocks out of the way, continue east and send cyclones to clear out the dense poison fog ahead. Clear away all of the fog to reveal a floor switch, which in turn reveals a hidden chest.

Open the chest for a precious treasure, then smack the nearby switch to open a door back to the west. Ignore the Gossip Stone; you've pillaged every chest on this floor.

Dungeon Chest 6: Treasure

Treasure

You found a treasure! Check it out on the Collection screen!

Speed past the Blastworms and run through the door you've just opened. There are more Blastworms here, along with a switch that you can't reach due to a pit and a wall of bomb blocks. You know what to do: smack a Blastworm to curl it up, then send it northward on a cyclone to smash through the bomb blocks.

With the bomb blocks out of the way, launch another Blastworm at the switch to activate it. This opens the floor's northeast door, exposing a very special key.

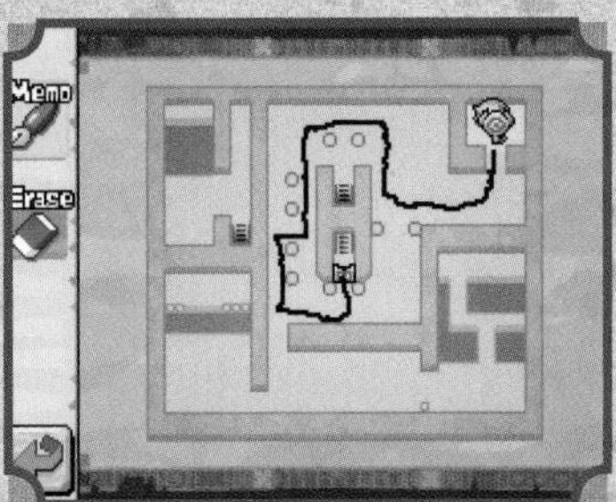

Before collecting the Boss Key, check out the map on the wall behind it. It shows some sort of path through this floor. Copy down this route on your own map for reference, then tap the Boss Key to make Link lift it over his head.

Carry the Boss Key along the exact route shown on the map, and you'll reach the Boss Key door without incident. Stray from the path, and a pair of dangerous Key Masters will materialize to stop you!

Key Master

Hits to Defeat: 3
Attack Type: Contact
Power: Strong
Damage: 1/2 heart

Threat Meter

If the Key Masters appear, tap anywhere near Link to make him set the Boss Key down, then attack the villains without mercy. The Key Masters' goal is to capture the Boss Key and return it to its holding chamber, so don't let them past your guard. The creatures aren't difficult to defeat if you're quick with your tapping.

Carry the key to the Boss Key block and tap the object to make Link hurl the key into place. The block retracts, granting passage to the fourth floor.

Forest Temple: Fourth Floor

Smash the pots along the walls up here for precious hearts, then examine the stone sign to the north. This causes blue light to appear nearby, allowing you to warp back to the temple's station. Don't step into the light, though; you've got a boss to battle. Head up the north stairs instead to advance to the final fight.

Stagnox, Armored Colossus

Hits to Defeat: Multiple!
Attack Type: Contact
Power: Strong
Damage: 1/2 heart (charge); 1/4 heart (poison)

Threat Meter

Stagnox looks big and mean, but he's by far the easiest boss Link faces. Simply run circles around the monster and try to sneak behind it. Be careful not to touch the poison fumes pluming out from the creature's rear—use the Whirlwind to blow out the fumes instead!

Break the numerous pots along the arena's edge for hearts as needed, but try not to waste them!

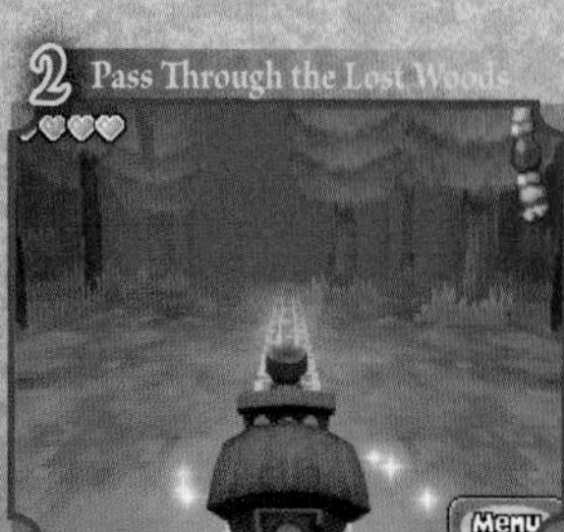

After you extinguish its poison fumes, Stagnox's behind is primed for stabbing. Bring the full weight of Link's steel to bear against it, landing as many blows as you can before the beast recovers.

Stagnox soon dives downward, attempting to snare Link. The minute you see Stagnox descend, send out a cyclone to snatch up a Blastworm. If you time this right, the bomb nails the boss, knocking it to its back!

Repeat this sequence until Stagnox takes flight, raining Blastworms down upon the arena. Quickly run around and stab each minion to curl it up into a spiky bomb—but remember not to touch them!

While Stagnox is down, rush forward and lay into its tender rump. Again, score as many hits as you can before the boss recovers. Repeat this process until Stagnox succumbs to the power of good.

After curling up all of the Blastworms, run toward the foreground, then turn to face Stagnox. Equip the Whirlwind and stand ready to blow.

With Stagnox defeated, the Forest Temple is at last cleansed of evil, and its flow of energy is restored. The Spirit Tracks linking the temple to the Tower of Spirits light up, and the lower portion of the tower stops spinning and locks back into place. Fantastic work!

As a reward for your valor, a giant treasure chest blinks into existence. Open the chest to claim a worthy prize: your very first Heart Container!

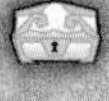

Dungeon Chest 7: Heart Container 1

Heart Container 1

You got a Heart Container! You increased your life by one and refilled your hearts!

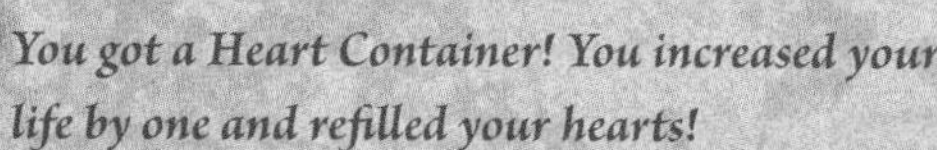

After claiming your Heart Container, step into the pool of blue light that has appeared nearby to return to the temple's station. Board the train and set a course for the Tower of Spirits—you've got to tell Anjean about your success!

To the Tower of Spirits

Enemies Encountered

Dark Train

Twisted Trolleys

Beware: Those harmless trolleys you saw running along the Forest Realm's tracks are no longer harmless; they've been transformed into frightening Dark Trains! These possessed transports are no joke, so adjust your course and keep far away from them. Monitor your map to see which direction they'll turn at junctions, and be sure you're not in their path. Don't be afraid to slam it into reverse if need be—for being rammed by a Dark Train instantly destroys your ride!

Dark Train

Hits to Defeat: N/A
Attack Type: Contact
Power: Strong
Damage: Insta-squish

Threat Meter

Missing Links

On your way back to the Tower of Spirits, consider stopping at these stations for a bit of optional plunder. There's no plunder like optional plunder, you know!

Forest Sanctuary

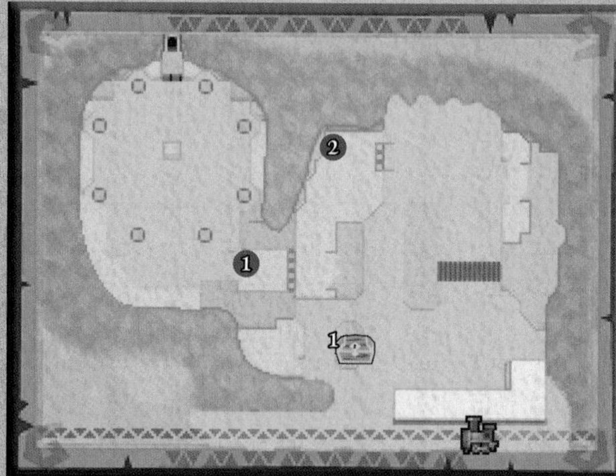

Forest Sanctuary

Legend

1 (chest)	Overworld Chest 4: Big Red Rupee
1	Air Stone
2	Stamp station

1 Visit Whittleton Village

2 Pass Through the Lost Woods

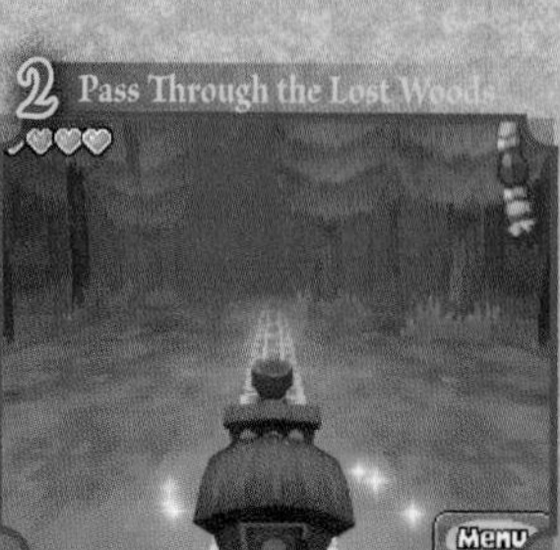

3 Speak with Gage

4 Clear the Forest Temple

Items to Obtain

Big Red Rupee

Enemies Encountered

Spinut
Crow
Red ChuChu

Make a stop at the Forest Sanctuary, for you now have a means of reaching the treasure chest you noticed before. Locate the chest, then climb onto the ledge to the west of it. Equip the Whirlwind and use it to knock the Cucco off the chest ledge.

Approach the Cucco slowly so as not to frighten it, then tap the little fowl to make Link lift it over his head. Nimbler than a Cucco, that boy is!

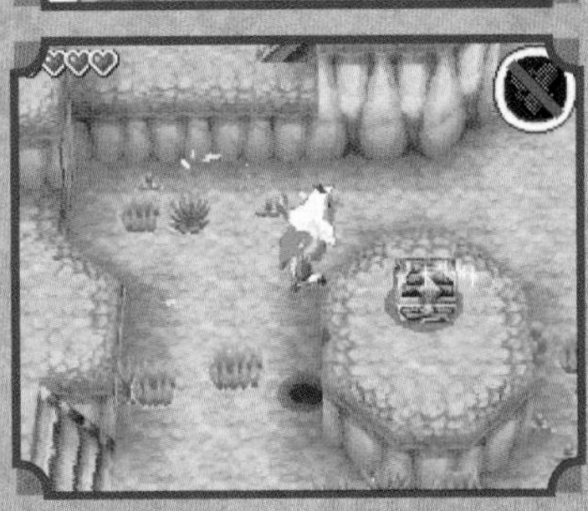

Return to the ledge that's west of the chest, and with Cucco in hand, run directly toward the chest. Link automatically jumps when he reaches the ledge's edge, and due to the Cucco's crazed flapping, he clears the distance and sails over to the chest ledge.

Way to fly! Now open that chest to score a Big Red Rupee and be on your way. (There's no point in visiting Gage; he has nothing new to say.)

Overworld Chest 4: Big Red Rupee

Big Red Rupee

You got a Big Red Rupee! It's worth 200 Rupees!

Whittleton Village

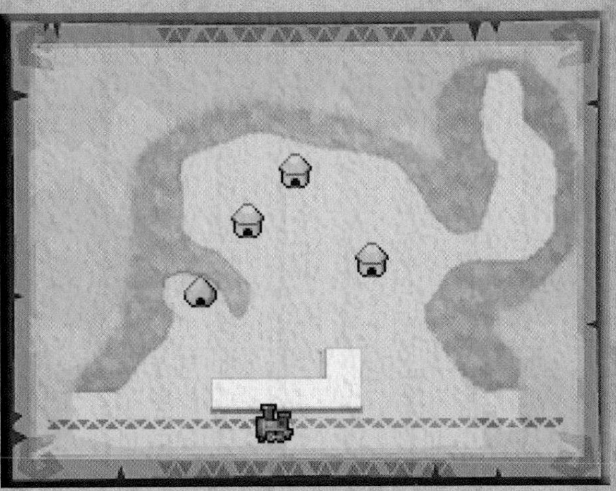

Whittleton Village

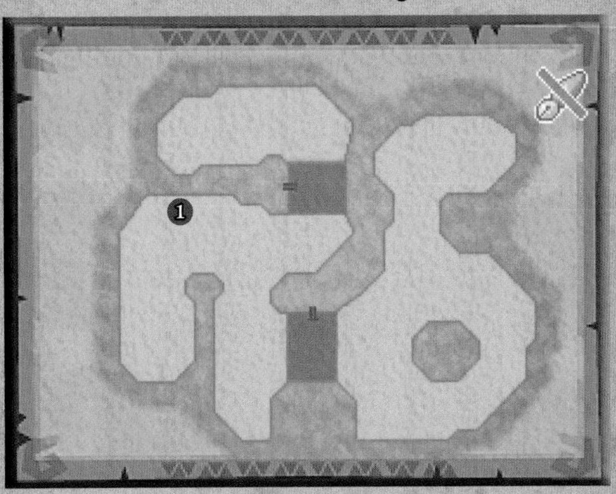

Whittleton Village North

Legend

1	Stamp station

Enemies Encountered

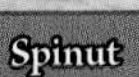

Spinut

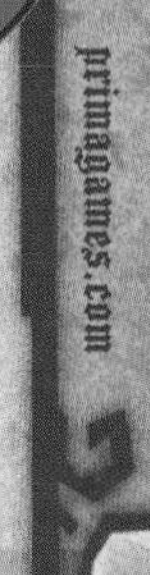

For even more loot, swing by Whittleton Village and put the Whirlwind to good use. Blow away all those piles of leaves on the ground to uncover all sorts of valuables. Leaves often conceal Blue and Red Rupees, and many hide valuable treasures, so it's well worth doing a little environmental cleanup whenever you see them. Visit the village's northern region for even more leaves!

Castle Town

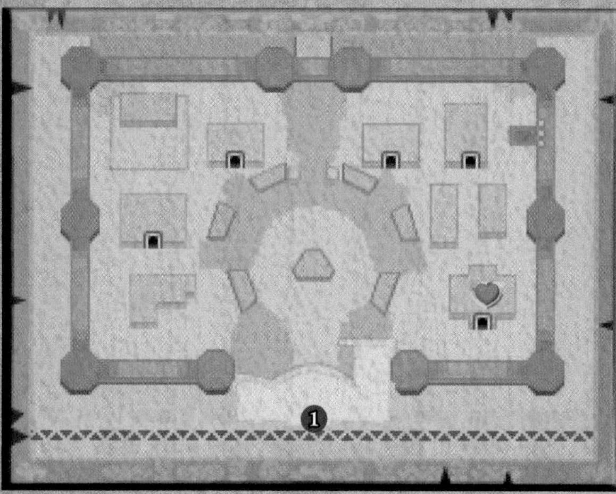

Castle Town

Legend

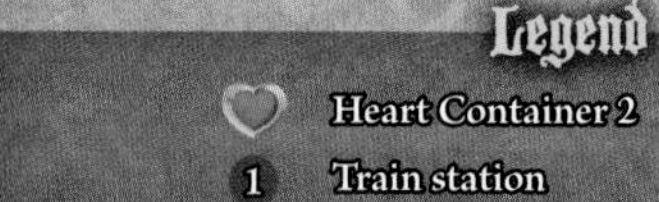

- Heart Container 2
- 1 Train station

Items to Obtain

Heart Container 2

Enemies Encountered

Blastworm, Spinut, Bubble, Mothula, Keese, Octorok, Rat, Red ChuChu, Stagnox, Armored Colossus

Definitely make a stop at Castle Town before going back to the Tower of Spirits. It's right on your way, and for just 50 Rupees, you can try a fun challenge that can earn you Heart Container 2.

Enter the building to the right of the station to enter the strange shop you noticed the first time you came to Castle Town. This time, the shop's mistress is more inviting and allows you to test your skills in her challenge. Pay the woman 50 Rupees to enter a monster-filled dungeon—Heart Container 2 will be yours if you can make it all the way through!

The dungeon consists of ten floors, each one a small arena-like chamber filled with different foes. You've seen all of these baddies before—except the Octoroks, which are easy to defeat. Just slash away at them.

1 Visit Whittleton Village

2 Pass Through the Lost Woods

3 Speak with Gage

4 Clear the Forest Temple

Octorok

Hits to Defeat: 2
Attack Type: Contact and Range
Power: Weak
Damage: 1/2 heart
Threat Meter

Stagnox, Armored Colossus

Fight your way to the top to face off against the boss of the challenge, Stagnox. The boss fight plays out exactly as it did back at the Forest Temple.

You got a Heart Container!

Clear this challenge, and you'll earn yourself that shiny new Heart Container, extending Link's Life meter to five hearts. Congratulations!

NOTE

You can't participate in the second level of this challenge until later in the adventure. We'll remind you when the time is right to return for more monster-slaying.

Heart Container 2

You got a Heart Container! You increased your life by one and refilled your hearts!

Onward and Upward: Tower of Spirits Revisited

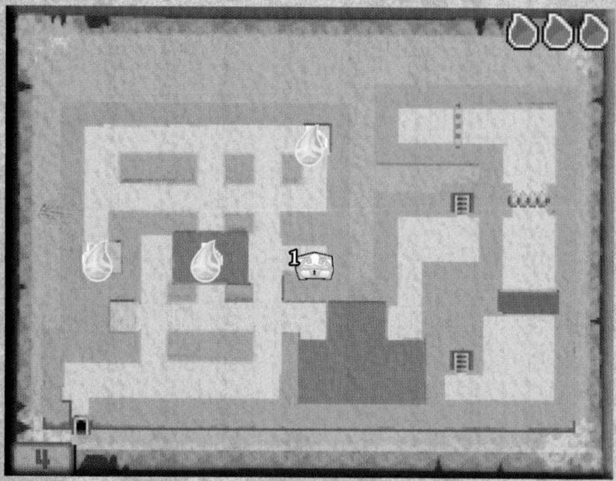

Tower of Spirits, Fourth Floor

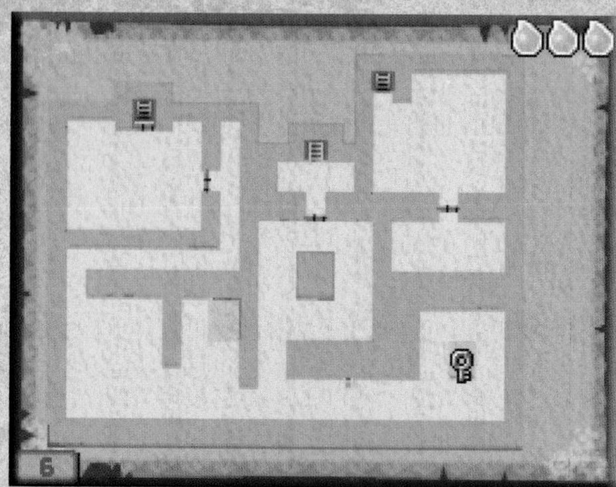

Tower of Spirits, Sixth Floor

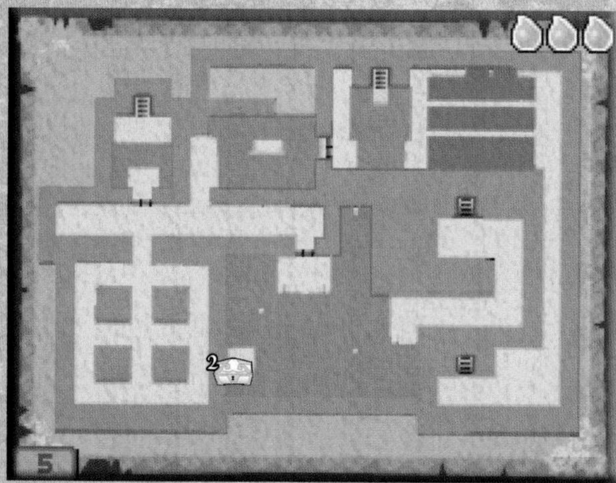

Tower of Spirits, Fifth Floor

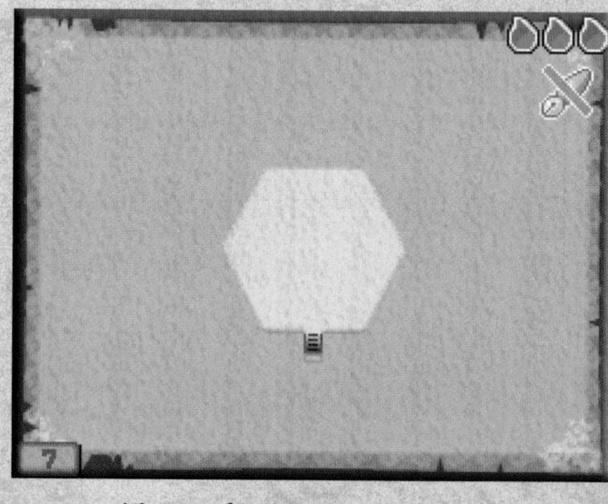

Tower of Spirits, Seventh Floor

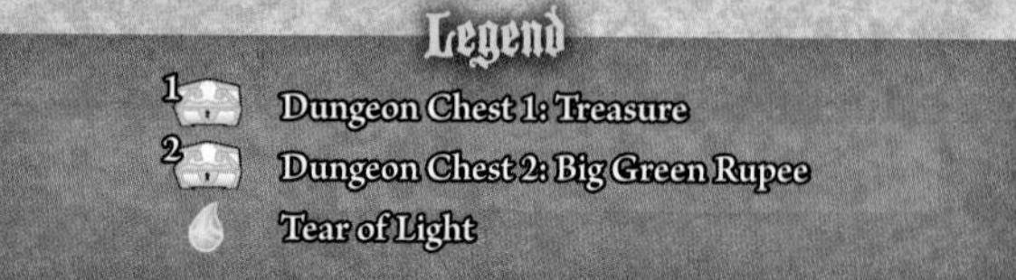

Legend

1 Dungeon Chest 1: Treasure
2 Dungeon Chest 2: Big Green Rupee
Tear of Light

Items to Obtain

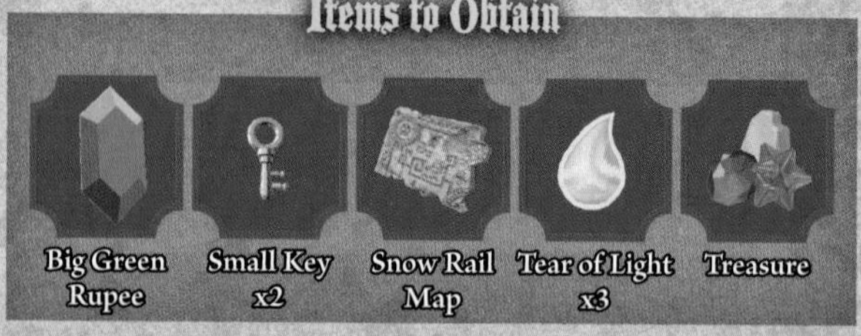

Big Green Rupee | Small Key x2 | Snow Rail Map | Tear of Light x3 | Treasure

1 Report Back to Anjean

2 Retrieve the Snow Rail Map

3 Acquire the Cannon

4 Journey to the Snow Realm

Stagnox has been felled and the Forest Realm's Spirit Tracks reenergized. Princess Zelda and her courageous companion, Link, now return to the Tower of Spirits. They seek council from the tower's sage guardian, Anjean, but what task might the noble Lokomo ask of them next?

A Link to the Present

Items Already Acquired

Enemies Encountered

Task 1: Report Back to Anjean

Back to the Tower

347
You can go farther up the tower to the level of the next rail map.
Menu

Returning to the Tower of Spirits, Princess Zelda and Link eagerly await their next assignment. Anjean asks her two heroic helpers to scale the tower once more—this time to recover the Snow Rail Map. For now, since the energy is once again flowing from the Forest Temple, you can explore more of the tower.

Go through the north door to reach the tower's main spiral staircase. This time, run past the door that leads to the first floor, and enter the next door above, which brings you to the tower's fourth floor.

Task 2: Retrieve the Snow Rail Map

Tower of Spirits: Fourth Floor

The tower's fourth floor is dangerous, filled with lava and fire traps. Dash past the first fire trap when it isn't spitting flames.

Two Phantoms patrol the fourth floor. Monitor your map and retreat to safe zones as needed.

Approach the Tear of Light that hovers amid the central lava, and use the Whirlwind to blow it within easy reach.

Tear of Light

You got a Tear of Light! Gather three of them to power up your sword!

Next, dash to the right and open a large chest to claim a rare treasure. Score!

Dungeon Chest 1: Treasure

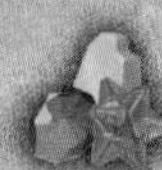

Treasure

You got a treasure! Check it out on the Collection screen!

When all's clear, sprint north and grab the northernmost Tear of Light. Beware the fire traps surrounding this Tear's safe zone.

Tear of Light

You got a Tear of Light! Gather three of them to power up your sword!

Now move for the final Tear to the west. Keep away from the northern Phantom, and wait patiently for the long stream of fire to cease from the northern fire trap before sprinting to grab the Tear.

Tear of Light

You got a Tear of Light! Gather three of them to power up your sword!

You've collected all three Tears, and Link's sword becomes infused with the power of light. Sneak up behind one of the two roaming Phantoms. Slash its back to stun it, then tap the brute to have Zelda take control.

To possess Phantoms with ease, hang out in a safe zone and whack Link's sword into the walls as a Phantom draws near. The brute will investigate the sound but won't find anything if you remain in the safe zone. When the Phantom turns to leave, nail it in the back!

As a Phantom, Zelda is immune to fire and lava. Move her into the lava to the east, then take control of Link and tap Zelda to make him leap on top of her.

1 Report Back to Anjean

2 Retrieve the Snow Rail Map

3 Acquire the Cannon

4 Journey to the Snow Realm

With Link riding on his Phantom Zelda, move Zelda across the lava. When you reach the far side, tap anywhere near Zelda to have Link hop down to solid ground. Scale the nearby stairs to reach the tower's fifth floor.

Tower of Spirits: Fifth Floor

Repeat the same trick up here, having Link ride on Zelda's back to cross the lava. Fluttering Keese make the trip somewhat risky; use the Whirlwind to blow them away and stun them.

Link can use items while riding on Zelda's back; just tap the Item icon to equip the tool.

Ferry Link over to the west platform to discover another large chest. Flip open its lid to pad your wallet with a Big Green Rupee.

Dungeon Chest 2: Big Green Rupee

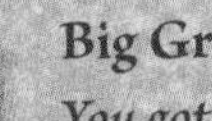

Big Green Rupee

You got a Big Green Rupee! It's worth 100 Rupees!

To open the north door, you must activate the lava lake's two Windmill Switches. Have Zelda escort Link to each one, and use the Whirlwind to get them spinning. Proceed through the door after it opens.

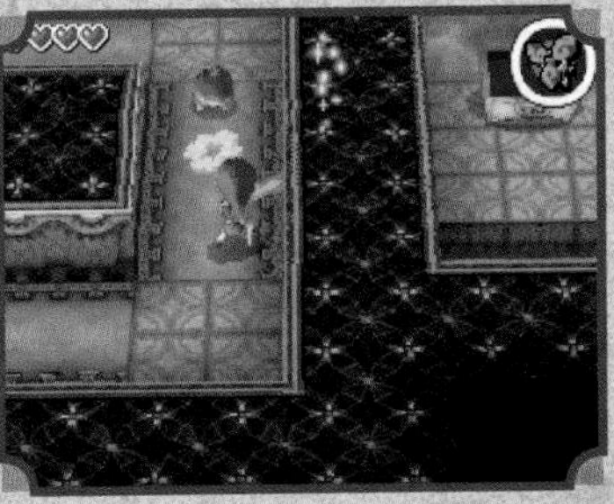

Ignore the northern lava pit and explore the floor's southwest corner. There, a speedy Spinut hurries about, fleeing from Link and Zelda whenever they approach. You must defeat the Spinut to obtain a Small Key.

This special Spinut appears as a Skull icon on your map. Corner the beast by tracing a patrol route for Zelda, then quickly taking control of Link. Keep working at cornering the little Spinut until it has nowhere to run, then slay the creature to claim its Small Key.

Small Key

You got a Small Key! Use this key to open locked doors!

Use your newfound key to open the north door. Have Zelda carry Link over the tiny pool of lava and proceed upstairs.

Tower of Spirits: Sixth Floor

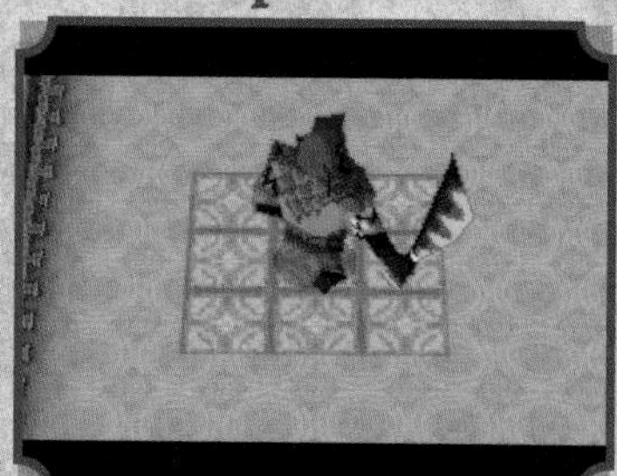

Entering the sixth floor, Link and Zelda become trapped in a room with a powerful new adversary: a Geozard! Teamwork is required to dispatch this dangerous foe.

TIP

Geozards are tough, so break the room's pots for hearts when you need them.

Geozard

Hits to Defeat: Multiple
Attack Type: Sword
Power: Strong
Damage: 1/2 heart

Threat Meter

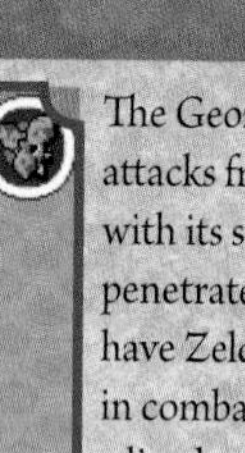

The Geozard blocks all attacks from the front with its sturdy shield. To penetrate its defenses, first have Zelda engage the fiend in combat by quickly tracing a line between her and the Zora.

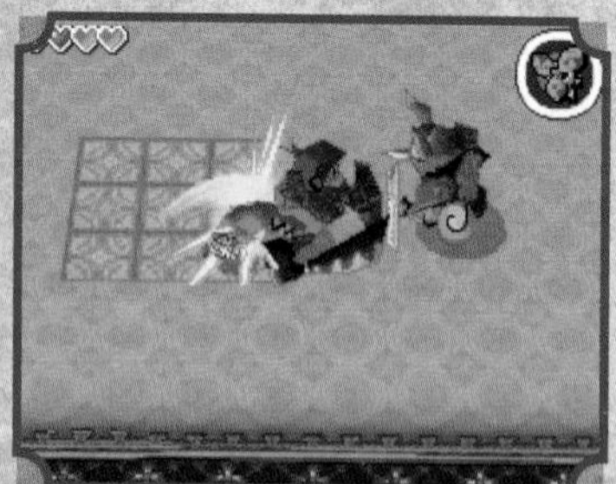

With the Zora's attention focused on battling Zelda, slip around behind it as Link and begin assaulting its vulnerable backside. Land as many hits as you can, and repeat this sequence until the creature finally falls.

Proceed to the south, where you encounter another new foe: a Mounted Miniblin! You're unable to defeat this enemy right now, so you must hurry past it. Fortunately, Mounted Miniblins are slow and easy to outmaneuver—*un*fortunately, a fire trap blocks your path!

Mounted Miniblin

Hits to Defeat: 1
Attack Type: Spikes
Power: Strong
Damage: 1/2 heart

Threat Meter

To advance past the Mounted Miniblin, position Zelda to block the fire trap's constant stream of flame. With Zelda in place, Link can sprint past safely. Call to Zelda afterward, and the flames will keep the Mounted Miniblin at bay.

TIP

Give yourself time to maneuver past the fire trap by luring the Mounted Miniblin to the north before attempting to cross.

Time for some payback. First, use the perch that's just beyond the fire trap to get Link onto Zelda's back as you've done before.

1 Report Back to Anjean

2 Retrieve the Snow Rail Map

3 Acquire the Cannon

4 Journey to the Snow Realm

Now backtrack to the Mounted Miniblin without fear of the fire trap. Use the Whirlwind to blow the Miniblin off its Armos steed, then trace a line to the stunned Miniblin to have Zelda finish it off with her massive sword. Once the Miniblin is defeated, the Armos quickly implodes.

You couldn't have blown the Miniblin off the Armos before, as Link wasn't elevated high enough. Only from the height of Zelda's back is Link able to target these high-riding foes.

Continue onward, keeping Link on Zelda's back so the two can take on more Mounted Miniblins to the east. No point in allowing the dangerous villains to roam about unchecked.

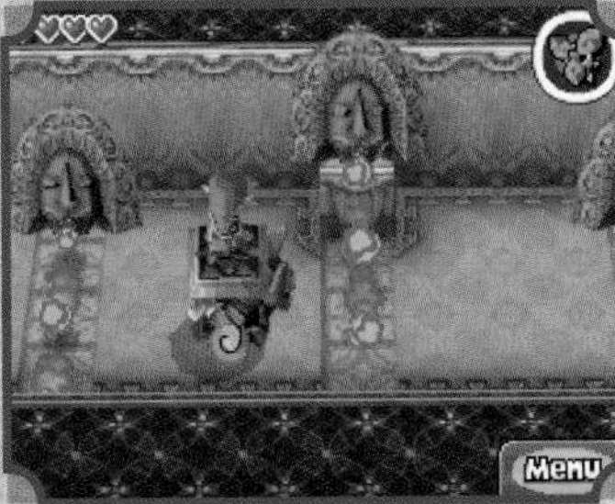

Cross the trio of fire traps in the southern hall, keeping Link on Zelda's back the whole while. Time your movement carefully past the elevated middle trap so the searing flames don't scorch Link.

A Small Key sits on a high platform in the southeast chamber. From atop Zelda's back, have Link blow the key into arm's reach with a toot from the Whirlwind.

Collect the Small Key, then make your way back across the fire traps. Unlock the door to the north to advance upstairs.

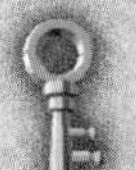

Small Key

You got a Small Key! Use this key to open locked doors!

Tower of Spirits: Seventh Floor

Link and Zelda come to a quiet chamber, and Zelda is cast out of her Phantom shell. The light fades from Link's blade—they must have reached the rail-map chamber!

Sure enough, the Snow Rail Map sits on the central platform. Collect the ancient tablet to restore more Spirit Tracks that link the Forest Realm to the Snow Realm up north.

Snow Rail Map

You got the Snow rail map! Some of the lost Spirit Tracks on it are reappearing!

You must go to the Snow Temple and restore the flow of energy to the tower!

With the Snow Rail Map in your possession, step into the blue light to return to the tower's base. Speak with Anjean for confirmation that you must now travel to the Snow Realm and speak with its spirit guardian, a Lokomo named Steem. He'll help you reach the Snow Temple, which you must clear to restore more of the tower's sacred energy.

Task 3: Acquire the Cannon

Back to Castle Town

Enemies Encountered

Bullbo

Besieged by Boar

Moments after leaving the Tower of Spirits, our heroes' train is assaulted by a pair of Bullbo. Sounding the whistle does nothing to stop these beasts from ramming into the locomotive, and Zelda suggests a quick stop at Castle Town to seek advice from the master engineer, Alfonzo.

461
Maybe we should go back to Castle Town and see if Alfonzo can help us.
MENU

The Bullbos will make short work of your train if you don't hurry to Castle Town. Shift up to second gear for maximum speed, and apply the emergency brake to stop short at Castle Town Station. Then shift into park to detrain. You'll take a couple of hits, but you'll get there!

Bullbo

Hits to Defeat: 3 (need cannon)
Attack Type: Contact
Power: Strong
Damage: 1 heart

Threat Meter
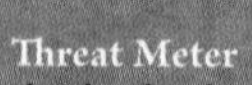

Castle Town and Hyrule Castle

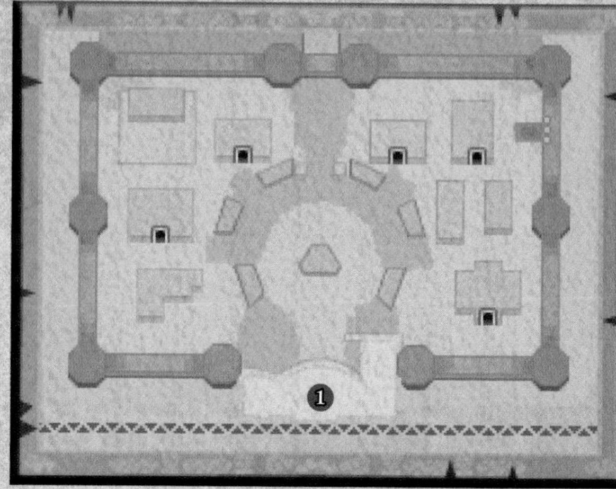

Castle Town

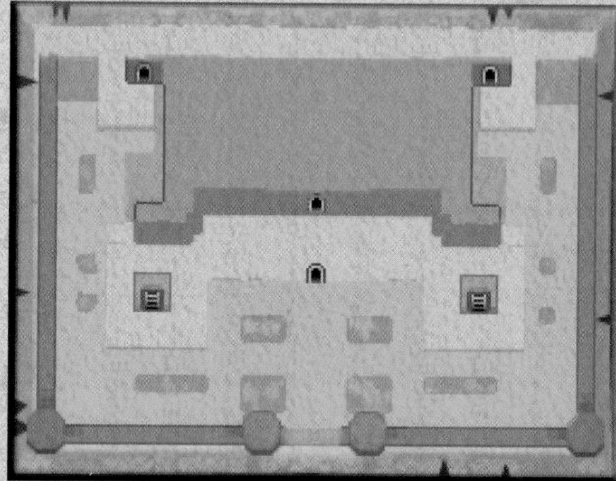

Hyrule Castle Grounds

Legend

1 Train station

Items to Obtain

Letter ("From Alfonzo")

1 Report Back to Anjean
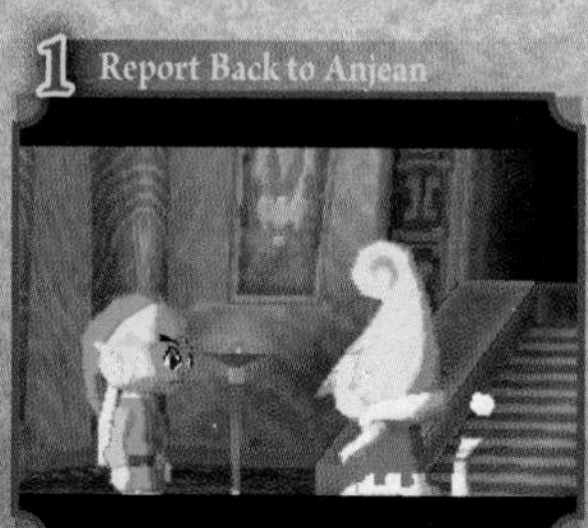

2 Retrieve the Snow Rail Map

3 Acquire the Cannon

4 Journey to the Snow Realm

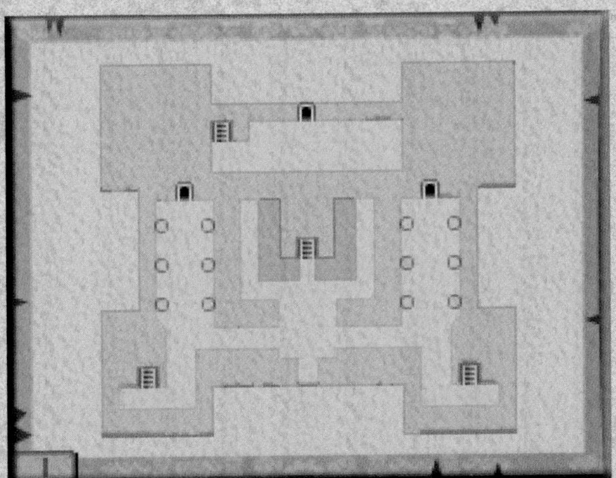

Hyrule Castle, First Floor

Mail Call

Greetings. I'm here with a letter from Mr. Alfonzo to Link!

Sprint north toward Hyrule Castle, but don't speed past that wiggling postbox! Tap the box to receive a letter from Alfonzo, who urges you to come visit him. One step ahead of you, old buddy!

Letter

You got a letter from the postman! Go to the Collection screen to read it!

Proceed to Hyrule Castle and go to the first floor. Visit the northeast room to find Alfonzo up and about, good as new. What a relief!

461
Oh, I have an idea! But we have to go back home to Aboda Village first.
Menu

Alfonzo is shocked to learn that Princess Zelda's spirit is intact and following Link. He believes the young lad's sincerity and asks Link to take him back to Aboda Village so he can help him in his quest. What a pal!

Troubled Teacher

Link bumps into Teacher as he hurries out of the castle. The old man is fraught with worry over the princess and doesn't believe Link's story that Zelda's spirit is right nearby. Poor Teacher! Perhaps you can help lay his fears to rest a little later.

Alfonzo awaits Link at the Castle Town Station. Tell him you're ready to go, and he'll hop aboard your train. Next stop: Aboda Village!

461
All right, let's get back to Aboda Village!
Menu

The Road to Aboda

Enemies Encountered

Moink	Snurgle	Dark Train

Aboda, Ho!

The Dark Trains are running the tracks, so plot a course that avoids them. No Bullbos will attack you during this trip, but you may need to sound the horn to scatter some cattle and pesky Snurgles.

Aboda Village

Aboda Village

Legend

1. Stamp station
2. Train station

Items to Obtain

Practical Cannon

Stamp Book

In the Books

461
Let me rig something up for you...
Menu

Arriving at Aboda Village, Alfonzo tells Link it'll take some time to make the necessary adjustments to the train. In the meantime, he suggests Link visit his old roommate, Niko. What a good idea!

Go to Link and Niko's house to speak with your old friend. Niko congratulates Link on becoming a full-fledged engineer but is surprised to see Link in his Recruit's Uniform, saying he looks just like a friend of his from his youth. He then gives Link a special item called a Stamp Book and asks his friend if he wouldn't mind bringing him stamps from places he visits during his travels. Score!

Note

Do you recognize Niko? He was a good friend to Link—that is, the Link who starred in *The Legend of Zelda: The Wind Waker*. When that Link was just cutting his teeth as a rookie pirate, Niko showed him the ropes—quite literally. He taught that Link how to swing on ropes, just like a real buccaneer!

Stamp Book

You got the Stamp Book! Get stamps from every part of the world for Niko!

Now that you've got the Stamp Book, you can start using those stamp stations you've been seeing everywhere. In fact, there's one right here in Aboda Village! Find the stamp station, which stands near Alfonzo's house, and tap it to use it. When Link opens the Stamp Book, simply tap on any blank page to imprint Aboda Village's unique stamp.

Note

There are 20 stamps to find in all. Return to Niko when you find 10, 15, and 20 stamps; you'll receive a variety of very special rewards. Don't worry—we'll remind you!

1 Report Back to Anjean

2 Retrieve the Snow Rail Map

3 Acquire the Cannon

4 Journey to the Snow Realm

Train Upgrade

With your first stamp in the books, speak to the rest of the villagers if you wish, then head to the train station. Alfonzo greets you there, rolling out a new-and-improved train that's now armed with a powerful cannon!

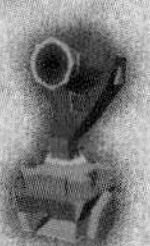

Practical Cannon

You got a Practical Cannon! Now you can smash boulders and defeat enemies while driving the train!

Blast trackside boulders to discover Rupees, which you automatically collect. When your train is damaged, you may also uncover blue hearts that will repair it!

Some enemies are challenging to hit, and some require several hits to defeat. If you ever feel overwhelmed, try slowing down to make lining up shots a little easier.

Task 4: Journey to the Snow Realm

To the Snow Realm

Enemies Encountered

Moink	Snurgle	Dark Train	Skulltula	Bullbo

Bombs Away

Armed with the cannon, you're now ready to make the arduous journey to the Snow Realm. Set a course running north, past the Forest Sanctuary, and up into the great unknown.

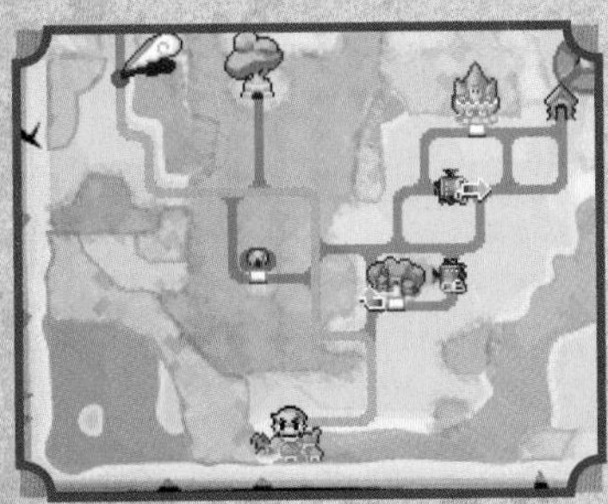

Use your new cannon to blast everything you see on your way to Snow Realm. Just tap anywhere to fire the cannon in that direction with remarkable accuracy. You can destroy signposts, boulders, and, of course, enemies! The only things you should avoid shooting are Moinks, because they become enraged and will chase you down. Better to blow the whistle than batter a bovine! You should also avoid Dark Trains, for you can only stun them with sustained fire—you cannot destroy them.

A monstrous rock blocks the tracks just beyond the Forest Sanctuary. Pound this obstacle with cannon fire until you destroy it and can safely pass. Then keep on truckin' to the Snow Realm.

Missing Links

Before rushing up to the Snow Realm, consider taking on this optional jaunt. Trust us; it's worth the trouble!

Rabbitland Rescue

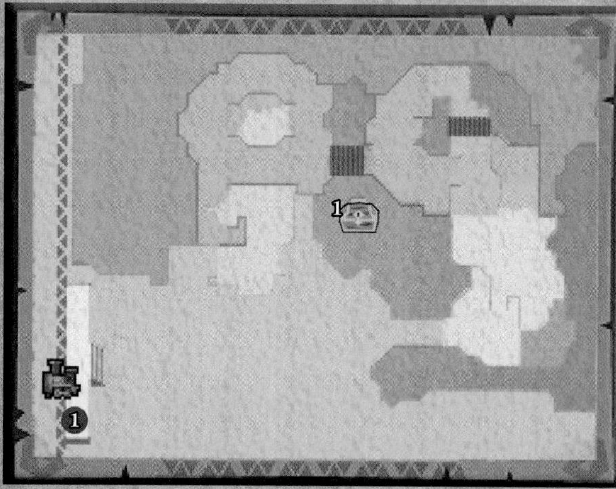

Rabbitland Rescue

Legend

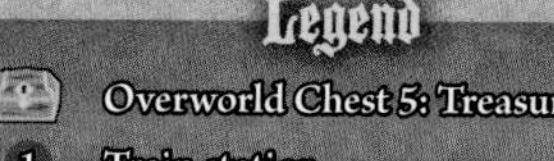

1 (chest)	Overworld Chest 5: Treasure
1	Train station

Items to Obtain

A train station tempts you to stop as you head to the Snow Realm. It's just past the big boulder you need to blast. Pull up to this station to visit a special place called the Rabbitland Rescue.

The owner of the rescue is an odd fellow, but he's harmless enough. Bunnies are his passion, and if you humor this odd fellow, he'll gladly hand over a special item called a Rabbit Net.

Rabbit Net

You got the rabbit net! Try using it while you're riding the train!

The rescue's owner goes on to explain how to catch rabbits. While riding the train, look for the furry critters hiding behind boulders. If you think you've spotted one, you can blow the whistle and it'll jump up high. Once you've tracked down a rabbit, simply blast its boulder to expose the little fellow, then use the net to swoop it up. Sounds simple enough!

Before leaving the rescue, locate a treasure chest sitting in the middle of the central pond. You can reach this chest with a leap from the high, rocky cliff to the northeast. It's a tough jump to land, but it's doable!

Inside the chest, you discover a rare treasure. Worth the risk!

1 Report Back to Anjean

2 Retrieve the Snow Rail Map

3 Acquire the Cannon

4 Journey to the Snow Realm

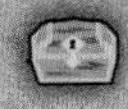

Overworld Chest 5: Treasure

Treasure

You got a treasure! Check it out on the Collection screen!

Forest Realm Rabbits 1–3

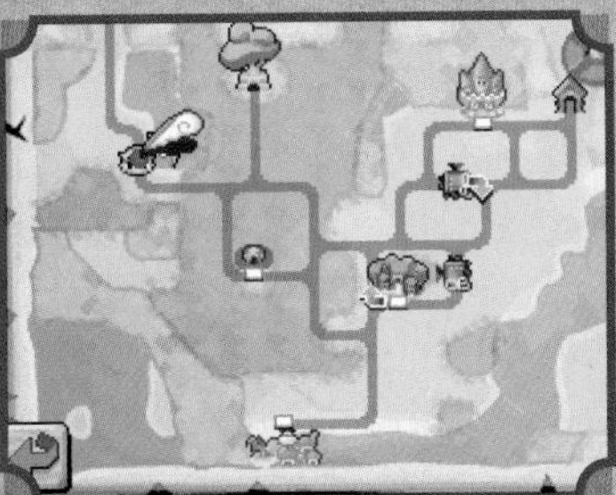

Now that you've obtained the Rabbit Net, why not hunt a few of those rascally rabbits? You can nab three of the little critters right here in the Forest Realm before setting foot in the frigid north; simply check the Overworld map to find their locations.

Since this is your first rabbit hunt, let's go over the basics. First, there's no need to sound the whistle; just blast each boulder you see—particularly the ones with rabbit ears sticking up!

After destroying a rabbit's boulder, a brief minigame event begins in which you have only a few seconds to catch the rabbit as it hops about. Tap anywhere to throw down your net, and if you time it right, you'll catch the rabbit!

It helps to wait for the rabbit to pause before throwing your net. It may also help to aim just in front of the bunny's nose so that you'll capture it even if you're a little slow, and it starts to hop again. If you miss the rabbit and time expires, it will flee; you won't be able to try for it again until you've stopped at a station or left the current realm and then returned. Doing either resets all rabbits in the realm, allowing you to try for them again.

Why catch those rabbits? Because the owner of Rabbitland Rescue has fabulous rewards to hand out! Your first reward comes after you've landed five of the furry fellows; we'll remind you when it's time to claim your prize.

Stamp Seeker

While searching around for rabbits, why not visit all those stamp stations you've seen as well? There's one at the Forest Temple, the Forest Sanctuary, and Whittleton Village. Collect all of these and you'll have 4 out of 20 stamps in your book before visiting the Snow Realm!

There's also a stamp station at Castle Town, but you can't reach it just yet.

Forest Temple

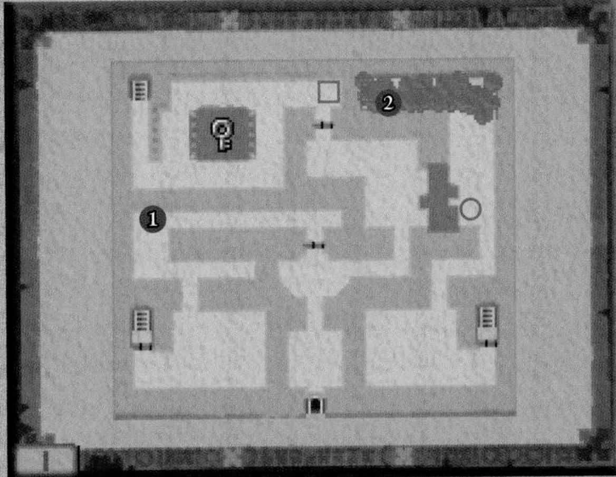

Forest Temple, First Floor

Legend

- Floor switch
- 1 Gossip Stone
- 2 Stamp station
- Switch

Enemies Encountered

Vengas

The Forest Temple's stamp station is right on the first floor, so it's not hard to reach. Use the Whirlwind to clear out all that poison fog from the northeast corner; this exposes the stamp station. Tap it to record the stamp.

Forest Sanctuary

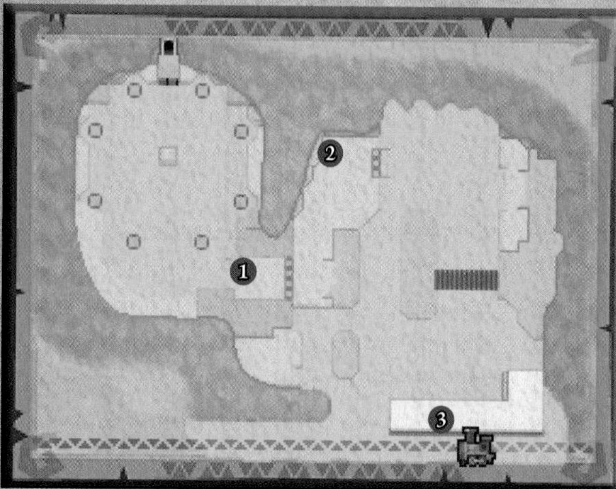

Forest Sanctuary

Legend

1 (chest)	Overworld Chest 4: Big Red Rupee
1	Air Stone
2	Stamp station
3	Train station

Enemies Encountered

Spinut

Crow

Red ChuChu

Use bomb flowers to cross the elevated bridges as you did before, and reach the stamp station here at the Forest Sanctuary.

Whittleton Village

Whittleton Village

1 Report Back to Anjean

2 Retrieve the Snow Rail Map

3 Acquire the Cannon

4 Journey to the Snow Realm

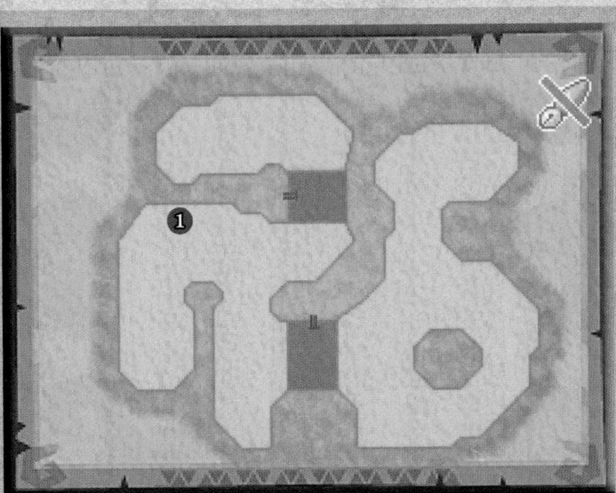

Whittleton Village North

Legend

1. Stamp station
2. Train station

Enemies Encountered

Spinut

Sprint to the northern region of Whittleton Village and lay waste to a few Spinuts on your way to the town's stamp station. Scatter all those leaves again to uncover more Rupees and treasure!

Chillin' Out: The Snow Realm

Armed with a powerful cannon and the will to blow stuff up, Link and Princess Zelda make their way north, into the cold embrace of the Snow Realm. What awaits them in this frigid place remains to be seen, but one thing's for certain: It's *cold* up here

A Link to the Present

Items Already Acquired

Engineer Certificate	Forest Rail Map	Practical Cannon	Rabbitland Rabbits (3)	Recruit's Sword
Recruit's Uniform	Snow Rail Map	Song of Awakening	Song of Healing	Spirit Flute
Stamp Book (4 Stamps)	The Whirlwind	Wooden Shield		

Enemies Encountered

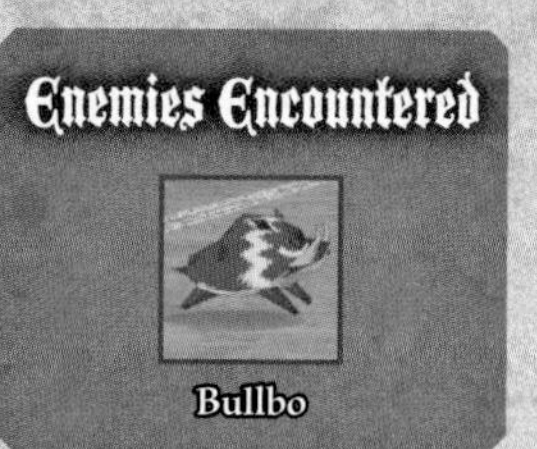
Bullbo

Task 1: Explore the Snow Realm

To Anouki Village

Crossing into the Snow Realm, Princess Zelda is excited to see fluffy flakes drifting down from the sky. Chancellor Cole had her cooped up in the castle for so long, she'd forgotten the simple joy of watching the snow fall.

1 Explore the Snow Realm

2 Speak with Steem

3 Navigate the Blizzard

4 Clear the Snow Temple

A glance at your map shows the western tunnel is sealed off, so chug along to the north instead, heading for the only visible landmark. As you near the station, look for a rabbit hiding behind a boulder to the left. Try to catch your first snow rabbit before putting it in park.

Missing Link: Warp Gate A

348
Let's see... "Pass through...the gate...steam whistle...will not open...
Menu

Make a slight detour and explore the south tracks to encounter a curious stone arch built around the tracks. This object is known as a warp gate. Blast the triangle atop the stone arch to activate the warp gate, which links to a similar stone arch back in the middle of the Forest Realm. Now you may simply blow your train's whistle as you pass through either of these arches to instantly travel between them! See the overworld map to discover the locations of every warp gate.

Anouki Village

Anouki Village

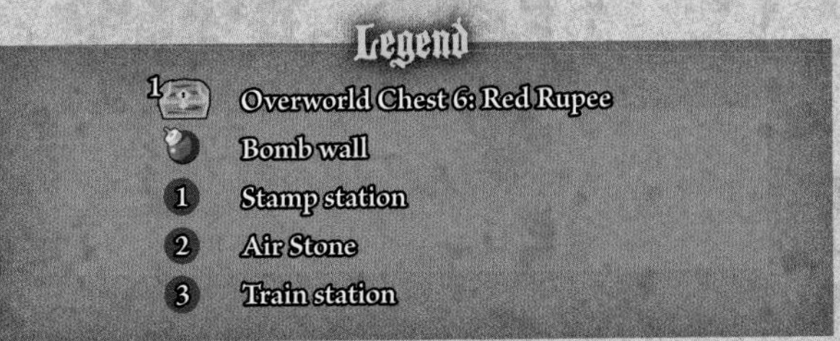

Items to Obtain

Red Rupee x2

Song of Discovery

Snow Folk

Stepping off the train, Link and Zelda find themselves in a quaint village covered in snow. This place holds its share of danger, however: Dangerous Ice ChuChus pop up from the ground to the west! Don't touch these frosty foes, or you'll be encased in ice and forced to rub the stylus across the screen to break free. Avoid them, or use the Whirlwind to stun them and then dispatch them with Link's sword.

Ice ChuChu

Hits to Defeat: 1 (after stunning)

Attack Type: Contact

Power: Strong

Damage: 1/2 heart (contact); 1/4 heart (freeze)

Threat Meter

Check behind the trees to the northeast to discover Anouki Village's stamp station. Manuever through the trees and use the station to plant your fifth stamp into Niko's book.

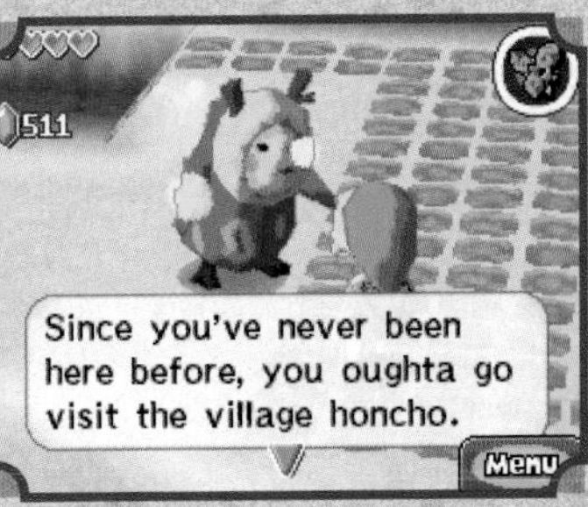

511
Since you've never been here before, you oughta go visit the village honcho.
Menu

Next, take a moment to meet the locals, a unique race of characters called Anouki. Like the villagers you met at Whittleton, these simple folk are suffering from the recent vanishing of their realm's Spirit Tracks. Most advise you to speak with the village "honcho," who lives at the top of the hill.

The honcho is happy to see a new face, because his village is in trouble. After the Spirit Tracks vanished, monsters started popping up everywhere. You've already seen some of them!

Grouping Anoukis

The honcho wants to put together a village watch to keep the monsters in check, but he's having trouble grouping his people into teams. Agree to help him; it's the only way to learn how to reach Steem and the Snow Sanctuary.

The honcho asks you to speak with his people so you can learn their preferences when it comes to teaming up. Run around talking to the Anouki to gather clues; then speak to the honcho to coordinate the groups. When the honcho shows you his work board, trace lines that connect the Anouki villagers into their preferred teams (as pictured in the screenshot above) to solve this little puzzle.

Thrilled with the teams you've picked out, the honcho hands over a Red Rupee and is now prepared to help you reach the Snow Sanctuary. He points out the sanctuary's location on your map but warns you that the tunnel you must take to get there is home to some sort of ginormous monster. Hoo boy...

Red Rupee

You got a Red Rupee! It's worth 20 Rupees!

Before leaving Anouki Village, find a Air Stone near the honcho's hut, and imitate its tune on your Spirit Flute. This teaches you the Song of Discovery, which you can use to reveal hidden objects. Handy!

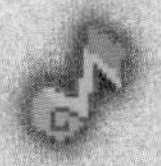

Song of Discovery

You got the Song of Discovery! Play it to find hidden objects.

The Air Stone rockets skyward after you learn its tune, leaving a small chest behind. Crack open the chest to claim another Red Rupee!

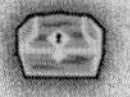

Overworld Chest 6: Red Rupee

Red Rupee

You got a Red Rupee! It's worth 20 Rupees!

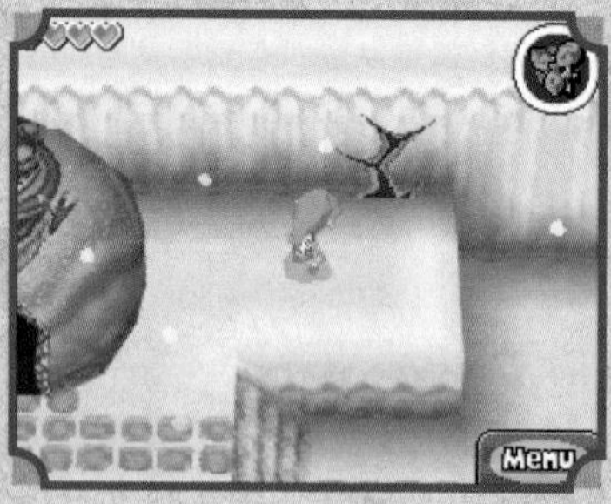

Lastly, note the giant crack running up the wall north of the honcho's hut. This is a bomb wall, but there are no bomb flowers about to help you blast through. You'll need a special item to bomb it open.

Return to the train station, and speak with Zelda to set off for the Snow Sanctuary.

Try for that snow rabbit again if you missed it on your way to Anouki Village.

To the Snow Sanctuary

Enemies Encountered

Bullbo

Boss: Rocktite

Tunnel Tyrant

The western tunnel is now open, so plot a direct course to the Snow Sanctuary and set off at high speed. You may face a few Bullbo on your way to the tunnel, but that's nothing compared to what awaits you inside.

Entering the tunnel, Link and Zelda catch a glimpse of *something* clinging to the ceiling. After they pass by, the object springs to life, landing behind them with a thunderous crash and quickly giving chase. Time for a boss fight!

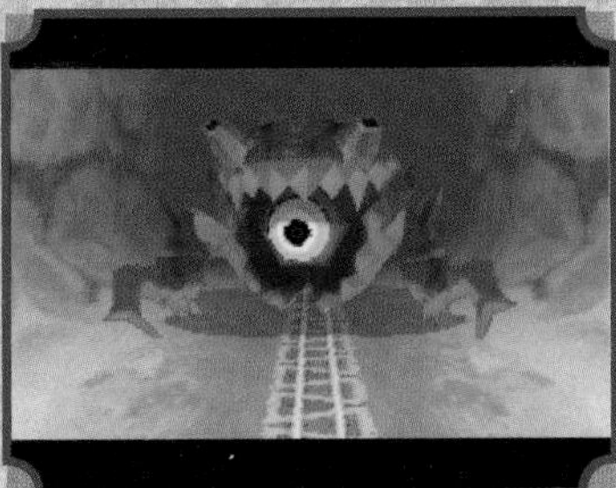

Rocktite

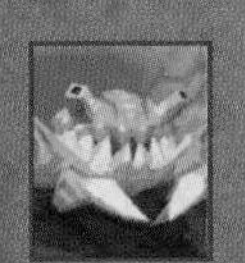

Hits to Defeat: Multiple
Attack Type: Contact
Power: N/A
Damage: 1 heart

Threat Meter

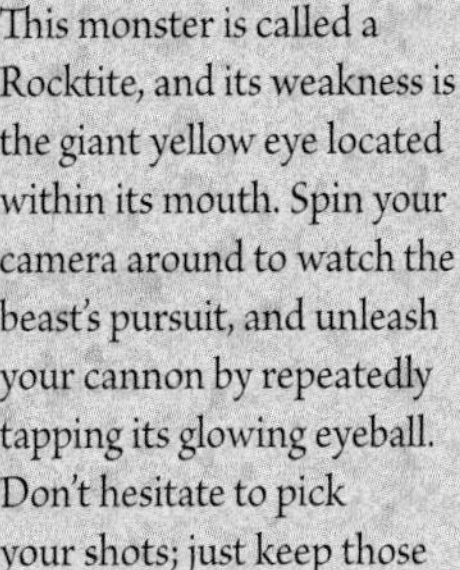

This monster is called a Rocktite, and its weakness is the giant yellow eye located within its mouth. Spin your camera around to watch the beast's pursuit, and unleash your cannon by repeatedly tapping its glowing eyeball. Don't hesitate to pick your shots; just keep those cannonballs flying.

After suffering several direct hits, the Rocktite collapses in a heap, giving you a chance to catch your breath. The monster is far from defeated, however; watch for that glowing eyeball to appear in the distant darkness, and resume fire the moment you see it.

The Rocktite will eventually trudge along the tunnel's ceiling and walls, making itself a more challenging target. It can't harm your train unless it's allowed to get close, so just keep hammering away at its eyeball to keep it from catching up.

After you stun the Rocktite several times, it collapses for the last time. What a battle! No wonder the Anouki kept far away from this treacherous tunnel.

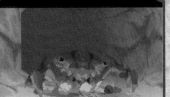

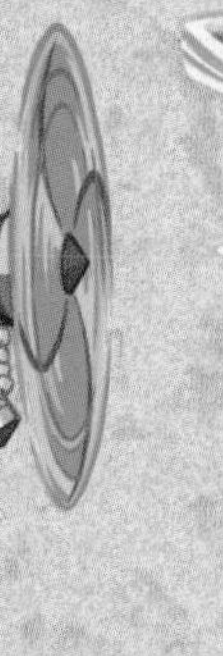

Task 2: Speak with Steem

Snow Sanctuary

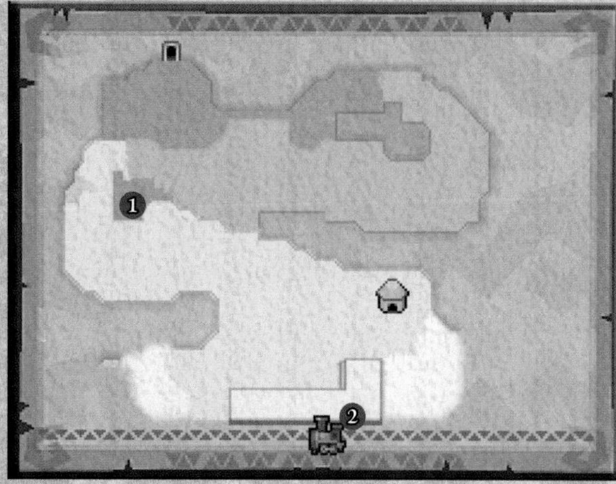

Snow Sanctuary

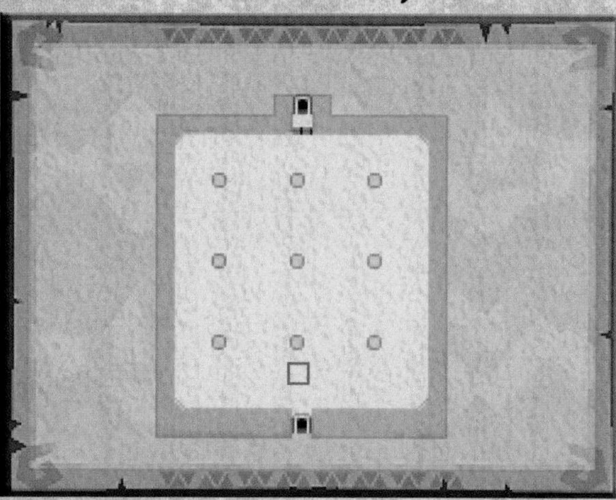

Snow Sanctuary Cave

Legend

- Floor switch
- 1 Stamp station
- 2 Train station

Enemies Encountered

Howling Mad

The Snow Sanctuary is home to the Snow Realm's Lokomo guardian, Steem. Unfortunately, it's also home to dangerous enemies known as White Wolfos! Like trouble itself, these hungry hunters always come in threes, popping up from the powder to surround Link in a blink. Unleash spin attacks by tracing circles around Link to best these beasts in short order.

White Wolfos

Hits to Defeat: 2 each
Attack Type: Contact
Power: Weak
Damage: 1/4 heart

Threat Meter

Snow Sanctuary Shop

Pop into the hut near the train station to visit a shop. Here you may purchase a variety of items, but the real eye-catcher is a Heart Container! Unfortunately, the precious item costs a whopping 2,000 Rupees, and there's little chance you've got that kind of scratch on you. Don't worry; it won't be long before you can trade in your treasures and buy it!

TIP

Consider buying a Red Potion or two if you haven't already. The coming Snow Temple is tough, and it's nice being able to replenish your hearts!

1 Explore the Snow Realm

2 Speak with Steem

3 Navigate the Blizzard

4 Clear the Snow Temple

Proceed up the snowy trail, making for the northern cave. Pause to add another stamp to Niko's book on your way up.

More White Wolfos attack you farther up the trail, along with some Ice ChuChus. Remember to use the Whirlwind to stun the Ice ChuChus before swinging Link's sword. Keep pressing forward, fighting your way into the northern cave.

Cold Stares

You must solve a tricky puzzle if you wish to speak with Steem. Think of it as a really, really good way of keeping unwanted solicitors at bay. Read the stone tablet as you enter the cave for a clue on how to proceed: You must navigate the cavern in a special fashion to reach the far door without being "seen."

Explore the cave to notice a collection of stone statues, each one facing in a certain direction. These are the watchers whose gazes you must avoid on your path to the far door.

It helps to draw each statue's line of sight on your map—this reveals the route you must follow. When you're all finished, your map should look something like the one pictured here. The route you must walk becomes obvious once you're done.

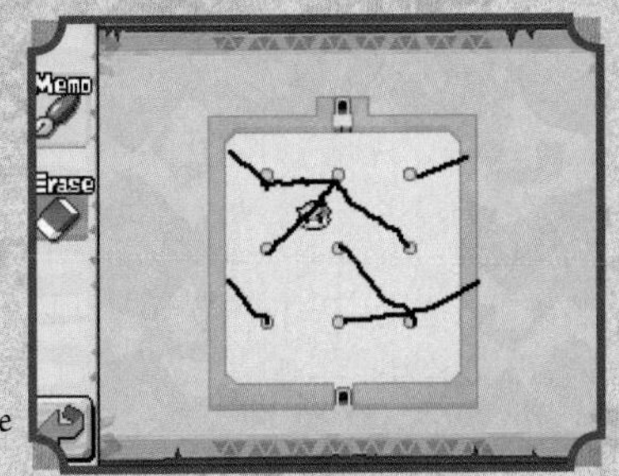

Return to the stone tablet and step on the nearby floor switch to open the far door. A timer then begins to tick; quickly make your way to the far door, keeping well out of the statues' sight. Hug the central statues as you go to avoid being spotted.

Jammin' with Steem

Steem awaits you in the chamber beyond the cave's north door. Like Gage, this little Lokomo asks you to play a song with him in order to reenergize the Snow Realm's Spirit Tracks.

Practice the song with Steem to learn your part before attempting the real thing. Again, it helps to nod your head a little to keep the timing as you play.

Complete the duet to warm Steem's heart and reenergize the realm's Spirit Tracks. Now you can travel all the way north and enter the Snow Temple!

The Snow rail map has started glowing! New tracks have appeared!

Steem's delighted to have helped, but he cautions Link about ferocious blizzards that have set in up north. You'll cross that bridge when you come to it; for now, return to the train station and set off for the Snow Temple.

Ferocious blizzards have been savaging the area around the temple.
Menu

To the Snow Temple

Enemies Encountered

Sir Frosty

Wicked Weather

Set a course for the Snow Temple and be on your way. As you roll eastward from the Snow Sanctuary, scan the right side of the tracks to find the second snow rabbit. Do your best to catch it.

Missing Link

Rabbitland Rescue

Rabbitland Rescue

Legend

1	Overworld Chest 5: Treasure
	Heart Container 3
1	Train station

Items to Obtain

Heart Container 3

Now that you've found five rabbits, make a quick stop at Rabbitland Rescue for a precious prize: Heart Container 3! Simply speak with the rescue's owner to receive this righteous reward.

1 Explore the Snow Realm

2 Speak with Steem

3 Navigate the Blizzard

4 Clear the Snow Temple

You must have collected all 10 available rabbits by this point to claim Heart Container 4. If you haven't found them all, check this guide's overworld map, then get out there and bag Forest Realm rabbits 1 through 3, along with Snow Realm rabbits 1 through 7.

Heart Container 3

You got a Heart Container! You increased your life by one and refilled your hearts!

Snowmen have a rep for being friendly and fun, but the ones you encounter on your trip north are neither. They toss their heads at your train, trying to derail your plans! Listen well for the telltale sound of Snowmen springing up, and blast their inbound heads from the sky. Nail their torsos afterward to put these immobile foes on ice.

Sir Frosty

Hits to Defeat: 2 (head and torso)
Attack Type: Range
Power: N/A
Damage: 1 heart

Threat Meter

It's not long before you're caught up in the intense blizzard that Steem warned you about. The track ahead becomes difficult to see, and before long, you find yourself right back where you started, near the place where you first entered the blizzard. Zelda advises you return to Anouki Village to seek advice. She's so smart!

Task 3: Navigate the Blizzard

Anouki Village Revisited

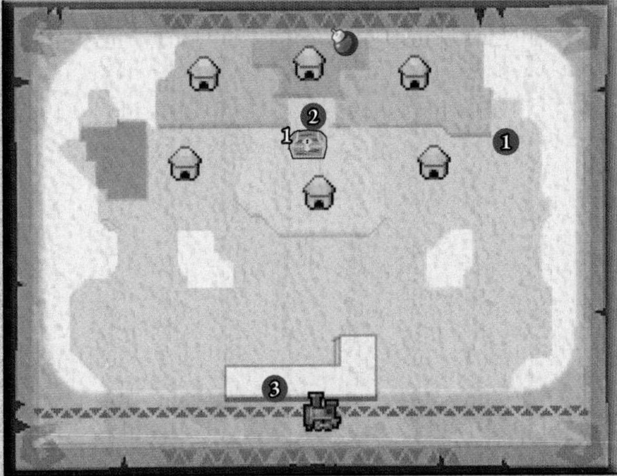

Anouki Village

Legend

- 1 (chest) Overworld Chest 6: Red Rupee
- Bomb wall
- 1 Stamp station
- 2 Air Stone
- 3 Train station

Enemies Encountered

Ice ChuChu

Heed the Honcho

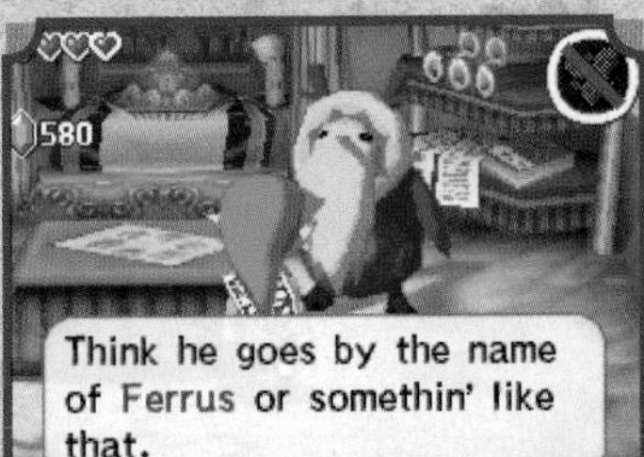

Speak with the Anouki honcho to learn that the blizzards have been around ever since the Spirit Tracks vanished. He doesn't know how to get through, but he may know someone who might: a man named Ferrus, who's nuts about trains and lives somewhere to the east. It's not much to go on, but at least it's something!

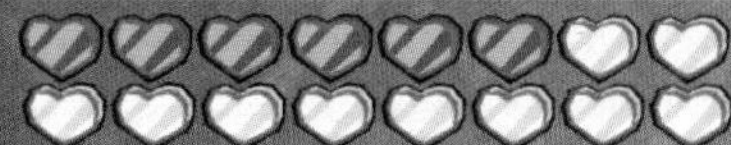

Finding Ferrus, Phase One

Enemies Encountered

Dark Train

Sir Frosty

Eastern Fields

Return to your train and set a course for the tracks to the east, where your map shows a Dark Train is on the loose. Great, something *else* to worry about!

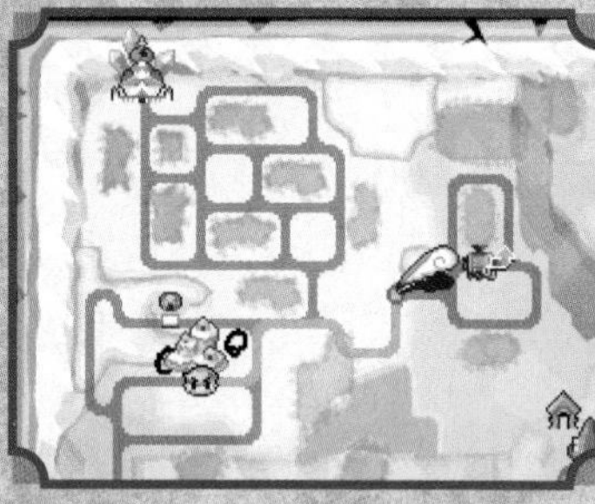

Aside from encountering a few Snowmen, the trip east is largely uneventful. No additional bunnies to catch just yet.

You come to a station as you draw near the eastern fields. This must be where Ferrus lives! Roll up to the station and put your train in park.

Wellspring Station

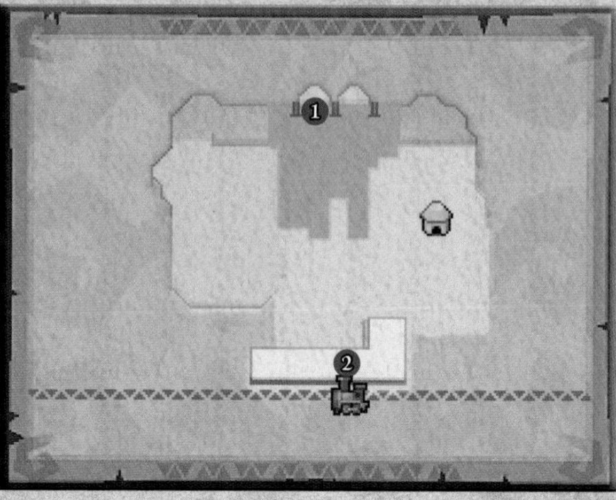

Wellspring Station

Legend

1. Stamp station
2. Train station

Enemies Encountered

Crow

White Wolfos

Nobody's Home

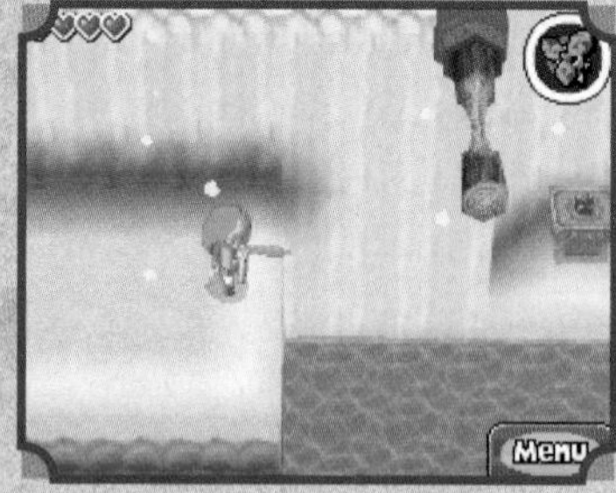

Wellspring Station gets its name from the giant freshwater spring located near the center. There are White Wolfos to the west and Crows in the treetops, and if you stand on the northwest ledge, you can just make out a stamp station tucked away in a northern nook. You can't reach the stamp station just yet, but mark its location for future reference.

1 Explore the Snow Realm

2 Speak with Steem

3 Navigate the Blizzard

4 Clear the Snow Temple

Enter the area's lone house, but don't get too excited—nobody's home. The place definitely feels like the abode of a train aficionado, though, what with all the photos of trains lying around. There's no doubt about it; this *must* be Ferrus's house!

Tap the drawing on the table for a closer look. It's some sort of map, and the title reads "Map of Good Places to Shoot Hot New Trains." Hmm...perhaps Ferrus is out in the field, indulging in his favorite hobby?

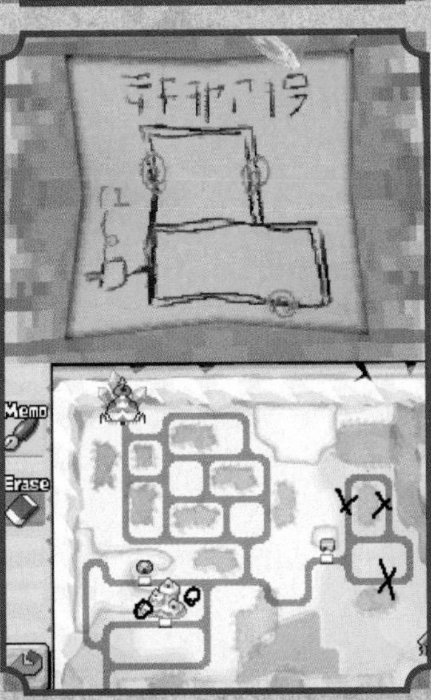

Tap the little Map icon to call up your rail map. Say, Ferrus's drawing looks just like the tracks to the east! Mark those three red circles on your map so you know where to look for Ferrus, then return to your train and set off in search of the man with answers.

Finding Ferrus, Phase Two

Enemies Encountered

Dark Train

Sir Frosty

One-in-Three Chance

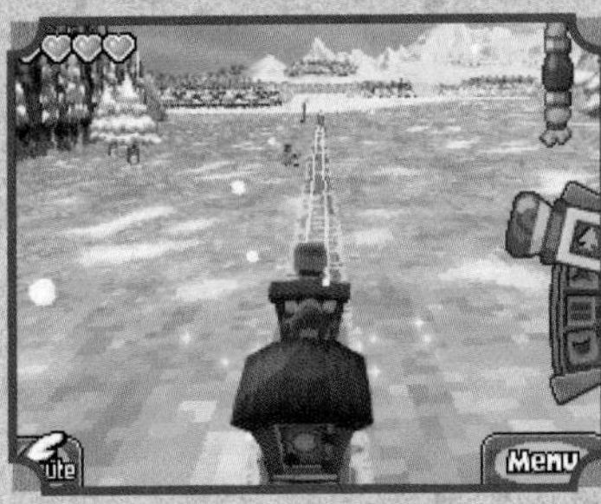

Ferrus will be at one of those three locations, so travel to each one. When you hear a clicking sound, you know you're close—for that is the sound of a choo-choo enthusiast's camera!

Be very careful while searching for Ferrus; that Dark Train can bring your hunt to a crashing halt. Monitor your map closely, kick it into high gear, and make sure the Dark Train never has a chance to derail you.

Ferrus will be standing trackside and is easy to spot, thanks to his camera flash. Once you see him, park nearby for a quick chat.

The excitable man can't believe you actually stopped and seems to know all about Link and the Spirit Train. More importantly, he knows the safest route through the blizzard, and he even has a map that shows it!

595
OH! I just remembered I have an old map of the tracks around that area

Ferrus's map is pretty old, so you'll need to blow away the dust. Blow on your screen to clear the stuff off, then copy the route that's shown onto your own map.

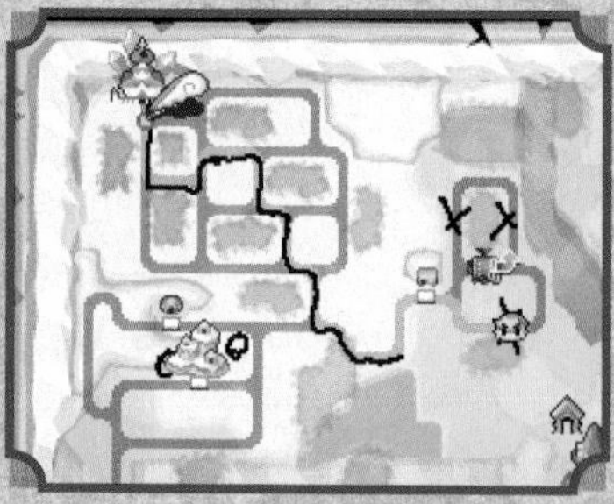

Great work! Now you can get through that awful blizzard! There's no time to waste; set a course to the temple, following the exact route you've just discovered.

The storm sets in just as before, but if you follow Ferrus's map, you won't be turned around. Snowmen attack you on your way, however, so stay sharp as you go.

NOTE

Though this guide's map shows several snow rabbits on the tracks near the temple, these bunnies are all hiding from the blizzard. Don't worry; you'll have a chance to nab them after you've finished your work in the Snow Temple.

Legend

- 1 Dungeon Chest 1: Red Rupee
- 2 Dungeon Chest 2: Red Rupee
- 3 Dungeon Chest 3: Boomerang
- 4 Dungeon Chest 4: Red Rupee
- 5 Dungeon Chest 5: Small Key
- 6 Dungeon Chest 6: Big Green Rupee
- 7 Dungeon Chest 7: Red Rupee
- 8 Dungeon Chest 8: Red Rupee
- 9 Dungeon Chest 9: Heart Container 4
- Floor switch
- 1 Stamp station
- Switch

Task 4: Clear the Snow Temple

Snow Temple

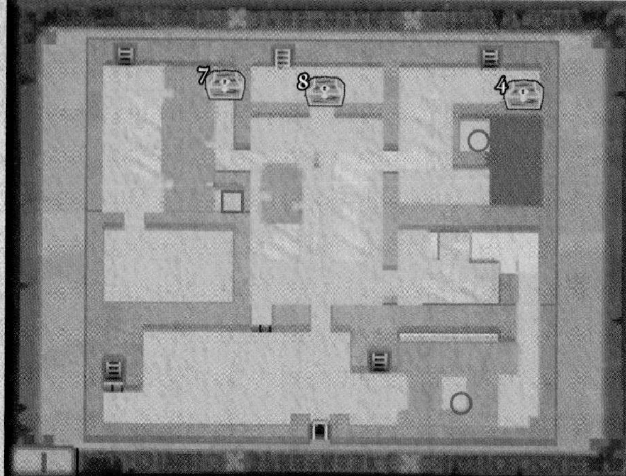

Snow Temple, First Floor

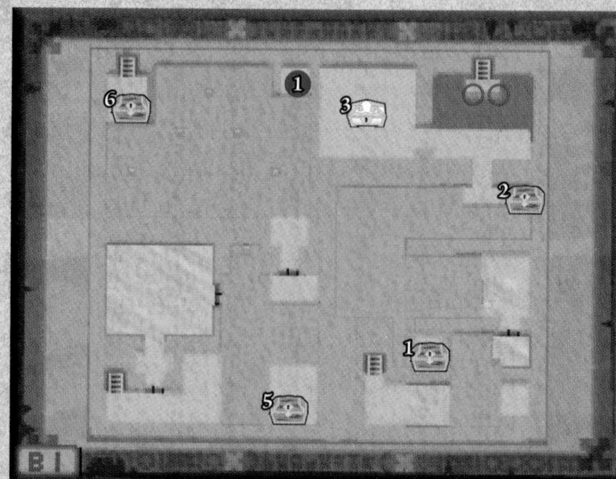

Snow Temple, Basement First Floor

Items to Obtain

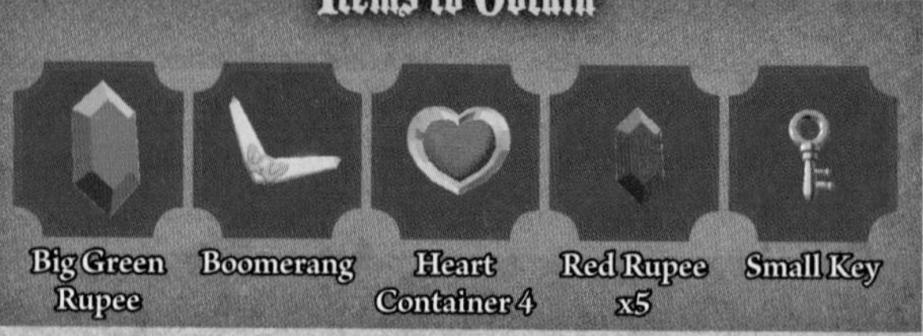

1 Explore the Snow Realm

2 Speak with Steem

3 Navigate the Blizzard

4 Clear the Snow Temple

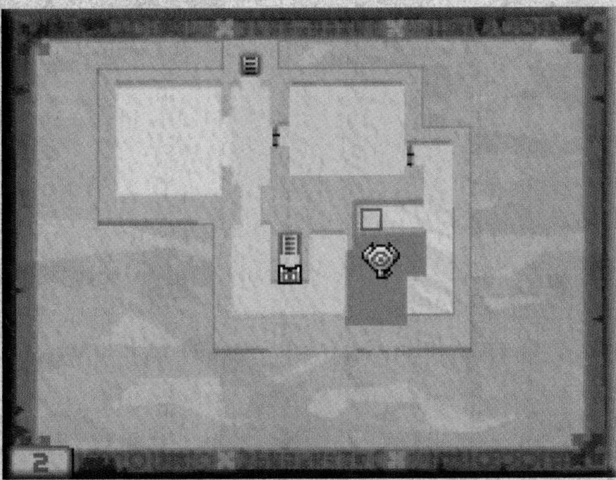

Snow Temple, Second Floor

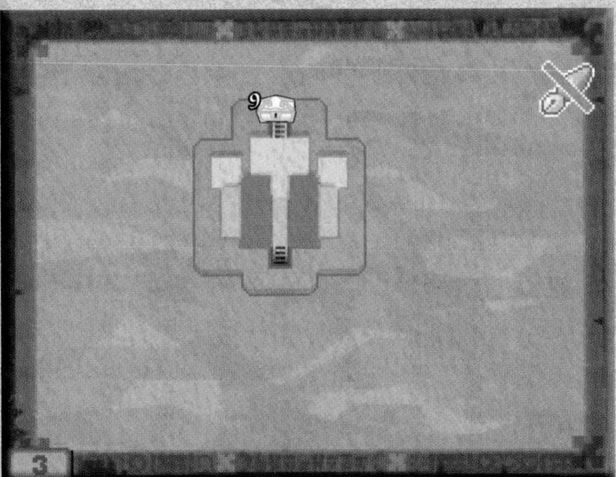

Snow Temple, Third Floor

Enemies Encountered

Snow Temple: First Floor

The Snow Temple's frozen stillness is indeed foreboding, but there's no sense turning back. Hack down the frozen grass for goodies and dispatch the roaming Keese in the temple's entry courtyard. Then proceed through the north door to reach the first floor's interior.

It's not much warmer inside the temple—in fact, much of the floor is covered in slippery ice! Dispatch the roaming Ice ChuChus, using the Whirlwind to stun them first.

After besting the monsters, note the unusual central block. A large bell is affixed to it. Slide this block north along the ice and situate it on the large floor plate. The weight of the block depresses the plate, putting the bell within Link's reach.

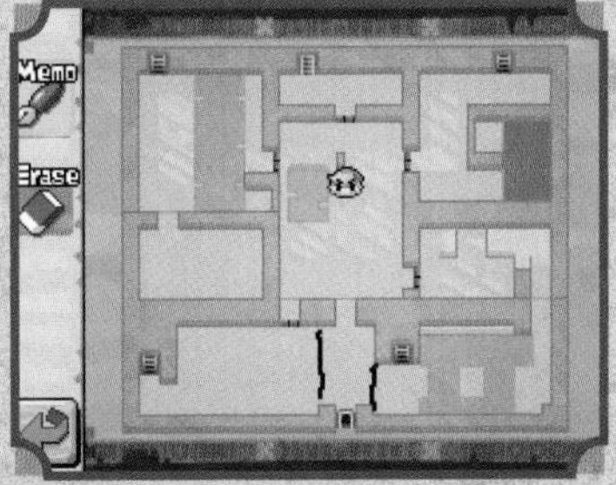

Tap the nearby sign for a clue: it shows a musical graph with two big bell icons on it. Tap the bell twice to make Link whack it with his sword, sounding the bell two times. This opens the southeast door.

A sliding-block puzzle awaits you beyond the door, but it's an easy one to solve. Slide the block down, then over to the left. Slide it up and then over to the right to land it between the two stone floor tiles. From there, simply slide the block up to position it right in the middle of the room's north wall.

If you need to reset the block, simply exit to the temple's courtyard and return; the block will be back in its original position.

With the block in place, run up the steps and leap onto the block. Then jump from the block to reach the high east ledge. Proceed through the south doorway to return to the courtyard.

An odd creature known as an Octive is lounging in the chilly water out here, relentlessly spitting spiky balls at the south wall. What a weirdo! Equip the Whirlwind and blow a cyclone to catch one of the balls and send it crashing into the switch to the west. This extends a bridge across the water; carefully dash past the Octives and proceed downstairs.

Octive

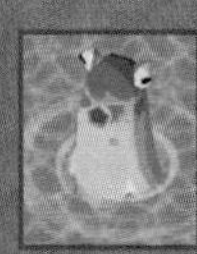

Hits to Defeat: 1
Attack Type: Range
Power: Weak
Damage: 1/2 heart

Threat Meter

Snow Temple: Basement First Floor

The temple's basement is flooded, so you must proceed with care—remember, Link doesn't like getting wet! Slide the wooden block into the first pool of water and then hop on top.

Bust out the Whirlwind and cast out a cyclone to activate the Windmill Switch to the east. Notice that the box drifts west when you blow the Whirlwind due to the force of the air current.

Once activated, the Windmill Switch opens a door to the north. Use the Whirlwind to get there, blowing cyclones south to sail to the north.

Careful—a Freezard patrols the icy ground near the door. Drift close and tap the creature to whack it with Link's sword, sending it crazily spinning around the ice. Try to rebound the monster off the far wall so that it slides into the water. Then leap over to the ice when it's safe.

Normally, smacking Freezards is the last thing you want to do, especially in a confined space. Avoid these creatures whenever possible, at least until you discover a means of defeating them.

Freezard

Hits to Defeat: 2 (once melted)
Attack Type: Contact
Power: Weak
Damage: 1/2 heart

Threat Meter

1 Explore the Snow Realm

2 Speak with Steem

3 Navigate the Blizzard

4 Clear the Snow Temple

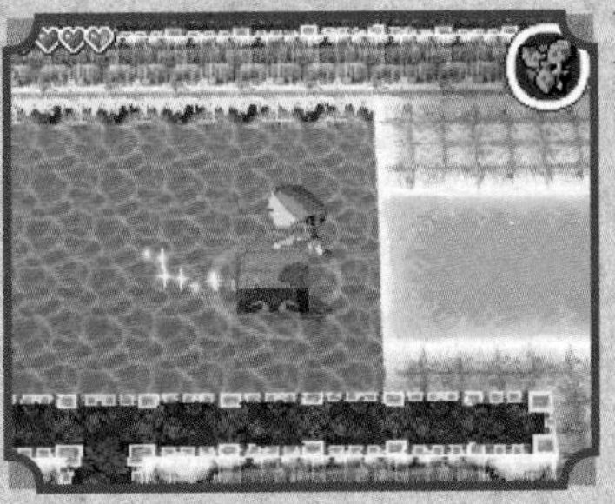

You find another wooden box just beyond the door. Shove it into the water and leap onto it, but stand ready to block spiky balls fired from the Octive to the west.

After blocking one of the Octive's projectiles, quickly take up the Whirlwind and use it to repel the next spiky ball back at the monster. This defeats the foe, allowing you to safely advance.

Maneuver into the narrow channel to the south to reach a small chest. Hop off your tiny vessel and open the chest to score a Red Rupee.

Dungeon Chest 1: Red Rupee

Red Rupee

You got a Red Rupee! It's worth 20 Rupees!

Return to your flotation device and dispatch the remaining Octives in this pool. Doing so reveals a hidden chest on the northern landing. Shore up and open the chest to claim another Red Rupee.

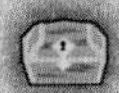

Dungeon Chest 2: Red Rupee

Red Rupee

You got a Red Rupee! It's worth 20 Rupees!

Ignore the twin switches that stand beyond the northern pit, and enter the room to the west. You become trapped in this room with a host of fluttering Ice Keese! Stun each of these little pests with the Whirlwind, and then follow up with Link's cold, hard steel.

Ice Keese

Hits to Defeat: 1
Attack Type: Contact
Power: Strong
Damage: 1/4 heart (freeze)

Threat Meter

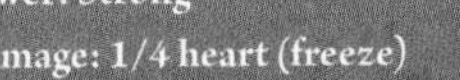

You got the boomerang!
This item follows the path
you draw on the screen!

Clear the room of Ice Keese to unseal its door and reveal a giant chest. Lift the chest's lid to obtain an extremely cool tool: the boomerang!

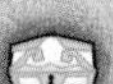

Dungeon Chest 3: Boomerang

Boomerang

You got the boomerang! This item follows the path you draw on the screen!

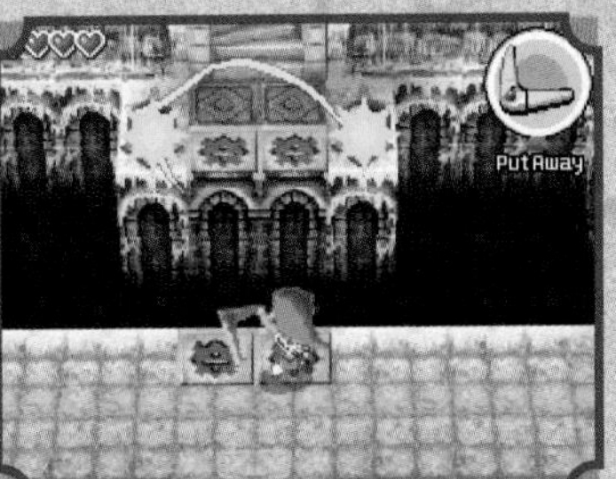

The boomerang is incredibly awesome, and you're about to find out why. Return to the twin switches you noticed a moment ago and equip the boomerang, which now appears in your screen's upper-right corner. With the boomerang in hand, trace a single line from one switch to the other, ensuring yellow "target" icons appear on each switch.

Now simply lift the stylus off the screen to make Link hurl the boomerang. The item flies through the air and quickly whacks both switches, activating both. A bridge then extends over the pit, allowing you to venture upstairs.

To switch between your equipable items, first tap Menu, then tap the item you wish to ready. The item you tap will appear in the screen's upper-right corner and will be ready to be equipped at a moment's notice.

Snow Temple: First Floor Revisited

You're back on the first floor, right near another odd block with a bell sticking up from its top. Ignore the block for a moment, and stand near the southern pit. Equip the boomerang and trace a line over the pit, aiming to strike the two Ice Keese fluttering above the abyss.

The boomerang bests the Ice Keese with just one hit each, making it a better weapon to wield against them than the Whirlwind, which only stuns the wee beasties. With both Ice Keese defeated, a hidden chest blinks into view up north. The chest contains a Red Rupee—your third thus far.

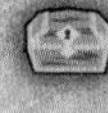

Dungeon Chest 4: Red Rupee

Red Rupee

You got a Red Rupee! It's worth 20 Rupees!

Return to the pit and equip the boomerang once more. This time, trace a line up and around to strike the switch on the ledge. Only the boomerang can activate this switch, which opens the door to the west.

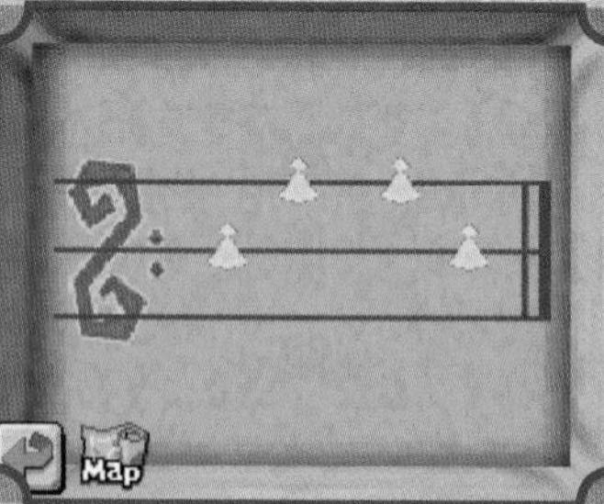

Now you may shove the bell block to the floor's center, where the first bell block still rests. But before you do, glance at the nearby sign on the wall. It's a musical chart that shows the order in which you must sound the bells.

Grab the bell block and slide it south; then shove it west, through the now-open doorway and into the floor's central chamber. From there, slide the block in the following order to get it onto its floor plate:

1. North
2. West
3. South
4. East
5. South
6. West
7. South

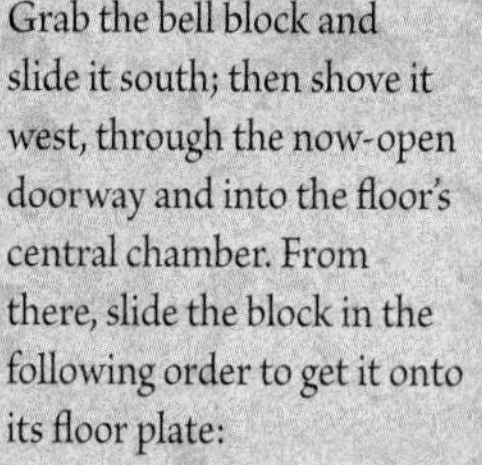

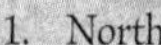

Presto! The block's little bell is now within reach of Link's sword—but it's the boomerang you must use to solve this puzzle, for the bells must be rung in quick succession. Trace a line from the big bell to the little one, then loop around and target the little bell a second time before going back up to the big bell and releasing. This causes the boomerang to ring the big bell once, the little bell twice, and the big bell for a second time, completing the sequence you saw on the wall.

Ringing the two bells in the proper order opens the southwest door. Go through to reach an as-yet-unexplored region of the courtyard, where four unlit torches surround one that's burning bright.

You must use the boomerang to light all four torches, but you must light them in a specific order. The pattern is hidden beneath the snow on the ground. Target the lit torch with the boomerang, then continue tracing the line all around the snow.

The boomerang catches fire as it passes through the lit torch's flames, then delivers its heat wherever it travels, melting the snow and revealing special tiles on the floor. Each tile sits near an unlit torch, and each has a different number of dots. The dots indicate the order in which you must light the torches: northeast, southeast, northwest, southwest.

Now simply target the lit torch and trace a line that connects all of the unlit torches in the proper order. With all five torches burning bright, the door to the west opens, allowing you to continue downstairs.

NOTE

No need to melt the rest of the snow; there's nothing else hidden around here.

Snow Temple: Basement First Floor, Revisited

Ignore the Gossip Stone on this floor; you've already discovered every hidden chest down here. That's not to say there aren't any more chests; one sits on the ledge to the right, seemingly out of reach due to the obstructing pool.

The boomerang is the key to crossing this pool. Equip it and trace a line to the blue torch that stands in the middle of the water; continue tracing the line back toward Link and then over to the chest.

The boomerang becomes infused with frost as it passes through the blue torch, spreading ice around the water's surface wherever it travels from there. The ice won't last, so dart across and open the chest to acquire a Small Key.

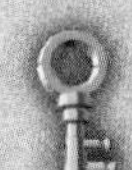

Dungeon Chest 5: Small Key

Small Key

You got a Small Key! Use this key to open locked doors!

Use the boomerang and blue torch to return across the water; then open the locked door near the stairs you took to get down here. Pass through the door to trigger a mandatory fight against four dangerous Freezards.

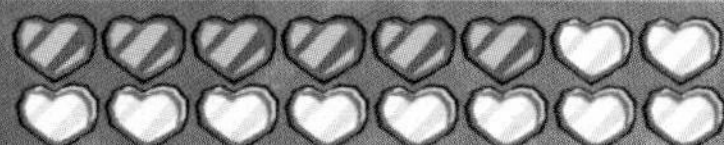

Do not attack the Freezards or you'll have utter chaos. Instead, lure them away to a corner, then run to the room's opposite side and equip the boomerang. Trace a line to the central torch, and continue tracing the line about the room, aiming to scorch each of the Freezards with searing heat.

One touch from your flaming boomerang melts the ice off these baddies, reducing them to your garden-variety Octorok. Now you may dispatch these villains with a few swipes from Link's trusty blade.

NOTE

You can use the boomerang to stun the Octoroks, but it alone won't defeat them.

Eliminating the Octoroks yields no treasure chests, but it does unseal the room's east door. Now you can use the boomerang to melt the ice that's covering a nearby Windmill Switch. Stand near the doorway and trace a line from the room's torch to the frozen Windmill Switch at the pool's north end.

With the Windmill Switch thawed, use your boomerang and the pool's blue torch to freeze the water's surface again. Then quickly ready the Whirlwind by tapping Menu and then the Whirlwind icon. Cross the ice to get within range of the Windmill Switch. Tap the Whirlwind icon in the screen's upper-right corner to equip the Whirlwind; then blow into your DS mic to cast a cyclone at the Windmill Switch. This opens the northeast door; retreat to solid ground and refreeze the pool before attempting to cross over.

Ready your Whirlwind again before passing through the door. The floor's final pool is filled with Octives. The first one pops up and spits a spiky ball at you the moment you move through the doorway. Block the first projectile, then quickly equip the Whirlwind and blow the next ball back at the Octive to sink it.

The pool sports many more Octives and several blue torches. Crossing through here is treacherous; you must light the torches and freeze the water with the boomerang to advance. The boomerang will only stun the Octives, so you'll need to switch back to the Whirlwind and repel their spiky balls if you wish to defeat them. There's good reason to dispatch them all, too—doing so spawns a chest near your destination, the northwest stairs.

As you cross the pond, pause at the ledge to the northeast, which sports a stamp station. Record your seventh stamp here, then complete your arduous trek toward the northwest staircase, lighting torches and besting Octives as you go.

If you defeated all the Octives here, open the chest your efforts have revealed to claim a Big Green Rupee. Not bad for a day's work!

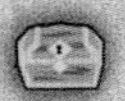

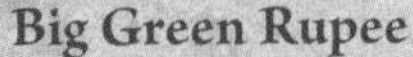

Dungeon Chest 6: Big Green Rupee

Big Green Rupee

You got a Big Green Rupee! It's worth 100 Rupees!

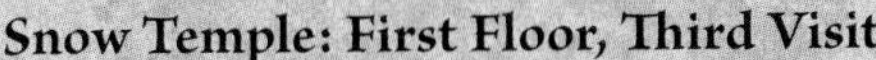

Snow Temple: First Floor, Third Visit

You emerge from the basement near another bell block; this one's got a huge bell on top. Sprint past the block and head through the southern doorway to reach the snow-covered courtyard.

Fire Keese swarm this section of the courtyard, but they're no match for your boomerang. Work to eliminate all of the pests.

TIP

You can also use the Whirlwind to stun the Fire Keese and extinguish their flames, making them vulnerable to Link's sword.

Fire Keese

Hits to Defeat: 1
Attack Type: Contact
Power: Strong
Damage: 1/4 heart

Threat Meter

After dispatching the Fire Keese, use the torches and the boomerang to melt the surrounding snow, revealing a musical graph on the ground. Sneaky! Scribble the notes down on your map before returning to the bell block.

First things first: use a blue torch and the boomerang to freeze the water near the bell block so you may cross and open the small chest in the northeast corner. A Red Rupee is the prize inside.

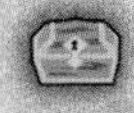

Dungeon Chest 7: Red Rupee

Red Rupee

You got a Red Rupee! It's worth 20 Rupees!

Now freeze the water and move to the southwest ledge, where you find a floor switch. Step on the switch to open the west door.

For your next trick, you must slide the bell block across the water. First, get the block into the proper position by sliding it in the following order:

1. North
2. East
3. South
4. West
5. North

Right! Now to cross the water. Freeze the surface with the boomerang, making an icy bridge for the block. Quickly circle around and shove the block east, across your icy bridge, through the door you recently opened, and into the floor's central chamber.

You're nearly finished. Freeze the entire small pond that lies south of where the bell block eventually comes to rest. Then quickly slide the block as follows to maneuver it onto its floor plate:

1. South
2. West
3. South
4. West
5. North
6. East

Excellent! Now that all three bells are in place, you can open this floor's final door. Use the boomerang to ring the bells in the following order, based on the chart you found beneath the courtyard snow: huge bell first, then big, big, small, and big. As before, you must ring the bells in this sequence with just one toss of the boomerang.

The north door opens, but before you head through, light the torches near the door, using the lit torch in the room to the west. This causes the floor's final hidden chest to appear to the north.

Venture north and avoid the lone Freezard. Open the chest you just exposed to claim your fifth Red Rupee from this temple; then proceed up the nearby staircase.

Dungeon Chest 8: Red Rupee

Red Rupee

You got a Red Rupee! It's worth 20 Rupees!

Snow Temple: Second Floor

Ignore the torches in the west chamber as you enter this small floor. Proceed south, cracking Ice ChuChus with your boomerang and finishing them off with cold steel.

Loop around the Boss Key door and inspect the sign on the wall. It shows a ring of red and blue flames, arranged in a specific pattern. Copy this pattern down on your map, using a simple system to keep it straight, such as Xs for red and Os for blue.

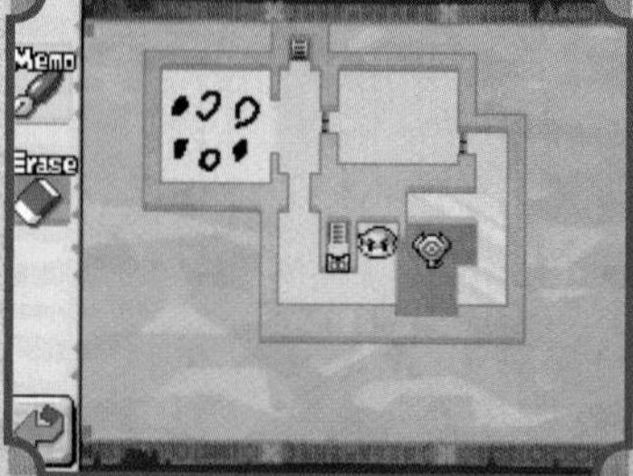

1 Explore the Snow Realm

2 Speak with Steem

3 Navigate the Blizzard

4 Clear the Snow Temple

Now return to the west chamber and light its torches with the boomerang. You must light all the torches in one toss, and you must light them in the sequence you saw on the sign. Doing so opens the east door.

Explore the east chamber to trigger a showdown with a pack of voracious White Wolfos. A series of spin attacks puts the beasts down rather quickly.

Navigate the icy floor to the south and step on the floor switch to extend a bridge. Cross the bridge and use the Whirlwind to blow the Boss Key off its pedestal and into your reach.

Collect the Boss Key and hurl it into the Boss Key door's lock. With this final obstacle cleared from your path, scamper upstairs toward the final showdown.

Snow Temple: Third Floor

There isn't much going on up on the third floor. Read the stone tablet to make the blue light appear, but don't enter it unless you wish to warp back to the temple's entrance. Ready the boomerang and proceed upstairs to face the temple's boss instead—but only after you've steeled yourself for a challenging battle.

TIP

If you're injured, toss the boomerang over to the third floor's side ledges to smash some distant pots and retrieve hearts.

Fraaz, Master of Icy Fire

Hits to Defeat: Multiple
Attack Type: Contact and Range
Power: Strong
Threat Meter
Damage: 1/2 heart (fire); 1/2 heart (ice); 1/4 heart (freeze)

Fraaz is a far more worthy adversary than Stagnox was. He's able to assault Link with both fire and ice, and his attacks can be tough to avoid.

Keep your distance and watch Fraaz as he inhales, becoming rotund and charged with power. Fraaz's color determines his forthcoming attacks, as well as his current vulnerability. Expect ice attacks when he's glowing blue and expect fire attacks when he's red.

The first stage of the battle is simple enough. Avoid Fraaz's attacks and wound him by tossing your boomerang into either the blue or red torch, then hitting him. Strike Fraaz with a fiery boomerang when he's glowing blue and a frosty boomerang when he's glowing red.

Hitting Fraaz with the boomerang stuns him for a moment. Take full advantage and assault the boss with rapid sword strikes, dealing as much damage as you can.

Repeat this sequence to harm Fraaz when he glows the other color. After damaging Fraaz when he's red and blue, the boss splits into two smaller Fraazes.

Harming the smaller Fraazes works a bit differently. One is vulnerable to ice and the other to fire. Glance at your map screen to see which is which, and hit each one with the appropriate attack.

After successfully striking both little Fraazes, the two re-form into the full-size Fraaz. At this point, the boss becomes wise to Link's tricks and destroys both torches. Foul!

Now the fight gets really tricky. You must wait for Fraaz to attack, dodge the attack (ideally), and then quickly make use of the lingering substance. For example, if Fraaz launches an ice ball, dodge the projectile (which explodes on the floor) and then ready the boomerang. Trace a line to the remnants of the ice, waiting for Fraaz to turn red before connecting the line to him and releasing the boomerang. The flames left behind by Fraaz's fireballs must be exploited in just the same manner; wait for Fraaz to turn blue, then strike.

Again, you must repeatedly stun Fraaz, attacking him afterward with Link's sword. Only when you've hit him enough times (up to three times depending on your speed) will Fraaz devolve into his twin microselves.

The second mini-Fraaz encounter is a bit more challenging as well. This time, you must strike both Fraazes with the boomerang, all in one toss. Wait for the little villains to attack, then quickly trace a line from the first lingering substance back to the appropriate mini-Fraaz, then back to the other substance and over to the other mini-Fraaz. Again, check your map to see which Fraaz is which.

Fraaz re-forms one final time, and, of course, he's worse than ever. Now you must strike him twice with one toss of the boomerang, using the appropriate substance to wound him. To do this, trace a line from the substance over to Fraaz, then draw a quick loop to target Fraaz again. You don't need to retarget the substance after striking Fraaz the first time; just draw a quick loop and retarget Fraaz so that you strike him twice in a row.

1 Explore the Snow Realm

2 Speak with Steem

3 Navigate the Blizzard

4 Clear the Snow Temple

As always, you must stun Fraaz, follow up with Link's sword, then stun him again, hacking away once more. When you're not attacking, stay mobile and do your best to avoid Fraaz's far-reaching attacks. Don't relent until the boss finally goes down for the count.

TIP

The pots around the arena contain hearts, but even still, Fraaz is one tough customer. If you can't beat him without running out of hearts, consider leaving the temple to purchase a potion or two from the Anouki shop you saw back at the Snow Sanctuary. When you return to the temple, you can use the blue light to warp right back to the boss fight, better equipped to quell Fraaz's wrath.

Dispatching Fraaz certainly isn't easy, but the ends justify the means. The temple's flow of energy is restored, and another portion of the Tower of Spirits is locked back into place. Well done!

Be sure to claim your hard-earned Heart Container from the large chest that appears after defeating Fraaz. Step into the blue light afterward to return to the temple's entrance.

Dungeon Chest 9: Heart Container 4

Heart Container 4

You got a Heart Container! You increased your life by one and refilled your hearts!

With the temple's energy flow restored, your next task is clear: Return to the Tower of Spirits and let Anjean know of your incredible accomplishment!

Missing Links

Anjean's used to waiting around for you by now, so why not take the time to complete these optional asides? You'll certainly enjoy the rewards!

Snow Rabbits 3–7

As you exit the Snow Temple, you'll be surprised to find warm sunlight greets you—the blizzard has cleared up! Now you can hunt down five more snow rabbits, all of them hiding around the tracks near the temple. See the overworld map for their exact locations, and collect every one of those bunnies to bring your total to ten! Keep reading; we'll take you there.

Beedle's Air Shop

Items to Obtain

Beedle Club Card	Bomb Bag 1	Letter ("Beedle Club Mailing")	Letter ("From Beedle")	Letter ("From Russell")

I've got a letter for you here from one Mr. Beedle!

Keep your eyes on the sky as you cruise about in search of rabbits. From now on, a special soul known as Beedle travels the land in his wondrous hot-air balloon! You receive a letter ("From Beedle") after clearing the Snow Temple, inviting you

to come and visit Beedle's Air Shop. Just visit any location with a postbox to find it wiggling away, then tap the box to receive the letter.

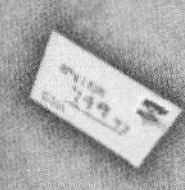

Letter

You got a letter from the postman! Go to the Collection screen to read it!

Mail for Link
from the guard captain!

You'll get another letter in the mail if you leave the scene and then return. Just enter a house or board your train and then immediately cancel, and you'll find the postbox a-wiggling once more. This time you get a letter from Russell, captain of the guard at Hyrule Castle, entitled (you guessed it) "From Russell." In his letter, the good captain invites you to visit him for some training. We'll steer you there in a bit, but there's more to say about Beedle right now.

Letter

You got a letter from the postman! Go to the Collection screen to read it!

Menu

The funny-face icon you see drifting about the map as you chug around in your train represent's Beedle's Air Shop. Beedle really gets around, so you need to catch him if you want to see his goods. And you do! So blow your train's whistle whenever you're close to Beedle, and he'll set down nearby. Then just park near his balloon to visit his shop.

899
Quit
Buy

Beedle has all sorts of interesting goods to sell you. The first thing you'll want to buy is the Bomb Bag, which allows you to use and carry bombs. Now you can blow stuff up even when there are no bomb flowers for miles!

Bomb Bag 1

You got bombs! You can hold up to 10 in your Bomb Bag.

You got a Beedle Club
Card! Now you can collect
points at Beedle's shop!

Beedle also has a special membership program that you should definitely sign up for. Tell him you're interested and he'll mail you his patented Beedle Club Card. The next time you pull up to a friendly station, find the local postbox and check your mail for another letter from Beedle ("Beedle Club Mailing")—one that contains your special card!

NOTE

Beedle's membership program has different levels of membership status, each with special perks, such as discounts on stuff you buy at Beedle's Air Shop. For every 10 Rupees you spend with Beedle, you earn one membership point. Become a gold member by spending over 5,000 Rupees with Beedle, and you'll earn that shiny Heart Container he's so proudly displaying up on his wall. It'll take quite a while to earn that coveted prize, which is why this guide considers it to be Heart Container 13—the final Heart Container you'll get.

Letter

You got a letter from the postman! Go to the Collection screen to read it!

Beedle Club Card

You got a Beedle Club Card! Now you can collect points at Beedle's Air Shop!

1 Explore the Snow Realm

2 Speak with Steem

3 Navigate the Blizzard

4 Clear the Snow Temple

Wellspring Station

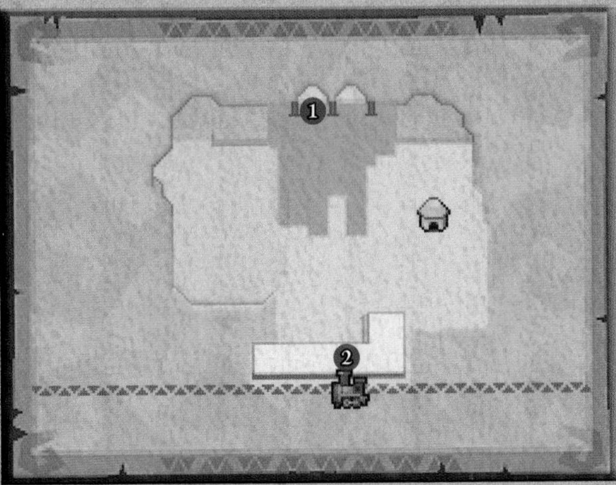

Wellspring Station

Legend

1 Stamp station

2 Train station

Enemies Encountered

Crow

White Wolfos

After nabbing all those snow rabbits, swing by Wellspring Station to claim another stamp for Niko. Stand near the water behind Ferrus's house, and toss your boomerang north to spy a blue torch. Target the torch and then trace a line west to the stamp station and then back down to Link.

After freezing the water's surface with the blue torch and boomerang, cross over and claim your eighth stamp from the stamp station. Nice one!

Anouki Village

Anouki Village

Legend

1 Overworld Chest 6: Red Rupee

2 Overworld Chest 7: Big Red Rupee

3 Overworld Chest 8: Big Green Rupee

Bomb wall

1 Air Stone

2 Train station

Items to Obtain

Big Red Rupee

Big Green Rupee

Enemies Encountered

Ice ChuChu

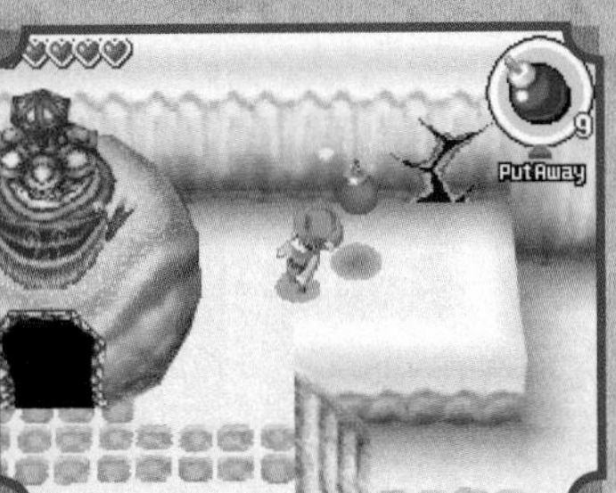

If you'd like to score a Big Red Rupee, use your newfound bombs to blow a hole through the cracked wall near the honcho's hut. This reveals an entrance to a long-forgotten cave.

You must solve a tricky sliding block puzzle to claim the Big Red Rupee. Here's how to slide the block so you can reach the chest on the high left ledge:

1. West
2. North
3. East
4. North
5. East
6. North
7. East
8. South
9. East
10. South
11. West
12. North

Overworld Chest 7: Big Red Rupee

Red Rupee

You got a Big Red Rupee! It's worth 200 Rupees!

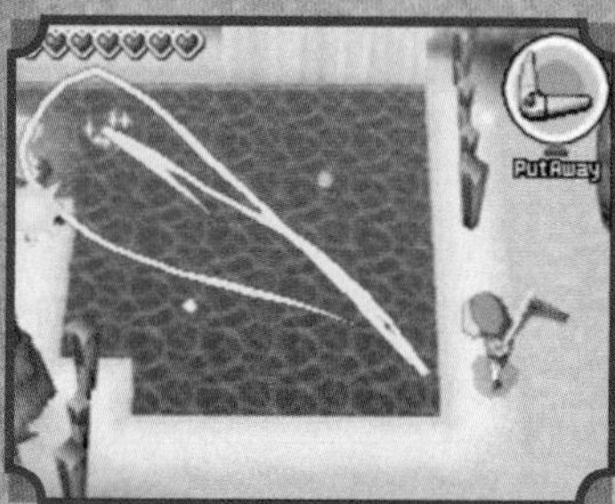

For another Rupee reward, go to the village's northwest corner of town. Use the boomerang and ice torch up here to freeze the pond so you may cross over and claim a Big Green Rupee from a tucked-away chest.

Overworld Chest 8: Big Green Rupee

Big Green Rupee

You got a Big Green Rupee! It's worth 100 Rupees!

Castle Town and Hyrule Castle

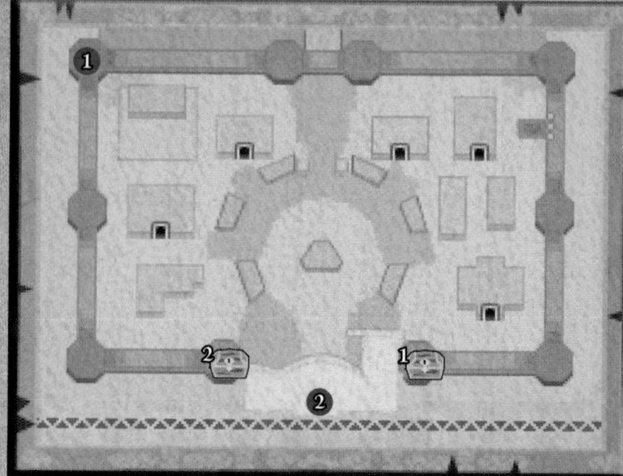

Castle Town

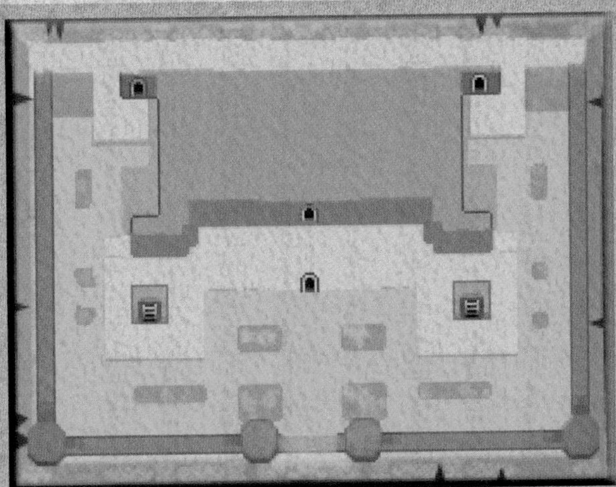

Hyrule Castle Grounds

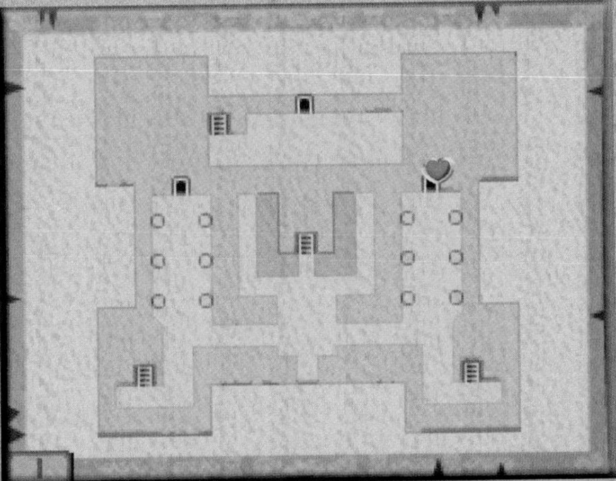

Hyrule Castle, First Floor

Legend

1 Overworld Chest 9: Red Rupee
2 Overworld Chest 10: Red Rupee
Heart Container 5
1 Stamp station
2 Train station

Last stop, Castle Town! There's quite a lot to do here, assuming you've purchased bombs from Beedle's Air Shop. If you have, use one to blow away the bomb blocks at the northeast corner of town so you may sprint up onto the surrounding ramparts.

Run south along the ramparts to reach a small chest on the high tower near the train station. Open this chest for a sparkly Red Rupee!

Overworld Chest 9: Red Rupee

Red Rupee

You got a Red Rupee! It's worth 20 Rupees!

Backtrack along the ramparts and go north, then west, to discover the town's stamp station. So that's where they've been hiding it! Grab that stamp to bring your total number to nine—just one more and it's time to visit Niko for a reward!

Continue along the ramparts to reach another small chest on the other tower near the station. This chest also holds a Red Rupee, and it's every bit as sparkly as the other.

Overworld Chest 10: Red Rupee

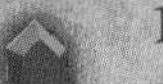

Red Rupee

You got a Red Rupee! It's worth 20 Rupees!

1002
Welcome back, Recruit!
How's your sword training
coming?
Menu

That's all the looting you can do from the ramparts for now. Time to put all those newfound Rupees to good use! Drop down and run to Hyrule Castle, heading for the first floor's northeast room. It's time to take Russell up on his generous sword-training offer!

For a mere 50 Rupees, Russell will be happy to let you whale away on his trio of troops. The boys fight back, of course, so you'll need to master both attack and defense. Land 60 hits or more in one session, and Russell will reward your hard work with an invaluable Heart Container!

You can always tell when one of the soldiers is about to strike—they begin spinning their spear in preparation for the blow. Since Link can suffer only three hits before the training session ends, avoiding these attacks is paramount. Don't overcommit to hitting the guards; strike once or twice, then dart out of harm's way. Slow and steady wins this challenge!

Heart Container 5

You got a Heart Container! You increased your life by one and refilled your hearts!

1 Explore the Snow Realm

2 Speak with Steem

3 Navigate the Blizzard

4 Clear the Snow Temple

Into the Darkness: Tower of Spirits 3

Link and Princess Zelda have now cleansed the evil from two sacred temples, and even more energy is flowing into the Tower of Spirits. Another chunk of the tower has locked into place, and the two have a good idea of what that means: another climb up the tower is in order!

A Link to the Present

Items Already Acquired

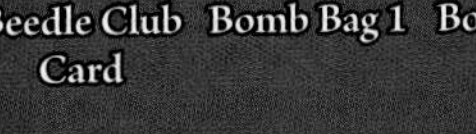

Beedle Club Card
Bomb Bag 1
Boomerang
Engineer Certificate
Forest Rail Map
Practical Cannon
Rabbitland Rabbits (10)
Recruit's Sword
Recruit's Uniform
Snow Rail Map
Song of Awakening
Song of Discovery
Song of Healing
Spirit Flute
Stamp Book (9 stamps)
The Whirlwind
Wooden Shield

Task 1: Report Back to Anjean

Tower of Spirits: Third Visit

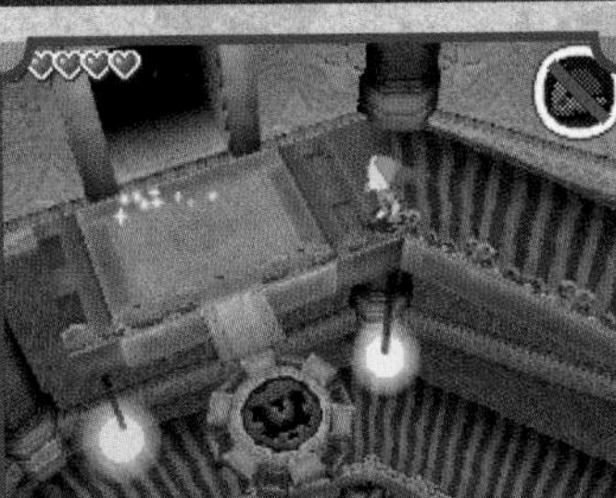

982
Once again, you must climb the tower and retrieve the next rail map.
Menu

Anjean awaits Princess Zelda and Link at the tower's entry hall, overjoyed that they've managed to restore even more energy to the tower. She bids them climb even higher now, braving the tower once more in search of a third rail map.

Dash all the way up the spiral staircase, entering the highest door you can reach to enter the tower's eighth floor.

Missing Links

Hold up, now! If you've bought bombs from Beedle, you can use them to score some very valuable loot from previous floors of the tower. Keep reading if you're up for a bit of treasure hunting, or skip this sidebar if you'd rather just carry on with the main adventure.

Tower of Spirits: First-Floor Secrets

Tower of Spirits, First Floor

Legend

Dungeon Chest 1: Treasure
Switch

Items to Obtain

Treasure x3

Enemies Encountered

Phantom

Dodge the first floor's Phantom and hurl the Boomerang at the floor's remote northwest switch to reveal a hidden chest on the northern safe zone. Open the chest for a very nice treasure you couldn't have scored before.

Dungeon Chest 1: Treasure

Treasure

You got a treasure! Check it out on the Collection screen!

Tower of Spirits: Second-Floor Secrets

Tower of Spirits, Second Floor

Legend

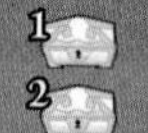
Dungeon Chest 1: Treasure

Dungeon Chest 2: Treasure

Dungeon Chest 3: Treasure
Bomb wall
Floor switch

Items to Obtain

Treasure x3

Enemies Encountered

Spinut

Phantom

Enter the Tower of Spirit's first floor, collect the three Tears of Light, and possess the Phantom. Go up to the second floor and visit its northeast corner; here, a wide pit kept Link from reaching a big treasure chest during your first trip through here. This time, position Zelda near the pit, then use the Whirlwind to blow her across.

1 Report Back to Anjean

2 Retrieve the Ocean Rail Map

3 Repair the Bridge

4 Journey to the Ocean Realm

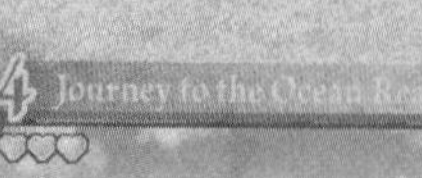

Once across, direct Zelda onto a floor switch, which extends a bridge that covers the pit. Switch to Link and have him open that big chest to score a super-rare treasure.

Dungeon Chest 1: Treasure

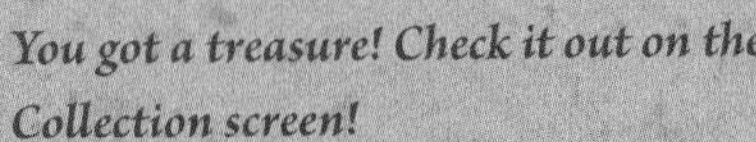

Treasure

You got a treasure! Check it out on the Collection screen!

Next, move Zelda west, having her drop from the nearby ledge. Leave her near the ledge so that Link can hop onto her back.

With Zelda carrying Link, steer the princess south to locate another big chest near the floor's center. Link must jump from Zelda's back to reach the elevated chest and claim the precious treasure inside.

Dungeon Chest 2: Treasure

Treasure

You got a treasure! Check it out on the Collection screen!

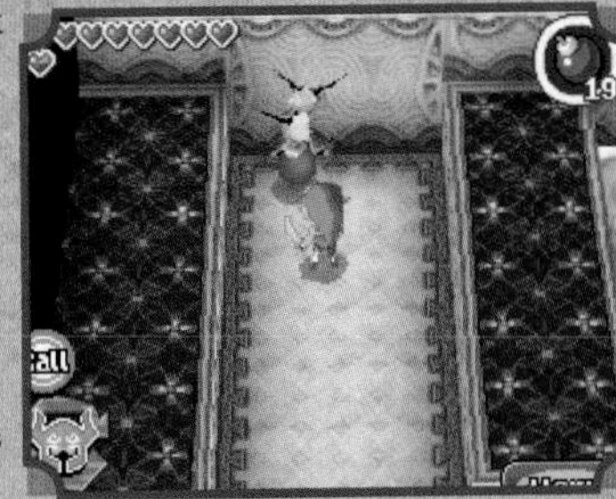

Last but not least, guide Link and Zelda over to the floor's northwest corner, ensuring the stationary Phantom doesn't see you. Drop a bomb by the cracked wall to blast an opening, then quickly dart inside before the alerted Phantom catches you. Zelda must be close, or Link won't be able to flee through the wall!

The small chamber beyond the wall contains another huge treasure chest. Open the chest for yet another super-rare treasure.

Dungeon Chest 3: Treasure

Treasure

You got a treasure! Check it out on the Collection screen!

Tower of Spirits: Fourth-, Fifth-, and Sixth-Floor Secrets

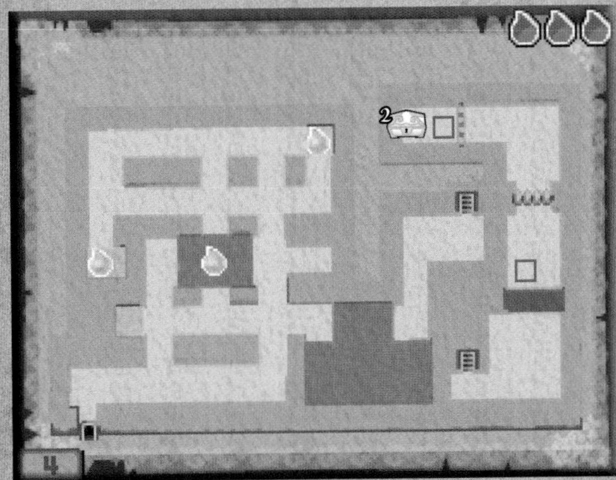

Tower of Spirits, Fourth Floor

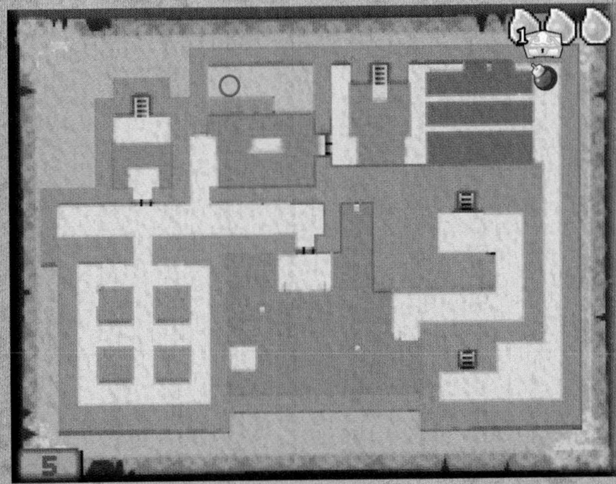

Tower of Spirits, Fifth Floor

Tower of Spirits, Sixth Floor

Legend

- Dungeon Chest 1: Treasure
- Dungeon Chest 2: Treasure
- Dungeon Chest 3: Treasure
- Dungeon Chest 4: Treasure
- Dungeon Chest 5: Treasure
- Dungeon Chest 6: Treasure
- Bomb wall
- Floor switch
- Switch

Items to Obtain

Treasure x6

Enemies Encountered

Fire Keese

Phantom

Geozard

To score even more loot, return to the tower's spiral staircase and enter the second door on your way up to the tower's fourth floor. Possess a Phantom and have Zelda carry Link across the lava, heading up to the fifth floor.

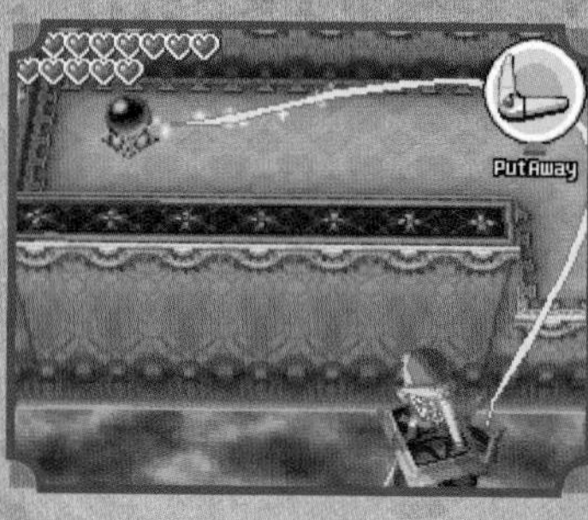

Cross the fifth floor's giant central lava pond, then visit the smaller lava pool to the north. Stand Zelda atop the central rise; with Link on her back, hurl the boomerang up around to the north, activating a switch you couldn't have triggered on your first trip through here. This opens the east door.

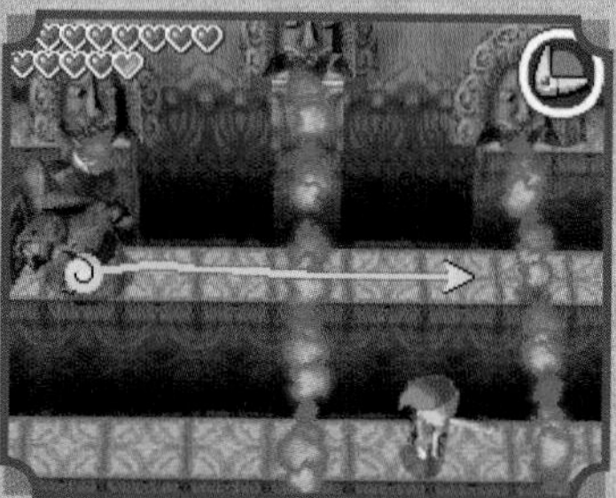

For now, ignore the stairs leading up, and cross the fire traps to the east. Have Zelda move along the central path, blocking the flames so that Link can sprint across the lower route. Don't worry about blocking the middle fire trap; its flames are too high to strike Link.

Bomb the cracked wall past the fire traps and head into the small chamber beyond to discover a big chest. Lift its lid to score a prized treasure worth mucho Rupees.

Dungeon Chest 1: Treasure

Treasure

You got a treasure! Check it out on the Collection screen!

Next, take the southeast stairs leading back down to the fourth floor. Use the old Whirlwind trick again to blow Zelda across the wide pit you encounter down here.

Once across the pit, move Zelda onto the nearby floor switch, which causes one of the two nearby torches to flare up. Toss the boomerang to spread the flame to the other torch, extending a bridge across the pit for Link.

Flames block the hall beyond the pit. Have Link pull out a bomb, then tap Zelda to make him hand it over. Don't worry; the bomb's fuse won't ignite.

Move Zelda past the flames and into contact with one of the bomb blocks plugging up the hall beyond. Zelda places the bomb, and a few seconds later, the bomb blocks are no longer an obstacle.

Now steer Zelda onto the floor switch beyond the bomb blocks. The switch shuts off the flames, allowing Link to join Zelda and open a large treasure chest for a shiny treasure.

Dungeon Chest 2: Treasure

Treasure

You got a treasure! Check it out on the Collection screen!

That takes care of this floor. Backtrack up to the fifth floor, cross the fire traps again with Zelda's help, then scale the fifth floor's northeast stairs to reach an unexplored area of the sixth floor.

Two Geozards assault you as you enter the sixth floor. Have Zelda distract each one so that Link can hack away at their unprotected backsides. Defeat both fiends to open the south door, which leads to a room full of treasure chests.

You've hit the mother lode! Crack open every chest in this small room to score a variety of treasures. After pocketing all your loot, make your way back to the temple's spiral staircase, and proceed up to the highest door to carry on with your quest.

Dungeon Chest 3: Treasure

Treasure

You got a treasure! Check it out on the Collection screen!

Dungeon Chest 4: Treasure

Treasure

You got a treasure! Check it out on the Collection screen!

Dungeon Chest 5: Treasure

Treasure

You got a treasure! Check it out on the Collection screen!

Dungeon Chest 6: Treasure

Treasure

You got a treasure! Check it out on the Collection screen!

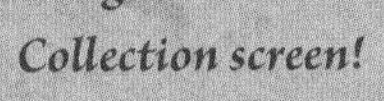

Task 2: Retrieve the Ocean Rail Map

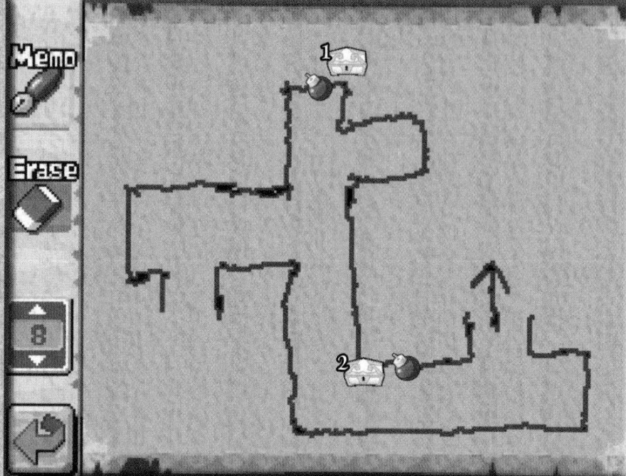

Tower of Spirits, Eighth Floor

Tower of Spirits, Ninth Floor

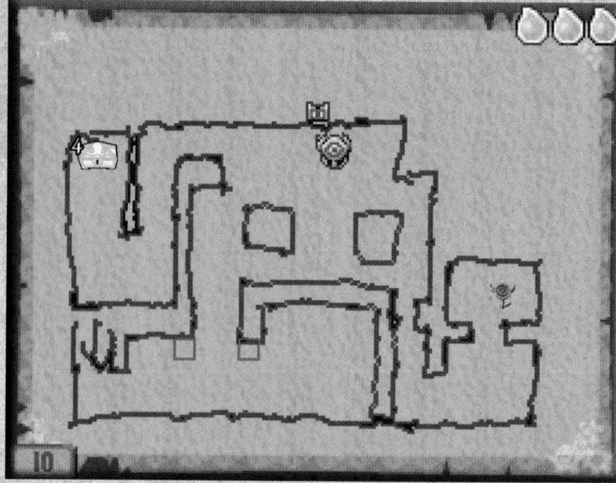

Tower of Spirits, Tenth Floor

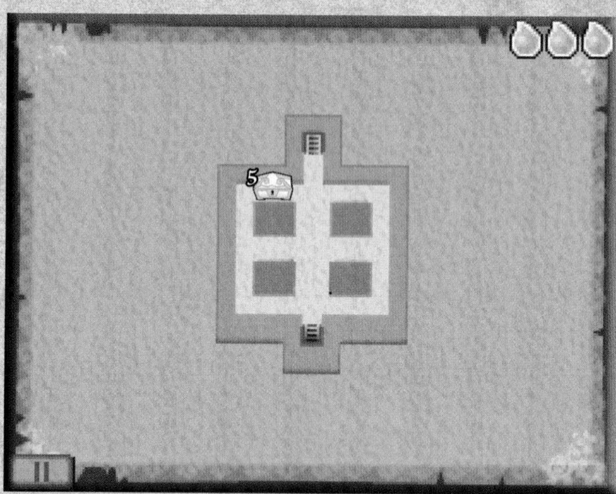

Tower of Spirits, Eleventh Floor

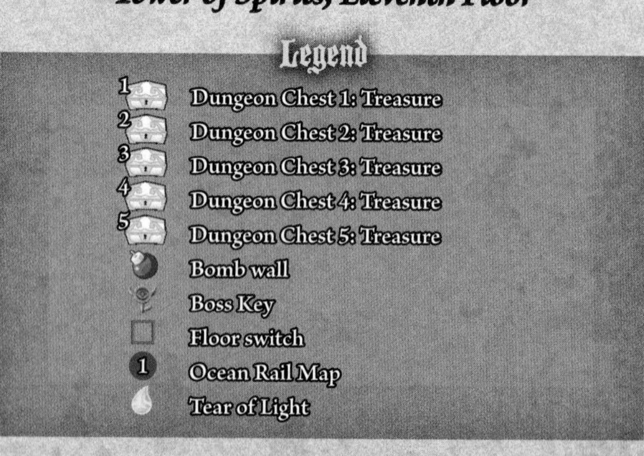

Tower of Spirits, Twelfth Floor

Tower of Spirits: Eighth Floor

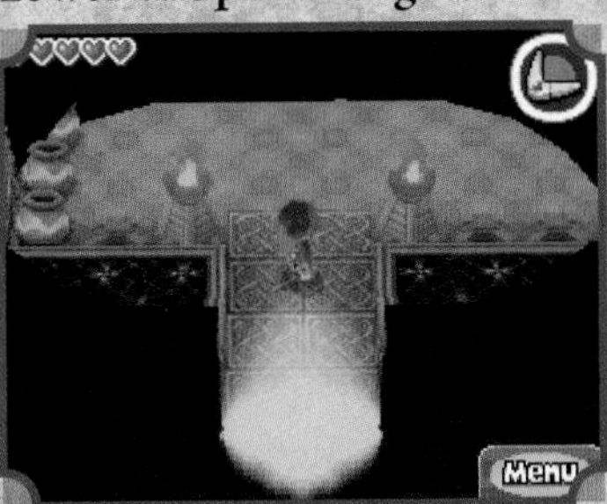

Hey, who turned out the lights? Apparently, all that energy you just restored to the tower wasn't enough to pay the electric bill—the whole eighth floor is pitch dark! Sparse torches are the only means of illumination, so you'll need to tread carefully up here.

Link can momentarily light his surroundings by smacking his sword on a wall, generating sparks. Just be certain no Phantoms are about, or they'll investigate the noise!

Though you have no map for darkened floors, Phantoms will still appear as icons on your map screen. There are no Phantoms on the eighth floor.

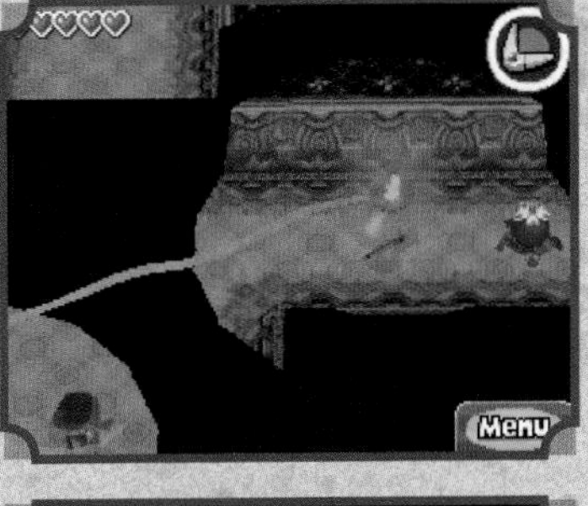

Blundering around in the dark's no fun, so use Link's boomerang to transfer fire between torches, helping to light up the place a bit. Lighting one of the floor's torches reveals a nearby bomb flower you couldn't see in the dark.

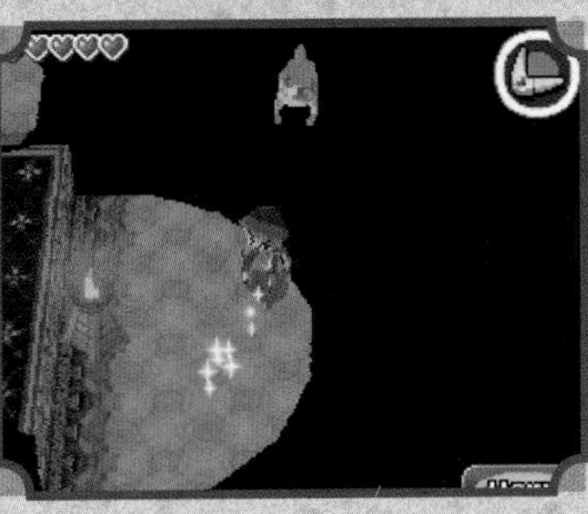

Run around lighting the floor's torches, but beware of roaming Nocturns! The darkness is home to these poor lost souls, and they'll attack Link ferociously if he wanders near. You're unable to lay these evil spirits to rest at present, so avoid the Nocturns and seek shelter in the light of torches. Nocturns don't like the light!

Nocturn

Hits to Defeat: 1 (once stunned)
Attack Type: Contact
Power: Strong
Damage: 1/2 heart
Threat Meter

Lighting every torch gives you a good sense of the eighth floor's layout and allows you to find the only set of stairs leading up to the ninth floor. However, don't climb the stairs just yet; pluck a bomb from the bomb flower and toss it at the northern wall, right between two torches.

Blammo! The bomb blasts a huge hole in the wall. Step through to reach a tiny chamber with only one object of interest: a giant treasure chest! Flip the chest's lid to claim a super-rare treasure.

Dungeon Chest 1: Treasure

Treasure

You got a treasure! Check it out on the Collection screen!

Back out of the treasure chamber and sidestep Nocturns as you make your way from torch to torch, heading for the stairs leading up to the ninth floor.

See that wall three steps to the right? It's kind of thin.

But wait, another wall can be bombed down here! Check the stone tablet in the south hall for a tip about a weak wall to the right. Bomb the wall to blast your way to another chest with a worthy treasure.

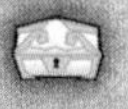

Dungeon Chest 2: Treasure

Treasure

You got a treasure! Check it out on the Collection screen!

Tower of Spirits: Ninth Floor

Look, Link!
That Phantom has a light!

The ninth floor is also pitch-black, but it's even more dangerous than the eighth. Your map shows two Phantoms patrolling the halls, each armed with a flaming sword! These are Torch Phantoms, and they're similar to regular Phantoms in every way—except that the fiery blades they carry provide them a bit of light in dark areas.

Torch Phantom

Hits to Defeat: 1 (with powered-up sword)
Attack Type: Contact
Power: Strong
Damage: 1 heart
Threat Meter

Be very careful not to alert the Torch Phantoms as you light the floor's torches. If you ever alert a Torch Phantom, run like crazy, backtracking down to the eighth floor or over to a safe zone you've discovered. There are indeed safe zones up here, but they aren't shown on your Map screen.

CAUTION

Nocturns roam about the ninth floor too—you must avoid them!

Fortunately, the Tears of Light you must gather *are* shown on your Map screen. They also appear on this guide's maps. Use the combination of the two to track down the two visible Tears of Light, which each hover above tiny safe zones.

Tear of Light

You got a Tear of Light! Gather three of them to power up your sword!

Tear of Light

You got a Tear of Light! Gather three of them to power up your sword!

A stone tablet stands near a southern torch; read it once the torch is lit. It hints that, if you blow out a "lonely torch" in a corner on this floor, you'll see a "faint light." Sounds like a clue!

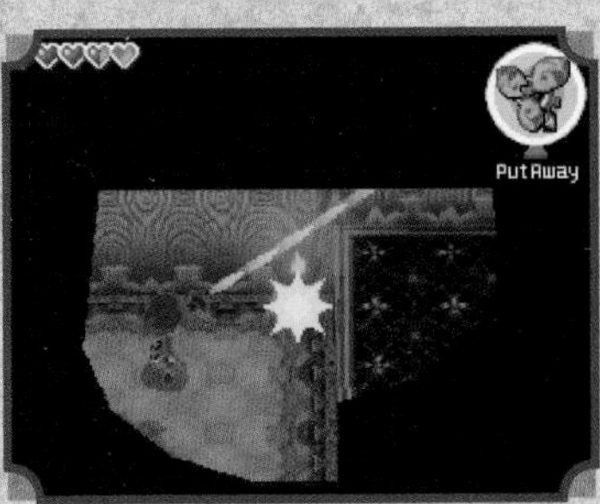

The torch you're after stands in the floor's northeast corner. Go there and use the Whirlwind to blow out the torch. This reveals a large crack in the nearby wall, which is only visible due to the faint light trickling in from the other side.

Pluck a bomb from the bomb flower to the west, near the large safe zone; use it to blast open the wall. Or simply use one of your own bombs if you've purchased the Bomb Bag from Beedle. Hurry through the opening you create after bombing the wall; those Torch Phantoms are sure to come running when they hear the blast!

You discover the third and final Tear of Light in the small chamber beyond the bomb wall. Now you can help Zelda possess one of those Torch Phantoms!

Tear of Light

You got a Tear of Light! Gather three of them to power up your sword!

Get to a safe zone and whack Link's sword into a wall to lure a Torch Phantom. When the guardian turns to leave, strike its back to stun it, then tap the Torch Phantom to make Zelda possess it.

As a Torch Phantom, Zelda now assists you by lighting up her surroundings. Lead her down to the narrow footbridge to the southwest, and have her light the way as you navigate the bridge. Be careful not to fall into the surrounding abyss—it's a long way down!

Just keep directing Zelda to lead the way until you discover a sealed door in the floor's southwest corner. Trace a line from Zelda to the unlit torch near the door to make her light it with her sword, triggering the door to open. You're all done here; sprint upstairs to the tenth floor.

Tower of Spirits: Tenth Floor

Great, *another* dark floor! At least you have Torch Phantom Zelda at your side. Begin exploring the area, targeting Nocturns with Zelda to make her dispatch them with her flaming steel.

Locate a floor switch near a sealed door, and leave Link standing on this floor switch. Steer Zelda eastward, continuing your probe into the darkness.

Another floor switch sits just to the east. Move Zelda onto it. With both floor switches depressed, the sealed door near Link opens.

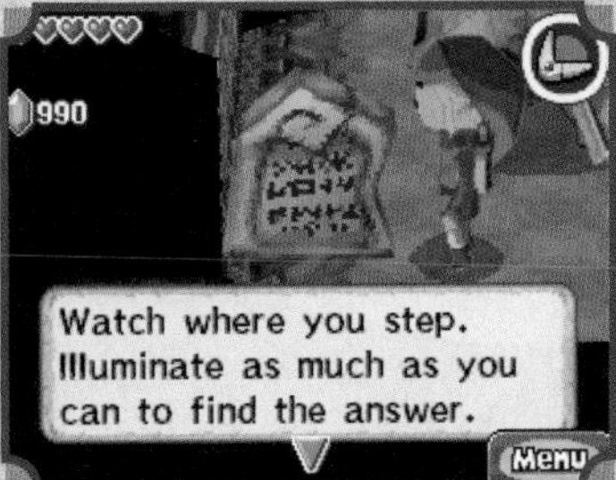

A stone tablet stands in the hall beyond the door, giving you important clues: watch where you step, and illuminate as much as you can to find "the answer." A bit cryptic, but you'll realize its meaning soon enough.

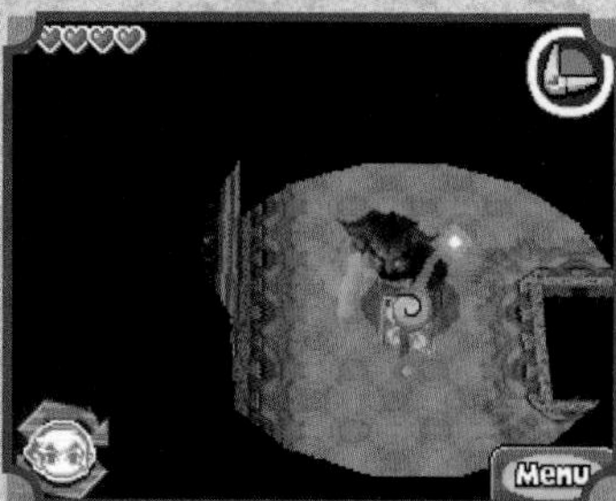

Continue exploring the floor, using Zelda to light things up and to defeat Nocturns. There are pits in the floor up here, so be careful when moving Link. You may find it easiest to simply leave him near a torch while Zelda looks around.

The Boss Key is visible on the Map screen, but a unique door bars access to its holding chamber. Tap the door, and you're asked to draw a symbol on it. The door opens only after you draw the proper symbol, which you've yet to discover.

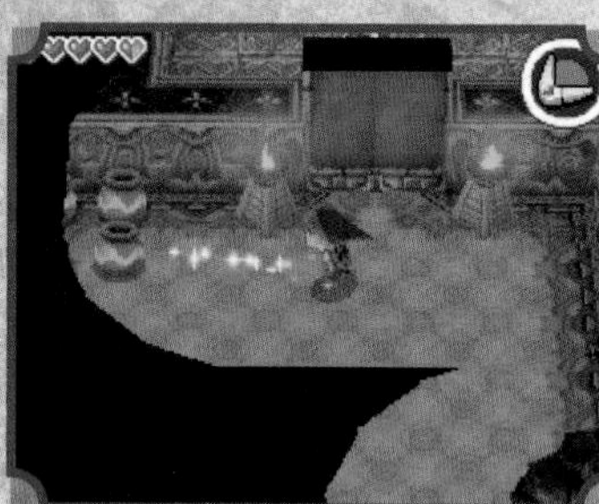

The symbol you must trace is shown by special floor tiles near the center of the floor. The tiles form a Z. But before you return to the door, explore the northwest corridor to find a large chest that contains a rare treasure.

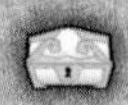

Dungeon Chest 3: Treasure

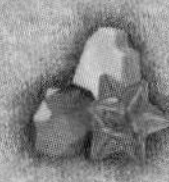

Treasure

You got a treasure! Check it out on the Collection screen!

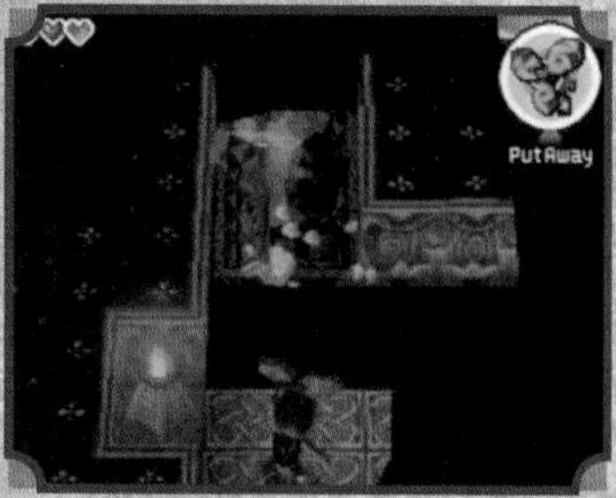

To score another treasure, use the Whirlwind to blow Zelda across a nearby pit, landing her on a secret path. Explore the path to discover a chest and floor switch. Stand Zelda on the floor switch to extend a bridge for Link, allowing him to cross over and open the chest.

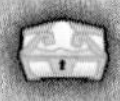

Dungeon Chest 4: Treasure

Treasure

You got a treasure! Check it out on the Collection screen!

With your loot all tucked away, return to the door near the Boss Key and tap it. Trace a Z across the face of the door to solve the riddle and gain access to the key.

The electricity might not be flowing up here, but the Boss Key sure is juiced up! Link can't touch the charged Boss Key; it'll zap him for damage. Have Zelda collect the key instead by tracing a line between her and the key.

The lights come on, and three Key Masters appear near the floor's center the moment Zelda takes up the Boss Key. Leave Zelda behind and send Link to secure the area.

When the Key Masters are no more, call to Zelda and then direct her to the Boss Key door. Draw a line between Zelda and the door to make her heave the Boss Key into its lock, opening the way to the eleventh floor. Ready yourself for a challenging showdown and then climb upstairs.

Tower of Spirits: Eleventh Floor

Entering the eleventh floor, Link and Zelda become sealed in a pit-filled chamber, forced to battle a dangerous Geozard Chief. Tackle this worthy foe as you would a Geozard, directing Zelda to attack the creature from the front, then quickly circling Link around to punish its rear.

Geozard Chief

Hits to Defeat: Multiple
Attack Type: Contact and Range
Power: Strong
Damage: 1/2 heart (both attacks)

Threat Meter

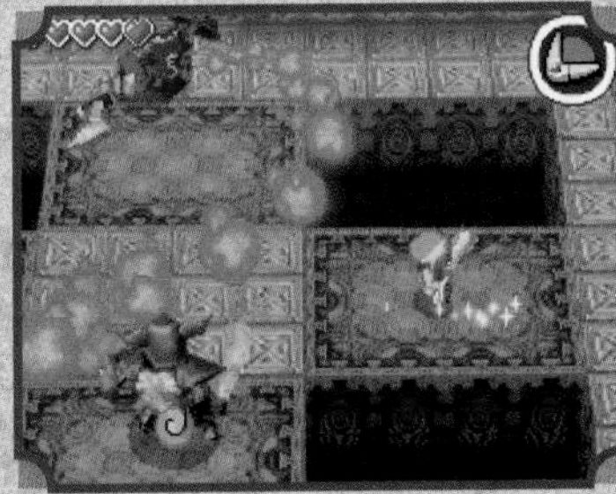

In addition to fierce sword attacks, Geozard Chiefs can also breathe long streams of fire that are tough to avoid. When you see the monster leap away, run to a far corner of the room—it's about to unleash its far-reaching fire breath!

Zelda can block the Zora's flames, protecting Link from being burned to a crisp.

Repeat the attack sequence until the Geozard Chief falls. A large chest appears in the room's corner, and its doors become unsealed. Open the chest to collect another super-rare treasure before scampering upstairs to claim an even more valuable prize.

Dungeon Chest 5: Treasure

Treasure

You got a treasure! Check it out on the Collection screen!

Tower of Spirits: Twelfth Floor

A familiar scene plays out as Link and the princess enter the twelfth floor. Zelda is cast out of her Phantom host, and the light in Link's sword dims. They've found the rail map chamber!

You got the Ocean rail map!

Climb up and grab the Ocean Rail Map, which restores a stretch of track running eastward from the Forest Realm, linking it to the Ocean Realm. Now you can explore a whole new realm!

Ocean Rail Map

You got the Ocean Rail Map! Some of the lost Spirit Tracks on it are reappearing!

Step into the blue light to return to Anjean at the tower's base. She informs you that the Ocean Realm's guardian is a Lokomo named Carben and goes on to say that you'll need to cross a bridge to reach the Ocean Realm. Without further ado, Link boards the Spirit Train and departs.

1001
The guardian of that realm is a Lokomo named Carben.
Menu

To the Bridge

Enemies Encountered

Snurgle	Dark Train	Bulblin	Bullbo

Chugging Southward

The Ocean Realm awaits, so what are you waiting for? Set a course south, heading straight for the bridge that Anjean pointed out. Avoid those Dark Trains and blast other enemies you encounter on your way. There's a good chance you'll come across new foes known as Bulblins. To eliminate these threats, blast their bomb arrows from the sky and punish their Bullbo mounts with multiple cannon shots.

NOTE

Attacking a Bulblin while it's preparing to launch a bomb arrow often cancels its attack. If you face two or more Bulblins at the same time, alternate your shots, pounding one and then the other to keep them both from firing.

Bulblin

Hits to Defeat: 3
Attack Type: Contact and Range
Power: Strong
Damage: 1 heart (both attacks)
Threat Meter

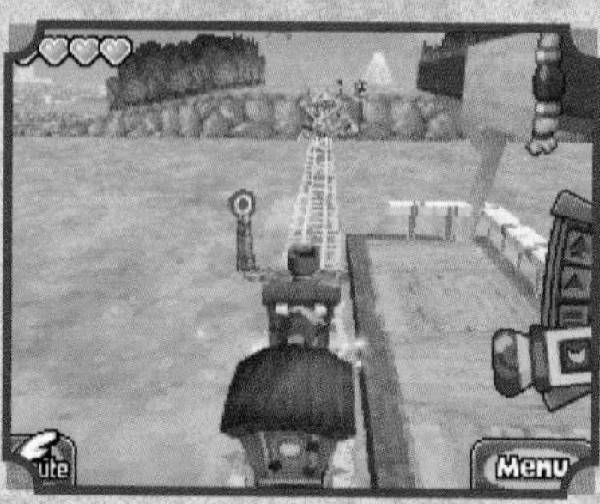

As you near the bridge, you can see that it's not in service. Someone has boarded up the tracks! You've come all this way, so you might as well pull up to the nearby station and see if anyone can lend a hand.

Trading Post

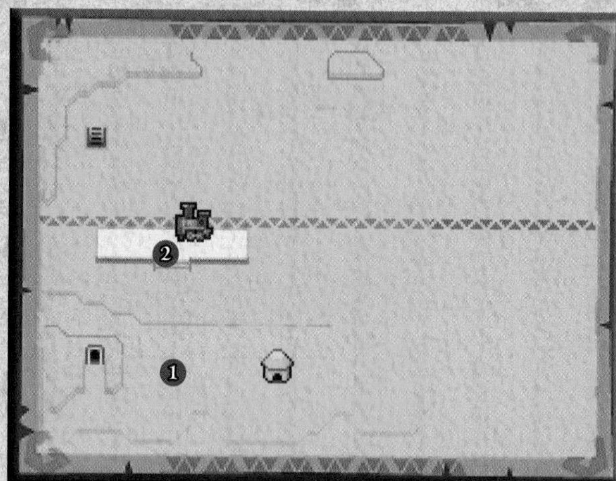

Trading Post

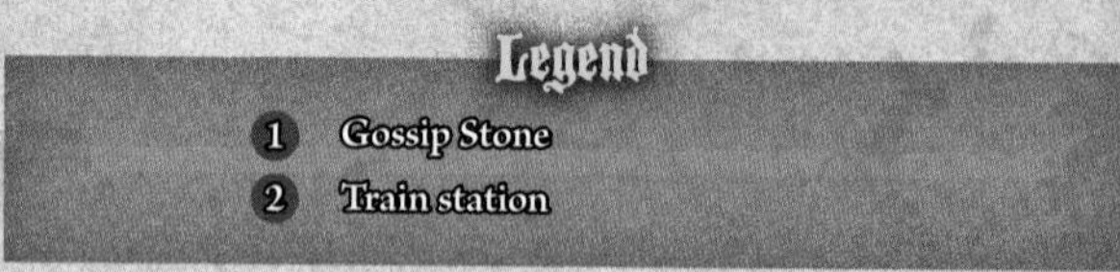

Legend

1. Gossip Stone
2. Train station

1 Report Back to Anjean

2 Retrieve the Ocean Rail Map

3 Repair the Bridge

4 Journey to the Ocean Realm

Third Time's the Charmer

I was going to call a bridge worker I know in the Snow Realm to fix the mess.

Enter this area's only building to meet a real charmer of a fellow named Linebeck III, president of Linebeck Trading. Treasures are this haughty fellow's trade, but with the bridge in such a sorry state, his business is less than booming. Fortunately, Linebeck knows of a bridge worker who lives in the Snow Realm. Maybe he can help!

For those who don't recognize Linebeck III, he's the direct descendant of Link's cowardly companion in *Phantom Hourglass*. Not much has changed through the generations!

There's little else to do here, so return to your train. Set a northward course for the Snow Realm.

Task 3: Repair the Bridge

To the Bridge Worker's Home

Enemies Encountered

Snurgle

Dark Train

Bulblin

Sir Frosty

Bullbo

Seeking Repairs

If you activated Warp Gate A during your first trek to the Snow Realm, use its sister gate, located north of Whittleton, to reach the Snow Realm with all speed. Check the overworld map for its exact location, and blow the whistle as you pass through the gate to warp. If you didn't activate the warp gate, plot a course to the Tower of Spirits instead, and tell Anjean you wish to travel to the Snow Realm once you get there.

If the Dark Trains are giving you grief on your way to the Tower of Spirits, take the scenic route and head north past Rabbitland Rescue. It doesn't really matter how you get to the Snow Realm, just so long as you arrive.

As you round the first bend on your way back north, look left to spy a forest rabbit hiding behind a boulder. Blast that boulder and bag the bunny to bring your total catches to eleven (you can get more prizes if you catch them all. There are 50 to find altogether.

The bridge worker's home is located just south of Wellspring Station. Explore the tracks there to find a station that doesn't appear on your map; then park and detrain.

Bridge Worker's Home

Bridge Worker's Home

Legend

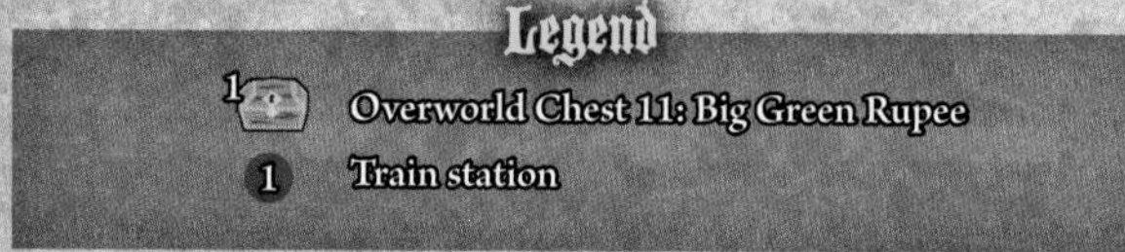

Items to Obtain

Enemies Encountered

Ready to Work

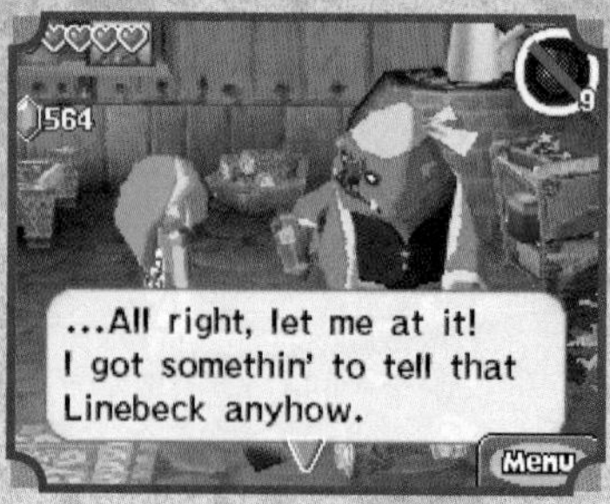

Dodge or dispatch the local hostiles on your way to the only house in this small area. The bridge worker is home, and he'll gladly go with you to help fix the bridge. He seems to have a history with Linebeck and is eager for a chance to speak with him anyway.

The bridge worker heads to the train station, where he says he'll wait for you. Before heading there, check near his house to discover a collection of boulders.

Throw the boulders aside, then play the Song of Discovery you learned from the Air Stone at Anouki Village to reveal a hidden treasure chest. The chest contains a Big Green Rupee. Score!

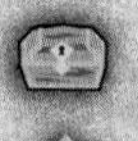

Overworld Chest 11: Big Green Rupee

Big Green Rupee

You got a Big Green Rupee! It's worth 100 Rupees!

Or if you don't follow the signs telling you to speed up or slow down...

Now make for the train station, but along the way, pause to speak with Ferrus, who's now standing near the platform. The well-meaning train enthusiast warns you that the bridge worker will get upset if you don't drive carefully, saying you must do the following:

1. Obey all signposts you pass.
2. Don't get hit by enemies.
3. Avoid slamming on the brakes (don't quickly throw the train into reverse).
4. Stop right at the station platform when you arrive.

The bridge worker is already on board your train, so simply approach the platform and speak with Zelda to begin the journey back to the Trading Post.

Back to the Bridge

All Aboard

From the bridge worker's home, plot a course to the Tower of Spirits, which you may pass through to quickly reach the Forest Realm. You pass by a whistle sign on the way; toot your whistle as you approach the sign to impress your burly passenger.

NOTE

Your passenger's mood is indicated by a special icon that appears on your train. Passengers always begin each trip happy and excited for the journey at hand; strive to keep them that way by following Ferrus's sound advice.

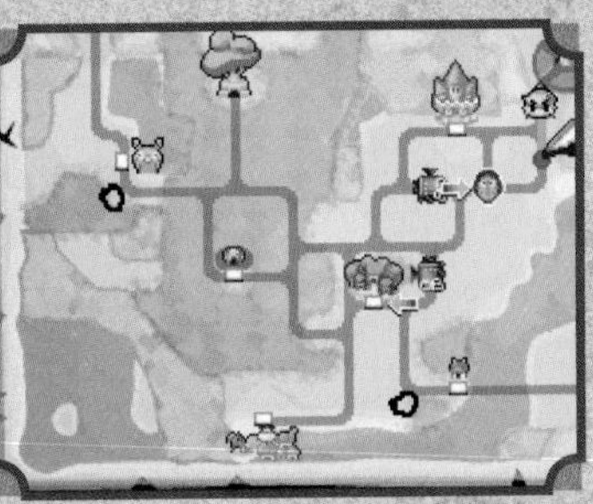

As you exit the Tower of Spirits, note the Dark Trains to the south and plot a course that doesn't take you near them. It's better to go a little out of your way than to risk a confrontation with those menacing locomotives.

Don't hesitate to slow down and reverse if a Dark Train is headed your way. You won't upset your passenger as long as you slow down a bit before reversing. Of course, if worse comes to worst, it's always better to slam on the brakes and jostle your passenger than to hit an oncoming train!

You'll pass more whistle signs on your way to the bridge, along with slow signs (orange) and speed-up signs (blue). Put your train into first gear when approaching a slow sign, and kick it up to second gear when nearing a speed-up sign. Remain in gear until the bridge worker expresses his joy at your skill. You must slow down when passing the orange signs, but you don't have to speed up at the blue signs—they're just letting you know it's OK to go faster!

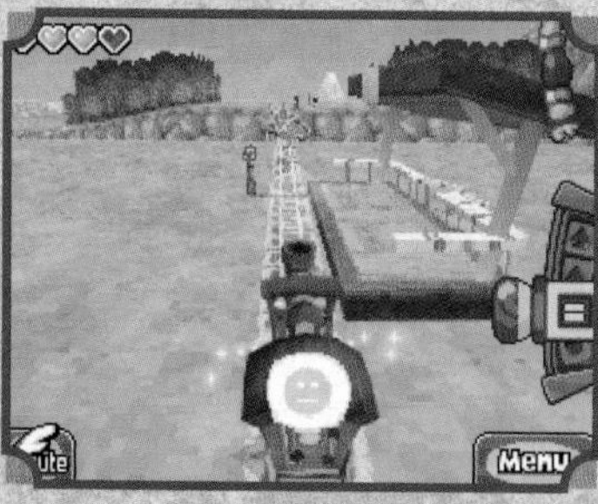

Reaching the platform with an elated bridge worker isn't easy, but don't worry if he's a little upset; it's your first time driving under these strenuous conditions! You're doing fine as long as he hasn't demanded to be let off. Just slide into first gear as you approach the Trading Post station, then put it in park as you draw even closer, doing your best to come to a stop right beside the platform. If need be, switch to reverse and then quickly put it back into park to stop a little faster and avoid drifting past the stop bar.

Trading Post Revisited

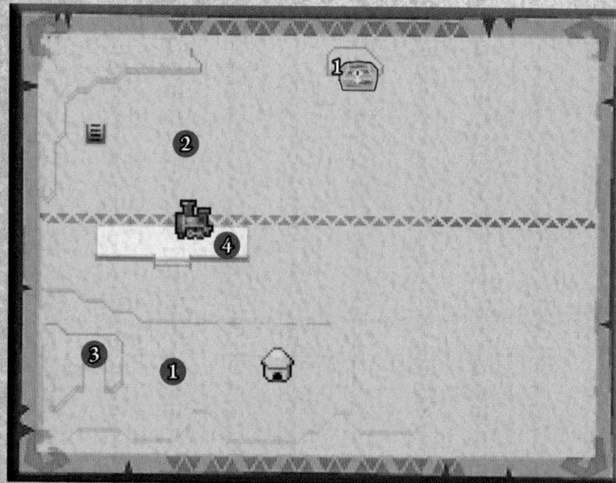

Trading Post

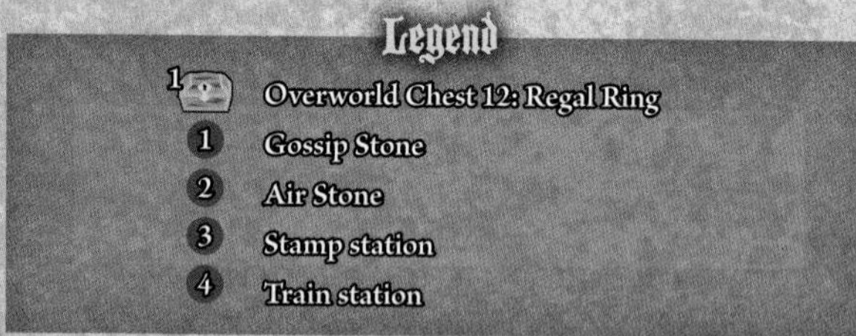

Legend

1 (chest)	Overworld Chest 12: Regal Ring
1	Gossip Stone
2	Air Stone
3	Stamp station
4	Train station

Hard Bargain

It'll take a while, so go kill some time and come back later.

The bridge worker comments on your driving skills, then walks off to inspect the bridge. Follow him to get his professional analysis: the bridge is certainly damaged but is not beyond repair. What a relief!

Five...THOUSAND?! Surely you must be joking!

Linebeck arrives, happy to hear the bridge can be fixed. However, his tone changes when the bridge worker mentions his fee. Between the bridge and some other repairs the bridge worker made to Linebeck's house in the past, he demands 5,000 Rupees in payment for his services.

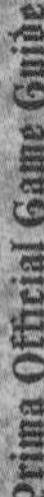

He's the one who wanted the bridge fixed in the first place, after all.

Linebeck balks at the figure, then quickly passes the buck to Link, saying he'll foot the bill. Yeah, right!

The bridge worker doesn't really care who pays him and quickly sets about his task. The repairs will take time to complete; before returning to his shop, Linebeck suggests Link use that time to figure out a means of payment.

Family Fortune

580
10
I've heard whispers about some high-value loot that was hidden here long ago.
Menu

You can't let that crafty Linebeck get away with this! Go to his shop and give him a piece of your mind. But before you can really lay into him, Linebeck says he's got a plan: if you're up for a little treasure hunting, he believes he knows where you can find a special treasure worth well over 5,000 Rupees—and it's right nearby!

Linebeck says his grandfather, Linebeck I, hid a precious treasure called a Regal Ring somewhere in the area. He left his grandson a letter with hints on how to find it, but Linebeck III could never solve the letter's riddles. He hands Link the letter, hoping the young lad will have better luck.

Letter

You got a letter from Linebeck! Go to the Collection screen to read it!

580
10
The ring seems to be near Gramps's grave. You can get there through here.
Menu

Linebeck next points to a nearby cave, saying that's where Link should begin his search for the Regal Ring. Read the letter he gave you for the following cryptic clues on the ring's whereabouts:

5. To enter the hiding spot, sound the light and follow its beam.
6. Once inside, go four steps north and six steps west from where the lights cross.

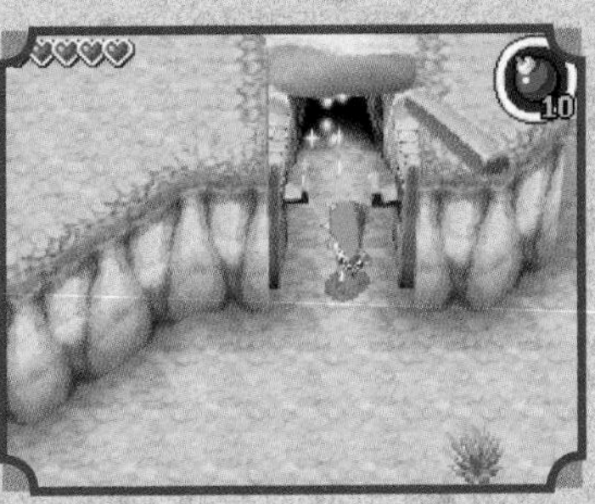

There's no point arguing with Linebeck—no one's won an argument with a Linebeck in ages! Leave the shop and run west to locate the cave Linebeck pointed to. Head inside to begin your search for the Regal Ring.

Trading Post Cavern

There's no map for this little cavern, but it's small enough that you won't get lost. Take heed of the sign as you enter: It warns of shield-gobbling monsters ahead and says that new shields can be procured at Linebeck Trading. Will Linebeck do anything to make a buck?

Ready your bombs if you've bought them from Beedle; if you haven't, prepare your boomerang. The monsters Linebeck's sign warned you of await just ahead: Like Likes! These wormlike foes will suck Link up if he gets too close, so toss bombs at them from afar instead. If bombs aren't an option, use the boomerang to stun the Like Likes before moving close to attack with Link's sword.

Being swallowed by a Like Like can cost you your shield. These things will eat *anything*! Keep away from alert Like Likes and quickly rub your stylus across the screen if you're gobbled; this will break you free before the creature consumes your shield.

Like Like

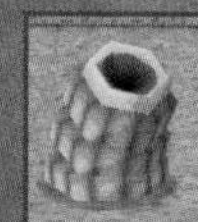

Hits to Defeat: Multiple
Attack Type: Range (inhale)
Power: Strong
Damage: 1/4 heart (digest)

Threat Meter

Beware when breaking the pots near the north stairs: The one that's jiggling actually contains another Like Like! Don't break this pot or you risk being swallowed up.

Before scampering upstairs, hop across the small rocks to the left to locate a stamp station. Stand on the first rock and toss a bomb over to the second to blast away an obstructive bomb block; then hop over and use the stamp station to record your tenth stamp.

NOTE

You've found ten stamps! When you've finished here, you should pay Niko a visit to receive a cool reward. Don't worry; we'll remind you!

Light Marks the Spot

The stairs lead back up to the surface, only now you're standing on the opposite side of the tracks, able to explore the Trading Post's northern area. Beware the Crows in the treetops, and pay your respects to Captain Linebeck I, whose grave stands nearby.

Locate a nearby Air Stone and imitate its tune on the Spirit Flute to learn the Song of Light. This causes the Air Stone to blast off, revealing a light crystal that shines a laser beam off to the northeast.

Song of Light

You got the Song of Light! Play it to activate beacons.

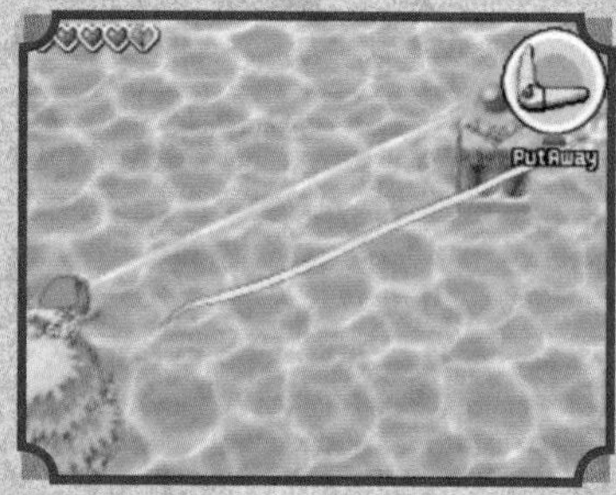

Follow the laser beam to discover that it shines directly at a remote switch. Link can't reach the tree due to surrounding water, but his boomerang can! Target the switch and give it a whack with the boomerang to extend a bridge leading to the northeast isle.

Beware the Bees in the trees around here! Flee to the cavern or leap into the water if you happen to anger them, and they'll buzz off.

Snatch a bomb from the isle's bomb flowers, and place it by the large crack in the nearby wall. After the blast, head through the hole that remains to move one step closer to obtaining the Regal Ring.

Tricky Chests

The cavern you enter is filled with Octoroks, so take a moment to clear out the place. Whatever you do, don't open the chest to the north: It's a fake and contains only a shield-swallowing Like Like!

Two dark crystals stand in the cavern. You know what to do! Play the Song of Light near each to activate them, causing laser beams to shoot out.

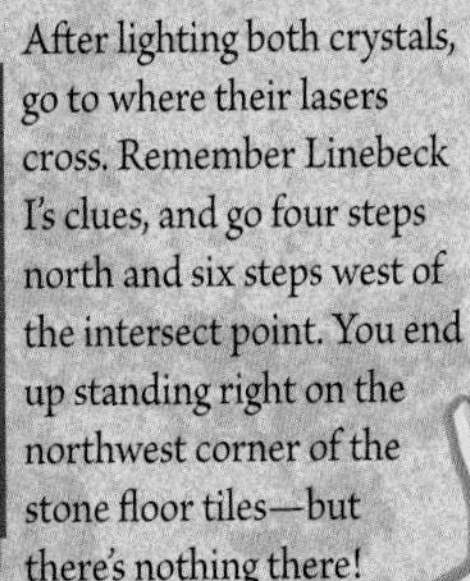

After lighting both crystals, go to where their lasers cross. Remember Linebeck I's clues, and go four steps north and six steps west of the intersect point. You end up standing right on the northwest corner of the stone floor tiles—but there's nothing there!

Not everything is what it seems. You're in the right spot, so play the Song of Discovery you learned from the Air Stone back at Anouki Village. A treasure chest appears—the very chest you've been searching for! Open it to at last obtain the Regal Ring.

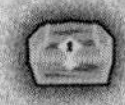

Overworld Chest 12: Regal Ring

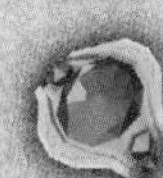

Regal Ring

You got a Regal Ring! It's been passed down by generations of nobility.

Paid in Full

You bet it is! It's gotta be
worth a cool 8,000

You've got what you came here for, so backtrack to Linebeck's shop and tell him of your success. The old treasure hound can't contain his glee, but his celebration is short-lived.

So this little doodad's
worth 8,000 Rupees?
Coulda fooled me.

Having finished his job, the bridge worker appears and swipes the Regal Ring from Linebeck's paws. Happy to have received his payment, the bridge worker departs, finding his own way home.

Linebeck is heartbroken but is also quite happy to have the bridge back in working order. He's grateful to Link and invites the lad to bring any treasure he finds to Linebeck's Trading, where he can trade them in for Rupees and custom train parts. Sounds like you've just made a valuable connection!

Ooh! Tell you what--from here on out, bring any treasure you find to me!

Task 4: Journey to the Ocean Realm

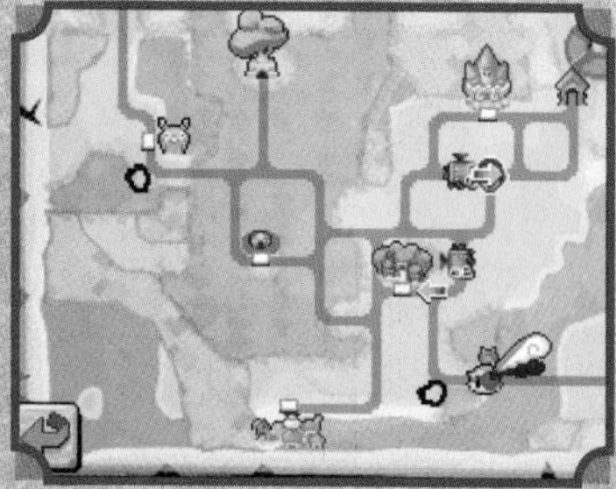

Great work, you're now able to cross the bridge and visit the Ocean Realm! Set an eastward course if you're in a rush, or check out the Missing Links sidebar if you'd prefer to score some optional goodies.

Missing Links

Now that Linebeck's shop is open for business, you can finally trade in all those flashy treasures you've been hoarding. You don't have to trade any right now, of course, but if you're willing to part with a few treasures, you can earn enough scratch to buy that Heart Container you saw back at the Snow Sanctuary's shop!

Linebeck will buy treasures off you at fair market value, paying 50 Rupees for common treasures, 150 Rupees for rare treasures, and 500 Rupees for those special ultrarares. Some treasures he will pay 2,500 for! He'll also sell you custom train parts in exchange for treasures; just ask him what treasures you need to make each part, or see "The Legendary Checklist" at the back of this guide for a full listing.

Aboda Village

Aboda Village

Legend

1. Shield of Antiquity
2. Stamp station
3. Train station

Items to Obtain

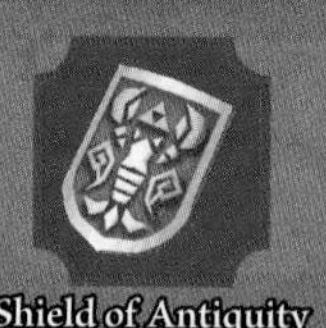
Shield of Antiquity

1730
Great to see you're back, Link!
Menu

Regardless of whether you choose to trade with Linebeck, board your train and set a course for Aboda Village. The village isn't far, and Niko is sure to be thrilled when he hears you've already found ten stamps for his Stamp Book.

1 Report Back to Anjean

2 Retrieve the Ocean Rail Map

3 Repair the Bridge

4 Journey to the Ocean Realm

You got the Shield of Antiquity!

Visit Link and Niko's house to speak with Niko, who perks up when he hears you've found ten stamps. As a reward for your hard work, he hands over a unique item: the Shield of Antiquity! This shield functions the same as the Wooden Shield but has a look all its own and it cannot be eaten by Like Likes. However, if you prefer the Wooden Shield, know that Niko will gladly swap your shields at any time. Just ask!

Shield of Antiquity

You got the Shield of Antiquity! Niko received this precious shield from an old, dear friend.

Snow Sanctuary

Snow Sanctuary Legend

♡	Heart Container 6
1	Stamp Station
2	Train Station

Enemies Encountered

Ice ChuChu

White Wolfos

Sell treasures to Linebeck until your wallet bursts with over 2,000 Rupees; then travel to the Snow Sanctuary. Pop into the Anouki shop to at last purchase that Heart Container that tempted you so long ago. You've got so many hearts now, they've started appearing on a second row!

2585
Quit
Buy

Tip

Consider buying a couple of Purple Potions from the Anouki shop as well. Now that you've cultivated a respectable Life meter, Purple Potions will come in very handy, automatically saving Link from the brink of defeat and restoring eight of his hearts should his Heart meter become empty. Better yet, take the time to track down Beedle, who also sells Purple Potions, and you'll earn a few membership points from the purchase!

Heart Container 6

You got a Heart Container! You increased your life by one and refilled your hearts!

Forest Rabbit 5

You've accomplished everything you can do in the Forest and Snow Realms for now, so set a course across the bridge and into the Ocean Realm. Keep an eye to your left as you cross the bridge, and try to nab the forest rabbit hiding on the other side. This should be your twelfth bunny!

Menu

Surf and Steam: The Ocean Realm

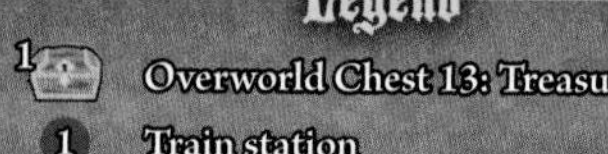

Papuchia Village

Legend

1 (chest)	Overworld Chest 13: Treasure
1	Train station

It took some doing, but the princess and her stalwart guardian have at last arrived at the Ocean Realm. Now they just need to track down the local Lokomo, Carben. The sooner the two can restore the Ocean Temple's flow of energy to the Tower of Spirits, the better!

A Link to the Present

Items Already Acquired

Beedle Club Card

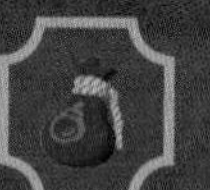
Bomb Bag 1

Boomerang

Engineer Certificate

Forest Rail Map

Practical Cannon

Rabbitland Rabbits (12)

Recruit's Sword

Recruit's Uniform

Shield of Antiquity

Snow Rail Map

Song of Awakening

Song of Discovery

Song of Healing

Song of Light

Spirit Flute

Stamp Book (10 stamps)

The Whirlwind

Wooden Shield

1 Explore Papuchia Village

2 Find Carben and Complete the [illegible]

3 Open the Way to the Temple

4 Clear the Ocean Temple

Items to Obtain

Treasure

Task 1: Explore Papuchia Village

Just Visiting

The Spirit Tracks certainly don't stretch very far into the Ocean Realm—you'll have to find Carben if you want to get very far. Detrain at the first station you encounter and see if Carben's around.

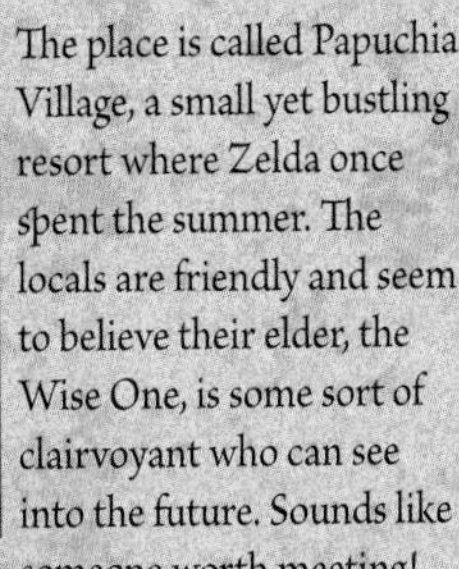

The place is called Papuchia Village, a small yet bustling resort where Zelda once spent the summer. The locals are friendly and seem to believe their elder, the Wise One, is some sort of clairvoyant who can see into the future. Sounds like someone worth meeting!

Other villagers speak of pirates who often show up to harass the populace. Apparently, they've kidnapped all of the men, taking them away to their hideout. Perhaps you can lend these poor women some assistance and find a way to bring their husbands home.

The Wise One

Enter the central hut to speak with the Wise One, an old mystic. She'll read your fortune for free; speak into the microphone and answer her questions.

Though interesting, the Wise One's tellings are somewhat vague and unhelpful. Perhaps she'd make more sense if you knew what to ask.

Leave the Wise One's hut and make your way to the northern isle, where you find a small chest just sitting in the open. Crack it open to add another treasure to your collection.

Overworld Chest 13: Treasure

Treasure

You got a treasure! Check it out on the Collection screen!

There's little else to do at Papuchia Village for now; Carben is not here. Visit the southwest shop if you like, and when you're ready to leave, board your train and set off to explore what little track there is left in the Ocean Realm.

Task 2: Find Carben and Complete the Duet

To the Ocean Sanctuary

Barrels of Fun

Your trip east takes you across the briny blue. Blast the drifting barrels to score Rupees, and just for fun, sound your whistle to thrill the exotic dolphins that swim by.

There's one final station within your reach, right near the end of the available track. Pull up to the station to continue your search for the realm's Lokomo guardian.

Ocean Sanctuary

Ocean Sanctuary

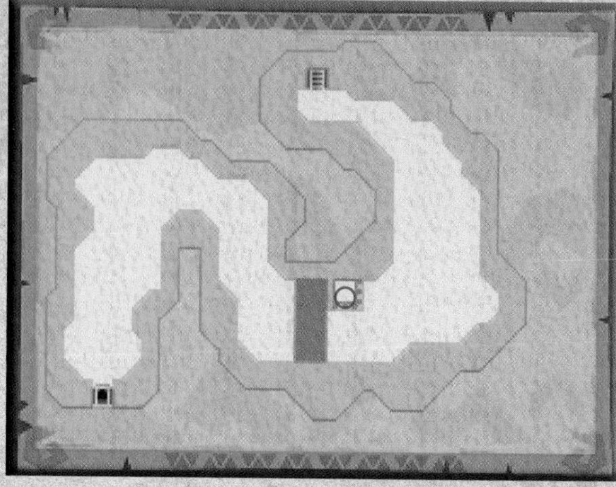

Ocean Sanctuary Cavern

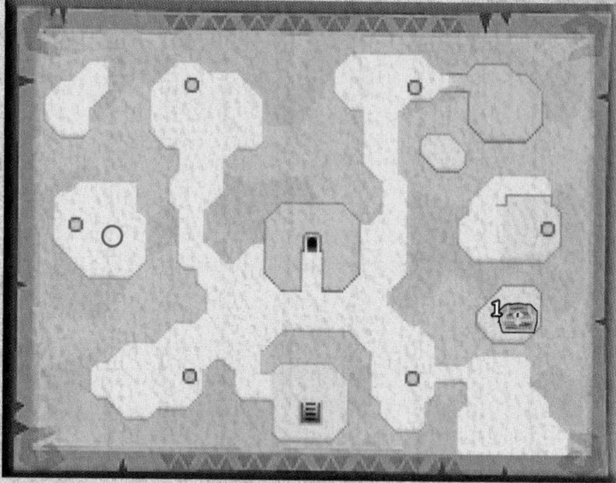

Ocean Sanctuary North

Legend

1 Overworld Chest 14: Treasure

Floor switch

Switch

Enemies Encountered

Lobarrier · Octorok

Questing for Carben

Skip off the station platform and head for the northeast cave. A new enemy confronts you on your way: a Lobarrier! Hiding behind their one massive claw, these guys act like impenetrable roadblocks. Keep your distance and toss your boomerang around Lobarriers, whacking them from behind to knock them silly; then get behind them and finish them off with swipes of Link's sword.

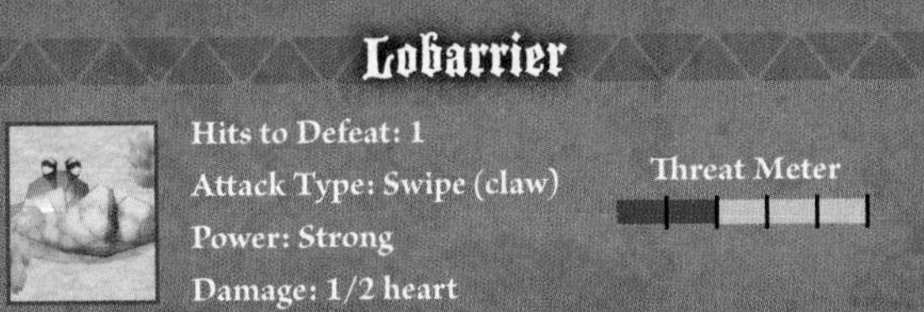

Lobarrier

Hits to Defeat: 1

Attack Type: Swipe (claw)

Power: Strong

Damage: 1/2 heart

Threat Meter

Dispatch more Lobarriers on your way through the cave, using the boomerang each time to help you stun and defeat them.

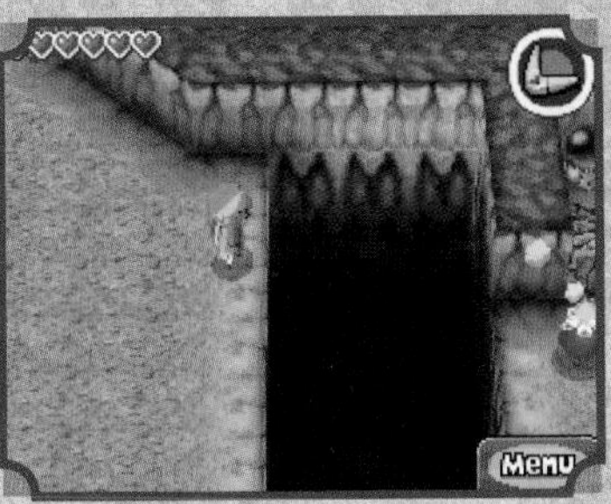

When you come to a wide pit, note the switch that's surrounded by bomb blocks on the pit's other side. Pluck a bomb from one of the two bomb flowers, and toss it carefully, aiming to land it close to the nearest bomb block.

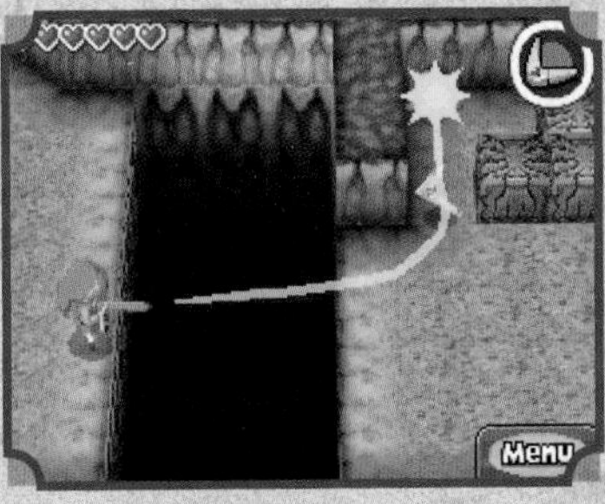

Keep tossing bombs until you destroy one of the bomb blocks; then guide your boomerang through the opening and trigger the switch. This extends a bridge across the chasm, allowing you to proceed.

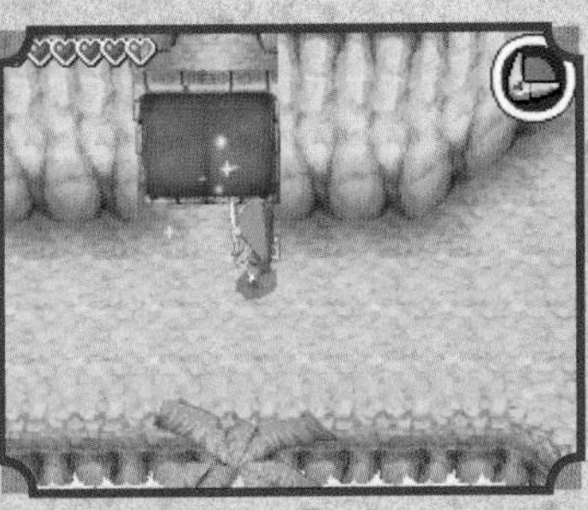

Defeat another Lobarrier on your way to the far stairs, which lead back up to the surface. You're now standing at the Ocean Sanctuary's northern region. Inspect the unusual door at the area's center. You must trace a special symbol to open the door. An inscription on the door hints that the answer lies within the gazes of the surrounding statues.

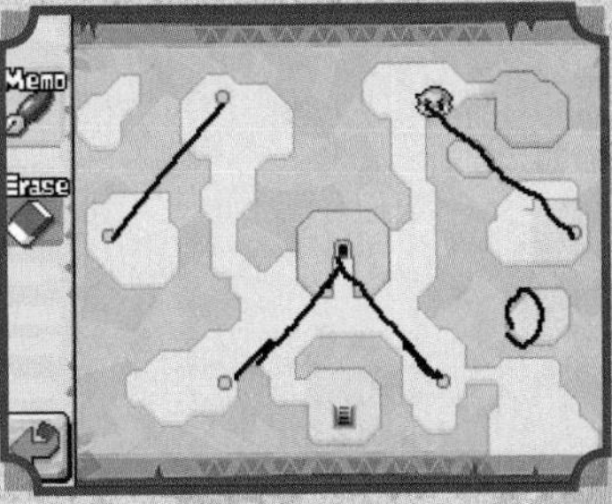

Run around and explore the area, looking for stone statues. They appear as little dots on your map. Whenever you find a statue, draw a line on your map outward from the statue's location, following the direction of its "gaze." Keep in mind that you're trying to discover some sort of symbol that you need to trace on the central door.

While searching for the statues, snatch a Cucco from the northeast cliff and leap south, gliding over to a nearby isle.

A little chest sits on the second isle. Open it to score another worthy treasure.

After you land on the isle, step on a floor switch to extend a bridge back to the mainland.

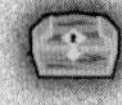

Overworld Chest 14: Treasure

Treasure

You got a treasure! Check it out on the Collection screen!

Mark the gaze of the isle's next statue, then grab the Cucco you used to get here and leap over to the next isle to the south.

To the west, a gang of angry Octoroks repeatedly spit stones westward, making it dangerous to advance. Hurl your boomerang to stun these fiends, and hit the switch near the Octoroks to extend a bridge. Cross over the bridge and finish them off.

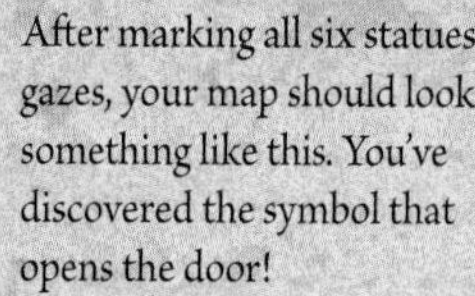

After marking all six statues' gazes, your map should look something like this. You've discovered the symbol that opens the door!

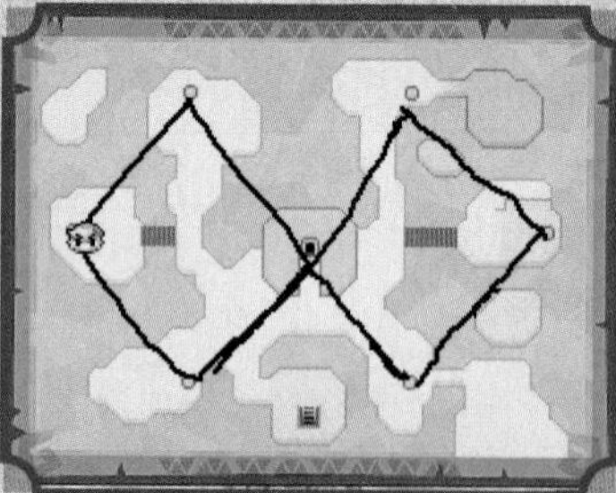

Return to the door and trace the symbol the statues showed you. The door opens, granting you passage to Carben's abode.

1 Explore Papuchia Village

2 Find Carben and Complete...

3 Open the Way to the Temple

4 Clear the Ocean Temple

Nobody's Home

You've found Carben's sanctuary all right, but there's no Lokomo in sight. Fortunately, Carben has left a message that he's at Papuchia Village, visiting his "sky friends." No way!

After inspecting Carben's sign, leave the sanctuary and take a shortcut back to your train—just follow the southeast trail to a floor switch. Step on the switch to extend a bridge that lets you skip the tunnel and return to the station a little quicker. Board your train and make the short trip back to Papuchia Village.

Papuchia Village

Papuchia Village

Legend

- 1 (chest) Overworld Chest 13: Treasure
- 1 Air Stone (hidden)
- 2 Train station

Items to Obtain

The Sky Friends' Song

After arriving at Papuchia Village, run south from the train platform to at last find Carben. He's way up in the sky, flying around on a giant bird! No wonder you never saw him before.

Carben doesn't seem to hear you, but you've just got to speak with him. Zelda wonders if maybe the Wise One would know what to do. You might as well ask and find out!

Visit the Wise One's hut, and have her read your fortune again. This time, her cryptic message is much more helpful: There's a hidden Air Stone near a lonely tree below the place where the "sky dwellers" gather. She must be talking about those giant birds!

Bid the Wise One farewell and return to the place where you found Carben. Sure enough, a palm tree stands beneath them, all by its lonesome. Play the Song of Discovery near the tree to reveal a hidden Air Stone!

Reproduce the Air Stone's melody as you've done before to learn a new tune: the Song of Birds! The statue blasts off, interrupting Carben's trancelike flight and bringing the Lokomo back down to earth.

Song of Birds

You got the Song of Birds! Play it to call a bird over!

Carben isn't thrilled to have his "me" time brought to an end, but he realizes the importance of the interruption. He motors off to the train, asking Link to bring him back to his sanctuary so they may conduct the ritual. What are you waiting for? Head for the train and set a course for the Ocean Sanctuary, posthaste!

Don't bother playing the Song of Birds to attract the "sky dwellers" above. You need to find another special item before you can really interact with them.

Back to the Sanctuary

Enemies Encountered

Miniblin

Big Blin

Waylaid at Sea

The trip back to the Ocean Sanctuary is more dangerous than you might expect. As you cross the sea on your way to the Sanctuary, a fearsome pirate ship shores up, its crew of scurvy sailors intent on boarding your train!

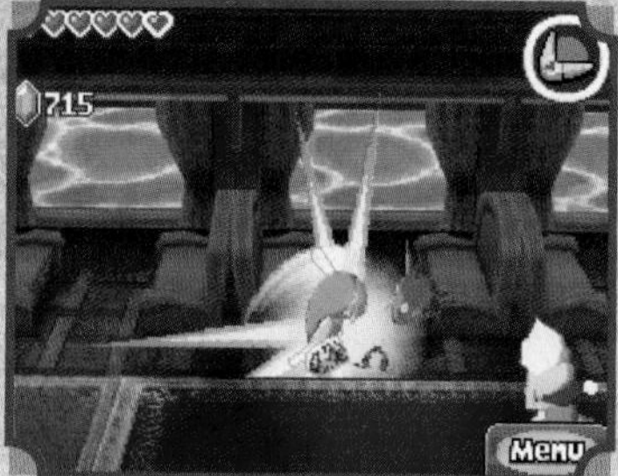

Carben is all alone in the passenger car, so Link must stop the train, go back to Carben's car, and protect the vulnerable Lokomo. Quickly dispatch each Miniblin that leaps into the car, ensuring no harm comes to your ward.

The Miniblins just keep on coming, soon pouring into the train almost faster than you can defeat them. Use the spin attack to wipe out several Miniblins at once whenever they begin to surround Carben.

Miniblin

Hits to Defeat: 1
Attack Type: Swipe (pitchfork)
Power: Strong
Damage: 1/2 heart

Threat Meter

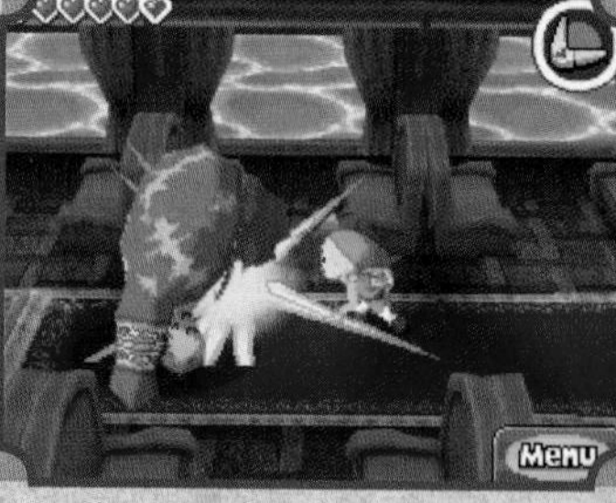

Eventually, the pirates bring in the big guns, sending a giant Big Blin to finish the job that the Miniblins started. This guy's a tough customer, able to throttle Link with his massive club. However, his attacks are slow to wind up, so dart in and rough him up, fleeing before the Big Blin takes his swing.

Big Blin

Hits to Defeat: Multiple
Attack Type: Swipe (club)
Power: Strong
Damage: 1/2 heart

Threat Meter

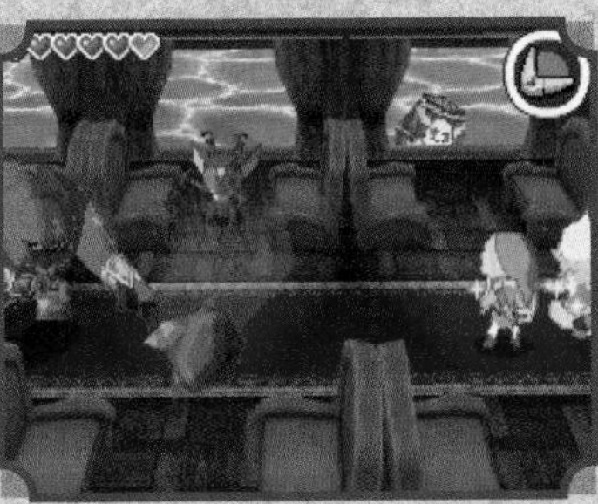

Don't get greedy while battling the Big Blin. Slip in, land a few hits, then dart out of range. Repeat this sequence to keep the Big Blin at bay and eventually drop the brute. Disheartened by the loss of their champion, the pirates retreat when at last the Big Blin falls.

Ocean Sanctuary Revisited

Ocean Sanctuary

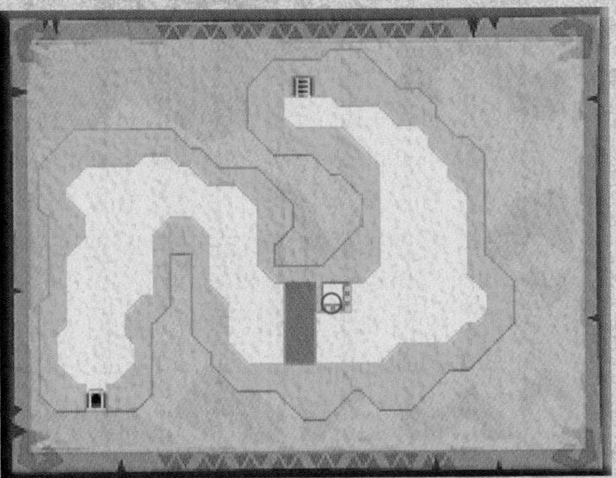

Ocean Sanctuary Cavern

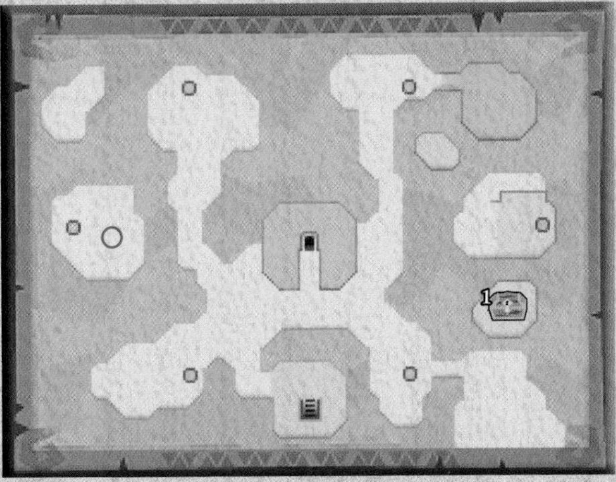

Ocean Sanctuary North

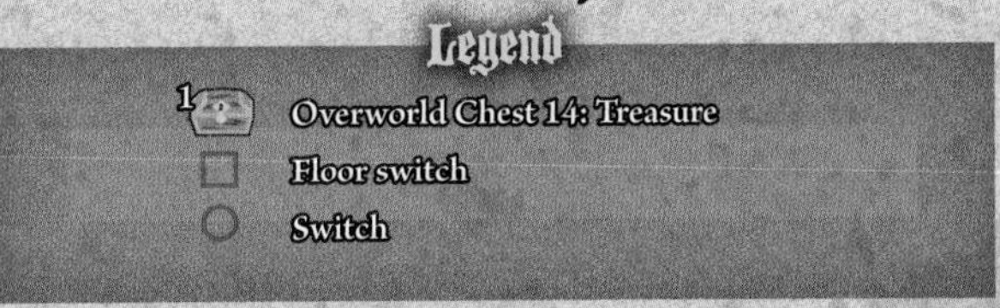

Items to Obtain

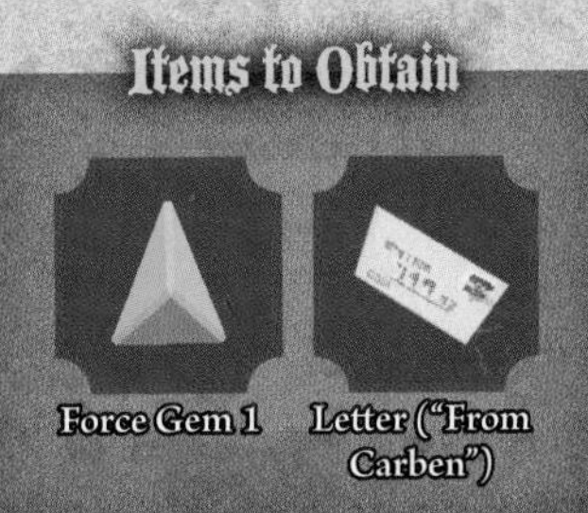

Enemies Encountered

Happy Thoughts

Energy lives in the hearts of everyone, even feeble old fellows like me...

Arriving at the Ocean Sanctuary, Carben is overjoyed to have made the trip in one piece. He gives Link a very special item called a Force Gem, explaining its nature: Every person has an energy inside of them, much like the energy that flows through the Spirit Tracks. When a person's heart is especially happy or grateful, their energy grows stronger and may manifest in the form of a Force Gem.

Force Gems carry so much good energy, they actually restore energy to the Spirit Tracks, which in turn restores lost portions of track. This first Force Gem you receive from Carben is no exception; the moment Link takes it, a small stretch of track materializes back in the Forest Realm!

You got a Force Gem!
The Forest rail map has started glowing!

NOTE

There's no pressing need to explore the new tracks that have appeared; they lead to a warp-activation gate that links back to the Snow Realm. We'll remind you about it when the time is right!

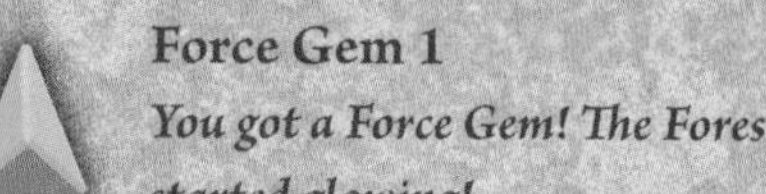

Force Gem 1

You got a Force Gem! The Forest Rail Map has started glowing!

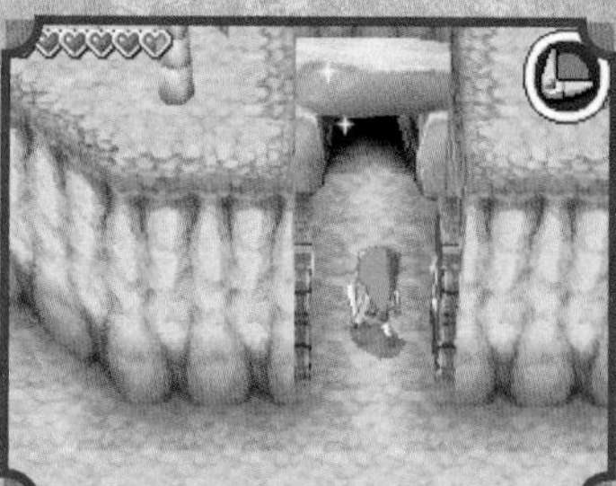

Carben putters off to his abode, bidding Link come find him. Make your way to the north region of the Ocean Sanctuary and return to Carben's lair.

Rockin' with Carben

This time, you find Carben waiting for you in his abode, ready to complete the duet. As always, practice your part before attempting the real thing.

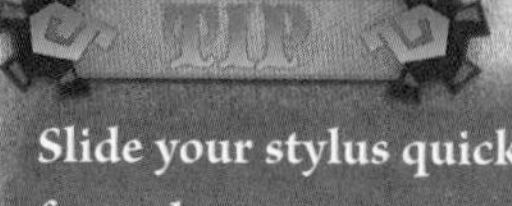
TIP

Slide your stylus quickly, and you can jump from the orange note to the purple one without sounding the yellow note that lies between them.

After a bit of practice, it's time for the real thing. Complete the song with Carben, making sure to keep the timing and not let his part confuse you. To nail the timing, sound your first note just as Carben is finishing his last.

1 Explore Papuchia Village

2 Find Carben and Complete the Duet

3 Open the Way to the Temple

4 Clear the Ocean Temple

Completing the ballad restores a significant portion of the Ocean Realm's Spirit Tracks. However, Carber. bursts your bubble a bit when he says that the Ocean Temple itself resides deep on the ocean floor. To get there, you'll need to find some way of exploring the ocean floor!

Carben goes on to say that there is a network of tracks underneath the water that lead to the Ocean Temple, but he can't recall how to get down to them. Then he remembers that he wrote down the method so he wouldn't forget! Carben hands you a letter and says the information you need is found inside.

811
To go to the Ocean Temple, you must first head to the ocean floor.
Menu

Letter

You got Carben's Letter! It has instructions on how to reach the ocean floor!

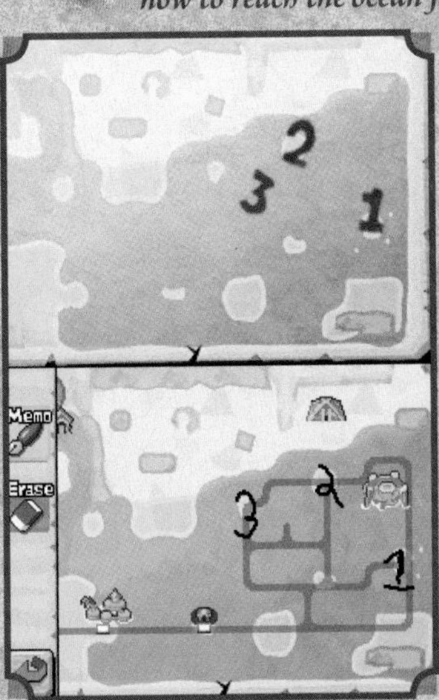

Read Carben's letter to discover an important clue: There's a map of the Ocean Realm inside, with the numbers 1, 2, and 3 written on it. Copy these numbers onto your map in the exact same places that they appear on Carben's.

It may have taken some effort to track down Carben, but the Lokomo has been a great help. Return to your train and set a course for those numbered locations.

Task 3: Open the Way to the Temple

To the Ocean Temple

Enemies Encountered

Armored Train

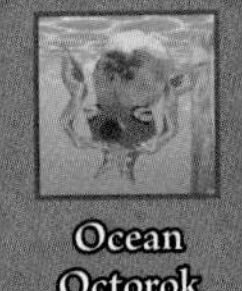

Ocean Octorok

Whistle for Service

As you head east from the Ocean Sanctuary, blast a barrel to your right to expose the first ocean rabbit. Believe it or not, these special bunnies can actually hop across water! That means they're pretty fast—but not too fast for your net, right?

You can bag a total of six ocean rabbits right now if you wish. Check the overworld map for their exact locations, and try to catch each one as you speed along, heading for the destinations indicated on Carben's map.

You hear the sounds of clicking before you get much farther—Ferrus is at his craft again, taking photos near the tracks! Take a moment to talk to Ferrus, who has a hot tip: There are mysterious statues around the Ocean Realm that react to loud noises. Sounds like something worth investigating!

812
They say there are statues that react to big noises out there too!

Head for the isle marked "1" on Carben's map. As you approach this area, scan the tall rock spires to spy an unusual statue with a giant red orb on top. It must be one of the statues that Ferrus was talking about!

Blow your whistle loud and clear as you pass the statue. Sure enough, the orb begins to glow and suddenly changes to blue. How about that!

Continue chugging along, heading for the isle marked "2." Spy another orb off to the right and sound your whistle to activate it.

Only one statue left! Take a moment to catch all six of those ocean rabbits if you like, then head for the area marked "3." The third and final statue sticks up from the water on your left as you approach; blow the whistle one final time to activate it.

With all three orb statues activated, the entrance to the Ocean Realm's underwater rail system emerges from the depths. There's no sense turning back now; head for those underwater tunnels, and hope your train is waterproof!

Under the Sea

Due to its otherworldly nature, the Spirit Train is somehow able to travel underwater just as easily as it does on dry land. Fire at the black sea urchins that float up from the depths, blasting them for Rupees just like boulders and barrels.

Beware of giant Ocean Octoroks as you cruise toward the Ocean Temple; they like to spit dark clouds of ink at your train, blotting your vision. Defeat these potential menaces by pounding them with three cannon shots before they have a chance to ink you over.

Ocean Octorok

Hits to Defeat: 3
Attack Type: Range (ink)
Power: N/A
Damage: None

Threat Meter

Track Terror

Ocean Octoroks are mere annoyances compared to the terrible Armored Train that appears as you approach the final junction before the temple. This thing's a lot like a Dark Train, only it pursues you with greater speed and tenacity, often stopping and reversing direction if you manage to give it the slip. Also, as its name implies, the Armored Train is covered in thick plating and is completely immune to your cannon.

Armored Train

Hits to Defeat: N/A
Attack Type: Contact
Power: N/A
Damage: Insta-squish

Threat Meter

The Armored Train is in your way, so you've got to outsmart it. Don't turn at the junction after the Armor Train appears; keep going straight, but bring your train to a screeching halt just after passing through. This will prompt the Armored Train to turn right when it reaches the junction. The moment your Map screen indicates that the Armored Train is turning right, reverse so you round the junction and go right, making a dash for the Ocean Temple. You've got to be quick in this stunt, because it won't take long for the Armored Train to reverse course and run you down. You can also briefly slow the Armored Train with cannon fire.

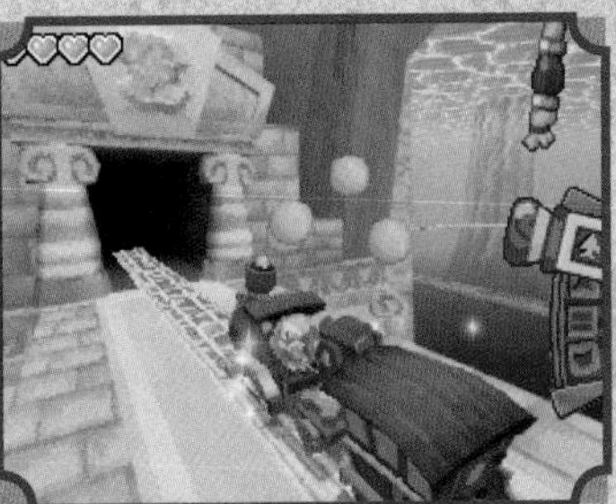

There it is, the entrance to the Ocean Temple! Race inside before the Armored Train catches up. You'll worry about how to get back out later!

Task 4: Clear the Ocean Temple

Ocean Temple

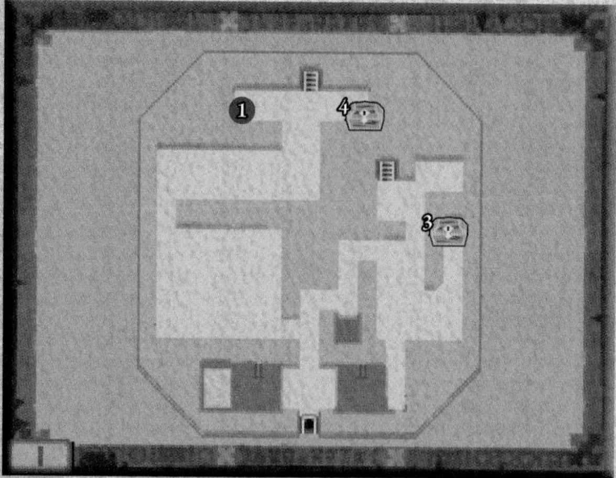

Ocean Temple, First Floor

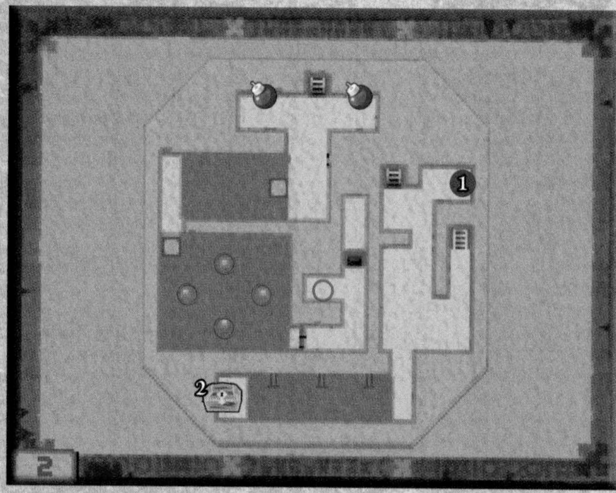

Ocean Temple, Second Floor

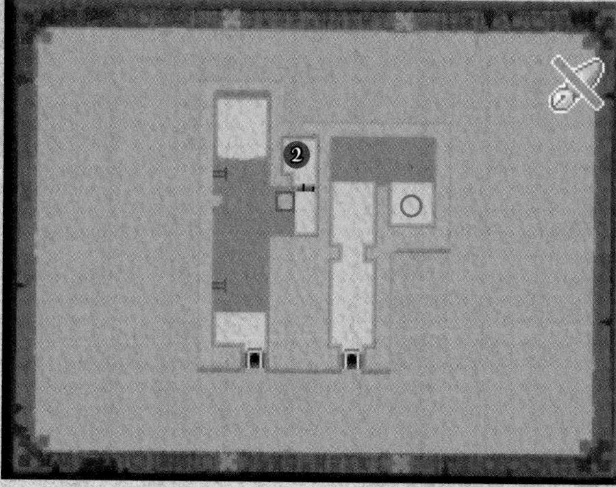

Ocean Temple, Second Floor North

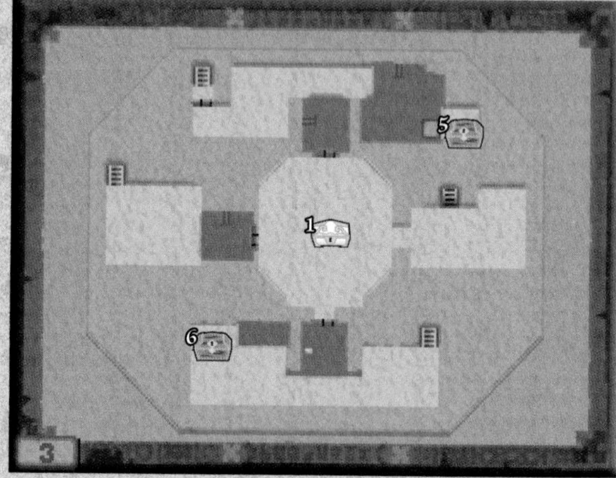

Ocean Temple, Third Floor

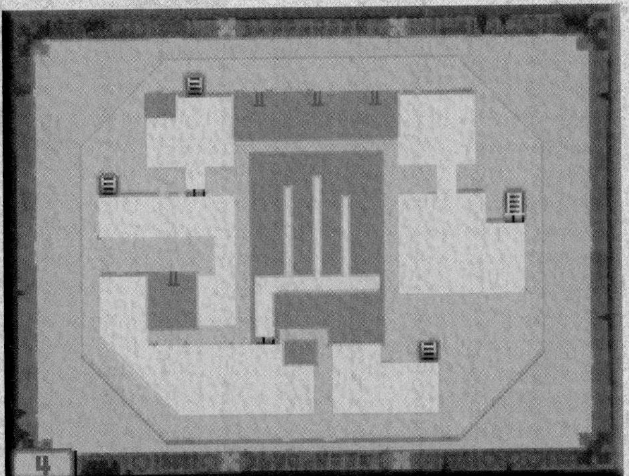

Ocean Temple, Fourth Floor

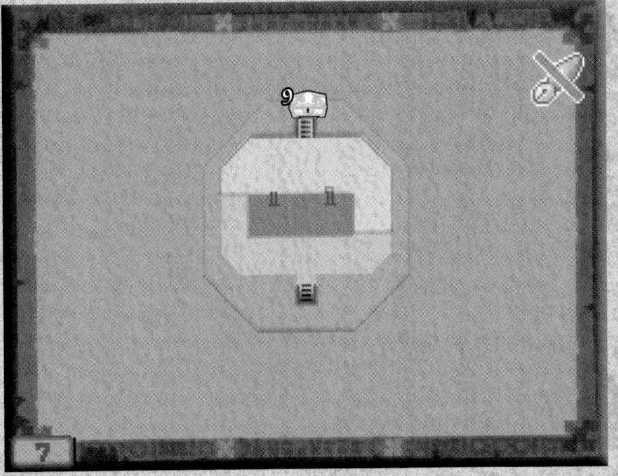

Ocean Temple, Seventh Floor

Ocean Temple, Fifth Floor

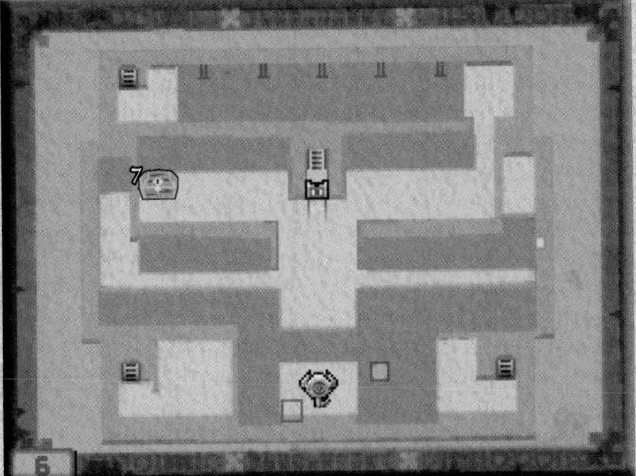

Ocean Temple, Sixth Floor

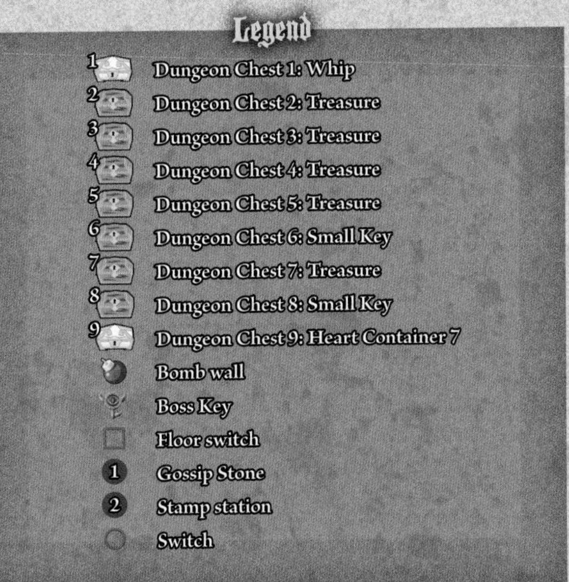

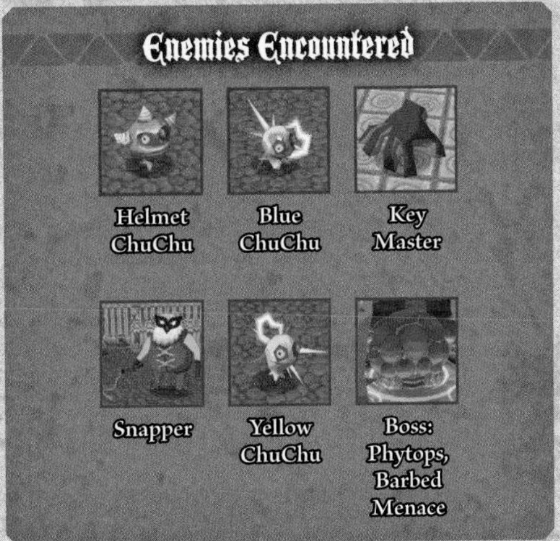

Enemies Encountered
Helmet ChuChu
Blue ChuChu
Key Master
Snapper
Yellow ChuChu
Boss: Phytops, Barbed Menace

Ocean Temple: First Floor

At last, you've made it to the Ocean Temple. An endless tide of rolling boulders leaves you no hope of exploring the eastern hall, so explore west instead.

Four stone tablets stand in the west chamber; each one has a number on it. Make a note of each stone tablet's number on your map; it'll soon prove useful.

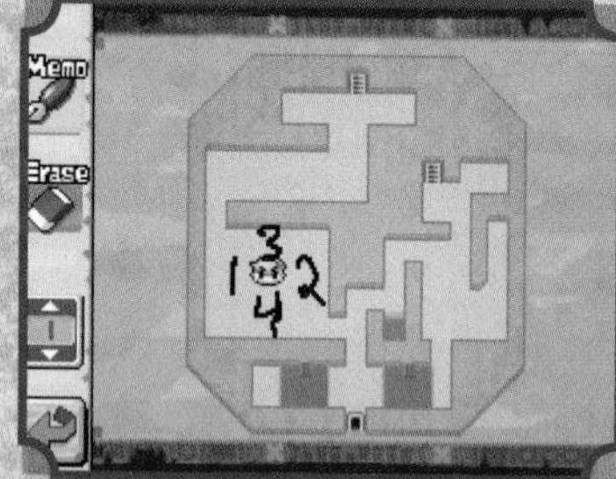

Take care while checking the tablets; Yellow ChuChus roam this area. These baddies become electrically charged, zapping Link if he touches them while they're all sparked up. Wait for their current to fade before striking, or stun them with the boomerang if you're in a hurry.

Yellow ChuChu

Hits to Defeat: 1
Attack Type: Contact
Power: Strong
Damage: 1/2 heart

Threat Meter

Sprint past the arrow traps in the following corridor, keeping close to the south wall so that you dash past without being hit.

Wake the Gossip Stone near the northern staircase to discover the locations of two hidden chests on this floor. Mark the chests' locations on your map so you don't forget where they are, then hurry upstairs.

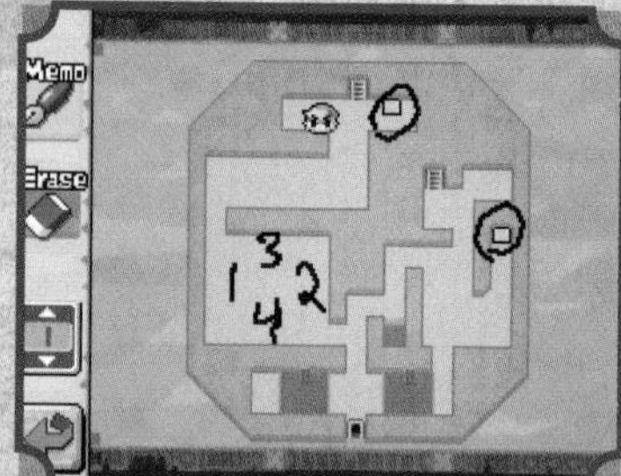

Ocean Temple: Second Floor

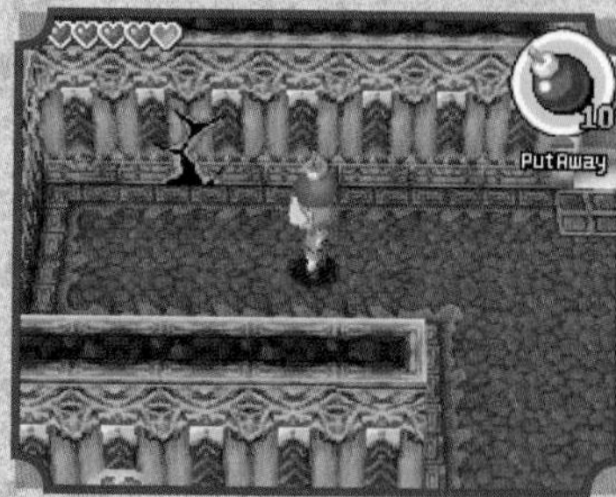

If you've bought bombs off of Beedle, use one to blast through the cracked wall to your left as you enter the second floor. This reveals the entrance to a secret northern portion of the floor.

Step through the opening and check out the second floor's northern region. You can't do much here at present, but you'll soon return.

1 Explore Papuchia Village

2 Find Carben and Complete the Duet

3 Open the Way to the Temple

4 Clear the Ocean Temple

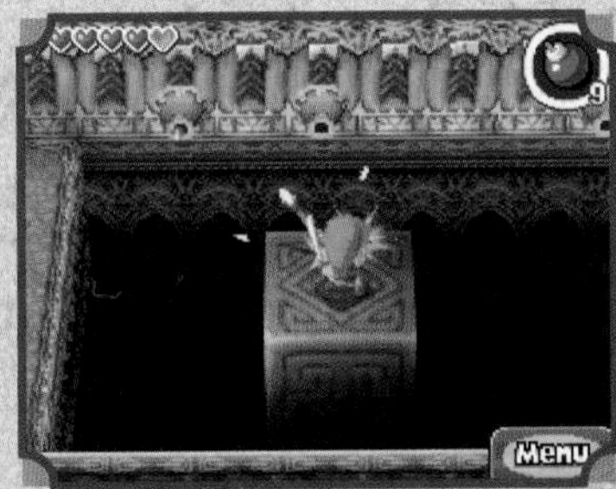

Step onto the large block to the south, and it will ferry you across a wide pit. Face north as you ride the block so that Link deflects the arrows shot by the northern traps with his shield.

Ride the next moving block diagonally across the second pit, noticing four switches as you go. These switches are in the same position as the stone tablets you noticed on the first floor. Hit all four switches with the boomerang as you move across the pit, triggering them in the following order: west, east, north, south. This opens the southeast door.

Find a switch in the following hall, and whack it with the boomerang to close a nearby trapdoor. This redirects the flow of boulders; perhaps now you can explore the east half of the first floor.

Backtrack to the first floor, again facing north as you ride one of the moving blocks to deflect inbound arrows.

Ocean Temple: First Floor, Revisited

Sure enough, those boulders are no longer an obstacle. Search the first floor's east half, where you notice a strange collection of thorny brambles. Don't touch the brambles or you'll be pricked for damage. Soon you'll find a means of dealing with them.

There isn't much else to see over here, so scale the nearby staircase to return to the second floor.

Ocean Temple: Second Floor, Revisited

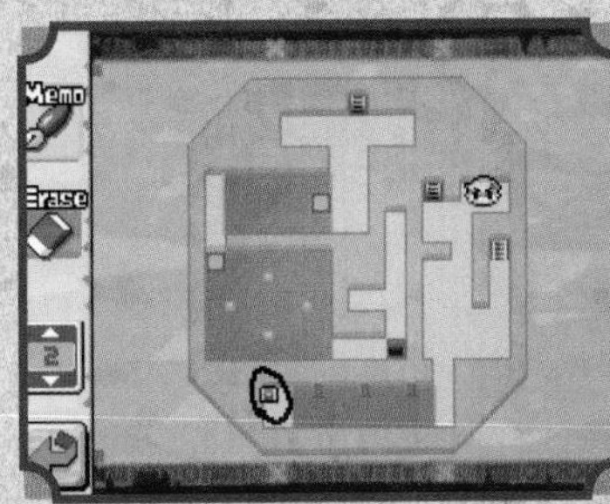

Go right as you enter the second floor, and wake the Gossip Stone to find the floor's only hidden chest. Mark it down on your map, then explore south.

Dispatch two Yellow ChuChus before scampering up more stairs that lead to the third floor.

Ocean Temple: Third Floor

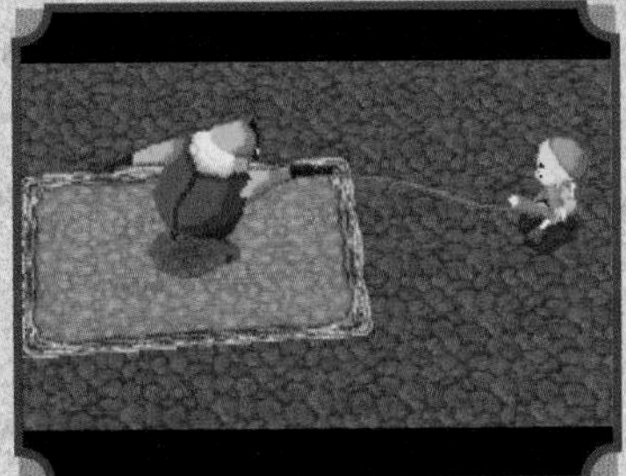

Go left and enter the third floor's central chamber. The room's doors seal after you enter, trapping you inside with a dangerous Snapper. The fiend lashes out at Link with its whip, snaring our hero by the waist. Not good!

Snapper

Hits to Defeat: Multiple
Attack Type: Contact and Range
Power: Strong
Damage: 1/2 heart
Threat Meter

Don't struggle to run away from the Snapper when he's got a hold of Link; he'll just yank on the whip, pulling Link back toward him. Instead, wait for the Snapper to pull Link in close, then deliver a short-range punch.

While Link is being pulled forward, swipe your stylus directly at the Snapper, tracing straight lines from Link to the villain to make Link stab straight forward with his sword. Do this quickly and Link will stab the Snapper as he's being reeled in, breaking free of the whip's grip.

Don't give the Snapper a chance to snare Link again. Stay right on top of him, slashing away with Link's blade. Straight stabs seem to work best. If you run away from the Snapper to collect hearts or the like, he'll try to tie you up again. If that happens, you'll need to be patient and break free as you did before.

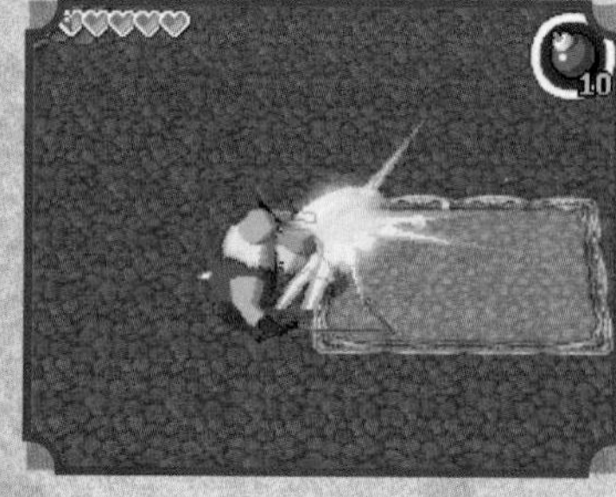

Keep attacking the Snapper while Link's free from his grip until the villain can withstand no more. A giant chest appears in the room's center, and all of its doors open. Open the chest to claim a new and versatile tool: the whip!

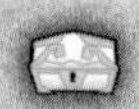

Dungeon Chest 1: Whip

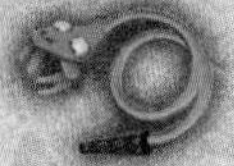

Whip

You got the whip! Tap the screen to give it a crack!

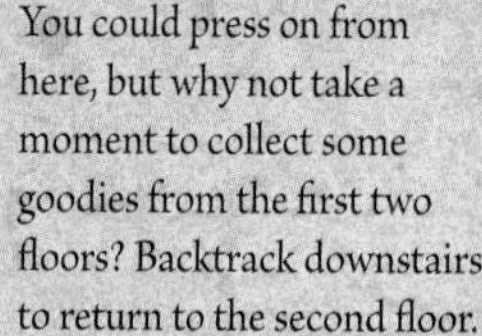

You could press on from here, but why not take a moment to collect some goodies from the first two floors? Backtrack downstairs to return to the second floor.

Ocean Temple: Second Floor, Third Visit

Now that you've found the whip, you can cross this floor's long southern pit. Stand near the brink and equip the whip; then tap the wooden post near the ceiling. Link lashes out and snags the post, swinging out over the chasm!

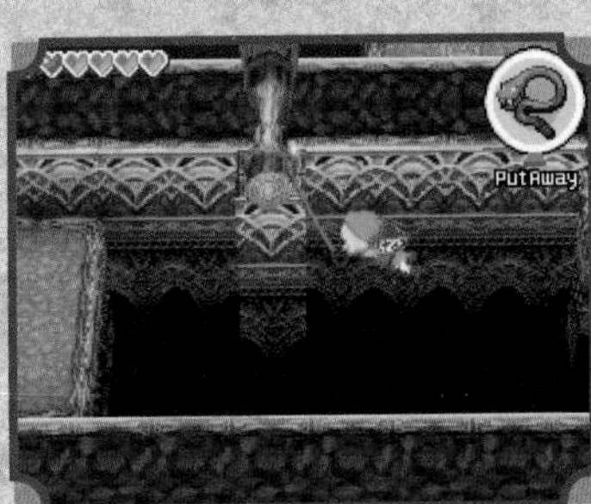

Quickly tap each post in the series to keep Link swinging. Cross the pit in this fashion to reach the far ledge, where you discover a small chest.

The chest contains a treasure. Pocket the prize and then swing back across the pit. Continue backtracking down to the first floor.

Dungeon Chest 2: Treasure

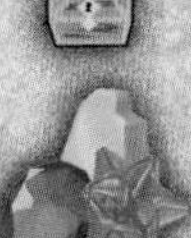

Treasure

You got a treasure! Check it out on the Collection screen!

Ocean Temple: First Floor, Third Visit

Remember those thorny brambles you noticed earlier? Return to them and use the whip to remove them from your path. Just lash at the big thorns near the floor to grab them, then swing the whip again to toss them away. Remove both thorny bits to make it safe to advance.

A small chest awaits beyond the thorns. Lift its lid to score another treasure.

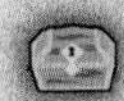

Dungeon Chest 3: Treasure

Treasure

You got a treasure! Check it out on the Collection screen!

Now run south and use the whip once more to swing across a wide pit. Again, simply target the overhead post to swing.

Whip-swing across the next pit to the left, and you reach a ledge with an odd fish sculpture affixed to the wall. Lash the whip at the fish sculpture to grab and pull the cord in its mouth. This causes the floor's remaining hidden chest to appear to the north.

Make your way north and crack open the chest for a rare treasure. Climb the nearby stairs afterward to reach the northern portion of the second floor.

Dungeon Chest 4: Treasure

Treasure

You got a treasure! Check it out on the Collection screen!

Ocean Temple: Second Floor, Fourth Visit

You're back near the wall you bombed. Step through again to reach the floor's northern region; this time, take a close look at your map. It shows another doorway to the east! This is an important clue; backtrack out of the secret area and plant a bomb in the east nook, right about where the other doorway should be.

Boom! Even though the wall had no large crack, it still proves vulnerable to your bomb. Head through the opening to reach the secret area's east half.

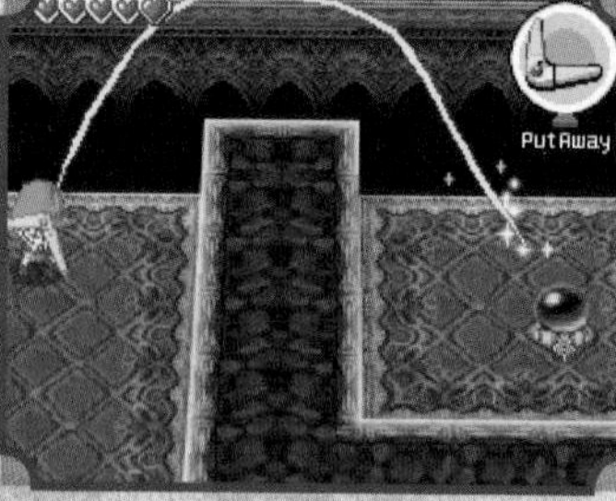

Lash some brambles out of your way, then use your boomerang to trigger a switch near the northeast pit. This extends a whip post to the west. Backtrack out and go through the west bomb wall.

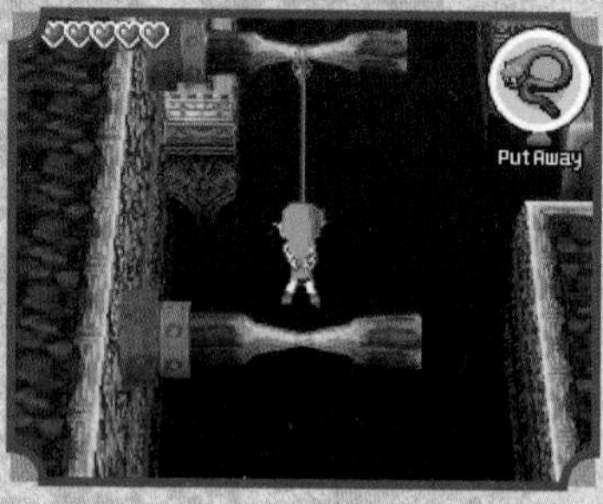

With the post extended, you're now able to whip-swing across the secret area's long pit. Tap those overhead posts to reach the far ledge.

You land near a fish sculpture. Use the whip again to tug on its cord. This opens a nearby door to the east.

Wait patiently for the nearby moving block to slide beneath the nearest whip post; then swing from the post to land on the block before it moves away. Ride the block to the east, then step off and go through the door you've just opened.

Ah, you've discovered the temple's stamp station! Plant a stamp on your book for Niko. That's your eleventh stamp so far!

Ocean Temple: Third Floor, Revisited

Now that you've completely pillaged the temple's first two floors, make your way back up to the third floor's central chamber, where you first discovered the whip. You can proceed north or west. Head north first, whip-swinging across the pit.

Wipe out the Yellow ChuChus to the north; these foes are easier to handle now that you possess the whip. It takes a few extra hits to defeat them with the whip, but you won't ever be shocked for damage, even when they're all lit up.

A locked door bars your progress, but that's okay; there's treasure nearby! Stand near the east pit and watch your map, waiting for the nearby moving block to slide up to the north wall. When it does, whip-swing over and land on the block; ride it south to reach a small ledge with a chest.

The chest holds another sparkly treasure. You're growing quite the collection!

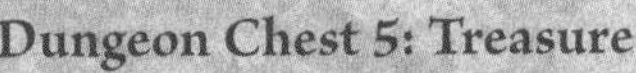

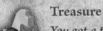

Dungeon Chest 5: Treasure

Treasure

You got a treasure! Check it out on the Collection screen!

That's all you can do up north for now. Return to the floor's central chamber, swing across the west pit, and scale the stairs beyond. You can't cross the south pit at present.

Ocean Temple: Fourth Floor

After emerging on the fourth floor, check the nearby stone tablet for a strange message: When three handles sit before you, pull only the one that's farthest from your grasp. Don't worry, it'll soon make sense!

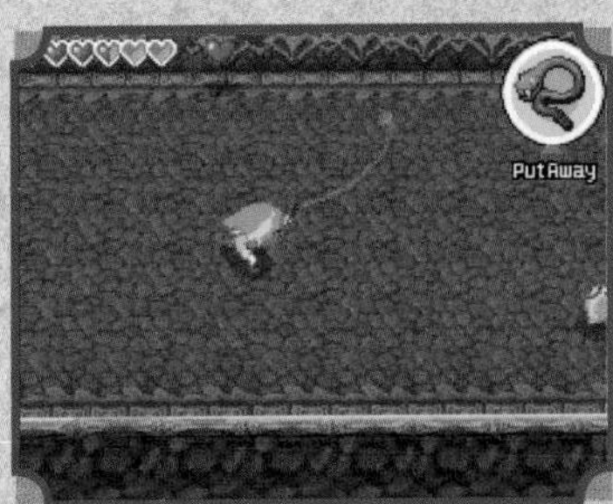

Go south and swing across a pit. Lash away at the Yellow ChuChus that follow to defeat them without risk of injury.

Find a fish sculpture in the nearby wall, and yank its cord with your whip to open the door ahead. Now you may proceed to the floor's central area, where three fish sculptures are affixed to the northern wall.

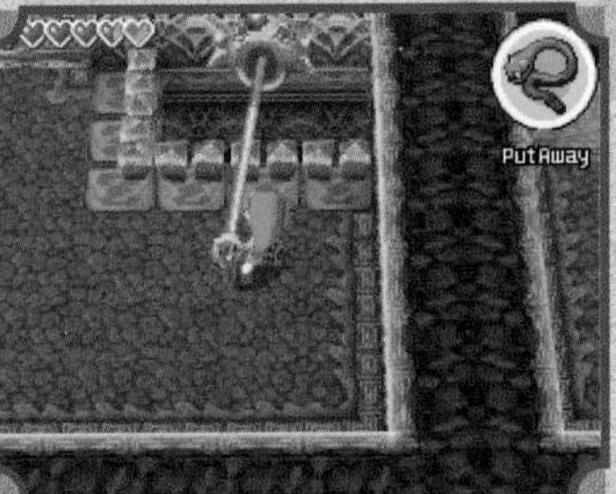

Remember the stone tablet's clue, and pull only the cord of the fish sculpture on the far right, which is farthest away from you. This extends a bridge to the south, allowing you to return downstairs.

Pulling either of the other two fish-sculpture cords will either trigger the surrounding arrow traps or cause a giant boulder to fall down on Link. Leave them be!

Ocean Temple: Third Floor, Third Visit

You've reached the third floor's south area, which you couldn't access before. Two fish sculptures stick out from the wall here, one with a handle sticking out from its mouth. Whip the handle to yank out a giant sword, then tap the other fish sculpture to toss the sword into its mouth. This causes a chest to materialize nearby and raises a whip post so you may reach the central chamber.

Flip open the chest's lid to obtain a Small Key. All right! Now you can open that locked door to the north.

Dungeon Chest 6: Small Key

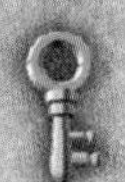

Small Key

You got a Small Key! Use this key to open locked doors!

Swing north to unlock the northwest door, crossing two pits on your way. Scale the stairs beyond to reach a portion of the fourth floor you haven't seen yet.

Ocean Temple: Fourth Floor, Revisited

Upon entering the fourth floor, pull the cord of the nearby fish sculpture to open the door to the south. This simply makes it easier to navigate between the floors you've been to.

There's no reason to head south—you've already explored that area. Instead, swing across the series of whip posts to the east.

Beyond the whip posts, Link becomes trapped in a room with a pair of Helmet ChuChus. These little creeps are practically invincible in their giant helmets, so use the whip to relieve them of their defensive gear. After snatching off a Helmet ChuChu's helmet, it's reduced to a garden-variety Red ChuChu—easy pickings!

Helmet ChuChu

Hits to Defeat: 1
Attack Type: Contact
Power: Weak
Damage: 1/2 heart

Threat Meter

1 Explore Papuchia Village

2 Find Carben and Complete the Duet

3 Open the Way to the Temple

4 Clear the Ocean Temple

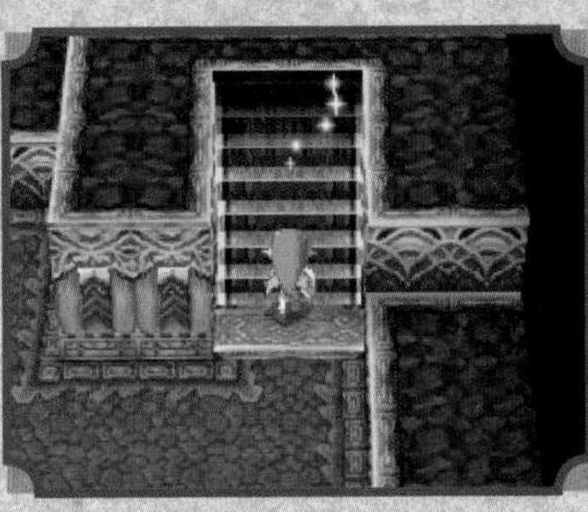

The room unseals after you best the Helmet ChuChus. Proceed up the nearby stairs to reach the fifth floor.

Ocean Temple: Fifth Floor

1014
Three blades sit in a row. Retrieve them all, and the path may open.
Menu

Nice work; you've made it all the way to the fifth floor! Whip away the dangerous brambles to the north, then inspect the stone tablet near the pit beyond. The tablet hints that by retrieving "three blades that sit in a row," a path may open. Sounds like something worth remembering!

You can't cross the pit near the tablet, because a few of its whip posts are missing. Go south instead, ignoring the row of fish sculptures on the nearby wall. You'll use them in a bit.

Two villainous Snappers patrol near the floor's center, eager for a fight. These two won't tie you up like the last one, so give them a taste of their own medicine and whip them both repeatedly. Whipping the Snappers keeps them stunned and will eventually defeat them if you keep lashing out.

You'll notice many more fish sculptures lining this floor's walls, some with handles, some without. Soon you'll learn how to use them; for now, investigate the floor's westernmost corridor to locate a strange device. Whip the device to make a propeller spring up and begin fluttering off.

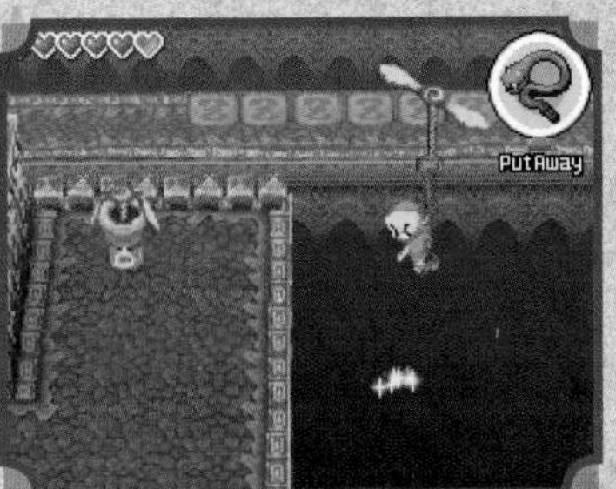

Quickly whip the propeller's handle to make Link latch on, hitching a ride to the floor's southwest corner. You must hold the stylus on the screen to keep a hold of the propeller.

Once Link's feet are over solid ground, release the propeller by removing your stylus from the screen. What a ride! Go up the nearby stairs for a quick visit up to the sixth floor.

Ocean Temple: Sixth Floor

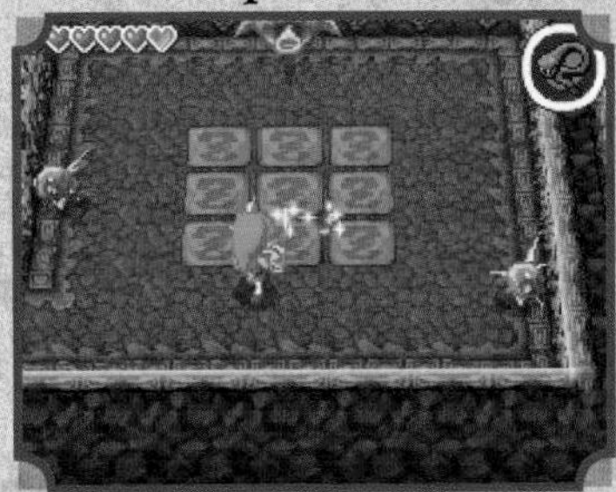

The temple's sixth floor has a similar layout to the fifth. If you have bombs, ready them and enter the nearby room, where Link becomes trapped with a pair of dangerous Blue ChuChus!

Blue ChuChu

Hits to Defeat: 1
Attack Type: Contact
Power: Strong
Damage: 1/2 heart

Threat Meter

These charged-up foes can be tough to handle, but not if you have bombs. Just heave a bomb at each monster to destroy them in short order. If you don't have bombs, you'll need to snag the large sword from the north fish sculpture, then quickly tap one of the Blue ChuChus to toss the sword at it and defeat it. This may take a few tries, but it's the only way to defeat them without bombs.

Wiping out the Blue ChuChus unseals the room and extends a whip post over the floor's far-east pit. This will come in handy later; for now, return to the fifth floor, and use another propeller to get back to the floor's central area.

Ocean Temple: Fifth Floor, Revisited

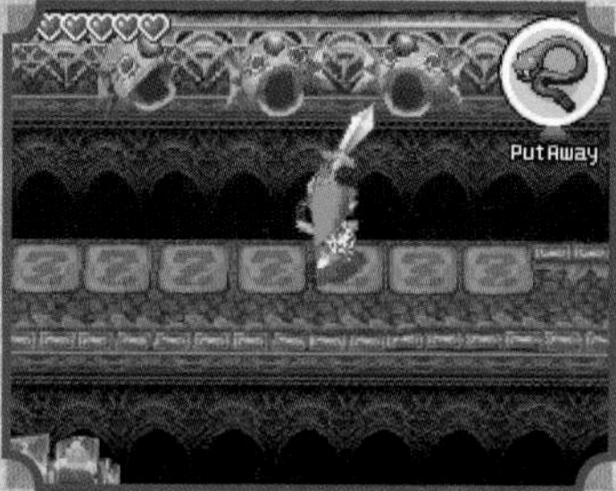

Back on the fifth floor, the propeller drops you off right near a row of three fish sculptures, each with a handle in its mouth. Remember the clue you recently read from a stone tablet, and yank all three handles, pulling swords out of the fish sculptures' mouths. This extends a series of whip posts along the north pit.

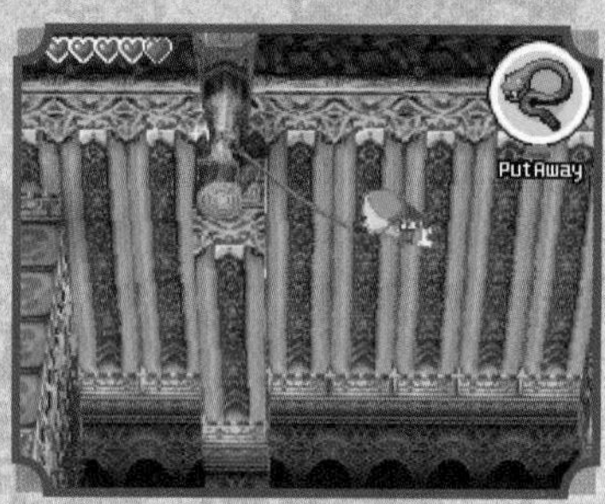

Hurry north and use the whip to swing across the long pit. Race up the staircase you land near to return to the sixth floor.

Ocean Temple: Sixth Floor, Revisited

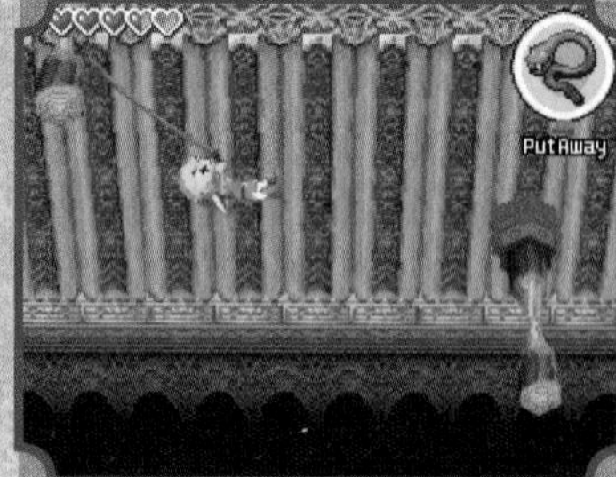

Back on the sixth floor, swing across the long nearby pit. Stay sharp, because some of the whip posts are set higher or lower than the others, making it easy to miss one and fall.

Whack the switch located on the far ledge to extend another whip post along the pit. Now it'll be easier going back across.

Read the stone tablet near the switch for a clue: Take note of how the blades are placed ahead. Roger that!

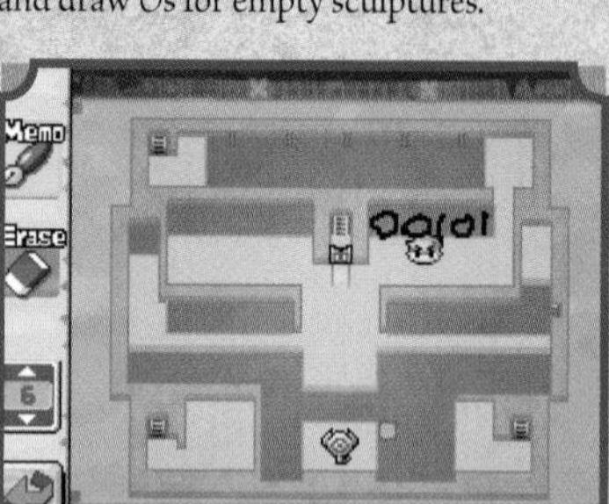

Go south and wipe out a Helmet ChuChu, yanking off its helmet to expose it to attacks. Examine the fish sculptures on the nearby wall afterward, noting on your map which ones have swords in their mouths and which ones don't. Draw lines for the sculptures' swords and draw Os for empty sculptures.

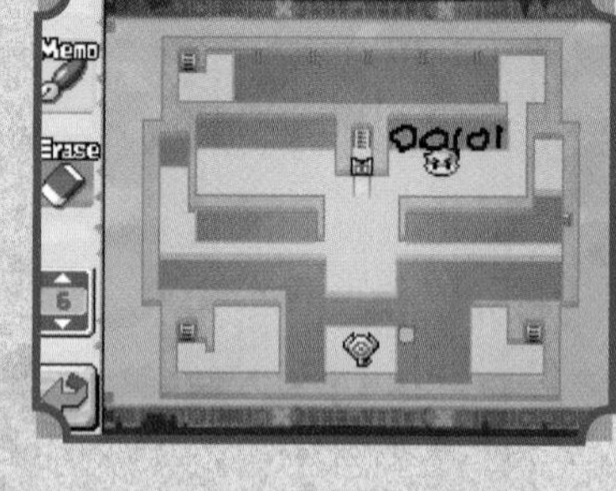

Continue exploring the sixth floor, noting the exact patterns of the fish sculptures. There are four separate rows of sculptures to find and note down.

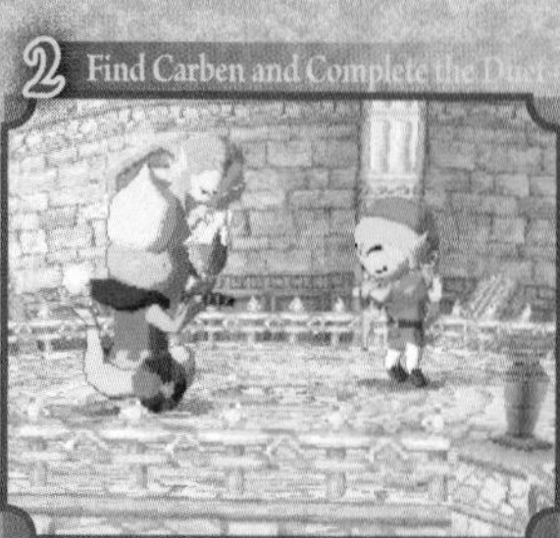

While seeking out the sculptures, remove the thorns from the west corridor, and tug the cord of the fish sculpture beyond to expose a hidden chest. Loop around to reach the chest, which contains another treasure for your collection.

Dungeon Chest 7: Treasure

Treasure

You got a treasure! Check it out on the Collection screen!

Now visit the floor's east corridor, where the whip post you raised by besting the Blue ChuChus can at last be put to good use. Swing across the whip post to reach a chest that contains a Small Key.

Dungeon Chest 8: Small Key

Small Key

You got a Small Key! Use this key to open locked doors!

You're all finished up here for now. Swing back across the north row of whip posts and go back down to the fifth floor.

Ocean Temple: Fifth Floor, Third Visit

Now that you know how to arrange the fish sculpture's swords, run around and put them in their proper order. Just imitate the patterns you saw up on the sixth floor. When all four rows of fish sculptures have their swords in their proper mouths, a door at the floor's southeast corner opens.

TIP

While viewing your map, you may scroll through the different floors of the dungeon. Just tap the little arrow icons on the left. This lets you call up the sixth-floor map and verify the locations of the fish sculpture swords (assuming you noted them down).

Use the Small Key you recently found up on the sixth floor to open the locked door to the south. Swing across the southeast pit afterward to pass through the door you just opened by manipulating the fish-sculpture swords. Run up the large staircase that follows to return to the sixth floor.

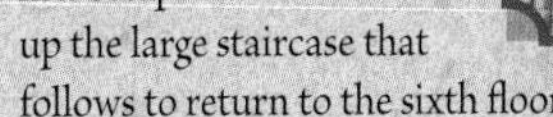

Ocean Temple: Sixth Floor, Third Visit

Use the whip to yank the handle of the propeller device you find up here, starting the propeller in motion. Latch on and hitch a ride west, letting go when Link passes over a moving block.

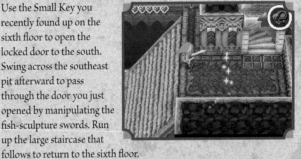

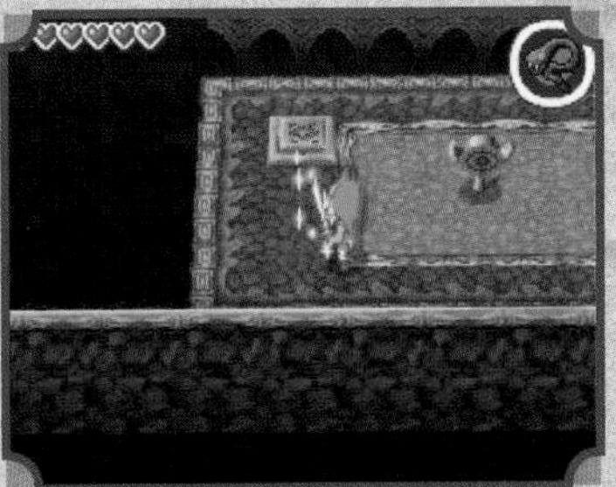

Ride the moving block to reach the southern platform, where the Boss Key sits. Step on the nearby floor switch to extend a bridge to the north; then pick up the Boss Key.

On cue, four creepy Key Masters materialize and begin stalking after Link. Quickly turn and toss the Boss Key behind Link; then make your stand on the bridge and wipe out the Key Masters as they creep close.

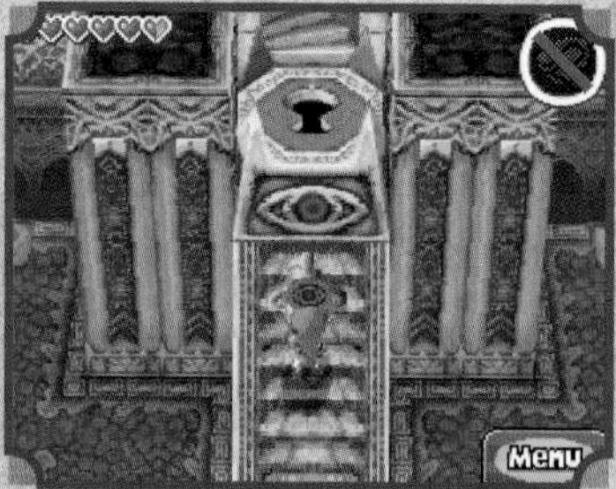

When all's clear, take up the Boss Key and carry it north. Hurl the key into the Boss Key door to banish the obstacle and open the way to the final showdown.

Ocean Temple: Seventh Floor

Swing across this small floor's pit, and lash away the brambles so you may advance to face the temple's boss. Smash the pots for hearts if need be, and read the tablet to make the blue warp light appear, just in case you need to leave and come back. When you're ready for the fight at hand, take a deep breath and head upstairs.

Phytops, Barbed Menace

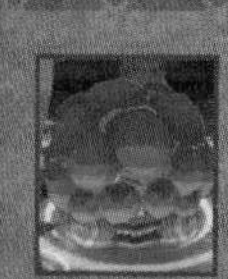

Hits to Defeat: Multiple
Attack Type: Contact
Power: Strong
Damage: 1/2 heart

Threat Meter

Link must scale a tall cliff before Phytops reveals itself. Use the whip to swing along the posts, and watch out for Phytops to periodically spew toxic gunk, which will rain down around you. Be patient if the gunk lands in your way; it'll evaporate after a moment.

Phytops's giant tentacles block your progress at several points. Each time you face one, use the whip to rip off one of its thorns, then toss the thorn at the tentacle's yellow eye. When the eye is struck, the tentacle retracts, allowing you to continue swinging.

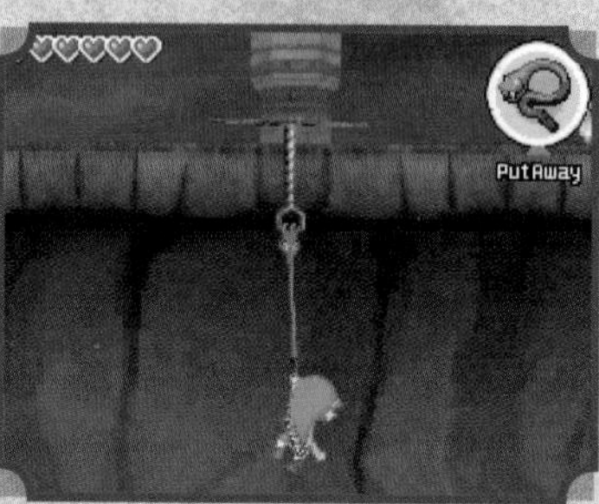

When you near the summit of the cliff, lash the propeller device and hitch a ride up to the top. Phytops awaits!

Phytops attacks with great fury, slamming the arena with its overgrown tentacles. Its defenses are somewhat lax, though, and the boss is fairly easy to stun and damage. Dodge the toxic gunk it continues to spit, and avoid being crushed by the tentacles. After a tentacle crashes to the ground, quickly lash it with the whip to tear off a thorn.

The moment you snare a thorn, toss it at one of the two purple sacs just above Phytops's purple mouth. Burst both sacs with thrown thorns to expose the fiend's weak spot: its eye!

1 Explore Papuchia Village

2 Find Carben and Complete the Duet

3 Open the Way to the Temple

4 Clear the Ocean Temple

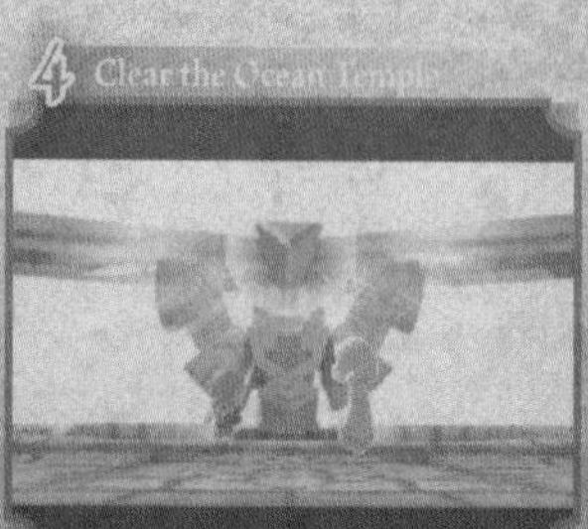

Continue avoiding Phytops's attacks until you can snare one more thorn from a fallen tentacle. Heave this third thorn at the creature's eye to stun the brute, causing its head to crash down nearby.

The moment Phytops's head touches down, race over and bring the full weight of Link's sword to bear on the exposed eyeball. Keep hacking and slashing the eye until Phytops recovers and pulls away.

That's all there is to beating Phytops—just keep repeating the same sequence until you achieve victory. The monster attacks with greater fury as the battle wages on, so stay mobile and keep a close eye on where its tentacles and gunk will land. Smash the surrounding pots and gobble down potions if you need to replenish Link's health.

With Phytops destroyed, the Ocean Temple is at last cleansed of evil. Its flow of energy comes back online, sending a current of power back along the Spirit Tracks and into the Tower of Spirits. A third hunk of the tower locks into place, leaving just one more spinning around. Excellent work!

Collect your prized Heart Container from the large chest that appears. If you've been following this walkthrough carefully, Link now has a whopping ten hearts! Step into the blue light to return to the temple's entrance, then board the Spirit Train and make ready to return to the Tower of Spirits.

You got a Heart Container!

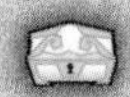

Dungeon Chest 9: Heart Container 7

Heart Container 7

You got a Heart Container! You increased your life by one and refilled your hearts!

Missing Links

Armed with the whip, Link is now able to perform several optional side quests for both fun and profit. Read on to discover all the plunder you can grab before returning to the Tower of Spirits.

Ocean Sanctuary

Ocean Sanctuary

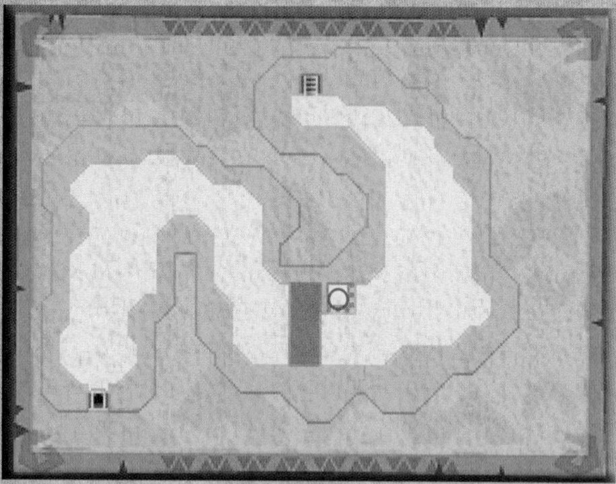

Ocean Sanctuary Cavern

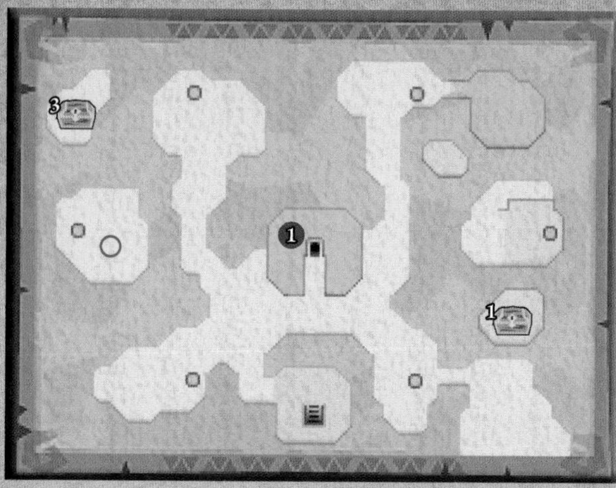

Ocean Sanctuary North

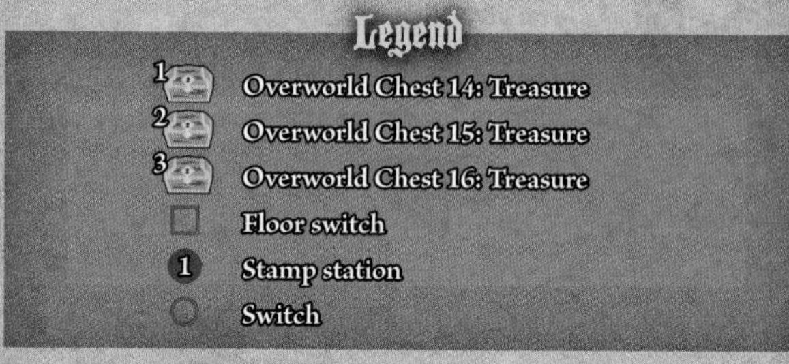

Since you're already hanging around the Ocean Realm, let's start with the stuff you can do around here. Swing by the Ocean Sanctuary and stand just south of the little isle that's north of the train station. Wait until you see a giant bird fly past, and play the Song of Birds to attract it. Then use your whip to latch on to the bird and hitch a ride over to the little isle.

1 Explore Papuchia Village

2 Find Carben and Complete the Duel

3 Open the Way to the Temple

4 Clear the Ocean Temple

Hey, there's a chest over here! Flip open the chest's lid to score a treasure.

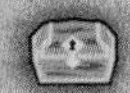

Overworld Chest 15: Treasure

Treasure

You got a treasure! Check it out on the Collection screen!

Play the Song of Birds again, and ride back over to the mainland. Your next stop is Carben's lair, located in the north region. Stand near the doorway leading to Carben's abode, and play the Song of Birds to attract another flying transport.

This bird brings you to the Ocean Sanctuary's stamp station. Record your twelfth stamp here, then make your way back to the train and set off for Papuchia Village.

Before leaving for Papuchia Village, move to the northwest corner of the Ocean Sanctuary's northern region and play the Song of Birds to attract some overhead transportation. Ride on a bird to the remote northwest isle, where you discover a chest with a sparkly treasure inside.

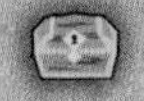

Overworld Chest 16: Treasure

Treasure

You got a treasure! Check it out on the Collection screen!

Papuchia Village

Papuchia Village

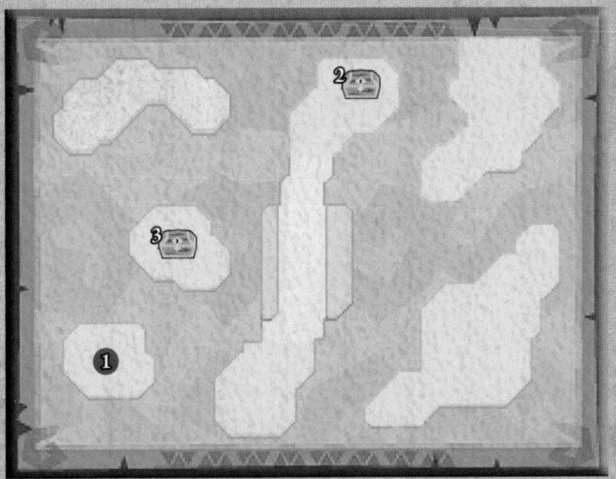

Papuchia Village South

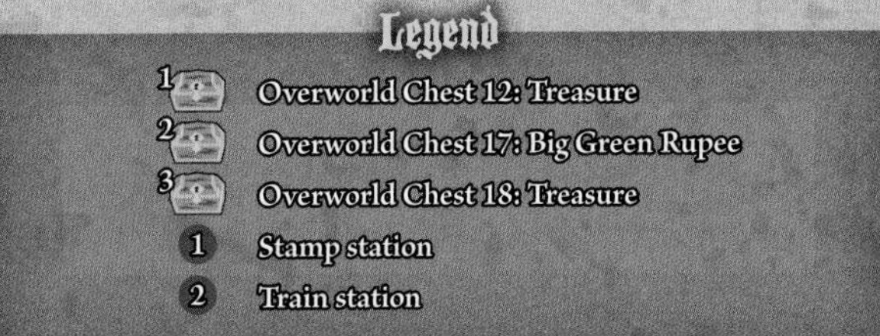

Legend

1 Overworld Chest 12: Treasure
2 Overworld Chest 17: Big Green Rupee
3 Overworld Chest 18: Treasure
1 Stamp station
2 Train station

Items to Obtain

Big Green Rupee — Force Gem 2 — Treasure

Enemies Encountered

Lobarriers

Go to the place in Papuchia Village where Carben had been frolicking with the giant birds. Use the whip to latch on to one of the circling birds' handles so you can hitch a ride to the east isle; then run south to reach the village's southern region.

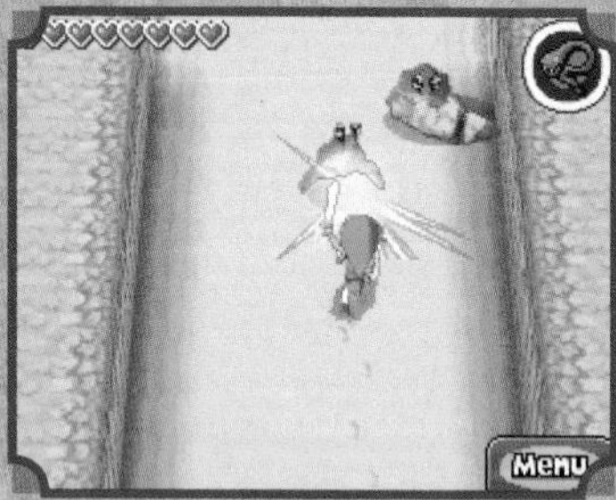

Use more giant birds to reach the south region's individual isles. If no birds are about, play the Song of Birds to attract them. Go to the southeast isle, then over to the central isle. Use your whip to quickly disarm and defeat any Lobarriers that get in your way.

Open the small chest you find at the central isle's north end to score a Big Green Rupee.

Overworld Chest 17: Big Green Rupee

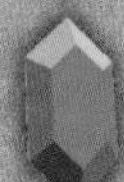

Big Green Rupee

You got a Big Green Rupee! It's worth 100 Rupees!

Continue using the birds to reach the west and southwest isles. On the west isle, you find a small chest containing a sparkly treasure, and Papuchia Village's stamp station is way down southwest. Open the chest and record the stamp (your thirteenth so far); then head back to the village proper, calling birds as needed.

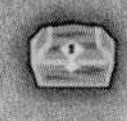

Overworld Chest 18: Treasure

Treasure

You got a treasure! Check it out on the Collection screen!

Before leaving Papuchia Village, enter one of the huts and speak with a woman who's desperate to find a husband. She says she'd like to meet someone with a beard; a large nose; and a burly, rugged appearance. Sounds like just about everyone you know from Whittleton... Let's go there real quick!

Out of all the burly hunks who live at Whittleton Village, only one will set the Papuchia woman's heart on fire. And it's none other than the village chief himself! He may be a little old, but there's no one more rugged or with manlier facial hair.

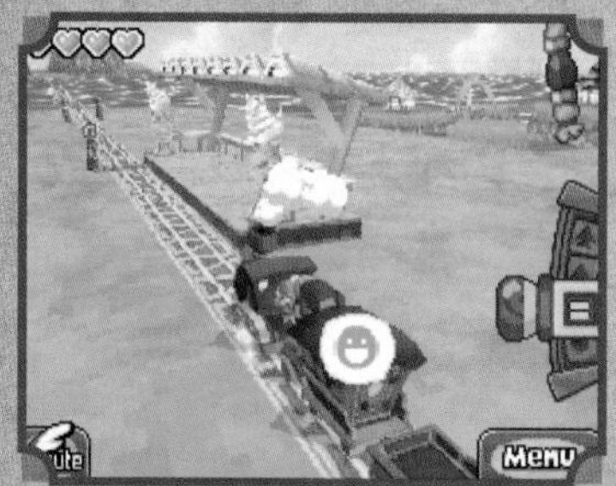

Board your train and ferry the Whittleton elder to Papuchia Village. Remember to obey all signposts, avoid getting hit, and pull up at the station without slamming on the brakes. Papuchia isn't far, so this is an easy trip to make.

1 Explore Papuchia Village

2 Find Carben and Complete the Duet

3 Open the Way to the Temple

4 Clear the Ocean Temple

2295
I think I've finally found my Mr. Right!
Menu

When you arrive at Papuchia, the elder goes ahead to speak with the woman, who falls head over heels for her new stud. The two are so happy that a Force Gem materializes from thin air! This is the second Force Gem you've found, and it opens up new tracks back in the Forest Realm. Return to Whittleton Village for even more surprises.

Force Gem 2

You got a Force Gem! The Forest Rail Map has started glowing!

Whittleton Village

Whittleton Village

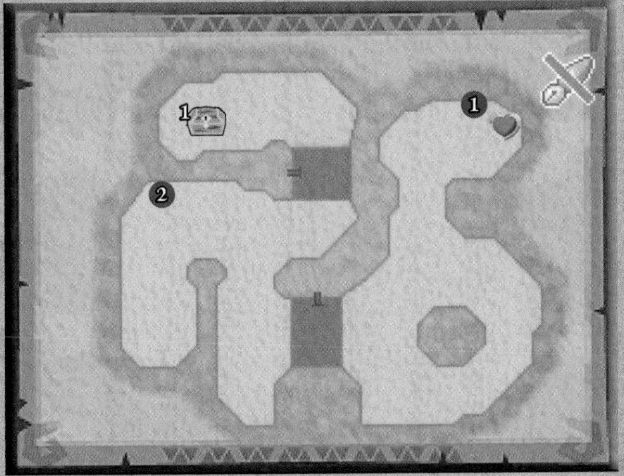

Whittleton Village North

Legend

1 (chest)	Overworld Chest 19: Treasure
1	Bomb Bag 2
(heart)	Heart Container 8
2	Stamp station
3	Train station

Items to Obtain

Bomb Bag 2 · Heart Container 8 · Treasure

Enemies Encountered

Spinut

Before speaking to the villagers (you can bring any of them back to Papuchia), go north and use the whip to swing across the northern region's north pit. This lands you near a small chest; open it for a treasure.

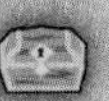

Overworld Chest 19: Treasure

Treasure

You got a treasure! Check it out on the Collection screen!

1168
Try your hand at a whip race? It's just 50 Rupees to prove what you got!
Menu

Now cross the south pit and sprint north to speak to a friendly fellow who runs a whip-race challenge. Pay the man 50 Rupees to attempt the game.

The whip race is similar to the climb you experienced before the Phytops showdown. Lash out and swing along the series of posts that stick out from the cliff, working your way ever upward. Tap each post the instant you see it to make Link swing from one to the next at top speed.

Each time you land on a ledge, hurry and move Link into range of the next stretch of posts. Run right up to the ledge's edge, equip the whip, and start swinging again as fast as you can.

Thorny brambles block the last few stretches of posts. Lash and toss away two thorns from each, then bolt onward. Getting past the brambles quickly is paramount to finishing in record time.

Reach the final platform in under one minute, thirty seconds to receive a Bomb Bag as a reward. Now you can hold even more bombs! Finish the race in under one minute and fifteen seconds to score an even greater prize: Heart Container 8!

You can also win treasures from the whip race as consolation prizes. Remember this if you're ever on the hunt for more treasure!

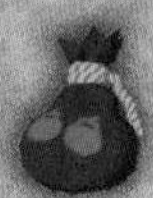

Bomb Bag 2

You got another Bomb Bag! Now you can carry twice as many bombs!

Heart Container 8

You got a Heart Container! You increased your life by one and refilled your hearts!

1078
Yeah!
No.
Oh, do you want to take the train out of here?
Menu

That's all the excitement Whittleton Village has to offer. Return to your train and plot a course to the south—it's time to explore the southern tracks that Carben's Force Gem opened up.

Hey, it's another warp gate! Blast the triangular symbol atop the gate to activate Warp Gate B. Now you can quickly travel to the east side of the Snow Realm! Take the gate for a test spin and warp there now; then set a course for Wellspring Station, which isn't far from where you emerge.

Wellspring Station

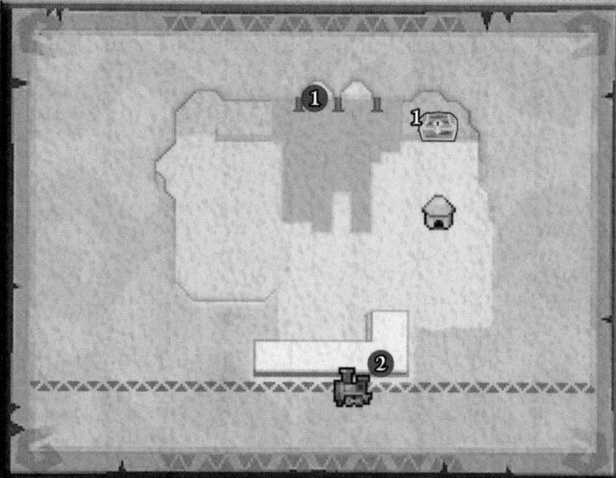

Wellspring Station

Legend

1 (chest)	Overworld Chest 20: Big Green Rupee
1	Stamp station
2	Train station

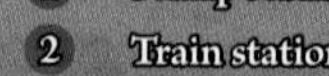

1 Explore Papuchia Village

2 Find Carben and Complete the Duet

3 Open the Way to the Temple

4 Clear the Ocean Temple

Items to Obtain

Big Green Rupee

Enemies Encountered

Crow

White Wolfos

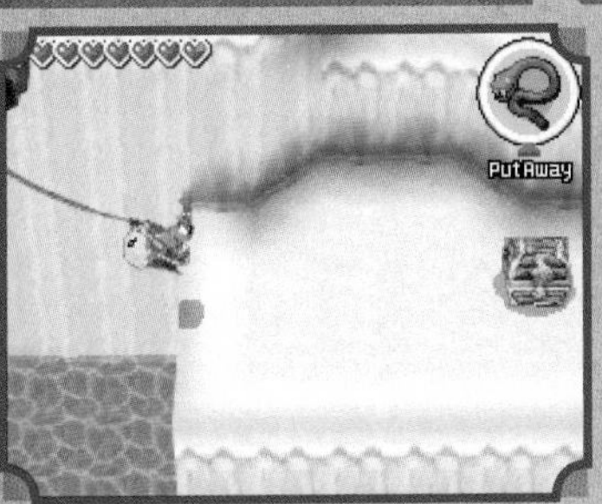

This is just a quick visit to Wellspring. Run to the region's northwest corner, and use your whip to swing across the overhead posts.

Your swinging lands you near a small chest. Crack it open to claim a Big Green Rupee! You can also use your boomerang and the blue torch to freeze the lake and reach the stamp station if you haven't done so already. When you're ready to go, return to your train and set a course for the Tower of Spirits. Cut through the tower and head back to the Forest Realm, making the short trip to Castle Town.

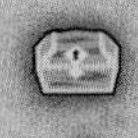

Overworld Chest 20: Big Green Rupee

Big Green Rupee

You got a Big Green Rupee! It's worth 100 Rupees!

Castle Town

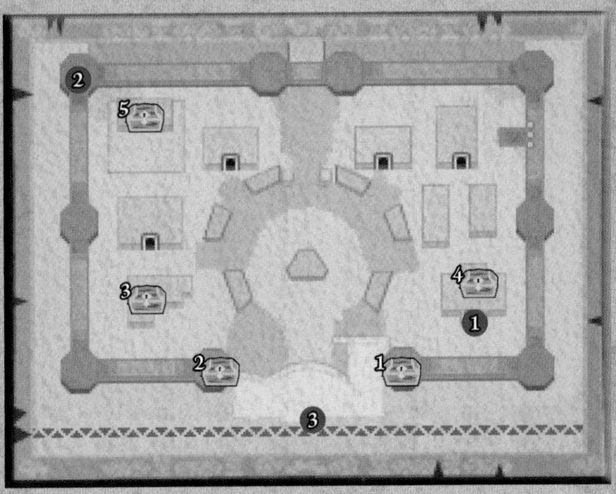

Castle Town

Legend

1 (chest)	Overworld Chest 9: Red Rupee
2 (chest)	Overworld Chest 10: Red Rupee
3 (chest)	Overworld Chest 21: Treasure
4 (chest)	Overworld Chest 22: Treasure
5 (chest)	Overworld Chest 23: Treasure
1	Bomb Bag 3
2	Stamp station
3	Train station

Items to Obtain

Bomb Bag 3

Treasure x3

Enemies Encountered

Spinut

Ice ChuChu

Freezard

Keese

Octorok

Rat

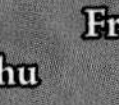

White Wolfos

Octive

Snapper

Geozard Chief

Geozard

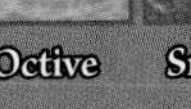

First Boss: Stagnox, Armored Colossus

Second Boss: Fraaz, Master of Icy Fire

Final Boss: Phytops, Barbed Menace

865
One.
Two.
Forget it.
OK then, what level do you want to try?
Menu

When you arrive at Castle Town, go to the "Take 'Em All On" challenge, which you beat after clearing the Forest Temple and scoring Heart Container 2. You're now able to attempt the challenge's second level, delving far deeper into a much longer dungeon.

You face a slew of enemies, so make sure you've got plenty of life before you head in. You may even want to bring a potion or two.

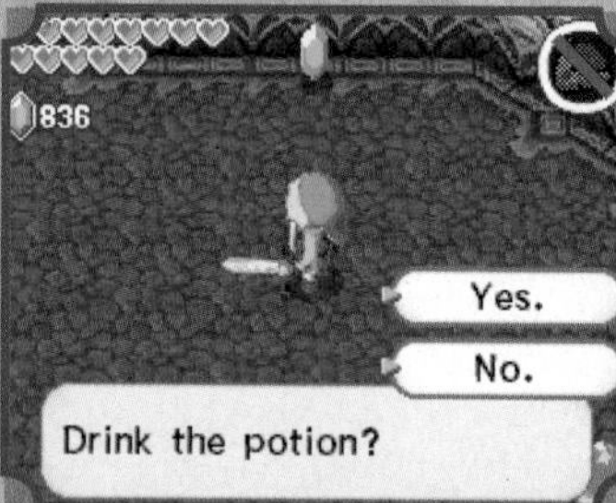
836
Yes.
No.
Drink the potion?

This time, the boss of the challenge is Phytops—though you also face Stagnox and Fraaz again. Best these three brutish bosses to clear the challenge and win the third and final Bomb Bag!

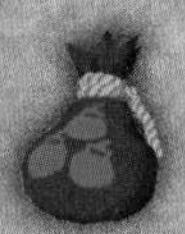

Bomb Bag 3

You got another Bomb Bag! Now you can carry maximum bombs!

Next, exit the challenge shop and go east. Find a building with a Cucco on top, and play the Song of Birds to lure the Cucco down within reach. Grab the Cucco and run to the ramparts.

With Cucco in hand, you're able to glide over to a few chests that have been tempting you since you first came to Castle Town. Simply jump from the south rampart wall to glide over to the southeast and southwest buildings; each has a chest sitting atop them. Both chests contain valuable treasures.

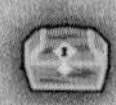

Overworld Chest 21: Treasure

Treasure

You got a treasure! Check it out on the Collection screen!

Overworld Chest 22: Treasure

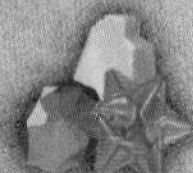

Treasure

You got a treasure! Check it out on the Collection screen!

The chest sitting atop the building near the Cucco stable isn't quite so easy to reach. Carry a Cucco back up to the ramparts, but this time, leap from the north wall, gliding to the roof of the northeast building.

Jump to the neighboring building to the west, and from there, make a daring leap onto the stone statue of a lion near the town's center.

1 Explore Papuchia Village
Menu

2 Find Carben and Complete the Duet

3 Open the Way to the Temple

4 Clear the Ocean Temple

There's not much margin for error when leaping to the stone statue; do your best to stick the landing. Leap to the other lion statue to the west, and from there, jump to the building with the last remaining treasure chest.

You got the ancient gold piece! Check it out on the Collection screen!

All this crazy Cucco hopping has been worth the effort: The chest contains a super-rare treasure!

Overworld Chest 23: Treasure

Treasure

You got a treasure! Check it out on the Collection screen!

1080
My husband has vanished! Where could he have gone?
Menu

For your next trick, enter the building south of the Cucco stable to speak with a woman whose rabbit-lover of a husband has vanished. She must be married to the guy who runs Rabbitland Rescue! Tell her you know where her husband is and agree to take her there. It'll be worth the trip!

Rabbitland Rescue

1
1

Rabbitland Rescue

Legend

1 Overworld Chest 5: Treasure

1 Train station

Items to Obtain

Force Gem 3

Thank you so much for bringing me all this way to meet him!

Drive with care as you ferry the woman to Rabbitland Rescue. It's not far, and you should be well accustomed to driving with passengers by this point. When you arrive, the woman streaks off in search of her husband without delay.

Sure enough, the rescue's owner is indeed the woman's husband. He gets an earful, and the woman walks away in a huff, demanding to be taken home.

I can't begin to understand your obsession with them!

You got a Force Gem! The Forest rail map has started glowing!

Return to the train to find that the woman's had a change of heart. She suddenly realizes how important this hobby is to her husband and is actually overjoyed to share this unusual love of fluffy bunnies with him. In fact, the woman becomes so happy that a Force Gem appears. That's your third Force Gem so far!

Force Gem 3

You got a Force Gem! The Forest Rail Map has started glowing!

Scoring Force Gem 4

Items to Obtain

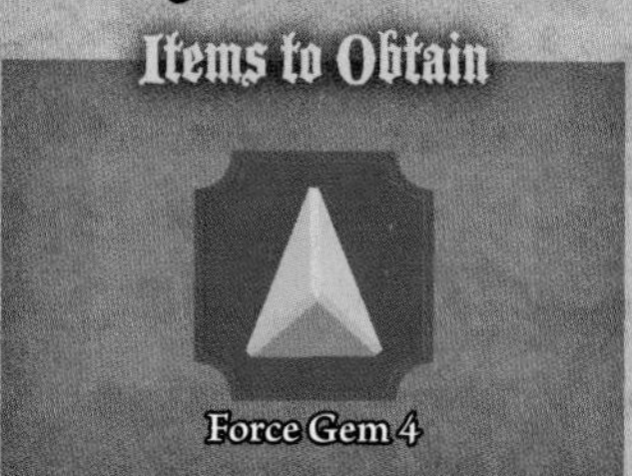

Force Gem 4

Enemies Encountered

Snurgle	Dark Train	Bulblin	Skulltula	Bullbo

You're able to find one more Force Gem before returning to the Tower of Spirits. Begin by visiting Aboda Village, the place where it all began. Find and speak to the boy there who tricked Link into stirring up a beehive at the start of this adventure.

The boy has a dream of seeing the world from way up in the sky, like a bird. He could get a view like that from Beedle's Air Shop! Tell the boy you know a place where he can fly like a bird, then start out in search of Beedle's balloon. Do your best to keep the rides smooth and steady as you track Beedle down.

Tip

Remember: Beedle's Air Shop appears on your map while you're cruising the overworld. Follow that merchant!

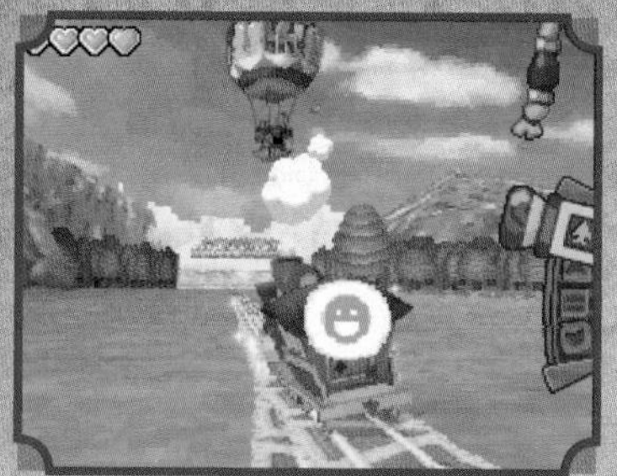

When you get close to Beedle's balloon, toot your whistle to make him land nearby. Then simply pull up and park to complete your task. The boy is thrilled to board the balloon—so thrilled that a Force Gem suddenly appears!

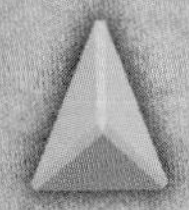

Force Gem 4

You got a Force Gem! The Forest Rail Map has started glowing!

Rabbit Roundup

You've done just about all you can before returning to the Tower of Spirits. Finding all those Force Gems has opened up a lot more track. With Force Gems 1 through 4 obtained, and much of the Ocean Realm open to exploration, you're now able to track down a few more bunnies. Check the overworld map and make sure you've collected forest rabbits 1 through 9, snow rabbits 1 through 7, and ocean rabbits 1 through 7 for a grand total of 23 rabbits. You don't have to find them all right now, of course, but the option's there!

1 Explore Papuchia Village

2 Find Carben and Complete the Duel

3 Open the Way to the Temple

4 Clear the Ocean Temple

Climbing Higher: Tower of Spirits 4

The Ocean Temple has been purified, its sacred energy made to flow into the Tower of Spirits once more. With a large new portion of the great tower to explore, Link and Princess Zelda can hardly wait to return to Anjean for their next assignment!

A Link to the Present

Items Already Acquired

Enemies Encountered

Task 1: Report Back to Anjean

Back to the Tower

Take care during your voyage back to the Tower of Spirits, for battalions of Cannon Boats now patrol the Ocean Realm's waters. The land hasn't gotten any safer, either; you may now encounter groups of deadly Tanks in other realms. These two new adversaries are somewhat similar, always appearing in threes to bombard your train with heavy cannon fire. Blast their inbound cannonballs from the sky, and counter at once to destroy these dangerous threats.

Cannon Boats

Hits to Defeat: 3 each
Attack Type: Range
Power: N/A
Damage: 1 heart

Threat Meter

Tanks

Hits to Defeat: 3 each
Attack Type: Range
Power: N/A
Damage: 1 heart

Threat Meter

1045
Yes, the next temple is hidden in a mountain of fire.
Menu

Keep a steady course and return to the Tower of Spirits to seek council from Anjean. The old Lokomo says the next realm is one of fire, and as usual, you must obtain its rail map from the tower's new top floor. Better get a move on, then! Run all the way up the staircase and enter the highest door.

Task 2: Retrieve the Fire Rail Map

Tower of Spirits, Fourth Visit

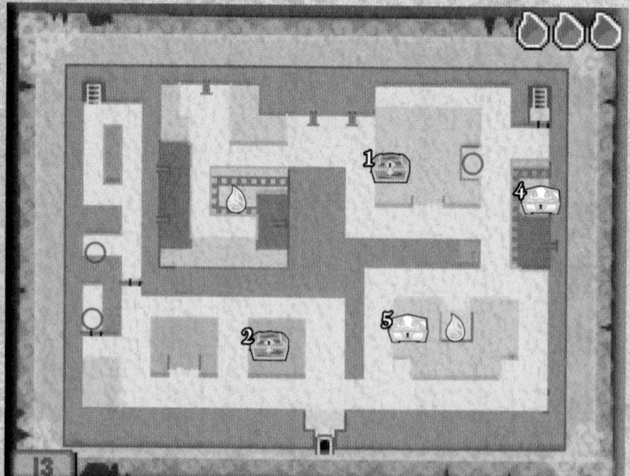

Tower of Spirits, Thirteenth Floor

Tower of Spirits, Fourteenth Floor

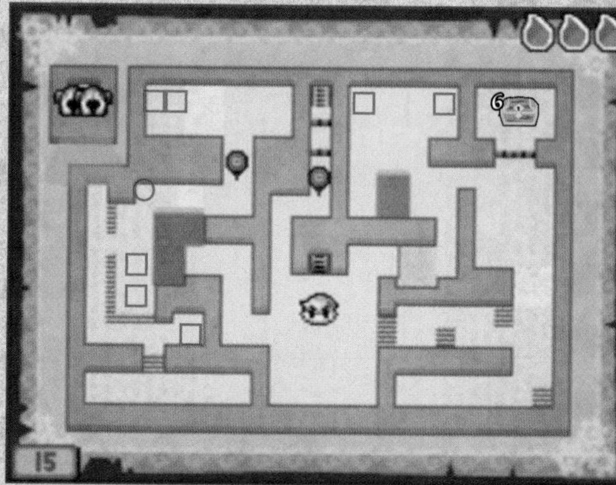

Tower of Spirits, Fifteenth Floor

Legend

- 1 Dungeon Chest 1: Small Key
- 2 Dungeon Chest 2: Small Key
- 3 Dungeon Chest 3: Treasure
- 4 Dungeon Chest 4: Treasure
- 5 Dungeon Chest 5: Treasure
- 6 Dungeon Chest 6: Small Key
- Floor switch
- 1 Fire Rail Map
- Switch
- Tear of Light

1 Report Back to Anjean

2 Retrieve the Fire Rail Map

3 Endure Encounter with Byrne

4 Journey to the Fire Realm

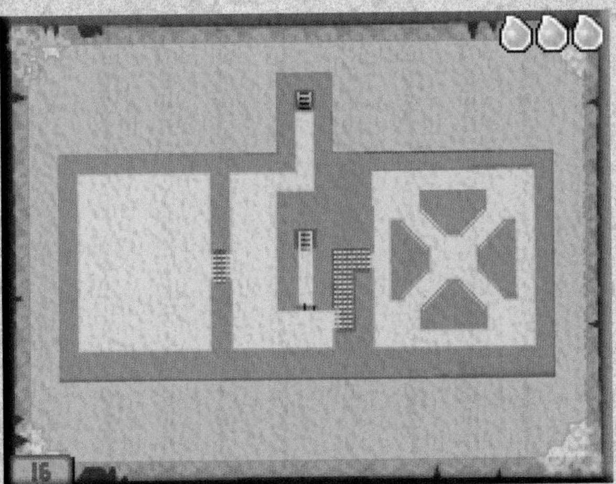

Tower of Spirits, Sixteenth Floor

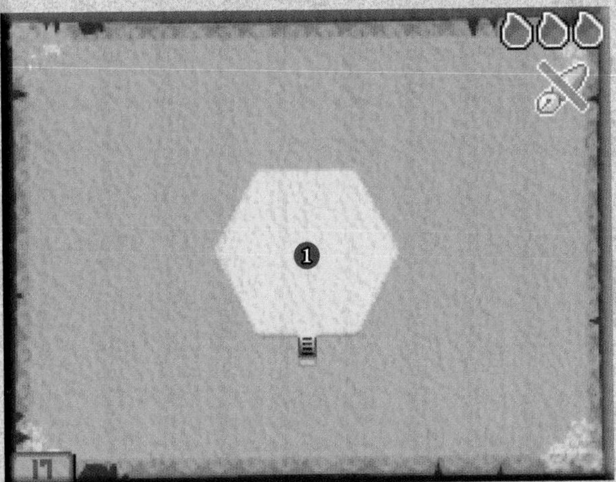

Tower of Spirits, Seventeenth Floor

Items to Obtain

Fire Rail Map
Small Key x3
Tear of Light x3
Treasure x3

Enemies Encountered

Tower of Spirits: Thirteenth Floor

Beware all those little eyeballs you see on your map when you enter the thirteenth floor. They represent new adversaries called Phantom Eyes, which act as sentries for Warp Phantoms. As their name implies, Warp Phantoms can instantly teleport to any Phantom Eye the moment it catches sight of an intruder—so keep well out of sight!

If you need to defeat a Phantom Eye, try stunning it by tossing the boomerang from around a corner. The Whirlwind can also stun a Phantom Eye. Stunned Phantom Eyes can't call for backup, allowing you to safely slip past or dispatch them with Link's sword.
Many Phantom Eyes reincarnate, returning to duty mere moments after you defeat them.

Phantom Eye

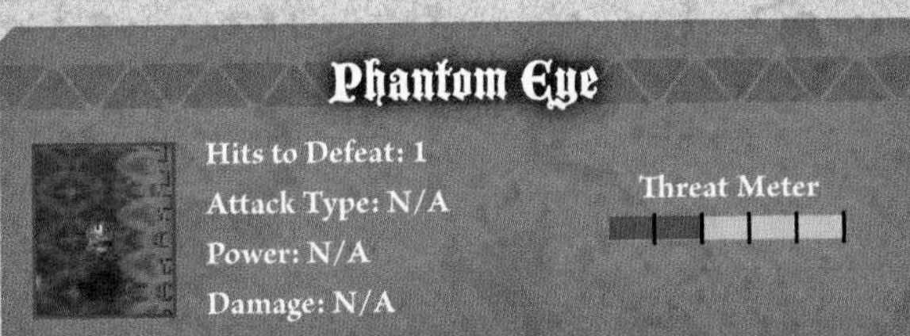

Hits to Defeat: 1
Attack Type: N/A
Power: N/A
Damage: N/A
Threat Meter

Warp Phantom

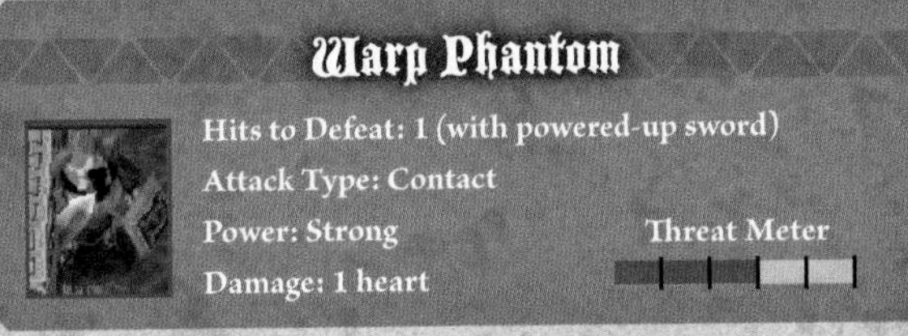

Hits to Defeat: 1 (with powered-up sword)
Attack Type: Contact
Power: Strong
Damage: 1 heart
Threat Meter

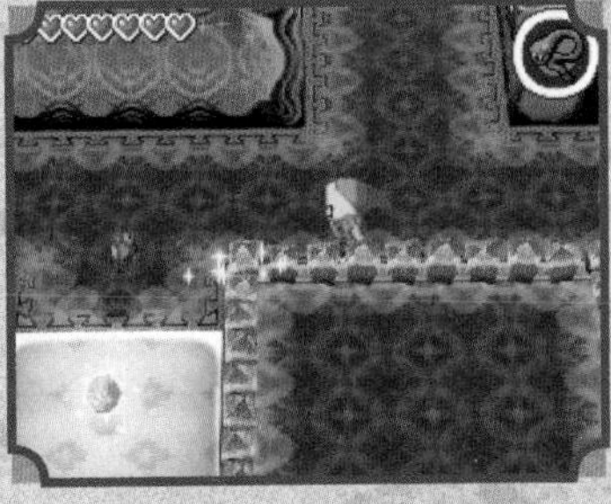

Go east and follow behind the patrolling Warp Phantom, keeping a safe distance. With the boomerang, stun from range the Phantom Eye near the southeast Tear of Light; then hurry over and collect the Tear of Light without being seen.

Tear of Light

You got a Tear of Light! Gather three of them to power up your sword!

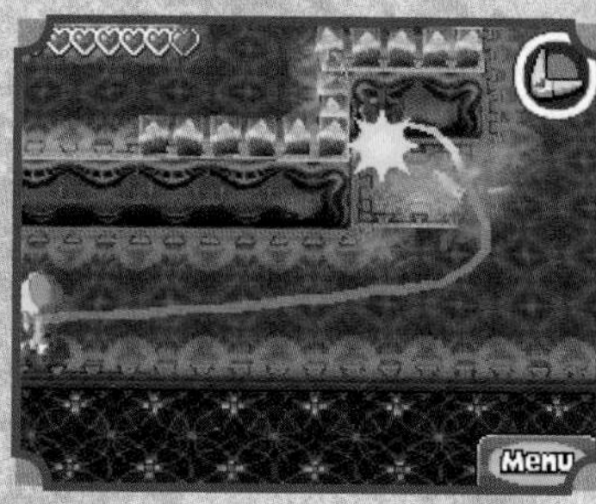

After grabbing the Tear of Light, note the big treasure chest you see on the high ledge close by. Then move to the south corridor and quickly use your boomerang to carry one torch's light to another. With the two torches lit, a hidden chest appears up north.

Make your way north without being noticed. Open the chest you just revealed to score a Small Key.

Dungeon Chest 1: Small Key

Small Key

You got a Small Key! Use this key to open locked doors!

Next, run to the northeast safe zone. Hit the switch you find there to extend a bridge linking two elevated platforms to the southwest. Note the large chest you see on the high ledge to the right of the safe zone.

Loop around and scale the nearby steps to climb onto the northeast platform. From this height, you can use the whip to yank out the sword from the fish sculpture in the north wall. Pull out the sword and toss it into the mouth of the fish sculpture to the right. This exposes another hidden chest on a high southwest platform.

Don't toss the sword into the fish sculpture on the left; doing so summons another Warp Phantom to the floor!

Use the whip to swing across the overhead posts to the left, landing on a high platform. Continue swinging across the subsequent gaps, turning south and working your way toward the second Tear of Light.

Swing over to the Tear of Light—get there quickly, before the Phantom Eye can alert a Warp Phantom. Snag the Tear of Light and remain in the safe zone as you dispatch the Phantom Eye, ending its threat.

Tear of Light

You got a Tear of Light! Gather three of them to power up your sword!

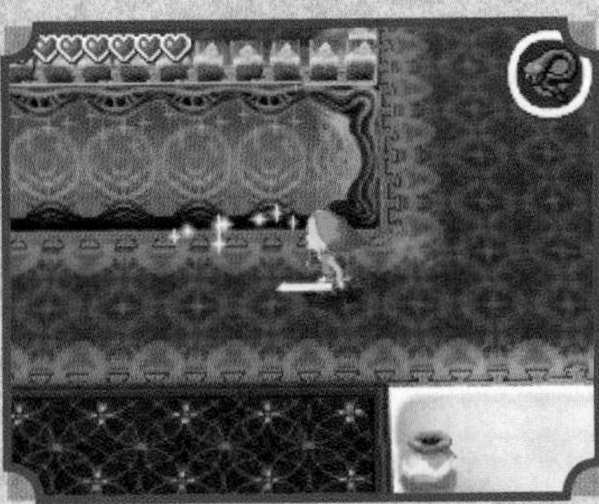

Swing back around and out of this area, running clockwise around the floor to return to the entry door. Wait until the time is right, then make a break for the southwest platform's steps.

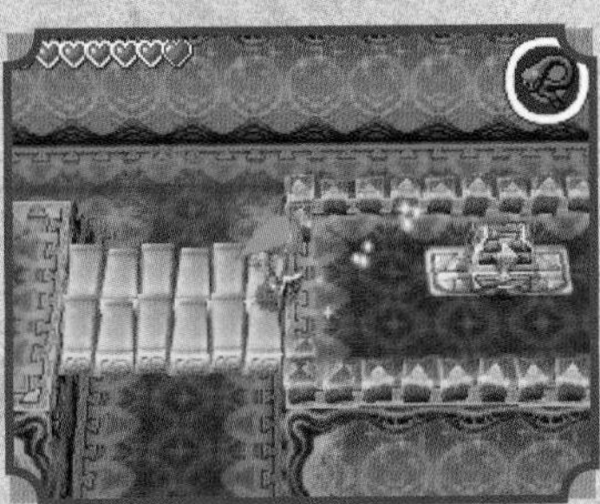

Cross the bridge you extended earlier, and open the chest you recently revealed to collect another Small Key. That makes two!

Dungeon Chest 2: Small Key

Small Key

You got a Small Key! Use this key to open locked doors!

Run back down the steps when it's clear, and open the locked door to the left. This leads to a small room with a switch. You can hit the switch, but it won't have any effect. You need to trigger the one above simultaneously, but there's a sealed door in the way.

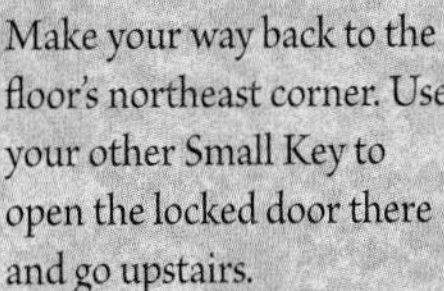

Make your way back to the floor's northeast corner. Use your other Small Key to open the locked door there and go upstairs.

Tower of Spirits: Fourteenth Floor

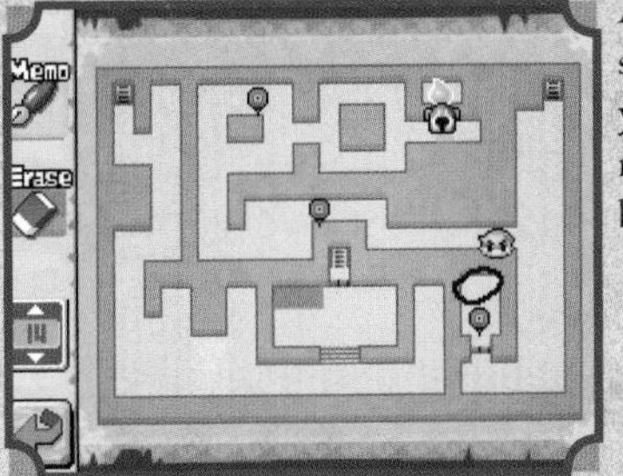

As you cross this floor's first safe zone, note the big chest you can see in the sealed room to the south. You'll be back for this soon.

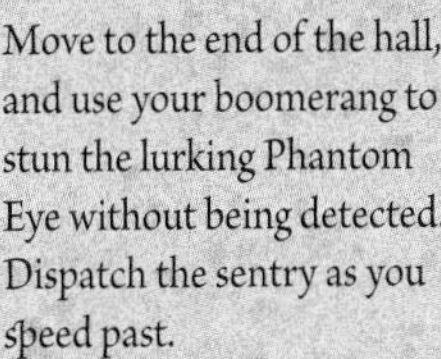

Move to the end of the hall, and use your boomerang to stun the lurking Phantom Eye without being detected. Dispatch the sentry as you speed past.

Stun the northern Phantom Eye in the same fashion, and defeat it as you advance toward the final Tear of Light.

A Warp Phantom stands watch over the third Tear of Light, and he isn't going anywhere. Lure the guardian away from his post by whacking a nearby wall with the sword.

When the Warp Phantom moves to investigate, circle around the corridor and dart into the safe zone he was blocking. Collect the third and final Tear of Light to power up Link's blade.

Tear of Light

You got a Tear of Light! Gather three of them to power up your sword!

Remain in the safe zone until the Warp Phantom returns to its post, then strike its back and have Zelda take possession. Cool, your very own Warp Phantom!

Now that Zelda's become a Warp Phantom, she can teleport to any Phantom Eye on the floor. Just draw a line from Zelda's marker to any Phantom Eye, and blink! Zelda warps there instantly and slays her unsuspecting beacon.

Use Zelda's new talent to warp to each Phantom Eye in turn, having her dispatch them so Link can backtrack out.

Make your way back down to the previous floor, pausing only to warp Zelda into the room with the big chest you noticed on your way in. Position Zelda on the room's floor switch to open its door so that Link may join her.

The large chest is yours for the taking. Open it with Link to collect a super-rare treasure.

Dungeon Chest 3: Treasure

Treasure

You got a treasure! Check it out on the Collection screen!

Tower of Spirits: Thirteenth Floor, Revisited

Back on the thirteenth floor, move Link onto the northeast platform so he may leap onto Zelda's back. Dispatch the roaming Phantom Eye first if you want to simplify the task of getting onto her back.

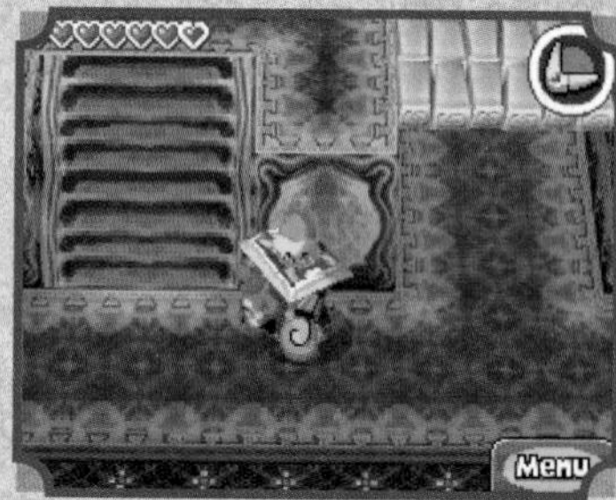

From the height of Zelda's back, Link can swing from the high whip post above the floor's east pit.

Open the chest you find on the pit's far ledge to score another precious treasure.

1 Report Back to Anjean

2 Retrieve the Fire Rail

3 Endure Encounter

4 Journey to the Fire Realm

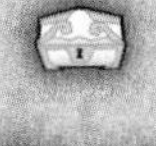

Dungeon Chest 4: Treasure

Treasure

You got a treasure! Check it out on the Collection screen!

Swing back across the pit and exploit the northeast platform again to return Link to Zelda's back. This time, mosey over to the floor's southeast platform and have Link leap onto it.

Now Link can open the large chest you noticed earlier, which contains yet another ultra-rare treasure.

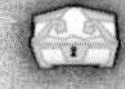

Dungeon Chest 5: Treasure

Treasure

You got a treasure! Check it out on the Collection screen!

You've looted this floor; now let's leave it. Make your way to its southwest corner. Leave Link near the switch you discovered earlier, and warp Zelda to the roaming Phantom Eye to the north.

Now Link and Zelda can trigger the twin switches together. Draw a line from Zelda to the switch on her side of the door, then quickly switch to Link and whack the other switch. Trigger both switches at the same time to open the door.

With the door open, Link is free to join Zelda on the other side. Reunite the two and proceed up the northwest stairs.

Tower of Spirits: Fourteenth Floor, Revisited

CAUTION

Beware: Blue ChuChus spring up from the ground on this half of the fourteenth floor, hoping to shock Link by surprise. Have Zelda take point and she'll neatly dispatch these minions.

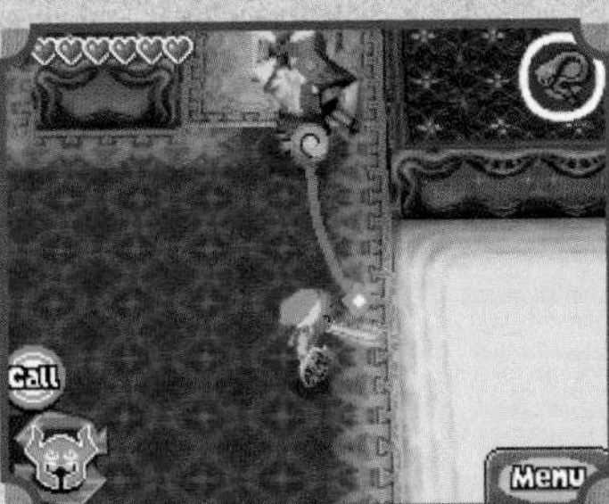

Uh-oh, Zelda can't cross the sandy patch of floor over here—her heavy armor makes her sink like a rock! Link's light enough to sprint across the sand, though; position Zelda onto the nearby floor switch and have Link go on alone.

Move Link onto another floor switch just beyond the sand pit. With both floor switches activated, a bridge extends over the sand for Zelda.

Advance Zelda past the floor spikes in the following hall. Place her on the red circle floor tile you discover to make it light up.

Switch to Link and have him stand on the matching red circle tile. This activates both tiles, causing Link and Zelda to trade positions.

Now use Link's whip to yank out a sword from one of the two fish sculptures in the nearby wall. Feed the sword to the other fish sculpture to open a nearby door, granting you access to the fifteenth floor.

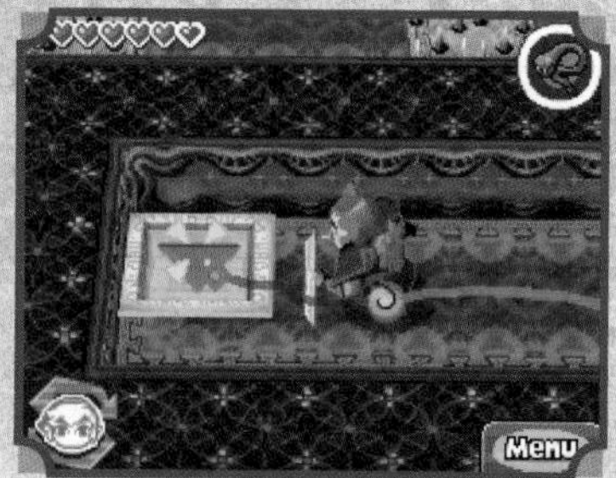

Loop Zelda around to the end of the southeast hall, where she finds a yellow triangle tile. Leave Zelda on the tile to make it light up, then switch to Link.

You guessed it: Move Link onto the matching floor tile to make him switch places with Zelda. Thanks, Princess!

Now explore the floor's east half with Link. Keep bombs at the ready so you can blow apart any Blue ChuChus that get in your way.

Tower of Spirits: Fifteenth Floor

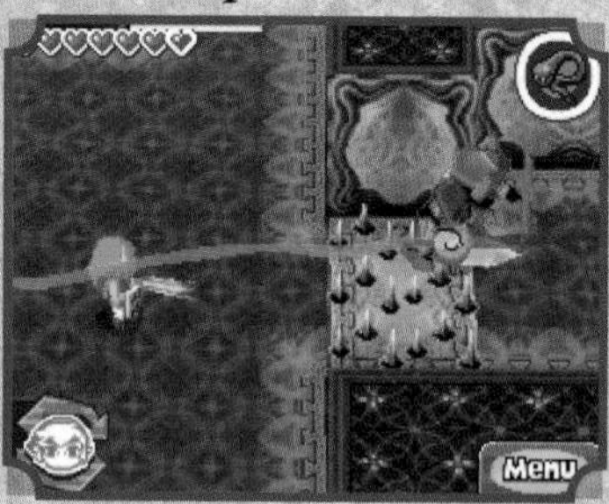

The tower's fifteenth floor is a bit confounding, so take it one step at a time. Begin by sending Zelda across the spikes to the east, where Link cannot follow.

Ready the whip as you cross some sand that would've sunk Zelda. A Geozard confronts you beyond the sand, and since Zelda's not around to help, Link has to get creative. Lash at the Zora's shield to strip it away, and unleash a furious series of attacks to quickly dispatch the beast.

1 Report Back to Anjean

2 Retrieve the Fire Rail Map

3 Endure Encounter with Byrne

4 Journey to the Fire Realm

Grab and shove the nearby block to the left, then slide it north, onto one of two floor switches. With the block in place, move Link onto the nearby blue square tile, lighting it up.

Take control of Zelda and move her onto the adjacent blue square tile. The princess and Link swap places once more.

Once Zelda's in the northern chamber, guide her onto the other floor switch. With Zelda and a block holding both switches down, the central hall's spikes retract, allowing Link to join Zelda on the floor's east half.

United again, Link and Zelda can open the giant northeast door. Order Zelda to shove one half of the door, then switch to Link and tap the other half to have him lend a hand. The two work together and shove the door wide open.

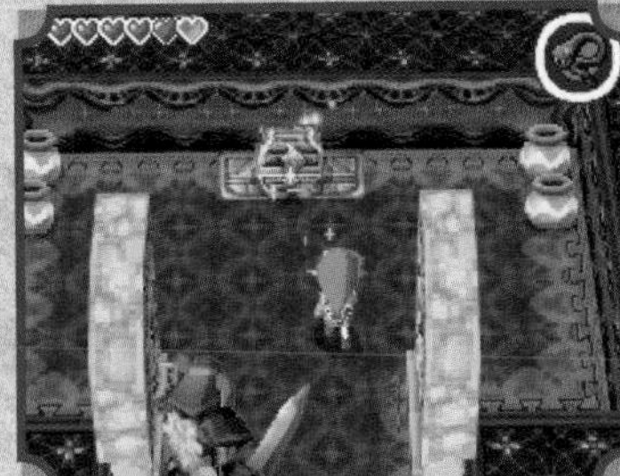

That great big door leads to a real small room. Smash the pots for hearts and items, and open the little chest here to obtain a Small Key.

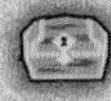

Dungeon Chest 6: Small Key

Small Key

You got a Small Key! Use this key to open locked doors!

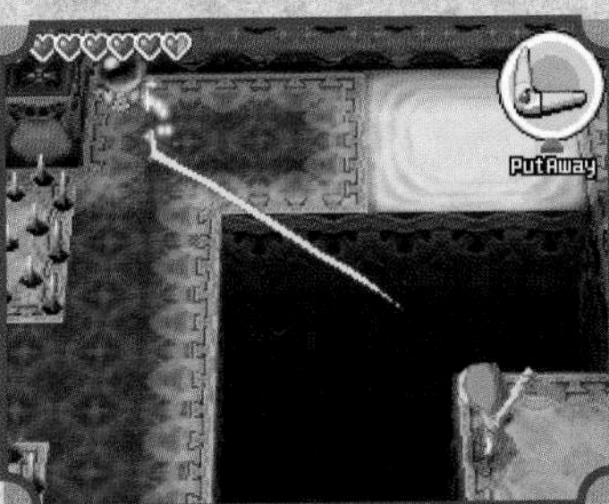

Get Link and Zelda back over to the entry stairs, then head down the west hall, which winds north and ends at a pit. Toss Link's boomerang across the pit to whack a distant switch.

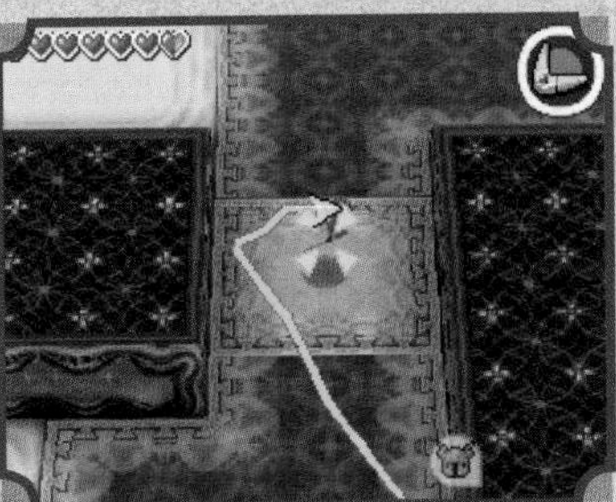

The switch extends a bridge across the nearby sand patch, which could only benefit Zelda. You must bring her there. Do so by tracing a line up to the northwest Phantom Eye. She's a Warp Phantom, remember?

Once Zelda's up north, steer her across the sand pit and down past the floor spikes. Keep going until you can position her atop the red circle floor tile located at the end of the southwest hall.

You know what to do: Move Link onto the matching red circle tile to swap his position for Zelda's. This puts Link on the floor's west half, but he's trapped by some floor spikes. That won't do at all!

Warp Zelda back up to the northwest Phantom Eye, and lead her across the sand patch once more. Have her stand on the floor switch near Link, which retracts the spikes and frees him from captivity.

Move Link past the spikes, then take control of Zelda. Have her cross the spikes to the north, and then move the princess in front of the tumbling boulders to the west.

Hurry Link up the west passage while Zelda does her best to block the boulders. Get Link past the spikes quickly, but don't move him too close to that Phantom Eye! Step on the nearby pair of floor switches to extend a bridge that soon comes in handy.

Call to Zelda after Link is safely past the spikes and out of harm's way. Use the boomerang to stun the nearby Phantom Eye without alerting it, but don't defeat it.

Quickly switch to the Whirlwind and use it to blow the dazed Phantom Eye north and then west, past some sand and over to a pair of floor switches. Don't worry, the Whirlwind's cyclones will keep the Phantom Eye stunned.

Once the Phantom Eye is beyond the sand and close to the floor switches, quickly switch to Zelda and trace a line to warp her over, bypassing the sand. Eliminate the Phantom Eye afterward to ensure that it doesn't sound the alarm.

Now position Zelda and Link on the two floor switches. This opens a door in the central hall. A switch to the south, near the rolling boulders and spikes, extends a bridge.

You're outta here! Cross that new bridge, and have Zelda wipe out the central Phantom Eye. Then advance Link and use the Small Key you found earlier to unlock the way upstairs.

1 Report Back to Anjean

2 Retrieve the Fire Rail Map

3 Endure Encounter with Byrne

4 Journey to the Fire Realm

Tower of Spirits: Sixteenth Floor

The sixteenth floor is a giant puzzle whose secrets are revealed by its map. The stone tablet in the central hall instructs you to move from "the green tile to the red," saying that the "path you walk will create a special symbol." What could it mean?

Get another clue by warping Zelda over to the east Phantom Eye. Have her speak with the patrolling Warp Phantom to learn that the pattern he's walking holds special meaning.

Now warp Zelda over to the west Phantom Eye. The chamber she appears in is dominated by a massive square of floor tiles; the nearest one is green, and the farthest one is red.

Have you figured it out? Move Zelda onto the green floor tile, then watch your map. Watch the east Warp Phantom's patrol route and steer Zelda around the floor tiles in the same pattern. From the green tile, move Zelda in the following fashion to solve the puzzle:

1. Directly south
2. Diagonally northeast
3. Directly west, back to the green starting space
4. Diagonally southeast, down to the red ending space

Completing the pattern with Zelda opens the central door, allowing you to advance to the next floor. You're all finished here; reunite Link and the princess, and head upstairs.

Tower of Spirits: Seventeenth Floor

The Fire Rail Map is housed in the lone chamber that is the tower's seventeenth floor. You've made it! After Zelda is banished from her Warp Phantom body and the light fades from Link's sword, race onto the platform and snatch up that rail map.

Fire Rail Map

You got the Fire Rail Map! Some of the lost Spirit Tracks on it are reappearing!

Task 3: Endure Encounter with Byrne

Sadly, the celebration is cut short when an unwelcome visitor crashes the party: Byrne has returned! After a brief spat with Anjean about their past relationship as master and student, Byrne soon unleashes his power against the princess and Link. Anjean acts fast, shielding Link and Zelda from her former student's assault.

Anjean urges Link and Zelda to rush to the Fire Realm before suddenly transporting them down to the tower's base. Left alone with her twisted student, the old Lokomo prepares to defend herself.

Link crashes down at the base of the tower, right next to the Spirit Train. Anjean's bought him time to reach the Fire Realm—better get rolling!

Task 4: Journey to the Fire Realm

To the Fire Realm

Jump in the Fire

To reach the Fire Realm, you must go east from the Snow Realm. At the tower's base, tell Zelda you wish to go to the Snow Realm, then set an eastward course when you get there.

Missing Link: Teacher Trolly

Hang on, there's no need to rush off to the Fire Realm just yet. Swing by Castle Town and you can ease an old friend's fears—and make a tidy profit in the process!

Pull up to Castle Town Station and you'll now find Teacher waiting at the platform. At least we *think* it's Teacher. That *is* a pretty cunning disguise he's got on.

Teacher wishes to search for the princess and asks if you'll take him to his detination, saying he'll make it worth your while. Accept the offer, and the old man steps on board without delay. Where he wants to go changes every day. He may want to go to Aboda Village, Papuchia, or Anouki Village. Later, his options will include Goron Village and Castle Town.

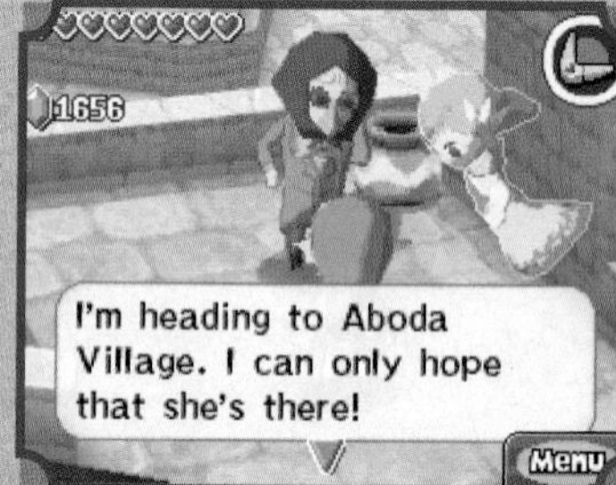

Ferry Teacher to his destination as you've done with many others in the past: Obey the signposts; avoid taking damage; and make a slow, safe stop at the station platform when you arrive. Above all, keep away from those pesky Dark Trains!

Teacher is grateful to be out in search of his beloved princess and rewards Link handsomely for his trouble. The amount of Rupees he hands over depends on how happy Teacher is when he arrives. Do your best to make it a smooth journey, for dropping off a delighted Teacher can net you a fast 300 Rupees!

1669
And here's your fee--300 Rupees. See you next time, young man.
Menu

1 Report Back to Anjean

2 Retrieve the Fire Rail Map

3 Endure Encounter with Byrne

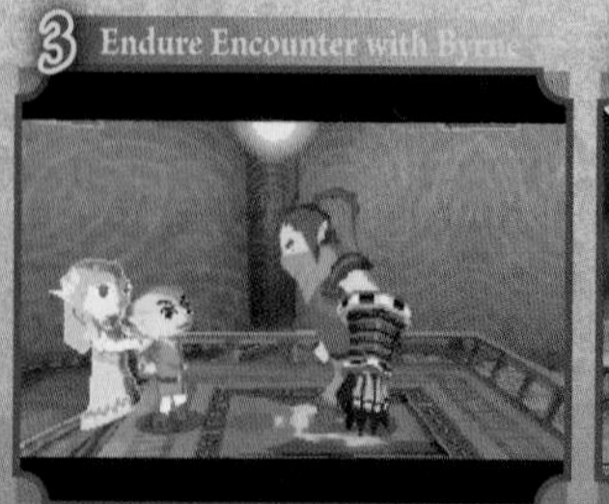

4 Journey to the Fire Realm

Boiling Point: The Fire Realm

Byrne's sneak attack on Link and Princess Zelda couldn't have come at a worse time. The evil henchman appeared just as the two had finally discovered the Fire Rail Map! Fortunately, Anjean showed up in time to distract Byrne and help Link and the princess escape. If only she'd also been able to tell them the Fire Realm guardian's name!

A Link to the Present

Items Already Acquired

 Task 1: Explore the Fire Realm 

Fire in the Sky

A terrible sound booms from the horizon as Link and Zelda ride into the Fire Realm. The local volcano is active, and it's spewing fiery debris!

Flaming boulders rain down everywhere as you delve into this foreboding place. Be prepared to blast them out of your way, for some will crash down right on the tracks!

If you like, you can pull up to the northern of the two visible stations on your map—but there's no pressing reason to do so at present. This is the Goron Target Range, but it's closed at the moment due to the frightening volcanic activity.

Set a course to the east station instead, passing through a mountain tunnel on your way. The station platform is right outside the tunnel, so begin to slow as you near the tunnel's exit. Put it in park and explore this new location.

Goron Village

Goron Village

Goron Village West

Legend

1 (chest)	Overworld Chest 24: Treasure
2 (chest)	Overworld Chest 25: Treasure
3 (chest)	Overworld Chest 26: Treasure
1	Stamp station
○	Switch
2	Train station

1 Explore the Fire Realm

2 Aid Goron Village

3 Find the Fire Sanctuary

4 Clear the Fire Temple

Items to Obtain

Treasure x3 Trusty Freight Car

Enemies Encountered

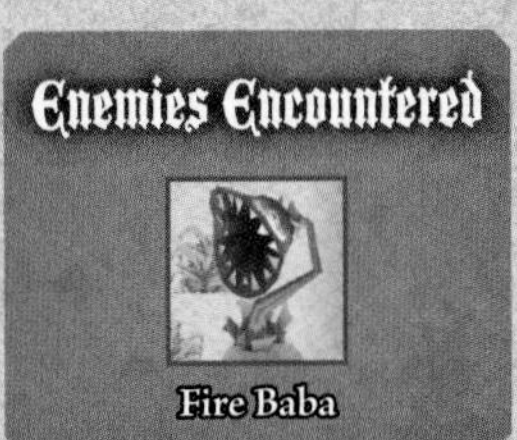

Fire Baba

Burning City

Link and the princess have come to a city of rugged mountain folk known as Gorons. The place is in chaos due to the volcano's sudden awakening; several paths are blocked off by fiery debris, separating many Gorons from their homes.

Pop into the local shop if you're low on bombs or potions, and pick some up. Notice that the shop also sells a quiver. You can't buy this valuable item until you've found a bow, but don't forget where you saw it!

Speak to the villagers gathered near the flaming debris. They inform you that the debris is cutting off all access to the village proper. One suggests that you speak with a Goron sage named Kagoron, who is praying at his altar at the top of the mountain path. Make your way down the west path to begin your search for Kagoron.

At the east side of the village, scale the steps and speak with a Goron merchant who deals in iron. You can't trade with the merchant, but you can open the little chest hidden behind his stock to score a treasure!

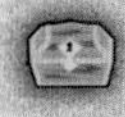

Overworld Chest 24: Treasure

Treasure

You got a treasure! Check it out on the Collection screen!

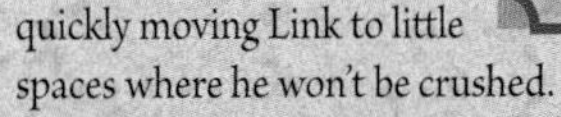

Rolling Boulders

Getting to Kagoron's altar won't be easy, for the Goron Village's west half is filled with danger. Huge boulders tumble down the tight passages, forcing you to dart from one safe spot to the next. Be patient and watch how the boulders roll, quickly moving Link to little spaces where he won't be crushed.

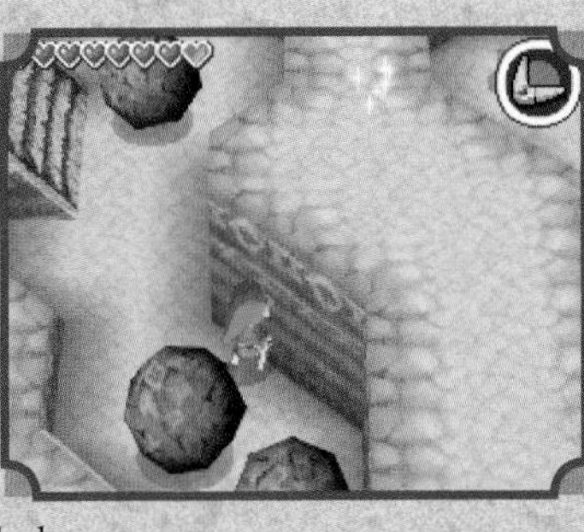

You eventually reach a small clearing where patches of grass are growing. Hack down the grass for hearts if you need them, then use the whip to swing across the north lava.

Climb up the steps on the far ledge and whip-swing again to reach the region's northwest corner. Beware: Two terrible Fire Plants spring up when you land! Sprint up the steps to get away from these dangerous local life-forms.

Fire Baba

Hits to Defeat: 2
Attack Type: Contact and Range
Power: Strong
Damage: 1/2 heart (both attacks)

Threat Meter

Fire Plants are rooted to the ground but spit searing flames at Link from range. The flames can't be blocked, so you've got to stay mobile. Hurling bombs at these menaces is a quick way to eliminate them, but if you're quick to target them, you may find it easier to defeat them with Link's Power Leap attack.

NOTE

Link automatically leap-attacks when you tap enemies that are a bit out of his reach. Like spin attacks, leap attacks deal twice the sword's normal damage. This means just one well-timed leap attack can defeat a Fire Baba.

Defeat the two Fire Plants on the ledge, then use the nearby stamp station to record your fourteenth stamp. One more and you can return to Niko for another present!

Swing back across the lava and whack a nearby switch. This extends a bridge up north and starts a timer.

Quickly switch back to the whip and swing across the lava. Turn right and sprint across the bridge you extended before it retracts. If time runs out, you'll need to swing back across the lava and try again.

Beyond the bridge, a wooden sign points to a shortcut leading back down the mountain. You haven't found Kagoron yet, but head north to find him at his prayer altar.

Kagoron the Wise

Kagoron is surprised to see Link and doesn't feel comfortable saying much to an outsider. Tell Kagoron you wish to speak with the Goron elder, and he'll ask you to meet him at your train.

Back Down the Mountain

Leave Kagoron's altar and run down the east path, taking the shortcut down the mountain. Swing across a couple of whip posts to clear a long pool of smoldering lava.

You discover a small chest up the stairs past the lava. Crack it open for another lovely treasure.

Overworld Chest 25: Treasure

Treasure

You got a treasure! Check it out on the Collection screen!

Remain on the high cliff and run past the Goron iron merchant without dropping down. Go north and drop onto the next cliff below, near the rolling boulders.

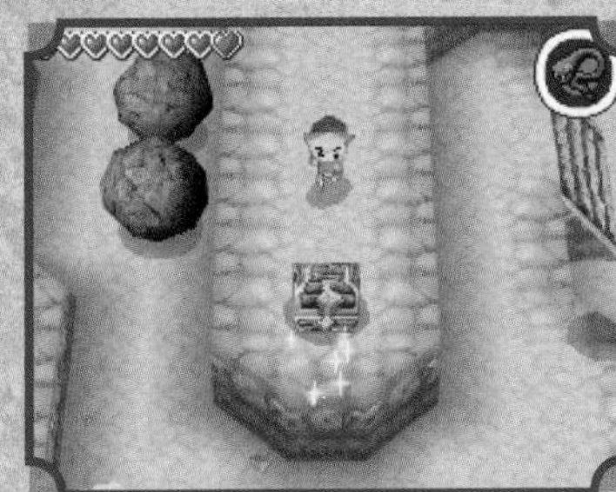

Run to the cliff's south end and open yet another small chest to score your third treasure from this area.

Overworld Chest 26: Treasure

Treasure

You got a treasure! Check it out on the Collection screen!

Now return to the village's train station. Kagoron greets you by rolling out a new addition for your trolley: a handy Freight Car!

Trusty Freight Car

You got a Freight Car! Now you can transport goods from one location to another!

2003
Use that freight car to bring something that can cool down the lava.
Menu

Kagoron entreats Link to bring something cold to the village, something that could cool the lava and debris that's blocking up the main trail. He advises that Link speak with merchants in villages he's been to and see if anyone can sell him something that might do the trick. Since it's something cold you're after, there's no better place to begin your search than Anouki Village! Set a course and be off at once, expecting to encounter the usual enemies along the way.

Task 2: Aid Goron Village

Anouki Village

Anouki Village

Legend

Symbol	Description
1 (chest)	Overworld Chest 6: Red Rupee
2 (chest)	Overworld Chest 7: Big Red Rupee
(bomb)	Bomb wall
1	Stamp station
2	Train station

Enemies Encountered

Ice ChuChu

Slimed

Step off the platform when you arrive at Anouki Village and run northwest, whipping any Ice ChuChus that pop up to block you. Speak with the little Anouki near the pool, who's excited to hear you've acquired a Freight Car.

2026
And ever since, there's been a gooey film floatin' on the surface... It's revoltin'!
Menu

The Anouki merchant deals in Mega Ice, which sounds like just the thing you need. Unfortunately, the local spring has recently been fouled by an Ice ChuChu that decided to hop in for a soak. Now there's a gooey film on the water's surface—it's no longer fit for making Mega Ice!

2026
Thank ya kindly! I owe ya one, guy! OK, I'll be waitin' for ya on the train.
Menu

The Anouki is also excited to hear that Link's train has a passenger car, and he asks to be taken somewhere with a more pure water source. Agree to take the Anouki someplace new, and he'll hurry off to board your train.

Think about where you could find a new source of water while running to the train station. The saltwater of the Ocean Realm certainly won't do; you need to find a pure source. Something like a natural spring or water from a well. Wait, that's it: Wellspring Station!

Wellspring Station

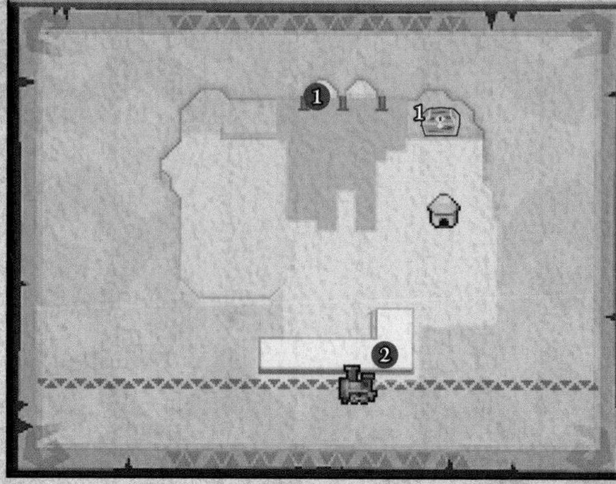

Wellspring Station

Legend

Icon	Description
1 (chest)	Overworld Chest 20: Big Green Rupee
1	Stamp station
2	Train station

Enemies Encountered

Crow, White Wolfos

Items to Obtain

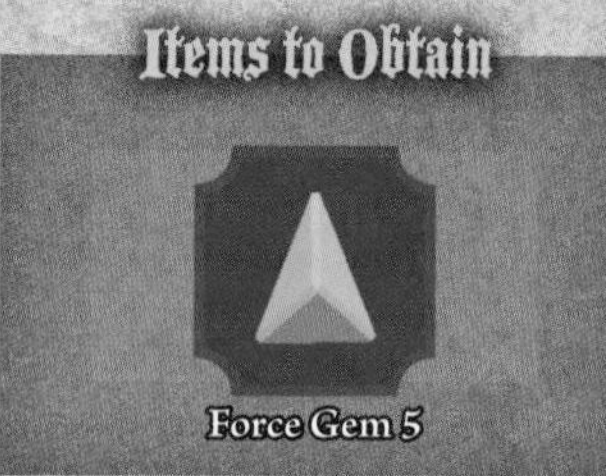

Force Gem 5

Mega Water Source

Arriving at Wellspring Station, the Anouki merchant is thrilled by your problem-solving prowess. His business saved, the little Anouki becomes overjoyed as he inspects the giant spring, and a Force Gem appears! This is the fifth Force Gem you've found, and it adds tracks to the Snow Realm's southern region.

Force Gem 5

You got a Force Gem! The Snow Rail Map has started glowing!

Getting a new Force Gem is all well and good, but you came here for Mega Ice. The Anouki doesn't want you seeing how he crafts his unique export and asks you to go away for a moment. Warm up inside Ferrus's house, then return to the Anouki to find a whole bunch of Mega Ice ready to go.

The Language of the Deal

The Anouki merchant may be grateful for your help, but he isn't in the business of just giving away Mega Ice. He'll fill your Freight Car for 25 Rupees, but you can haggle him down to 10 if you take the time. Keep telling him the cost is too steep and that you want it cheaper, and he'll eventually break down. Haggle long enough and you'll get it for free.

Once you've struck a bargain, the Anouki merchant loads 20 units of Mega Ice into your Freight Car. Great work! Now you've just got to bring the stuff back to Goron Village.

Back to Goron Village

Precious Cargo

Set a course for the Fire Realm and roll out. Be aware that you'll lose Mega Ice if you allow monsters to damage your train.

Snurgles are especially pesky, often swarming around your goods and attacking the freight directly—watch out for these beasts and don't let them ruin your cargo!

Because Mega Ice is a frozen commodity, it'll start to melt once you enter the heat of the Fire Realm. It doesn't melt all that quickly, but you still shouldn't dally. Put it in high gear and make for Goron Village.

Train Game

As you approach the first corner in the Fire Realm, you'll discover a Dark Train has been waiting for you on the track ahead. Great, it's blocking your route to Goron Village! There's no easy way past this Dark Train; you'll just have to reverse and turn left at the previous junction, taking the scenic route to your destination.

After making your turn, set a new course on the north rails, taking the shortest possible route to Goron Village. There are two more Dark Trains up here, but these two roam about haphazardly and can be outmaneuvered with a bit of care.

Your cargo won't be affected by sudden stops, so don't hesitate to slam it into reverse if you need to escape a Dark Train.

Mercifully, only one unit of Mega Ice is needed to cool the lava at Goron Village. Get there and speak with Kagoron, who stands near the train platform, to tell him of your success.

If you run out of Mega Ice, you can always return to Wellspring Station and pick up some more. Make sure to bargain with the Anouki merchant so you get the best deal.

Task 3: Find the Fire Sanctuary

Goron Village and Fire Sanctuary

Goron Village

Goron Village West

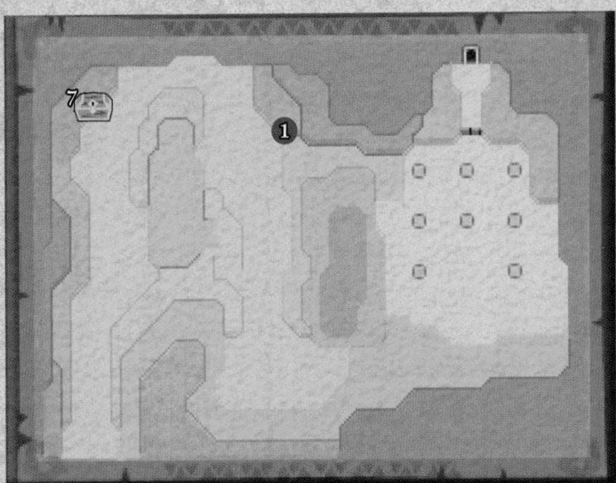
7
1

Fire Sanctuary

Legend

1 Overworld Chest 24: Treasure
2 Overworld Chest 25: Treasure
3 Overworld Chest 26: Treasure
4 Overworld Chest 27: Treasure
5 Overworld Chest 28: Treasure
6 Overworld Chest 29: Treasure
7 Overworld Chest 30: Treasure
Floor switch
1 Stamp station
Switch
2 Train station

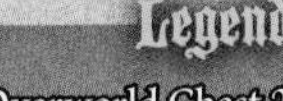

Items to Obtain

Treasure x4

Enemies Encountered

Fire Keese
Fire Baba

Like Like

Treasure Hunter

2142
Oh! Wonderful! We can use this to chill the lava that is keeping us from crossing.
Menu

The Mega Ice does its work on the lava, cooling it down and opening the way to the center of town. Now you can explore more of Goron Village! Kagoron is so pleased that he lets you keep the Freight Car as a token of his gratitude. Score!

NOTE

Ignore the Goron villager near the station who asks for a ride to Anouki Village. We'll get to him in a moment!

2250
Sure.
I'm busy.
Will you please bring more of the cold stuff?
Menu

With the lava out of your way, sprint north and explore the northern half of Goron Village. Run up the steps to the east and assure a Goron villager that you'll bring more Mega Ice to cool the remaining lava that's keeping the Goron from returning to his home.

You'll have a chance to transport more Mega Ice soon. For now, leave the poor Goron to his plight and run up the north steps, exploring the higher cliffs. Cross an elevated footbridge to find a chest that contains a treasure.

Overworld Chest 27: Treasure

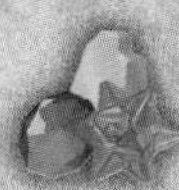

Treasure

You got a treasure! Check it out on the Collection screen!

Continue south and notice three pots sitting close together. Play the Song of Discovery here to expose a hidden chest, which also holds treasure.

Overworld Chest 28: Treasure

Treasure

You got a treasure! Check it out on the Collection screen!

Meeting the Elder

That's all the loot you can get from the village for now. Drop to the main ground and enter the northernmost house to at last speak with the Goron tribe's elder.

The elder is surprised by Link's intrusion at first, but he finds reason to trust the young hero when his grandson recounts how Link helped out the village. He agrees to let Link pass, saying the tunnel behind him leads to the Fire Sanctuary. Thanks, Gramps!

To the Fire Sanctuary

You must pass through a short cavern to reach the Fire Sanctuary. This cavern is small enough to be considered part of Goron Village. Use the whip, the Whirlwind, or boomerang to safely dispatch the Fire Keese that flutter about.

Swing across the northern lava to reach a collection of pots and a floor switch. Break the pots for prizes and then step on the switch to extend a couple of bridges.

You can't yet reach the small chest that tempts you from a high ledge, so cross the bridge you just extended to reach another group of pots. Three of the pots are jiggling—don't break them or you'll release some Like Likes! Smash the others for loot, then scamper up the steps to the north.

After scaling the steps, run to the left to locate the chest you saw earlier. Open it to score a rare treasure, then backtrack and go up more steps to return to the surface.

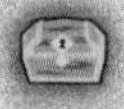

Overworld Chest 29: Treasure

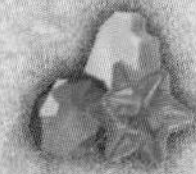

Treasure

You got a treasure! Check it out on the Collection screen!

Taming the Fire Sanctuary

The Fire Sanctuary is anything but a safe haven. Searing fireballs fall from the sky, and the trail you must navigate is lined with dangerous Fire Plants. Take it nice and slow, moving just close enough to each Fire Baba to make them emerge from their pods; then tap their heads to deliver fast, fatal leap attacks.

Pluck bombs from the surrounding bomb flowers and heave them at baddies for explosive results.

1 Explore the Fire Realm

2 Aid Goron Village

3 Find the Fire Sanctuary

4 Clear the Fire Temple

Torches stand along the trail as well, some lit and some not. Use the boomerang to spread fire to each and every torch, dispatching even more Fire Plants as you go.

Even if you're eager to visit Niko, you might as well finish exploring this area first. From the stamp station, drop off to the south and land on the ledge below, then run east to visit a clearing full of stone statues.

Lighting all of the torches extends three elevated footbridges to the north. After extending all three bridges, scale the nearby steps and begin exploring the cliffs you've been circling.

Read the nearby stone tablet, which tells a long tale full of clues on how you must proceed. The key hint is found at the story's end: something about a light shining.

Use the bridges to reach a northwest chest. Kick it open and claim yet another treasure.

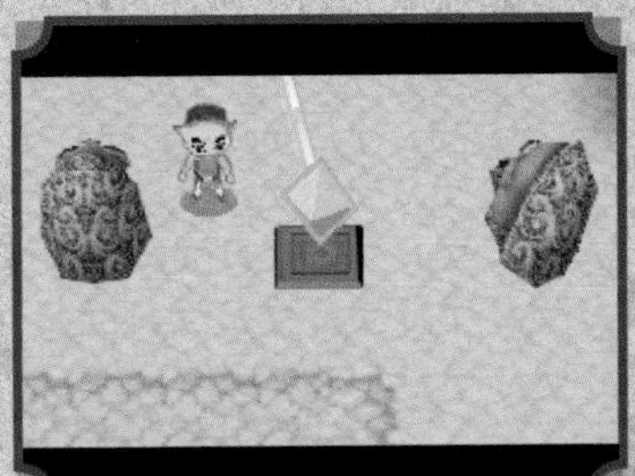

To solve this little riddle, move between the center and center-east statues, and play the Song of Light. This reveals a hidden crystal that emits a laser beam that points at the north door, opening the way forward.

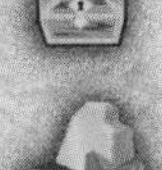

Overworld Chest 30: Treasure

Treasure

You got a treasure! Check it out on the Collection screen!

Continue exploring the cliffs, crossing the northernmost footbridge to discover a stamp station. Slap that stamp into your book to record your fifteenth stamp—enough to merit another reward from Niko!

The Fire Realm's Guardian

At long last, you've found this realm's resident Lokomo. The guardian's name is Embrose, and he's ready to teach you your part in the duet that restores more of the Fire Realm's Spirit Tracks.

As ever, practice your part thoroughly before attempting the real song. Focus on the metronome to help you keep the timing, and don't let Embrose's part interfere with yours.

After a righteous jam session, Link's Fire Rail Map starts to glow. New tracks have appeared, running all the way to the Fire Temple! Embrose congratulates Link on a job well done, then warns him of danger surrounding the temple. His parting words are to seek advice from the Gorons.

The Fire rail map has started glowing! New tracks have appeared!

Goron Advisors

1709
There is a gate to the Fire Temple that is protected by three locks.
Menu

Trek out of the Fire Sanctuary, through the shot cavern, and back to the Goron elder's home. The elder is glad to hear of Link's success in finding Embrose, but he informs Link that the Fire Temple is protected by three locks. This was done to keep the curious at bay, but the plan has backfired: Mischievous monsters have stolen the keys to the locks, and now no one can enter!

Speak to other Goron villagers to learn key pieces of advice: The monsters who've taken the keys must be tackled head-on, and they don't enjoy loud noises. Good to know! File this information away in your head and board your train, plotting an eastward course to the Fire Temple.

Missing Links

Hang on now; before you get carried away with cleansing the Fire Temple, know that a whole lot of optional tasks are now open for exploring. After all, folks who own trains with both passenger and freight cars are hard to come by! Check out these optional exploits now if you like, or skip this sidebar and return to it after you've cleared the Fire Temple. You'll have even more optional stuff to explore by then!

Items to Obtain

Force Gems 6-14

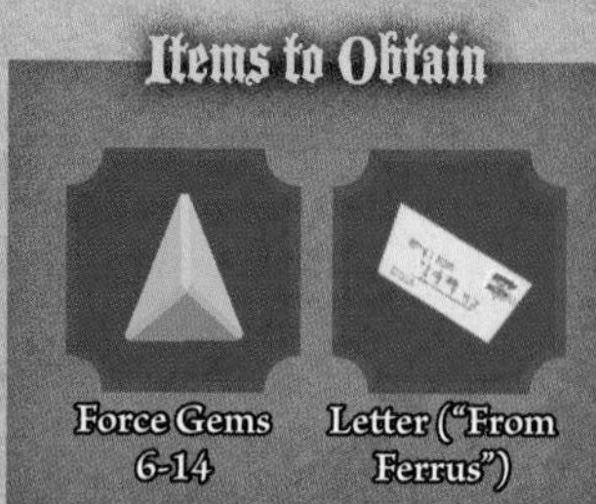
Letter ("From Ferrus")

1 Explore the Fire Realm

Menu

2 Aid Goron Village

2143
Menu

3 Find the Fire Sanctuary

Menu

4 Clear the Fire Temple

Force Gem 6

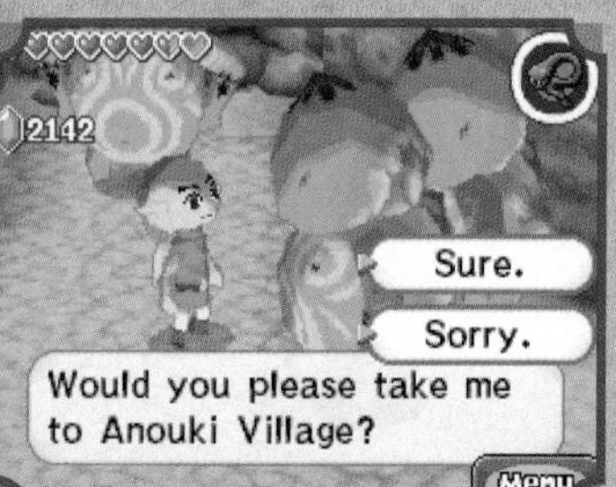

Remember that Goron who wanted to visit Anouki Village? He's still waiting for a lift down by Goron Village's train station. Speak with the Goron and agree to ferry him to see the Anoukis.

NOTE

You'll be transporting lots of passengers and cargo throughout these Missing Links. Remember to always keep your cargo safe from monsters and to obey signposts while ferrying passengers.

Arrive at Anouki Village without upsetting your passenger, and the Goron will be so pleased that a Force Gem will appear. Nice one! Claim this sixth Force Gem to restore some tracks to the Snow Realm.

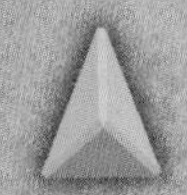

Force Gem 6

You got a Force Gem! The Snow Rail Map has started glowing!

Force Gem 7

Since you're already visiting Anouki Village, speak to the locals to discover that a certain Anouki would love to visit someplace warm, like Goron Village. No problem, friend! Agree to bring the Anouki to Goron Village, then board your train and depart.

Make the trip back to Goron Village with minimal drama, and your Anouki passenger will be overjoyed. A Force Gem materializes, restoring even more of the Snow Realm's lost tracks.

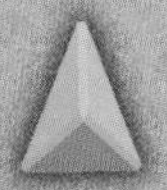

Force Gem 7

You got a Force Gem! The Snow Rail Map has started glowing!

Force Gem 8

Since you're in the neighborhood, why not douse the rest of the lava here at Goron Village? The Gorons would certainly approve. Roll for Wellspring Station and buy a full load of Mega Ice when you get there.

Ferry your Mega Ice back to Goron Village without delay. Keep enemies away from your cargo and set a direct course for Goron Village once you reach the Fire Realm.

You must bring ten units of Mega Ice to Goron Village in order to douse the remaining lava. To complete the task, speak to the Goron villager who stands near the lava, delighting the Goron and scoring your eighth Force Gem.

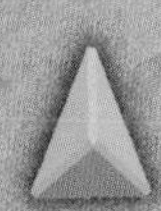

Force Gem 8

You got a Force Gem! The Fire Rail Map has started glowing!

Force Gem 9

During one of your many visits to Whittleton Village, you may have overheard that the place is in need of iron to forge new axes. Speak to the Goron merchant on the west side of town, and purchase some pricey iron from him.

Now simply transport the iron down to Whittleton Village, ensuring that at least five units survive the trip. Speak to Whittleton's lumber merchant afterward to hand over the iron, and the man becomes joyous enough to generate another Force Gem.

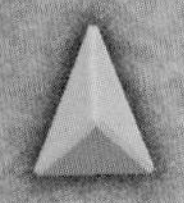

Force Gem 9

You got a Force Gem! The Forest Rail Map has started glowing!

Force Gem 10

You may also have overheard the Anoukis bemoan their need for lumber and for a gifted builder to help them construct a monster-repelling fence around their village. Whittleton's got lumber, so buy some from the local merchant and bring it up to Anouki Village, using Warp Gate A to hasten the trip.

Now you just need to find a handyman—the bridge worker should fit the bill! You won't find the bridge worker at home, however; he's still hanging out at the Trading Post, admiring his recent handiwork on the bridge. Warp back to the Forest Realm and pick up the lumber and the bridge worker, then bring him to the Anoukis.

With both lumber and the bridge worker delivered to the Anoukis, the villagers become overjoyed at their newfound sense of security. Speak to them to score your tenth Force Gem, restoring even more lost Spirit Tracks.

Force Gem 10

You got a Force Gem! The Snow Rail Map has started glowing!

Force Gem 11

You've no doubt received a letter from Ferrus by now, asking you to come find him at a certain location shown to you in a photo that Ferrus included in his letter. If you don't have this letter, check any postbox to get it. (Ferrus mails you the letter after you bring your first load of Mega Ice to Goron Village.)

Letter

You got a letter from the postman! Go to the Collection screen to read it!

1 Explore the Fire Realm

2 Aid Goron Village

3 Find the Fire Sanctuary

4 Clear the Fire Temple

The place Ferrus awaits is along the vertical stretch of track that is south from the vertical tracks to the right of Snow Temple. Go there to find Ferrus snapping photos by the tracks as usual. Park next to him to chat with him.

Ferrus asks you to bring him to meet his idol: the great engineer Alfonzo. It's a long way to Alfonzo's workshop at Aboda Village, but it's worth making the trip! Take Warp Gate A back to the Forest Realm, and set a course for Aboda Village, obeying every signpost as you go.

When you at last arrive at Aboda, head to Alfonzo's shop and introduce Ferrus. The conversation is a bit odd, but Ferrus is thrilled to at last meet the greatest engineer in the land. Naturally, it doesn't take long for another Force Gem to materialize!

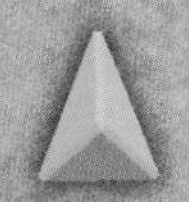

Force Gem 11

You got a Force Gem! The Forest Rail Map has started glowing!

Force Gem 12

Make the scenic trip from Aboda to Papuchia Village and speak to the fish merchant, who stands near a cart by the local shop. Buy a full load of fish off the woman and return to your train.

Have you talked to that woman in Castle Town who keeps yapping about fish? That's where you're headed! Make the trek to Castle Town, making sure at least ten fish survive the journey. Speak to the woman to delight her with your cargo and spawn another Force Gem.

Force Gem 12

You got a Force Gem! The Forest Rail Map has started glowing!

Force Gem 13

While you're here visiting Castle Town, take the opportunity to speak with the Cucco merchant, who stands amidst his flock in the northwest Cucco stable. That farmer you met at Aboda Village really wanted some Cuccos, so buy some from the merchant and see if you can't make his day.

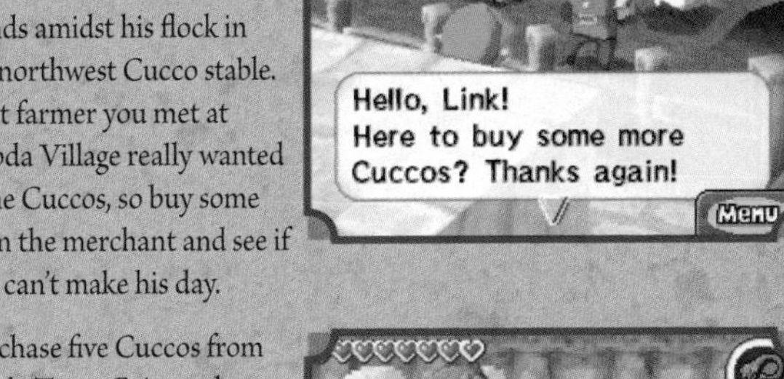

Purchase five Cuccos from Castle Town. Bring at least ten Cuccos to Aboda and speak with the farmer to blow him away with your generosity. The man's dream of owing lots of Cuccos is at last fulfilled, and a Force Gem suddenly appears.

Force Gem 13

You got a Force Gem! The Forest Rail Map has started glowing!

Force Gem 14

Believe it or not, there's one more Force Gem you can acquire before setting foot inside the Fire Temple. Return to Papuchia Village and speak with the Wise One. Tell her you're having bad luck, and she'll offer to sell you a special vessel that brings good luck. The vessel is pricey, but go ahead and buy it anyway.

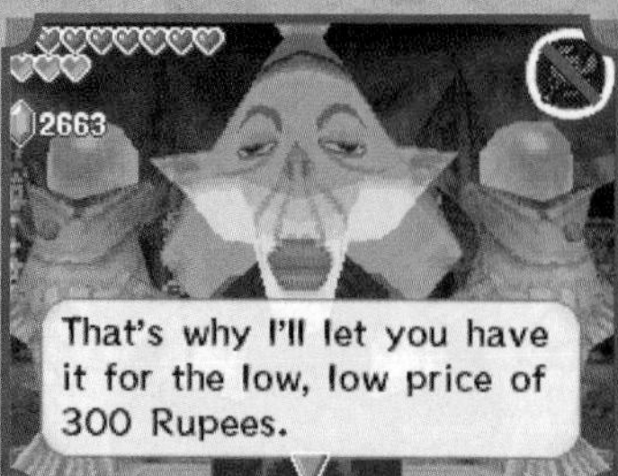

2663
That's why I'll let you have it for the low, low price of 300 Rupees.

Return to your train and set a course for the Forest Realm, aiming to take Warp Gate A up to the Snow Realm. You must not allow any monster to hit you on your way, or the expensive vessel you're carrying will break!

Once you've arrived at the Snow Realm, set a course for the Snow Sanctuary, which isn't far. Defend your precious cargo the whole way there.

When you at last arrive at the Snow Sanctuary, you find Steem eagerly awaiting you at the station platform. The Lokomo guardian was looking for a lucky charm, as well as a decorative object for his abode. He gladly takes the vessel off your hands and places a Force Gem in your mitts in trade!

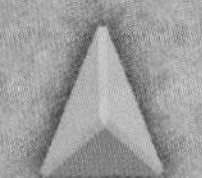

Force Gem 14

You got a Force Gem! The Snow Rail Map has started glowing!

Warp Gate Activation

After acquiring all those Force Gems, you have a whole bunch of new track to explore. Check the overworld map included in this guide to find that you can now access and activate Warp Gates C, D, E, and F. Travel to each activation gate and blast the green triangle atop the arch to activate the gates. This makes navigating the overworld a whole lot easier!

Rabbit Roundup

Now that you've restored so much track, several more fluffy bunnies are yours for the catching. Check this guide's overworld map, and hunt down these rabbits; then speak to the dude at Rabbitland Rescue for your rewards (treasures and/or Rupees).

- Forest rabbit 10
- Snow rabbits 8-10
- Ocean rabbit 8

Snowdrift Station

One of the Force Gems you've found has restored the tracks leading to a new area called Snowdrift Station. Visit the northwest corner of the Snow Realm, riding to the very end of the line to discover this remote destination. Park and investigate the place—if you dare.

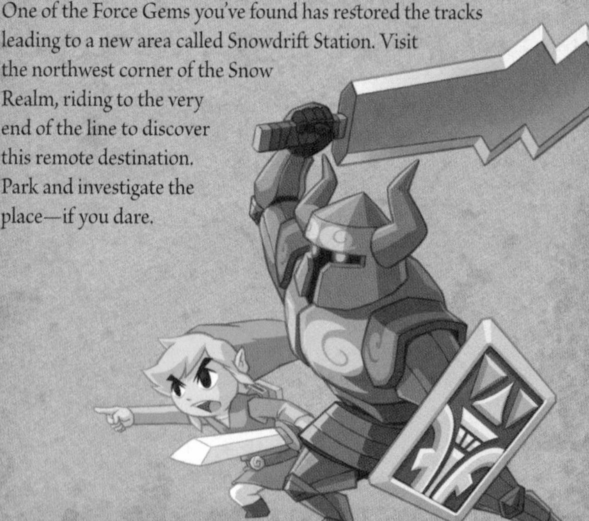

1 Explore the Fire Realm

2 Aid Goron Village

3 Find the Fire Sanctuary

4 Clear the Fire Temple

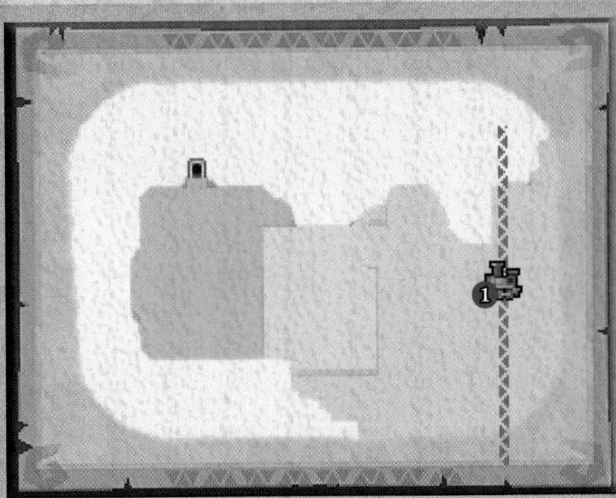

Snowdrift Station

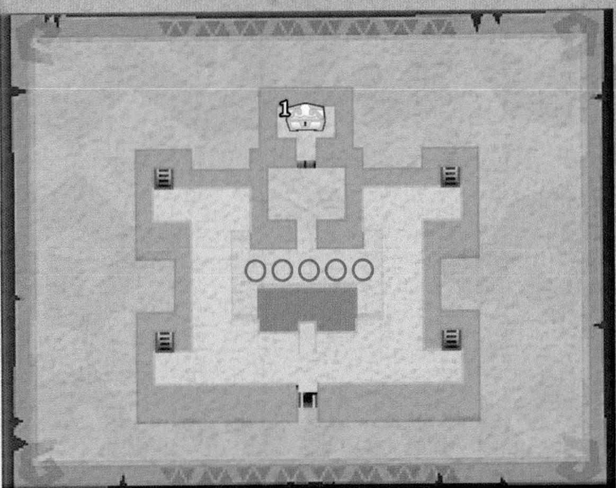

Snowdrift Station Dungeon

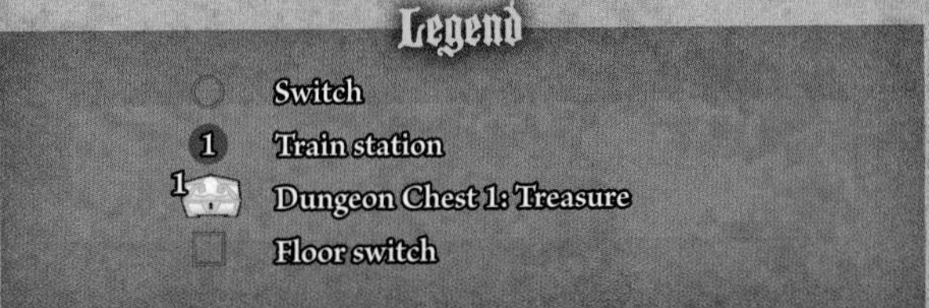

Don't let the peaceful surroundings catch you off guard. Several White Wolfos lurk below the freshly fallen snow. Consider dazing these beasts with your boomerang before dispatching them with your sword. There are no treasures to be found outside, so dash to the northwest to reach the dungeon's icy interior. Take care while maneuvering through the mazelike set of fences along the way. If you're not careful, you can get cornered by a trio of White Wolfos.

Once inside, heed the advice on the stone tablet near the entrance: Those who get the order wrong will fall into darkness. This refers to the five switches in the room's center. Don't touch them! You must activate the switches in a certain order to unlock the treasure chamber to the north.

Ignore the switches for now and search for clues on the activation order. Start your search by descending the northeast stairs—watch out for the Freezards along the way.

On this floor, you must activate a series of ice torches while heading across a pool of water. Equip your boomerang and target the lit ice torch near the water's edge; then trace a line to the unlit torch to the west. As the icy boomerang travels over the water, it creates an icy path for you to walk on.

Continue lighting torches and traveling west until you can reach the stone floor to the northwest. Here you find a stone tablet containing your first clue: Don't hit the false one in the middle. Ah, so the switch in the middle doesn't need to be hit at all. Good to know! Follow the adjoining lit path back to the room's entrance and return upstairs.

Next, descend the steps in the southeast corner of the main chamber. A door slams shut behind Link, trapping him in a water-filled room packed with ice torches, as well as several Spitter Slugs and Ice Keese. Keep your boomerang in hand and get busy dazing the nearby Spitter Slugs before they have an opportunity to fire. Next, create an ice bridge across the water by targeting one of the ice torches with your boomerang.

If you can get close enough to the dazed Spitter Slugs, attack them with your sword. Otherwise, prepare your Whirlwind and blow their projectiles back at them. The Ice Keese are more a nuisance than a threat, but they can still knock you in the water, so keep your distance. Once all the enemies in this room are down for the count, the door to the north opens, allowing you to escape.

Another clue is inscribed on the stone tablet in the next room, offering the following advice: The second switch from the left is the third switch to hit. Got it? You're one step closer to figuring out this puzzle. Retrace your steps back to the stairs to return to the main chamber.

Now head for the southwest steps and scour this room for more clues. Stand to the right of the floor switch ahead and prepare to dash across the icy course to the west. As you dash over the switch, a door opens to the north, accompanied by the ticking sound of a timer—you need to reach the northern chamber before the door closes!

There's no time to spare, so keep moving along the slippery path, avoiding contact with walls along the way. It may take a few attempts to get it just right, but you'll eventually get the hang of it and reach the chamber before the door slams shut.

As expected, another stone tablet awaits in the chamber, offering the following clue: The first and the last are on the ends. It's beginning to make sense now, but you don't quite have all the pieces to figure out this puzzle. Fortunately there's one more clue. Return to the main chamber upstairs, then descend the steps in the northwest corner.

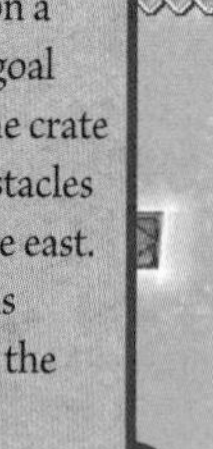

Here Link is greeted by a wooden crate placed on a large floor of ice. The goal here is to maneuver the crate through a series of obstacles to reach the pool to the east. Follow these directions to move the crate into the proper position:

1. North
2. East
3. South
4. West
5. South
6. East
7. North
8. East

1 Explore the Fire Realm

2 Aid Goron Village

3 Find the Fire Sanctuary

4 Clear the Fire Temple

Now you're ready to ride the crate across the pool of water. But beware of the Spitter Slugs on the other side of the pool. Use the Whirlwind to blow their projectiles back at them.

But even with the Spitter Slugs gone, you must turn your attention to the arrows shooting out of the walls. With the Whirlwind equipped, propel yourself east. Quickly stow the Whirlwind and face north to use your shield to deflect the incoming arrows. When you reach the pool's opposite side, hop off the crate.

Here you find the fourth and final clue written on another stone tablet. This one advises the following: The second one and the fourth one are next to each other. That's it! You should have enough information to deduce the order in which the switches must be activated. Head upstairs and give it a shot.

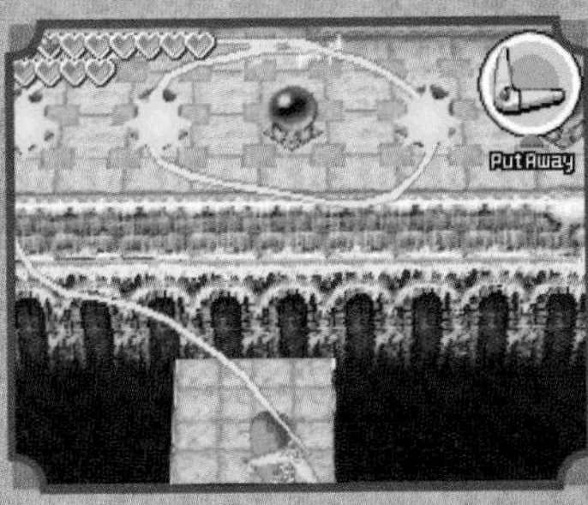

In the main chamber, climb the central steps (near the entrance) and stand on the small platform so you have a clear view of all five switches. Now it's time to put those clues to use! With your boomerang in hand, do the following:

- Target the first switch on the left first.
- Guide the boomerang's trajectory over to the fourth switch from the left.
- Loop back and hit the second switch from the left.
- Finally, loop around again and strike the fifth switch from the left.

You must hit all switches with one boomerang toss, so make sure you have the order correct. If you got the sequence down, a bridge to the north extends, allowing you to enter the now-open door beyond the switches.

What gives? This room isn't filled with treasure! It's filled with Freezards! Don't lose your cool. Instead, move to a corner of the room with your shield facing toward the center. This will cause the pesky creatures to bounce off your shield while protecting your flanks from attack. As each Freezard approaches, slash at it with your sword. Each hit you score on these creatures causes it to shed some of its protective ice. But it also makes it bounce all around this compact room. Remain vigilant and keep your back to the corner while continually slashing at these frozen creatures.

Once a Freezard has lost its protective armor, you can finish it off in one sword strike. But don't get overconfident. Stay in your corner and take it nice and slow. When you've eliminated all the Freezards, the door to the north opens, finally allowing you to reach that hard-earned treasure.

That seemed like a lot of work for one treasure chest, but the effort is well worth it once you see what's inside. Admire your new loot, then head back to the train station. There's nothing more for you to do here.

Dungeon Chest 1: Treasure

Treasure

You got a treasure! Check it out on the Collection screen!

Slippery Station

In addition to Snowdrift Station, your Force Gem collect-a-thon has also paved the way to another lost region of the Snow Realm called Slippery Station. Venture to the end of the Snow Realm's farthest northeast track to discover this unusual place.

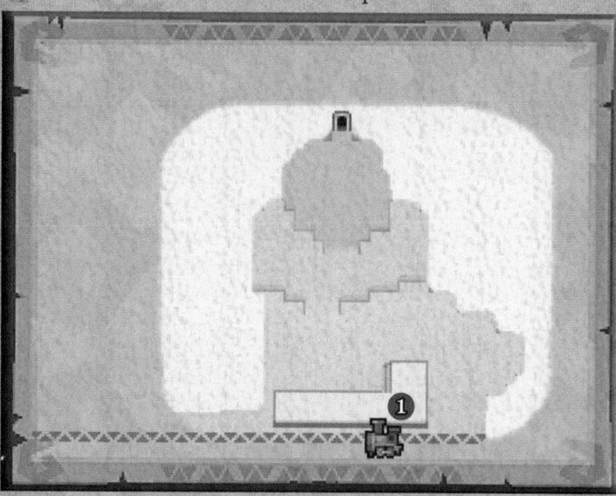

Slippery Station

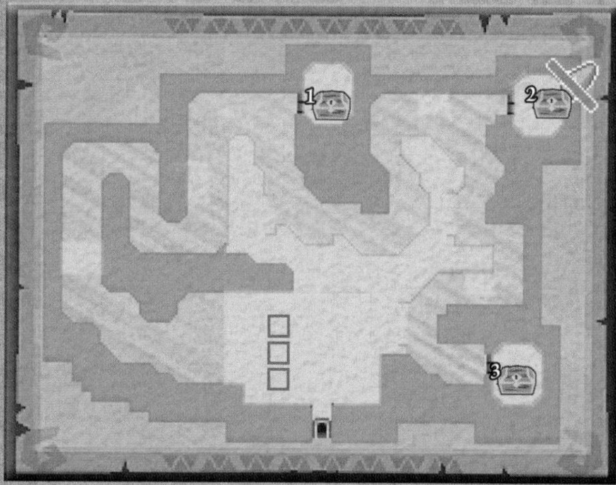

Slippery Station Dungeon

Items to Obtain

Enemies Encountered

This station sure looks cold and desolate, but there's a few pesky creatures who call this home. Before stepping off the platform, equip your boomerang and prepare to confront several Ice ChuChus. Whack these critters with the boomerang, then strike with your sword while they're still dazed. Continue fighting off the Ice ChuChus while moving toward the dungeon entrance to the north.

Inside the dungeon are three floor switches next to three lanes, each adorned by a stone tablet. Judging by the amateur, pro, and champion course inscriptions, it looks like some sort of race. Trigger the southernmost floor switch to see what happens.

As you step on the floor switch, a door to the north slides open, and a ticking sound commences. Yep, you guessed it: You have to run to the northern chamber before time expires. If you haven't started dashing along the ice to the west, simply chill out and wait for the time to expire. You'll need every fraction of a second to reach the northern chamber before the door slams shut.

1 Explore the Fire Realm

2 Aid Goron Village

3 Find the Fire Sanctuary

4 Clear the Fire Temple

1814
15
The pitfalls here mirror those on the other side, so make note of them.
Menu

The doors open after you clear the room. Go south and read a stone tablet for a tip that should entice you to jot down the nearby pits on your map.

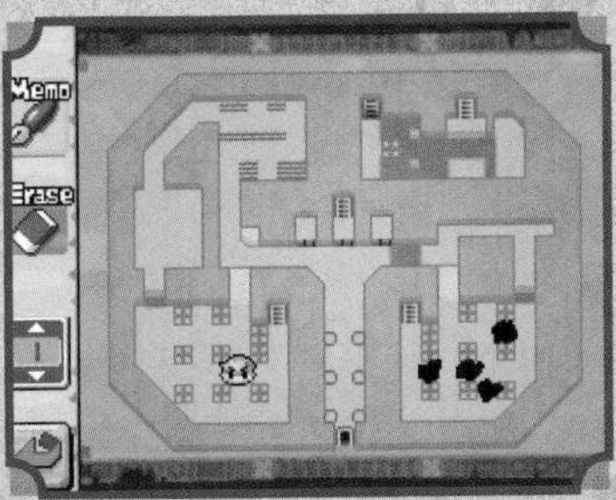

Note each pit's location on your map as you move about this dangerous area. Keep away from the Winders that slink along the walls; you've no means of defeating them at present.

Moldola

Hits to Defeat: N/A
Attack Type: Contact
Power: Strong
Damage: 1/2 heart

Threat Meter

Scale some nearby steps to gain some height, then toss your boomerang to the north to activate a high switch. This causes a large stone disc to drop into the corridor below.

Ignore the stone disc for now and climb the next set of stairs to reach the temple's second floor.

Fire Temple: Second Floor

As you enter the second floor, play the Song of Awakening to wake the nearby Gossip Stone. Pay the 20-Rupee fee, and then mark down the locations of each hidden chest on this floor.

Zelda notices an unusual contraption nearby. It's an old mine cart! Tap the cart to make Link hop aboard and speed off.

The cart deposits Link near a treasure chest. Flip the chest's lid to score a Small Key.

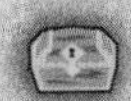

Dungeon Chest 1: Small Key

Small Key

You got a Small Key! Use this key to open locked doors!

That's it for now. Use the cart to return to the stairs and head back down to the first floor.

Fire Temple: First Floor, Revisited

Backtrack around the pits, spikes, and fire traps, moving back toward the entry hall. Tap the stone disc that fell from the ceiling before to make Link lift it overhead.

Carry the disc to the right and tap the odd object in the nearby pit to toss the disc on top. Now Link can hop across!

Beyond the pit sits a movable block. Slide the block south twice so that you can shove it one space to the right; then maneuver the block to plug up the fire trap that's spewing flames down the hall.

Navigate the southeast area with care—there are invisible pits all around! As the aforementioned stone tablet hinted, the pits are found in the same places they appear in the similar area to the west. Wake the Gossip Stone here to discover the locations of all hidden chests on this floor.

An exposed chest sits right nearby. Crack it open to pad your wallet with a Big Green Rupee, then proceed up the nearby stairs to reach the second floor.

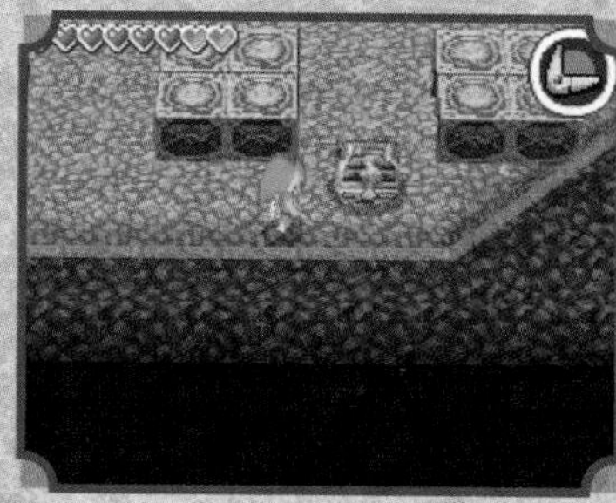

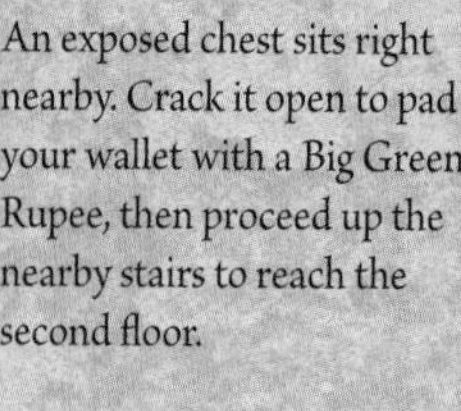

Dungeon Chest 2: Big Green Rupee

Big Green Rupee

You got a Big Green Rupee! It's worth 100 Rupees!

Fire Temple: Second Floor, Revisited

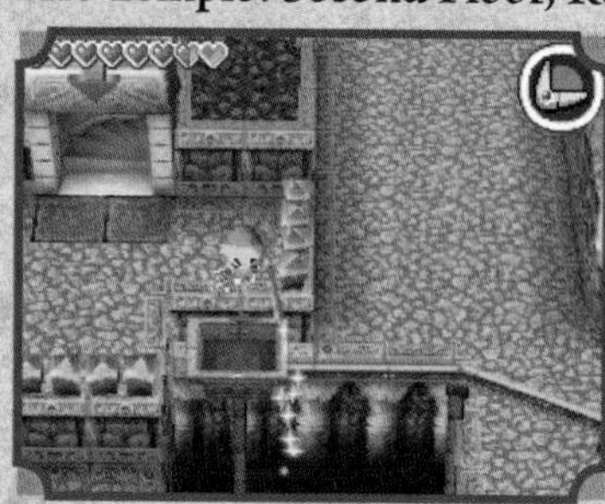

Another mine cart awaits you on this side of the second floor. Hop aboard to speed off on a new stretch of track.

Whack a switch with Link's sword as you speed along the track. This switches the rail, keeping you moving. You hit a dead end if you miss the switch; ride back to the entry stairs and try again.

If you don't hit the second switch, you'll land near an isolated chest. Open this one for a nice little treasure.

1 Explore the Fire Realm

2 Aid Goron Village

3 Find the Fire Sanctuary

4 Clear the Fire Temple

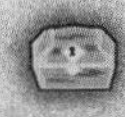

Dungeon Chest 3: Treasure

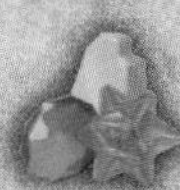

Treasure

You got a treasure! Check it out on the Collection screen!

PutAway

Ride all the way back to the entry stairs, then take the mine cart for one more spin. Whack both switches this time to reach a northeast ledge, where a Stalfos springs to life. Dispatch the Stalfos with the whip or a bomb, then open the nearby chest to score another Small Key.

Dungeon Chest 4: Small Key

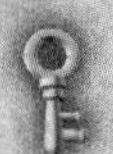

Small Key

You got a Small Key! Use this key to open locked doors!

That about wraps things up. Return to the first floor with your loot.

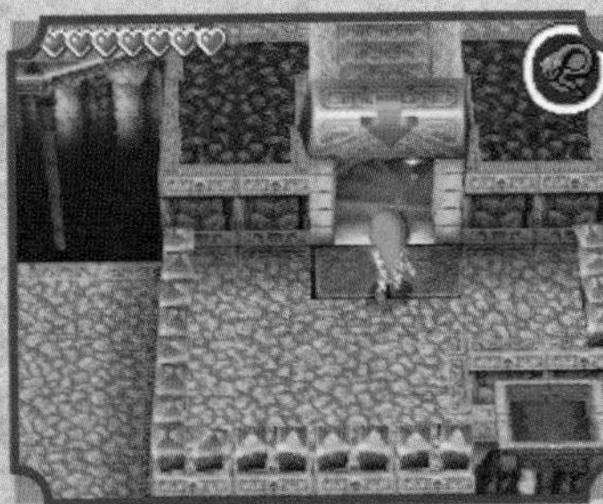

Fire Temple: First Floor, Third Visit

Menu

Use the two Small Keys you've pilfered from the second floor to open the two locked doors at the first floor's center. This exposes a pair of switches.

Menu

Stand between the switches, and use your boomerang to activate both in one toss. This opens the central door, allowing you to venture back upstairs.

Fire Temple: Second Floor, Third Visit

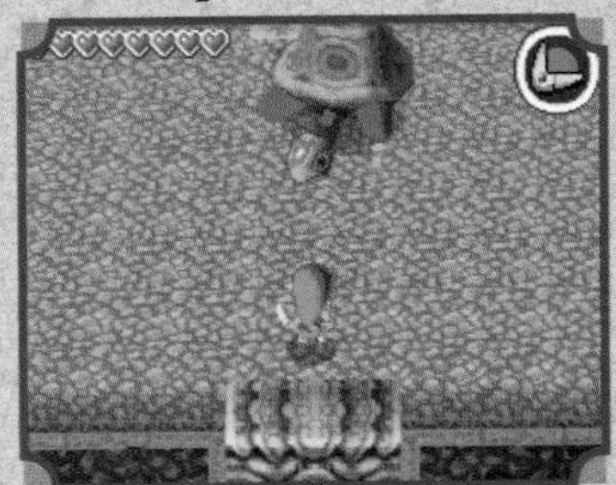

Link becomes trapped in a room as he enters the second floor. A formidable Heatoise lurks here and must be defeated to advance.

Heatoise

Hits to Defeat: Multiple
Attack Type: Contact
Power: Strong
Damage: 1/2 heart

Threat Meter

You can't damage the Heatoise directly, but it's easy enough to outsmart. The Winders on the walls are your friends in this fight; trick the Heatoise into charging at you, then dodge so that he gets a nasty jolt from one of the rolling wall-huggers.

The Heatoise becomes stunned after suffering a zap from a Moldola, and its head flops to the floor. Hurry up and attack its vulnerable head to deal some damage before the monster perks back up.

Menu

You got the bow and arrow! Tap the Touch Screen and release to fire.

Repeat this sequence until the Heatoise has been fully shell-shocked. The room's doors then open, and a giant chest appears. Open the chest to claim a new and awesome weapon: the bow and arrow!

Dungeon Chest 5: Bow and Arrow

Bow and Arrow

You got the bow and arrow! Tap the touch screen and release to fire.

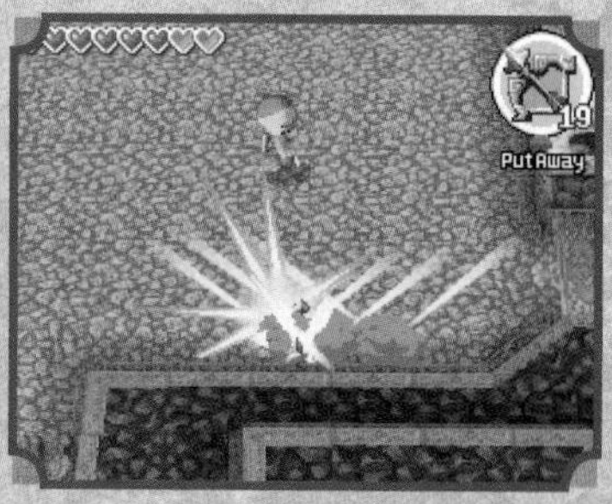

Test out your new bow on the roving Winders. It dispatches them with a single shot—from a nice, safe range. Handy!

Run east and smash an Item Bulb to score more arrows. Then use the bow to launch one across the north pit, striking the eye switch on the wall to extend a bridge. Cross over and head back downstairs.

TIP

The bow requires arrows to use. Link can't carry more than 20 arrows at present, so don't waste them. You can acquire more arrows by breaking Item Bulbs and other item-yielding objects.

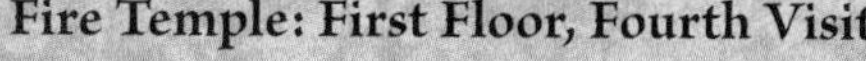

Fire Temple: First Floor, Fourth Visit

You've explored the whole first floor, except for this northeast corner. Equip the bow and fire an arrow south, into the strange object on the nearby ledge.

The object is known as an arrow aimer, and it redirects your arrow, firing it east into a second arrow aimer. The second arrow aimer fires the arrow north, into an eye switch. Once you hit the eye, a bridge extends.

Cross the bridge, then leap to the east ledge and open the small chest you find there to claim a worthy treasure.

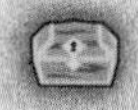

Dungeon Chest 6: Treasure

Treasure

You got a treasure! Check it out on the Collection screen!

Return to the first arrow aimer and smack it with Link's sword. Each whack rotates the arrow aimer, changing its direction of fire. Whack the aimer until it's pointing due north.

Now tap the arrow aimer to make Link lift it over his head. Move to the platform's west edge, and tap the tiny platform to the west to heave the arrow aimer over there.

1 Explore the Fire Realm

2 Aid Goron Village

3 Find the Fire Sanctuary

4 Clear the Fire Temple

If you throw the arrow aimer before you rotate it, use the boomerang to change its firing angle from afar.

With the arrow aimer rotated and placed, fire a single arrow at it to strike another eye switch to the north. This extends yet another bridge.

Cross the bridge and whack the arrow aimer until it faces west. Toss the arrow aimer to the north tiny platform, then shoot another arrow to trigger a third eye switch. Cross the bridge that extends and scamper downstairs to visit the temple's basement.

Fire Temple: Basement First Floor

Your first trip through this floor is a short one. A stone tablet near a locked door reminds you that only a key will open it. No kidding! You're fresh out of keys, so head down the nearby staircase to delve even deeper into this unusual place.

Fire Temple: Basement Second Floor

Link falls under fire when he enters the second basement floor: Rows of Stalfoses on either side of the entry chamber spring to life and begin tossing sharp bones! Dispatch these out-of-reach villains quickly with the bow, firing one arrow to collapse their bodies and another to wipe out their hopping skulls.

Smash the nearby Item Bulb for more arrows, refilling Link's quiver. Then venture south and fire an arrow into the aimer that sits across the west lava pit. The arrow ends up striking an eye switch, temporarily shutting off the lava geysers to the east.

The clock is ticking; hurry across the east lava, using the whip to swing along the overhead posts. Get across before the geysers kick back up or you'll take a nasty fall and have to try again.

The posts on this side of the lava are too high to reach, so ignore them and go north. Defeat a pair of Stalfoses here and wake the Gossip Stone to discover the locations of this basement floor's hidden chests.

The statue reveals that one of the floor's chests is right nearby—on the high ledge across the east lava. Hop across the lava's stone discs, crossing the first three while their geysers aren't active.

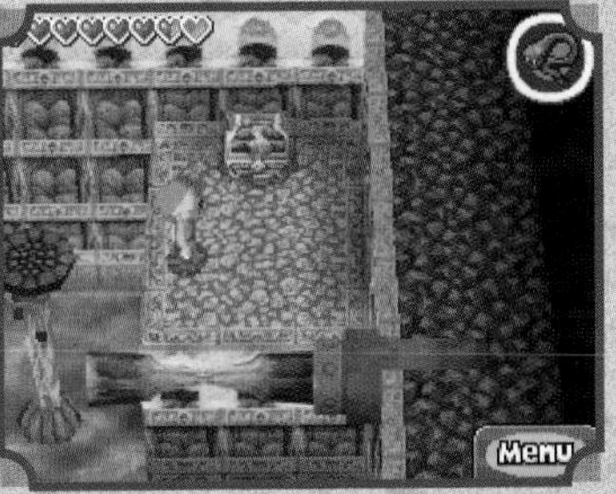

Wait on the third disc until its geyser shoots you skyward; then leap across the final disc and onto the chest ledge. Open the chest to pocket another treasure.

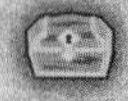

Dungeon Chest 7: Treasure

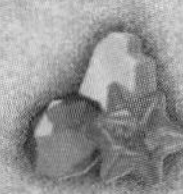

Treasure

You got a treasure! Check it out on the Collection screen!

Link can reach the overhead whip posts from the height of this ledge. Swing south along them, bypassing a sealed door. Step on the floor switch after you land to open the door and make it easier to move about the floor.

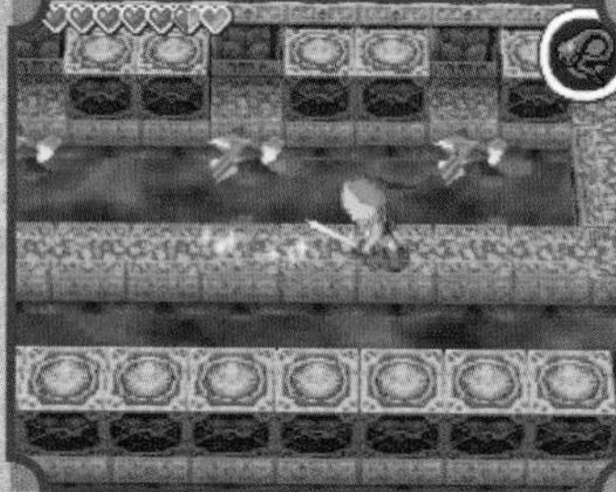

Sharp blades fly back and forth across the narrow hall that follows. Dart past each blade in turn, stopping at the safe spots between them.

The final blade takes longer to complete its course. Wait for it to fly past, then chase after the blade as it travels south. Duck to the west when possible so you avoid the blade during its return trip.

Open the little chest you find beyond the blade traps to add another valuable treasure to your collection.

Dungeon Chest 8: Treasure

Treasure

You got a treasure! Check it out on the Collection screen!

Fire Keese flutter above the lava to the right, and no matter how many times you defeat them, more just keep popping up. That's because you need to use them! Target a Fire Keese with the boomerang, then continue tracing the line into contact with the two nearby torches. The boomerang catches fire after dispatching a Fire Keese, spreading its heat to the torches and lighting them up.

When both torches are lit, a stone disc falls to the west. Use the disc to hop across the lava and reach a staircase leading up.

Fire Temple: Basement First Floor, Revisited

Link is ambushed by two Giant Turtles as he enters the floor. There are no Winders to exploit this time, so fire arrows at the creatures' heads to stun them—that is, when they're not busy charging you!

Follow up with Link's sword after stunning the Giant Turtles with an arrow, and repeat this sequence until both monsters are down for the count. You can acquire more arrows from the Item Bulb in the room's corner.

1 Explore the Fire Realm

2 Aid Goron Village

3 Find the Fire Sanctuary

4 Clear the Fire Temple

A chest appears after you dispatch both Giant Turtles. Swipe a nice little treasure from the chest, then inspect the nearby stone tablets.

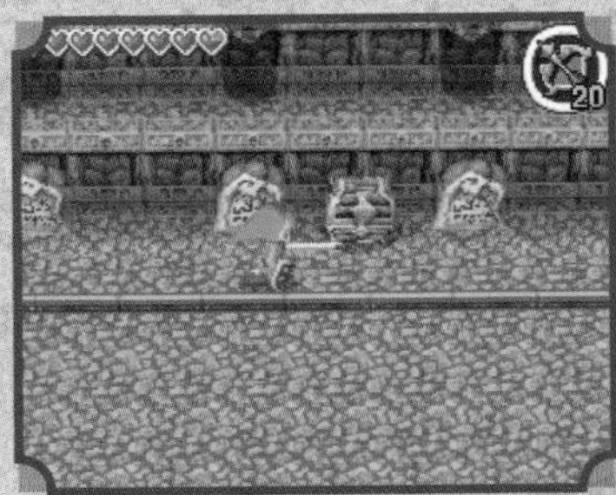

Dungeon Chest 9: Treasure

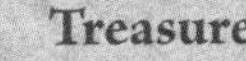

Treasure

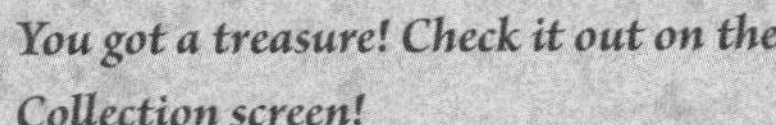

You got a treasure! Check it out on the Collection screen!

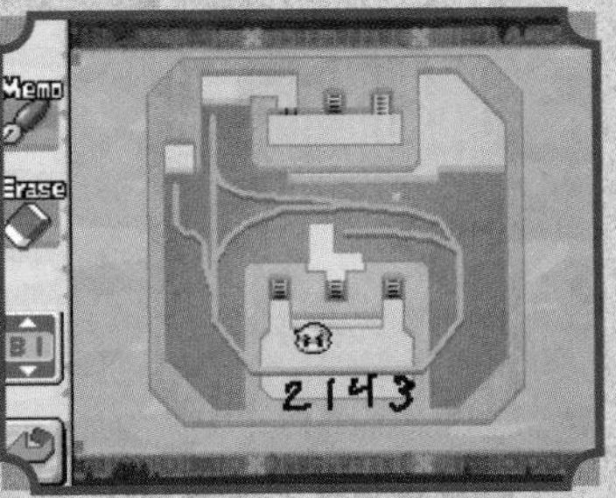

Each tablet instructs you to aim at the eye switch that lies above in a specific order. This comes in handy later, so scribble down the sequence on your map before proceeding down the nearby staircase.

Fire Temple: Basement Second Floor, Revisited

Clear the hall of Stalfoses as you explore this half of the basement's second floor. Step on a floor switch to open a door, but the door closes when you step off the switch. That's no good!

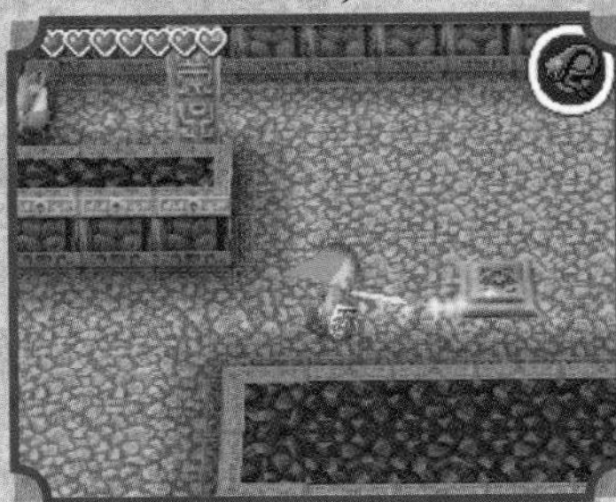

Head north to discover an arrow aimer. Collect the arrow aimer and carry it back down to the floor switch. Place the aimer to the switch's north, and ensure it's facing west, right at the door.

With the arrow aimer in place, step onto the floor switch again to open the door, then fire an arrow at the aimer. The device redirects the arrow, sending it past the open door and into an eye switch. Nice shot!

Triggering the eye switch causes a stone disc to fall nearby. Carry the disc north and place it on a fire geyser so you can ride up to the higher area.

Whack the switch you find on the higher area to extend a whip post over the lava pit to the east. This will help you leave the scene when you're done here.

Wipe out the flapping Fire Keese to secure the upper area, then whack the other switch to activate three fire geysers up here.

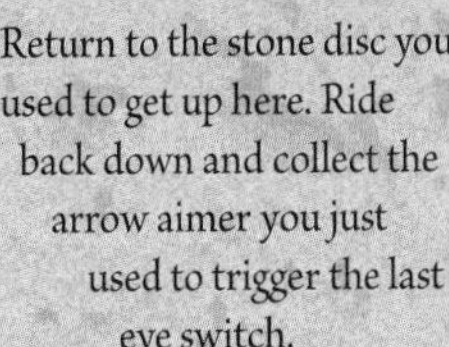

Return to the stone disc you used to get up here. Ride back down and collect the arrow aimer you just used to trigger the last eye switch.

Carry the arrow aimer up to the higher area, once again riding the stone disc like an elevator. Place the arrow aimer on the east fire geyser up here, ensuring that it's facing west, right at an eye switch.

Now collect the arrow aimer that's already up here, which fires only at diagonal angles. Set the aimer to face northeast and then place it onto the south fire geyser.

You're almost finished here! Approach the stone disc you've been using to reach this elevated area, and tap the disc while the geyser is shooting it upward. Link deftly snatches the object away from the geyser.

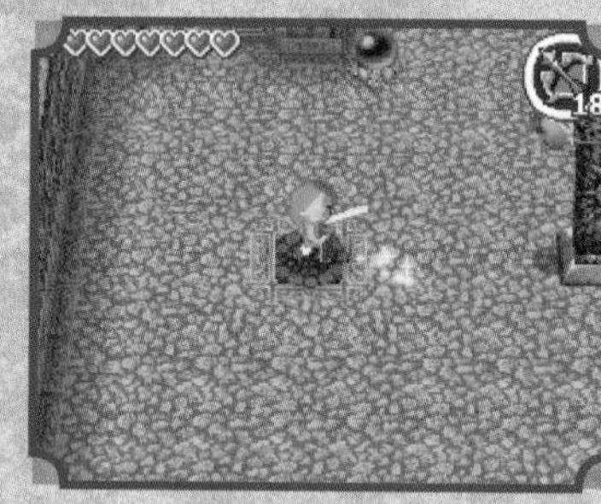

Carry the stone disc over to the west geyser, and place it there to create another makeshift elevator. Whack the nearby switch to shut off the fire geysers up here, then move Link onto the stone disc.

Now you can solve this little puzzle. Fire an arrow at the switch to reactivate the fire geysers, then launch an arrow into the eye switch across from Link. A timer sounds; quickly shoot another arrow at the south arrow aimer, which redirects the shot to the second arrow aimer, and from there, it shoots an arrow into the second eye switch.

With both eye switches activated, the nearby door opens. Run up the steps beyond and claim a Small Key from a little chest.

Dungeon Chest 10: Small Key

Small Key

You got a Small Key! Use this key to open locked doors!

Time to open that door you noticed a while ago. Ensure there's a whip post over the east lava pit (whack the switch if there isn't one) and then swing across. Scale the north stairs to return to the first basement floor.

Fire Temple: First Basement Floor, Third Visit

Now that you've found another Small Key, you can open this floor's locked door and explore the rest of it. Collect arrows from the Item Bulb beyond the door, then hop into the mine cart.

1 Explore the Fire Realm

2 Aid Goron Village

3 Find the Fire Sanctuary

4 Clear the Fire Temple

The mine cart rushes you past four eye switches—the very switches the stone tablets told you how to activate. Ready the bow and make as many passes as you need to strike all four switches. It may help to tap and hold the stylus on the screen, readying an arrow for flight.

Hit the eye switches in the following order to activate them properly: center-left, far left, far right, center-right.

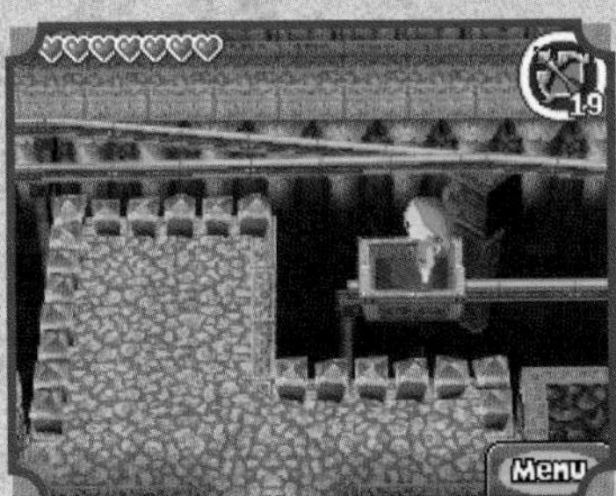

With all four eye switches activated in the proper order, the track changes, allowing you to reach the floor's central staircase. Don't go downstairs just yet; return to the mine cart and ride back toward the cart's starting point.

Ready your bow as you speed along the rail, and hold the stylus on the screen to take aim. Scan the southwest corner of the floor as you race past, and hit the distant switch with an arrow.

Trigger the switch while moving from south to north, and you'll veer off to the left, landing near a stamp station. Sneaky! Plant a quick stamp on Niko's book, then return to the central staircase and go downstairs. When you reach the second basement floor, proceed down the next set of stairs to delve even deeper.

Fire Temple: Basement Third Floor

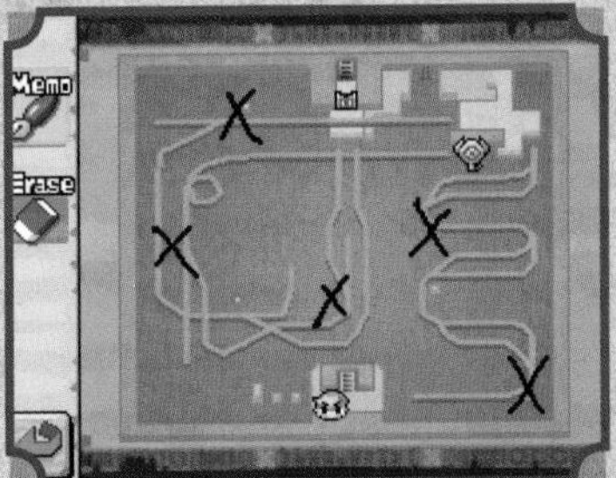

As you enter the third basement floor, check out the map on the wall, which shows a diagram of the floor's mine rail. Five burst designs are labeled on the map; copy them down on your own map in the same locations for future reference.

Next, hop across the little platforms to the west, and pluck a bomb from the bomb flower at the far end. Carry the bomb back across and place it near the boulder to the right.

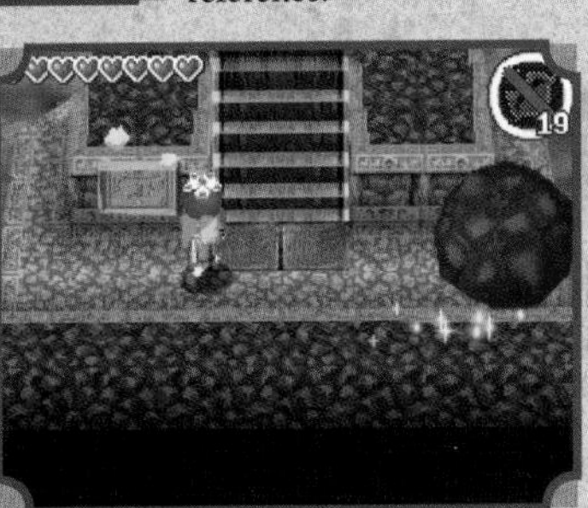

The bomb blasts the boulder, reducing it to a stone disc. How convenient! Toss the disc onto the nearby fire geyser; then ride up and hop into the mine cart.

Whack two switches on this first cart ride—the two that were labeled on the wall map. If you don't hit both switches, or if you whack ones that you're not supposed to trigger, Link's ride will be brought to an unpleasant halt when he speeds into an active fire geyser.

The mine cart drops you near the Boss Key, but it's currently out of reach. There's a mine cart just to the key's left, however; use the Whirlwind to blow the key into that cart.

Now run north and whip-swing across a lava pit to reach a small chest, which contains a rare treasure. Might as well grab this before you move on!

Dungeon Chest 11: Treasure

Treasure

You got a treasure! Check it out on the Collection screen!

Swing back over the lava, and use the nearby Item Bulb to restock your arrows. Then ready your bow and climb into the mine cart that's adjacent to the one you've recently loaded with the Boss Key.

You must strike three switches during this wild ride, but the last one's out of sword reach. Hit it with an arrow instead, readying your bow in preparation for the shot the moment after you hit the second switch.

Hit all the right switches to land near the Boss Key door. The other cart made the ride as well, delivering the Boss Key right nearby. Collect the key and toss it into the Boss Key door to open the way to the temple's final level.

Fire Temple: Basement Fourth Floor

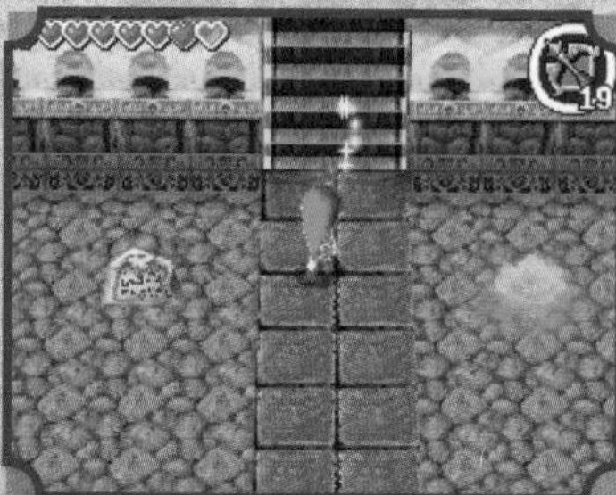

Collect hearts and items from this small floor's pots, then read the stone tablet to summon the blue warp light. Save your game and head upstairs to face one of the coolest boss fights yet.

Cragma, Lava Lord

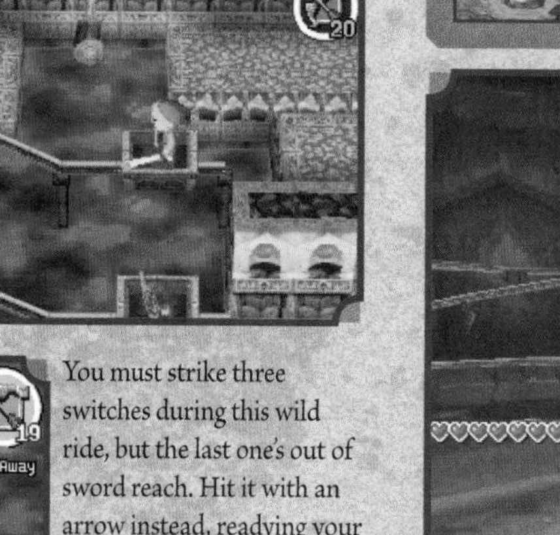

Hits to Defeat: Multiple

Attack Type: Contact

Power: Strong

Damage: 1/2 heart

Threat Meter

Cragma is a furious golem of rock and fire. The boss attacks by slamming the ground with its gigantic stone fists. Run to one side or the other, double-tapping the screen to make Link somersault away from these crushing blows.

1 Explore the Fire Realm

2 Aid Goron Village

3 Find the Fire Sanctuary

4 Clear the Fire Temple

As Cragma lifts a fist in preparation to strike, he reveals a weak spot somewhere along the base of his torso. Watch for a glowing patch of skin, and quickly strike this area with an arrow from Link's bow.

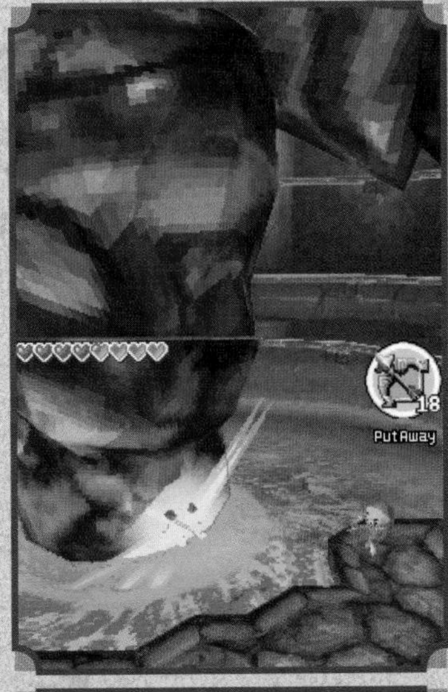

Quickly lift and carry the stone disc to the northeast, heading directly for a fire geyser. If you're too far away, you may need to drop the disc and flee another attack from Cragma before you can complete the journey.

Run away the moment you hit Cragma's soft spot. The boss retaliates by slamming the ground with both fists, covering a wide area that's tough to escape. Regardless of whether you dodge this attack, run around and locate a boulder that has fallen due to the intense impact.

Drop the stone disc onto the geyser, then tap the disc to make Link leap onto it. From here, Link can reach the nearby mine cart.

Hang out near the boulder until Cragma is just about to hammer the ground again, then dart to one side and somersault away. Trick the boss into smashing the boulder with a heavy blow, reducing the boulder to a stone disc.

Hop into the cart to begin circling Cragma at high speed. As you circle the boss, look for more glowing weak spots and strike each one with an arrow. Do your best not to miss or you'll need to make multiple trips around the boss and will risk running out of arrows before you reach the top.

NOTE

If you run out of arrows, you can acquire more from the ground level. Run around and wait for rocks to fall from the ceiling, then collect the arrows that are often left behind.

If Cragma ever holds a palm out while you're circling him, immediately shoot the glowing weak spot in his palm's center. This interrupts a nasty attack that often knocks Link out of his cart, forcing you to start over.

Make it all the way up to the highest rail by striking all of Cragma's weak spots. When you reach the top, take aim and fire an arrow into Cragma's giant eyeball. Time this well or your arrows may be deflected when Cragma raises an arm or blinks.

TIP

Hold your stylus on the screen to line up shots, removing the stylus when you wish to fire.

Cragma collapses when you shoot his eye, and Link is deposited onto the arena's floor. Now's your chance! Run up to Cragma and unleash the full fury of Link's blade against the glowing weak spot located atop the boss's head.

Repeat this sequence a second time, following the exact same steps to stun and collapse Cragma so you can deliver more punishment. The boss fights with greater fury as the fight wages on, so stay mobile and try not to miss your shots. Become one with the mine cart and the bow to at last bring the Lava Lord down.

1 Explore the Fire Realm

2 Aid Goron Village

3 Find the Fire Sanctuary

4 Clear the Fire Temple

With the great foulness banished from the Fire Temple, the place is once again free to send its current of righteous energy back along the Spirit Tracks and into the Tower of Spirits. The final portion of the tower locks into place, and the forces of good move one step closer to foiling the schemes of evil.

Congratulations, you've beaten the Fire Temple! Crack open the giant chest that appears to collect your ninth Heart Container, then ride the blue light back down to your train.

Dungeon Chest 12: Heart Container 9

Heart Container 9

You got a Heart Container! You increased your life by one and refilled your hearts!

 Missing Links 

The urge to return to the Tower of Spirits is strong indeed, but consider making time for these optional asides. Between these and the Missing Links that preceded the Fire Temple, you can open up nearly every stretch of Spirit Track around the overworld and can visit several new and exciting places where all manner of plunder awaits.

Items to Obtain

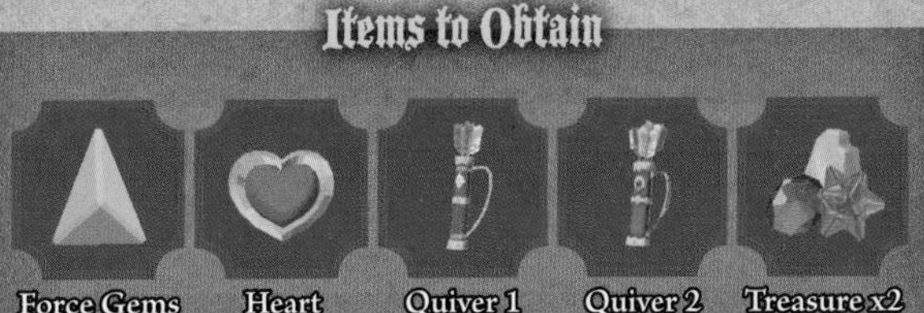

Quiver 1

You'll certainly want to tell the Gorons of your rousing success in clearing the Fire Temple, but there's another reason to visit Goron Village: to purchase that quiver you noticed at the local shop! Round up 2,000 Rupees (you may need to sell a few treasures to Linebeck at the Trading Post) and buy that quiver to increase your maximum arrow capacity.

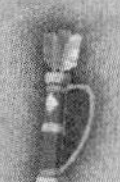

Quiver 1

You got a quiver! Now you can hold more arrows. Check the Collection screen.

Goron Target Range

1960
Welcome! This is the Goron Target Range! As you can see, it is a special place.
Menu

Remember that station you visited before arriving at Goron Village, the one that was closed due to volcanic activity? Well, the shop's open now, so feel free to swing by for an exciting challenge that can earn you super-rare treasures.

Pay the 20-Rupee fee to attempt the Goron's game, and you'll enter a roller-coaster track full of targets for you to blast with your cannon. Blue targets are worth 10 points each, and you can shoot red targets up to three times, earning you 30 points per shot (90 points total). Don't shoot the Goron targets or you'll lose 30 points!

The ride is pretty steady, but there is the occasional twist, turn, and sudden drop. Do your best to hit each target, striving to blast those red ones three times each. Beware of targets that spin around to reveal Goron faces, and learn not to shoot those ones—at least until after they've spun around again to show the target's other side once more.

Set a new high score of over 1,000 points, and the Goron will add even more track to the ride, allowing you to go for maximum pointage! When riding the longer track, spin the camera behind you during the final stretch and blast targets you've passed by, because many will continue to rotate, revealing extra point opportunities.

The Goron always gives you a choice between two chests at the end of each game, and you never really know what you'll get. The rule goes like this: The better your score, the better your odds of winning super-rare treasures! Have fun with this distracting minigame, and see how many treasures you can earn.

Force Gem 15

Since you're already kickin' it with the Gorons, return to Goron Village and speak to the Goron child near the elder's house to learn that he'd like to see the splendor of Castle Town. Tell the kid you'll take him there, and he'll board your train without delay.

The shortest route to Castle Town is to cut through the Tower of Spirits. Deliver the Goron child to Castle Town in one piece, and his joy at traveling abroad will score you a sparkly Force Gem.

Force Gem 15

You got a Force Gem! The Fire Rail Map has started glowing!

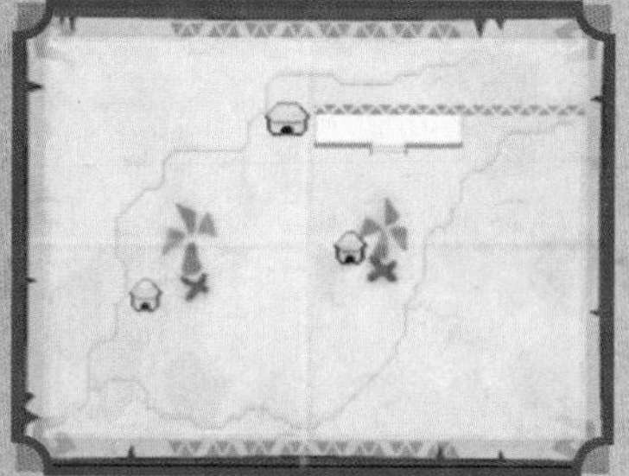

Now that you've cleared the Fire Temple, visit any postbox to receive a letter from your old pal, Niko. He hints that you should return to Aboda Village and search for some hidden treasure!

Go to Aboda and play the Song of Discovery near the two special palm trees as shown on Niko's map. Each chest contains a valuable treasure.

1 Explore the Fire Realm

2 Aid Goron Village

3 Find the Fire Sanctuary

4 Clear the Fire Temple

Overworld Chest 31: Treasure

Treasure

You got a treasure! Check it out on the Collection screen!

Overworld Chest 32: Treasure

Treasure

You got a treasure! Check it out on the Collection screen!

Force Gem 16

When you bought fish off the merchant in Papuchia, did she happen to tell you how badly she needed ice to keep her stock fresh? You're not far from Wellspring Station; set a course there and buy some Mega Ice off the friendly Anouki merchant. You're becoming his best customer!

To shorten the journey to Papuchia, consider taking Warp Gate B to the south corner of the Forest Realm. Mega Ice melts outside of the Snow Realm, so the quicker the trip, the better.

Make sure at least ten units of Mega Ice survive the trek, and the fish merchant will be overjoyed that you've helped her. A Force Gem appears, and all is right in the world.

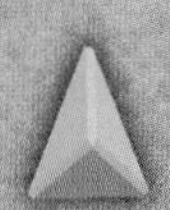

Force Gem 16

You got a Force Gem! The Ocean Rail Map has started glowing!

Pirate Hideout

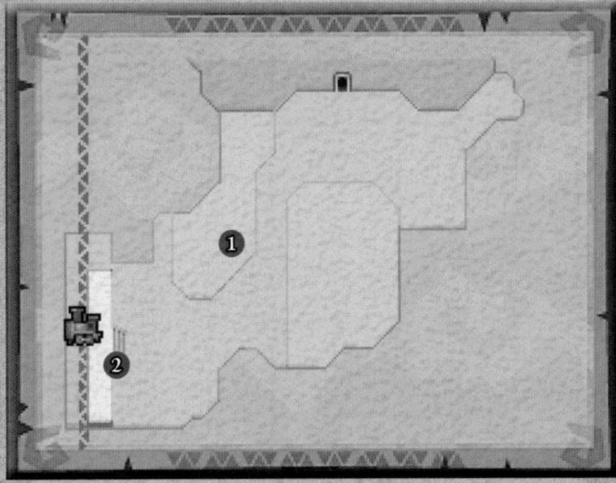

Pirate Hideout

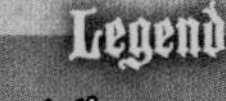

Legend	
1	Stamp station
2	Train station

Items to Obtain

Enemies Encountered

Explore the tracks you've just restored by delivering Mega Ice to Papuchia Village, and you'll discover a special location called the Pirate Hideout. Pull up to the station, then explore the grounds to spy a stamp station atop a high ledge. There's a circling shadow up there, so play the Song of Birds to attract some flying transportation.

Use the whip to ride on the bird, which deposits you on the high ledge. Record a new stamp for Niko, then return to the lower ground. Enter the north cave for a unique experience.

Hey, it's one of the Papuchia villagers! The pirates have the poor man all locked up, and they aren't about to let him go. Miniblins begin pouring out from the east and west, taunting Link and tossing large nets at him from across a pit! It's game-over if the Miniblins snare you, so make any inbound nets your primary target.

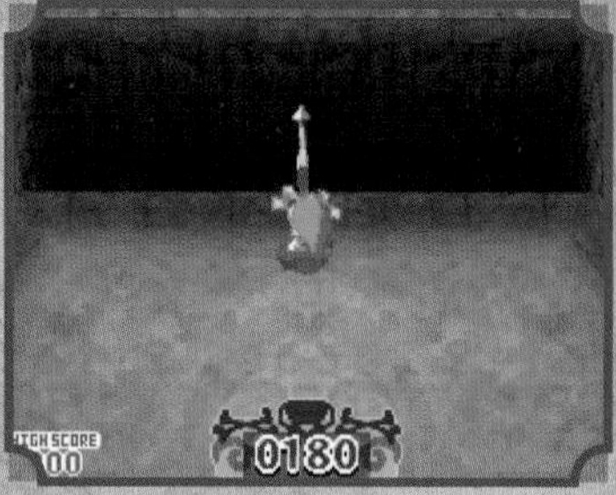

What unfolds is an exciting minigame from which you can earn a variety of rewards. You'll find you have an unlimited supply of arrows for this challenge; use them to dispatch the distant Miniblins, earning points for each one you shoot. Avoid missing the Miniblins to crank up your score multiplier, earning more and more points for each Miniblin you defeat in a chain.

Shooting down the nets the Miniblins throw breaks your score multiplier, so don't give them the chance to toss anything at you. Pick off each little scallywag as soon as they creep into view.

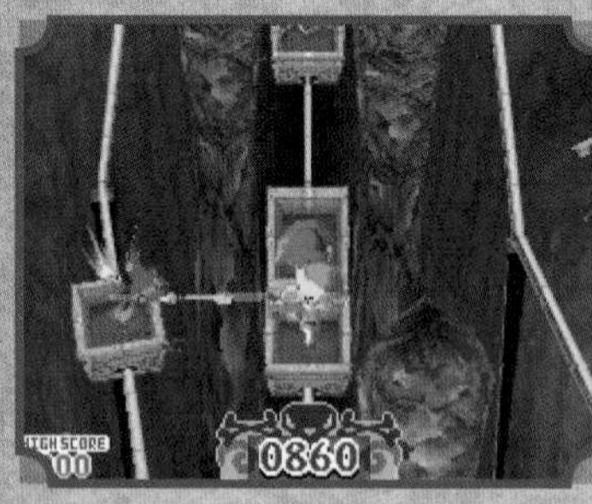

After wiping out a host of Miniblins, Link succeeds in freeing the prisoner, and the two board a mine cart in hopes of making a daring escape. You must continue dispatching Miniblins with arrows, but now you must do so from a moving mine cart! Again, do your best not to miss a Miniblin to keep your score multiplier running strong.

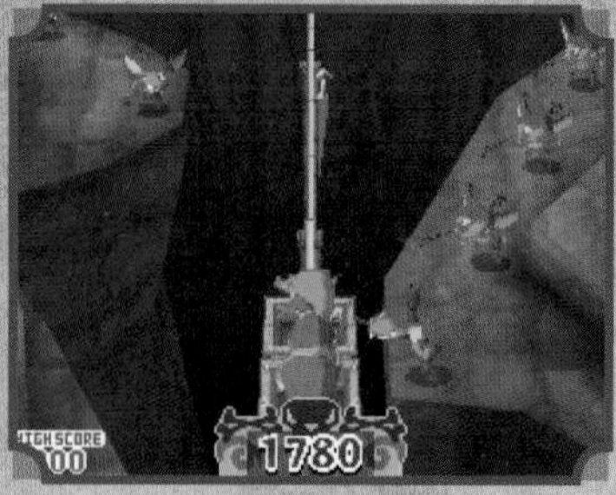

During the final leg of the ride, you speed through a cavern filled with Miniblins, and a giant Big Blin stands in your path. Ignore the Miniblins and unload on the Big Blin—you must strike him with several arrows to clear the way to freedom.

Get past the Big Blin to escape the pirates' clutches. The Papuchia man couldn't be happier to see the light of day and asks you to do him one last favor by taking him back home. You certainly can't leave him here, so agree to return him to Papuchia Village.

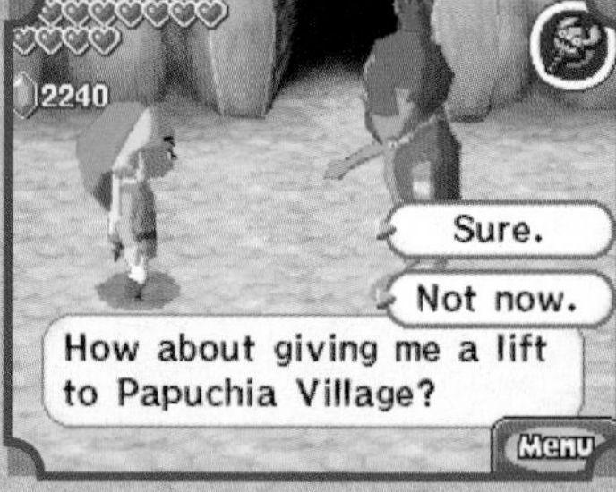

2240
Sure.
Not now.
How about giving me a lift to Papuchia Village?
Menu

Beware the pirate ships that attack you during the short trip back to Papuchia. If the larger ship gets close enough, its crew of vicious scallywags will board your train, and you'll have to fight them off!

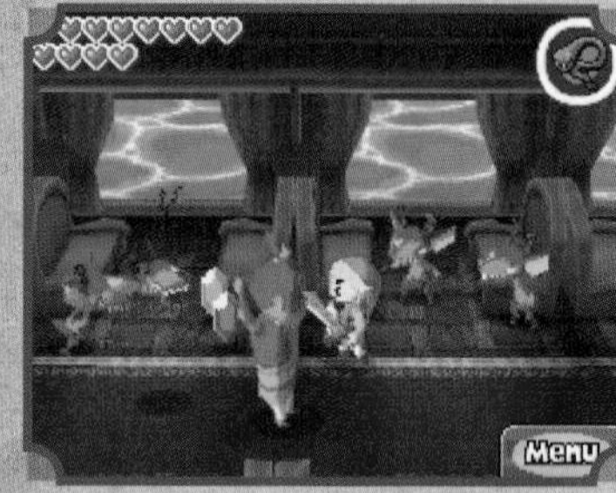

If the pirates board your train, defend the Papuchia man from the swarm of Miniblins just as you protected Carben, the Ocean Realm's Lokomo guardian, when you escorted him back to the Ocean Sanctuary. Stand near the villager and use fast sword attacks to wipe out the Miniblins as they pour into the car.

1 Explore the Fire Realm

2 Aid Goron Village

3 Find the Fire Sanctuary

4 Clear the Fire Temple

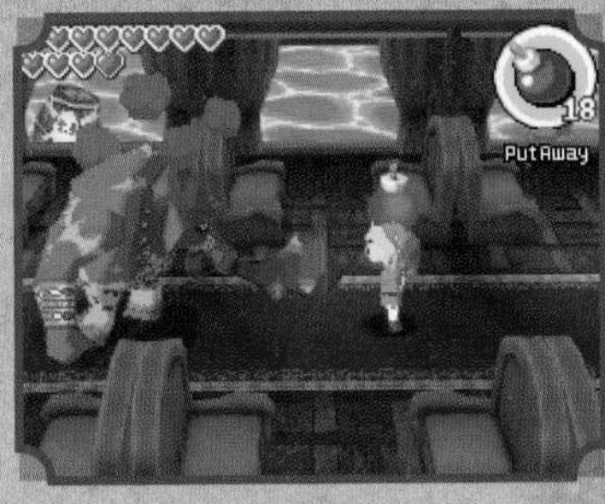

Eventually, a massive Big Blin joins the fight. Hit him with everything you've got—bombs, arrows, you name it—and don't let him near the villager. Also beware of additional Miniblins that sneak in and try to capture the man while you're busy fighting the Big Blin.

Reach Papuchia without allowing your passenger's recapture, and he'll be eternally grateful. His great relief and boundless gratitude manifest themselves in the form of a Force Gem.

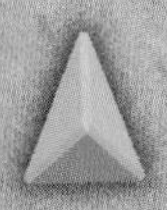

Force Gem 17

You got a Force Gem! The Ocean Rail Map has started glowing!

After rescuing the Papuchia villager, return to the Pirate Hideout to try the minigame challenge again—for you're now able to win fabulous prizes! To keep a healthy score multiplier going throughout the game, do your best not to miss your shots. Finish the challenge with a score of over 4,000 points to win a new Heart Container. Scoring more than 3,500 points but less than 4,000 points will earn you a new quiver, so it's well worth giving the game another shot!

Quiver 2

You got a quiver! Now you can carry the maximum number of arrows!

Heart Container 10

You got a Heart Container! You increased your life by one and refilled your hearts!

Warp Gate G

You're not far from the tracks that unlocked when you rescued the Papuchia villager from the Pirate Hideout, so set a course and explore these new rails. You discover a new warp gate over here; activate it to bring Warp Gate G online.

Rabbit Roundup

Your newfound Force Gems have restored even more track, and you know what that means: More bunnies are available for hunting! Go round and grab these furry friends if you feel like killing some time, making good use of the seven warp gates you've activated to this point to bounce around the overworld with greater speed.

- Ocean rabbit 9
- Mountain rabbits 1-9
- Desert rabbit 1

Disorientation Station

Your recently acquired Force Gems have restored Spirit Tracks leading to a long-lost destination of the Fire Realm called Disorientation Station. Explore the realm's farthest northwest tracks to find the station platform. Pull up here to explore this curious place.

Disorientation Station

Legend

1 Overworld Chest 33: Treasure
2 Overworld Chest 34: Red Rupee
3 Overworld Chest 35: Treasure
4 Dungeon Chest 1: Treasure
1 Train station

Items to Obtain

Red Rupee | Treasure x2 | Treasure

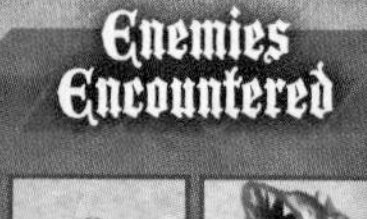

Spinut | Fire Baba

Hold on a second!
Is that...a soldier from
Hyrule Castle?

Upon your arrival at the station's platform, Zelda notices a soldier from Hyrule Castle standing on the cliff to the northwest. What is he doing here? Before rushing toward the out-of-place soldier, scour the area for three treasure chests.

The first chest is located on the low mesa to the west, but it's out of reach. Maybe the birds flying above can give you a lift? Equip your flute and play the Song of Birds. When a bird flies within view, equip your whip and latch on for a ride. Don't let go until you're directly over the mesa where the first chest awaits. Open the chest to receive your reward.

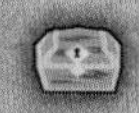

Overworld Chest 33: Treasure

Treasure

You got a treasure! Check it out on the Collection screen!

Don't drop off the mesa once you've opened the chest. Instead, play the Song of Birds again to hitch another ride. This time, hold on until you reach the low mesa to the east.

Move to the right side of the eastern mesa until you can spot an overhead post. Equip your whip and swing across to the ledge on the right. Once on the other side, you can follow a series of ledges and steps to the west, where the solider is standing.

While scurrying along the narrow ledge, watch your step. A number of Spinuts occupy the ledges and can knock you off if you're not careful. Before climbing the last set of steps, open this nearby chest to acquire a Red Rupee. Climb up the steps and rush past the soldier to open a third chest on a ledge to the east.

Overworld Chest 34: Red Rupee

Red Rupee

You got a Red Rupee! It's worth 20 Rupees!

Overworld Chest 35: Treasure

Treasure

You got a treasure! Check it out on the Collection screen!

785
See, I came here with my
friend to uncover a golden
treasure.
Menu

Finally, return to the soldier and find out what he's doing here. Apparently he came here with his friend to find a golden treasure. But they were attacked by a plant monster, causing them to become separated. The soldier managed to escape, but he hasn't seen his friend since. The soldier would like Link to enter the dungeon and perform a little reconnaissance. But he warns the place is a maze and offers a cryptic clue to find the treasure: From a room that knows no south, follow the rocky trail north and north....

1 Explore the Fire Realm

2 Aid Goron Village

3 Find the Fire Sanctuary

4 Clear the Fire Temple

Take the soldier's advice and head inside. As the soldier warned, this dungeon is tricky, so pay close attention to where you're going. Start by smashing the four pots in the center of this chamber to stock up on hearts and Rupees. You can travel in four directions from this room, but instead of searching this maze endlessly, follow these directions to reach the rumored golden treasure:

1. East
2. South
3. North
4. North

As you head north for the first time, you find a stone with an inscription—it's a note from the soldier's friend. He was never able to find the treasure or an exit. In his final note, he urges his friend to go on without him. Leave the stone behind and head north again.

The chamber ahead is occupied by two Fire Plants. Take on one plant at a time, attacking with your sword. As you sever the stem, the vicious bud hops on the ground, still alive. Be ready to slash it too.

Once the chamber is free of carnivorous flora, step on the small square stone in the northeast corner. Equip your flute and play the Song of Discovery to conjure a large chest from the ground—this must be the golden treasure the soldier was telling you about! Open the chest to acquire a rare treasure.

Dungeon Chest 1: Treasure

Treasure

You got a treasure! Check it out on the Collection screen!

Now that you've found the treasure, there's nothing else for you to do here. Exit the dungeon by heading south, then east to make your way outside, where the soldier is still waiting. Knowing that you found the treasure doesn't seem to cheer the soldier up—he's more concerned about his lost friend. If you read the stone sign left by the soldier's friend and then talk to the soldier, he says that he will do as his friend says and then gives you a Big Green Rupee. When you're finished speaking with the soldier, return to the train station and continue your journey.

Over the Top: Tower of Spirits 5

Through great courage and effort, Link and Princess Zelda have succeeded in purifying the great Fire Temple. With this fourth and final seal restored, the Tower of Spirits has been made whole once more. Fearing Anjean's unknown fate, Link and Zelda hurry back to the tower, anxious to discover what lies at its summit.

A Link to the Present

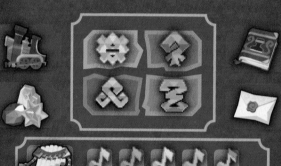

Items Already Acquired

Beedle Club Card | Bomb Bag 1 | Bomb Bag 2 | Bomb Bag 3 | Boomerang

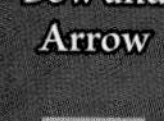

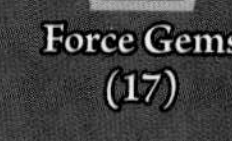

Bow and Arrow | Engineer Certificate | Engineer's Clothes | Fire Rail Map | Force Gems (17)

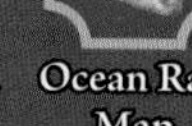

Forest Rail Map | Ocean Rail Map | Practical Cannon | Quiver 1 | Quiver 2

Rabbitland Rabbits (39) | Recruit's Sword | Recruit's Uniform | Shield of Antiquity | Snow Rail Map

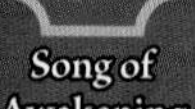

Song of Awakening | Song of Birds | Song of Discovery | Song of Healing | Song of Light

Spirit Flute | Stamp Book (17 stamps) | Whip | The Whirlwind | Wooden Shield

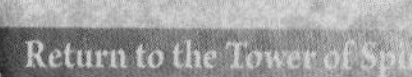

1 Return to the Tower of Spirits

2 Climb to the Tower's Top

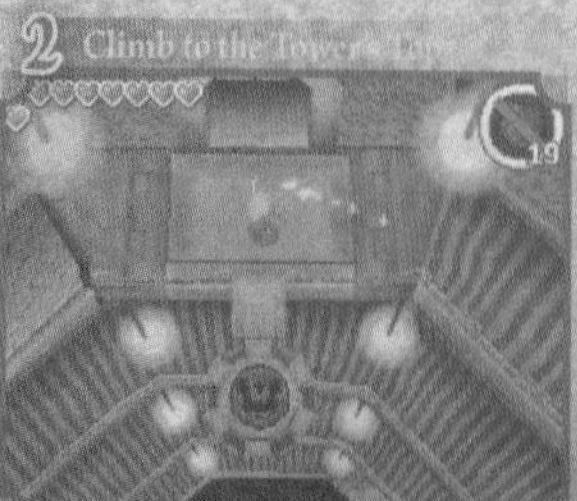

3 Defeat Byrne

4 Journey to the Sand Realm

Task 1: Return to the Tower of Spirits

Back to the Tower

Wherever you are, set a course for the Tower of Spirits, expecting to encounter the typical overworld enemies en route. If you're coming straight from the Fire Temple, you'll be happy to find that Spirit Tracks now lead from the Fire Realm directly into the tower—they materialized when you restored the Fire Temple's energy flow.

Arriving at the tower, Link and the princess find no trace of Anjean. Hope she's okay! Zelda suggests they press on and explore the top of the tower, where they're sure to find some answers.

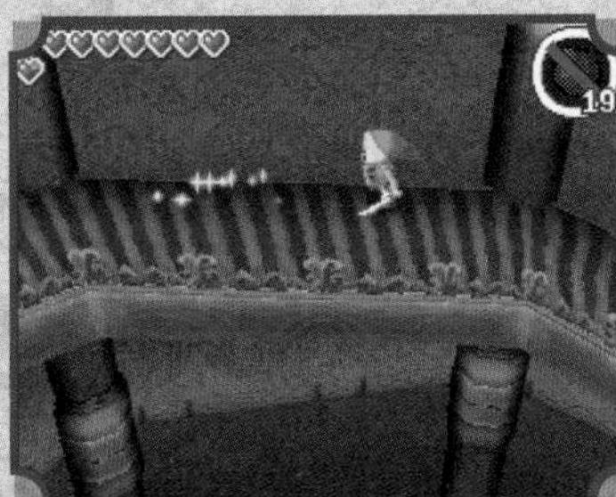

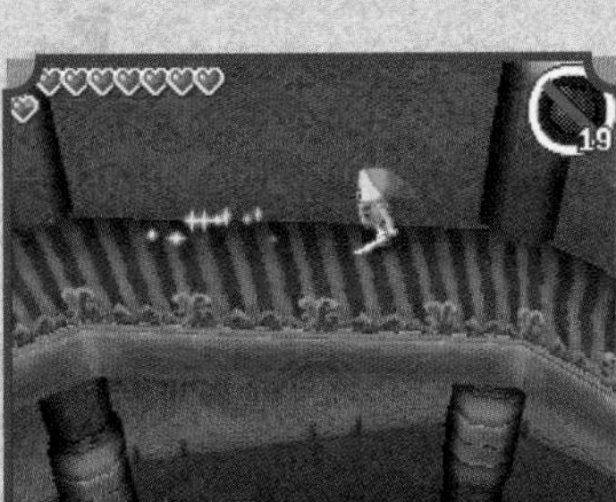

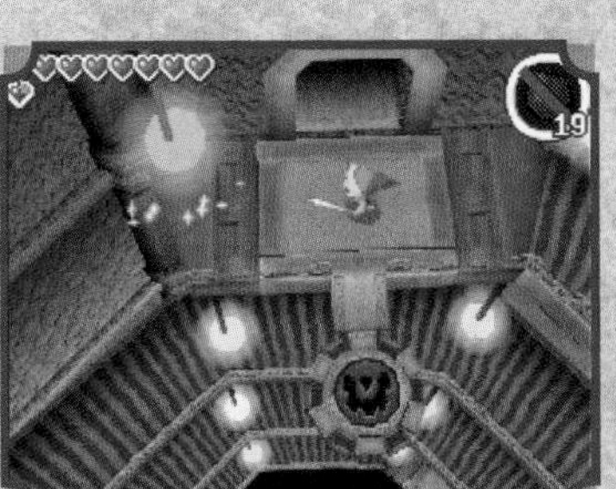

Check your vertigo at the door and climb the spiral staircase, entering the highest door. No need to revisit previous floors; if you've been following this walkthrough carefully, you've fully explored each section of the tower below this point.

Task 2: Climb to the Tower's Top

Tower of Spirits

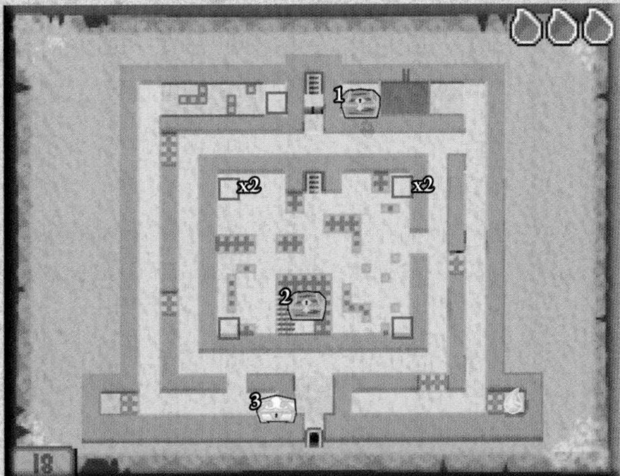

Tower of Spirits, Eighteenth Floor

Tower of Spirits, Nineteenth Floor

Enemies Encountered

Key Master, Mounted Miniblin, Phantom, Stalfos, Wrecker Phantom, Geozard, Boss: Byrne

Tower of Spirits, Twentieth Floor

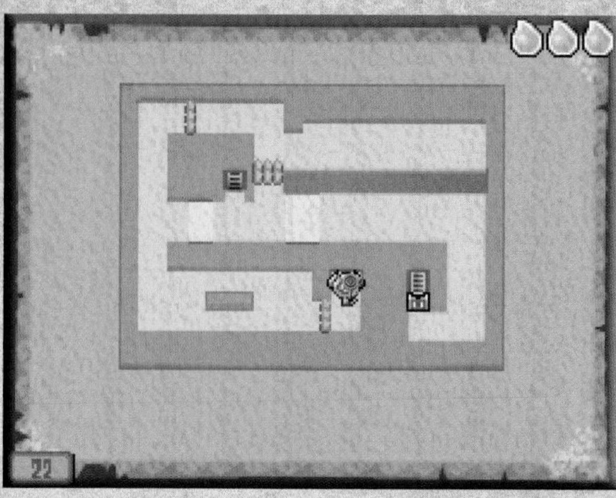

Tower of Spirits, Twenty-second Floor

Tower of Spirits, Twenty-first Floor

Tower of Spirits, Twenty-third Floor

Legend

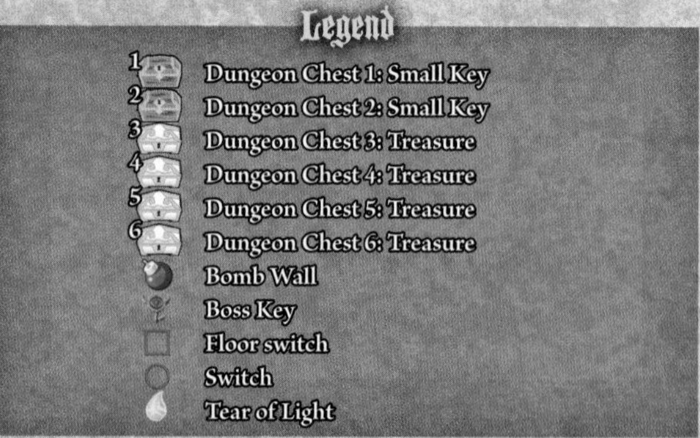

Items to Obtain

1 Return to the Tower of Spirits

2 Climb to the Tower's Top

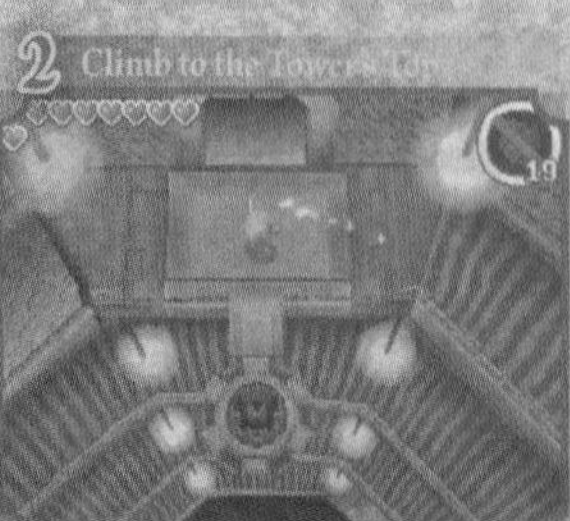

3 Defeat Byrne

4 Journey to the Sand Realm

Tower of Spirits: Eighteenth Floor

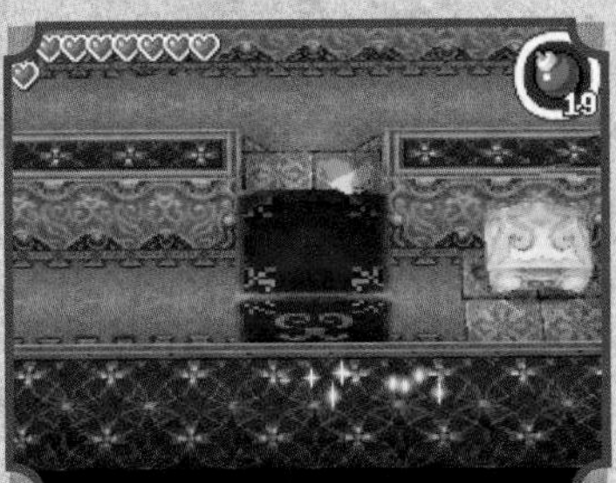

This is it: the final climb to the top of the tower. Run left from the start zone and note a big treasure chest sitting in the eighteenth floor's southwest corridor. A giant block stands in your way, but mark the chest's location for future reference.

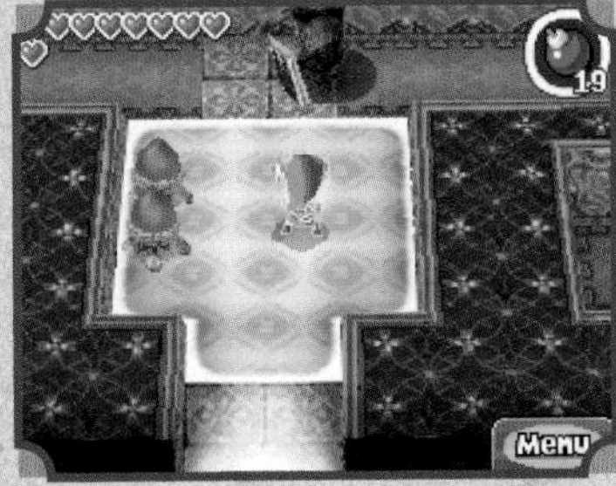

Return to the entry safe zone and wait for a nearby roaming Phantom to pass by. These are a new type of Phantom called Wrecker Phantoms. They chase Link down with great speed by rolling up into huge wrecking balls! It's best to keep well out of sight when one of these rolling guardians lurks nearby.

Double-tap the screen to perform somersaults that can help you escape Wrecker Phantoms who are hot on your heels.

Wrecker Phantom

Hits to Defeat: 1 (with powered-up sword)
Attack Type: Contact
Power: Strong
Damage: 1 heart
Threat Meter

After the Wrecker Phantom has gone, dash to the right and use one bomb followed by another to blast through the nearby cluster of bomb blocks. Be ready to retreat to the entry safe zone if a Phantom is drawn to the noise.

TIP

Fresh out of bombs? Trick a Wrecker Phantom into smashing the bomb blocks for you! Just stand near some bomb blocks, attract a Wrecker Phantom, then sidestep away before the rolling guardian bowls you over. It's riskier than using bombs, but it does the job!

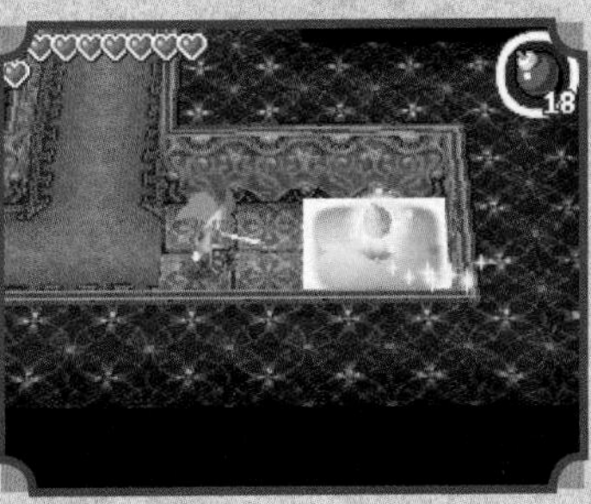

Use more bombs to blast through the southeast blocks, exposing a safe zone with a Tear of Light. Rest here for a moment and collect your first Tear. Two more to go!

Tear of Light

You got a Tear of Light! Gather three of them to power up your sword!

Since you're getting rid of all these blocks, you might as well do away with the bomb blocks in the east corridor. Blast through to make navigating the floor a little easier—handy when you're trying to outrun a Wrecker Phantom!

Now make your way up and around so you can bomb the floor's west blocks. Seek shelter at the northern and southern safe zones as needed.

Next, head to the northwest safe zone, where you discover a few movable blocks. Pull the first one backward to get it out of your way, then pull the second block backward and to the south. This lets you reach a floor switch; step on the switch to make a small chest appear on a northeast ledge.

Head for the northeast safe zone, then use the whip to swing across the wide pit and reach the chest you've just revealed. It contains a Small Key!

Dungeon Chest 1: Small Key

Small Key

You got a Small Key! Use this key to open locked doors!

That's all you can do here for now. Use your newfound key to open the north door and proceed upstairs in search of more Tears.

Tower of Spirits: Nineteenth Floor

Run right as you enter this floor, and collect an arrow aimer from atop the floor's northeast stairs. Ignore the hopping Mounted Miniblins, and carry the aimer back to the west.

Set the arrow aimer down on the unique floor tile to the right of a sealed door on the floor's west side. Stand on the floor switch to the north to open the door, then ready the boomerang. Toss the boomerang past the door, and whack the arrow aimer on the other side, setting it to fire north.

If necessary, use the boomerang to point the other aimer west, then fire an arrow at it. The arrow is redirected between the two aimers and is sent into an eye switch beyond the door.

Activating the eye switch extends a bridge across the floor's southeast pit. Loop up and around to reach the bridge, and cross it without engaging the Mounted Miniblins on patrol.

Beware: a Wrecker Phantom materializes to the east as you explore the floor's south hall and immediately starts rolling after you! Sprint west through the bomb blocks, taking a direct route to the far safe zone.

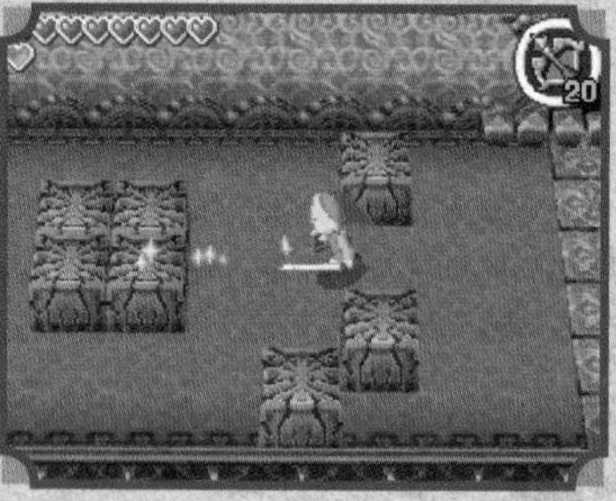

1 Return to the Tower of Spirits

2 Climb to the Tower's Top

3 Defeat Byrne

4 Journey to the Sand Realm

You need to possess one of those Phantoms if you're going to cross that lava you saw downstairs. Wait until the guardians return to their patrol routes, then work to stun one with a strike from behind. Quickly possess the Phantom and return to the twentieth floor. Skip the lava for the moment and continue backtracking to the nineteenth floor.

Tower of Spirits: Nineteenth Floor, Fourth Visit

Now that Zelda's no longer a giant rolling behemoth (she's now just a plain old, garden-variety behemoth), she's able to carry Link around on her back. Go to the northeast platform, ignore its arrow aimer, and have Link leap atop his Phantom partner.

Carry Link to the floor's center; it's time to use those elevated arrow aimers. Have Link scale the tiny steps and stand on a floor switch to open a nearby door. Have Zelda pick up one of the arrow aimers, then move her onto the unique floor tile beyond the door. Fire two arrows, relaying them northward into two eye switches.

Activating the eye switches causes two chests to appear nearby. Open them both to score two more worthy treasures for your collection, then return to the twentieth floor.

Dungeon Chest 4: Treasure

Treasure

You got a treasure! Check it out on the Collection screen!

Dungeon Chest 5: Treasure

Treasure

You got a treasure! Check it out on the Collection screen!

Tower of Spirits: Twentieth Floor, Third Visit

Return to the lava and have Link hop onto Zelda's back. Cross to the far door, where you find an arrow aimer.

Have Link leap off Zelda's back and collect the aimer. Have him ride Zelda once more and go east.

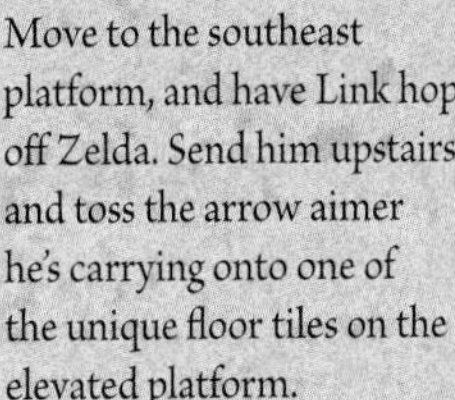

Move to the southeast platform, and have Link hop off Zelda. Send him upstairs, and toss the arrow aimer he's carrying onto one of the unique floor tiles on the elevated platform.

Point the arrow aimer to the east and fire an arrow into it. The arrow strikes a distant eye switch, opening an elevated door to the west. The door closes after a short time, but at least you've figured out how to open it.

Return Link to Zelda's back and backtrack out of the lava. From the height of Zelda's back, Link can reach an overhead post with his whip. Swing back across the lava to reach a high north ledge.

Another arrow aimer sits on the high ledge. Pick it up, then have Zelda move close so that Link can leap down onto her back. Ferry Link back out of the lava again.

Have Link dismount from his Phantom steed once they're back on solid ground. Drop the arrow aimer, then get Link back on top of Zelda. Whip-swing across the lava again, landing Link on the high north platform.

Switch to Zelda and move her into contact with the arrow aimer Link left on the ground. Zelda lifts the aimer high overhead; have her carry it back across the lava. Next, position Zelda on the unique floor tiles atop the southwest platform.

Now you're all set to solve this little puzzle. If necessary, use the boomerang to ensure Zelda's arrow aimer is facing due west, then fire an arrow into the other aimer—the one you left on the southeast platform.

The clock is ticking, so quickly shoot another arrow at Zelda's aimer to send it flying through the elevated door before it closes. The arrow strikes a remote aimer that sends it northward, right into contact with an eye switch that opens the lower door, granting access to some stairs.

Great work! That was tricky. Swing Link back across the lava, and move Zelda close by, then hit Zelda with just about anything (whip, boomerang, etc.) to make her drop the aimer she's carrying. Return Link to Zelda's back, and make one last trek across the lava, heading for the staircase.

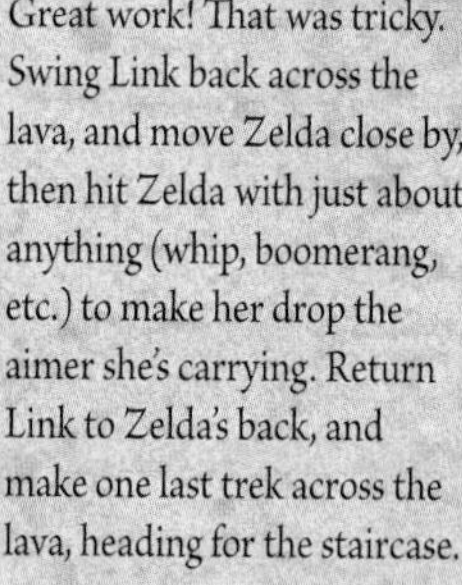

Tower of Spirits: Twenty-first Floor, Revisited

This is just a quick trip up to the next floor above. Smash pots and Item Bulbs for hearts and ammo as you make for the next set of stairs.

One of this floor's southern Phantoms gives a clue about a weak wall up here. Before heading upstairs, go to the twenty-first floor's northeast corner and place a bomb there to blast into a small room with a long-lost treasure chest.

Dungeon Chest 6: Treasure

Treasure

You got a treasure! Check it out on the Collection screen!

1 Return to the Tower of Spirits

2 Climb to the Tower's Top

3 Defeat Byrne

4 Journey to the Sand Realm

Tower of Spirits: Twenty-second Floor

You've reached the floor with the Boss Key, but this item is not easy to claim. Begin by sending Zelda north, moving her past the flames on the ground. Guide her counter-clockwise around the floor, heading for the Boss Key. Link can take a shorter route to the key by sprinting across the sand.

Smash the Item Bulbs near the Boss Key to ensure Link has a quiver full of arrows, then move Zelda past the flames and have her pick up the electrified key. On cue, a gang of Key Masters pop up, intent on keeping their treasure far away from the Boss Key door.

Switch back to Link and call to Zelda; you need her close. Wipe out the Key Masters you encounter as you return to the floor's center. Link must cross the sand while Zelda moves through the northern flames.

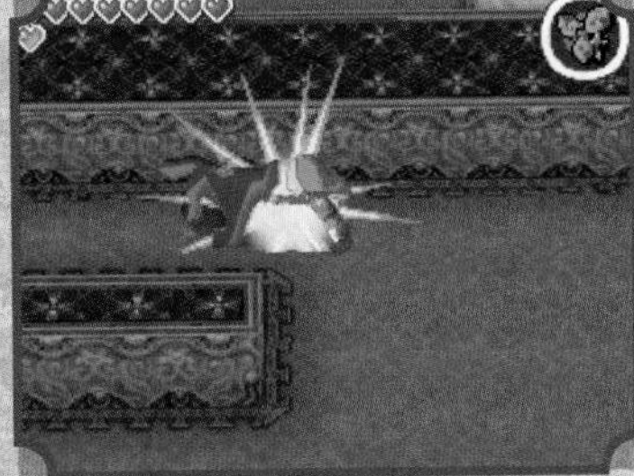

Once Zelda is safely beyond the first set of northern flames, leave her there and switch to Link. Move Link within sight of the two remaining Key Masters to the northeast, then quickly pick off both monsters with arrows from afar.

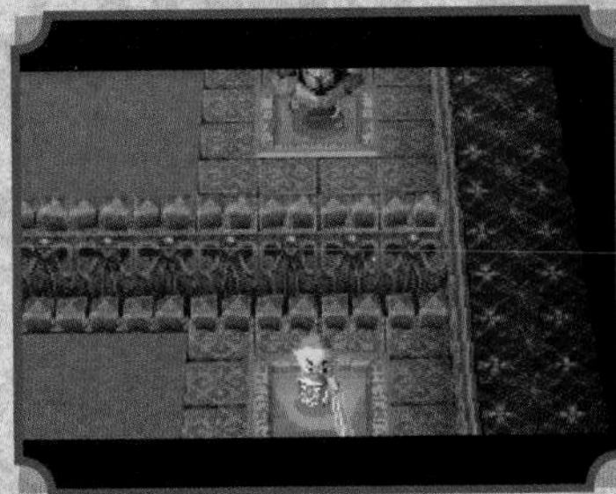

The Key Masters reappear after a short time, so you've got to move quick! Place Link on the red circle floor tile to the right, then switch to Zelda and get her onto the matching tile up north. Do this quickly or the s will appear and snatch the Boss Key away.

Zelda's in the clear after she trades places with Link. Steer her toward the Boss Key door, and she'll heave the key into its lock. Way to go!

With the Boss Key door opened, the floor's flames extinguish, allowing Link to join his partner. Climb the staircase the Boss Key door was blocking to advance even closer toward the tower's apex.

Tower of Spirits: Twenty-third Floor

The twenty-third floor is pretty bare, but there are a few pots along the walls that beg for a good smashing. After looting the place, have Link and Zelda work together to shove open the giant double door. This causes a blue warp light to appear and opens the way upstairs.

CAUTION

A difficult boss fight lies ahead. If you're wounded or lacking potions, consider warping back out of the temple and making a quick run to Castle Town for supplies.

Task 3: Defeat Byrne

Byrne

Hits to Defeat: Multiple
Attack Type: Contact and Range
Power: Strong
Damage: 1/4 heart (all attacks)

Threat Meter

If Byrne hits Zelda, Link must attack the gauntlet to break Byrne's grip, and vice versa. When Link is grappled, he'll steadily lose health until Zelda breaks the hold.

Entering a majestic stained-glass hall, Link and Princess Zelda find none other than Byrne waiting for them. An intense fight breaks out after a few heated words; Byrne jumps atop a high pillar, leaping around to several others and firing beams of evil energy down at his prey.

During the first stage of this challenging fight, keep control of Link and run about, avoiding Byrne's ranged attacks. Zelda will block his energy beams, so try to keep her between Link and Byrne. Hearts may appear if the princess blocks several beams in a row.

Eventually, the camera will pan down low, and Byrne will prepare to launch his retractable gauntlet. A targeting crosshair appears over Link or Zelda, showing who Byrne is aiming for. Run around as Link and try to get Byrne to fire and miss.

Make Byrne miss, then quickly switch to Zelda and direct her to grab his gauntlet while it's stuck in the ground. Just trace a line from Zelda to the gauntlet and she'll move to grab it.

Zelda pulls Byrne to the ground, bringing the fiend down to Link's level. Switch to Link and assault Byrne with rapid sword strikes.

Repeat this sequence to bring Byrne down a second time and inflict more damage. Byrne adds a new attack during the second phase, firing a slow-moving energy ball that knocks Zelda for a loop if it hits her. Have Zelda follow Link and keep moving to avoid and block Byrne's ranged attacks.

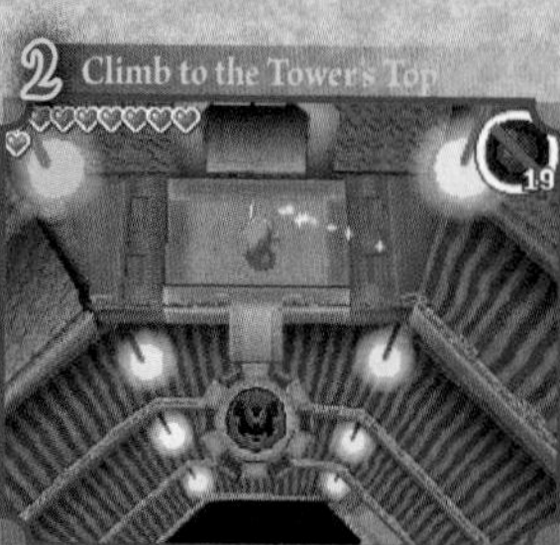

After walloping Byrne for a second time, the battle moves to its third phase, during which Byrne remains on the ground and swipes furiously at Link with his heavy gauntlet. Keep moving and stay out of range of Byrne's fast attacks.

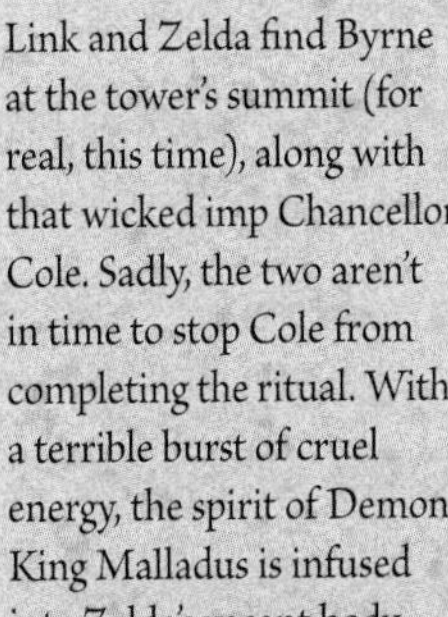

Wait for a moment when Byrne isn't attacking, then unleash a fast sword combo with Link. Byrne will block every blow, but then he'll leap back and begin to glow with villainous power.

Quickly move Link behind Zelda while Byrne is preparing his next attack. The villain soon streaks forward, rushing at Link. Ensure Zelda is in the way and she'll lock up with Byrne, interrupting the attack.

Now's your chance! While Zelda and Byrne are locked together, circle Link behind Byrne and whale away on his vulnerable backside. Repeat this sequence if needed—it won't be long before Byrne has had enough.

Beaten—but far from broken—Byrne flees through a far doorway. You can't let him escape!

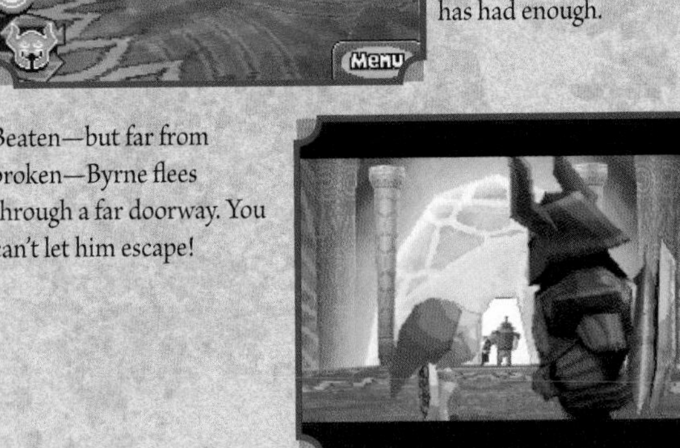

Chase after Byrne, climbing a long, winding staircase that runs along the tower's exterior. Thought you were at the top, didn't you!

Link and Zelda find Byrne at the tower's summit (for real, this time), along with that wicked imp Chancellor Cole. Sadly, the two aren't in time to stop Cole from completing the ritual. With a terrible burst of cruel energy, the spirit of Demon King Malladus is infused into Zelda's vacant body.

Malladus may be reborn, but he's far from fully recovered—all those years of captivity have taken their toll. Still, the Demon King is easily able to knock Byrne for a loop, punishing him for his inability to stop two mere children from meddling in his affairs.

Suddenly, that terrible, demonic train that Link and Zelda glimpsed during their first run-in with Cole and Byrne appears, soaring past the tower and whisking Cole and Malladus away from danger. With a hysterical cackle, Cole assures his foes that the whole world will suffer once Malladus's revival is complete.

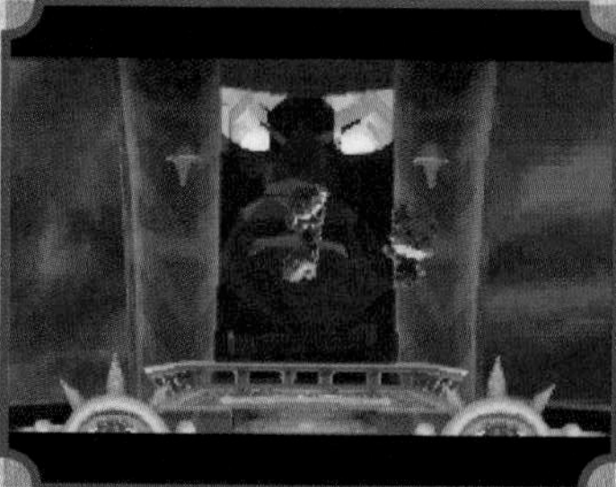

Things seem grim indeed, but a ray of light peeks through the clouds when Anjean suddenly putters into view. The old Lokomo must have had a few tricks left up her sleeve, because she's alive and well—and ready to help once more.

With nothing else to do atop the tower, the party heads downstairs and boards the Spirit Train for a group chat. Feeling sorry for Byrne, they even decide to carry him along.

Anjean explains that Malladus is close to full revival but that there's still time to stop him. A legendary artifact known as the Bow of Light holds the key to the Demon King's undoing. Armed with the Bow of Light, Link should be able to rid Zelda's body of Malladus's wicked presence.

Anjean goes on to say that the Bow of Light is kept deep inside a foreboding place called the Sand Temple. The whole place was built to protect the Bow of Light, so it's filled with all sorts of devious traps. No matter—the Bow of Light must be obtained!

Go to the final temple, the Sand Temple.

Zelda points out that the Spirit Tracks don't lead to the desert, but Anjean has another surprise: the old Lokomo hands over a Force Gem she's been hoarding all this time. This special Force Gem restores a bunch of track in the Ocean Realm, granting passage up to the northern desert. Perfect!

Though this is indeed a Force Gem, it's not counted as one of the 20 you can collect to open up optional tracks. Nope, this one's special!

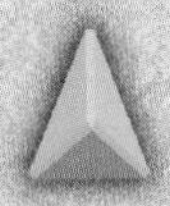

Force Gem

You got a Force Gem! The Ocean Rail Map has started glowing!

1 Return to the Tower of Spirits

2 Climb to the Tower's Top

3 Defeat Byrne

4 Journey to the Sand Realm

Task 4: Journey to the Sand Realm

With Malladus's revival imminent, Link and Zelda waste no time speeding out of the tower and rolling into the Ocean Realm. If you've been following this walkthrough carefully, there are no extra side quests for you to carry out at this point. Set a course for those sandy dunes to the north and be on your way to the Sand Realm!

The Sand Realm is a special place that's found mostly in the Ocean Realm, but it also stretches up north into the Fire Realm. You could say that it's a realm amongst realms!

Dunes of Doom: The Sand Realm

Though they succeeded in defeating Byrne, Link and Princess Zelda were not able to prevent Chancellor Cole from reviving his master, the great Demon King Malladus. It will take time for the Demon King to fully revive—but time is short indeed. Link and the princess must hurry to the Sand Realm, a desolate place where the mythical Bow of Light is said to be kept. If this sacred weapon can be retrieved, the forces of darkness may yet be repelled!

A Link to the Present

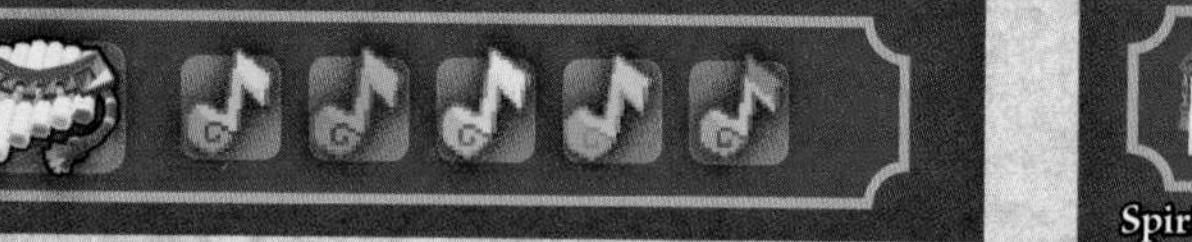

Items Already Acquired

Beedle Club Card	Bomb Bag 1	Bomb Bag 2	Bomb Bag 3	Boomerang
Bow and Arrow	Engineer Certificate	Engineer Clothes	Fire Rail Map	Force Gems (17)
Forest Rail Map	Ocean Rail Map	Practical Cannon	Quiver 1	Quiver 2
Rabbitland Rabbits (39)	Recruit's Sword	Recruit's Uniform	Shield of Antiquity	Snow Rail Map
Song of Awakening	Song of Birds	Song of Discovery	Song of Healing	Song of Light
Spirit Flute	Stamp Book (17 stamps)	Whip	The Whirlwind	Wooden Shield

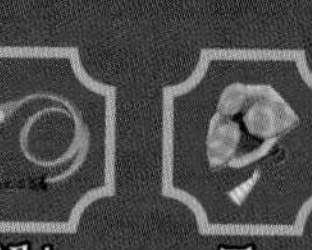

1 Explore the Sand Realm

2 Find the Lokomo Guardian

3 Reach the Sand Temple

4 Clear the Sand Temple

Task 1: Explore the Sand Realm

To the Sand Sanctuary

Enemies Encountered

Malgyorg

Danger in the Dunes

Go carefully while traveling in the Sand Realm, for dangerous Malgyorgs survive this desolate place by preying upon the unwary. Whenever you see shark fins emerge from the sand near your trolly, you know that Malgyorgs are on the hunt!

Malgyorg

Hits to Defeat: 1
Attack Type: Contact
Power: N/A
Damage: 1 heart

Threat Meter

Malgyorgs are immune to attacks while traveling underground, and they strike very suddenly by leaping out of the ground and slamming your train. Blast a Malgyorg while it's airborne to defeat it before its attack lands. Better yet, sound your train's whistle to force all nearby Malgyorgs to jump, giving you a chance to blast them before they strike.

Look at your map and notice that the Sand Realm's tracks come to a sudden end at one point near the middle. Set a course for that spot, and you'll discover a station when you reach the end of the line. Park there to visit the Sand Sanctuary.

Task 2: Find the Lokomo Guardian

Sand Sanctuary

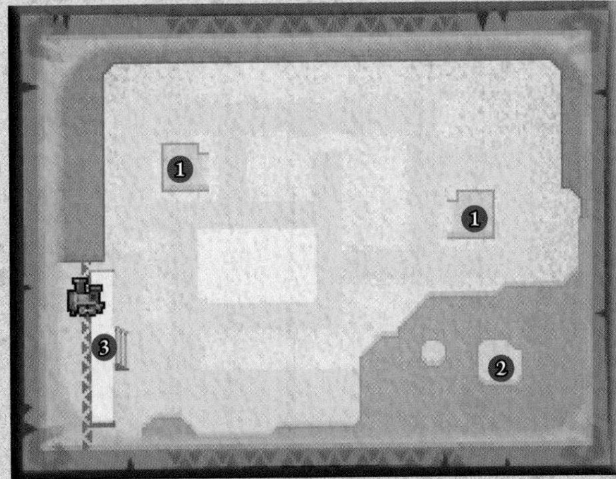

Sand Sanctuary

Legend

1. Gossip Stone
2. Stamp station
3. Train station

Puzzling Place

Sadly, there's no Lokomo guardian to be seen at the Sand Sanctuary. Instead you find two Gossip Stones, each one standing next to a bomb flower. A stone tablet stands in the middle of the place as well, and cobblestone roads cover much of the terrain.

NOTE

Don't bother trying to reach the stamp station on the south isle—you can't just yet.

Wake the statues and read the tablet for three cryptic clues. After reading them all, you should realize that the entire sanctuary has been fashioned in the form of the Sand Realm itself—its cobblestone roads mimic the realm's Spirit Tracks. Another clue hints that something "sleeps" where the "gazes of the statues meet." Huh? But there are no gazing statues around here—just lazy, sleeping ones!

Armed with this somewhat confounding knowledge, leave the Sand Sanctuary and set a course that takes you all around the Sand Realm's tracks. It's time to check out the local scenery!

Roll around enough and you're bound to notice one of the Sand Realm's many large statues. These giant sculptures are all staring at the same thing: the realm's southern plateau. This must mean something, but you can't seem to visit that plateau—there are no stations around.

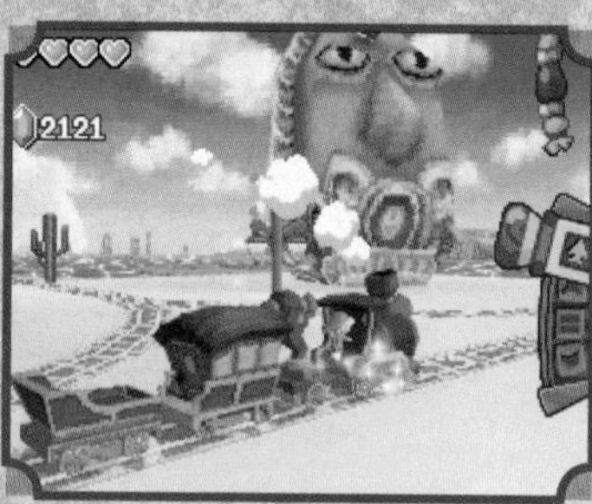

Missing Link: Rabbit Roundup

As long as you're surfing the Sand Realm, you might as well go after some of its native desert rabbits. These bunnies can be pretty elusive, but try your best and you can catch desert rabbits 2 through 5 right now. Just check the overworld map to see where they're hiding.

Have you figured it out? Return to the Sand Sanctuary and take a good look at its map. Remember that the sanctuary is a representation of the Sand Realm itself, its roads mimicking the Spirit Tracks. Go to the place where all the realm's statues were looking: the patch of sand between the cobblestone roads, right where the southern plateau would be located.

There's no plateau here, but the answers you seek must be close! Perhaps they lie underground? Pluck a bomb from one of those bomb flowers, or use one of your own if you like, and place it on the ground on the "southern plateau's" east side.

Blammo! Bomb the right spot, and you destroy a hidden trapdoor, revealing a staircase. It must lead to the guardian's chamber! Scamper downstairs and see what's what.

1 Explore the Sand Realm

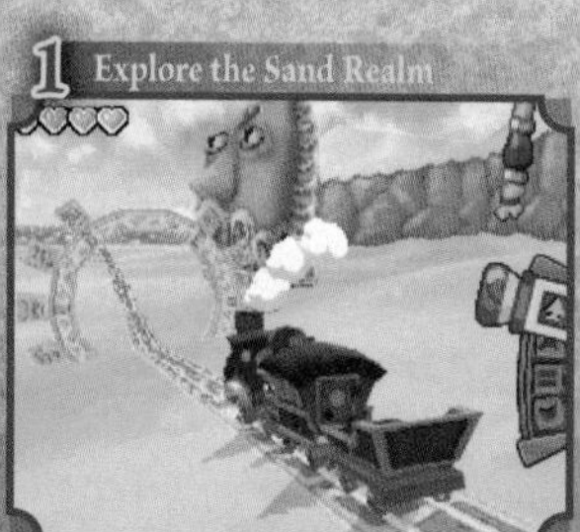

2 Find the Lokomo Guardian

3 Reach the Sand Temple

4 Clear the Sand Temple

Rockin' with Rael

Sure enough, the Sand Realm's humble Lokomo guardian awaits you in a private chamber beneath the surface. This one's name is Rael, and, boy, has he got a mean Lokomo song to teach you! This is by far the toughest tune yet, demanding you make a fast stylus swipe at the end to skip from the teal note to the green. Practice the melody until you've got it down, then go for the real thing.

Rock out with Rael as you've done with so many other Lokomos, completing a rousing duet. The sweeping song generates positive vibes, reenergizing the rest of the Sand Realm's missing Spirit Tracks. Now you can travel to the Sand Temple!

2372
And finally, you will face the impenetrable temple
Menu

Rael thanks you for acing his righteous ballad, then issues a grave warning: you must pass three trials en route to the Sand Temple. Hey, passing trials is what you do best! Bid Rael a fond farewell and hop aboard your train. The Sand Temple awaits!

Task 3: Reach the Sand Temple

To the Sand Temple

Enemies Encountered

Malgyorg — Boss: Rockite

Eye in the Dark

Set a northward course out of the Sand Sanctuary, taking the newly energized Spirit Tracks up north toward the Fire Realm. Well, actually, you're heading to the northern portion of the Sand Realm, which just happens to spill into the Fire Realm a teensy bit. Try and keep it straight!

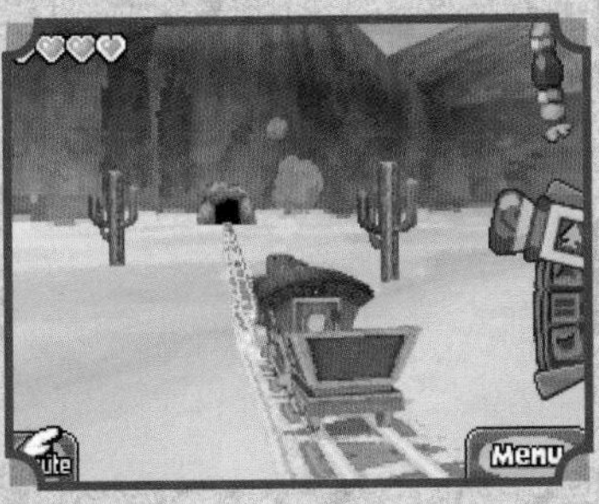

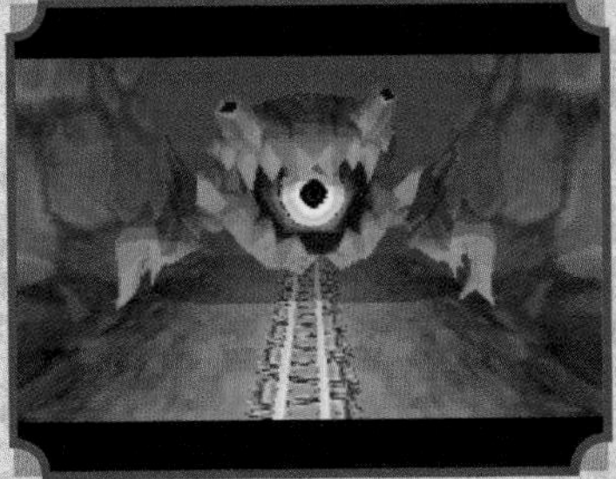

As you pass through the first long tunnel, a massive creature drops from the ceiling, landing behind your train. Oh no, it's another Ghoma! You mean there's more than one of these things?!

Rocktite

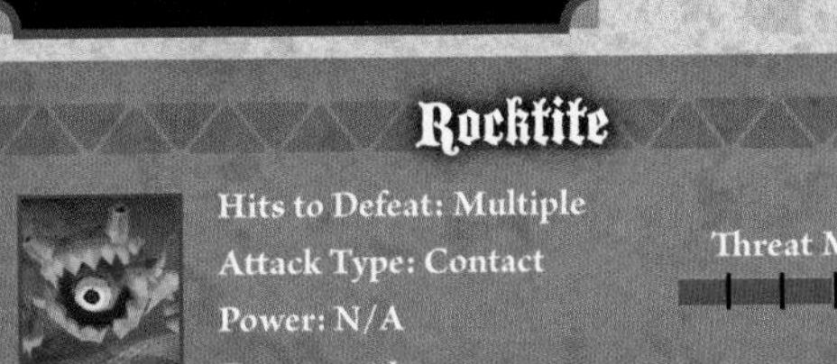

Hits to Defeat: Multiple
Attack Type: Contact
Power: N/A
Damage: 1 heart

Threat Meter

Tackle this giant cave crawler just as you did the first: pound its glowing eyeball with relentless cannon fire! Keep whaling away on the Rocktite's eye until it collapses, falling behind into the pitch. Be ready to resume fire the moment you see its eye start to glow again.

Eventually, you begin passing explosive barrels that are lodged in the cave wall. At this point, the Rocktite closes its mouth, and you must catch the beast with at least one explosive barrel to make it open up and expose its eye again. Just blast each barrel you pass to detonate it, hoping to harm the Rocktite. Then feed its eye a steady diet of cannonballs.

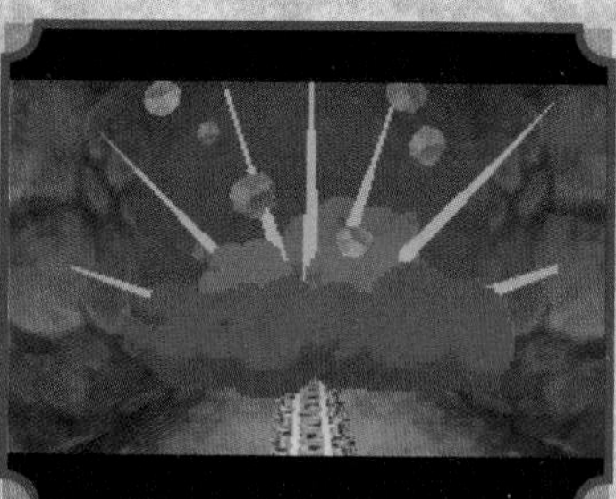

The Rocktite's a tough customer, but keep it up and you'll eventually drop the brute. Moments later, you exit the tunnel, finding yourself in new surroundings.

Forgotten Tunnels

Great, there's another tunnel ahead! Don't worry; there are no scary cave monsters in this one. This is the entrance to the Forgotten Tunnels, and you'll understand the meaning behind the name once you try driving through.

The Forgotten Tunnels make no sense, spitting you out great distances from where you should emerge from each tunnel. Invariably, you'll end up back where you started. Trial and error seems to be the only way through.

Missing Link: More Desert Rabbits

While struggling to navigate the Forgotten Tunnels, keep an eye out for three more desert rabbits alongside the tracks. These are desert rabbits 6 through 8.

To get through the Forgotten Tunnels without all the hassle, drive around until you're sent back to the start. (Zelda will point this out when it occurs.) From the Forgotten Tunnels' entrance, do the following to get through:

1. Enter the Forgotten Tunnels through the main entrance (from the start).
2. When you emerge, immediately go in reverse as if to backtrack out.
3. You emerge up north instead. Immediately go in reverse as if to backtrack out.
4. You emerge to the east instead. Turn right at the junction and enter the south tunnel.
5. You emerge down south. Congratulations, you made it!

Having navigated the Forgotten Tunnels, only one trial remains. Continue south to return to the Sand Realm's southern half, not far from the Sand Temple.

1 Explore the Sand Realm

2 Find the Lokomo Guardian

3 Reach the Sand Temple

4 Clear the Sand Temple

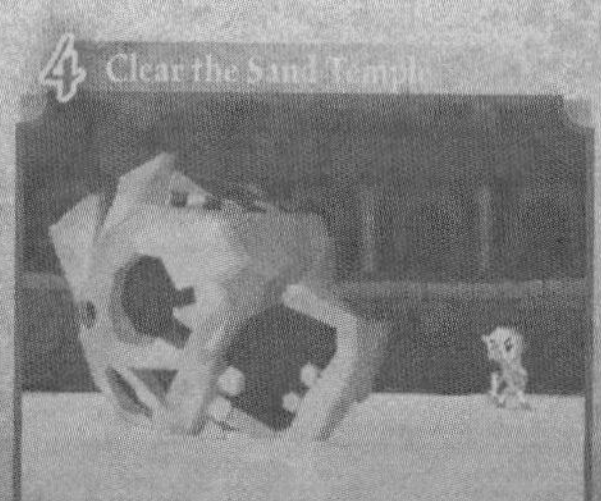

Impenetrable Temple

As you return to the Ocean Realm (don't get us started...), turn left at the first junction and ride to the end of the line to discover Warp Gate H. Activate the gate with a round from your cannon to bring the overworld's eighth and final warp gate online.

Reverse back around the turn again, and this time, bear right at the junction to speed toward the Sand Temple. Beware: The whole temple is covered in cannons that open fire as you make your approach!

Missing Link: Final Desert Rabbits

We know you're getting shot at from every angle, but could you do us a huge favor? Would you mind picking up desert rabbits 9 and 10 as you circle the temple? That'd be great. Thanks!

Teach these wannabe cannons a lesson in how to really blow stuff up. Blast back with your own trusty cannon, knocking inbound fire from the sky and destroying each and every gun emplacement as you circle the structure. If you're fast, you can destroy most of the cannons before they even have a chance to fire on your train.

When all its defensive cannons have been obliterated, the Sand Temple's front door opens. If this place was this tough to get into, just think of how nasty it's gonna be inside!

Task 4: Clear the Sand Temple

Sand Temple

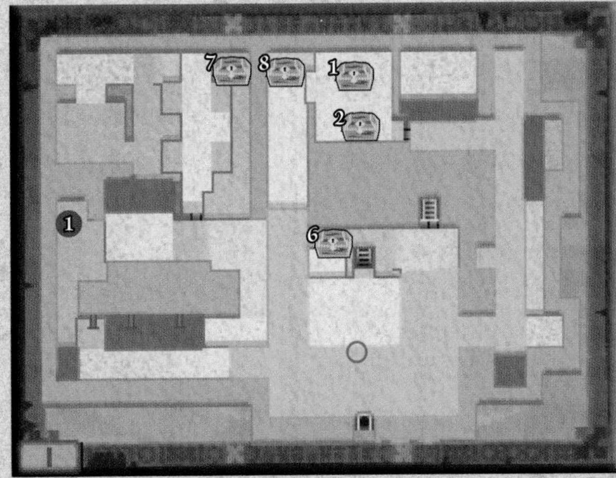

Sand Temple, First Floor

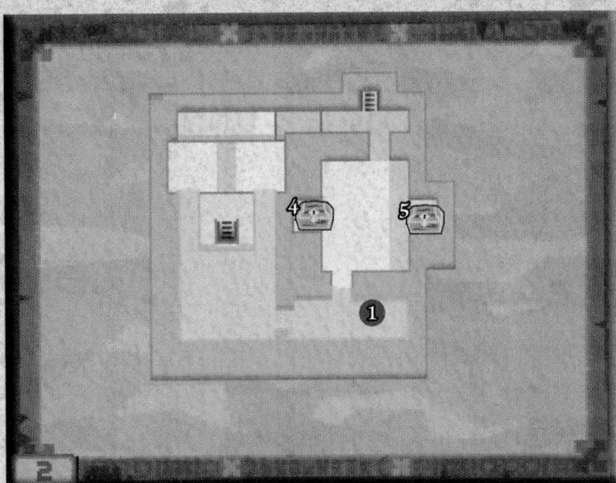

Sand Temple, Second Floor

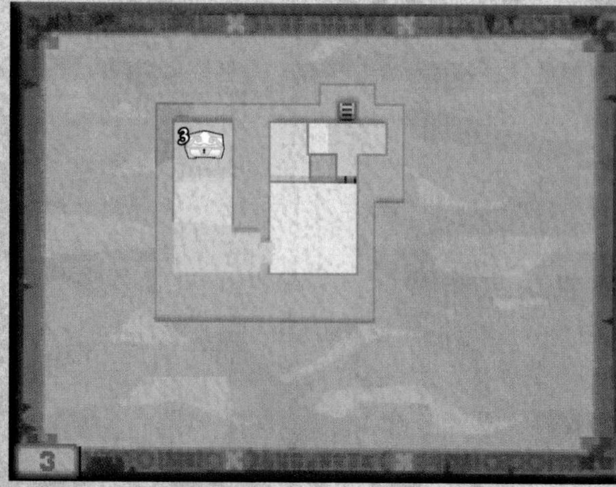

Sand Temple, Third Floor

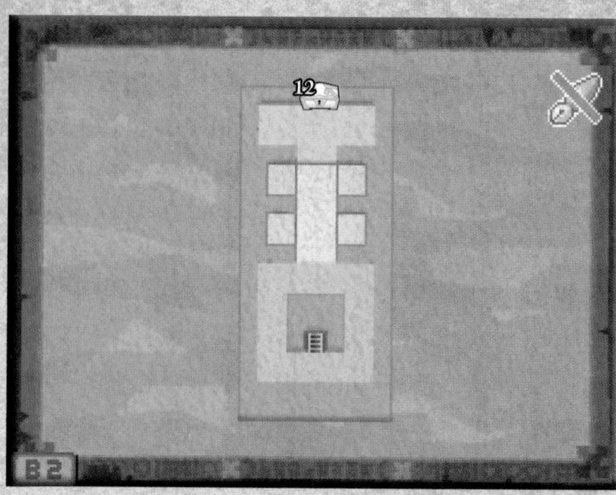

Sand Temple, Basement Second Floor

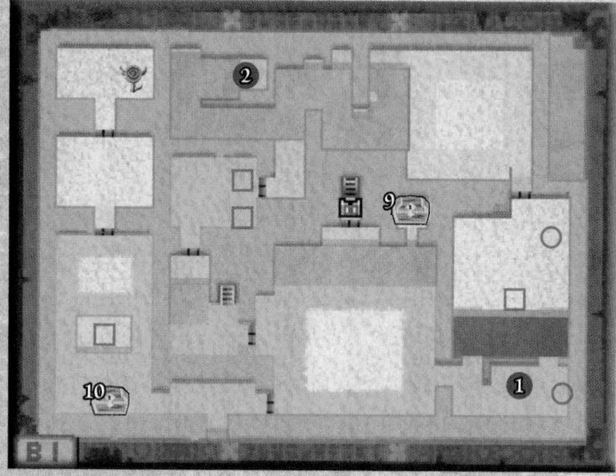

Sand Temple, Basement First Floor

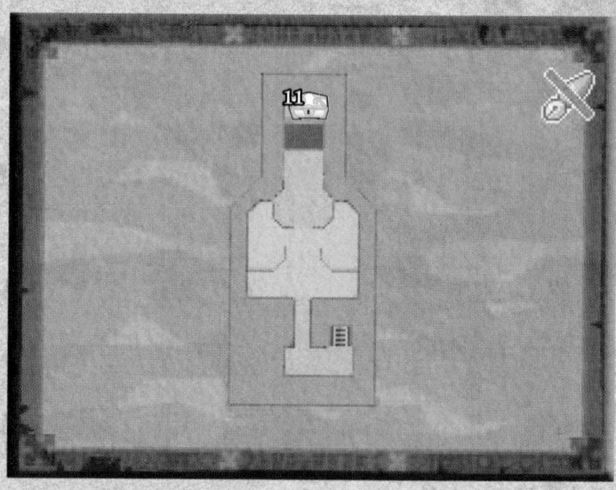

Sand Temple, Basement Third Floor

1 Explore the Sand Realm

2 Find the Lokomo Guardian

3 Reach the Sand Temple

4 Clear the Sand Temple

Legend

1 Dungeon Chest 1: Green Rupee
2 Dungeon Chest 2: Small Key
3 Dungeon Chest 3: Sand Wand
4 Dungeon Chest 4: Red Rupee
5 Dungeon Chest 5: Treasure
6 Dungeon Chest 6: Treasure
7 Dungeon Chest 7: Red Rupee
8 Dungeon Chest 8: Red Rupee
9 Dungeon Chest 9: Red Rupee
10 Dungeon Chest 10: Treasure
11 Dungeon Chest 11: Heart Container 11
12 Dungeon Chest 12: Bow of Light
Boss Key
Floor switch
1 Gossip Stone
2 Stamp station
Switch

Sand Temple: First Floor

The Sand Temple is a cunning place full of deadly traps and difficult monsters. You can explore much of the first floor's central area, but there's only one path to travel: Make your way up the east corridor, darting back and forth between the tumbling boulders to avoid being crushed.

Dive into the side hall up north, and pull out the bow. Hold your stylus on the screen, and aim at the eye switch on the far north wall. Fire an arrow between the rolling boulders, slipping it between them and activating the eye. This opens the nearby door.

A chest sits on the sand beyond the door. Kick it open for a Green Rupee. No, not a Big Green Rupee—just a plain old Green Rupee.

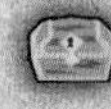

Dungeon Chest 1: Green Rupee

Green Rupee

You got a Green Rupee! It's worth 1 Rupee!

Opening the chest triggers a trap: several Stalfoses spring up from the sand and begin stalking Link. Quickly dispatch these foes with bombs or the bow, or conserve ammo and punish them with the whip if you like.

Another chest appears after you dispatch all the Stalfoses. This one holds a much better prize: a Small Key!

Dungeon Chest 2: Small Key

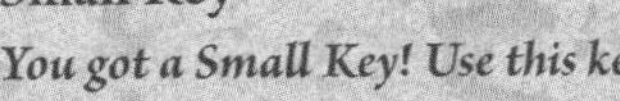

Small Key

You got a Small Key! Use this key to open locked doors!

With key in hand, backtrack to the floor's central area, sidestepping boulders as you go. Open the only locked door within reach and then venture upstairs.

Sand Temple: Second Floor

Cross the odd footbridge up here without touching its pointy edges. Smash a few pots for hearts on the other side. There's no fence over here; drop down to the lower area.

Beware: Foul demons known as Sandmen roam the room to the south. You can't harm these creepy fiends at present, so hurry past them; they won't chase you very far.

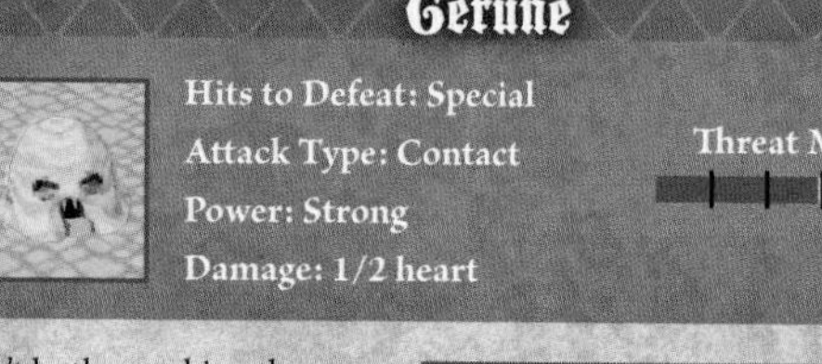

Gerune

Hits to Defeat: Special
Attack Type: Contact
Power: Strong
Damage: 1/2 heart
Threat Meter

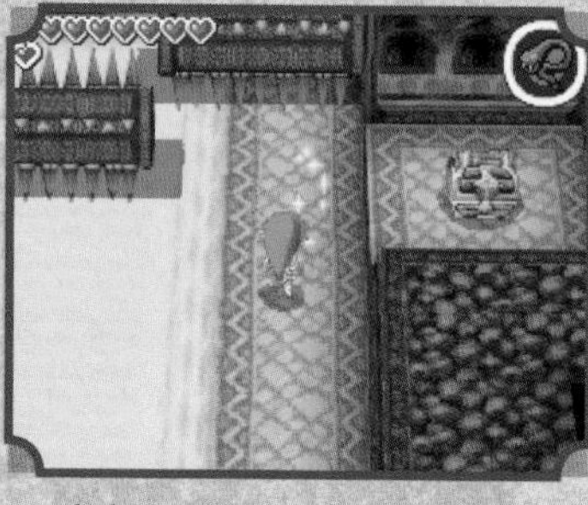

Don't bother waking the Gossip Stone at the end of the south hall; the two chests it reveals are plainly visible as you navigate the next sandy chamber. Avoid the rolling spike traps, and make a note of both chests, which sit on high ledges and are currently out of reach. Scamper up the north stairs to reach the temple's top floor.

Sand Temple: Third Floor

The top floor is small, but it houses an ancient and valuable artifact. However, you must defeat the artifact's guardians if you wish to claim the prize: three challenging Stalfos Warriors bound up from the earth, ambushing Link!

Stalfos Warrior

Hits to Defeat: Multiple
Attack Type: Contact (sword)
Power: Strong
Damage: 1/2 heart
Threat Meter

Unlike regular Stalfoses, these fiends are too aggressive to easily handle with the whip. They stalk Link relentlessly and unleash fast, sweeping sword combos. Use bombs or the bow to dispatch them with speed, doing your best to keep your distance the whole time.

You got the Sand Wand! Tap any sandy area to raise the sand into a wall!

Best the Stalfos Warriors to gain access to a large, ornate chest. Lift its lid to obtain the Sand Wand—a very handy tool to carry in this dusty place!

Dungeon Chest 3: Sand Wand

Sand Wand

You got the Sand Wand! Tap any sandy area to raise the sand into a wall!

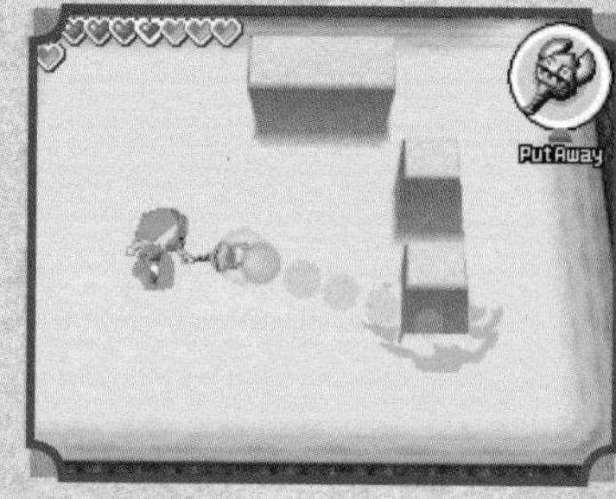

Test your new toy out on the sandy floor where you fought the Stalfos Warriors. Equip the Sand Wand and then trace your stylus around the sand. The sand rises up wherever you point it, creating temporary walls that collapse after a few seconds. Neat!

You've cleared out this floor, now you must use the Sand Wand to escape this place. Raise the sandy floor, including the patch beneath Link's feet. Then quit using the Sand Wand and hurry across the sand you've raised to reach the high north ledge, circumventing the sealed door. Drop to the ground and return to the previous floor.

1 Explore the Sand Realm

2 Find the Lokomo Guardian

3 Reach the Sand Temple

4 Clear the Sand Temple

That statue said a chest should be here, but there's none around. Maybe you just haven't revealed it yet. Go south and roll the pin once more so you may cross back over to the west, circumventing the fence that stood in your way.

Put Away

Battle two scary Sandmen after crossing the pin, again using the Sand Wand to freeze them before smashing them up. Beat both Sandmen to reveal the hidden chest back across the stone pin. Those Gossip Stones never lie!

Backtrack and open the small chest to score a Red Rupee; then cross the pin again and return to the place where you fought the Sandmen.

Dungeon Chest 7: Red Rupee

Red Rupee

You got a Red Rupee! It's worth 20 Rupees!

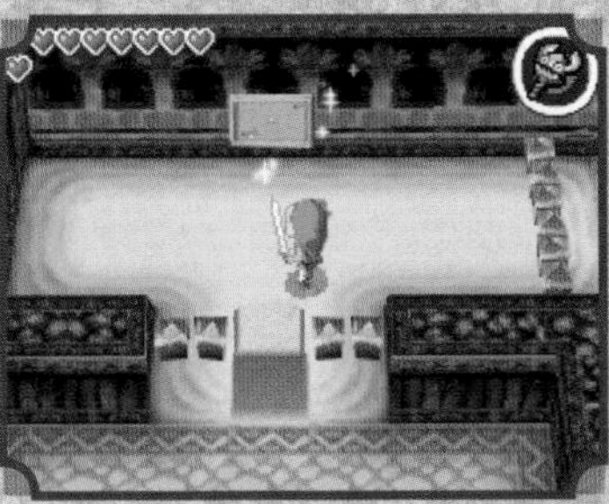

There's something on the far north wall, but a fence keeps you from getting close enough to read it. Raise Link over the low fence with the Sand Wand, then tap the sign to see what it says.

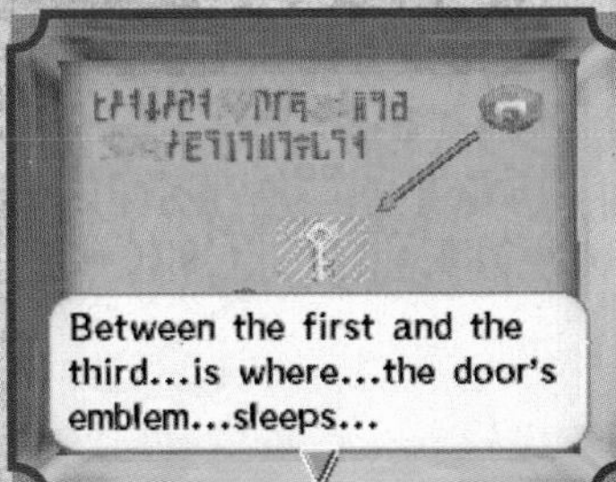
Between the first and the
third...is where...the door's
emblem...sleeps...

The sign shows a drawing of a single eye to the northeast and a trio of eyes to the southwest, with a key between them. It hints that "between the first and the third is where the door's emblem sleeps." What could it mean? A hidden key?

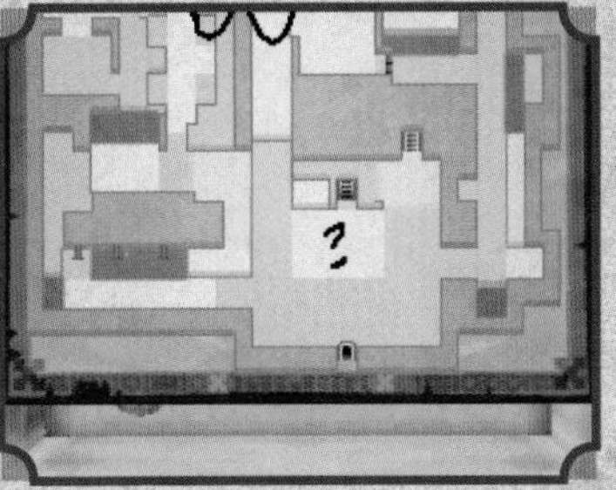

Have you solved the riddle? The sign is referring to this very floor—more specifically, its eye switches. Remember the first eye switch you shot here—the one to the northeast, near the rolling boulders. From there, trace a line on your map toward the trio of eye switches you recently activated on the floor's west side. You'll find a key in the center of that line!

Backtrack all the way around the floor, returning to the east hall with the rolling boulders. This time, use the Sand Wand to raise Link onto the east balcony, running past the boulders with less trouble. Leap from the corner of the balcony, and dart into the north side hall when the time is right. The breaks between the boulders are few and far between now, so this can be a tricky move to pull off.

17
Put Away

The door beyond the boulders has somehow sealed itself again, so you'll need to shoot the northern eye switch once more to open it. Two boulders sit in front of the eye switch now, blocking your shot. Use the Sand Wand to move the boulders out of your way, then strike the eye with an arrow and head through the door.

17
Menu

As you enter the sandy room beyond the door, the room seals, and new enemies emerge from the ground: Ergtoroks! These creatures are similar to Octives, rising up to fire spiky balls at Link from afar. In addition, Ergtoroks can move about underground, and they're smart enough to retreat when you send their projectiles back at them with the Whirlwind.

Ergtorok

Hits to Defeat: Multiple
Attack Type: Range
Power: Weak
Damage: 1/2 heart
Threat Meter

Link can block the Ergtoroks' projectiles with his shield, but because they often circle behind him, it's better to just keep moving. To damage an Ergtorok, you must first stun it: Use the Sand Wand to raise the sand beneath the creature while it's moving underground—target the telltale puffs of sand. After stunning an Ergtorok, raise Link up and then quickly close on the creature, hacking away at it before it recovers.

With the Ergtoroks down for the count, the floor's other hidden chest materializes on the west ledge. Raise Link up there and open the chest to score another glimmering Rupee.

Dungeon Chest 8: Red Rupee

Red Rupee

You got a Red Rupee! It's worth 20 Rupees!

You're right near the spot where the key you seek should be. Raise the sand to the south to discover the key, which was lost beneath the earth. Collect the key, then raise Link over the fence at the path's south end and hop down to the ground floor.

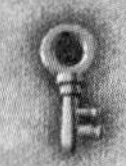

Small Key

You got a Small Key! Use this key to open locked doors!

You're almost done here. Go to the boulder that rests near the floor's central sand pit, and push it around by raising sand walls near it. Maneuver the boulder onto the seat of the strange southern device, which sports a hammer.

Once the boulder's locked in place, hit the nearby switch to activate the device, swinging the hammer and driving the boulder into the far wall with furious force. The boulder shatters when it strikes the wall, but it also smashes the wall to bits, revealing a staircase! Head downstairs to begin exploring the temple's basement.

Sand Temple: Basement First Floor

Smash the pots down here and solidify the quicksand to make it safe to cross. Use your newfound key to open the nearby door, and step through.

A pair of Sandmen attack you beyond the door, but you can use these enemies for a specific purpose. Freeze them both with your trusty Sand Wand, then quickly lift and place each frozen foe onto the room's pair of floor switches. When both switches are depressed, the east door opens—hurry through before the Sandmen recover!

1 Explore the Sand Realm

2 Find the Lokomo Guardian

3 Reach the Sand Temple

4 Clear the Sand Temple

The next stretch is a bit cruel, demanding fast reflexes. The passage's whole floor is made of quicksand, which you must freeze with the Sand Wand to cross. However, deviously placed arrow traps also fire pointy things at you from the walls, making this journey even more perilous. Begin by freezing the quicksand to the west and heading for the nearby stamp station.

Arrows are firing from the corner ahead, so you can't risk using the Sand Wand after you round the bend. Pause near the edge of the corner, and create a path to walk on that takes you past the arrows and over to the stamp station.

Your sand walls won't dissipate if you keep using the Sand Wand to keep them around. Make sure the one beneath Link's feet never vanishes!

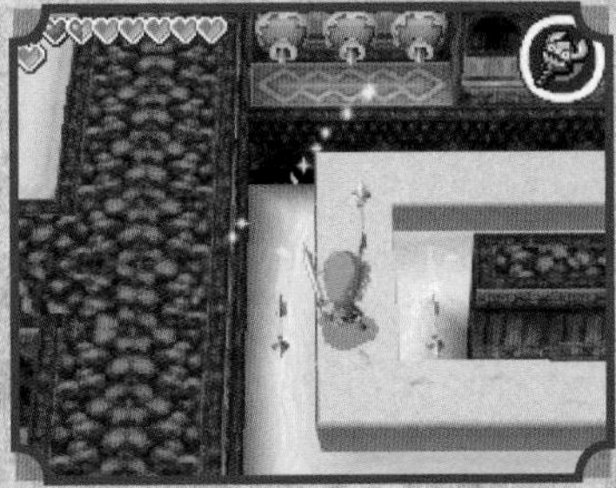

There's little need to fear these arrows while running along the sand; Link will block them with his shield as he sprints north. Of course, the return trip is a different story!

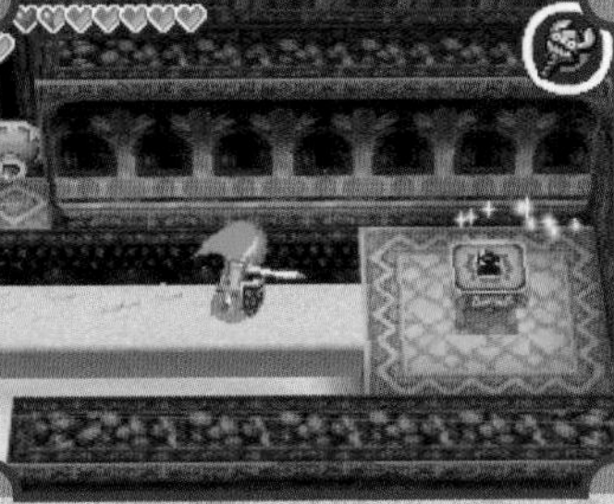

Plant a new stamp into Niko's stamp book, then take a moment to catch your breath. When you're ready to go, head back to the passage's starting point, moving quickly past those arrows and doing your best to time your run so you aren't shot in the back.

Now you must voyage east along the quicksand passage. Repeat the same tactics, pausing before each set of arrows to get the timing before dashing across. Remember: The sand won't vanish from beneath Link if you keep using the Sand Wand to hold it there. Pause at each available landing to gather your wits before pressing on.

When the quicksand passage mercifully ends, you arrive at an odd chamber with a giant block in its center. The block's top features a blue gemstone, and there's a blue tile with an indentation on the ground nearby. You must use the Sand Wand to tip the block several times, manipulating it so that its blue gemstone lands atop the blue tile.

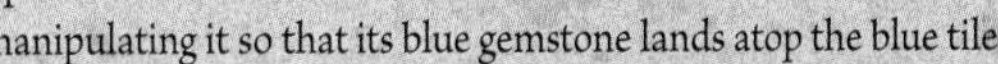

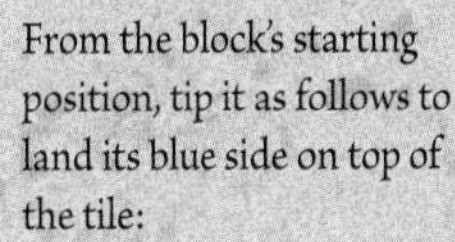

From the block's starting position, tip it as follows to land its blue side on top of the tile:

1. South
2. East
3. South
4. East
5. North
6. West

The south door opens when the block is put in place. Run south to discover another hammer device and a steady stream of rolling boulders. Step on the nearby floor tile to extend a bridge across the south pit, which retracts the moment you step off the tile.

This one's easy. Use the Sand Wand to stop a boulder, then maneuver the boulder onto the hammer device. Step on the floor tile, and then chuck the boomerang to trigger the switch that swings the hammer. The boulder is knocked across the bridge, bashing through a thick stone wall.

With the stone wall gone, you're able to strike the switch beyond the pit with the boomerang or an arrow. Trigger the switch to extend another bridge across the pit—one that stays put!

2457
All right! Here are all the treasures chests on this floor!
Menu

Wake the Gossip Stone beyond the bridge to learn the whereabouts of two hidden chests on this floor. Note them down and then go west to discover a second, more challenging block puzzle.

Before attempting to solve the block puzzle, use the Sand Wand to cross the north quicksand and reach a small chest that contains another Red Rupee.

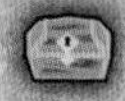

Dungeon Chest 9: Red Rupee

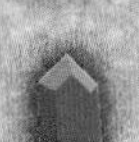

Red Rupee

You got a Red Rupee! It's worth 20 Rupees!

Now for the block puzzle. This time, you must maneuver two blocks onto two colored floor tiles. Shift the blocks as follows to land their blue gemstones on the two blue floor tiles:

Left block:

1. East
2. East
3. South
4. West
5. South
6. East
7. East

Right block:

1. West
2. West
3. South
4. East
5. South
6. West
7. North
8. West

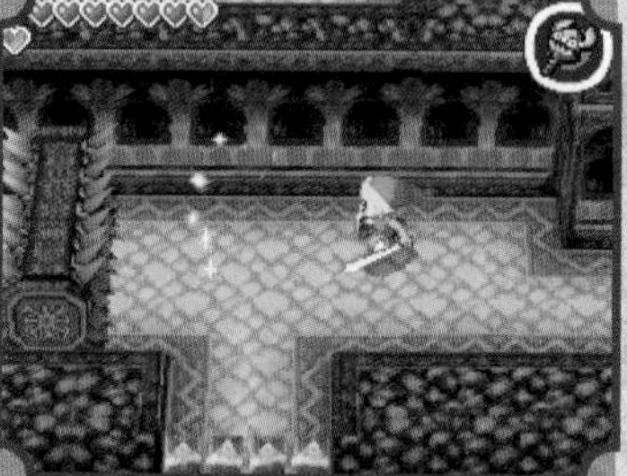

With both blue floor tiles activated, the blue door to the west opens. Head through and duck into a little nook to help you slip past a rolling spike trap.

Stalfos Warriors patrol the next room. Wipe them all out to reveal a treasure chest that contains another prized treasure.

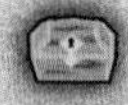

Dungeon Chest 10: Treasure

Treasure

You got a treasure! Check it out on the Collection screen!

Two rolling spike traps are at work to the north, and you must use one of them to open the north door. Freeze the southern spike trap with a wall of sand, then raise Link up and onto it. You can safely walk onto this object only from the north, so it may help to seal off the northern spike trap with a sand wall as well.

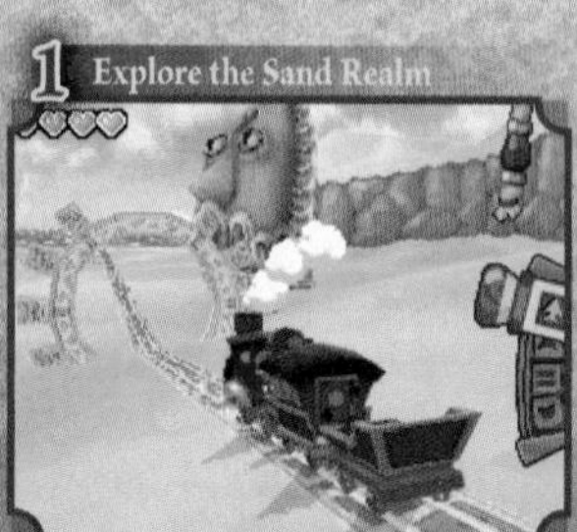

Cross the south spike trap to reach an elevated floor switch. Step on the switch to open the north door; then drop down and sprint through when it's safe to do so (halt the spike traps again if need be).

Link is trapped in the room beyond the spike traps, sealed in with a host of sneaky Ergtoroks. Raise these monsters up when they're moving underground to stun them, and then hack them apart as you did before. Clear the room to open its doors and continue onward.

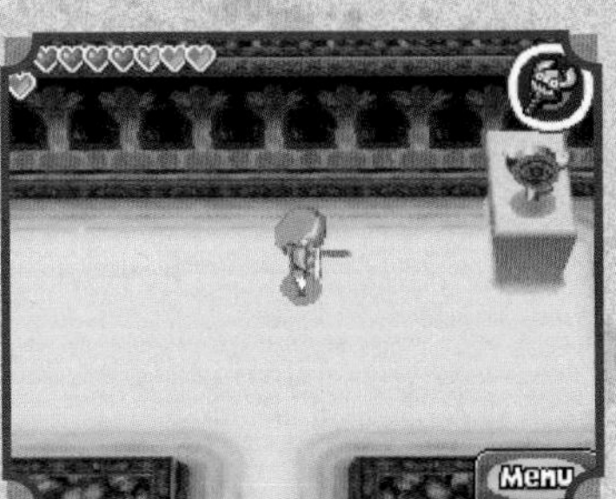

You've reached the floor's northwest chamber, but there seems to be nothing here. Not so! Raise up the sand here to discover two valuable items: a Big Green Rupee and, even better, the Boss Key!

Big Green Rupee

You got a Big Green Rupee! It's worth 100 Rupees!

With the Boss Key held high, make your way back to the double-block puzzle you solved before. You may need to toss the key and use the Sand Wand at times to get past traps. No Key Masters are about, so there's no harm in heaving the key.

Back at the block puzzle, move the blocks as follows to land their red circular knots atop the red circular tiles. Note that this pattern may only work if you followed the previous steps to place the blocks on the blue tiles:

Right block (originally the left block):

1. West
2. South
3. East
4. North
5. West
6. South
7. East

Left block (originally the right block):

1. North. That's it!

Now that both red floor tiles are activated, the red door across the north quicksand opens, exposing the Boss Key door. Solidify the quicksand with the Sand Wand, then quickly carry the Boss Key to its door, and toss it into the lock to open the way downstairs.

Sand Temple: Basement Second Floor

If you like, raise Link up to smash the pots that sit atop high nooks down here. Read the stone tablet at the hall's far end to reveal the blue warp light, then proceed through the door to face the Bow of Light's final guardian.

Skeldritch, Ancient Demon

Hits to Defeat: Multiple
Attack Type: Contact and Range
Power: Strong
Damage: 1/2 heart (all attacks)

Threat Meter

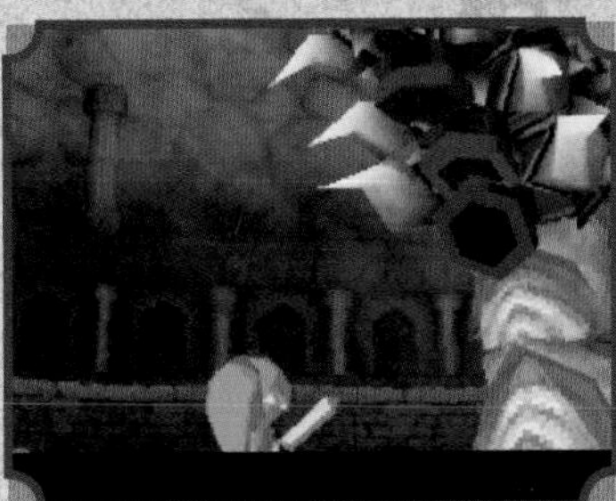

Skeldritch is a monstrous skeletal skull with a spinal cord that protrudes from the center of a sandy arena. To best this big bad boss, you must knock out each of its vertebrae, steadily lowering its head down to Link's level.

To knock out a vertebra, first run circles around Skeldritch, waiting for the fiend to fire a series of boulders at you. Get the timing down, and then use the Sand Wand to raise a thick wall that stops the last boulder in its tracks.

Quickly maneuver the boulder you've captured onto one of the many hammer devices that border the arena. Stop rolling the boulder and run to dodge Skeldritch's attacks as necessary.

Once the boulder is in place, whack the trigger switch to send it flying at Skeldritch, smashing the first of its many vertebrae.

Repeat this same sequence to destroy Skeldritch's vertebrae, one after the other. Skeldritch adds laser attacks and fires boulders with greater ferocity as the fight wages on; each of these attacks can be dodged by simply running circles around the boss, somersaulting whenever an extra burst of speed is needed.

Get close to Skeldritch to circle it at greater speed, avoiding its attacks more easily.

Skeldritch's upper vertebrae are covered by thick armor, but each one is missing a chink. Circle the boss to find those weak points, which are usually on its spine's backside.

Once you've discovered a chink in Skeldritch's armor, load a hammer device with a boulder and then circle around the boss, tricking Skeldritch into turning away from the loaded device. The idea is to lure Skeldritch into exposing its rear weak spot to the boulder. When Skeldritch is facing in the proper direction, wait for a lull between its attacks and then quickly hurl the boomerang around the boss, striking the hammer device's switch. If your aim is true, the boulder crashes into the exposed bone, destroying another vertebra.

Skeldritch's final vertebra's weak spot is not directly behind the boss, but slightly off to the side.

The fight changes drastically after you've severed all vertebrae. Skeldritch's massive skull starts hopping around on its own, chasing Link down and trying to gobble him up!

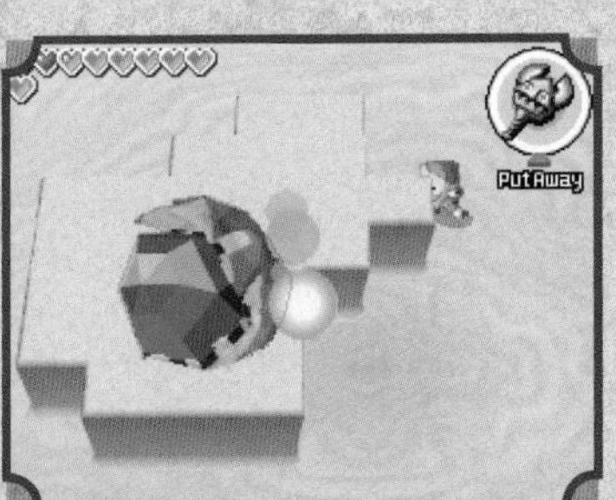

Don't let Link become Skeldritch's snack. Run away to gain some distance, then use the Sand Wand to raise the earth, surrounding your foe in solid walls of sand.

When Skeldritch is completely surrounded, the boss starts struggling to free itself. Now's your chance! Raise Link up and then dart behind Skeldritch, whaling away on the giant jewel atop its massive skull.

It doesn't take Skeldritch long to break free. Get behind the boss the moment you get it stuck!

Skeldritch speeds up after each assault on its skull's weak spot, chasing Link with greater tenacity. Don't give up; keep freezing Skeldritch in place so you may unleash Link's blade on its vulnerable jewel.

When Skeldritch finally calls it quits, you've passed the last test. The sand drains from the arena, revealing a staircase. Open the large chest that materializes to obtain another Heart Container, then go downstairs.

Dungeon Chest 11: Heart Container 11

Heart Container 11

You got a Heart Container! You increased your life by one and refilled your hearts!

Sand Temple: Basement Third Floor

It's quiet down here—almost peaceful. Break the silence by smashing the surrounding pots for goodies, then sprint up the north stairs to discover an ornate chest. Open this final chest to at last obtain the legendary Bow of Light.

Dungeon Chest 12: Bow of Light

Bow of Light

You got the Bow of Light! Tap and hold to charge and fire bolts of divine light!

A blue warp light appears after you collect the sacred weapon, but it's across a wide pit. Equip the Bow of Light and aim at the ornate eye switch on the far wall. Hold the stylus on the screen until the bow becomes charged with pure energy, then lift the stylus to loose the arrow—striking the eye switch and extending a bridge to the warp light.

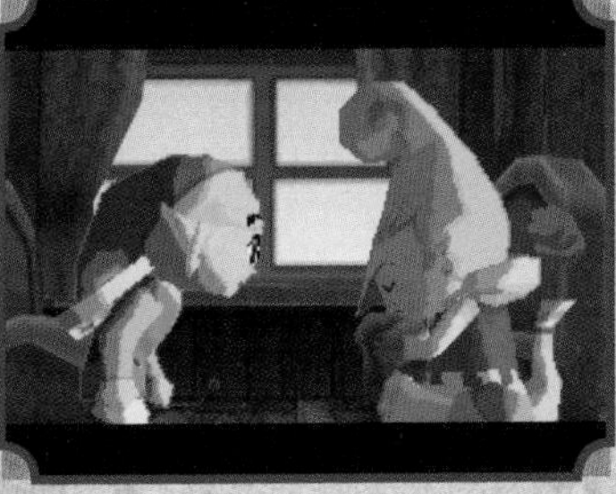

Congratulations! You've acquired the only weapon capable of ousting Malladus from Zelda's spiritless body. Return to the Spirit Train to inform Anjean of your success. You may now rush off to the Tower of Spirits to continue your journey, or you may check out the following Missing Links if you're up for grabbing some bonus loot.

Missing Links

This is it, dear friends: the last of the Missing Links. Well, not exactly. There is just one more side venture, even after these. So...yeah. Forget we said anything.

Items to Obtain

Enemies Encountered

Force Gem 18

You've no doubt received a second letter from Ferrus by now, asking you to pick him up at another vague location. This time, Ferrus is snapping photos along the Fire Realm's northwest tracks, almost directly north of the Goron Target Range. Go there and park near Ferrus for another trackside chat.

Letter

You got a letter from the postman! Go to the Collection screen to read it!

2496
Oh, yeah. Will you let me off at the Ocean Temple? I've always wanted to go.

This time, Ferrus asks you to bring him to the Ocean Temple. That's all the way down on the ocean floor! Well, anything for a friend. Agree to bring Ferrus to his desired destination, keeping in mind that you'll need to respect all signposts along the way.

Set a course for Warp Gate F and engage at maximum speed, Captain. If you haven't activated this particular warp gate, you'll find it on the overworld map, at the Fire Realm's southwest corner. Just head due south from the Goron Target Range—you can't miss it.

Warp Gate F spits you out just east of the entrance to the Ocean Realm's underwater rail system. Make the short trip west and enter the briny blue.

There's no scary Armored Train to worry about down here anymore, so simply ferry Ferrus to the Ocean Temple, enjoying the spectacular scenery along the way.

1 Explore the Sand Realm

2 Find the Lokomo Guardian

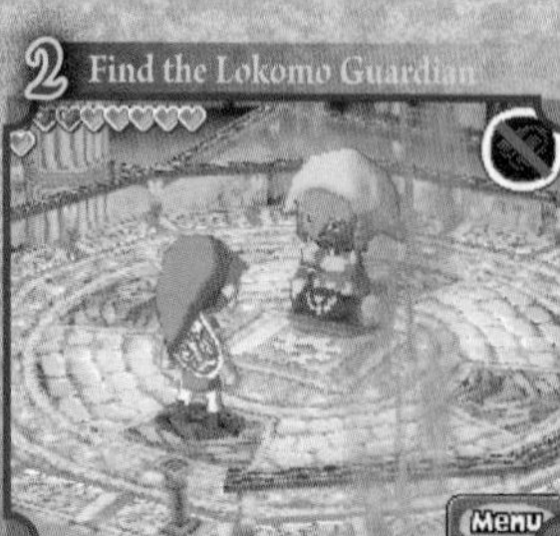

3 Reach the Sand Temple

4 Clear the Sand Temple

As a token of Ferrus's "ginormous" gratitude, he hands over a sparkly Force Gem that restores a long stretch of track on the Fire Realm's east side and links down to the Sand Realm. Not a bad haul!

Force Gem 18

You got a Force Gem! The Fire Rail Map has started glowing!

Force Gem 19

This next Force Gem is a tough one to get, but the tracks it unlocks lead to a very interesting place, making it well worth the effort. Ensure you've activated every warp gate on the overworld, then explore the track you've just revealed by acquiring Force Gem 18. There, you'll discover a unique station called the Dark Ore Mine.

Have you received Kagoron's letter yet? It hints of a treasure hidden around this strange place. Enter the mine and take the right passage, heading north until you reach a dead end. Play the Song of Discovery near two torches here to reveal Kagoron's treasure chest. Score!

Overworld Chest 36: Treasure

Treasure

You got a treasure! Check it out on the Collection screen!

Enter the mine's central cavern to meet a Goron who will sell you a rare commodity known as Dark Ore. Buy some of this special substance; someone who values the unique is sure to appreciate this item.

Your destination is the Trading Post located at the Forest Realm's southeast corner. Dark Ore melts in the sunlight, so you must use warp gates and tunnels to reach the place with your cargo intact. You have ten units of Dark Ore but need to complete the trip with only five. Go south from the Dark Ore Mine and enter the tunnel that leads into the Sand Realm.

Passing through this first tunnel is the most challenging part of the journey, for the place is home to another monstrous Rocktite. Fight this one just as you did the last, pounding its giant eye with cannonballs and detonating barrels along the sides of the tunnel to force the monster to open up whenever its mouth is closed.

Unfortunately, this bad crab isn't alone. Little Tektites also join in the fun, running up from behind and leaping at your train. Blast these little creeps in addition to whaling on the Rocktite.

Tektite

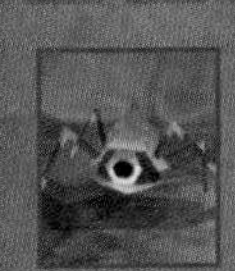

Hits to Defeat: 1
Attack Type: Contact
Power: N/A
Damage: 1 heart

Threat Meter

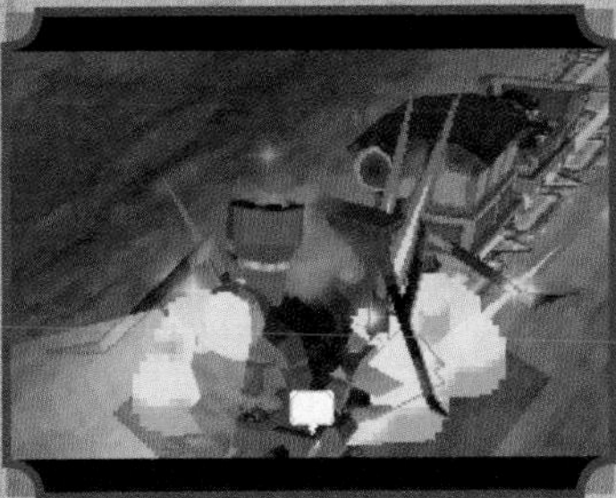

You must pass through the Rocktite's tunnel with no less than nine units of Dark Ore intact. Any less, and you won't be able to reach the Trading Post with the five units needed to get the job done—you lose four units to the sunlight. This means you can only suffer one hit during the entire trip through the tunnel. If you're hit more than once, you may want to let the monsters defeat you so you can restart from the Dark Ore Mine and try again.

Once you succeed in making it out of the tunnel, it's just a matter of taking the right warp gates to reach the Trading Post as quickly as possible. Keep your train in top gear and set a course for Warp Gate H, located just east of the Sand Temple.

After emerging from Warp Gate H's sister gate, plot a route down to Warp Gate G, which is just to the south. Passing through this gate lands you in the Forest Realm, just west of the Trading Post.

Get to the Trading Post with at least five units of Dark Ore to spare, and you've all but completed your task. Just speak with Linebeck at his shop, and the savvy salesman will be floored that you scored him so much ore. Five units of the precious substance is easily worth the Force Gem Linebeck parts with in trade—and it's sure to do more good in your hands than his!

887
Wh-what's this? You actually brought me some Dark Ore?!
Menu

Force Gem 19

You got a Force Gem! The Ocean Rail Map has started glowing!

Force Gem 20

2593
It does!
Nah.
Five birds for 300 Rupees. Sound good?
Menu

Don't worry, the twentieth and final Force Gem is much easier to grab than that last one. To get this one, you only need to buy five Cuccos from the merchant at Castle Town, then bring the birds to Rael, the Sand Realm's Lokomo guardian.

Swing by the Sand Sanctuary with your load of Cuccos and you'll thrill Rael, who's been yearning to study the curious animals. Give Rael five Cuccos and your good deed will be rewarded with a glowing Force Gem!

Force Gem 20

You got a Force Gem! The Fire Rail Map has started glowing!

Sand Sanctuary

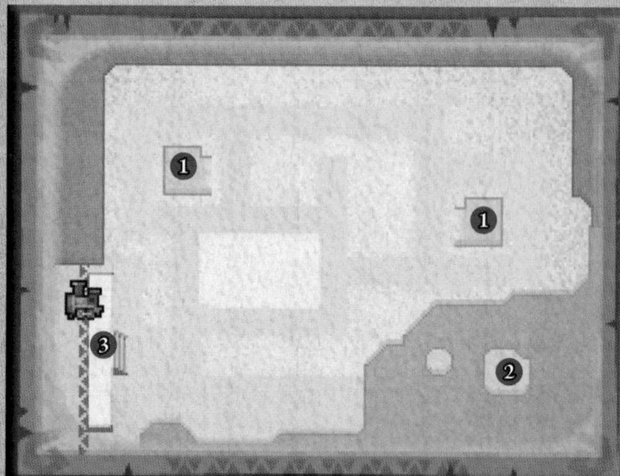

Sand Sanctuary

Legend

1. Gossip Stone
2. Stamp station
3. Train station

After bringing Cuccos to Rael and acquiring the final Force Gem, use one of the hapless animals to reach the area's stamp station. Just pluck up a Cucco and leap along the southeast isles to find the station, and record your nineteenth stamp. Only one more to find, and Niko's book will be full!

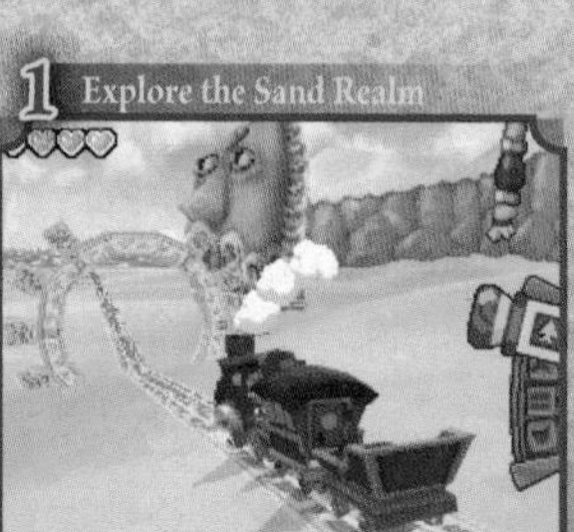

Rabbit Roundup: Sword Beam

If you've followed this walkthrough faithfully, you've now restored every last stretch of Spirit Track across the entire overworld. This means you can finally capture every rabbit! You should have only two left to get: ocean rabbit 10 and mountain rabbit 10.

970
Ooh! It looks like you've managed to catch every variety of rabbit out there.
Menu

Confirm that you've found all 50 rabbits by calling up the Collection screen. Once you've caught 'em all, visit the dude at Rabbitland Rescue for the ultimate reward: Swordsman's Scroll 1, which grants you the awesome ability to use the Sword Beam!

NOTE

The Sword Beam is a classic attack that allows Link to launch beams of energy out of his sword, striking and defeating remote foes. Link uses this attack automatically whenever he swings his sword, but only when his Life meter is full. A tremendous attack, indeed!

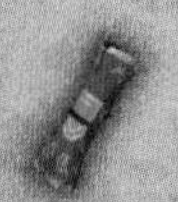

Swordsman's Scroll 1

You got the Swordsman's Scroll! Memories of veteran swordsmen flow through it.

Heart Container 12

Remember that Heart Container you saw at Beedle's Air Shop? Well, after all this adventuring, you should be able to attain that precious prize by now. All you need to do is spend over 5,000 Rupees at Beedle's—enough to merit an upgrade to Gold Card status! Sell some treasures if you need to hit the 5,000 mark, then buy lots and lots of stuff off Beedle. Purple potions are always welcome, and you can even buy treasures off Beedle to restock your collection! Just keep spending until you earn Gold Club status, at which point Beedle finally decides to reward your loyalty with a Heart Container.

Heart Container 12

You got a Heart Container! You increased your life by one and refilled your hearts!

Lost at Sea Station

Finding Force Gem 19 has paved the way to a mysterious new station. Travel the Ocean Realm's southeasternmost tracks to find this peculiar place, where many precious treasures await discovery.

Lost at Sea Station

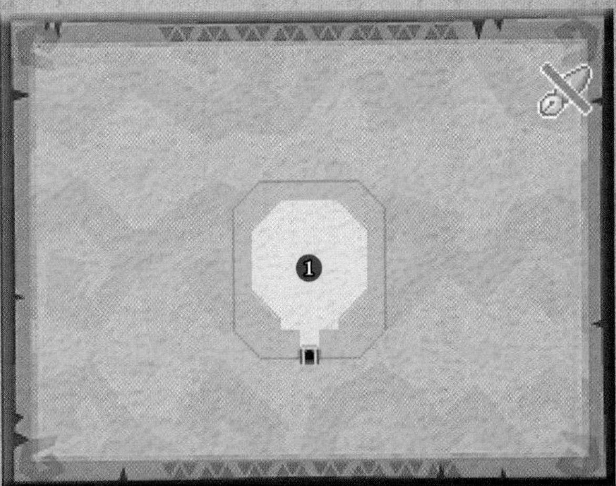

Lost at Sea Station Cave

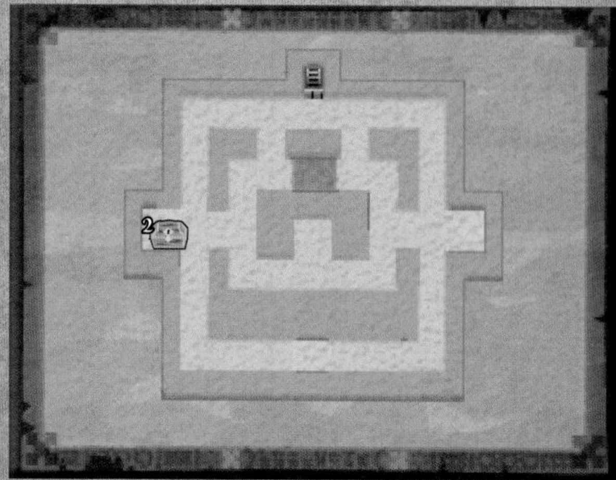

Lost at Sea Temple, First Floor

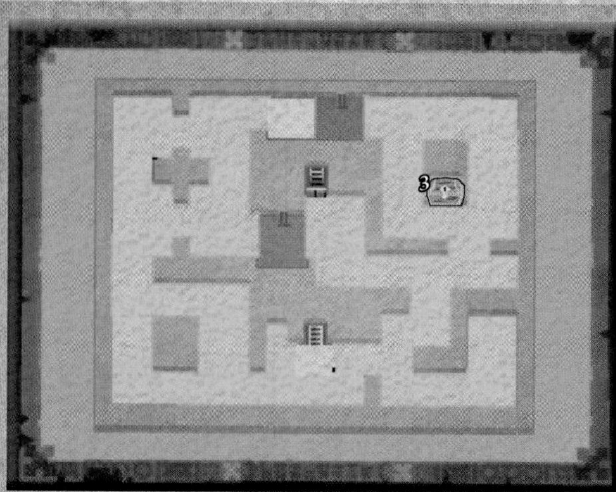

Lost at Sea Temple, Third Floor

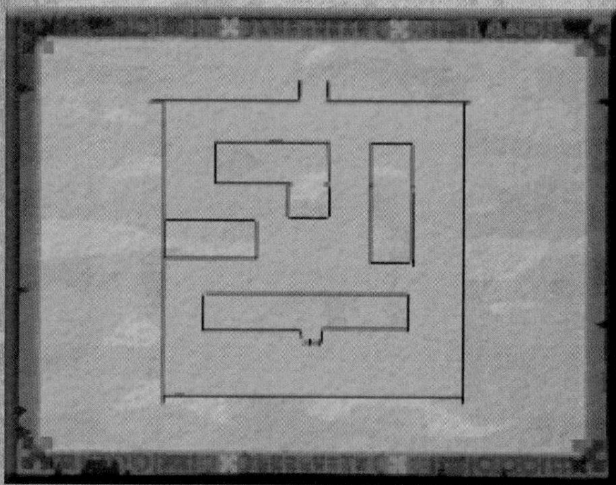

Lost at Sea Temple, Second Floor

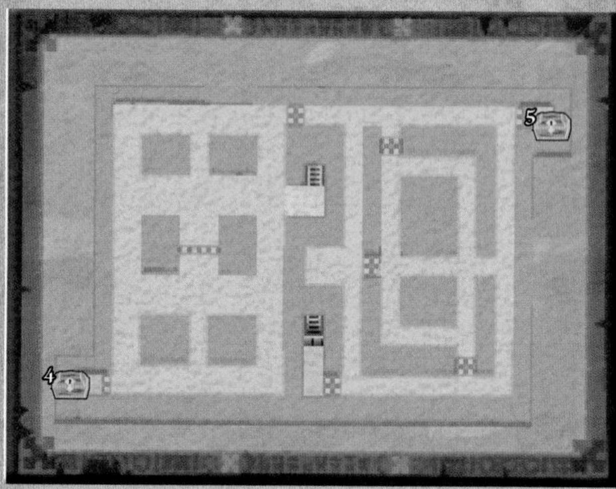

Lost at Sea Temple, Fourth Floor

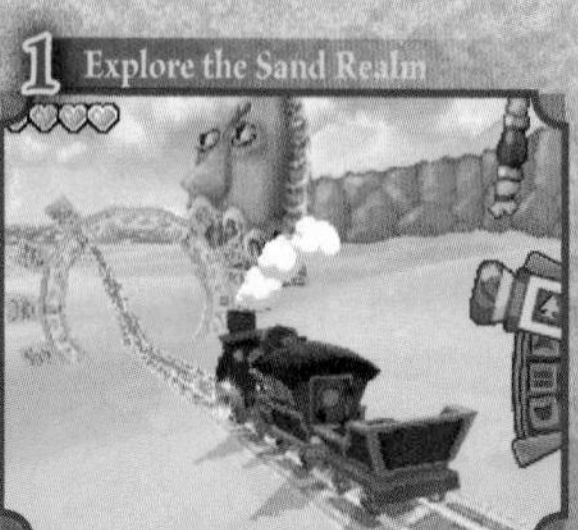

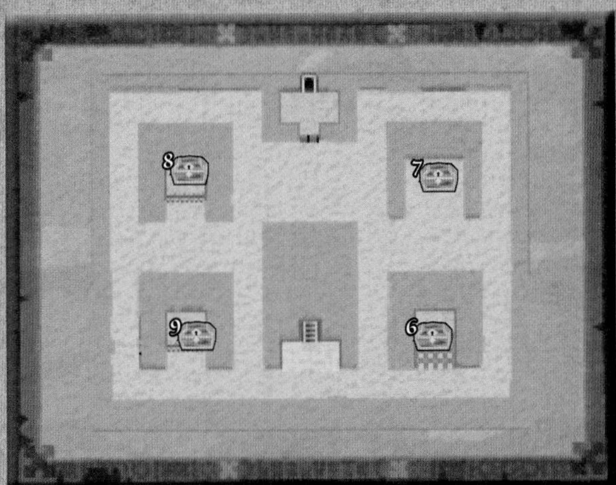

Lost at Sea Temple, Fifth Floor

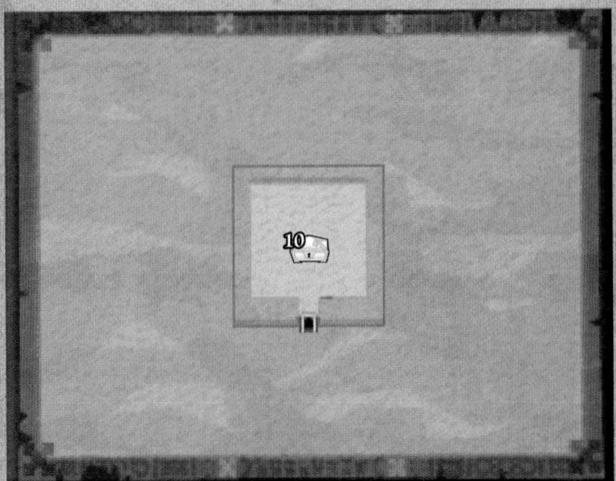

Lost at Sea Temple, Sixth Floor

Legend

1 Overworld Chest 37: Treasure
2 Dungeon Chest 1: Treasure
3 Dungeon Chest 2: Treasure
4 Dungeon Chest 3: Treasure
5 Dungeon Chest 4: Treasure
6 Dungeon Chest 5: Treasure
7 Dungeon Chest 6: Treasure
8 Dungeon Chest 7: Treasure
9 Dungeon Chest 8: Treasure
10 Dungeon Chest 9: Treasure
Bomb wall
1 Gossip Stone
2 Train station

Soon after stepping off the train, head west to locate a dark crystal. Equip your flute and play the Song of Light. As you complete the tune, a blue beam of light shoots out of the object in an eastward direction. Ignore the light for now and look for a similar dark crystal in the northeast.

Locate this second crystal and play the Song of Light again. This object emits a light pointing to the south. Follow the blue light south to the point where the two beams intersect.

When you reach the spot where the two beams form an X, play the Song of Discovery. This causes a small chest to emerge from the ground. Open it to retrieve a treasure.

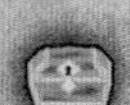

Overworld Chest 37: Treasure

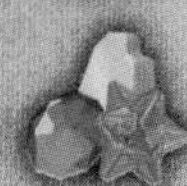

Treasure

You got a treasure! Check it out on the Collection screen!

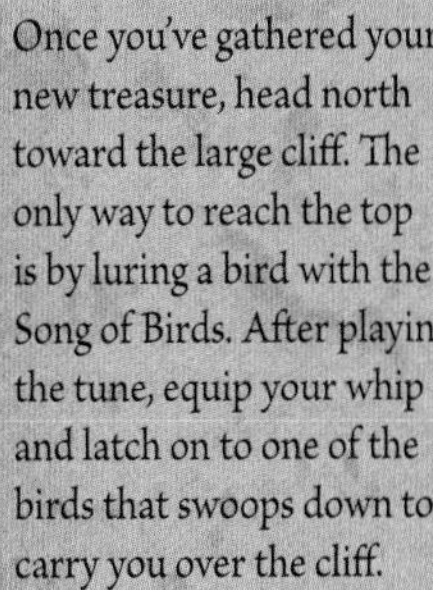

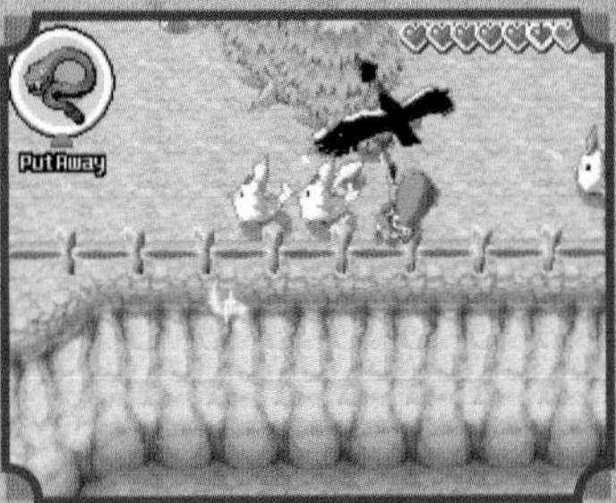

Once you've gathered your new treasure, head north toward the large cliff. The only way to reach the top is by luring a bird with the Song of Birds. After playing the tune, equip your whip and latch on to one of the birds that swoops down to carry you over the cliff.

Once you're over the high cliff, drop down, but beware of Crows nesting in the nearby trees. Ignore them and look for another gray diamond object to the east. Once again, play the Song of Light to make it emit a blue beam. This time the beam shoots north at a point in the cliff wall. What's it trying to tell you?

Grab a bomb from the nearby Bomb Flower, and toss it at the wall at the point where the blue beam is shining. Once the dust settles, a hole in the wall is revealed. Step through and see what's on the other side.

At the center of this small cave is a Gossip Stone. Play the Song of Awakening to rouse this statue from its slumber. The statue informs you that you're about to enter a replica of a temple from a distant kingdom. The treasures within are guarded by several Phantoms, and if you choose to enter, you cannot use your sword or your bow—sounds like a challenge! Agree to the statue's conditions to be transported to the temple's first floor.

Lost at Sea Temple: First Floor

The statue transports you to the first floor of the temple, where a nearby stone tablet instructs you to light all of the torches. Sounds easy enough.

Before lighting any torches, head west to locate a small chest. Open it to retrieve a new treasure. Don't worry about Phantoms here—they can't touch you as long as you stay in the safe zone.

Dungeon Chest 1: Treasure

Treasure

You got a treasure! Check it out on the Collection screen!

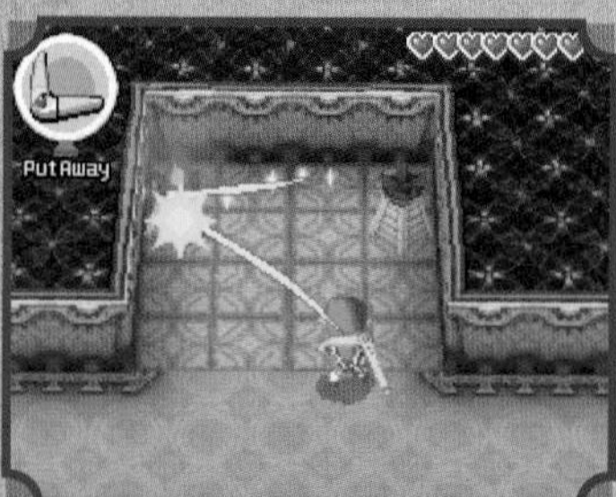

Now it's time to light some torches. The first torch is located in the center of the map. Wait for the Phantoms to clear out of this area, then dash in and light this torch with your boomerang by attaining flame from the adjacent torch. Make it quick, though, as a Phantom is likely to return to this area soon. Only two more torches to go.

The next two torches are located in the northwest and northeast corners. This area is frequented by at least one patrolling Phantom, so wait for the right moment to strike. For your fire source, target one of the lit torches flanking the doorway. Stand near the center of the northern corridor and light one torch at a time, being careful to avoid the nearby fire traps. Once you've lit both torches in the corners, the door opens, allowing you to access the next floor.

1 Explore the Sand Realm

2 Find the Lokomo Guardian

3 Reach the Sand Temple

4 Clear the Sand Temple

Lost at Sea Temple: Second Floor

The second floor is dark. Even worse, you're tasked with extinguishing all the lit torches on this level, all while avoiding the Phantoms. Equip your Whirlwind and get busy blowing out the torches by the floor's entrance. More torches are located in the northwest and northeast corners.

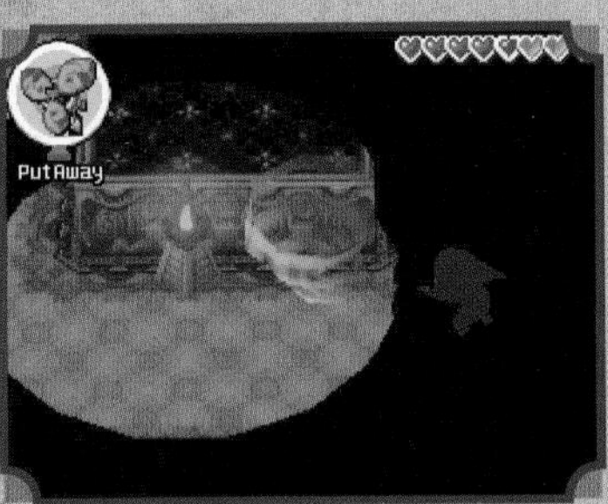

Take your time searching this floor for lit torches, and steer clear of the Phantoms. If they catch you, you'll have to start all over. The floor resembles a figure eight with torches lining each corridor. After extinguishing the northern torches, work the eastern and western passages before heading south. The final few torches are in the southern corridor—quickly blow them out to open the door to the next floor.

Lost at Sea Temple: Third Floor

Step back into the light on the third floor, where the nearby stone tablet offers the following vague advice: In each pair, one switch is correct. What does this mean? In addition to two Phantoms patrolling this floor, there's also a Phantom Eye. From the entrance, head northeast toward this nook, where a small chest is waiting. Grab the loot, then head to the floor's northeast corner.

Dungeon Chest 2: Treasure

Treasure

You got a treasure! Check it out on the Collection screen!

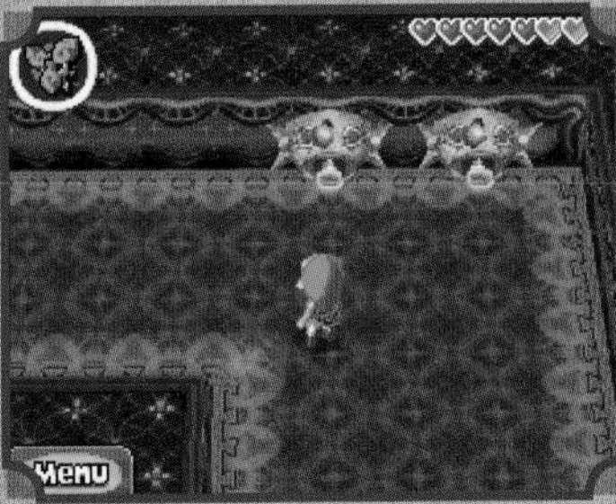

Here you find two fish sculptures set into the wall, each with a yellow switch in its mouth. This is exactly what that clue on the stone tablet was referring to. You need to pull one of these switches with your whip. Pulling the correct switch helps unlock the door leading to the next floor. But if you pull the wrong switch, a new Phantom Eye spawns, making it even more difficult to get around on this floor. In all, there are four sets of these handles. For this particular set, pull the switch on the right.

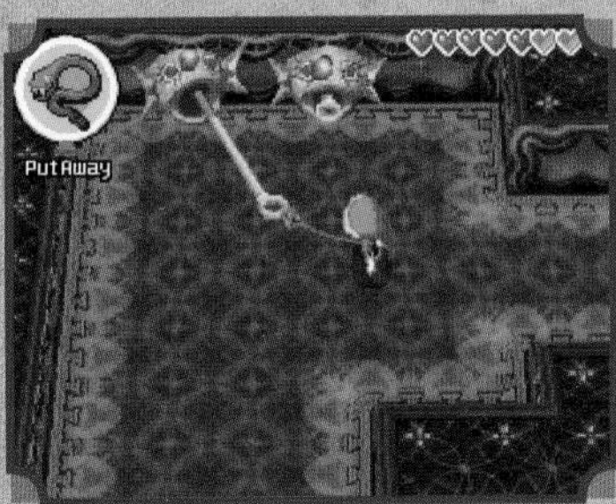

Swing across the pit to the west, and approach the northwest corner, where two more fish sculptures await your decision. This time, pull the switch on the left.

Now turn south and approach the next set of switches in the southwest corner. Pull the switch on the right.

Finally, sneak to the southeast corner, where the last set of switches is located. Yank the switch on the right, and make a break for the now-open doorway at the floor's center.

Lost at Sea Temple: Fourth Floor

Your task on this floor is to destroy all of the blocks. This is easy if you have enough bombs. If not, you'll need to play matador with the Phantoms and let them roll through the blocks for you. Start by taking out the blocks in the southwest corner, where a treasure chest is waiting for you. After placing a bomb, consider walking away until it explodes. The sound of an exploding bomb may draw the attention of nearby Phantoms, prompting them to investigate. So it's a good idea to toss a bomb and leave the area to avoid getting caught. However, it's important to go back and get the treasure.

Dungeon Chest 3: Treasure

Treasure

You got a treasure! Check it out on the Collection screen!

Another treasure chest is located in the map's northeast corner. Drop some bombs at blocks on your way to stay one step ahead of the Phantoms—while they're busy investigating old explosions, get busy staging new ones. If necessary, take a break in this corner to catch your breath. Once you've destroyed all the blocks, proceed to the newly opened doorway to the south.

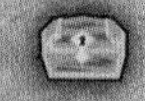

Dungeon Chest 4: Treasure

Treasure

You got a treasure! Check it out on the Collection screen!

Lost at Sea Temple: Fifth Floor

Four Phantoms patrol the fifth floor of the temple, making it difficult to pull off your final task. To escape this floor, you must open all the treasure chests. Start by heading to the southeast corner, and use bombs to blast away the blocks concealing the first chest. It takes at least four bombs to get through this barrier, so head back to the safe zone by the door if necessary to avoid being spotted by a nosy Phantom. Once a path is clear, rush through and open the chest.

Dungeon Chest 5: Treasure

Treasure

You got a treasure! Check it out on the Collection screen!

The next chest is located in the northeast corner, situated between two fish sculptures. Open the chest, then pull the fish switch on the left—this retracts the spikes protecting the next chest to the west.

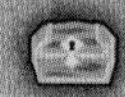

Dungeon Chest 6: Treasure

Treasure

You got a treasure! Check it out on the Collection screen!

Now that the spikes are retracted, accessing the next chest is a breeze. Rush forward and open the chest to retrieve your treasure.

Dungeon Chest 7: Treasure

Treasure

You got a treasure! Check it out on the Collection screen!

Accessing the chest in the southwest corner can be tricky, especially if you conjured a Phantom Eye by pulling the wrong switch earlier. The chest in the southwest is protected by spikes. To retract the spikes, you must light the torch to the north—the one by the closed door. Avoid the fire traps and use your boomerang (and the fire from the nearby lit torch) to light this fire.

If a Phantom Eye is standing guard near the closed door, stun it with your boomerang before attempting to light the torch.

1 Explore the Sand Realm

2 Find the Lokomo Guardian

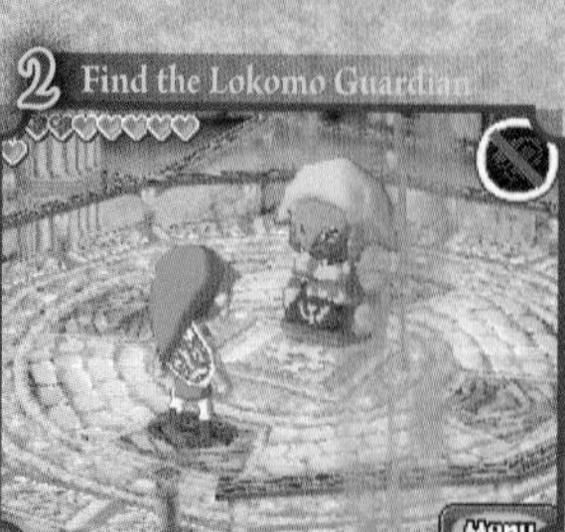

3 Reach the Sand Temple

4 Clear the Sand Temple

Lighting the torch causes the spikes to drop, giving you a clear path to the final chest. Rush to the southwest alcove and claim your treasure!

Dungeon Chest 8: Treasure

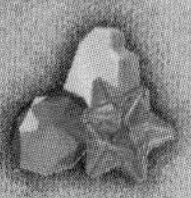

Treasure

You got a treasure! Check it out on the Collection screen!

With all four chests opened, the door to the north opens, clearing a path for your escape. Make sure no Phantoms are on your tail, and make a break for the open doorway. Don't worry about the Phantom Eye standing guard by the door—you can dash past it and escape before the Phantoms can catch up.

Lost at Sea Temple: Sixth Floor

You made it! Open the large chest in this room's center to claim the grand prize for all your hard work. Once you've grabbed the loot, step into the blue light to return to the cave where you began this journey. Time to head back to the train station, as you've completely plundered this location.

Dungeon Chest 9: Treasure

Treasure

You got a treasure! Check it out on the Collection screen!

The Lost at Sea Temple's treasures regenerate after you clear the temple. Brave the temple's challenges again and again for even more precious loot!

Ends of the Earth Station

The final Force Gem, given to you by Rael, has restored the Fire Realm's northeasternmost Spirit Tracks. Venture there to visit the very ends of the earth—quite literally!

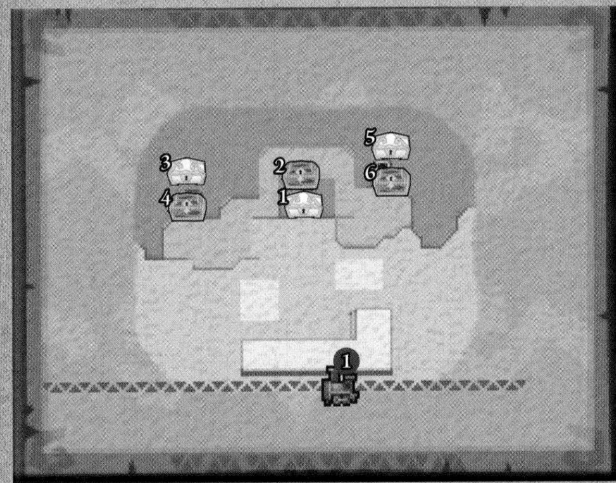

Ends of the Earth Station

Legend

- 1 Dungeon Chest 1: Treasure
- 2 Dungeon Chest 2: Big Green Rupee
- 3 Dungeon Chest 3: Heart Container 13
- 4 Dungeon Chest 4: Big Green Rupee
- 5 Dungeon Chest 5: Treasure
- 6 Dungeon Chest 6: Big Green Rupee
- 1 Train station

Items to Obtain

Big Green Rupee x3	Heart Container 13	Treasure x2

As its name implies, this barren landscape has little to offer at first glance. But don't dismiss this station too quickly. There are three dungeon entrances set into the cliffs to the north. Head for the center entrance first, and read the stone tablet near the doorway. Apparently, a set of brain-teasing block puzzles awaits inside. There are three sets of puzzles in all, each contained within one of these three entrances. Step inside the central doorway first.

TIP

If you just want to grab Heart Container 13, skip the central and eastern dungeons, and focus on completing the block puzzles in the western dungeon.

Proceed to the first chamber, blocked by a large stone doorway. To open the door, you must solve this first block puzzle. Before beginning, notice the blue diamond-shaped nodule at the block's top. You must rotate the block until this nodule fits inside the blue socket in the floor to the south. Equip your Sand Wand and manipulate the sand beneath the block to begin rolling it. Experiment rolling the block in different directions until you get the nodule facedown inside the socket. This opens the door to the north, where another block puzzle awaits.

When rolling blocks, always stand to the side of the room. If you stand on the sandy floor, there's a chance you'll inadvertently roll a block on top of yourself, inflicting minor damage. You can achieve all block manipulation from the room's perimeter walkway.

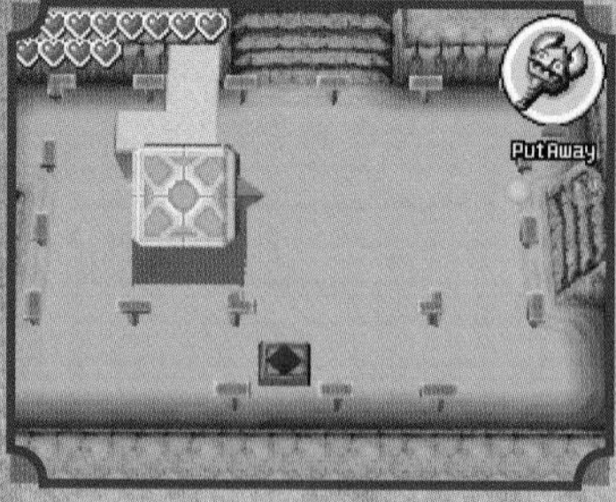

In this puzzle, you must roll the block from the northwest corner toward the socket on the floor's south side. But this time there are obstructions preventing you from making a direct approach. Instead, you must move the block to the east side of the socket, then roll it west to secure the nodule to open the door leading to the third and final chamber.

The last puzzle in this set is a bit more difficult, given the lack of space to maneuver the block. First, get the block on the floor's east side, with the blue nodule facing west. Then roll it into position over the socket to unlock the door to the north.

The chamber ahead contains a large chest that holds a rare treasure item. Grab your loot, then exit through the doorway to the east.

Dungeon Chest 1: Treasure

Treasure

You got a treasure! Check it out on the Collection screen!

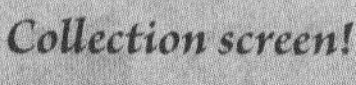

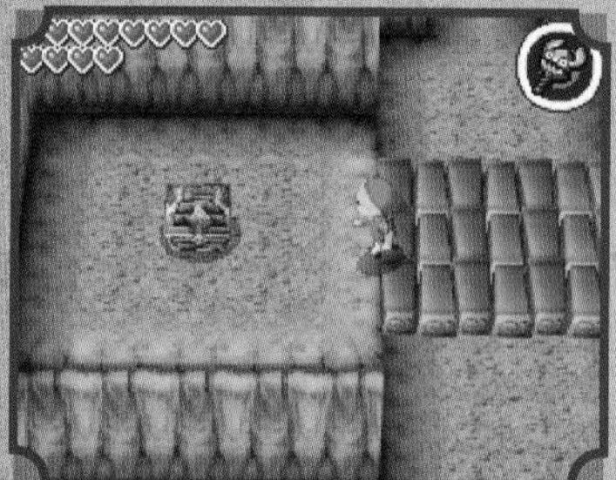

Before completely exiting this dungeon, cross the bridge to the west to find a small chest resting on a ledge. Open it to retrieve a Big Green Rupee!

Dungeon Chest 2: Big Green Rupee

Big Green Rupee

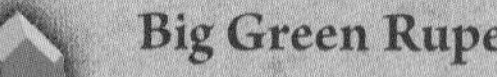

You got a Big Green Rupee! It's worth 100 Rupees!

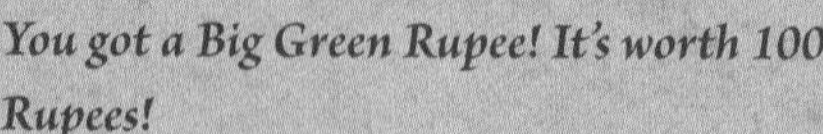

1 Explore the Sand Realm

2 Find the Lokomo Guardian

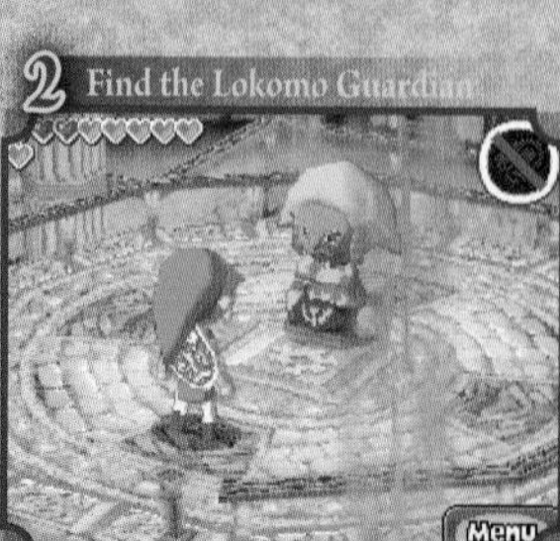

3 Reach the Sand Temple

4 Clear the Sand Temple

Eager to find more treasure? Head west to the next set of puzzles. The stone tablet outside the door warns of the brain twisters that await inside.

Put Away

Proceed to the first chamber, and get ready to turn more blocks. This time, there are two blocks to maneuver into two separate sockets. This puzzle isn't too challenging if you take it one block at a time. Once both blocks are properly situated, the northern door opens, giving you access to the next puzzle.

Put Away

Once again, you must maneuver two blocks into sockets to exit this room. Although the space is rather confined, you can still take it one block at a time. Roll the northern block into the eastern socket, then roll the southern block into the western socket. Once complete, continue to the next chamber.

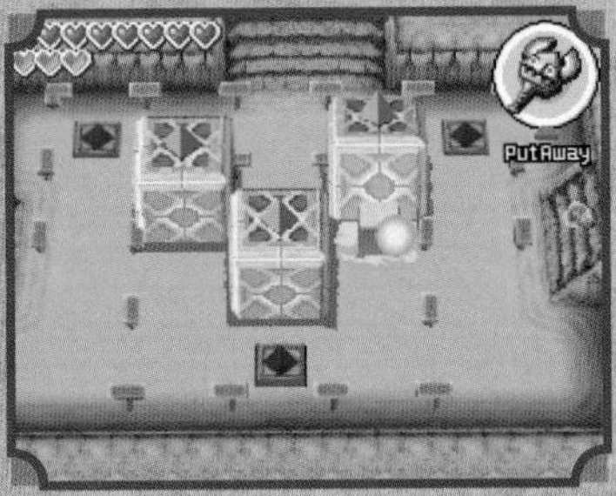
Put Away

This is the last puzzle of this set, and it's the most difficult you've faced thus far. Now you have three blocks to roll around, and the bracketlike obstructions prevent you from rolling them in any direction you please. Fortunately, there's still plenty of room to maneuver. Start by spreading out the blocks to provide a bit more space, then go to work on one block at a time. Once you've situated a block into a socket, you won't need to move it again, essentially giving you more space to move the remaining two blocks. Keep working the puzzle until you've fitted all blocks over a socket.

You got a Heart Container!

Rush north into the northern chamber to get your prize, which waits in a large chest. Inside is a Heart Container!

Dungeon Chest 3: Heart Container 13

Heart Container 13

You got a Heart Container! You increased your life by one and refilled your hearts!

You got a big green Rupee!
It's worth 100 Rupees!

Once again, pay close attention on your way out of this dungeon, and remember to open the small chest on the ledge before exiting. It contains a Big Green Rupee.

Dungeon Chest 4: Big Green Rupee

Big Green Rupee

You got a Big Green Rupee! It's worth 100 Rupees!

Surely you're not tired of block puzzles yet. There's one more set of puzzles located in the dungeon to the east. Yikes! The stone tablet outside this doorway describes the puzzles inside as brainmashers. Enter if you dare!

Put Away

Don't let the sign outside intimidate you. While the puzzles here are more difficult, you're now well prepared to deal with these challenges. This time, you have three blocks in a very confined space. Still, it's not all that difficult. Just remember that you may have to move a situated block north temporarily in order to roll a neighboring block into position.

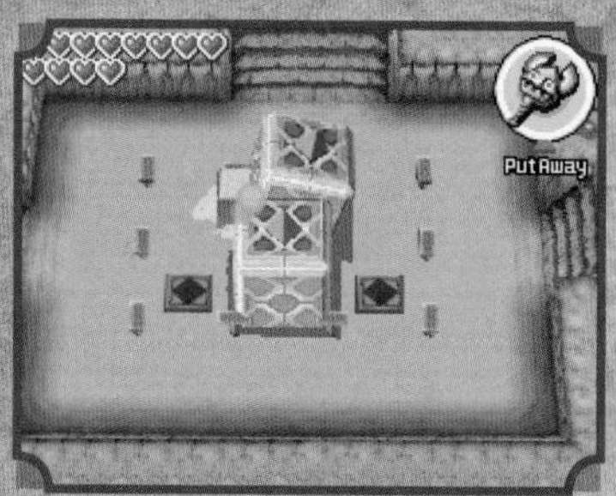

There's only two blocks to roll around in the second puzzle, but there's very little room to maneuver, making it difficult to properly orient the blue nodules with the sockets. Focus on getting one block situated first, then maneuver the second block into position. While moving the second block, it will be necessary to temporarily dislodge the already situated block. Just be extra careful when moving it out of the way to ensure you keep the nodule correctly oriented.

Okay, this last puzzle is a doozy. You have three blocks packed into the tightest space yet. Is it even possible? Don't worry—it's not as hard as it looks. It's important to remain flexible in this puzzle, especially once you get your first block situated. Be ready to move that situated block out of the way so you can maneuver the other two into position. Likewise, you will also need to move your second situated block so you can get the final block into a socket. Now, more than ever, it's very important to move the Sand Wand with great care to prevent the blocks from getting all jumbled.

Now it's time for your reward! Head through the open doorway to the north, and unlatch the big chest to acquire a rare treasure.

Dungeon Chest 5: Treasure

Treasure

You got a treasure! Check it out on the Collection screen!

In all your excitement (and relief), don't forget to open the small chest on your way out of this dungeon to retrieve another Big Green Rupee. Having completed all the puzzles here, head back to the train and say farewell to the Ends of the Earth Station. It's been a lucrative visit!

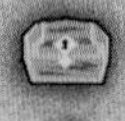

Dungeon Chest 6: Big Green Rupee

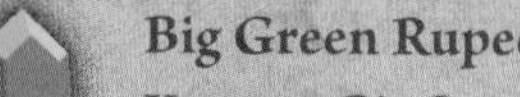

Big Green Rupee

You got a Big Green Rupee! It's worth 100 Rupees!

Diabolic Descent: Tower of Spirits 6

Braving immeasurable hardships, Link and Zelda have succeeded in retrieving the Bow of Light from the depths of the Sand Temple. Now armed with this sacred weapon, our heroes continue to cling to a sliver of hope that evil may yet be allayed. Anjean holds council aboard the Spirit Train, where the forces of good begin to plot their next move...

A Link to the Present

Items Already Acquired

Beedle Club Card, Bomb Bag 1, Bomb Bag 2, Bomb Bag 3, Boomerang

Bow and Arrow, Engineer Certificate, Engineer's Clothes, Fire Rail Map, Force Gems (20)

Forest Rail Map, Ocean Rail Map, Practical Cannon, Quiver 1, Quiver 2

Rabbitland Rabbits (50), Recruit's Sword, Recruit's Uniform, Sand Wand, Shield of Antiquity

Snow Rail Map, Song of Awakening, Song of Birds, Song of Discovery, Song of Healing

Song of Light, Spirit Flute, Stamp Book (19 stamps), Swordsman's Scroll 1, Whip

The Whirlwind, Wooden Shield

Items to Obtain

Lokomo Sword

Task 1: Report Back to Anjean

Aboard the Spirit Train

But the evil ones have hidden it too well...

Elated by their recent success, Link and Princess Zelda can't wait to report back to Anjean. The old Lokomo reassures them that the Bow of Light should indeed fell Malladus, but she drops a bombshell when she says she has no idea where the great Demon King could be hiding.

Having overheard the conversation, a groggy Byrne interjects, saying he knows how to find his former lord. He tells his new associates that there are yet more floors of the Tower of Spirits to be explored and that a magical object called the Compass of Light is located somewhere in the tower's highest floors. Only this special compass can point the way to the Dark Realm, where evil resides.

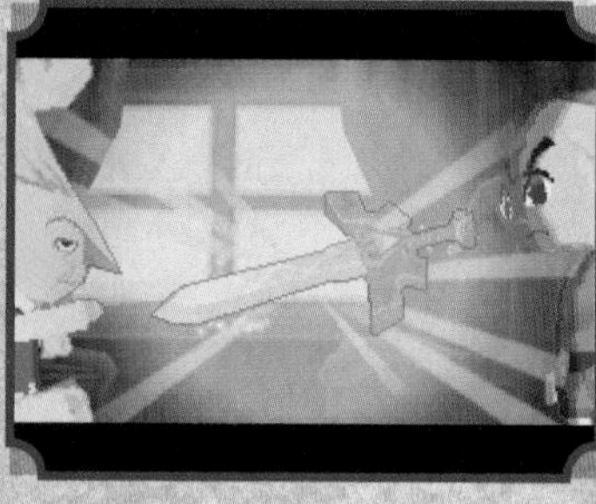

Our heroes' task is now clear: They must make one final trip to the tower, braving its highest floors in search of the Compass of Light. Knowing full well the dangers that lie ahead, Anjean bestows one final gift to Link: the Lokomo Sword, the most powerful blade ever forged by the spirits of good! Armed with this divine weapon, Link is now ready to battle the worst evil has to offer.

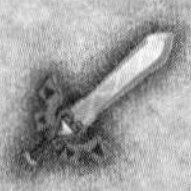

Lokomo Sword

You got the Lokomo Sword! This sacred blade was a gift from the spirits.

Task 2: Return to the Tower of Spirits

Back to the Tower

If you're coming directly from the Sand Temple, hop through Warp Gate H, then set a course to the Tower of Spirits. If you're anywhere else, simply scan the overworld map and plot out your preferred route to the tower.

Climb the tower's spiral staircase as you've done so often by now, heading to the top. Don't enter the highest door, though; instead, step into the blue warp light near the door to warp to the tower's twenty-third floor. Next, run upstairs to return to the place where you battled Byrne.

Run through the arena's background doorway just as you did when chasing Byrne after the fight. This brings you outdoors, to the spiral steps that wind up around the tower. Sprint up the steps to reach the altar at the tower's apex, where Cole held the ritual that revived the Demon King.

Hang on, there's a stamp station up here! Link hadn't noticed it before. Use the station to press the twentieth and final stamp into Niko's book. Now you can return to Niko for his final gift!

1 Report Back to Anjean

2 Return to the Tower of Spirits

3 Obtain the Compass of Light

4 Venture to the Dark Realm

Before rushing off to see Niko, fire the Bow of Light at the two gilded eye switches on the altar's base. You couldn't have done much with these before, but now you've got the Bow of Light. Shoot each eye switch with a fully charged light arrow to activate them; this raises a secret door from the altar's base that leads back down into the tower. Enter this door to begin the arduous quest for the Compass of Light.

Missing Link: Great Spin Attack

Items to Obtain

Swordsman's Scroll 2

Before you run off questing for the compass, consider returning to the Spirit Train and setting course for Aboda Village. It's not all that long of a journey, and Niko has a precious prize to hand out for filling his stamp book: Swordsman's Scroll 2, which grants Link the use of the great spin attack!

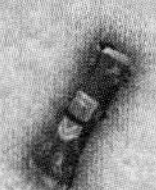

Swordsman's Scroll 2

You got a Swordsman's Scroll! Memories of veteran swordsmen flow through it.

The great spin attack certainly lives up to its name. Execute the attack by tracing three circles around Link as if to make him perform three regular spin attacks in a row. On the third spin, Link begins to whirl around with greater fury, becoming a deadly tornado of doom! While Link is executing the great spin attack, you may move him around with the stylus, wiping out anything and everything in sight. The great spin attack is sure to come in handy during the coming battles. Now get back to the Tower of Spirits and find that Compass of Light!

Task 3: Obtain the Compass of Light

Tower of Spirits

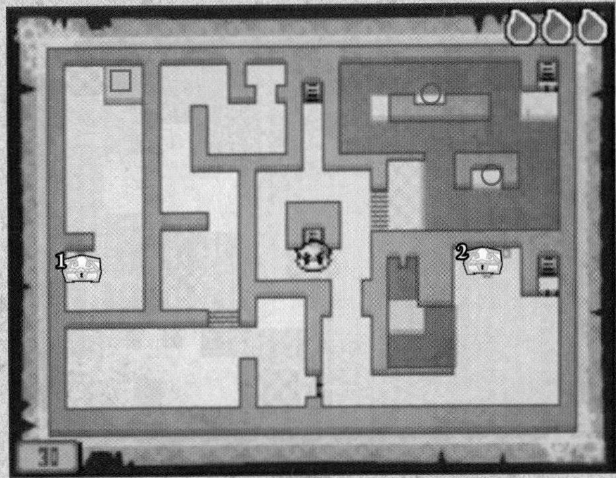

Tower of Spirits, Thirtieth Floor

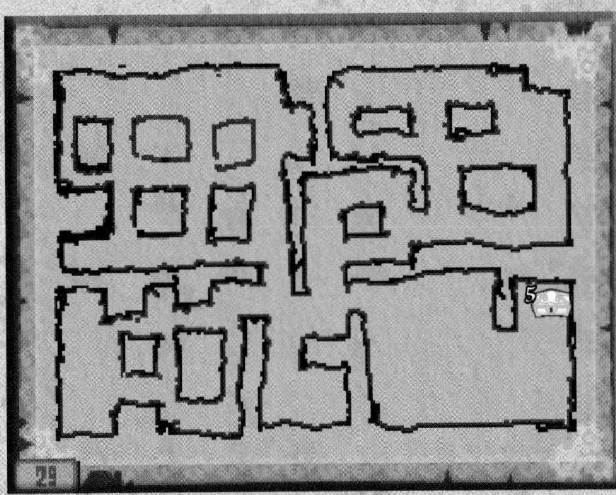

Tower of Spirits, Twenty-ninth Floor

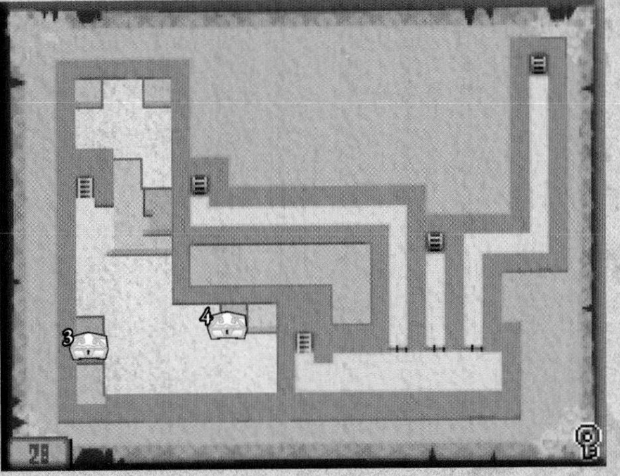

Tower of Spirits, Twenty-eighth Floor

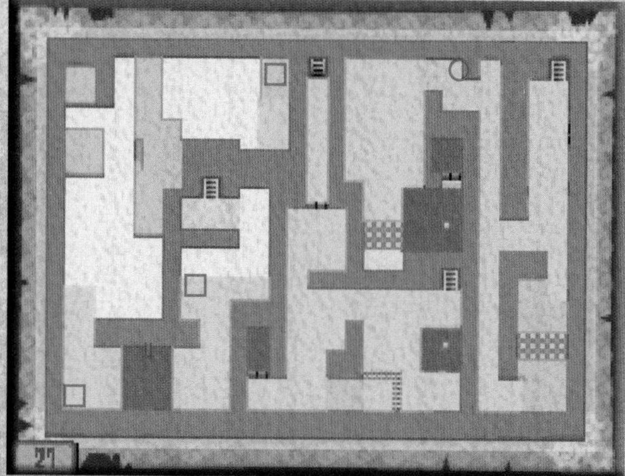

Tower of Spirits, Twenty-seventh Floor

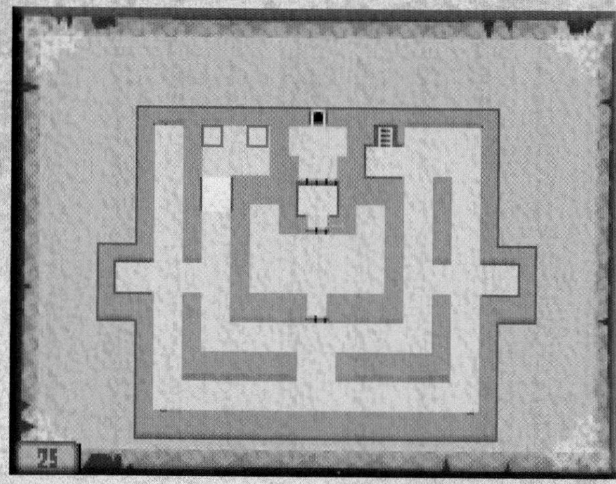

Tower of Spirits, Twenty-fifth Floor

Tower of Spirits, Twenty-sixth Floor

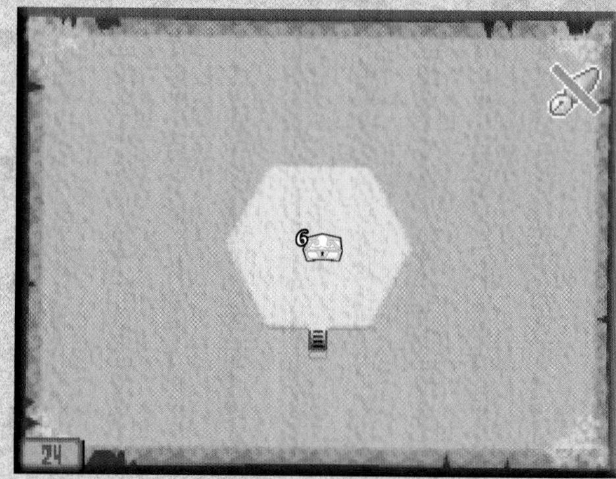

Tower of Spirits, Twenty-fourth Floor

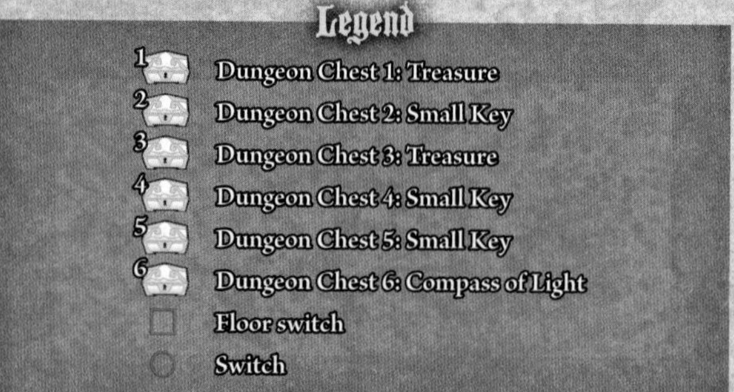

Tower of Spirits: Thirtieth Floor

No, not "thirteenth." *Thirtieth*. You've been climbing the tower this whole time, only to have to delve back into its highest floors now that you've reached the top. Such is the life of a world-saving hero! Or was that royal engineer? No matter—after entering the altar door, proceed through the small entry chamber, breaking pots on your way to the thirtieth floor.

You begin near the thirtieth floor's center. Armos statues block the south passage, and sharp spikes lie to the east, leaving you no choice but to proceed down the north staircase.

Tower of Spirits: Twenty-ninth Floor

Oh no, it's all dark down here! There's no map for the twenty-ninth floor, so you'll need to tread lightly.

2601
It's pitch black in here, Link...
Menu

Luckily, Link's new blade is already infused with magical energy—he no longer needs to collect Tears of Light to power his sword! Lure one of the two roaming Phantoms over to the entry safe zone, then stab its back when it loses interest and turns away. While the Phantom is stunned, tap it to have Zelda take control.

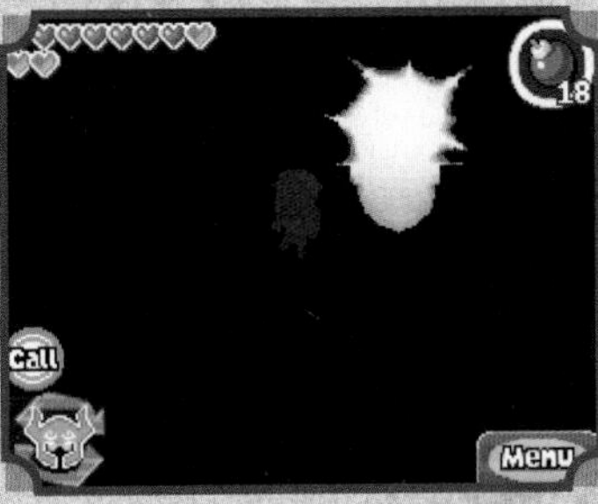

After possessing one Phantom, have Zelda speak with the other for a clue: There's a weak wall at the floor's northwest corner! Make your way there, and plant a bomb at the corner to blast a hole through the north wall, exposing a secret passage.

Smash pots for loot as you maneuver through the short passage, which leads upstairs and spits you out at the thirtieth floor.

Tower of Spirits: Thirtieth Floor, Revisited

First things first: Plant bombs near the stacked bomb blocks to the south, blasting them all away to uncover a hidden chest. Open the chest to claim the Compass of Light! Just kidding, it's just a treasure. But a nice one!

Dungeon Chest 1: Treasure

Treasure

You got a treasure! Check it out on the Collection screen!

Next, use the Sand Wand to raise Link up so he can leap onto Zelda's back. Carry Link over to the nearby ledge so he may leap off and reach a floor switch.

Stepping on the switch causes a pair of Phantom Eyes and a Warp Phantom to appear on the floor. That's all you can do from this side of the thirtieth floor, but you're far from finished up here. Retrace your steps back down to the pitch-dark twenty-ninth floor, then lure the Warp Phantom over to a safe zone so you can safely possess it. Then continue backtracking, returning to the thirtieth floor's central area, where you first began.

Back at the center of the thirtieth floor, guide Zelda past the east spikes, and have her step on the nearby floor switch to remove this obstacle from Link's path. Move Link past the spikes and purposely alert the Phantom Eye, then rush back to the central safe zone before the Warp Phantom appears.

Lure the Warp Phantom over to the safe zone, then stun the brute and make Zelda possess it. That's all for now; return to the thirtieth floor's west side by way of the twenty-ninth floor's secret passage.

Once you're back on the floor's west side, move Link onto the red circle floor tile that lies to the south. Switch to Zelda and trace a line from her to the adjacent red circle tile. Hang your stylus above the tile and wait for the Phantom Eye to pass by, then target the sentry and have Zelda warp to its location.

Land Zelda safely on the tile, and she and Link will swap positions. Quickly move Link into the nearby safe zone, and switch back to Zelda.

Wait until the south Phantom Eye respawns if need be, then trace a line from Zelda to the east spikes. Warp Zelda to the spikes when the Phantom Eye drifts past them.

Next, guide Zelda onto the yellow triangle floor tile that lies to the north, beyond the spikes. Switch to Link and move him to the matching tile when the Phantom Eye isn't looking. Trade places with Zelda again.

1 Report Back to Anjean

2 Return to the Tower of Spirits

3 Obtain the Compass of Light

4 Venture to the Dark Realm

Have Link run north to discover a gilded eye switch. Charge up a light arrow and strike the eye to open a door down south.

Use the yellow triangle tile to swap Link and Zelda around again. Now the two can explore the floor's east side together. Before venturing through the door you've just opened, use the nearby sand to lift Link onto Zelda's back.

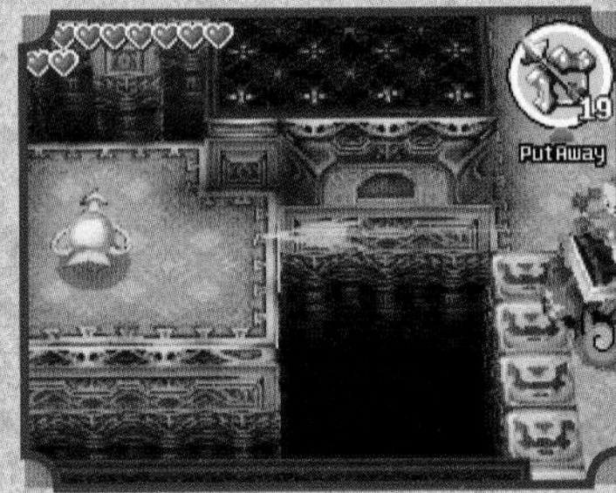

From his elevated position, have Link wipe out the Mounted Miniblin beyond the door with the whip or an arrow. Then move close to the nearby pit, and use the boomerang to whack the remote arrow aimer, pointing it north. Fire a fully charged light arrow into the aimer to strike a fancy eye switch; this opens another door that leads to some stairs. Go down to reach the southeast corner of the twenty-ninth floor.

Ignore the stacked bomb blocks here for now; you'll destroy them soon enough!

Tower of Spirits: Twenty-ninth Floor, Revisited

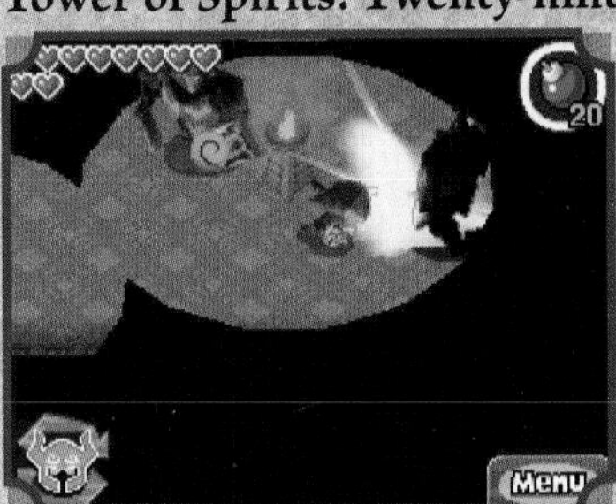

You're here for only one purpose: to possess the roaming Wrecker Phantom. Lure the guardian over to your safe zone, and have Zelda possess it after it turns to resume its patrol. Return to the thirtieth floor.

Tower of Spirits: Thirtieth Floor, Third Visit

As a Wrecker Phantom, Princess Zelda has no problems bashing down the bomb blocks up here. Smash them, along with the Armos statues they were covering, to expose a large chest. Have Link crack it open to score a Small Key.

Dungeon Chest 2: Small Key

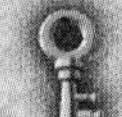

Small Key

You got a Small Key! Use this key to open locked doors!

Have Zelda continue onward and smash through more Armos statues that block the route back to the floor's center. Now you can move about this place more easily. Take the north stairs down to the twenty-ninth floor, possess a regular Phantom down there, then return to this floor.

Back on the thirtieth floor, have Zelda dispatch the Phantom Eye to the east, then move her into the lava. Quickly leap Link onto her back and be off before the sentry respawns.

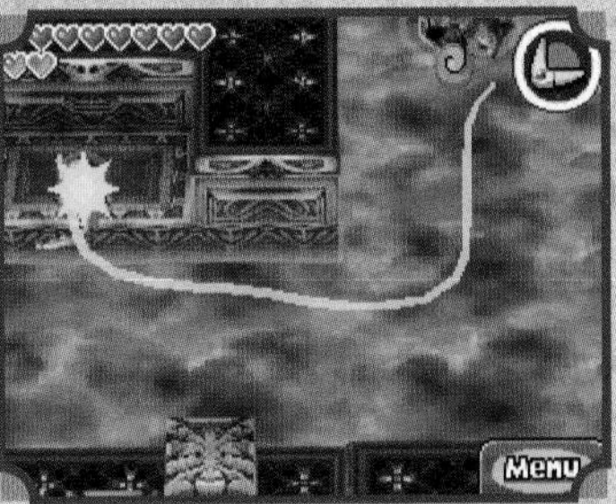

Cross the lava, moving close to the northeast stairs. From here, have Link hurl his boomerang at two elevated switches, striking them both in quick succession to open the way downstairs.

Tower of Spirits: Twenty-ninth Floor, Third Visit

Run west from where you enter, hugging the floor's north wall to discover a stone tablet. The tablet hints that "Phantoms like us like the dark." Perhaps you should dim the lights?

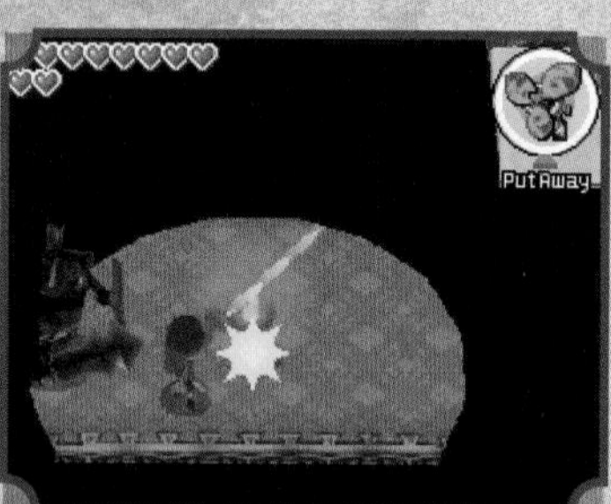

Run around this northeast section of the floor, avoiding Nocturns and using the Whirlwind to blow out every lit torch. A sealed door opens after you extinguish all nearby torches, allowing you to explore more of this dark floor.

Beware: You're now within reach of this floor's patrolling Torch Phantom. That's actually a good thing, because he's your next target. Get behind the Torch Phantom and stun it so Zelda may take the reins.

Ah, that's better! As a Torch Phantom, Zelda's flaming blade lights up the place a bit. Now you must backtrack to the thirtieth floor, go back across the lava, and take the north stairs down to the twenty-ninth floor's northwest area.

Back at the twenty-ninth floor's northwest region, guide Zelda southwest and locate a pair of unlit torches near a door. Have Zelda light both torches with her flaming sword by tracing lines to them, then proceed downstairs to reach the twenty-eighth floor.

Tower of Spirits: Twenty-eighth Floor

Now you're getting somewhere! Unfortunately, that somewhere is a very challenging floor full of hazardous sand. Have Link scale the nearby steps, and drop to the northwest sandy area. Use arrows or toss a bomb to quickly wipe out the Stalfos Warrior that springs to life up here.

This next part's tricky. Link must raise the sand here so that Zelda can cross and light two torches near the north wall. Quickly switch between the two, trading off between moving Zelda and keeping the sand solidified.

Lighting both torches causes a pair of chests to appear to the south. Help Zelda return across the sand and make for those chests.

1 Report Back to Anjean

2 Return to the Tower of Spirits

3 Obtain the Compass of Light

4 Venture to the Dark Realm

Send Link south to dispatch more Stalfos Warriors, securing the area. Afterward, use the steps back near the entry stairs to land Link on top of Zelda.

With Link riding on Zelda's back, equip the Sand Wand and use it to raise the south sands. Have Link continue to hold the wand, and steer Zelda south across the sand. Anywhere you tap while not steering Zelda will make Link use the Sand Wand there, so it's somewhat easier to move this way.

Reach the south ledge and have Link dismount on the higher plateau, near the chest. Quickly move Zelda onto the lower portion of the ledge, before the sand she's standing on melts away. Open the chest to score a rare treasure, then leap Link back onto his partner's shoulders.

Dungeon Chest 3: Treasure

Treasure

You got a treasure! Check it out on the Collection screen!

Don't let Link fall from the chest ledge! If he does, you'll have to bring both him and Zelda back to the starting area to return Link to Zelda's back.

Have Link and the princess work together as before to cross the sand and reach the other chest. This one contains a Small Key. Return Link to Zelda's shoulders, and journey back upstairs with your loot.

Dungeon Chest 4: Small Key

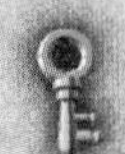

Small Key

You got a Small Key! Use this key to open locked doors!

Tower of Spirits: Twenty-ninth Floor, Fourth Visit

Back in the twenty-ninth floor's dark halls, take the northeast stairs up to the thirtieth floor, then go south and take the southeast stairs to reach the twenty-ninth floor's southeast corner. Have Torch Phantom Zelda shed some light on the north wall here to discover an ornate eye switch, which Link must hit with a fully charged light arrow.

After triggering the eye switch, go directly west to find a sealed door. Light the nearby torch with Zelda to open the door, along with the last remaining sealed door on this floor. Now you may move freely through the inky darkness.

Continue west until a Warp Phantom appears at the floor's southwest corner. Maneuver Zelda to the Warp Phantom's left, and then speak to the creature to make it turn and expose its back. Stun and possess the Warp Phantom to remove this dangerous obstacle.

With the Warp Phantom out of the way, aim and loose a charged light arrow at the gilded eye switch on the wall that the creature was formerly guarding. With this second eye switch activated, a chest appears back across the floor to the east.

On your way to the chest, stun and possess the roaming Wrecker Phantom—this will soon come in handy. Open the chest to score a Small Key—your third and final one.

Dungeon Chest 5: Small Key

Small Key

You got a Small Key! Use this key to open locked doors!

With three Small Keys in your possession (check the Map screen's lower-right corner to ensure this is the case), backtrack toward the Warp Phantom and take this floor's southwest stairs to reach the twenty-eighth floor.

Tower of Spirits: Twenty-eighth Floor, Revisited

You've found three keys, and now you've discovered the three locked doors they open. All three doors are lined up in a row; open all of them, then head through the right door and venture down the northeast staircase.

Tower of Spirits: Twenty-seventh Floor

You're shown three eye switches as you enter the twenty-seventh floor for the first time. You'll probably need to activate all three of them somehow. Roll Zelda north up the hall of rolling boulders, smashing them to bits. Have the princess whack the switch she finds at the hall's north end to deactivate the boulders and allow Link to catch up.

Next, have Zelda smash through the bomb blocks and Armos statues to the south, getting them all out of the way. This will be helpful later.

Scope out the arrow aimer that's poised above a nearby pit, and ensure it's facing due north. You're all done over here after that. Backtrack to the twenty-eighth floor; this time, take the door on the left to reach the stairs leading down to the twenty-seventh floor's west half.

Once you're on the floor's west side, have Link head south and step on a floor switch, extending a bridge across the sand for Zelda. Such a gentleman!

Now use the sand to raise Link up and onto Zelda's back. Trudge southward and spy a high whip post over a nearby pit.

1 Report Back to Anjean

2 Return to the Tower of Spirits

3 Obtain the Compass of Light

4 Venture to the Dark Realm

Link can only reach the whip post from the height of Zelda's shoulders. Swing him across the pit in heroic fashion, and step on the floor switch you land near to extend another bridge for your Phantom friend.

As you continue, a Warp Phantom and a Phantom Eye materialize ahead of you up north. Sneak Link over to the Warp Phantom's ledge, and monitor these two enemies closely. When the Phantom Eye is elsewhere and the Warp Phantom is moving north, raise Link onto the platform with the Sand Wand and quickly stun the Warp Phantom from behind.

Immediately possess the Warp Phantom before the Phantom Eye notices Link. Then move Link up the tiny staircase located near the middle of this ledge.

Leave Link atop the staircase so the Phantom Eye won't notice him. Use the Sand Wand to raise a path for Zelda to cross over and collect the west arrow aimer. Leave Zelda on the west platform after she lifts the aimer overhead.

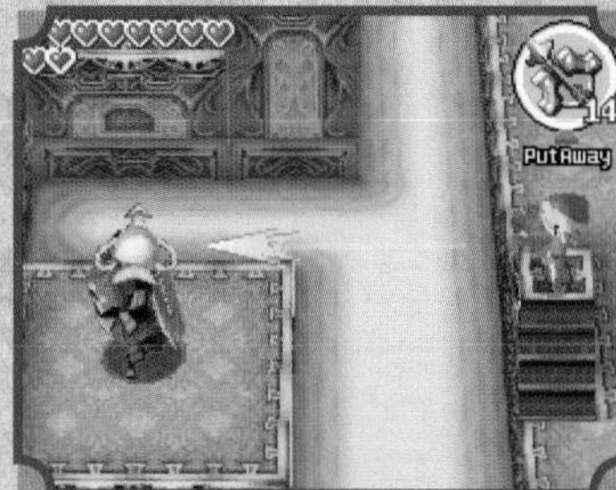

From the height of the tiny staircase, Link can lodge a light arrow into the aimer Zelda's holding. Ensure the aimer is pointing north, and your fully charged arrow will end up striking an eye switch. One down, two to go!

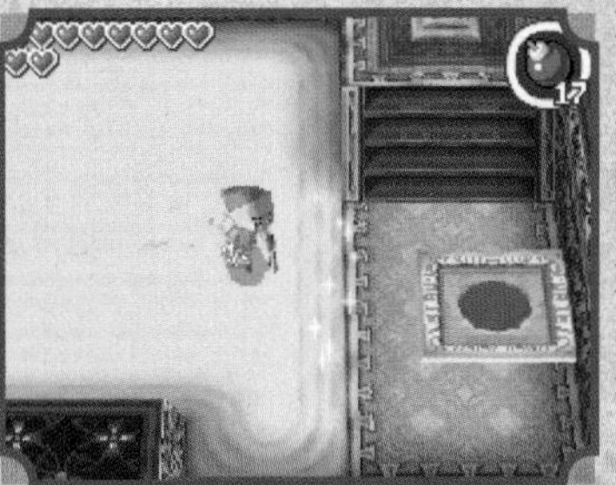

Next, have Link drop down and explore the sandy area to the east. Use bombs or arrows to clear out the Stalfos Warriors around here, then leave Link standing atop a red circle floor tile.

Switch to Zelda and warp her to the floor's easternmost Phantom Eye. From there, Zelda can move north and reach the matching red circle tile. Send her there to trade places with Link.

Once Link and Zelda have swapped spots, send Zelda up the nearby stairs and leave her standing on a floor switch. This opens a door back near Link.

Take control of Link and aim at the arrow aimer you noticed before, which is poised atop a nearby pit. Ensure the aimer's pointing north and loose a light arrow at it to activate the second eye switch.

Warp Zelda back over to Link and then go east, deactivating the rolling boulders so you may safely reach the northeast stairs leading back to the twenty-eighth floor. Make a quick trip up to the twenty-ninth floor to possess a Torch Phantom, then return to the twenty-eighth floor, and take the middle door this time. Go down the central stairwell to reach the twenty-seventh floor's central area.

Back on the twenty-seventh floor, have Zelda use her fiery blade to light a nearby torch. Then have Link carry the torch's fire to the southeast and northeast torches. Finally, have Zelda cross some spikes and light a southwest torch. You must light the torches in this order; any other sequence won't work.

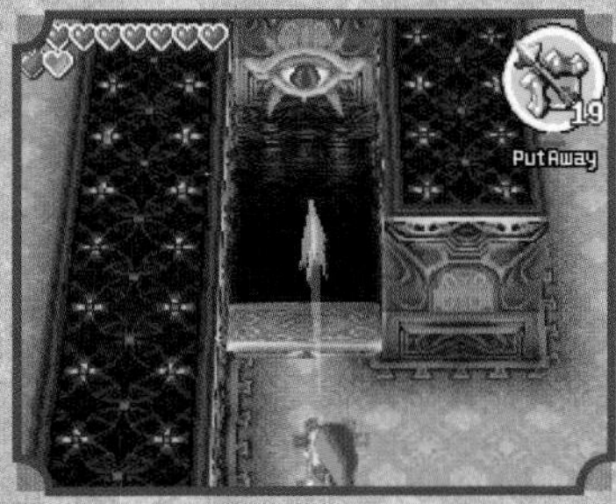

Lighting the four torches opens a nearby door, exposing the floor's final eye switch. Launch a light arrow into this third eye to open the central passage. Now you may proceed north and take the stairs down to the twenty-sixth floor.

Tower of Spirits: Twenty-sixth Floor

Your wits have been well tested thus far, but now you must prove your skill with the sword. Link and Zelda become trapped as they enter this tiny floor, forced to battle several waves of powerful enemies. If you have plenty of bombs, use some to wipe out a few enemies at the start of each wave. This gives you a bit of breathing room. Don't forget that Zelda can join in the fight, too!

First you face Blue ChuChus, then come several Stalfoses and Stalfos Warriors, followed by a trio of fire-breathing Geozard Chiefs. Zelda is great at hacking up ChuChus, but the Stalfoses prove too fast for her—use Link's arrows or bombs on them instead.

Keep Link moving when the final wave of Zoras arrive. Remember that he can hide behind Zelda to take cover from their fiery breath. Whip away those shields and then punish the Zoras with sword combos to survive this frantic fight!

Zelda and Link take a moment to congratulate each other after the dust settles. The room's doors have opened, so proceed downstairs to face the final challenge.

2730
We're unstoppable when you put us together. We can take on any monster!
Menu

Tower of Spirits: Twenty-fifth Floor

This is it: you just have to get past this last floor full of Phantoms. No problem! Leave Zelda near the entry stairs and run Link south. Hang out near the outer wall's south opening, and wait for the Torch Phantom to walk past.

When the Torch Phantom moves by, slip behind and stun it, then quickly possess it. Do this without alerting the Wrecker Phantom that patrols the outer hall.

1 Report Back to Anjean

2 Return to the Tower of Spirits

3 Obtain the Compass of Light

4 Venture to the Dark Realm

Once Zelda's in control of the Torch Phantom, have her light both torches on either side of the central door. The door then opens, granting you access to the interior chamber. Unfortunately, lighting the torches also prompts a Phantom Eye to appear to the east!

Possessing the Warp Phantom beyond the door is your next goal, but the stationary Phantom won't stop staring in your direction. Retreat Link to a safe zone, then have Zelda speak with the stationary Phantom, tricking it into looking away from the south doorway.

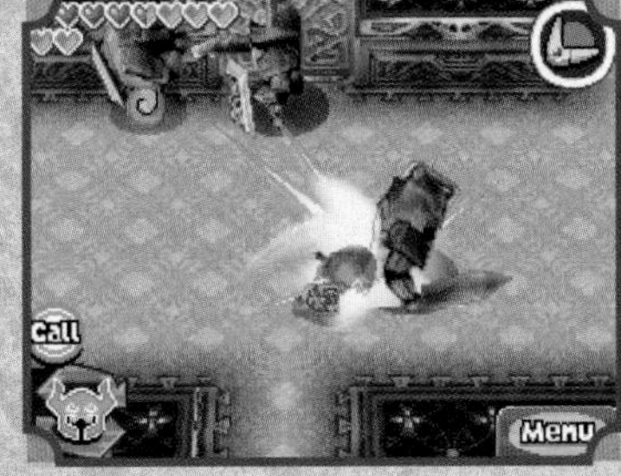

With the Phantom distracted, sneak Link back into the interior chamber and slip behind the patrolling Warp Phantom. Stun the brute and have Zelda possess it, but beware: the moment she does, the stationary Phantom will no longer be distracted! Immediately take Link to a safe zone before he's captured.

For your next trick, you must use the Whirlwind to blow the roaming Phantom Eye across the northeast sand pit. Wait until the Phantom Eye moves close to the sand, then dart out from hiding and start casting cyclones. The Whirlwind keeps this sentry stunned, so you don't need to worry about raising the alarm.

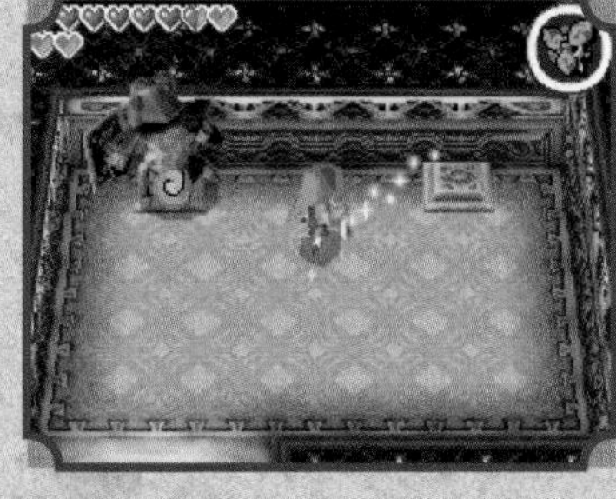

After blowing the Phantom Eye past the sand, switch to Zelda and quickly warp her over to the Phantom Eye. Dispatch the little troublemaker, then move both Link and Zelda onto the two floor switches to open the door that the stationary Phantom is guarding.

You've opened all the doors; now you just need to reach the northern doorway. The easiest way to accomplish this involves possessing the Wrecker Phantom, then sending him rolling north, into the stationary Phantom and through the Armos statues beyond.

Trace circles around the Phantom so that Zelda just keeps smacking into it and the Warp Phantom, when it reappears. With these two guardians dazed and confused, switch to Link and make a break for the northern safe zone.

All right, you made it! Now simply shove open the double door and pass through the doorway beyond.

Tower of Spirits: Twenty-fourth Floor

You got the Compass of Light!

Zelda is cast out of her Phantom form as she and Link enter the twenty-fourth floor. Scale the steps ahead and open the tower's final chest to at last acquire the item you seek. You've done it—you've found the Compass of Light!

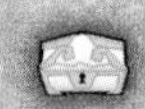

Dungeon Chest 6: Compass of Light

Compass of Light

You got the Compass of Light! It shines light upon the world, revealing places linked to the Dark Realm.

The compass goes to work immediately, restoring the very last portion of Spirit Tracks. Rail now runs to a tiny isle in the Forest Realm's southwest corner—it must be the entrance to the Dark Realm! How about that? All this time and the entrance to the Dark Realm was just a few miles away from Link's home.

The Compass of Light has revealed a track leading into the darkness!

Task 4: Venture to the Dark Realm

Into the Darkness

You've found the entrance to the Dark Realm, and there's nothing left for you to accomplish in the overworld. Set a course for the Forest Realm's tiny southwest isle, where the Spirit Tracks suddenly end. Pass through the ancient warp gate you discover there to at last visit the Dark Realm. It's high time Cole and Malladus were made to pay for the tremendous suffering they've caused.

TIP

The Dark Realm is not a friendly place, so do yourself a favor and stock up on potions before you go. Castle Town is right on the way!

1 Report Back to Anjean

2 Return to the Tower of Spirits

3 Obtain the Compass of Light

4 Venture to the Dark Realm

Final Battle: The Dark Realm

Princess Zelda has been through a lot lately, and she kindly asks that you help her defeat the great Demon King Malladus so that her spirit may at last return to her body. What do you say, hero? You busy?

A Link to the Present

Enemies Encountered

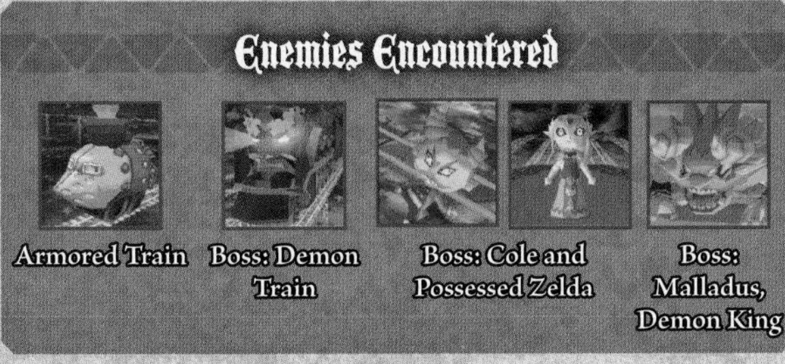

Items Already Acquired

Task 1: Destroy the Armored Trains

The Dark Realm

Passing through the overworld portal, you emerge in the Dark Realm, a twisted place full of rickety train tracks and multiple warp holes. A Tear of Light lies in the track dead ahead. As you collect it, your train becomes supercharged with divine energy, rushing forward at top speed!

Hang on, did we say top speed? Pull your train's whistle and you'll see what this baby can really do! As long as you hold down the cord, your train surges forward at a truly dizzying velocity. Use this incredible speed burst to cover lots of track!

Your purpose here is to destroy all six Armored Trains. To do this, you must ram them while your train is supercharged by a Tear. It's therefore best to follow a route through the realm that leads you from one Tear of Light to another. You do *not* want to be caught without the power of a Tear on your side!

Since Armored Trains often change direction on a whim, it's tough to give advice on an exact path through this area. If you're having trouble, try the following:

1. Collect the first Tear of Light, sound the whistle, and surge forward at top speed without altering course. Defeat the first Armored Train.
2. Continue speeding along, catching up to and destroying a second Armored Train just before your first Tear of Light's effects fade.
3. Immediately turn left after smashing the second Armored Train, veering north to snag another Tear of Light.
4. After collecting the second Tear, immediately reverse, swinging back around the junction. Tug the whistle while reversing to back out at top speed.
5. Kick it up into high gear again and plot a course that takes you east, along the realm's southern track, and then north, directly toward two more Armored Trains. Hold the whistle to close the distance quickly.
6. Grab the northeast Tear of Light while chasing down and destroying both northeast Armored Trains—you don't want to run out of juice around here!
7. After destroying both northeast Armored Trains, set a course for the middle warp hole on the realm's east side. Pass through to emerge from the middle warp hole to the west.
8. Continue straight, grabbing another Tear of Light and entering a warp hole. This one spits you out up north, near the northwest Armored Train.
9. Hurry and smash the northwest Armored Train before your Tear of Light wears off. Then go through the northwest warp hole to emerge back east.
10. Grab the nearest Tear of Light (the one to the northeast), and chase down the final Armored Car. But beware: The last Armored Car breaks from its normal cycle and tries to hunt *you* down as well! Make sure you've always got a Tear of Light on your side, and you derail this final adversary in a matter of time.

1 Destroy the Armored Trains

2 Catch the Demon Train

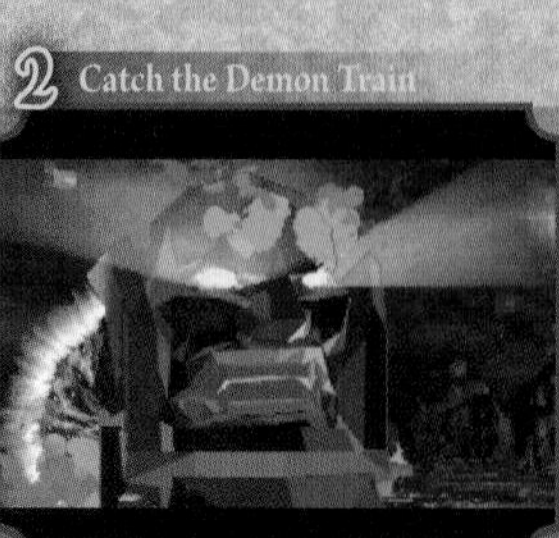

3 Banish Malladus from Zelda

4 Defeat the Demon King

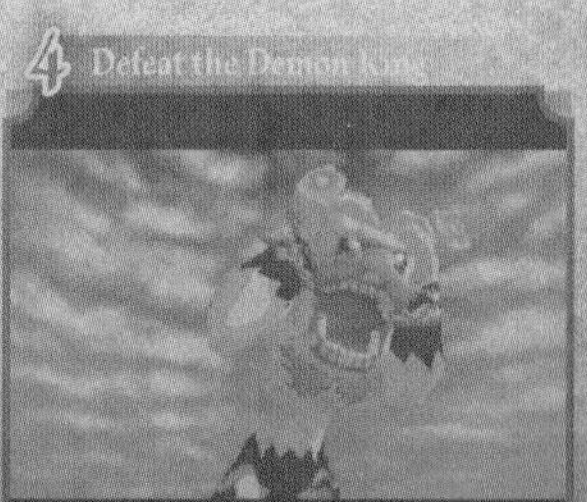

Task 2: Catch the Demon Train

Runnin' Down a Demon

When you've destroyed all six Armored Trains, Link is at last able to pursue the Demon Train directly. The Demon Train runs along four parallel stretches of track; ride up close to the Demon Train and batter its explosive barrel launchers with your cannon to damage the mechanical monstrosity.

Demon Train

Hits to Defeat: Multiple
Attack Type: Contact and Range
Power: N/A
Damage: 1 heart
Threat Meter

Be ready to slam on the brakes at any moment—the Demon Train can cross between the tracks at will, and you don't want to be running alongside it when it moves over! Zelda shouts out a warning each time the Demon Train switches tracks. If necessary, throw it into reverse to slow down so you aren't rammed.

Blast all of the barrel launchers on one side of the Demon Train, then blast all the ones on the other side. To advance to the next stage of the battle, destroy them all before you run out of track.

The battle's second phase is much like the first, with you racing alongside the Demon Train and destroying its weapon systems. This time, the Demon Train employs laser cannons that are quick to fire. The lasers have a limited firing arc, however, so simply keep back a bit and you should be able to blast each one without exposing yourself to danger.

Destroy all of the Demon Train's laser cannons to advance to the third and final phase. Now the Demon Train has abandoned all defenses and unleashes a wide spread of rotating laser beams that strike out in all angles. Do your best to avoid being sliced by the lasers as you race alongside the Demon Train, blasting the blue crystals from which the lasers emanate.

Remain on one side of the Demon Train, and wipe out every active blue crystal. You can accomplish this without shifting sides, because each crystal rotates within firing view. The Demon Train shudders and slows dramatically once you've hit all the crystals. Race forward and unload on the fiend's face!

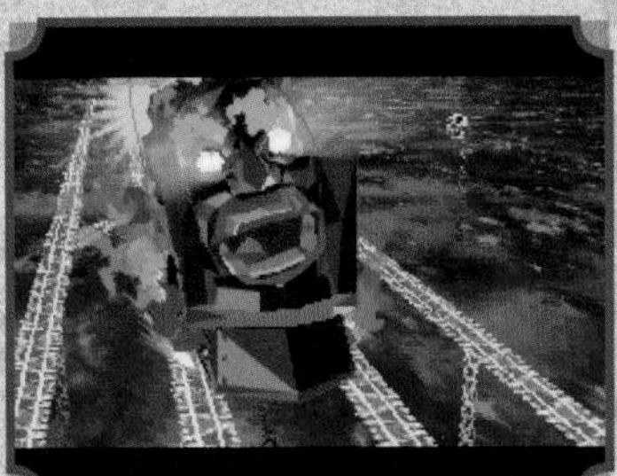

Keep your train in high gear and just keep pounding the Demon Train's face. Don't relent until the terrible train is at last derailed.

Task 3: Banish Malladus from Zelda

Two on Two

Having tamed the Demon Train, Link and Zelda are at last able to board the vile vehicle—but not before Anjean kindly summons a suit of Phantom armor for Zelda to occupy. The two find Chancellor Cole waiting for them on the Demon Train's roof, along with the Demon King himself, who's still using Zelda's body as his vessel.

Cole

Hits to Defeat: N/A
Attack Type: Summon (Rats)
Power: Strong
Damage: 1/2 heart (Rat)

Threat Meter

Possessed Zelda

Hits to Defeat: 1 (Bow of Light)
Attack Type: Range
Power: Strong
Damage: 1/2 heart

Threat Meter

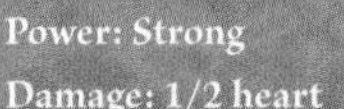

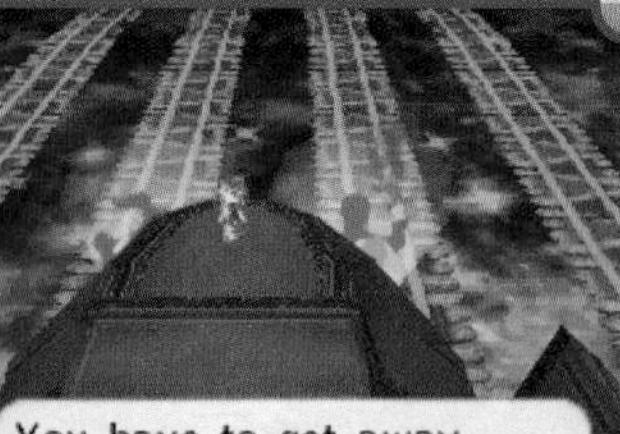

This segment is brutal until you realize how simple it is. For the most part, just ignore Malladus—Cole is the real threat here. Direct Zelda to walk north along the train, then switch to Link and focus on repelling Cole's attempts to interfere.

Cole primarily attacks by summoning magical Rats that encircle Zelda, scaring the wits out of her. Keep Link close by, and be quick to wipe out each Rat that Cole spawns. If you can succeed in this effort, this stage of the battle becomes relatively simple.

It's bad news if one of Cole's Rats manages to touch Zelda. Cole seizes control of the princess when this occurs, steering her actions like a puppeteer. Whenever Cole takes control of Zelda, immediately toss out the boomerang, guiding it around and behind the princess, with the intent of severing the magical strings Cole's using to control her. Cut the cords and Zelda returns to normal. (Well, as normal as she can be these days.)

1 Destroy the Armored Trains

2 Catch the Demon Train

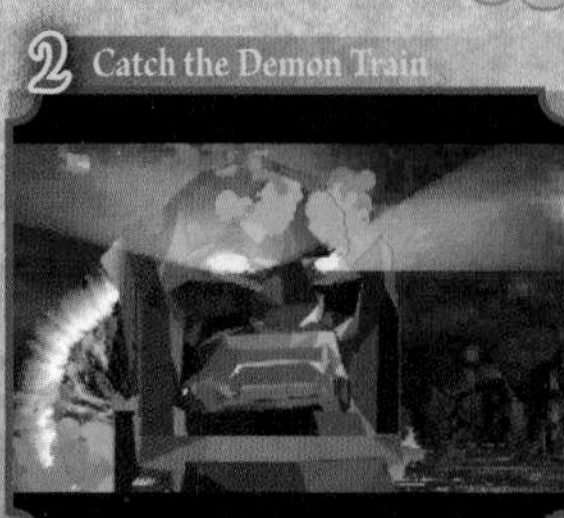

3 Banish Malladus from Zelda

4 Defeat the Demon King

The idea is to prevent Cole from possessing Zelda while also keeping Zelda moving north, toward her possessed body. Zelda must lead the way, because only she can withstand the powerful laser Malladus fires as you approach. Keep Link behind Zelda at all times, and keep his sword swinging away at those Rats!

Now's your chance! While Zelda and Malladus are locked in a struggle, whip out the Bow of Light and hold the stylus on the screen to charge up an arrow. Aim at Malladus and fire when he spins around and you have a clear shot. Whatever you do, don't be fazed by the fact that you're currently shooting arrows at the body of the princess!

The Demon Train's roof compartments commonly shift from side to side. Keep to the roof's middle to avoid taking a nasty tumble.

Battle all the way up to Malladus, then steer Zelda into contact with her possessed body. Zelda grabs hold of Malladus tightly, and the two soar off into the sky.

Hit Zelda's possessed body with a single light arrow to bring this stage of the finale to its close. The Demon Train's run of terror is at last brought to a halt, and everyone's deposited at a remote clearing somewhere back in the real world.

The Bow of Light works exactly as advertised, ousting Malladus from Princess Zelda's body. Seizing the opportunity she's longed for, Zelda wastes no time in merging with her body, at long last becoming whole again.

The princess's great gain becomes Chancellor Cole's ultimate loss. In need of a new host, Malladus takes possession of his loyal impish underling. The Demon King knows he can't last long in such an unfit vessel, but he vows to destroy the world in the short amount of time he has left. And so begins the ultimate clash!

Task 4: Defeat the Demon King

Mess with the Bull

Malladus, Demon King

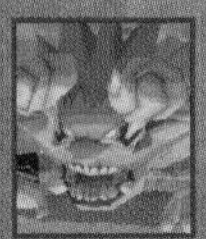

Hits to Defeat: Multiple
Attack Type: Contact and Range
Power: Strong
Damage: 1/2 heart (all attacks)
Threat Meter

As the battle begins, Princess Zelda implores Link to protect her from Malladus while she concentrates on channeling her family's sacred power. Stand before Zelda and swing Link's sword to batter away each demonic fireball Malladus spits forth. While you're getting down the timing, try swinging in advance of each fireball—swing just after you see it appear at the top of the Touch Screen.

Malladus gets tricky as you deflect more and more of his fireballs. Pairs of fireballs that veer out to either side will eventually curve back in to strike Zelda from the sides, so you must quickly dash from one side to the other to swat them away. You might also try unleashing several spin attacks in a row to deflect them. The great spin attack is excellent here—assuming you've learned the move from Niko!

The Demon King also bounds to the sides and spits fireballs at odd angles. Worse, he'll eventually spew out a volley of four fireballs, all at once, which quickly spread out and then converge as they near their target. Only a perfectly timed spin attack performed at the very last second can repel all four fireballs. Again, the great spin attack is ideal.

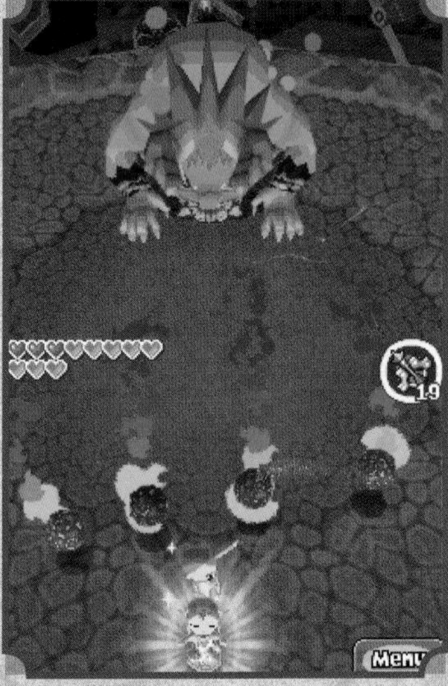

2559
Let's combine my sacred power with the power of the Spirit Flute!

Just keep knocking those fireballs away from Zelda until she finally summons the power she needs. Zelda says she must combine her power with that of the Spirit Flute, hoping the effect will amplify and weaken the Demon King.

Hey, it's worth a shot! Take up the Spirit Flute and play a challenging song with Zelda that demands quick strokes of the stylus to skip past certain notes as you steadily blow into the microphone.

Ace the song to summon the spirits of the many Lokomo guardians you've met on your travels: Gage, Steem, Carben, Embrose, and Rael. All of the Lokomos appear, adding their sacred instruments to Zelda's divine ballad.

The song has the desired effect, wounding Malladus with its purity and revealing a shimmering weak point on his back. *Now* we've got a boss fight on our hands!

I'll shoot him in the back

Zelda pulls Link into one final huddle, advising that he distract the Demon King while she shoots his weak point from behind with the Bow of Light. Sounds like a plan, Princess!

All right, *this* is the final battle. For real now, you guys. The goal is simple: Run up to Malladus and assault him with a barrage of sword strikes until he finally rounds on Link. Then run away screaming and glance at the top screen to view the world through Zelda's eyes. When at last the Demon King's back is within her sight, Zelda's purple targeting crosshair changes to a yellow burst. Now! Tap the Bow of Light icon at the bottom of your screen to make Zelda fire, striking Malladus's weak spot with a light arrow full of pure, wholesome juju.

Now, Link!
Give him your worst!
18
Menu

Repeat this sequence, pumping Malladus full of light arrows until the villain at last collapses. Then sprint to the glowing red gemstone on Malladus's head, and hack at it with Link's sword until the Demon King regains his senses.

Malladus adds a few new attacks, but you've seen worse. He offers nothing you can't easily dodge, so just keep focusing on landing those light arrows. Whale away on the boss's gemstone each time he goes down.

Eventually, Malladus's gemstone cracks open a bit—enough for Link's blade to become lodged inside. You can't give up! Rub the stylus back and forth across the screen as fast as you can, helping Link wedge his sword deeper and deeper into Malladus's head. Even Zelda rushes over to lend a hand, because defeating evil's a team effort!

Keep rubbing that stylus until our heroes are at last able to shatter Malladus's precious gemstone. The Demon King rears back in terrible agony, then bursts apart in a violent shower of light. Congratulations, hero, you've done it!

With no reason left to linger around the land of humans, the Lokomo guardians bid Zelda and Link a fond farewell, then depart into the heavens to be with the rest of their kin—the noble spirits of good. Link and the princess watch in awe as the Lokomos' spirits rise into the red, dusky sky, soon drifting away to mere twinkles. The two clasp hands as they enjoy the moment, sharing a well-deserved sense of relief and harmony. For now, they know that the spirits of good will always be there, watching over and protecting them.

1 Destroy the Armored Trains

2 Catch the Demon Train

3 Banish Malladus from Zelda

4 Defeat the Demon King

Multiplayer

Even after you've restored the Tower of Spirits and opened every chest, the fun is far from over, thanks to *Spirit Tracks'* multiplayer modes. In Battle Mode, go head-to-head with your friends and other opponents in a frantic search for Force Gems. Or simply trade treasures with friends using Chance Encounter Communication in Tag Mode. So what are you waiting for? Find a friend and get busy!

Battle Mode

In Battle Mode, up to four players can tackle each other in a series of six mazes, battling for supremacy over a collection of Force Gems. It's a wild game that offers hours of laughs and entertainment as you try to collect as many gems as possible, all while sabotaging the efforts of your opponents. It's a fast-paced game in which fortunes can change in an instant.

Getting Started

To play Battle Mode, each player must have a Nintendo DS and at least one copy of *Spirit Tracks* for Single-Card Play. When you start the game, select your save file and then choose "Battle" from the Main menu screen. This shuttles you into the Main menu for Battle Mode.

From the Battle Mode setup screen, you can create or join a group. This screen also displays your profile's stats, showing your number of wins, battles, rank points, and your current rank. At the screen's bottom is the Player List, which tracks all the players you've encountered in Battle Mode. If you wish to join a group of players, choose the Join Group option. Or if you'd prefer to start a group of your own, select Create Group.

When creating or joining a group, you must wait a few seconds for new players to show up before the battle can begin. If you've created a group, it's up to you to choose when to close the room, preventing other players from joining. If you want a two-player match, close the room after only one other player has joined. If you want a bigger group, wait around for more players to join—a maximum of four players can take part in Battle Mode. Once you select the Close Room button, no other players can join your game.

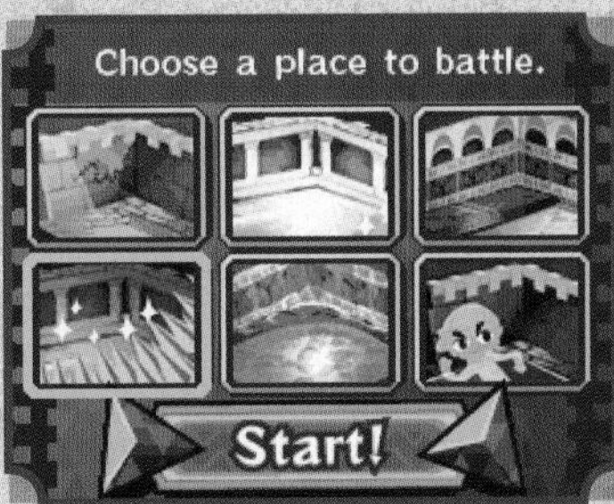

Next, it's time to select a stage. There are six different stages, each with unique layouts and hazards. Browse through the options to view the map layouts until you find one that looks appealing. If you're new to Battle Mode, consider choosing from the three maps on the top row, as they're geared toward beginners. Once you've selected a stage, the game begins. Get ready to grab some Force Gems!

How to Play

The object of the game is simple: acquire more Force Gems than your opponents. Force Gems appear as triangles of varying sizes—they also appear on the map. Small Force Gems are worth one point each, a regular-sized Force Gem is worth two points, and a large Force Gem is worth three points. These Force Gems materialize throughout the match, so keep an eye on your map to locate and grab them before your opponents can. The number of Force Gems in your possession is indicated by a number above your character's head. The tally of each player's Force Gem count is also shown in the top screen, allowing you to see who has the lead with a quick glance at the map. Each round lasts for three minutes and is tracked by the timer at the screen's bottom.

But there's more to Battle Mode than simply gathering Force Gems. Look for opportunities to attack and steal from your opponents—especially if they're winning. Floor switches activate trapdoors, allowing you to drop your rivals down a deep, dark pit. As they plummet into the darkness, they leave behind a large share of their Force Gems, allowing you to steal them. Trapdoors are also a clever way to dispatch those pesky Phantoms.

Oh yes, there are Phantoms in Battle Mode too. As in the Tower of Spirits, these devoted sentries patrol the halls and will stop at nothing to prevent you and your opponents from gathering Force Gems. Pay close attention to the map to spot the locations of Phantoms, and do your best to stay out of their field of vision. You'll know a Phantom has spotted you when a Phantom Eye appears and hovers around your head. Take this as a clue to start running! All it takes is one hit from a Phantom's sword to make you fall, losing 50 percent of your Force Gems in the process. After a Phantom strikes, it disappears and respawns at a random location.

There are a few ways to get a Phantom off your tail. Phantoms will not climb or descend stairs. So if you change elevations, you can cut the chase short. Or, you can always get a Phantom to chase one of your opponents. Simply rush past one of your opponents to divert the Phantom's attention. With proper timing, the Phantom will then chase after your opponent instead of you. Be sure to grab your opponent's dropped Force Gems once the Phantom has struck.

All stages contain Bomb Flowers. This is the only offensive weapon you can use directly against your opponents. Simply grab a bomb, and toss it toward your opponent to knock them down, causing them to eject a large share of their Force Gems. However, don't bother using these bombs against Phantoms, as they have no effect. Quite the contrary in fact. A bomb will only draw the Phantom's attention toward you, initiating a frantic chase.

Be careful when tossing bombs! If you're too close to the explosion, you may incur damage, causing you to lose some of your Force Gems.

Bonus Pick-ups

Throughout the match, look for these colorful swirling medallions inscribed with a question mark icon. This is a bonus pick-up, and if you grab it, you can benefit from several powerful bonuses. Once acquired, the medallion appears in the bottom screen's top-right corner and rotates as several icons flash within its center. This functions much like the dial on a slot machine as the randomly selected bonus is determined.

Force Gem Bonus

There are three different types of Force Gem bonuses, differing only by the amount of gems showered down upon you. In its most modest iteration, three small Force Gems fall out of the sky near you—you still have to pick them up to acquire them. And in its most generous offering, a mix of small, medium, and large Force Gems shower over you. These gems are up for grabs, so be sure to pick them all up before your opponents rush in and steal your bonus.

Invincibility

This is one of the most powerful bonuses, rendering you invincible for a few seconds. While invincible, your character glows with a purplish hue, allowing you to confront most hazards without taking damage. So don't worry about Phantoms, bombs, or lava. While invincible, chase down your opponents and knock them down, stealing their dropped Force Gems in the process. However, invincibility does not protect you against trapdoors, so watch your step. If you fall into one of these pits, your invincibility run is over.

Thunder Storm

Summon a powerful thunderstorm with this bonus, striking down your nearby opponents with a shocking lightning strike. Once this is activated, you're given nine seconds to get an opponent within the storm's radius, as indicated by the yellow circle around your character. As the timer counts down to zero, any opponents within the yellow radius are knocked down, coughing up a large portion of their Force Gems in the process. If another player has activated this bonus, the screen turns purple and you're warned of the incoming storm, so do your best to stay outside your opponent's yellow radius.

Pitfalls

The pitfalls bonus is hazardous to all players, causing pits to open up all over the map without warning. However, the player who activates this bonus can see where the pits are, as they are represented by red boxes on the map. Simply avoid these red boxes while the bonus is active to avoid falling down these pits. Your opponents aren't so lucky and will have to watch their step.

Stages

Battle Mode offers six unique stages, each with its own hazards and challenges. In this section, we take an in-depth look at each stage, providing a detailed map as well as some vital gameplay tips to help you dominate each match.

Ancient Earth

Ancient Earth is a compact stage designed specifically for two-player matches. Other than the trapdoors and patrolling Phantoms, there aren't too many threats here, making it the ideal stage for beginners.

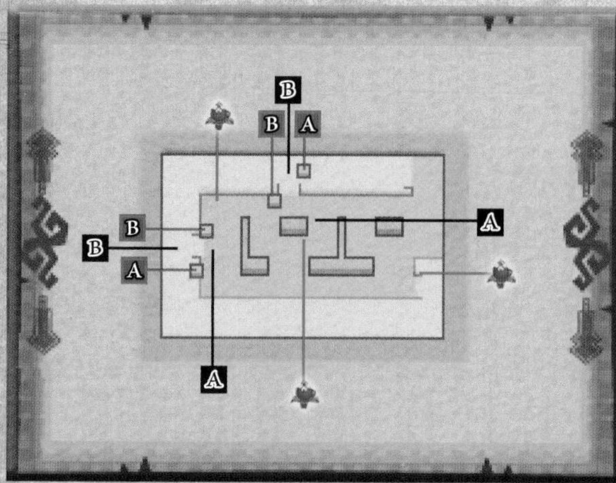

Legend

- A Floor Switch A
- B Floor Switch B
- A Trapdoor A
- B Trapdoor B
- Bomb Flower

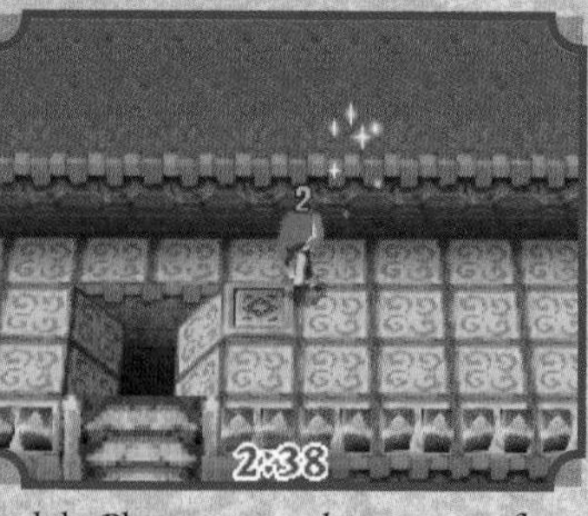

First thing to note on this stage are the trapdoors. The two floor switches on the upper level activate the two trapdoors on the lower level, and the floor switches on the lower level activate the trapdoors on the upper level. Keep an eye on the map to spot where your opponents and the Phantoms are; then step on a floor switch at the right time to send them plummeting through a trapdoor.

Given the upper and lower levels of this stage, it's easy to lose a Phantom during a chase. One Phantom patrols the upper level while the other patrols the lower level. If you're being chased on the lower level, simply race up the steps to the upper level to lose your foe. Likewise, if being chased on the upper level, head downstairs. This is by far the quickest and easiest way to end a chase. And no matter how courageous you feel, don't throw a bomb at a Phantom.

There are three Bomb Flowers in this stage, so don't forget to put their explosive fruit to good use. This is a great way to knock some Force Gems away from your opponents. An exploded bomb leaves behind a fire for a few seconds, so be careful not to tread directly into the aftermath of a blast; otherwise it will be you who's shedding Force Gems.

On the upper walkway, there's a barrier preventing players from dropping to the lower level. However, there is a gap in this barrier on the southern span. Just run off the walkway here to land on the stage's lower level. This is a great way to shake a Phantom off your tail or to simply transition to the lower level without using stairs.

Frozen Plains

Slip and slide your way to victory in this challenging frozen maze filled with Phantoms and a set of tricky trapdoors. Like Ancient Earth, this compact stage is best suited for small-scale two-player matches.

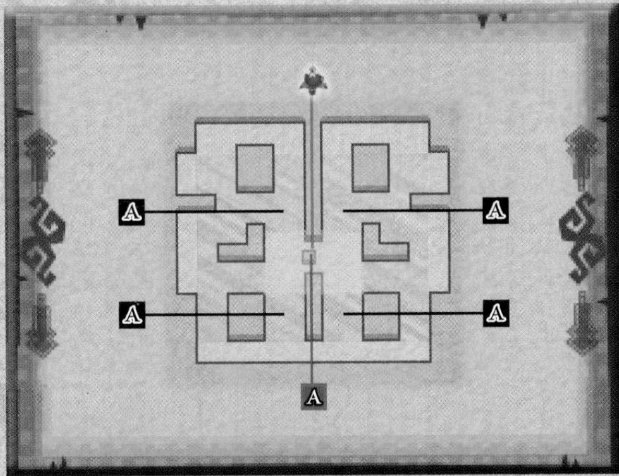

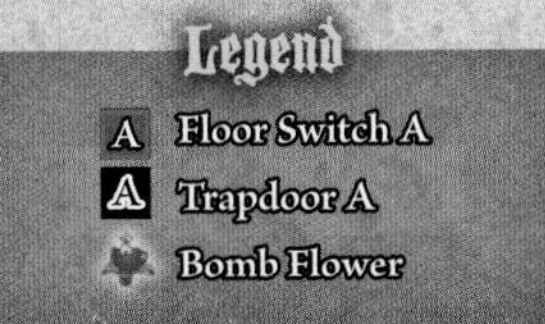

Legend
A Floor Switch A
A Trapdoor A
Bomb Flower

There is only one floor switch on this stage, but it's a very powerful one, capable of opening all four of the surrounding trapdoors. Try to take advantage of this switch as often as possible, but don't make a habit of camping the center of the map—unless you want a Phantom to chase you. Rather, cut through the map's center while seeking Force Gems. But watch your step if another player is standing near the floor switch—they may be waiting to drop you down a pit so they can steal your scattered Force Gems.

The icy portions of the floor make it difficult to maneuver, especially if you need to make a quick course correction. This can make it hard to avoid the gaze of an approaching Phantom. Therefore, play it safe and keep a close eye on the map, staying as far away from the Phantoms as possible. If you're spotted, you'll have a tough time getting away, as there are no upper or lower levels on which to take refuge. You'll either have to drop the pursuing Phantom down a pit or convince it to chase one of your opponents.

When possible, stick to the perimeter's stone walkways to limit your exposure to the icy floors. The stone floor provides more traction, resulting in greater speed and control. Consider using these stone floor pieces as your own personal racetrack to circle around the stage.

NOTE

Traveling around the perimeter isn't the fastest way to get around, but it allows you to quickly change direction while avoiding the trapdoors in the map's center.

The stage's only Bomb Flower is located in the map's center, right next to the floor switch. This gives some players even more incentive to camp the center, so watch out! If the trapdoors don't get you, a crafty opponent with a bomb just might. But if you're the one throwing the bomb, be careful, especially if you're running on the ice. Your forward momentum will make you slide directly into the explosion and resulting fire, causing you to lose several Force Gems.

Fire Arena

Race to gather Force Gems while avoiding the rising lava in this frantic stage. Although the map looks rather large, at any given time, half the floor is filled with lava, drastically reducing the playable area. So consider choosing this map during two-player battles.

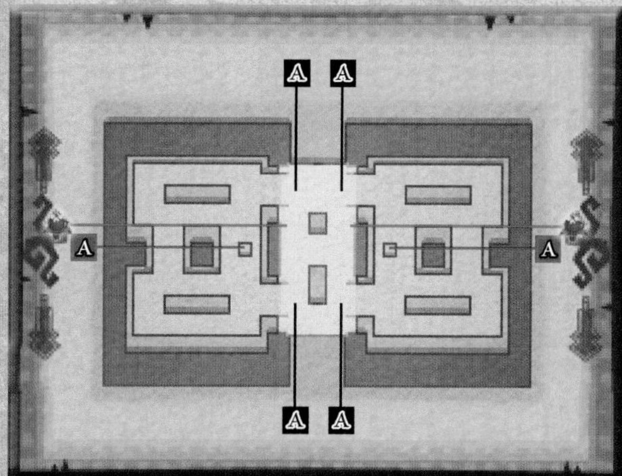

The first thing to note on this map is the lava. As the battle starts, the map's entire western half is filled with lava, making this area inaccessible. Approximately 30 seconds later, the lava drains from the western floor and fills the eastern floor. As the lava switches sides, you will hear a distinct ticking sound. Immediately head for higher ground in the center of the map. From there, you can access the opposite floor, now drained of lava. If you get trapped in the lava, you'll lose several Force Gems and respawn on the central island.

There are only two floor switches on this map, and they each open the four trapdoors on the central island. Each trapdoor is cleverly placed at the top of each set of stairs—four of the most high-traffic areas. Given their locations on the western and eastern floors, only one floor switch is accessible at any given time; the other one is covered with lava. This makes it relatively easy to monitor the switch on the top map, allowing you to see if any opponents are waiting to drop you down a pit. If playing larger-scale matches, the trapdoors become even more effective. Simply loiter near one of the floor switches and step on it when an opponent dashes up one of the staircases. Then grab their dropped Force Gems before they respawn.

Of all the stages, this is one of the easiest to avoid Phantoms. One Phantom patrols the lower floor while another paces around the central island. If you're being chased, simply race up or down one of the staircases to lose your pursuer. But pay close attention to other hazards while doing so. For instance, while running up the stairs, watch out for open trapdoors. Also, pay close attention to where the other Phantom is to avoid running directly into it.

The invincibility bonus has many great benefits on this map. Not only does it make you immune to the effects of lava, but you can also ignore any Phantoms chasing you. But don't waste time. Make a beeline directly for one of your opponents. If you can't catch them, at least try to chase them into the path of a Phantom or into a trapdoor. However, invincibility doesn't last forever, so make sure you're clear of any lava or pursuing Phantoms before time runs out.

Icy Plains

Beware of the slippery ice and sharp spikes in this challenging stage. Due to the hazards and compact layout, this arena is best suited for Battle Mode veterans. To ramp up the difficulty even more, try playing with four players.

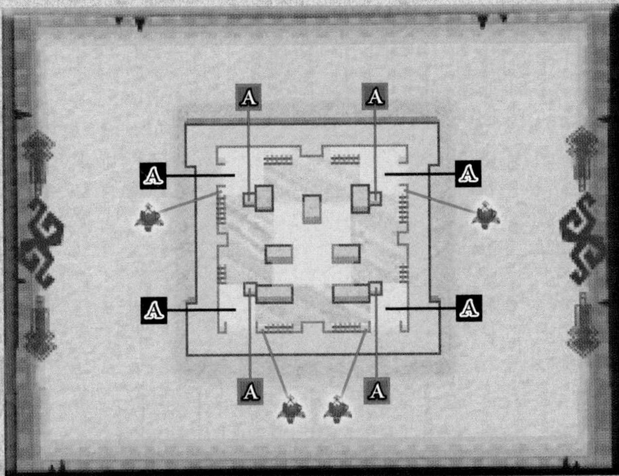

Legend

- A Floor Switch A
- A Trapdoor A
- Bomb Flower

Before you start searching for Force Gems, quickly study the map's layout. The large platform at the map's center is home to most of the stage's hazards, including the trapdoors, spikes, and Bomb Flowers. The stone walkway on the map's perimeter is relatively free of hazards, save for the occasional patrolling Phantom. But you'll never win by staying on the outer walkway, as most Force Gems are dropped on the central platform. Therefore, consider using the stone perimeter walkway to circle the map, then make short trips onto the central platform to retrieve Force Gems. Minimizing your exposure to the ice and trapdoors can make a big difference in the long run.

The patches of ice on the central platform are partially surrounded by sharp metal spikes, designed to impale out-of-control gem hunters. Therefore, exercise extreme caution while maneuvering on the ice. For one, slow down. The slower you move, the more control you have on the ice. But if you slide out of control, quickly adjust your course to avoid contacting the spikes. If you plan your turns early, you can maintain high speeds while preventing such collisions. Contact with the spikes will not knock you down, but it will cause you to lose some of your Force Gems, giving your opponents a chance to steal them.

This stage's trapdoors are located on the four corners of the central platform and are activated by the nearby switches—each switch activates the same four trapdoors. These four corners are high-traffic areas, making the position of these trapdoors very dangerous. Players skidding across the ice may not be able to stop in time and will fall through an open trapdoor. Use this to your advantage. When an opponent is racing across one of the icy patches, step on a floor switch as they near one of the corners. If they're moving too fast, they can't avoid falling into the open pit. In some instances, players may slide across the floor switch and fall directly into the trapdoor they just opened. Make sure such embarrassing mistakes don't happen to you.

While the ice, spikes, and trapdoors may seem like enough hazards to keep track of, don't neglect the stage's Phantoms. One Phantom patrols the ringlike stone floor on the lower level while the other occupies the icy central platform. The slippery ice can make it tough to avoid the Phantom in the center, sometimes causing you to slide directly into one of these bad boys. Therefore, it's extremely important to keep your distance, because you never know when the Phantom might suddenly turn in your direction. As usual, if you're spotted, dash toward one of the staircases. However, running on ice isn't easy, and the Phantom has a good chance of catching up before you establish the necessary traction to run away—Phantoms are not slowed by ice, nor do they slip.

Scorched Battlefield

Brave the fiery hazards of this lava-filled stage to come out on top in your quest for Force Gems. This is another stage designed for veteran players, and it is made even more difficult by increasing the player count. Start off playing one-on-one until you get familiar with the stage's layout and unique hazards.

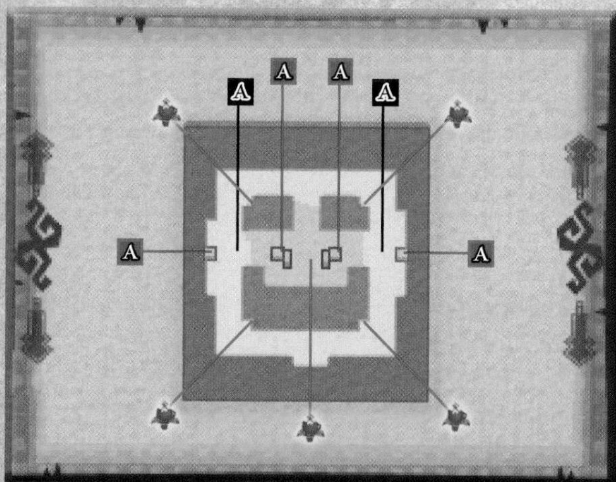

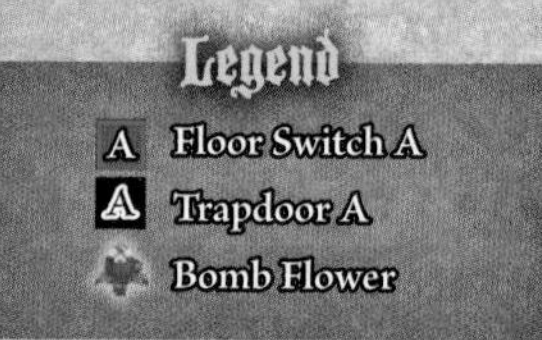

When the stage begins, the entire map is playable, including the central lower level. However, after only 15 seconds, the middle of the map begins filling with lava. If you want to grab some Force Gems on the lower level, make a quick dash for the map's center; then get out before the lava seeps onto the floor. Lava continually drains and fills this lower level throughout the duration of the match, so listen for that telltale ticking sound to avoid getting stuck in the middle at the wrong time. Force Gems are not dropped in the middle of the map while the lava is present, so simply stick to the upper walkway on the map's perimeter until the lava recedes.

The stage's only two trapdoors are located at the tops of the eastern and western steps; you can activate them by any of the four floor switches. To avoid getting dropped down a pit, make a habit of using the northern and southern staircases during your transitions from the lower and upper levels. Also, look for opportunities to drop your opponents down a pit as they carelessly use the eastern and western staircases.

There are no walls on the sides of the eastern and western upper walkways. Instead, each walkway is flanked by a black abyss. So watch your step when maneuvering through these areas. Stepping off the walkway's edge causes you to lose a large portion of your Force Gems.

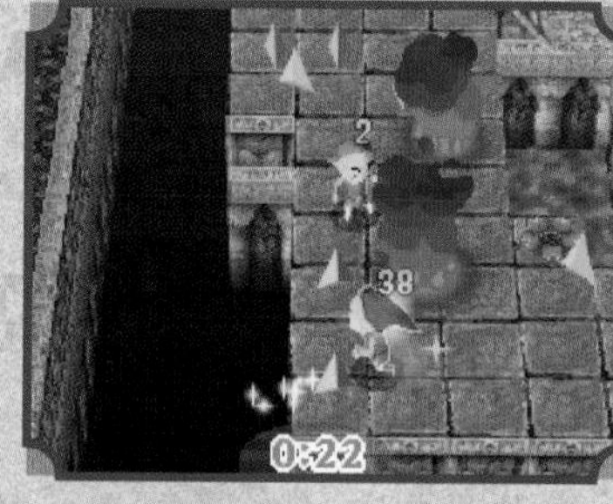

Bomb Flowers are spread throughout the map, making bomb-throwing duels a common occurrence on this map. Just don't pick a fight with an opponent who's invincible. Once the bomb's are thrown, pay extra attention to the fires left behind. These fires can be just as deadly as the bombs themselves, particularly if you keep running into them. So steer clear of the fires while collecting the dropped Force Gems from your victims.

The lava in the map's center presents a problem when a Phantom is chasing you. As long as the lava's present, you can't dash down the stairs to lose the Phantom. Your best bet is to activate a trapdoor in hopes that the Phantom steps into the open pit. Another option (albeit trickier) is to lead the Phantom toward one of your opponents. If the Phantom spots one of your opponents, it may stop chasing you in favor of your buddy. You can always outrun the Phantom, too, leading it in circles around the map until the lava clears, allowing you to head downstairs and end the chase.

Shadow Stage

Become invisible and covertly sneak around this watery stage to gather Force Gems while ambushing your unsuspecting opponents. This arena's unique layout and characteristics make it a fun stage for players of all skill levels.

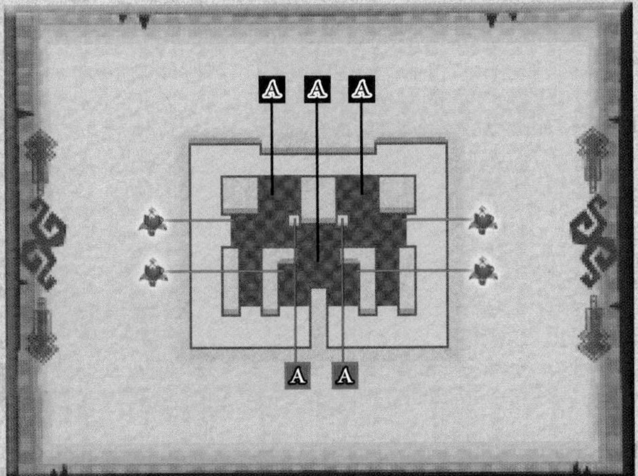

Legend

- A Floor Switch A
- A Trapdoor A
- Bomb Flower

The center of this map is filled with shallow water. Don't hesitate to jump in—don't worry, you won't sink. Instead, this water makes you invisible, causing you to disappear from your opponents' maps. But you're not completely invisible to your opponents. With each step you take, a small ripple appears behind you, allowing others to track your movements and vice versa. Still, the Phantoms don't need to see ripples to begin chasing you. Regardless of whether you are invisible, Phantoms will begin pursuing you as soon as you move within their field of view, so don't get too comfortable in the water.

There are plenty of Bomb Flowers scattered throughout this stage, but think twice before carrying a bomb into the shallow water. You'll still turn invisible as soon as your feet get wet, but the bomb carried high above your head remains visible. This simply makes it easier for your opponents to spot you. Even if you stay still (to avoid making ripples), when they see a bomb floating in midair, they're likely to deduce that an invisible opponent is carrying it.

The two floor switches in the map's center activate the same three trapdoors nearby. However, since the floor switches are in the watery area, it's difficult to tell when an opponent is poised to drop you down a pit, since anyone standing near a switch is invisible. The best way to prevent such treachery is to memorize the locations of the trapdoors and avoid the northwest, northeast, and southern passages. But if you're the one looking to ambush opponents, simply stand still next to a floor switch to avoid making ripples. Then when one of your opponents moves into position, step onto the floor switch to drop them down a pit. This can be a fun way to dispose of Phantoms too.

There are no upper or lower levels in this stage, so losing a pursing Phantom can be tricky. Once a Phantom Eye spots you, even turning yourself invisible won't halt the chase. Once again, rely on the trapdoors in the map's center to drop your pursuer down a pit. Or you can turn the Phantom onto one of your opponents, even if they're invisible. In any case, keep moving. The perimeter stone passages offer long stretches, making it easier to dash ahead and stay one step ahead of the Phantom's blade. Race around the perimeter until you have an opportunity to ditch the pursuing Phantom.

Tag Mode

Remember all those treasures you plundered from the dungeon and overworld chests? Instead of selling them off to Linebeck, consider trading your loot with friends using Tag Mode. This is a fun way to show off your treasures to friends and to help newer players by giving them rare treasures they can exchange for Rupees at the Trading Post. This form of power-leveling can give lower-level players a tremendous advantage, allowing them to attain vast amounts of Rupees and to buy items they would normally be unable to purchase.

To begin Tag Mode, first choose a save file, then select Start—make sure you choose a file that has treasure to trade. When this screen appears, select the Tag Mode option at the screen's bottom. Obviously, both parties involved in Tag Mode need a *Spirit Tracks* game and a save file that contains some treasure.

This inventory screen shows all the treasure you've acquired during your adventures. Select a piece with the stylus to reveal its name and its value in Rupees. Pay close attention to each treasure's value, as you probably don't want to trade your extremely rare items unless you're certain you're receiving something of equal value in return.

When you're ready to part with an item, select it with your stylus and drag it over to one of the three green cups on the screen's right side. You can place only one item in a cup at a time, for a total of three items per trading session. But you don't have to fill all the cups, either. If you just want to hand over one item, just fill one cup. When you're ready to make the trade, select the Exchange button at the screen's bottom.

Now it's time to find out what you've received! Every pink cup contains an item, while green cups are empty. Use the stylus to drag the lid off each pink cup to reveal your new treasure. Once you've removed all the lids and retrieved your new items, Tag Mode returns to the inventory screen, where you can prepare to make a new trade. As long as you have treasure, you can trade. Just be sure to keep your DS powered on during these trading sessions, or you may lose your treasure.

The Legendary Checklist

With so much to see and do in Link's world, it's easy to become lost if you don't keep track. That's why we've provided the following checklists. Use them to keep tabs on everything you've accomplished during the adventure.

TIP

These checklists correspond to the rest of the guide, including the walkthrough and the poster map. Use them all in conjunction to ensure you never miss a thing!

Force Gems

Whenever a person's heart is filled with joy, that profound feeling of happiness may manifest in the form of a Force Gem. By fulfilling side tasks that make people happy, Link can obtain Force Gems, which restore lost stretches of Spirit Tracks when acquired. A few Force Gems are required to complete the adventure. However, the majority of Force Gems are optional, the tracks they restore leading to noncritical areas that often hold special goodies.

Got It?	Number	First Chance to Get	How to Get
	1	Before Ocean Temple (required event)	Escort Carben back to the Ocean Sanctuary from Papuchia Village.
	2	After Ocean Temple	Bring the chief of Whittleton Village to the lady who is looking for a husband in Papuchia Village.
	3	After Ocean Temple	Bring woman from Castle Town to Rabbitland Rescue.
	4	After Ocean Temple	Bring the boy from Aboda Village to Beedle's Shop.
	5	After Ocean Temple (required event)	Escort Anouki Mega Ice merchant from Anouki Village to Wellspring Station.
	6	After obtaining the Trusty Freight Car	Bring the Goron near the train station in Goron Village to Anouki Village.
	7	After obtaining the Trusty Freight Car	Bring Anouki villager from Anouki Village to Goron Village.
	8	After obtaining the Trusty Freight Car	Bring 10 units of Mega Ice to Goron Village for a second time and speak with Goron near the remaining lava.
	9	After obtaining the Trusty Freight Car	Bring 5 units of iron from Goron Village to the lumber merchant in Whittleton Village.
	10	After obtaining the Trusty Freight Car	Bring lumber from Whittleton Village and the bridge worker from the Trading Post to Anouki Village.
	11	After obtaining the Trusty Freight Car	Find Ferrus after receiving his letter, and bring him to Aboda Village; then go to Alfonzo's house.
	12	After obtaining the Trusty Freight Car	Bring 10 units of fish from Papuchia Village to the lady near the fountain in Castle Town.
	13	After obtaining the Trusty Freight Car	Bring 10 Cuccos from Castle Town to the farmer in Aboda Village.
	14	After obtaining the Trusty Freight Car	Buy a vessel from the Wise One in Papuchia Village, and bring it to Steem at the Snow Sanctuary.
	15	After Fire Temple	Bring the Goron child near the elder's house in Goron Village to Castle Town.
	16	After Fire Temple	Bring 10 units of Mega Ice to the fish seller in Papuchia Village.
	17	After Fire Temple	Rescue the prisoner at the Pirate Hideout and bring him to Papuchia Village.
	18	After Sand Temple	Find Ferrus after receiving his second letter and bring him to the Ocean Temple.
	19	After Sand Temple	Bring 5 units of Dark Ore from the Dark Ore Mine to Linebeck at the Trading Post.
	20	After Sand Temple	Bring 5 Cuccos from Castle Town to Rael at the Sand Sanctuary.

 Heart Containers 

Link can find 13 Heart Containers if he searches far and wide. Each one he obtains adds a whole extra heart to his Life meter. Go out of your way to find every Heart Container as soon as they're available to gain a serious advantage over Link's foes.

Got It?	Number	Location	First Chance to Get	Items Required to Get	How to Get
	1	Forest Temple	During first visit	None	Clear temple to get Heart Container 1
	2	Castle Town	After Forest Temple	The Whirlwind	Beat "Take 'em All On" challenge at Level 1
	3	Rabbitland Rescue	After Snow Temple	Rabbit Net	Catch five or more rabbits, then speak to the owner of Rabbitland Rescue
	4	Snow Temple	On first visit	None	Clear temple to get Heart Container 4
	5	Hyrule Castle	After Snow Temple	50 Rupees or more	Get 60+ hits on Russell's sword-training challenge
	6	Snow Sanctuary	Before Ocean Temple	2,000 Rupees	Buy from Anouki shop
	7	Ocean Temple	On first visit	None	Clear temple to get Heart Container 7
	8	Whittleton Village	After Ocean Temple	Whip	Complete the whip Race in under 1:15.
	9	Fire Temple	On first visit	None	Clear temple to get Heart Container 9
	10	Pirate Hideout	After saving the Papuchia prisoner	None	Score over 4,000 points in the pirate minigame.
	11	Sand Temple	On first visit	None	Clear temple to get Heart Container 11
	12	Beedle's Air Shop	Toward the end of the adventure	5,000 Rupees	Become a Gold Club member (500 points) to get Heart Container 12
	13	Ends of the Earth Station	On first visit	Sand Wand	Solve block puzzle

 Items 

Link wouldn't get very far if he didn't have lots of clever tools on his side. Here's a list of the major items Link needs to complete his quest, along with any optional items that are well worth picking up.

Got It?	Item	Name	Location	First Chance to Get	Items Required to Get	Notes
		Engineer Certificate	Hyrule Castle	Before Forest Temple	None	Proves that Link is a full-fledged royal engineer
		Recruit's Uniform	Hyrule Castle	Before Forest Temple	None	Link's trademark adventuring clothes. Helps him blend in with castle guards.
		Spirit Flute	Hyrule Castle	Before Forest Temple	None	Royal family heirloom; used to play sacred songs
		Recruit's Sword	Hyrule Castle	Before Forest Temple	None	Link's first sword
		Forest Rail Map	Tower of Spirits	On first visit	None	Restores Spirit Tracks around the Forest Realm
		The Whirlwind	Forest Temple	On first visit	None	Allows Link to cast out cyclones for a variety of benefits
		Snow Rail Map	Tower of Spirits	During Tower of Spirits 2	None	Restores Spirit Tracks around the Snow Realm
		Stamp Book	Adobe Village	After Tower of Spirits 2	None	A gift from Niko. Used to collect stamps from stamp stations across the land.
		Rabbit Net	Rabbitland Rescue	On first visit	None	Used to catch trackside rabbits while riding train
		Boomerang	Snow Temple	On first visit	None	Handy tool that can be thrown for a variety of benefits

Got It?	Item	Name	Location	First Chance to Get	Items Required to Get	Notes
		Bomb Bag 1	Beedle's Air Shop	On first visit	500 Rupees	Lets Link carry and use up to 10 bombs
		Beedle Club Card	Beedle's Air Shop	After Snow Temple	None	Allows Link to accumulate membership points and earn special rewards
		Ocean Rail Map	Tower of Spirits	During Tower of Spirits 3	None	Restores Spirit Tracks around the Ocean Realm
		Shield of Antiquity	Aboda Village	Before Ocean Temple	10 stamps	Cannot be eaten by Like Likes
		Whip	Ocean Temple	On first visit	None	Multipurpose tool that grants Link a variety of benefits
		Bomb Bag 2	Whittleton Village	After Ocean Temple	50 Rupees	Lets Link carry and use up to 20 bombs
		Bomb Bag 3	Castle Town	After Ocean Temple	50 Rupees	Lets Link carry and use maximum bombs (30)
		Fire Rail Map	Tower of Spirits	During Tower of Spirits 4	None	Restores Spirit Tracks around the Fire Realm
		Freight Car	Goron Village	After Ocean Temple	None	Train add-on; used to haul goods
		Engineer Clothes	Aboda Village	Just before Fire Temple	15 stamps	Link's engineer uniform. Purely cosmetic.
		Bow and Arrow	Fire Temple	On first visit	None	Fires arrows to activate remote switches and defeat enemies
		Quiver 1	Goron Village	After Fire Temple	2,000 Rupees	Increases Link's arrow capacity to 30
		Quiver 2	Pirate Hideout	After rescuing the Papuchia prisoner	None	Increases Link's arrow capacity to its maximum (50)
		Sand Wand	Sand Temple	On first visit	None	Allows Link to raise walls of sand for a variety of benefits
		Bow of Light	Sand Temple	On first visit	None	Divine weapon needed to defeat the Demon King
		Compass of Light	Tower of Spirits	During Tower of Spirits 6	None	Points the way to the Dark Realm
		Lokomo Sword	Spirit Train	After Sand Temple	None	Divine blade needed to defeat the Demon King
		Swordsman's Scroll 1	Rabbitland Rescue	After Sand Temple	50 rabbits	Grants Link the Sword Beam ability
		Swordsman's Scroll 2	Aboda Village	Just before Tower of Spirits 6	20 stamps	Grants Link the great spin attack

Letters

See a wiggling postbox? Tap it to check Link's mail. Our hero can receive each of the following letters over the course of his adventure.

Got It?	Name	Location	First Chance to Get	Items Required to Get	Notes
	From the postmaster	Castle Town	During first visit	None	A friendly greeting from the postmaster
	From Princess Zelda	Hyrule Castle	Obtained during first meeting with Zelda	None	Asks Link to meet Zelda in secret
	From Alfonzo	Castle Town	After second visit to Tower of Spirits	None	Asks Link to come see Alfonzo
	From Beedle	Anywhere	After Snow Temple	None	Informs Link about Beedle's Air Shop and Bomb Bag 1.
	From Russell	Anywhere	After Snow Temple	None	Invites Link to visit Russell and practice his swordplay
	Beedle Club Mailing	Anywhere	After Snow Temple	None	Info about Beedle's membership club; includes Beedle Club Card
	From Linebeck	Trading Post	Before Ocean Temple	None	Hints about how to find the Regal Ring
	From Carben	Ocean Sanctuary	On Second Visit	None	Hints about how to enter the Ocean Temple
	From Ferrus	Any postbox	After bringing Mega Ice to Goron Village	None	Asks Link to come meet Ferrus at a pictured location
	From Ferrus 2	Any postbox	After Fire Temple	None	Asks Link to come meet Ferrus at a pictured location
	From Ferrus 3	Any postbox	After Sand Temple	None	Asks Link to come meet Ferrus at a pictured location
	From Niko	Any postbox	Obtained upon return to the Tower of Spirits after the Fire Temple	None	Contains a map showing the loction of two hidden treasures
	From Kagoron	Any postbox	After obtaining Force Gem 18	None	Kagoron tells link about a hidden treasure he had when he was a kid.
	Gold Membership	Any postbox	After getting 500 points (Total 5,000 Rupees Spent)	Beedle Club Card and Silver Membership	Beedle congratulates Link for obtaining 500 points.
	Silver Membership	Any postbox	After getting 200 points (Total 2,000 Rupees Spent)	Beedle Club Card	Beedle congratulates Link for obtaining 200 points.
	Platinum Membership	Any postbox	After getting 1,000 points (Total 10,000 Rupees Spent)	Beedle Club Card and Gold Membership	Beedle congratulates Link for obtaining 1,000 points.
	Diamond Membership	Any postbox	After getting 2,000 points (Total 20,000 Rupees Spent)	Beedle Club Club Card and Platinum Membership	Beedle congratulates Link for obtaining 2,000 points.

Overworld Chests

Goodie-holding chests aren't merely found in dungeons. Many also appear outdoors, in various regions of the overworld. Search far and wide for each of these chests so Link may benefit from their contents.

Got It?	Number	Location	First Chance to Get	Contents	Items Required to Get	How to Get
	1	Hyrule Castle	After Obtaining the Spirit Flute	Red Rupee	None	SW corner of Hyrule Castle 2F
	2	Hyrule Castle	After Obtaining the Spirit Flute	Treasure	None	NW rampart of Castle Grounds
	3	Hyrule Castle	After Obtaining the Spirit Flute	Red Rupee	None	Northern area of Hyrule Castle 1F
	4	Forest Sanctuary	After Forest Temple	Big Red Rupee	Whirlwind	Blow Cucco off ledge; use to reach.
	5	Rabbitland	On first visit	Treasure	None	sW corner of Hyrule Castle 2F

Got It?	Number	Location	First Chance to Get	Contents	Items Required to Get	How to Get
	6	Anouki Village	On first visit	Red Rupee	Song of Discovery	Learn Song of Discovery from song stone, revealing chest in the process.
	7	Anouki Village	After Snow Temple	Big Red Rupee	Bombs	Beyond north bomb wall.
	8	Anouki Village	After Snow Temple	Big Green Rupee	Boomerang	NW lake (freeze with ice torch).
	9	Castle Town	After Snow Temple	Red Rupee	Bombs	On rampart tower (destroy blocks to reach).
	10	Castle Town	After Snow Temple	Red Rupee	Bombs	On rampart tower (destroy blocks to reach).
	11	Bridge Worker's Home	After Snow Temple	Big Green Rupee	Song of Discovery	Play song near four boulders to reveal.
	12	Trading Post	After escorting the Bridge Worker	Regal Ring	Song of Discovery	Solve Linebeck's riddle; play song to reveal.
	13	Papuchia Village	After Snow Temple	Treasure	None	Just sitting in the open.
	14	Ocean Sanctuary	On first visit	Treasure	None	Use Cucco to reach.
	15	Ocean Sanctuary	After Ocean Temple	Treasure	Whip	Use whip to fly via bird and reach the center isle.
	16	Ocean Sanctuary	After Ocean Temple	Treasure	Whip; Song of Birds	Use whip to fly via bird and reach the chest at the northern region's northwest isle.
	17	Papuchia Village	After Ocean Temple	Big Green Rupee	Whip	Use whip to fly via birds and reach chest at south region of village.
	18	Papuchia Village	After Ocean Temple	Treasure	Whip	Use whip to fly via birds and reach chest at south region of village.
	19	Whittleton Village	After Ocean Temple	Treasure	Whip	Beyond north-most pit (swing across).
	20	Wellspring Station	After Ocean Temple	Big Green Rupee	Whip	On northeast ledge (swing across posts).
	21	Castle Town	After Ocean Temple	Treasure	Bombs; Song of Birds	On SE roof. Play Song of Birds to get Cucco; jump with Cucco from south rampart.
	22	Castle Town	After Ocean Temple	Treasure	Bombs; Song of Birds	On SW roof. Play Song of Birds to get Cucco; jump with Cucco from south rampart.
	23	Castle Town	After Ocean Temple	Treasure	Bombs; Song of Birds	On NW roof. Play Song of Birds to get Cucco; jump with Cucco from north rampart; cross buildings and lion statues to reach.
	24	Goron Village	After Ocean Temple	Treasure	None	West region, near iron merchant.
	25	Goron Village	After Ocean Temple	Treasure	None	West region, NE corner.
	26	Goron Village	After Ocean Temple	Treasure	Whip	On high ledge in west region (can only get on way back down the mountain).
	27	Goron Village	After bringing Mega Ice to Goron Village	Treasure	None	Village proper; on a high ledge.
	28	Goron Village	After bringing Mega Ice to Goron Village	Treasure	Song of Discovery	Play song near three pots on high cliff to reveal.
	29	Goron Village	After bringing Mega Ice to Goron Village	Treasure	None	In cave leading to Fire Sanctuary.
	30	Fire Sanctuary	After bringing Mega Ice to Goron Village	Treasure	Boomerang	On high NW ledge (light torches to reach)
	31	Aboda Village	After Fire Temple	Treasure	Letter: "From Niko"; Song of Discovery	Play song near palm tree in Aboda Village where indicated by Niko's map to reveal first hidden chest.
	32	Aboda Village	After Fire Temple	Treasure	Letter: "From Niko"; Song of Discovery	Play song near palm tree in Aboda Village where indicated by Niko's map to reveal second hidden chest.
	33	Disorientation Station	After Fire Temple	Treasure	Whip; Song of Birds	On low mesa to west.
	34	Disorientation Station	After Fire Temple	Red Rupee	Whip; Song of Birds	On west narrow ledge, near steps.
	35	Disorientation Station	After Fire Temple	Treasure	Whip; Song of Birds	Beyond a soldier, on east ledge.
	36	Dark Ore Mine	After Sand Temple	Treasure	Song of Discovery	Play song near the two torches at the mine's dead-end to reveal chest.
	37	Lost at Sea Station	After Sand Temple	Treasure	Song of Light; Song of Discovery	Activate crystals, play song near beam intersect point

Rabbitland Rabbits

Have you met the man at Rabbitland Rescue? He's a strange sort, but he's got a lot of great stuff to give you—provided you're up for a little rabbit hunting! Visit Rabbitland Rescue, located at the Forest Realm's northwest corner, and speak with the owner to obtain the Rabbit Net. Then blast trackside boulders and barrels, hoping to scare out a rabbit. Catch that rabbit before it runs off to add another bunny to your collection. Return to Rabbitland Rescue regularly to inform the owner of your progress and collect special prizes.

Forest Realm Rabbits	
Got It?	Number
	1
	2
	3
	4
	5
	6
	7
	8
	9
	10

Snow Realm Rabbits	
Got It?	Number
	1
	2
	3
	4
	5
	6
	7
	8
	9
	10

Ocean Realm Rabbits	
Got It?	Number
	1
	2
	3
	4
	5
	6
	7
	8
	9
	10

Fire Realm Rabbits	
Got It?	Number
	1
	2
	3
	4
	5
	6
	7
	8
	9
	10

Sand Realm Rabbits	
Got It?	Number
	1
	2
	3
	4
	5
	6
	7
	8
	9
	10

Spirit Flute Songs

Link can learn the following melodies from Air Stones he encounters along his travels. Simply whip out the Spirit Flute whenever you see an Air Stone and imitate its tune to learn the song.

Got It?	Name	Location	First Chance to Get	Notes
	Song of Awakening	Forest Sanctuary	On first visit	Sacred song that awakens Gossip Stones
	Song of Healing	Forest Temple	On first visit	Sacred song that summons a fairy who fully restores Link's hearts; one-time use
	Song of Discovery	Anouki Village	On first visit	Sacred song that reveals nearby hidden objects when played
	Song of Light	Trading Post	After Snow Temple	Sacred song that activates light beacons; must obtain Snow Rail map
	Song of Birds	Papuchia Village	After Tower of Spirits 3	Sacred song that calls nearby birds and Cuccos to Link

Stamp Stations

While Alfonzo's busy installing a cannon to the Spirit Train, take a break and speak with Niko to receive a nifty gift called a Stamp Book. Niko asks Link to fill his book with stamps, and he'll give out rewards as you collect more and more. Simply tap each stamp station you discover to plant a stamp in the book.

Got It?	Number	Location	Items Required to Get	How to Get
	1	Aboda Village	None	Near Alfonzo's house
	2	Whittleton Village	None	North portion of village
	3	Forest Sanctuary	None	Across bridge
	4	Forest Temple	The Whirlwind	First floor, northeast corner, covered by poison fog
	5	Anouki Village	None	Behind the northeast trees
	6	Snow Sanctuary	None	On a ledge along the trail
	7	Snow Temple	Boomerang	First basement floor, northeast corner of Octive lake
	8	Wellspring Station	Boomerang	Beyond the north lake (use ice torch to freeze the water)

Got It?	Number	Location	Items Required to Get	How to Get
	9	Castle Town	Bombs	Atop the ramparts, northwest tower
	10	Trading Post	Bombs	North area, within the cave
	11	Ocean Temple	Bombs, Whip	In secret northern area of the second floor (bomb two walls and use whip to reach)
	12	Ocean Sanctuary	Song of Birds, Whip	Play the Song of Birds near the entrance to Carben's abode; ride a bird up to the high ledge
	13	Papuchia Village	Song of Birds, Whip	Use birds to travel to village's south region, then use more birds to reach the southwest isle
	14	Goron Village	Whip	Use whip to rea ch northwest corner of the village's west region
	15	Fire Sanctuary	Boomerang	Light all of the torches, then cross the north bridge
	16	Fire Temple	Bow	First basement floor; shoot the southwest switch while riding the mine cart clockwise around the floor
	17	Pirate Hideout	Song of Birds, Whip	Play the Song of Birds and then fly up to the ledge near the train station.
	18	Sand Temple	Sand Wand	First basement floor; west end of quicksand passage
	19	Sand Sanctuary	Cuccos	After delivering Cuccos to Rael, use one to reach the southeast isle
	20	Tower of Spirits	None	Near the altar at the tower's apex

Train Parts

After you manage to repair the bridge that links the Forest and Ocean Realms, you'll find that Linebeck III is ready to start wheeling and dealing out of his shop at the Trading Post. Linebeck will gladly purchase treasures you've acquired at a fair price, but he also offers to trade you treasures for train parts! The following tables list the treasures needed to obtain each part—after trading with Linebeck, head to Aboda Village and ask Alfonzo to update your train.

Spirit Train

Got it?	Item	Name	Treasure 1	Qty	Treasure 2	Qty	Treasure 3	Qty
		Engine	—	—	—	—	—	—
		Cannon	—	—	—	—	—	—
		Passenger	—	—	—	—	—	—
		Freight	—	—	—	—	—	—

Wooden Train

Got It?	Item	Name	Treasure 1	Qty	Treasure 2	Qty	Treasure 3	Qty
		Engine	Wood Heart	2	Star Fragment	2	Dark Pearl Loop	1
		Cannon	Wood Heart	2	Stalfos Skull	1	Ruto Crown	1
		Passenger	Wood Heart	1	Bee Larva	1	Dragon Scale	1
		Freight	Wood Heart	1	Demon Fossil	2	Pearl Necklace	1

Steel Train								
Got It?	Item	Name	Treasure 1	Qty	Treasure 2	Qty	Treasure 3	Qty
		Engine	Pearl Necklace	2	Ruto Crown	1	Goron Amber	1
		Cannon	Pearl Necklace	2	Dragon Scale	2	Mystic Jade	1
		Passenger	Pearl Necklace	2	Pirate Necklace	3	Ancient Gold Piece	1
		Freight	Pearl Necklace	2	Dark Pearl Loop	2	Goron Amber	1

Skull Train								
Got It?	Item	Name	Treasure 1	Qty	Treasure 2	Qty	Treasure 3	Qty
		Engine	Stalfos Skull	4	Bee Larva	3	Ruto Crown	2
		Cannon	Stalfos Skull	2	Demon Fossil	3	Dragon Scale	1
		Passenger	Stalfos Skull	3	Star Fragment	2	Pearl Necklace	1
		Freight	Stalfos Skull	2	Wood Heart	4	Pirate Necklace	2

Stagecoach Train								
Got It?	Item	Name	Treasure 1	Qty	Treasure 2	Qty	Treasure 3	Qty
		Engine	Ancient Gold Piece	1	Dragon Scale	3	Bee Larva	8
		Cannon	Ancient Gold Piece	1	Dark Pearl Loop	3	Pirate Necklace	2
		Passenger	Ancient Gold Piece	1	Ruto Crown	3	Star Fragment	5
		Freight	Ancient Gold Piece	1	Pearl Necklace	2	Stalfos Skull	7

Dragonhead Train								
Got It?	Item	Name	Treasure 1	Qty	Treasure 2	Qty	Treasure 3	Qty
		Engine	Pirate Necklace	2	Mystic Jade	1	Demon Fossil	12
		Cannon	Pirate Necklace	2	Goron Amber	1	Wood Heart	9
		Passenger	Pirate Necklace	1	Dark Pearl Loop	3	Demon Fossil	8
		Freight	Pirate Necklace	2	Ruto Crown	2	Bee Larva	6

Sweet Train								
Got It?	Item	Name	Treasure 1	Qty	Treasure 2	Qty	Treasure 3	Qty
		Engine	Palace Dish	1	Mystic Jade	2	Ancient Gold Piece	1
		Cannon	Palace Dish	1	Pearl Necklace	5	Goron Amber	1
		Passenger	Palace Dish	1	Dragon Scale	3	Ruto Crown	4
		Freight	Palace Dish	1	Goron Amber	1	Dark Pearl Loop	3

Golden Train								
Got It?	Item	Name	Treasure 1	Qty	Treasure 2	Qty	Treasure 3	Qty
		Engine	Alchemy Stone	1	Ancient Gold Piece	2	Mystic Jade	3
		Cannon	Alchemy Stone	1	Palace Dish	3	Goron Amber	2
		Passenger	Regal Ring	1	Dragon Scale	4	Ancient Gold Piece	2
		Freight	Regal Ring	1	Pearl Necklace	4	Mystic Jade	1

Treasures

Speaking of treasures, here's the full list of every precious bauble Link can find, along with their values.

Got It?	Treasure	Name	Value
		Alchemy Stone	2,500
		Ancient Gold Piece	500
		Bee Larvae	50
		Dark Pearl Loop	150
		Demon Fossil	50
		Dragon Scale	150
		Goron Amber	500
		Mystic Sphere	500

Got It?	Treasure	Name	Value
		Palace Dish	500
		Pearl Necklace	150
		Pirate Necklace	150
		Regal Ring	2,500
		Ruto Crown	150
		Stalfos Skull	50
		Star Fragment	50
		Wood Heart	50

Contents

Using water

Water is essential for life. About 97% of the world's water is salty and cannot be used for drinking. Of the rest, 2% is frozen in the ice caps and in glaciers. This means that just 1% of all the water on the planet is suitable for drinking and other uses.

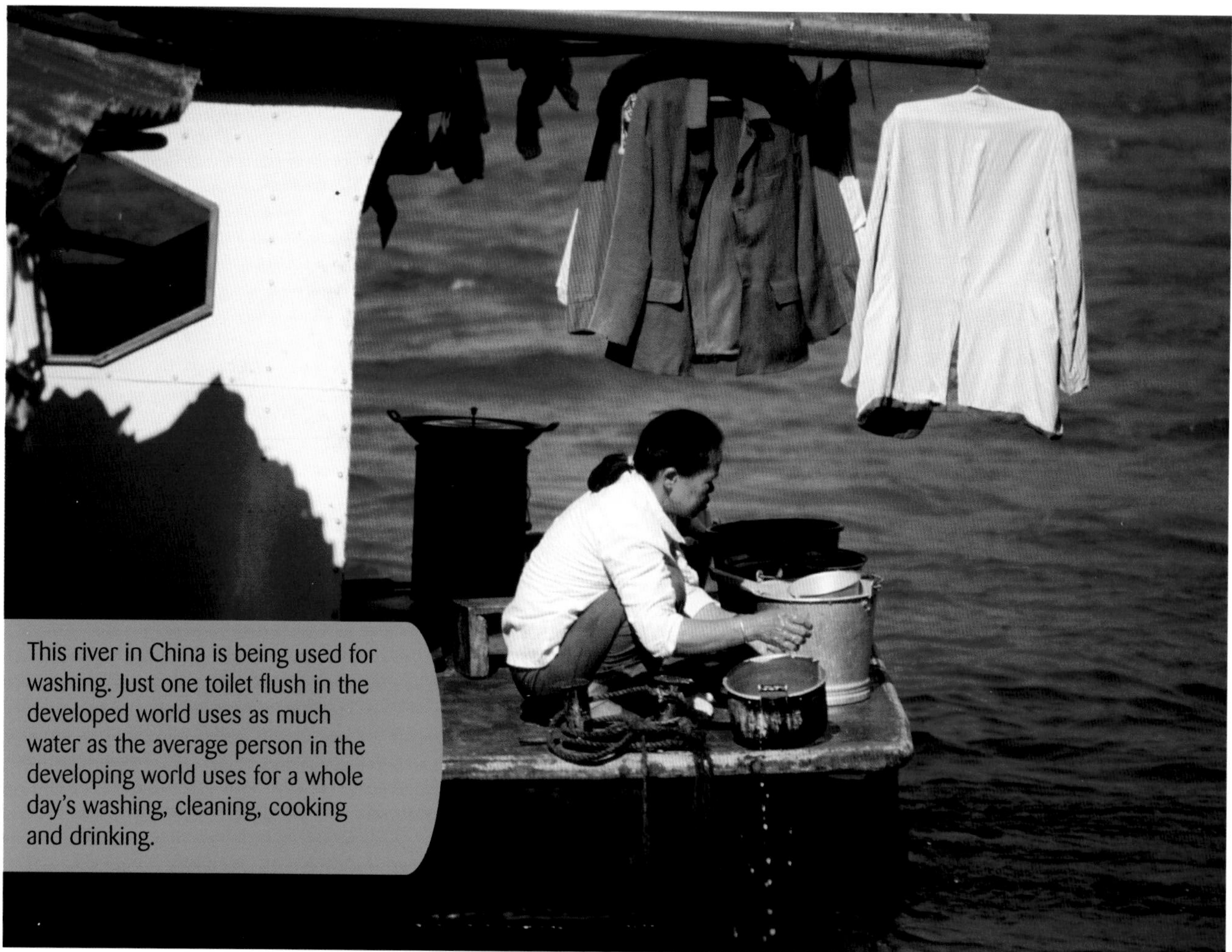

This river in China is being used for washing. Just one toilet flush in the developed world uses as much water as the average person in the developing world uses for a whole day's washing, cleaning, cooking and drinking.

Everyday uses

People use water every day for cooking, washing, cleaning and heating. Water is also used to water gardens and clean cars. Industry uses large quantities in manufacturing processes and farmers use it for their animals and to water crops. All these everyday uses create lots of waste water.

It's my world!

Think about the different ways that you use water each day. How would you cope if you had to collect your water from a tap in the street?

Did you know...?

The average American uses about 340 litres of water a day. That's much more than people living in other parts of the world. A European uses about 200 litres. Someone living in the dry parts of Africa, such as the Sudan, uses just 15 litres.

More people use more water

As the number of people in the world increases, so does the amount of water that is used. Many people do not think about the water they use. Every time they turn on a tap water pours out. However, in many of the hotter parts of the world this is not the case. There are shortages and even droughts when rain does not fall for months, sometimes years.

In this book you will read about the different ways that waste water can be treated and learn about ways in which everybody can help to reduce the amount of water that is used.

Watering a garden using a hose uses up far more water than a watering can and some water ends up on paths rather than on the soil.

Waste water

Waste water has to be treated or disposed of carefully so that it does not pollute (harm) the environment.

Types of waste water

There are different types of waste water. Water that has been used for washing or cleaning contains soaps and detergents. Water that has been used to flush the toilet is called sewage and it contains urine, faeces and toilet paper as well as harmful bacteria. Waste water that has been used in industry may contain chemicals. Water that runs off farmland in wet weather may contain fertilizers and pesticides.

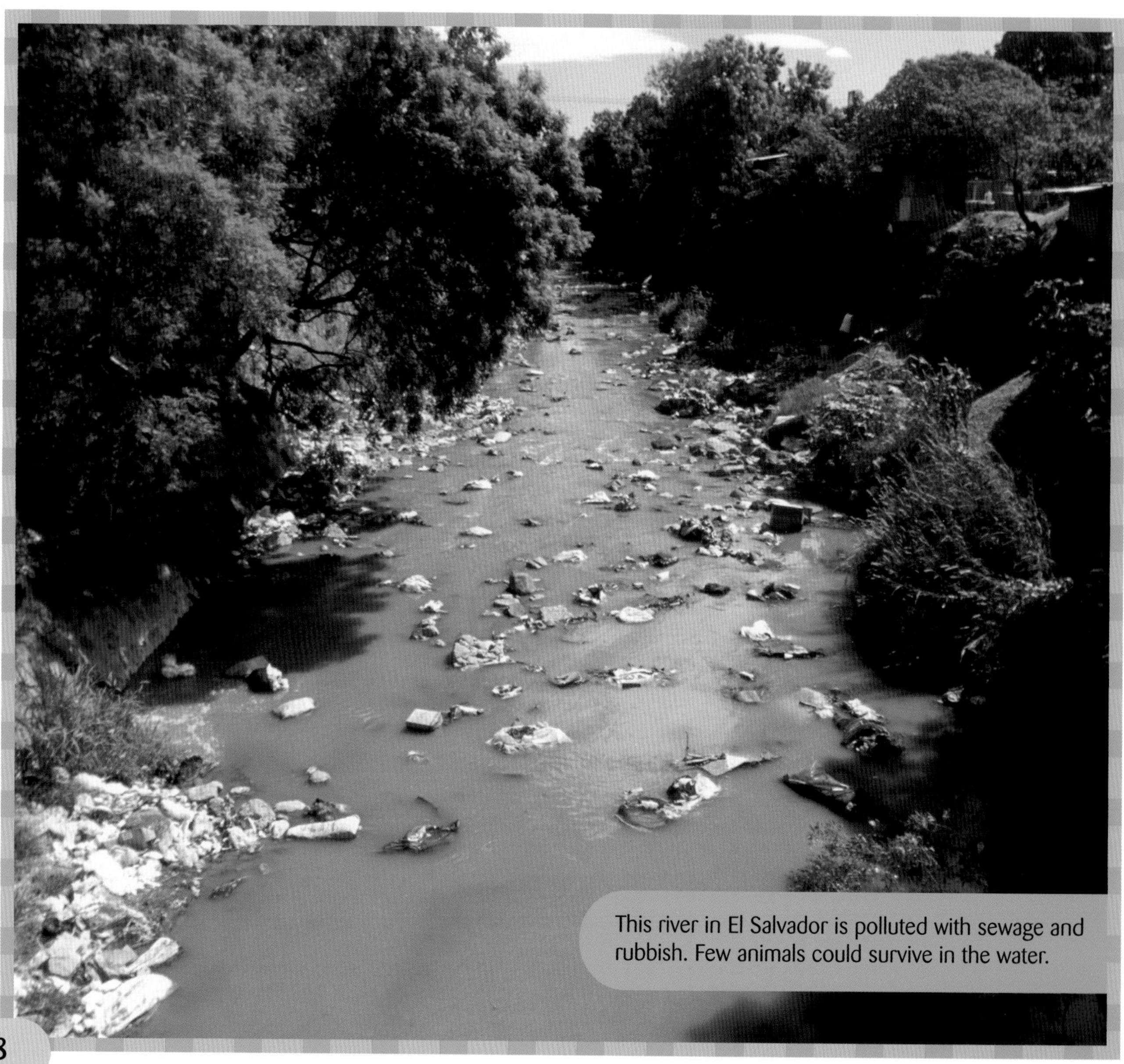

This river in El Salvador is polluted with sewage and rubbish. Few animals could survive in the water.

Water pollution

In the past, waste water was simply emptied into rivers and oceans and this caused water pollution. For example, huge piles of foam from detergents were seen floating on the surface of rivers. Nowadays this sight is less common, as modern detergents are biodegradable and they break down in the water. Also, less untreated water is put into rivers and oceans. However, in many developing countries untreated sewage and other dirty water is emptied straight into rivers and oceans. This kills fish and small animals that live in water.

Sewage has been emptied into the water through this pipe and it has killed all the fish in the water.

It's my world!

How clean is your local river or lake? The next time you walk past, have a good look at the water. Can you see any rubbish floating in the water? Occasionally, factories or farms have accidental spills of chemicals. If you see a number of dead fish floating in the water, contact the local water authority and let them know.

Street water

As well as waste water from sewage, there is urban runoff. This is water that flows down streets and into storm drains during wet weather. The water picks up rubbish and chemicals from the street, such as oil, paint and pesticides. During heavy rains, the waste water in the sewers may overflow and mix with rainwater in the storm drains. Unfortunately this waste water usually empties straight into rivers or oceans.

Treating sewage

Clean drinking water comes into homes through one set of pipes and leaves as waste water through another set, called sewer pipes. This waste water has to be treated.

Clearing the waste

All of the waste water produced by a city eventually ends up in a river, lake or ocean. On its way, this waste water flows through a sewage treatment plant. The sewage treatment plant treats the sewage so that the waste water is clean enough to be emptied into a river or ocean. The treatment plant separates the solids in the sewage from the liquid part. Then the liquid part is cleaned using living organisms.

Did you know...?

By the 19th century the population of London had reached two million and masses of sewage was emptied into the River Thames. The year 1858 was the year of the 'Great Stink' when the stench from the Thames was so bad that thousands of people had to flee the city and the streets were drenched in perfume in an attempt to hide the appalling smell. A bill was rushed through parliament to provide money to build a massive new sewer system.

Clean water from a sewage treatment plant in Florida is emptied into a marshy area.